ANTITRUST QUESTIONS AND ANSWERS

ANTITRUST
QUESTIONS AND ANSWERS

by

Edwin S. Rockefeller

THE BUREAU OF NATIONAL AFFAIRS, INC. • WASHINGTON, D.C.

Printed in the United States of America
Library of Congress Catalog Card Number: 73-93042
International Standard Book Number: 0-87179-183-8

Preface

In 1961, as I was about to leave the staff of the Federal Trade Commission, Adolph Magidson of The Bureau of National Affairs, Inc., asked me to assist him in the organization of a weekly news publication covering antitrust and trade regulation matters. Adolph's idea, which I enthusiastically accepted, was to use BNA's information gathering facilities to publish a report each week of Court, Commission, Justice Department, Capitol Hill, and other activities of interest to antitrust and trade regulation lawyers. The publication would not necessarily restrict itself to official case reports, but there was no idea that the Report should become some sort of "inside dope" sheet. To assist BNA's staff in their initial education in the field and to provide a continuing source of background and evaluation, an advisory board was created. The founding members were: Herbert A. Bergson, Robert A. Bicks, Leonard J. Emmerglick, Frazer F. Hilder, Ephraim Jacobs, Irving H. Jurow, Earl W. Kintner, Victor H. Kramer, S. Chesterfield Oppenheim, Worth Rowley, Louis B. Schwartz, William R. Tincher, F. Gerald Toye, Jerrold G. Van Cise, and Robert L. Wald.

Since July of 1961, this board, whose current membership is shown below, has met every month (except July or August) to discuss what appeared to be the most significant developments occurring in the field. For the first year or so, I prepared the agenda, with an initial memo to the members prior to the meeting, took notes during the discussion, and, following the meeting, where the subject seemed to warrant, drafted an analysis for publication in the weekly report. As the years went by, I was able to escape the burden of drafting and note taking. Also, we developed the habit of sending drafts of the analyses to selected members of the board before publication in order to avoid blunders and maintain balance in our comments.

This book has been developed from the board's published analyses, but in contrast to two previous volumes published in 1967 and 1969, which were simply verbatim collections of the previously published articles, I have now attempted to rework the entire body of material, to edit, eliminate, rewrite, and update into a single volume of questions and answers. This pulling together in one volume of the material resulting from more than a decade of discussions of the

v

ATRR Advisory Board has been a valuable experience for me. I expect that the book will be useful for reference and a quick refresher in my day-to-day law practice. I hope that it may be of similar use to others.

In addition to my debt to members of the ATRR Board, whose ideas have been freely used without attribution, it should be recognized that much of the material from which I worked was prepared by John C. Scott, who was the initial managing editor of ATRR and served for a number of years in that position; others who will recognize their words here are Mark H. Woolsey, Robert B. Greenbaum, William J. Barnhard, Terrence R. Murphy, Alan M. Frey, and Richard Haddad. Karen Bokat assisted in research, and Paul H. Karlsson read the galley proofs.

Glen E. Weston reviewed the entire manuscript. For his helpful suggestions I am particularly grateful.

Edwin S. Rockefeller

Washington, D.C.

ANTITRUST AND TRADE REGULATION REPORT

ADVISORY BOARD

Table of Contents

PART I

Trust and Antitrust—Some Fundamentals

1. Size and the Antitrust Laws

Question: *Do the antitrust laws limit the competitive aggressiveness and free business choice of big corporations?*

Justice Cardozo once wrote: "Mere size . . . is not an offense . . . but size carries with it an opportunity for abuse . . ." (*U.S.* v. *Swift & Co.,* 286 U.S. 106, 116 (1932)). Judge Learned Hand, in *U.S.* v. *Alcoa,* 148 F.2d 416, 430, 431 (2nd Cir. 1945), said that "the successful competitor, having been urged to compete, must not be turned upon when he wins." Judge Hand found illegal under Section 2 of the Sherman Act Alcoa's continuing efforts "progressively to embrace each new opportunity as it opened, and to face every newcomer with new capacity already geared into a great organization, having the advantage of experience, trade connections and the elite of personnel." He disapproved of the anticipation by Alcoa of increases in demand and preparation for supplying them by "doubling and redoubling capacity before competitors entered the field."

Large corporate enterprises may sometimes be said to be caught in a conflict between the Sherman Act, which prohibits restraints of trade (and monopolies), and the Robinson-Patman Act, which prohibits discriminating in price between different purchasers with many complex exceptions, provisos, and defenses. Some antitrust specialists, and some courts, have found inconsistency between "hard" competition favored by the Sherman Act and "soft" competition protected by the Robinson-Patman Act. The latter is said to offer protection to the wholesaler, or distributor, or retailer—to protect him where he cannot protect himself.

Some say that big companies *ought* to be less free than their small competitors. With size goes responsibility and obligation to serve the public without stepping too heavily on smaller competitors. The giant achieves a sort of public-utility status.

Some antitrust restrictions apply more tightly to large than to small competitors. Tying and exclusive-dealing agreements, for example, are unlawful only where they are shown to have substantial adverse effects on competition. They may, therefore, be less

1

available to giants than to smaller competitors because, when used by giants, they have a greater potential effect on competition.

Although the general doctrine for all is that the seller may choose his customers on any basis he wishes, or no basis at all, refusal to deal may be more dangerous for large than for small. A lease-only policy may be objectionable if followed by some (*U.S.* v. *United Shoe Machinery Corp.,* 110 F.Supp. 295 (D. Mass 1953), *aff'd per curiam,* 347 U.S. 521 (1954)). The Automobile Dealers Day in Court Act may put special limits on the freedom of automobile manufacturers. Here, Congress has apparently placed special obligations on those who have special power, requiring a kind of due process in the cancellation of a dealer's franchise. (See section VI-E, p. 445.)

Even where conduct is lawful, self-restraint may be dictated by considerations of vulnerability to political agitation, congressional investigation, and potential legislation. Giants, more than others, may have to operate within *prospective* legal prohibitions as well as within existing law. One direction in which our law could go is suggested by provisions of European law and treaties focusing on "abuse of economic power" by "dominant concerns." Senator Hart's bill, S. 1167, 93d Cong., 1st Sess. (1973), to break up "concentrated" industries and the FTC's proceeding in *Kellogg Co.,* D. 8883, to break up the cereal industry as a "shared monopoly" may be possible clues to future development.

There is probably a greater burden on giant corporations to establish a legitimate business motivation for any course of action that may result in tough competition. Like the professional prizefighter, the big corporation has to be careful whom it punches.

Pricing of products may present special problems for giant corporations. Although price is supposed to be determined by the competitive market, where there are only a few large sellers, each may have a measure of power over price. A producer who seeks to obtain too high a price may end up with fewer sales and an indignant public. On the other hand, offering at a price too low can be dangerous, too. Sales "at an unreasonably low price," coupled with facts from which intent to destroy competition or eliminate a competitor can be inferred, may constitute a criminal violation of the Robinson-Patman Act or a Sherman Act violation, if competitors are excluded or a market preempted. It is difficult to define "unreasonably low price." Cost may be the mark below which a price is "unreasonably low," but "cost" itself may be an elusive standard for the giant integrated producer. Few prosecutions have been brought under the "unreasonably low prices" ban in the Robinson-Patman Act, but the Supreme Court has held that the statute is not unconstitutionally vague (*U.S.* v. *National Dairy Prods. Corp.,* 372 U.S. 29, *rehearing denied,* 372 U.S. 961 (1963)). (See section IV-G, p. 347.)

Some experts see an important distinction between pricing to create a new market and pricing to preempt an existing one. Compare for example, *U.S.* v. *Jerrold Electronics Corp.,* 187 F.Supp. 545 (E.D.Pa 1960), *aff'd,* 365 U.S. 567 (1961), with *U.S.* v. *Eastman Kodak Co.,* 1954 Trade Cas. ¶67,920 (W.D.N.Y. 1954).

2. Interlocking Directorates

Question: *Is anything done by the Government about corporate interlocks?*

Section 8 of the Clayton Act contains a provision that "no person at the same time shall be director in any two or more corporations, any one of which has capital, surplus, and undivided profits aggregating more than $1,000,000 . . . if such corporations are or shall have been theretofore . . . competitors, so that the elimination of competition by agreement between them would constitute a violation of any of the provisions of any of the antitrust laws."

Interlocks in the banking industry are dealt with separately in the two preceding paragraphs of Section 8. In those provisions, the ban is against being "a director or other officer or employee" of more than one enterprise, either of which has "deposits, capital, surplus, and undivided profits aggregating more than $5 million." Like the provisions in the third paragraph with respect to ordinary industrial and commercial corporations, the two paragraphs on banking are aimed at "horizontal" interlocks—that is, common directors or employees in enterprises that compete with each other.

Provisions in Section 10 of the Clayton Act on "common carriers" concern "vertical" interlocks—those involving companies that deal with each other as buyer and seller rather than as competitors. "No common carrier engaged in commerce shall have any dealings . . . to the amount of more than $50,000, in the aggregate, in any one year, with another corporation, firm, partnership or association when the said common carrier shall have upon its board of directors or as its president, manager or as its purchasing or selling officer, or agent in the particular transaction, any person who is at the same time a director, manager, or purchasing or selling officer of, or who has any substantial interest in, such other corporation, firm, partnership or association," unless the deal is made by competitive bidding.

Although Sections 8 and 10 have been in effect since 1916, a report of the House Antitrust Subcommittee's staff (INTERLOCKS IN CORPORATE MANAGEMENT, Staff Report of House Antitrust Subcommittee, U.S. Government Printing Office, No. 26-188, March 12, 1965) declared that "widespread interlocks among corporate managements . . . have continued to be a characteristic of the way American business operates." The report presented a statistical study of a 74-company sample showing that these companies' 1,449 directorships were held by 1,206 individuals. And 182 of those individuals held 425 directorships.

Another set of figures given in the report was a Federal Trade Commission tabulation of multiple directorships in the 1,000 leading industrial corporations. The Commission also identified the products involved and reported: "There are some 400 interlocks, of which some may be in violation of Section 8 of the Clayton Act." But a sample "verification" of the products mentioned for 17 of the companies convinced the subcommittee staff that the Commission's source for the product identifications is "of little value" in determining whether the multiple directorships involved competitors.

The subcommittee staff made no attempt to study the social or economic effects of interlocks. In fact, the report stated that "there is a dearth of objective, factual information on the social and economic effects, as embodied in actual business transactions, of decisions made by linked corporate managements," but the subcommittee staff was convinced that "common sense, practical observation, and abstract reasoning all support the conclusion" that adverse competitive effects "should follow" decisions by interlocking corporate managements. "It would be naive to think that the ability of two corporations to compete is not impaired by common management members; that individuals who occupy top management positions in corporations that deal with each other will not have their judgments beclouded by considerations that affect their own financial interests; and that an individual who is too busy to appear at board meetings does not debase the management of the corporations he serves." "Of most concern" to the staff was "the fear that, by means of the interlocking management device, inordinate control over the major part of the U.S. commerce would be concentrated in the hands of so few individuals that the normal social and political forces relied upon to maintain a free economy would be ineffective to correct abuses."

A basic finding in the Antitrust subcommittee staff's report is that "enforcement of the Clayton Act's prohibitions against interlocking directorates" has been "neither prompt nor vigorous." Only the Justice Department has enforcement responsibility under all the Clayton Act's provisions on interlocks. In banking, the Department shares that duty with the Federal Reserve Board; in land transportation, with the Interstate Commerce Commission; in air transport, with the Civil Aeronautics Board; and, in other industries, with the Federal Trade Commission.

The FTC has filed about a dozen complaints under Section 8. Most were dismissed when the directors discontinued the challenged relationships. In *General Electric Co.,* FTC File No. 731 0129, 605 ATRR A-17 (3/20/73), issuance of the complaint forced the resignation of a GE director from the board of Chrysler Corp. (606 ATRR A-19), but the complaint alleged a violation of Section 5 of the FTC Act, as well as a violation of Section 8, and the complaint was not dismissed. On May 16, 1973, the Commission announced the acceptance of consent orders prohibiting interlocking directorates between Alcoa and Kennecott Copper Corp. and between Alcoa and Armco Steel Corp. (613 ATRR A-23 (5/15/73)). The orders (Dockets C-2415 through C-2418) were issued on July 10, 1973.

The Department of Justice did not undertake a systematic program against interlocking directorates until just after World War II, when it conducted a survey of 1,600 corporations and their more than 10,000 directors. Some 1,500 individuals were found to be holding interlocking directorships, but the Attorney General reported that when these individuals were informed of the results of the survey and of the possibility that their relationships violated Section 8, most resigned without further contest.

In February 1952, the Antitrust Division instituted four Section 8 cases challenging two groups of interlocking directorates. The first of these cases was decided for the Government (*U.S.* v. *Sears, Roebuck and Co.,* 111 F.Supp. 614 (S.D.N.Y. 1953)). The case involved interpretation of Section 8's ban on interlocks among "competitors, so that the elimination of competition by agreement between them would constitute a violation of any of the provisions of any of the antitrust laws." Defendant contended that this language means there must be a finding that merger of the two corporations would violate the Clayton Act. The district judge stressed the Act's reference to "any of the provisions of any of the antitrust laws" and decided that it is enough if the companies involved sell in competition with each other, raising the possibility of price-fixing or territory-splitting agreements.

The district judge directed the individual defendant to resign his directorship in one or the other of the two companies involved and directed the company chosen to accept his resignation, but the court turned down the Government's request for a broad injunction against future violations of Section 8, stating in an endorsement on the back of the judgment that such a decree "should be granted only where there is evidence showing a persistent purpose to violate or commit recurrences of the condemned act."

Three other Justice Department complaints were considered together in *U.S.* v. *W. T. Grant Co.,* 112 F.Supp. 336 (S.D.N.Y. 1952), *aff'd,* 345 U.S. 629 (1953). The issue in the district court was whether the director's discontinuance of the challenged relationships rendered the proceedings moot—that is, deprived the court of jurisdiction to prohibit a resumption of multiple directorships. After noting that mere cessation of an unlawful activity does not deprive a court of jurisdiction to prohibit its resumption, the district judge found not the "slightest threat" that the individual who held the directorships would attempt in the future any activity that would violate Section 8. The Supreme Court agreed with the test applied by the district judge and found no abuse of discretion in the refusal to award injunctive relief, despite a showing that the individual defendant had been involved in three distinct violations of Section 8, had expressly refused to concede their illegality, had failed to terminate the interlocks until after suit was filed following five years of administrative attempts to persuade him, and had refused to promise not to commit similar violations in the future.

When it announced the filing of four Section 8 cases in 1952, the Justice Department included a policy statement of the Assistant Attorney General in charge of the Antitrust Division: "The Antitrust Division will maintain a continuing watch over the directorship field and in cases in which individuals continue to serve on the boards of competing companies after notification by the Division that they are violating this statute, it will proceed to file legal actions to terminate such directorships."

In three injunction complaints, the Antitrust Division has added Section 8 charges to allegations that mergers violated Section 7 of the Clayton Act (*U.S.* v. *Thrifty Drug Stores Co., Inc.* (57 ATRR A-20, 8/14/62); *U.S.* v. *Richfield Oil Corp.* (66 ATRR A-4, 10/16/62); *U.S.* v. *Newmont Mining Corp.* (78 ATRR A-7, 1/8/63)). The complaint against Thrifty Drug Stores was dismissed (181 ATRR A-2, 12/29/64) after the companies severed their relationship. The complaint against Richfield was dismissed as moot and the one against Newmont terminated by a consent decree (1966 Trade Cas. ¶71,709 (S.D.N.Y. 1966)).

In *U.S.* v. *The Cleveland Trust Co.,* (1961–1970 Transfer Binder) Trade Reg. Rep. ¶45,070 (Case #2089) (pending in N.D. Ohio), (complaint reprinted in Congressional Record of April 6, 1970, H.2654, in extension of remarks of Rep. Patman), the Department of Justice is contending that Cleveland Trust Co., a corporation, is the "director" of competing companies in violation of Section 8 because the bank's separate "agents" are serving on the boards of directors of machine tool companies that are competitors. If the Government's novel legal theory is sustained, Section 8 will be applicable to many "indirect" interlocks previously thought to be unreachable under Section 8—particularly through financial institutions, insurance companies, and mutual funds. (The case is even more far-reaching in its Section 7 theories in alleging that stock held in a fiduciary capacity by financial institutions is subject to Section 7.) See also the two volume Staff Report on Commercial Banks and Their Trust Activities, House Committee on Banking & Currency, (Subcommittee on Domestic Finance), 90th Cong., 2d Sess. (1968).

Decisions under Section 10 of the Clayton Act are few. In *In re Missouri Pacific Ry. Co.*, 13 F.Supp. 888 (E.D. Missouri 1935), it was held that Section 10 completely forbids sales of securities to a railroad having a common director with the selling firm, since competitive bidding is economically impossible in securities transactions. "Any other view would render the provisions of Section 10, relating to securities, absolute nullities."

In 1963, criminal proceedings under Section 10 against the Boston & Maine Railroad and three of its officials were dismissed by the district judge on the theory that the three officials, not being officers or directors of the other corporation involved, had not been shown to have a "substantial interest" in the other corporation (*U.S.* v. *Boston & Maine R.R.*, 225 F.Supp. 577 (D.Mass. 1963)). To show a "substantial interest," the government alleged an agreement for "the purpose of producing profits for [the other corporation] from dealings by it in property acquired from the B&M . . . and pursuant to which [the B&M officials] were to and did receive substantial monies."

The Supreme Court, in *U.S.* v. *Boston & Maine R.R.*, 380 U.S. 157 (1965), agreed with the district judge that the Government's allegations were not enough to establish a "substantial interest" of the B&M officials in the other corporation, but it took issue with the district judge's requirement that the Government show "a then present legal interest in the buying corporation." The Supreme Court read the words "substantial interest" as presupposing "an existing investment of some kind . . . or the creation of [the other corporation] by the three individual appellees for their use, or a joint venture or continued course of dealings, licit or illicit, with [the other corporation] for profit sharing." The Court remanded the case to the district judge with instructions that the Government be given a chance to file a new bill of particulars satisfying the "substantial interest" test.

In its 1965 report (*supra*, p. 3), the staff of the House Antitrust Subcommittee stressed the "general ineffectiveness" of Section 8 "both with respect to halting interlocks within its terms and in its complete failure to reach interlocks with apparently equal significance." It was said that corporate procedures have changed significantly since the enactment of the Clayton Act. "Management functions have devolved to a cadre of professional staff officials. Directors in the larger corporations have tended to become removed from the actual decision-making process in business operations. In this context, interlocks of officers and other senior employees probably are of more consequence on matters of antitrust significance than are interlocks of directors."

The staff report recommended, "as a framework for further investigation," the preparation of a "model bill" designed to curb interlocks not only on boards of directors but also among officers and employees "with management functions." As envisioned by the staff, the model bill would "prohibit any person, directly or indirectly, at the same time, from being a director, officer, or employee with management functions, or having a representative or nominee for such purpose, in any two or more corporations, any one of which has capital, surplus, and undivided profits aggregating more than one million dollars." The prohibition would apply to all classes of corporations and to all types of business. It would forbid not only "horizontal interlocks between actual and potential competitors" but also "vertical interlocks between actual and potential customers, suppliers, and sources of credit or capital."

Despite this "model bill" recommendation, the staff report reached the conclusion that repeal of Sections 8 and 10 of the Clayton Act was not warranted. The staff did not feel that it had enough information to suggest results that might be anticipated from specific amendments to existing law. The subcommittee was told that additional investigation, including subcommittee hearings, should be made into the "social and economic consequences that have resulted from interrelated managements in business transactions in the recent past."

There are antitrust experts who, in the absence of concrete evidence that interlocking directorates produce anticompetitive decisions, do not regard such directorates as a major threat to the public interest. There is a tendency to disparage the argument—mentioned in the staff report—that interlocking directorates are the natural result of a scarcity of director talent and offer corporations an opportunity to obtain men of wider experience and more diversified background. There is a widespread view, buttressed by some of the situations the Antitrust Division encountered in the late 1940's, that the individuals who serve simultaneously on several big-company boards of directors are not doing much directing anyway.

It is not clear what basis the subcommittee staff had for its statement that Section 8 enforcement efforts have been "neither prompt nor vigorous." The Antitrust Division releases no data on the number of directorships that have been resigned voluntarily by individuals receiving admonitory letters from the Antitrust Division since its 1952 lawsuits. The Division's declared "surveillance" policy suggests a possibility that such letters are sent. The staff report recognizes that statistics on the overlapping personnel of big corporations must be viewed in the light of Section 8's inapplicability to "vertical" or "conglomerate" interlocks and to management or executive interlocks.

Whatever the need for additional legislation in this field, some lawyers are convinced that no statute will eliminate the types of interlocks that provide effective channels for coordinating the policies of corporations competing or dealing with each other unless the prohibitions are made more inclusive and more explicit than even those suggested in the subcommittee staff's "model bill." For example, there is precedent for the staff's suggestion that a director or officer of one corporation be forbidden to have a "representative or nominee" on the board or management staff of a competitor, supplier, or customer. Section 409 (a)(3) of the Civil Aeronautics Act makes it unlawful, without Civil Aeronautics Board approval, for a director of an interstate air carrier to have a "representative or nominee" on the board of another common carrier. In *Lehman* v. *CAB*, 209 F.2d 289 (D.C. Cir. 1953), that provision was applied to partners in an investment-banking business. The court's theory was that the business was operated in a way which made each partner a representative of the partnership and therefore of the other partners, but the court refused to hold that the community of interest attributable to mere membership in the same partnership is in and of itself sufficient to make the partners "representatives or nominees" of each other within the meaning of the Act.

Under reasoning like that of the *Lehman* case, it might be doubtful whether the statutory language suggested by the subcommittee's staff would prevent two corporations from having directors with family connections, or directors who represent the same large stockholder-principal, or directors who are fellow executives or fellow directors in the same financial or investment corporation.

Interlocking directorates do not seem to be in any trouble under other provisions of the antitrust laws, although attempts have been made to apply the unfair-methods-of-competition ban in Section 5 of the FTC Act against them, resulting in consent orders. (Cases cited above, p. 5.) The major effort to apply Sections 1 and 2 of the Sherman Act ended in failure when the district court held in *U.S.* v. *Morgan,* 118 F. Supp. 621 (S.D.N.Y. 1953), that the Government had not proven a conspiracy on the part of leading investment-banking houses to monopolize the securities business by maintaining banker representatives on the securities issuers' boards of directors.

One court decision which might be regarded as posing a threat to interlocking directorates is *Hamilton Watch Co.* v. *Benrus Watch Co.,* 114 F.Supp. 307 (D. Conn), *aff'd,* 206 F.2d 738 (2d Cir. 1953), holding that the acquisition of a minority block of stock in a competitor for the purpose of obtaining representation on the competitor's board of directors violated Section 7 of the Clayton Act.

3. Anti-Monopoly Decrees

Question: *If the courts find an unlawful monopoly, are they likely to do anything really effective about it?*

The Sherman Act adds nothing to the traditional powers of a court of equity; it merely extends them to Sherman Act violations. Section 4 says, "The several district courts of the United States are invested with jurisdiction to prevent and restrain violations of this Act; and it shall be the duty of the several United States Attorneys, in their respective districts, under the direction of the Attorney General, to institute proceedings in equity to prevent and restrain such violations."

"The problem of the district court does not end with enjoining continuance of the unlawful restraints nor with dissolving the combination which launched the conspiracy. Its function includes undoing what the conspiracy achieved" (*U.S.* v. *Paramount Pictures, Inc.,* 334 U.S. 131, 171 (1948)). In monopolization cases, the decree must "neutralize the extension and continually operating force which the possession of the power unlawfully obtained has brought and will continue to bring about" (*Standard Oil Co.* v. *U.S.,* 221 U.S. 1, 78 (1911)).

The Supreme Court has repeatedly indicated that dissolution or divestiture is the remedy the federal district court should try first as a means of undoing what an illegal monopoly has achieved (*Schine Chain Theatres* v. *U.S.,* 334 U.S. 110, 127–228 (1948); *U.S.* v. *Paramount Pictures Inc.,* 334 U.S. 131 (1948); *U.S.* v. *Crescent Amusement Co.,* 323 U.S. 173, 189 (1944)). In ANTITRUST POLICY, Kaysen and Turner called "for a widespread application of dissolution remedies, on the ground that an increase in numbers and reduction of concentration is the surest and most durable way of reducing market power" (pp. 113–114). (" 'Dissolution' is generally used to refer to a situation where the dissolving of an allegedly illegal combination or association is involved; it may include the use of divestiture and divorcement as methods of achieving that end. 'Divestiture' refers to situations where the defendants are required to divest themselves of property, securities or other assets" (Oppenheim & Weston, FEDERAL ANTITRUST LAWS, 3rd Ed., p. 858).

Since World War II there have been at least five fully litigated Sherman Act cases in which the Government has asked for a decree of dissolution or divestiture against tight oligopolies or dominant single firms (*U.S.* v. *Alcoa,* 148 F.2d 416 (2d Cir. 1945); *U.S.* v. *National Lead Co.,* 332 U.S. 319 (1947); *U.S.* v. *Paramount Pictures,* 334 U.S. 131 (1948); *U.S.* v. *Grinnell Corp.,* 384 U.S. 563 (1966); and *U.S.* v. *United Shoe Machinery Corp.,* 391 U.S. 244 (1968)). The Government succeeded in obtaining a divestiture decree in two of those cases—*Paramount Pictures* and *Grinnell.*

Divestiture was granted against Paramount Pictures on appeal after denial by the district court (*U.S.* v. *Paramount Pictures,* 66 F.Supp. 323 (S.D.N.Y. 1946)). The Government sought to separate motion-picture film production from distribution. The district court merely enjoined the producers from expanding their theater holdings in any manner and directed that all their films be marketed through competitive bidding. Because it considered the district court's findings on monopolization inadequate and the competitive-bidding procedure unworkable, the Supreme Court set aside both decree provisions and ordered the district court "to make an entirely fresh start on the whole of the problem." On remand, the district court granted the requested divestiture (334 U.S. 131, 175 (1948); 85 F.Supp. 881 (S.D.N.Y. 1949)).

The *Alcoa* case was litigated during World War II and was decided on appeal before it was possible "to say what will be 'Alcoa's' position in the industry after the war" (148 F.2d at 446), since much of Alcoa's business was being conducted in plants leased from the Government. Under the Surplus Property Act of 1944, 50 App. U.S.C.A. Sec. 1622, those leased plants were to be disposed of after the war in a manner designed "to discourage monopolistic practices and to strengthen and preserve the competitive position of small business concerns." Eventually (91 F.Supp. 333 (S.D.N.Y. 1950)), domestic divestiture was denied, although the district court saw danger in common control of Alcoa and Aluminium, Inc., a Canadian affiliate, and ordered their common stockholders to sell their shares in one or the other. The decree also struck down grant-back clauses in Alcoa's patent-licensing contracts. The district judge found the two domestic divestiture plans proposed by the Government unworkable and noted that the industry had in the meantime acquired two substantial new competitors in primary-aluminum production, "thousands of firms which fabricate aluminum products," and about 50 firms engaged in the production of secondary aluminum out of aluminum scrap.

In the *National Lead* case, the Government proposed that National Lead and duPont each be required to dispose of one of its two principal titanium-pigment plants. The Supreme Court pointed out that compulsory patent-licensing terms in the decree seemed likely to create two new competitors and saw in the record no showing that the plants to be divested were adapted for independent operation. There was no showing, the Court said, that four major competing units would be preferable to two. "Assuming, as is justified, that violation of the Sherman Act in this case has consisted primarily of the misuse of patent rights," the Supreme Court affirmed a decree directing nonexclusive licensing of the patents at a uniform, reasonable royalty.

Divestiture separating the Grinnell Corporation from three subsidiaries found to give it an illegal alarm-service monopoly was ordered by the district court (236 F.Supp. 244 (D.R.I. 1964)), but the Supreme Court agreed with the Government that further divestiture was appropriate, breaking up one of the subsidiaries, which was found to have a complete monopoly of burglar-protection and fire-protection central-station services in 92 of the 115 cities in which it was doing business (*U.S.* v. *Grinnell,* 384 U.S. 563 (1966)). The Supreme Court stressed "that adequate relief in a monopolization case should put an end to the combination and deprive the defendants of any of the benefits of the illegal conduct, and break up or render impotent the monopoly power found to be in violation of the Act." The decree entered on remand (315 ATRR A-8 (7/25/67)) also directed that subsidiary to reduce its five-year service contracts to two-year contracts. All the defendant companies were ordered to make their products available for purchase on nondiscriminatory terms.

The district court in *U.S.* v. *United Shoe Machinery Corp.,* 110 F.Supp. 295 (D. Mass. 1953), denied the Government's request that United Shoe Machinery be dissolved into three separate shoe-manufacturing companies. The proposal was labeled "unrealistic," since United did all its manufacturing at one plant that "cannot be cut into three equal and viable parts." (The district judge indicated he did not think the Government itself really took the proposal seriously.) The decree enjoined United from further monopolization, ordered it to offer its machines for sale instead of exclusively for leasing, limited the leases to five-year terms, banned restrictive lease conditions, required nonexclusive licensing of patents on reasonable nondiscriminatory royalty terms, restricted the acquisition of further patents, and prohibited the acquisition of any shoe-machinery manufacturer or any secondhand shoe machinery. The Government took no appeal from the decree, and when United took an appeal, the order was affirmed *per curiam,* 347 U.S. 521 (1954).

The decree in *United Shoe* provided that in 10 years "both parties shall report to this court the effect of this decree, and may then petition for its modification, in view of its effect in establishing workable competition." At the time, the district judge seems to have regarded his decree as a tentative one, for he remarked that the more severe relief sought by the government "would be undesirable, at least until milder remedies have been tried" (110 F.Supp. at 349). The defendant was "forewarned by the decree itself that if it abuses this flexibility, the court after the entry of this decree may modify it. Thus the decree invokes the precedent not of Draco, but of Damocles and Dionysius" (110 F.Supp. at 351).

Pursuant to the 10-year-trial clause, the Government reported on January 1, 1965, that United continued to dominate the shoe-machinery market and that additional relief was necessary. The court, asked to order United to submit a plan for dividing its business into two competing companies, decided it had no power to modify the original decree except on a clear showing of grievous wrong evoked by new and unforeseen circumstances (266 F.Supp. 328, 334 (D. Mass. 1967)).

According to the Supreme Court, the district judge misread *U.S. v. Swift & Co.*, 286 U.S. 106 (1932), as to his power to modify a decree. The *Swift* opinion rejected a plea by major meat packers that a 1920 Sherman Act consent decree be modified to readmit them to the businesses of meat retailing, stockyard operation, grocery manufacturing, and milk distribution. While the Court did not doubt "the power of a court of equity to modify an injunction in adaptation to changed conditions, though it was entered by consent," it found the packers' powerful economic position had not changed enough to warrant modification of the decree (391 U.S. 244 (1968)).

If the Government can prove its allegations that United Shoe still dominates its market and that "workable competition" has not been restored by the decree, "the present case is the obverse of the situation in Swift." Even if the district court had omitted from its decree the provision for a later report and petition for modification, Justice Fortas declared, it would still have been the court's duty to modify the decree on a showing that it had not achieved adequate relief. "The duty of the court to modify the decree so as to assure the complete extirpation of the illegal monopoly . . . is implicit in the findings of violation of Section 2 and in the decisions of this Court as to the type of remedy which must be prescribed."

Although Justice Fortas stressed the necessity of writing a decree that will both terminate the illegal monopoly and deny to the defendants the fruits of the violation and insure that there remain no practices likely to result in future monopolization, divestiture may not be required in every monopolization case. The district judge "may, if circumstances warrant, accept a formula for achieving the result by means less drastic than immediate dissolution or divestiture."

In neither *Grinnell* nor *United Shoe Machinery* did the Supreme Court dictate the terms of the decree to be issued; the Court left the details and precise scope to the district judge, directing "reconsideration" of certain government requests that appear to have been rejected for invalid reasons and taking pains to merely "suggest" an additional injunctive term. The Supreme Court appears to have wavered in the deference it has shown the district court's choice of remedies. In some Sherman Act decisions, the Court has stressed that "the fashioning of a decree in an antitrust case in such way as to prevent future violations and eradicate existing evils is a matter which rests largely in the discretion of the court" *(Associated Press* v. *United States,* 326 U.S. 1, 22 (1945). See also *International Salt Co.* v. *U.S.,* 332 U.S. 392, 400–401 (1947); *U.S.* v. *duPont,* 353 U.S. 586, 607–608 (1957)). In others, though, the Court simply ordered modification of district court judgments without discussing the weight to be assigned the trial judge's selection of the form of relief—action that was criticized in the dissenting opinion of Justice Frankfurter in the *Paramount* case. See also *Standard Oil Co.* v. *U.S.,* 221 U.S. 1 (1911); *U.S.* v. *American Tobacco Co.,* 221 U.S. 106 (1911); *Timken Roller Bearing Co.* v. *U.S.,* 341 U.S. 593 (1951); *Hartford-Empire Co.* v. *U.S.,* 323 U.S. 386 (1945).

In *U.S.* v. *U.S. Gypsum Co.,* 340 U.S. 76, 89 (1950), after citing the statement quoted above from the *Associated Press* case, the Court said: "We have never treated that power as one of discretion, subject only to reversal for gross abuse. Rather we have felt an obligation to intervene in this most significant phase of the case when we concluded there were inappropriate provisions in the decree." In its later opinion on relief in *U.S.* v. *E. I. duPont De Nemours & Co.,* 366 U.S. 316, 323 (1961), the Court said: "In sum, we assign to the district courts the responsibility *initially* to fashion the remedy, but recognize that while we accord due regard and respect to the conclusion of the district court, we have a duty ourselves to be sure that a decree is fashioned which will effectively redress proved violations of the antitrust laws." (Emphasis in original.) This time the Court gave a reason for assigning the district court's remedial rulings less weight in antitrust cases than in other litigation. "Our practice reflects the situation created by the congressional authorization, under Section 2 of the Expediting Act, of a direct appeal to this Court from the judgment of relief fashioned by a single judge. Congress has deliberately taken away the shield of intermediate appellate review by a Court of Appeals, and left with us alone the responsibility of affording the parties a review of his determination. This circumstance imposes a special burden upon us, for, as Mr. Justice Roberts said for the Court, '. . . it is unthinkable that Congress has entrusted the enforcement of a statute of such far-reaching importance to the judgment of a single judge, without review of the relief granted or denied by him,' *Hartford-Empire Co.* v. *United States,* 324 U.S. 570, 571 (1945)."

Regardless of the words the Supreme Court uses to define the scope of its review of the relief granted in Sherman Act cases, it is clear that the district courts have had, and probably will continue to have, an important voice in framing decrees. Although the decrees in significant cases are generally challenged on appeal by one side or the other, appeals as a rule attack only some parts of the relief awarded. It has been the district judges who, with the benefit of knowledge gained through the "painstaking process of adjudication" Justice Frankfurter referred to in the *Paramount* case, have developed such ingenious remedies as compulsory licensing of patents. Even divestiture is a remedy that originated in the district courts (*Standard Oil Co.* v. *U.S.,* 221 U.S. 1, 78 (1911)).

The emphasis the Supreme Court has repeatedly placed on divestiture or dissolution suggests to some antitrust experts that a decree like Judge Wyzanski's in *United Shoe Machinery* should be regarded as establishing, not a 10-year set of curbs on the defendant's commercial practices, but a 10-year moratorium on divestiture, while less drastic remedies are tested—i.e., while the defendant is given an opportunity to restore competitive conditions without drastic intervention by the court. That view of the decree is supported by the observation in the Supreme Court's opinion that the district court's reservation of jurisdiction was immaterial—that the district judge would have been bound to modify the decree in any event if 10 year's experience showed it had not achieved adequate relief.

While the Sherman Act does not add anything to the traditional remedial powers of a court of equity, some lawyers maintain that the courts can properly be regarded as having broader injunctive powers in Sherman Act cases than in other equity proceedings. They point out that Congress took unusual action when, having already made the Sherman Act a criminal law, it added enforcement powers based on the broad authority of a court of equity. Congress went even further to stress its reliance on antitrust injunctions when, in Section 6(c) of the FTC Act, it assigned the Federal Trade Commission responsibility to investigate compliance with decrees and report its findings to the Attorney General. And Section 7 suggests that the Commission be used "as a master in chancery, to ascertain and report an appropriate form of decree" in suits brought by the Justice Department.

The *United Shoe Machinery* opinion was read in some circles as contributing an important new weapon to the arsenal of the antitrust enforcement agencies. According to *Business Week,* May 25, 1968, the Justice Department acquired "a hefty fist," for it can now go back to court for additional relief in "a previously settled monopoly case." Some antitrust lawyers see, in Justice Fortas' discussion of the *Swift* case, a significant failure to distinguish between orders entered by consent and those entered after full litigation. He described *Swift* as teaching "that a decree may be changed upon an appropriate showing." While the absence of a record, of findings of fact, or even of an adjudication that a violation occurred would seem to be an insurmountable barrier to enlargement of a consent decree in the way Judge Wyzanski was asked to modify the *United Shoe Machinery* judgment, this is not the first time the Supreme Court has lumped consent judgments with litigated judgments in discussing subsequent modification. In *Swift* the Court said: "The result is all one whether the decree has been entered after litigation or by consent. *American Press Ass'n* v. *United States,* 245 F. 91. In either event, a court does not abdicate its power to revoke or modify its mandate, if satisfied that what it has been doing has been turned through changing circumstances into an instrument of wrong. We reject the argument for the intervenors that a decree entered upon consent is to be treated as a contract and not as a judicial act." (But see section VI-B-2, p. 458.)

4. Agreements Not to Compete

Question: *Do the antitrust laws allow an agreement between the seller of a business and the buyer to the effect that the seller will not compete with the buyer?*

The head of the Antitrust Division once expressed concern about the practice of "taking an overbroad covenant not to compete in connection with the purchase of a competitor" (Address of Assistant Attorney General William H. Orrick, Jr., January 27, 1965, before the New York Bar Association's Antitrust Section). Recognizing that this area of business activity "heretofore has been . . . largely relegated to a subdivision of the laws of the several states on unfair competition," he expressed the view that "in particular contexts an overbroad covenant not to compete can itself rise to the dignity of an antitrust violation, and certainly may be an anticompetitive effect on which a Section 7 or Section 2 case might turn."

Under the "subdivision" of the common law referred to by Mr. Orrick, anticompetitive restrictions ancillary to sale of a business are regarded as lawful if (1) necessary to secure to the purchaser of the business the full benefits of the transaction and (2) no more comprehensive than necessary with regard to the time and geographical area covered by the restriction (Restatement of Contracts, Sections 514–518). A general commitment by the seller not to compete with his buyer is regarded as contrary to public policy and therefore unenforceable. A covenant not to compete for a limited number of years or within a particular market or area is generally deemed reasonable and enforceable.

With the development of faster communication and transportation, the tendency has been to allow agreements not to compete to cover a broader area, but apparently there has been no similar extension of the time such a covenant may cover. A number of states, including California, Oklahoma, and the Dakotas, have enacted statutes specifying the permissible duration of a covenant not to compete. Elsewhere, many of the courts apply, as a rule of thumb, a three-year maximum.

In establishing common-law rules, the state courts were dealing with the enforceability of the covenants between the parties to them, rather than with the applicability of the antitrust laws, but under the Sherman Act basically the same reasoning has been applied. In *U.S.* v. *Addyston Pipe and Steel Co.*, 85 F. 271 (6th Cir. 1898), the court distinguished between naked covenants not to compete, which are per se Sherman Act violations, and covenants that are "merely ancillary to the main purpose of a lawful contract, and necessary to protect the covenantee in the employment of the legitimate fruits of the contract, or to protect him from the dangers of an unjust use of those fruits by the other party." If the ancillary covenant is to survive attack under the antitrust laws, the court said "the contract must be one in which there is a main purpose, to which the covenant in restraint of trade is merely ancillary. . . . If the restraint exceeds the necessity presented by the main purpose of the contract, it is void for two reasons: First, because it oppresses the covenantor, without any corresponding benefit to the covenantee; and second, because it tends to monopoly."

In its few decisions applying Sections 1 and 2 of the Sherman Act to covenants not to compete, the Supreme Court has also applied substantially the same rules as prevailed at common law. In *Cincinnati, P.B.S. & P. Packet Co.* v. *Bay*, 200 U.S. 179 (1906), the Court found no Section 1 violation in an agreement by the seller of river-transportation equipment that for five years he would not operate competing freight and passenger packets over the buyer's stretch of the Ohio.

The Supreme Court has found a Sherman Act violation in a covenant not to compete because it was one of a series of covenants obtained in business acquisitions and was part of a larger monopolization program (*Schine Chain Theatres* v. *U.S.,* 334 U.S. 110 (1948); *U.S.* v. *Crescent Amusement Co.,* 323 U.S. 173, 181 (1944); *U.S.* v. *American Tobacco Co.,* 221 U.S. 106, 174 (1911); *Shawnee Compress Co.* v. *Anderson,* 209 U.S. 423 (1908)).

Covenants not to compete can be ancillary to many types of agreements other than the sale of a business. The inclusion of such covenants in employment contracts is not unusual when the employee is to be given special training or trade secrets that would make it possible for him to go into business on his own. Such covenants are often required of franchised dealers or distributors, a practice the Federal Trade Commission prohibited in *Snap-On Tools Corp.,* 59 F.T.C. 1035 (1961), as "an integral part" of an illegal scheme to maintain prices and exclusive territories, but the Commission was reversed (*Snap-On Tools* v. *FTC,* 321 F.2d 825 (7th Cir. 1963)). The covenants may be for the term of the franchise ("in-term") or beyond it ("post-term"). The former may be more likely to be upheld. See *McDonald's System, Inc.* v. *Sandy's Inc.,* 45 Ill. App. 2d 57, 195 N.W. 2d·22 (1963) (in-term covenant upheld); *Pelton's Spudnuts, Inc.* v. *Doane,* 234 P.2d 852 (Sup. Ct. of Utah, 1967); *Shakey's Inc.* v. *Martin,* 430 P. 2d 504 (Sup. Ct. of Idaho, 1967).

A covenant can be given with the sale or lease of business property or equipment, as opposed to the sale of a going business with its good will. Shopping-center developers often give their tenants covenants that space will not be leased to competing merchants. See, for example, *Savon Gas Stations* v. *Shell Oil Co.,* 309 F.2d 306 (4th Cir. 1962). An analogous situation was dealt with in *National Cold Storage Co.* v. *Port of New York Authority,* 286 F.Supp. 1016 (S.D.N.Y. 1968). See also *Dalmo Sales Co.* v. *Tysons Corner Regional Shopping Center,* 308 F.Supp. 988 (D.D.C. 1970), *aff'd* 429 F.2d 206 (D.C. Cir. 1970) and FTC complaint in *Tysons Corner Regional Shopping Center,* D. 8886; *U.S.* v. *Wachovia Bank & Trust Co.,* 1972 Trade Cas. ¶74,109 (M.D.N.C. 1972).

In his address, *supra,* Mr. Orrick spoke of "an overbroad covenant not to compete in connection with the purchase of a competitor" —a type of covenant the Antitrust Division has met in some suits to terminate violations of the antimerger provisions in Section 7 of the Clayton Act. In *U.S.* v. *Hertz Corp.,* 1960 Trade Cas. ¶69,762 (S.D.N.Y. 1960), for example, the court directed Hertz to dispose of some of the car-leasing enterprises it had acquired and to refrain from such acquisitions in the future. The decree also limited Hertz's freedom to enter into and to enforce covenants not to compete. Hertz was forbidden to make any such covenant that covered a period of more than one year, unless the Justice Department consented to the acceptance of a covenant for a longer period in a specific instance. The complaint and judgment in that case were based entirely upon Section 7 of the Clayton Act and did not challenge the legality of any of Hertz's "noncompetition covenants" in and of themselves. In *U.S.* v. *Lima News,* Civil No. 64–178, complaint, (N.D. Ohio, November 19, 1964), a sale of a newspaper publishing business to the LIMA NEWS, together with an ancillary covenant of the seller not to engage in the newspaper-publication business for five years anywhere within 60 miles of a LIMA NEWS operation, was attacked under Sections 1 and 2 of the Sherman Act, as well as Section 7 of the Clayton Act. In addition, the complaint alleged that the covenant not to compete "is a contract in unreasonable restraint of trade in violation of Section 1 of the Sherman Act." A contract with another publisher that he would receive monthly payments for five years in return for a commitment not to publish in the markets occupied by LIMA NEWS was alleged to be a Section 1 violation. A consent judgment prohibited the challenged practices (1965 Trade Cas. ¶71,609 (N.D. Ohio 1965)).

It has been suggested that the impact of agreements not to compete is greatest in industries that are particularly dependent upon the supply of trained personnel for management. This is especially so of personal-service industries, where a small equipment plant outlay may be required to invade a new market or geographical area. Yet the invader is often bought out at a figure greatly in excess of the value of the assets involved and in return gives a commitment not to compete further in that territory. A similar situation can arise in a small, highly specialized industry that depends largely upon know-how and customer contacts. When one company buys the assets of a competitor, the buyer may have little intention of utilizing them but be primarily interested in a long-term covenant not to compete. Sometimes the acquiring and the acquired company are the only two competitors in a local market, so that the survivor achieves a monopoly through its acquisition.

In these situations, the Justice Department could take the position that the covenant not to compete represents the principal motivation for the transaction and therefore cannot be considered "ancillary to the main purpose of a lawful contract" within the meaning of the doctrine of the *Addyston Pipe & Steel* case. When it is clear that a covenant not to compete is ancillary to a lawful contract, there is little federal precedent for determining the "reasonableness" of time or geographical limitations. Cases like *Schine, Crescent*

Amusement, American Tobacco, and *Shawnee* are not much help, since the covenants involved there were found to be ancillary to illegal arrangements aimed at monopolization and market control.

Both the Justice Department and the FTC have approved specific covenants not to compete given in connection with the disposition of a corporation pursuant to a Section 7 Clayton Act divestiture order. Sometimes the Antitrust Division has agreed to consent judgments that spell out the permissible boundaries of covenants not to compete taken with purchases of other businesses. In the *Hertz* case, the time limit placed on such covenants was one year, and the geographical limit was expressed in terms of "leasing passenger automobiles . . . to customers of such acquired business." In *U.S.* v. *Philadelphia Association of Linen Suppliers,* Civil Action No. 35–168, consent decree (E.D. Pa. February 26, 1964), the covenant could extend for five years if limited to "the area of the business so sold" and for ten years if limited to catering to or soliciting the customers of the acquired business. Apparently the appropriate limitations will vary with the particular facts of each case.

5. Group Choice of Supplier

Question: *If several competitors agree to buy exclusively from a single supplier, have they violated the Sherman Act?*

Four of Philadelphia's largest department stores had been using a consolidated package-delivery service furnished by a single company. They found a consolidated delivery service to be the most efficient and economical method of delivering packages because such delivery service allowed a greater concentration of deliveries to any given area of the city. When labor difficulties stopped the delivery company's operations in April 1967, the department stores were forced to make other arrangements with independent delivery services. Eventually two of them worked out arrangements with one delivery service, and the other two with a second delivery service.

In December 1967, one of the delivery firms informed its two clients that, once the Christmas rush had passed, it would be unable to maintain efficient service at existing contract rates. The four stores then invited the two carriers to compete for a consolidated package service. The carriers were asked to present their respective capabilities and contract rates at a meeting of representatives from all four stores. After that meeting, the two largest stores chose one of the carriers and then tried to persuade representatives of the other two stores to use the same carrier, arguing that it was financially more stable and had better labor relations. A third store, having been influenced by the action of the first two, went along with their choice. Soon thereafter at a meeting of representatives of all four stores, the fourth store joined.

The second delivery service that had been doing business with two of the stores sued all four stores and their chosen delivery service for treble damages and an injunction, charging a concerted refusal to deal. The district court denied the complaining carrier's motion for a preliminary injunction (*Instant Delivery Corp.* v. *City Stores Co.,* 284 F.Supp. 941 (E.D. Pa. 1968)).

The district court did not deny the existence of an agreement among the four department stores but stated: "Their agreement was limited to the reestablishment of a consolidated delivery service with which they had earlier enjoyed a long and satisfactory experience, and to the selection of one of two competing carriers to perform that service." The complaining carrier "is a disappointed competitor, not the object of an illegal boycott."

Cases like *Klor's, Inc.* v. *Broadway-Hale Stores,* 359 U.S. 207 (1959), holding that group boycotts or concerted refusals to deal are per se violations of Section 1 of the Sherman Act, were distinguished by the court. In each of those cases, it was noted, the aim and purpose of the refusal to deal was either to force a change in the boycotted firm's trade practices or to exclude it from competition. Here, there was said to be no intent to discriminate against or exclude the complaining carrier. The complaining carrier "was invited to compete, and did so vigorously, for selection as the carrier to perform the consolidated delivery. . . . The decision that each of the stores made was to select [the successful carrier], not to exclude [the complaining carrier]." Exclusion of the complaining carrier was a mere "by-product of the decision to reinstitute consolidated delivery which necessarily involves the use of one carrier."

In its refusal to find a boycott in violation of the Sherman Act, the court relied on two precedents: *Interborough News Co.* v. *Curtis Publishing Co.,* 225 F.2d 289 (2nd Cir. 1955), and *Parmelee Transportation Co.* v. *Keeshin,* 186 F.Supp. 533 (N.D. Ill. 1960), *aff'd,* 292 F.2d 794 (7th Cir. 1961), *cert. denied,* 368 U.S. 944 (1961). In the *Interborough News* case magazine publishers were charged with combining to eliminate one wholesaler in favor of several new wholesalers. The trial judge found there had been no combination or conspiracy between any of the defendants. It apparently was not disputed that one of the publishers had initiated dealings with the new wholesalers and had then sent other publishers communications stressing the advantages of doing business with the new wholesalers. In the words of the court of appeals, that publisher "had a legal right to break away from a wholesaler whose service it considered unsatisfactory and to set up and encourage by subsidy new competing wholesalers; and there is no reason apparent to us why [the publisher] should not use every reasonable effort to influence and persuade other national distributors to patronize the new competing wholesalers." The court of appeals stressed a finding that "each defendant independently negotiated its agreements with its respective wholesalers."

The *Parmelee* opinion sustained the joint selection of an interterminal transfer service by a group of railroads using the terminals. Both the district court and court of appeals opinions stressed that in *Chicago* v. *Atchison T. & S.F. Ry. Co.,* 357 U.S. 77 (1958), the Supreme Court recognized the right of railroads under the Interstate Commerce Act to act as a group in selecting a transfer operator to provide interstation service.

Having put aside the rule of per se illegality in the *Instant Delivery* case, the Philadelphia Federal District Court announced that the question of whether consolidated delivery constitutes an unreasonable restraint of trade "can only be resolved at the trial . . . , after the parties have had an opportunity to develop fully the factual setting out of which consolidated delivery emerged." In view of the greater efficiencies made possible by a consolidated delivery service and in view of the widespread use of consolidated delivery by retail business establishments, the court did not feel that the complaining carrier had demonstrated a substantial probability that it would ultimately prevail on the issue of reasonableness. On appeal to the Court of Appeals for the Third Circuit, the complaining carrier's brief pressed the theory of per se illegality, but the case was settled prior to argument.

Some of the accepted principles of antitrust law can be put together to support a conclusion that an agreement by several competitors to buy exclusively from a single supplier—either a product or, as in *Instant Delivery,* a service—is a per se Section 1 Sherman Act violation. Business enterprises are as obligated to compete when they do their buying as when they do their selling (*Los Angeles Meat & Provision Drivers Union* v. *U.S.,* 371 U.S. 94 (1962); *Union Carbide & Carbon Corp.* v. *Nisley,* 300 F.2d 561 (10th Cir. 1962)). Competing sellers cannot lawfully combine in their decisions as to whom they will accept as customers (*U.S.* v. *General Motors Corp.,* 384 U.S. 127 (1966)).

An agreement by a single buyer to buy exclusively from one seller may violate Section 1 of the Sherman Act and Section 3 of the Clayton Act if shown to be anticompetitive (*Standard Fashion Co.* v. *Magrane-Houston Co.,* 258 U.S. 346 (1922)). When several enterprises combine in such an arrangement, the risk of monopolization or restraint of trade, it is arguable, may be great enough to make make unnecessary any inquiry as to anticompetitive effect. "An act harmless when done by one may become a public wrong when done by many acting in concert" (*Eastern States Retail Lumber Dealers Assn.* v. *U.S.*, 234 U.S. 600, 614 (1914)).

Use of common buying agencies by groups of competitors has been held lawful (*Arkansas Brokerage Co.* v. *Dunn & Powell*, 173 F. 899 (8th Cir. 1909); *Associated Greeting Card Distributors of America*, 50 F.T.C. 631 (1954)). In neither of those cases, however, was the buying agency restricted to dealing with a single source of supply. Nor was there an agreement among the competing buyers that they would rely exclusively on the common buying agency. In the *Arkansas Brokerage* case, each member of the parent group, acting on his own, did refuse to buy from any other firm unless it would match the price available through the common buying agency.

Application of a rule of per se illegality to the concerted choice of an exclusive supplier by four of the largest enterprises in a market may not mean that every group selection of an exclusive supplier is a Sherman Act violation. As stated by the Supreme Court, a "per se" rule is merely a "principle of per se unreasonableness" designed to bypass "incredibly complicated and prolonged economic investigation . . . to determine at large whether a particular restraint has been unreasonable" (*Northern Pacific R. Co.* v. *U.S.*, 356 U.S. 1, 5 (1958)). (In *Northern Pacific* "tying agreements" were held unreasonable per se only when the seller has control or dominance over the tying product and a "not insubstantial" amount of commerce is affected by his tying practice.)

What if the *Instant Delivery* case had gone to trial and the four department stores had been able to prove (1) that it is not economically feasible for them to supply delivery service for their customers unless they choose a single supplier and (2) that they made their choice after giving every available carrier a full and fair opportunity to compete for their contract? Some antitrust experts believe these two factors would take this concerted choice of a supplier outside the category of per se violations. They feel addition of these two factors would create the type of situation former Federal Trade Commissioner Philip Elman had in mind when he said: "A realistic analysis of competitive practices is necessary, therefore, not only when the question is whether the practice is illegal under the rule of reason, but equally (if not more so) when the question is whether one of the existing per se categories should be extended to embrace the practice. The categories are not self-defining; their bounds cannot be ascertained by reference to the semantic overtones of the verbal formula in which the rule is capsuled. To fix the rule's outer limits requires, above all, attention to its underlying rationale, which may be far narrower than the form of words in which the rule is expressed, and an understanding of the factual situation to which the rule is sought to be applied" (Elman, "Petrified Opinions and Competitive Realities," 66 COLUM. L. REV. 625, 626–27 (1966)).

Should one consider the effect of a consolidated delivery service upon only the market in buying and selling delivery services? Visible in that market are important consumer benefits that might outweigh the benefits of insisting on continuing competition among several delivery companies. But what about the effect of these economies on competition among retail stores? Are four of the largest department stores in a metropolitan market to be permitted to join forces in order to offer a service their competitors cannot match? The cases have not yet answered these questions.

6. Attempts and Conspiracies to Monopolize

Question: *Is evidence defining a relevant market essential to proof of an attempt or conspiracy to monopolize?*

Section 2 of the Sherman Act defines not one but three crimes, as the Supreme Court pointed out in *American Tobacco Co.* v. *U.S.,* 328 U.S. 781 (1946). It provides penalties for every person "who shall (1) monopolize, or (2) attempt to monopolize, or (3) combine or conspire with any other person or persons, to monopolize any part of the trade or commerce among the several States."

In *U.S.* v. *duPont,* 351 U.S. 377 (1956), a monopolization injunction suit in which it was held that the Government had to prove monopoly power over a broad "flexible packaging materials" market, the Supreme Court distinguished cases using narrower markets by noting that they involved charges of mere attempts to monopolize. Prior to heading the Antitrust Division, Donald F. Turner, in an article entitled "Antitrust Policy and the Cellophane Case," 70 HARV. L. REV. 281 (1956), commented: "As for definitions of market in attempt and conspiracy cases, there was good reason to conclude that Yellow Cab [332 U.S. 218 (1947)] and Columbia Steel [334 U.S. 495 (1948)] virtually eliminated the question altogether. 'Any part' [in Section 2 of the Sherman Act] meant not a properly defined market in the economic sense, but merely a substantial amount of commerce. Specific intent, as shown by coercive conduct or absence of 'normal business purpose,' apparently became a complete offense in itself, providing only that a substantial amount of commerce was affected."

In two federal district court opinions, Mr. Turner's thesis has been rejected. In *U.S.* v. *Johns-Manville Corp.,* 231 F.Supp. 690 (E.D. Pa. 1964), a district court held that proof of relevant market is indispensable in a criminal case charging a conspiracy to monopolize. The indictment alleged a conspiracy to monopolize trade in asbestos-cement pipe, but the court had evidence that the defendants' primary competitors were sellers of metal pipe. In support of its decision, the district court cited the 1955 Report of the Attorney General's National Committee to Study the Antitrust Laws (p. 47). According to the report, the concept of "the market" is not brought into the antitrust laws by the words "any part" in Section 2. Rather, the report asserts, "it is integral to the basic concept of 'monopolization' and the ideas of competition and monopoly on which it rests. Thus, Section 2 of the Sherman Act deals with monopolizations affecting markets which constitute 'any part' of the trade or commerce covered by the Act. . . . Without a finding as to the market involved, there is no way of determining whether or not the defendants have a given degree of market power."

In a suit charging an attempt to monopolize the citric acid market (*U.S.* v. *Chas. Pfizer & Co.,* 245 F.Supp. 737 (E.D.N.Y. 1965)), the district court saw no basis in the *Yellow Cab* or *Columbia Steel* opinions for Mr. Turner's proposition. The district judge found that proof of relevant market had been required in *American Football League* v. *National Football League,* 205 F.Supp. 60 (D. Md. 1962), *aff'd,* 323 F.2d 124 (4th Cir. 1963), an attempt-to-monopolize case.

The Government relied on *Lessig* v. *Tidewater Oil Co.,* 327 F.2d 459 (9th Cir. 1964), for the proposition that it is enough to prove an attempt to monopolize the manufacture and sale of citric acid—"any part of trade or commerce"—and a specific intent to monopolize that part of trade or commerce, but the district court regarded it as more significant that no case decided by the Court of Appeals for the Second Circuit had approved the principle stated in the *Lessig* case. In *U.S.* v. *Consolidated Laundries Corp.,* 291 F.2d 563, 573 (1961), the Second Circuit did indicate that relevant-market evidence is not essential in a conspiracy-to-monopolize case, citing Professor Turner's paper, but an attempt to monopolize and a conspiracy to monopolize were regarded as different. In *Bushie* v. *Stenocord Corp.,* 1972 Trade Cas. ¶73,896 (9th Cir. 1972), the contention that in attempted monopoly cases intent is the sole essential element was rejected.

The Justice Department filed a notice of appeal in the *Pfizer* case, and its time for docketing that appeal in the Supreme Court was later extended, but no appeal was ever filed.

In *Walker Process Equipment, Inc.* v. *Food Machinery and Chemical Corp.,* 382 U.S. 172 (1965), the Supreme Court said: "To establish monopolization or attempt to monopolize a part of trade or commerce under Section 2 of the Sherman Act, it would then be necessary to appraise the exclusionary power . . . in terms of the relevant market for the product involved. Without a definition of

that market there is no way to measure . . . ability to lessen or destroy competition. It may be that the device . . . does not comprise
a relevant market. There may be effective substitutes." The Court's
reference to "attempt to monopolize" was gratuitous, for the treble-
damage counterclaim reinstated by the decision did not allege a
mere attempt. It charged a patent owner with actual monopolization through enforcement of a fraudulently procured patent. See also
Panotex Pipeline Co. v. *Phillips Petroleum Co.*, 457 F.2d 1279 (1972),
cert. denied, 409 U.S. 845 (1972); *Kearney & Trecker Corp.* v. *Giddings & Lewis, Inc.*, 452 F.2d 579 (7th Cir. 1971); *Radzick* v. *Chicago-
land R.V. Dealers Ass'n,* 1972 Trade Cas. ¶74,167 (N.D. Ill. 1972).

As it developed in the criminal law, the concept of an attempt
to commit a crime has embodied the thought that, if the attempt
is to be punished, the result intended must constitute a crime.
Logically, a business enterprise that attempts to monopolize must
intend to monopolize something. Unless the defendant has in mind
an objective constituting the offense of monopolization, there is no
"dangerous probability" of occurrence of the substantive offense
(*Swift & Co.* v. *U.S.,* 196 U.S. 375 (1905)). In a prosecution for attempt the defendant's intent is always crucial, and in Section 2
cases apparently a "relevant market" is an indispensable element
of intent.

Every court that has found a violation of the attempt provision
in Section 2 of the Sherman Act has undoubtedly had in mind a
"something" or a "relevant market" the defendant intended to
monopolize, even if that market was never explicitly defined. The
ostensible dispute in cases like *Pfizer* over whether the Government
must prove relevant market might be more accurately termed a
division over how broad the "market" must be if the defendant's
attempt to control it is to be regarded as a Section 2 violation. The
Government argued that the production and sale of citric acid
alone constitute a "part" of commerce that can be monopolized and
that the Government had already presented ample evidence of
relevant market in its evidence that Pfizer controlled the production
and sale of citric acid. The district judge, thinking more like the
Attorney General's Committee, could not visualize a "monopoly"
that has competition—competition from producers of other acids.
The courts have tended to let the scope of the market vary in inverse proportion to the evil they have seen in the defendant's intent. For example, "a specific intention to exclude competitors and
to control prices" once led the Federal District Court for Southern
New York to adopt a market definition limited to the defendants'
own trademarked line of perfumes and toilet water (*U.S.* v. *Guer-
lain,* 155 F.Supp. 77 (1957), *probable jurisdiction noted,* 355 U.S.
937 (1958)). Later, the Justice Department submitted to a Supreme

Court order (358 U.S. 915 (1958)) vacating the district court judgment and dropped the suit for the stated purposes of seeking legislative resolution of an "intra-government conflict" over interpretation of a Tariff Act provision asserted as a defense in the district court.

If a sufficiently evil intent can be shown—to destroy or exclude a competitor, control prices, or coerce customers or suppliers—the Court might not look for any relevant market beyond the product immediately involved. The *Walker Process* dictum is not necessarily to the contrary, for the intent alleged in that case was to get a patent by fraud.

Anticompetitive attempts falling short of Section 2 violations might be proceeded against by the FTC as violations of the unfair-methods-of-competition ban in Section 5 of the FTC Act. In such a proceeding, the Commission's staff might not be required to show an attempt to control a broad market including substitute products.

7. "Bathtub" Conspiracies

Question: *Can a corporation's dealings with its subsidiaries or divisions subject it to antitrust liability?*

In contrast with Section 2, which makes monopolization an offense even when it is the act of a single person, Section 1 of the Sherman Act does not forbid a single person to impose a restraint on trade. The proscription in Section 1 against "every contract, combination . . . or conspiracy, in restraint of trade" presupposes the existence of two or more contracting, combining, or conspiring parties. In Section 1 cases involving corporations, (and their officials, their agents, their divisions, and their subsidiaries), the courts have been troubled by difficulties in ascertaining who and what are separate parties capable of contracting or conspiring with each other.

Employees of a single corporation have been convicted under indictments including Section 2 charges (*Patterson* v. *U.S.*, 222 F. 599 (6th Cir. 1915); *White Bear Theatre Corp.* v. *State Theatre Corp.*, 129 F.2d 600 (8th Cir. 1942)), but it has been held that a Section 1 charge, standing alone, cannot be sustained by proving joint action on the part of only a corporation and officers acting on its behalf (*Nelson Radio & Supply Co.* v. *Motorola*, 200 F.2d 911 (5th Cir. 1952); *Marion County Co-Op Assn.* v. *Carnation Co.*, 114 F.Supp. 58 (W.D. Ark. 1953)) on the theory that a corporation cannot conspire with itself any more than a private individual can, and it is the general rule that the acts of the agent are the acts of the corporation.

To be considered incapable of forming a Section 1 conspiracy with his corporation, an individual must be completely free of any separable personal interest in the outcome of the activity attacked (*Poller* v. *CBS,* 368 U.S. 464, 489 (1962)). Individuals cannot insulate a conspiracy from the Sherman Act by organizing a corporation as the instrumentality for carrying out their purpose (*Bascom Launder Corp.* v. *Farny,* 15 F.R.D. 277 (S.D.N.Y. 1950); *Beacon Fruit & Produce Co.* v. *H. Harris & Co.* 152 F.Supp. 702 (D. Mass. 1957)). "Any affiliation or integration flowing from an illegal conspiracy cannot insulate the conspirators from the sanctions which Congress has imposed" (*U.S.* v. *Yellow Cab Co.,* 332 U.S. 218 (1947)).

When a single business enterprise includes a complex of related corporate entities or when several incorporated businesses are operated and controlled by the same ownership, the courts have decided that the separate corporate entities are capable of making a Section 1 conspiracy with each other. The *Yellow Cab* case involved six corporations controlled by a single majority stockholder. In the Supreme Court's view, "an unreasonable restraint of interstate commerce . . . may result as readily from a conspiracy among those who are affiliated or integrated under common ownership as from a conspiracy among those who are otherwise independent. . . . The corporate inter-relationships of the conspirators, in other words, are not determinative of the applicability of the Sherman Act." In *U.S.* v. *Timken Roller Bearing Co.,* 83 F.Supp. 284 (N.D. Ohio 1949), *modified and aff'd,* 341 U.S. 593 (1951), corporations affiliated through controlling stockholdings were held to have conspired with each other in violation of Section 1.

When the Attorney General's Committee reviewed the *Yellow Cab* and *Timken* decisions in 1955, it concluded that they applied Section 1 to combinations and conspiracies among commonly owned or controlled corporations only when their purpose or effect is "coercion or unreasonable restraint on the trade of strangers to those acting in concert. . . . Where such concerted action restrains no trade and is designed to restrain no trade other than that of the parent and its subsidiaries, Section 1 is not violated" (Report of the Attorney General's National Committee to Study the Antitrust Laws, 1955, pp. 30–36).

A parent corporation's determination or approval of the prices to be charged by a subsidiary has been held not to be illegal price fixing (*U.S.* v. *Arkansas Fuel Oil Corp.,* 1960 Trade Cas. ¶69,619 (N.D. Okla. 1960)). Intra-enterprise conspiracy claims have been rejected when the existence of separate corporations has no real economic or competitive significance (*Syracuse Broadcasting Corp.* v. *Newhouse,* 319 F.2d 683 (2d Cir. 1963); *Sunkist Growers, Inc.* v.

Winckler & Smith Citrus Products Co., 370 U.S. 19 (1962)). On the other hand, a parent corporation's directions to its subsidiary may create a Sherman Act conspiracy when the directions require the subsidiary to interfere with competition from the parent's rival (*Aerojet-General Corp.* v. *Aero-Jet Products Corp.* 235 F.Supp. 341 (N.D. Ohio 1964)). See also *Perma Life Mufflers, Inc.* v. *Internat'l Parts Corp.,* 392 U.S. 134 (1968) and *Fortner Enterprises* v. *U.S. Steel,* 394 U.S. 495 (1969). Justice Department views were stated in a letter of February 22, 1971, to the Federal Reserve Board (516 ATRR D-1 (6/8/71)).

Some members of the Attorney General's Committee felt that there are no circumstances under which a parent and its separately incorporated subsidiary should be held guilty "of an offense that must be committed by more than one person." Everyone agreed that "there would concededly be no liability under Section 1, if a company does business through unincorporated branches, divisions or departments." The Committee's statement about unincorporated branches or divisions is supported by subsequent opinions on the capacity of unincorporated divisions to join with the parent corporation in a Section 1 conspiracy (*Poller* v. *CBS,* 284 F.2d 599 (D.C. Cir. 1960); *Deterjet Corp.* v. *United Aircraft,* 211 F.Supp. 348 (D. Del. 1962); *Kemwel Automotive Corp.* v. *Ford Motor Co.,* 1966 Trade Cas. ¶71,882 (S.D.N.Y. 1966); *Johnny Maddox Motor Co.* v. *Ford Motor Co.,* 202 F.Supp. 103 (W.D. Tex. 1960); *Nelson Radio & Supply Co.* v. *Motorola,* 200 F.2d 911 (5th Cir. 1952)). In the *Poller* case, a charge that CBS had conspired with one of its divisions was characterized by the court as "in reality a charge that CBS conspired with itself."

Each of the decisions upon corporation-division conspiracies was distinguished on its facts by the first recorded opinion dealing with charges of a horizontal Section 1 conspiracy among unincorporated divisions of a single corporation. In *Hawaiian Oke and Liquors, Ltd.* v. *Joseph E. Seagram and Sons, Inc.,* 272 F.Supp. 915 (D. Hawaii 1967), *rev'd,* 416 F.2d 71 (9th Cir. 1969), *cert. denied,* 396 U.S. 1062 (1970), District Judge Martin Pence instructed a jury that it could find a Section 1 Sherman Act violation in a conspiracy among Calvert Distilling Co., Four Roses Distilling Co., and Frankfort Distilling Co. to eliminate a wholesale distributor, even though each of these three companies was an unincorporated division of House of Seagram, Inc. Stressing the three divisions' use of separate and "pretty autonomous" sales organizations, Judge Pence saw a clear distinction between a "vertical" conspiracy involving a corporation and one of its divisions and a "horizontal" conspiracy among corporate divisions that otherwise act "entirely independently." In Seagram's setup, he emphasized, each division was responsible for establishing a distribution system for its brand of whisky—a responsibility that included the choice of one or more wholesale distributors for every geographical area. Seagram's conversion of Calvert, Four Roses, and Frankfort from incorporated subsidiaries into mere divisions came shortly after, and "apparently resulted from," the Supreme Court's decision in *Kiefer-Stewart Co.* v. *Seagram,* 340 U.S. 211 (1951). In refusing to attribute antitrust significance to the divisions' new "label," Judge Pence relied on the statement in *Simpson* v. *Union Oil Co.,* 377 U.S. 13 (1964), that "differences in form often do not represent 'differences in substance.'"

In reversing Judge Pence, the Court of Appeals for the Ninth Circuit concluded that Seagram's corporate divisions were not separate entities capable of conspiring with each other. The court found no evidence that the transformation was a sham. The court of appeals viewed the lower court's decision as an unnecessary interference with the need of today's corporations to divide themselves into departments or divisions and to delegate authority in order to function efficiently, without subjecting themselves to limitless antitrust liability.

The decisions applying Section 1 to "bathtub conspiracies" suggest that the courts tend to rely on that doctrine when they would otherwise be prevented from taking action against what they regard as a flagrant violation of the spirit of the Sherman Act. The use of separate and independent sales organizations, the use of apparently rival brands, and a previous record of antitrust litigation predicated on the existence of separately incorporated enterprises—where these elements are present, the "bathtub conspiracy" doctrine may yet have some life.

When subordinate branches or divisions—whether incorporated or unincorporated—are involved, the key may lie in the attitude shown toward the subordinate branches—whether they are treated, in the operation of their businesses, as separate enterprises. If, as Judge Pence thought was true in the Seagram organization, the separate divisions walk like competitors, talk like competitors, and look like competitors, some courts may be inclined to treat them as competitors forbidden to make agreements among themselves to limit competition.

8. Proof of Conspiracies Between Competitors

Question: *If competitors act alike and know it, are they violating the Sherman Act?*

The restraint-of-trade prohibition in Section 1 of the Sherman Act applies only to a "contract, combination in the form of trust or otherwise, or conspiracy" in restraint of trade. One of the major issues in Section 1 cases—particularly criminal prosecutions—has been the nature of evidence that will prove the existence of a "contract, combination . . . or conspiracy."

The Supreme Court dealt with the problem in *Eastern States Retail Lumber Dealers Ass'n.* v. *U.S.,* 234 U.S. 600 (1914). The Government's evidence established two facts. First, the association had systematically circulated among its members reports naming wholesale lumber dealers reported by association members to be selling directly to consumers. Second, upon receipt of these reports, a significant number of the members of the association had ceased doing business with the offending wholesalers. In holding the evidence sufficient to justify an inference of conspiracy, the Supreme Court said: "It is elementary . . . that conspiracies are seldom capable of proof by direct testimony and may be inferred from the things actually done, and when in this case by concerted action the names of wholesalers who were reported as having made sales to consumers were periodically reported to the other members of the association, the conspiracy to accomplish that which was the natural consequence of such action may be readily inferred."

In *Interstate Circuit, Inc.* v. *U.S.,* 306 U.S. 208 (1939), the Government's case consisted of evidence that a manager of a motion picture theater had sent to each of the defendant film distributors a letter listing the names of all his addressees and requesting the distributors to impose restrictions designed to help exhibitors maintain prices. The distributors later imposed the suggested restrictions. Although the evidence indicated that the exhibitors had never met with the distributors and the distributors had never discussed the matter with each other, the Supreme Court rejected a contention that there was no proof of an agreement among the distributors. "Acceptance by competitors, without previous agreement, of an invitation to participate in a plan, the necessary consequence of which, if carried out, is restraint of interstate commerce, is sufficient to establish an unlawful conspiracy under the Sherman Act." In *American Tobacco Co.* v. *U.S.,* 328 U.S. 781, 804–05 (1946), "circumstantial evidence of the existence of a conspiracy" was found in a simultaneous price increase by all three major cigarette producers at a time when sales were declining. Apparently there was no evidence of communication among the producers. In *FTC* v. *Cement Institute,* 333 U.S. 683 (1948), the Supreme Court sustained an FTC order under Section 5 of the FTC Act. The Commission's finding of conspiracy was based largely on industry-wide adoption and use of an identical basing-point pricing formula. Apparently on the basis of that case, the FTC in 1948 sent a notice to its staff announcing that mere "conscious parallelism of action" is an FTC Act violation.

Six years later, the Supreme Court rejected the notion that con-

scious parallelism alone can be considered a Sherman Act violation.
In *Theatre Enterprises, Inc.* v. *Paramount Film Distributing Corp.,*
346 U.S. 537 (1954), the Court said: "To be sure, business behavior
is admissible circumstantial evidence from which the fact finder
may infer agreement. . . . But this Court has never held that proof
of parallel business behavior conclusively establishes agreement or,
phrased differently, that such behavior itself constitutes a Sherman
Act offense. Circumstantial evidence of consciously parallel behavior
may have made heavy inroads into the traditional judicial attitude
toward conspiracy; but 'conscious parallelism' has not yet read
conspiracy out of the Sherman Act entirely."

The Attorney General's National Committee to Study the Antitrust Laws listed in its 1955 report (pp. 36, 39) some of the market
factors that may affect the weight to be given evidence of "conscious parallelism" as proof of the existence of an agreement
or conspiracy. "The significance of uniform action may depend, in
any one instance, on a variety of factors. How pervasive is the uniformity? Does it extend to price alone or to all other terms and
conditions of sale? How nearly identical is the uniformity? How
long has the uniformity continued? What is the time lag, if any, between a change by one competitor and that of the other or others?
Is the product involved homogeneous or differentiated? In the case
of price uniformity, have the defendants raised as well as lowered
prices in parallel fashion? Can the conduct, no matter how uniform,
be adequately explained by independent business justifications?
Upon the answers to questions like these depends the weight to be
accorded parallel action in any given case."

The question of the effect to be given evidence of "conscious
parallelism" came up in *Delaware Valley Marine Supply Co.* v.
American Tobacco Co., 297 F.2d 199 (3d Cir. 1961), a private treble-
damage action. The damage complaint alleged a conspiracy among
the major tobacco companies and a Philadelphia ship chandler to
refuse to do business with a new company setting up a chandlery
operation. The "conscious parallelism" apparent in all three tobacco
companies' refusal to deal with the new company was entitled to
little weight, the court explained, because the situation "was not
of a sort which allowed much scope of action to the participants."

The court saw only two possible answers to the new chandler's
request for supplies—"yes" and "no." The new chandler admitted
that a ship-chandlery operation can succeed only if the chandler
has available all major brands of cigarettes. If, as the chandler
argued, each of the tobacco companies knew the others would
not supply cigarettes, the court reasoned, then it would have been
a costly and futile gesture for any of them to accede to the request.
"Conscious parallelism," the court declared, is merely "circumstan-

tial evidence the probative value of which necessarily varies with the kind of parallelism and factual setting where it is found." ("*Interdependent* conscious parallelism" may be something more. See *Wall Products Co.* v. *Nat'l Gypsum Co.,* 326 F.Supp. 295 (N.D. Calif. 1971)).

In *Esco Corp.* v. *U.S.,* 340 F.2d 1000 (9th Cir. 1965), the court of appeals discussed circumstantial evidence of a Section 1 conspiracy. The defendant in that case admitted attending a meeting of competitors at which an attempt was made to define "stocking jobbers," a list of stocking and nonstocking jobbers was prepared, and a proposal to reduce the "stocking jobber" discount from 10 percent to 5 percent was made. Later the discount was reduced by the distributors who had attended the meeting. Defendant contended that the biggest of the competitors involved (who had pleaded nolo contendere to the criminal charges) had called the meeting "not to ask for agreement, but simply to announce" its own pricing plans. The court's reply: "Were we triers of fact, we might well ask if this were so, what purpose was to be served by a meeting of competitors?"

Written by Judge Stanley N. Barnes, former Assistant Attorney General in charge of the Antitrust Division, the *Esco* opinion had the following statement: "While particularly true of price-fixing conspiracies, it is well recognized law that any conspiracy can ordinarily only be proved by inferences drawn from relevant and competent circumstantial evidence, including the conduct of the defendants charged (*Daily* v. *United States,* 282 F.2d 818 at 820 (9th Cir. 1960)). A knowing wink can mean more than words. Let us suppose five competitors meet on several occasions, discuss their problems, and one finally states—'I won't fix prices with any of you, but here is what I am going to do—put the price of my gidget at X dollars; now you all do what you want.' He then leaves the meeting. Competitor number two says—'I don't care whether number one does what he says he's going to do or not; nor do I care what the rest of you do, but I am going to price my gidget at X dollars.' Number three makes a similar statement—'My price is X dollars.' Number four says not one word. All leave and fix 'their' prices at X dollars.

"We do not say the foregoing illustration compels an inference in this case that the competitors' conduct constituted a price-fixing conspiracy, including an agreement to so conspire, but neither can we say, as a matter of law, that an inference of no agreement is compelled. . . . We agree with appellant's contention that although 'a written or otherwise express agreement is not required to support a finding of a Section 1 violation;' and 'no consideration in a technical sense' is required, nevertheless 'the term 'agreement' does necessarily imply mutual consent,' i.e., 'an exchange of assurances to take or refrain from a given course of conduct.' With this we disagree if by it appellant means the existence of specific assurances. Written assurances it concedes are unnecessary. So are oral assurances, if a course of conduct, or a price schedule, once suggested or outlined by a competitor in the presence of other competitors, is followed by all—generally and customarily—and continuously for all practical purposes, even though there be slight variations."

A few days later, in an address to the Antitrust Division of the New York State Bar Association (186 ATRR A-14 (2/2/65)), Assistant Attorney General William H. Orrick, Jr., described the *Esco* opinion as one furnishing "impressive support" for the Government's "long-standing position that the prohibitions of Section 1 of the Sherman Act are violated even though there is no express exchange of mutual assurances. In our view, a common price increase following a discussion of such an increase is sufficient."

Despite the importance Mr. Orrick seemed to assign the *Esco* decision, many antitrust lawyers think the opinion added nothing to substantive antitrust law. Judge Barnes made clear that the court did not intend to outlaw "conscious parallelism" as such or to permit proof of the illegal price-fixing conspiracy from proof of mere price leadership. Following the portions of the opinion quoted above, the court said: "An accidental or incidental price uniformity, or even 'pure' conscious parallelism of prices is, standing alone, not unlawful. Nor is an individual competitor's sole decision to follow a price leadership, standing alone, a violation of law."

The burden of proving conspiracy beyond a reasonable doubt in a criminal case is said to be substantially greater than the preponderance of the evidence burden in a civil case. For example, in the "rock salt" case, the district court found the evidence of a price-fixing conspiracy adequate to justify the issuance of an injunction (*U.S.* v. *Morton Salt Co.,* 1964 Trade Cas. ¶71,198 (D. Minn. 1964)), although a jury had acquitted the same companies of criminal charges two years earlier (*U.S.* v. *Morton Salt Co.,* (1961–1970 Transfer Binder) Trade Reg. Rep. ¶45,061 Case 1614 (D.Minn. 1962)). Civil price-fixing cases rarely go to trial. In a criminal case, on the other hand, for the company that is willing to risk the expense and publicity of a criminal trial, there may be some chance for a successful defense. In *U.S.* v. *Standard Oil Co.,* for example, a second trial of the major gasoline refiners produced a jury verdict of not guilty ((1961–1970 Transfer Binder) Trade Reg. Rep. ¶45,058 Case 1418 (N.D. Ind. 1964)), even though another jury in another federal district had previously convicted the defendants, but the conviction was reversed on appeal (316 F.2d 884 (7th Cir. 1963)).

One clear lesson from the *Esco* opinion is the desirability of avoiding any discussions of price with one's competitors. Judge Barnes' question—"what purpose was to be served by a meeting of competitors?"—illustrates the attitude that has been taken by a number of federal courts. Another illustration is *Pittsburgh Plate Glass Co.* v. *U.S.*, 260 F.2d 397 (4th Cir. 1958). One of the defendants in this case was convicted on the basis of a telephone conversation of a sales executive with a member of a trade association to which the defendant did not even belong but at the annual meeting of which prices were discussed.

In price-fixing cases brought by the Federal Trade Commission under the unfair-methods-of-competition ban in Section 5 of the FTC Act, proof of a "conspiracy" may be dispensed with altogether. In *Triangle Conduit and Cable Co.* v. *FTC*, 168 F.2d 175, 181 (7th Cir. 1948), the court upheld an FTC finding of a Section 5 violation under a count that made no mention of any "combination" or "conspiracy." The court stressed evidence that "each conduit seller knows that each of the other sellers is using the basing point formula; each knows that by using it he will be able to quote delivered prices and thus present a condition of matched prices under which purchasers are isolated and deprived of choice among sellers so far as price advantage is concerned." The court found the question before it identical with that considered by the Supreme Court in the *Cement Institute* case and quoted the *Cement Institute* opinion's statement that "individual conduct . . . which falls short of being a Sherman Act violation may as a matter of law constitute an 'unfair method of competition' prohibited by the Trade Commission Act." What the Supreme Court denied in the *Theatre Enterprises* opinion was that it had "read conspiracy out of the Sherman Act." In *FTC* v. *Beech-Nut Packing Co.*, 257 U.S. 441 (1922), the Court said it had "no doubt of the authority and power of the Commission to order a discontinuance" of "suppression of the freedom of competition by methods in which the company secures the cooperation of its distributors and customers which are quite as effectual as agreements, express or implied, intended to accomplish the same purpose."

9. "Combinations" in Restraint of Trade

Question: *Is a "combination" different from a contract or a conspiracy?*

Section 1 of the Sherman Act outlaws "every contract, combination in the form of trust or otherwise, or conspiracy, in restraint of trade." Section 1 prohibits actions by two or more persons. As the Supreme Court once put it: "An act harmless when done by one may become a public wrong when done by many acting in concert, for it then takes on the form of a conspiracy . . ." (*Eastern States Retail Lumber Dealers' Assn.* v. *U.S.,* 234 U.S. 600 (1914)).

Some courts have drawn a distinction between contracts on the one hand and combinations or conspiracies on the other (*Rice* v. *Standard Oil Co.,* 134 F.464 (C.C. N.J. 1905); *U.S.* v. *American Linen Supply Co.,* 141 F.Supp. 105 (N.D. Ill. 1956)). The Supreme Court has drawn a distinction between contracts and conspiracies in holding that an express agreement need not be shown to establish an unlawful conspiracy. (*Interstate Circuit, Inc.* v. *U.S.,* 306 U.S. 208, 227 (1939); *American Tobacco* v. *U.S.,* 328 U.S. 781, 809 (1946); *U.S.* v. *Paramount Pictures, Inc.,* 334 U.S. 131, 142 (1948)).

For years no distinction was made between combinations and conspiracies. When the district judge gave his instructions to the jury panel in the *American Tobacco* case, he stated: "Thus you will see then an indispensable ingredient of each of the offenses charged in the information is a combination or conspiracy. Now, these terms as used in the Sherman Act have the same legal effect. I shall use them in these instructions interchangeably, without intending any distinction in their meaning" (ABA Antitrust Section, JURY INSTRUCTIONS IN CRIMINAL ANTITRUST CASES, 161, 169 (1965)). In *U.S.* v. *Baumgartner,* April 10, 1969, the Federal District Court for Northern Illinois charged a jury that "a combination is, in the nature of things, like any other agreement or conspiracy" (22, 24). To the same effect is the jury charge in *U.S.* v. *Local 36 of International Fishermen* (245, 247). A widely used antitrust casebook begins a chapter with the statement: "The concept of conspiracy, which is of ancient lineage in the law, is a chief concept under the Sherman Act. Apparently, not much legal significance has been attributed to any distinction which might inhere in the use of the different terms 'combination' or 'conspiracy' as used in Section 1 of the Sherman Act, and it seems clear that the element basic to both is some concert of action between two or more parties." (Oppenheim and Weston, FEDERAL ANTITRUST LAWS, CASES AND COMMENTS, 178 (1968)).

After the Supreme Court's opinion in *U.S.* v. *Parke, Davis and Co.,* 362 U.S. 29 (1960), however, lawyers began to suggest that the "combination" language of that opinion "indicates that you can prove a combination with a little less evidence than you can a conspiracy" ("Panel Discussion on New Theories of Price Conspiracy," 24 ABA ANTITRUST L.J. 76, 100 (1964)). Parke, Davis was found to have violated Section 1 of the Sherman Act by enlisting the aid of wholesalers, through refusal-to-deal threats, in enforcement of a resale price-maintenance program and by using some retailers' willingness to cooperate as a means of persuading other retailers to comply with the pricing policy. Parke, Davis was held to have "created a combination with the retailers and the wholesalers." Throughout the opinion, the Court relied more on the word "combination" than on the word "conspiracy." "An unlawful combination is not just such as arises from a price maintenance *agreement,* express or implied; such a combination is also organized if the producer secures adherence to his suggested prices by means which go beyond his mere declination to sell to a customer who will not observe his announced policy. . . . When the manufacturer's actions, as here, go beyond mere announcement of his policy and the simple refusal to deal, and he employs other means which effect adherence to his resale prices, this countervailing consideration is not present and therefore he has put together a combination in violation of the Sherman Act. Thus, whether an unlawful combination or conspiracy is proved is to be judged by what the parties actually did rather than by the words they used" (362 U.S. at 43, 44).

Parke, Davis reversed a district court (164 F.Supp. 827 (D.D.C. 1958)) that had dismissed the Government's complaint on the authority of *U.S.* v. *Colgate & Co.,* 250 U.S. 300 (1919). The Supreme Court insisted that it had already, in *U.S.* v. *Bausch & Lomb Optical Co.,* 321 U.S. 707 (1944) and *FTC* v. *Beech-Nut Packing Co.,* 257 U.S. 441 (1922), limited the Colgate Doctrine to mean "no more than that a simple refusal to sell to customers who will not resell at prices suggested by the seller is permissible under the Sherman Act." The Court said it would have been lawful for Parke, Davis to announce a "simple refusal without more to deal with wholesalers who did not observe the wholesalers' net price selling schedule," but that policy became "tainted with the vice of illegality . . . when Parke, Davis used it as the vehicle to gain the wholesalers' participation in the program to effectuate the retailers' adherence to the suggested retail prices."

In *Albrecht* v. *Herald Co.,* 390 U.S. 145, 149 (1968), the Supreme Court seemed to go all the way in separating the concept of a combination from that of a contract or conspiracy. "Section 1 of the Sherman Act . . . covers combinations in addition to contracts and conspiracies, express or implied. The Court made this quite clear in *United States* v. *Parke, Davis & Co.,* 362 U.S. 29 (1960), where it held that . . . a combination arose when Parke, Davis threatened its wholesalers with termination unless they put pressure on their retail customers."

On whether a "combination" may differ from a contract or a conspiracy, the Antitrust Bar seems to be divided. At the 1968 spring meeting of the American Bar Association's Antitrust Section, former Assistant Attorney General Donald F. Turner expressed confusion as to precisely what the Supreme Court had in mind when it indicated in *Albrecht* and *Parke, Davis* that a combination is something different from a conspiracy (An interview with the Honorable Donald F. Turner, 37 ABA ANTITRUST L.J. 290, 300–301 (1968)). But he made it clear he does not believe that the Court read the element of consent or agreement out of the word "combination." During Mr. Turner's service as its chief, the Antitrust Division probably never tried to give Section 1 of the Sherman Act any broader scope than it did in footnote 31 to its brief in *U.S.* v. *Arnold, Schwinn & Co.,* 388 U.S. 365 (1967). In a muted attack on the Colgate Doctrine, that footnote said: "The announcement plus the threat of cancellation would appear to create a tacit agreement with those distributors and dealers who comply—all Section 1 requires." Soon afterwards the question of whether there must be compliance or tacit agreement before a Section 1 violation can be found divided the judges of the Court of Appeals for the First Circuit (*Quinn* v. *Mobil Oil Co.,* 375 F.2d 273 (1st Cir. 1967)).

Some antitrust lawyers, looking at the facts of the *Albrecht, Beech-Nut, Bausch & Lomb,* and *Parke, Davis* cases, insist that there was ample basis in each of those records to support a finding of conspiracy and that the discussion in those opinions of "combination" is not significant. Even accepting the proposition that the "combination" language in the Supreme Court's opinion is not part of the logic of the decision, some would take at face value the Supreme Court's statement that the Sherman Act "covers combinations in addition to contracts and conspiracies, express or implied." If a "combination" arose "when Parke, Davis threatened its wholesalers with termination unless they put pressure on their retail customers," then the unilateral action of a single party can create a combination between that party and others who do not share his business interests or motives but are simply used to effect his unilateral policies. This seems to be something different from a conspiracy, which connotes a common purpose, intent, or design.

Treatment of a combination as something different from and less difficult to prove than an agreement or conspiracy could open important new avenues for expanding application of the Sherman Act. Two companies may more easily drift into a relationship that has all the elements of a conspiracy except for an agreement or a common design or purpose, such as reciprocal dealing. (See section II–E, p. 159.) The Court of Appeals for the Second Circuit has used the word "combination," without statutory basis, to describe and condemn, as "joint" action of affiliated companies in violation of Section 17(d) of the 1940 Investment Company Act, parallel conduct of two companies that could not be shown to have acted by agreement (*SEC* v. *Talley Industries, Inc.,* 399 F.2d 396 (2d Cir. 1968)).

If the unwilling acquiescence of a customer or supplier is enough to create a "combination" between him and the enterprise putting pressure on him, may the unwilling acquiescence of smaller members of an industry in a price change by that industry's dominant company also create a combination? In *U.S.* v. *Waltham Watch Co.,* 47 F.Supp. 524, 533 (S.D.N.Y. 1942), there is reasoning that implies antitrust responsibility on the part of an unwilling participant if he knows his action promotes the purposes of a conspiracy. See also *U.S.* v. *National Lead Co.,* 63 F.Supp. 513, 525-6 (S.D.N.Y. 1945).

Is it possible that a large multi-division corporation or a single family of commonly owned corporations might in and of itself be labeled a combination? Standard Oil of New Jersey was deemed a "combination" in *Standard Oil Co.* v. *U.S.,* 221 U.S. 1, 75 (1911). One former Assistant Attorney General in charge of the Antitrust Division indicated a preference for the "bathtub conspiracy" theory of proceeding against multicorporation enterprises, even in reciprocal-dealing situations (34 ABA Antitrust L.J. 122–123 (1967)) There are antitrust practitioners who believe there is no meaningful distinction between combination and conspiracy and that, even if there is, the Justice Department will never bring a case based on the distinction. But see FTC complaints in *Kellogg Co.* Docket 8883, and *Boise Cascade,* File No. 721 0014 (proposed complaint, 604 ATRR A-19 (3/13/73).

10. Joint Ventures

Question: *How are the antitrust laws applied to joint ventures?*

In a speech to the Economic Club of Detroit in March 1962, Paul Rand Dixon, who was at that time Chairman of the FTC, discussed joint ventures (55 ATRR A-12 (4/13/62)). In a joint venture two or more pool their financial resources and skills to engage in some business activity. The type of joint venture of primary concern to the FTC Chairman was the offspring of giant corporations with vast financial resources. Several industries, the Chairman declared, have many joint ownerships. Although the joint venturers generally claim that their partnership is limited to a specific purpose, Mr. Dixon said, there is justifiable doubt that business strategists can treat one another as belligerents in one market when they are allies in another. It is one thing, he said, for small retailers to pool their resources to survive against com-

petition provided by large chains, but it is another thing if two
firms, each with a sizeable share of the market for a commodity,
pool their resources to form a joint venture. For all practical purposes, the result is a merger, in Mr. Dixon's opinion. "It is really
the old 'trust' technique in modern dress. The damage to competition is clear-cut, and, if possible, the move should be quickly
halted."

According to Mr. Dixon, the four economic functions of modern
joint ventures are: "(1) To provide the amounts of capital needed
for the exploitation of raw material sources, particularly financial
resources. (2) To supply security in new industrial development, of
borderline concern to the major business of the corporate partners,
where considerable financial risk is involved. (3) To establish one
large, joint facility which is more economical in operation than
would be smaller, separate installations by the partners. (4) To
undertake research, or other experimental work, on a scale too
vast to be conducted by single companies." Frequently, the FTC
Chairman continued, it is difficult to relate joint ventures to the
asserted reason for their existence. Joint ventures in the glass industry, he said, have reached a stage of development unequalled in
any other industry of similar size. Another "fine maze" of joint
ownerships was attributed to the petrochemical industry, as well
as to the steel companies' mining and coke-producing operations.

Proceedings against purely domestic joint ventures have been
scarce. Decisions like *Timken Roller Bearing Co.* v. *U.S.,* 341 U.S.
593 (1951); *U.S.* v. *Minnesota Mining & Mfg. Co.,* 92 F.Supp.
947 (D. Mass. 1950); and *U.S.* v. *Imperial Chemical Industries,* 100
F.Supp. 504 (S.D.N.Y. 1951) found Sherman Act violations in
domestic manufacturers' operation of joint ventures in foreign
countries. Justice Department views on joint ventures were stated
in the Department's trial brief in the *Penn-Olin* case, an injunction
suit to break up a joint venture of the Pennsalt Chemicals Corp.
and Olin Mathieson Chemical Corp (*U.S.* v. *Penn-Olin Chemical
Co.,* 217 F.Supp. 110 (D. Delaware 1963), *vacated,* 378 U.S. 158
(1964); 246 F. Supp. 917 (D. Delaware 1965), *aff'd,* 389 U.S. 308
(1967)). Penn-Olin Chemical Co. was formed by the two parent
firms to manufacture sodium chlorate for the southeastern part of
the country. The Government brief urged two theories. First, it
argued that formation of Penn-Olin must be regarded, on either
or both of two theories, as an acquisition violating Section 7 of the
Clayton Act. Each parent's contribution of assets to the common
enterprise and purchase of stock in the new firm "was tantamount
to an indirect acquisition by Pennsalt and Olin of the assets of
the other," and the stock purchase alone falls within the scope of
Section 7. Second, the Government maintained, even if the joint

venture did not violate Section 7, it did violate the restraint-of-trade provision in Section 1 of the Sherman Act. Since both Pennsalt and Olin would have been able to compete in the sodium chlorate market on an individual basis, it was argued, the joint venture destroyed potential competition.

The Delaware District Court, which dismissed the action, found that the joint venture was not an instrumentality through which competitors sought to enlarge their economic power but was a means of breaking into a market and challenging the supremacy of two companies already there. According to the court, the test of legality is not whether the two joint venturers "could" but whether they "would" have competed individually. The real issue, in the district judge's view, was "whether, based upon relevant economic factors, the formation of Penn-Olin has resulted, or as a reasonable probability will result, in a substantial lessening of competition or tend to create a monopoly in sodium chlorate in the southeastern part of the United States." In deciding that issue, the court stressed the fact that Pennsalt and Olin Mathieson were not competitors. Pennsalt had been producing sodium chlorate for some time, but only for the Far West, and Olin Mathieson was a user, not a producer, of sodium chlorate. "Penn-Olin was the means by which the strength of the two companies was joined—not for the purpose of further pre-empting a market which they already occupied, but to break into a market to challenge the supremacy of two companies which were dominating it." The two existing producers in the southeast were Hooker Chemical Corp. and American Potash and Chemical Corp.

The Government's evidence was designed primarily to show an adverse effect upon potential competition, although it included an attempt to show impact on existing competition in a nationwide market. It was argued that the financial resources of Pennsalt and Olin Mathieson are so great in comparison with those of Hooker and American Potash that Penn-Olin would have competitive advantages enabling it ultimately to dominate the market. According to the Government, the size of the two parent firms was such that they would be able to use their combined buying power as a basis for making reciprocal arrangements with their suppliers who are sodium chlorate users. The district judge recognized that Pennsalt is "an acknowledged practitioner of reciprocity" but was not convinced that it was reasonably probable Penn-Olin would ultimately dominate the sodium chlorate market.

In its appeal to the Supreme Court the Government suggested it should prevail under Section 7 even if the district judge was correct when he said the most favorable assumption that could be made from the Government's point of view is "that one company would have decided to build while the other continued to ponder." Even that competitive result would be enough to condemn the joint venture, the jurisdictional statement asserted. "The formation of the joint subsidiary not only precluded the immediate entry of one of the parents, but also eliminated the prospect that the other parent, waiting in the wings, might have come into the market at some future time when competitive conditions invited. The very presence of one of the parents as a watchful potential, but not actual, competitor is a source of protection for purchasers and ultimately the consuming public."

The Supreme Court adopted the test urged by the Government and rejected the district court's standard of whether both companies would have entered the market, absent the joint venture. The Court remanded the case for a finding on whether there was a reasonable probability that, absent the joint venture, either of the parent corporations would have entered the market by building a plant, while the other would have remained a significant potential competitor. On remand, the district court found the Government failed to establish that either Olin or Pennsalt would have entered the chlorate market alone, absent the joint venture (246 F.Supp. 917 (D. Del. 1965)). This decision was affirmed by an equally divided Supreme Court (389 U.S. 308 (1967)).

The foreign venture cases, as well as *Penn Olin,* indicate that not all joint ventures, but only those with an adverse effect on competition, potential or existing, will be declared illegal. Joint ventures for producing or for exploration and producing may be viewed more favorably than joint marketing ventures. The Government's only plea for per se illegality in the *Penn-Olin* case was made in connection with its claim that a "sales agreement" and a "production agreement" made by Pennsalt and Olin Mathieson in advance of the joint venture violated the restraint-of-trade provisions in Section 1 of the Sherman Act. As a practical matter, some sort of customer-allocation arrangements may be by-products of many joint ventures. While there are antitrust lawyers who argue that arrangements of this type are not direct restraints and hence should not be subjected to a rule of per se illegality, understandings that have the effect of limiting or eliminating competition between the participants in the joint venture may be in for trouble.

More frequently, perhaps, the problem of determining "reasonableness" will arise in connection with restraints placed upon competition between the joint enterprise and one or more of its parents. With or without an actual agreement or understanding, it is not likely, some say, that the company established as a joint venture is going to feel free to compete with its parents. It would not seem realistic to expect parent companies to organize a joint venture with the intention of allowing it to compete with them. Advocates of a "rule of reason" for joint ventures would allow an agreement not to compete, provided it is limited in time and geographical scope in the same fashion as the traditional agreements not to compete that are extracted from sellers of going businesses. (See section I-4, p. 16.) One federal judge has held that a joint venture, coupled with a division of territories, was lawful when established, although a parent's later restraints on extension of the joint venture's operations became a Sherman Act violation (*U.S.* v. *Pan American World Airways, Inc.,* 193 F.Supp. 18 (S.D.N.Y. 1961), *rev'd on other grounds,* 371 U.S. 296 (1963)).

Some joint ventures, particularly those in research and development and in the missile and space industries, may not present these problems of inter-parent or parent-subsidiary competition. Where each participant joins the joint venture because it has only one of the essential skills or ingredients needed to produce the item the joint venture was organized to develop, it may be that no injury to either existing or potential competition can occur from mere organization of the joint venture, but even here there are antitrust lawyers who caution that the Sherman Act may require that the life of the joint venture—or at least of its freedom from competition—must be limited. Since this sort of arrangement would otherwise permit perpetuation of a monopoly, it is argued, the joint venturers should be expected to give up their ownership of the new enterprise once the development stage has been passed.

In addition to customer allocation and reciprocity arrangements, a joint venture might be accompanied by some sort of exclusive-dealing or requirements contract. For example, a group of small steel or aluminum fabricators might choose to build, as a joint venture, their own plant for manufacturing the primary metal. Such an enterprise might not be likely to succeed against existing competition unless it had, at least temporarily, a guaranteed market for its product—that is, unless the owners obligate themselves to buy from the joint venture. In this situation, application of the rule of reason might permit the fabricators to make a commitment to buy all their primary metal requirements from their offspring.

The Government's chance of successfully attacking joint ventures under Section 7 of the Clayton Act is a subject of disagreement among antitrust experts. Some consider it irrational to regard the formation of a joint venture as an acquisition of stock or assets. Others remind that Clayton Act counts given only secondary advance billing won for the Government such important Supreme Court decisions as that in the *duPont-General Motors* case, 353 U.S.

586 (1957), and the *Philadelphia National Bank* ruling, 374 U.S. 321 (1963). As one lawyer has put it, "the court that applied Section 7 to bank mergers can certainly apply it to joint ventures."

Application of Section 7 to joint ventures may require consideration of a seldom-discussed portion of the Clayton Act. There is a provision in the third paragraph that Section 7 does not "prevent a corporation engaged in commerce from causing the formation of subsidiary corporations for the actual carrying on of their immediate lawful business, or the natural and legitimate branches or extensions thereof, or from owning and holding all or part of the stock of such subsidiary corporations, when the effect of such formation is not to substantially lessen competition." This language ends with a clause that, unlike the first paragraph of Section 7, seems to speak in terms of actual, rather than merely threatened, injury to competition. In its *Penn-Olin* trial brief the Government cited the third paragraph as an indication Congress intended Section 7 to apply to the organization of companies such as Penn-Olin. Otherwise, it was claimed, the paragraph has no purpose.

If the FTC were to act against a joint venture, the legality of the venture and any concomitant intercompany arrangements might be judged by a different standard. In addition to Section 7 of the Clayton Act, the Commission might use the "unfair methods of competition" provision in Section 5 of the FTC Act. Some support for use of Section 5 may be found in the Supreme Court's opinion in the *Panagra* case, (371 U.S. 296) in which the Civil Aeronautics Board's authority to halt "unfair practices" and "unfair methods of competition" was regarded as broad enough to encompass plenary control over the joint venture and its relationships with the two parent firms.

For a violation of Section 7 of the Clayton Act there must be an acquisition of stock or of assets. In the formation of a joint venture, has anyone acquired anything? The Supreme Court skirted this question in its decision remanding *U.S.* v. *Penn-Olin Chemical Co.* The Court was addressing itself to defendants' contention as to commerce, concluding that the test is not whether the joint venture is engaged in commerce but whether the acquisition has any effect on commerce. The Court noted that in this instance the formation of Penn-Olin and the acquisition of its stock by the two parent companies inhibited competition between the parents or between a parent and Penn-Olin. The Court seemed to imply that when a new company is formed to carry out a joint venture and when the parents acquire its stock, there has been an acquisition to which Section 7 of the Clayton Act will apply. The Court did not reach the question of application of Section 7 to joint ventures when no new entity is formed.

II. Codes of Ethics

Question: *What are the antitrust risks in private group attempts to regulate industry practices?*

Some may regard as "unethical," "unfair," or "unconscionable" conduct which the antitrust enforcement agencies see as laudable techniques of hard competition. Efforts to achieve price uniformity—or even stability (*U.S.* v. *Gasoline Retailers Assn.*, 285 F.2d 688 (7th Cir. 1961))—are per se violations of the Sherman Act. Many trade associations have been proceeded against for price fixing. For example, the National Funeral Directors Association was sued by the state of Wisconsin (*State* v. *National Funeral Directors Association*, 1967 Trade Cas. ¶72,289 (Wisc. Cir. Court, Milwaukee County 1967)) and later by the Justice Department for an injunction against code provisions for expelling any member who does any price advertising (*U.S.* v. *National Funeral Directors Association*, 1968 Trade Cas. ¶72,529 (E.D. Wisc. 1968)). See also *U.S.* v. *Utah Pharmaceutical Association*, 201 F.Supp. 29 (D. Utah 1962), *aff'd per curiam*, 371 U.S. 24 (1962), and *Northern Calif. Pharmaceutical Association* v. *U.S.*, 306 F.2d 379 (9th Cir. 1962). "Price tampering" was the condemnatory label used by the district court in *U.S.* v. *Bakersfield Associated Plumbing Contractors*, 1958 Trade Cas. ¶ 69,087 (S.D. Calif. 1958) when it enjoined a group of associations of construction subcontractors from enforcing bid-depository rules that prohibited a discount on "combination" bids from exceeding 5 percent and imposed large bid fees and bid-withdrawal fees. In advisory opinions, the FTC informed trade associations they should not discuss a policy of requiring suppliers to give firm price quotations (FTC ADVISORY OPINION DIGEST 137 (1967)), agree upon fair profit levels (FTC ADVISORY OPINION DIGEST 115 (1967)), or distribute a standard service-pricing manual for electronics servicemen (FTC ADVISORY OPINION DIGEST 158 (1968)).

Consent decrees have barred professional associations from engaging in practices which may affect the fees received by their members. The American Society of Civil Engineers consented to a decree against any course of action that prohibits members from submitting price quotations for engineering services (561 ATRR A-8 (5/2/72)). The American Institute of Architects (564 ATRR A-6 (5/23/72)) and the American Institute of Certified Public Accountants (566 ATRR A-2 (6/6/72)) have consented to similar decrees. In a case which began in 1970, the Department of Justice announced that the Cleveland Real Estate Board consented to a decree which prohibits the fixing of brokerage fees, the publishing or recommendations of fee schedules, and the enforcement of fee schedules (567 ATRR A-7 (6/13/72)). The decree also prohibits any rule that members must accept only exclusive rights to sell.

Bruce Wilson, Deputy Assistant Attorney General in the Antitrust Division, told a group of Pennsylvania lawyers that the use of minimum legal fee schedules "is fraught with antitrust dangers and should be abandoned or at least radically changed if it is to remain outside the forbidden zone," and, at about the same time, the Department of Housing and Urban Development informed the Justice Department that the manner in which minimum fee schedules are applied in property settlements "may violate the Sherman Antitrust Act" (557 ATRR A-14 (4/4/72)). One private, treble-damage class action has challenged a lawyers' fee schedule as it applies to real estate transactions with some initial success (*Goldfarb* v. *Va. State Bar,* 595 ATRR H-1 (E.D. Va. 1973)).

If courts were to regard the use of lawyers' fee schedules as strictly a business practice, there would be serious doubt that the fee schedules could withstand an antitrust attack. Even where they are not enforced, it could be argued that they have a "chilling" effect on price competition. See *U.S.* v. *Container Corp. of America,* 393 U.S. 333 (1969). It would probably make no difference if it could be demonstrated that they have the effect of keeping fees down. See *Albrecht* v. *Herald Co.,* 390 U.S. 145 (1968). It could also be argued that the fee schedule is not analogous to the still permissible suggested retail price because the suggested retail price is a vertical measure while the fee schedule is horizontal in nature. It is doubtful that the interstate commerce requirement is much of a barrier to an antitrust action here in view of the expansion of the concept of interstate commerce in the last few decades.

One possible line of defense of fee schedules is suggested by the close relationship between the bar and the courts. To the extent that the courts are involved in enforcing the ethical rules of the profession, it might be argued that the rules are governmental action and thus exempt from the application of the antitrust laws under the doctrine of *Parker* v. *Brown,* 317 U.S. 341 (1943). (See section I-15, p. 70.)

Probably the critical question in assessing the lawfulness of fee schedules is whether they are reasonably ancillary to a legitimate professional purpose. In *U.S.* v. *Oregon State Medical Society,* 343 U.S. 326, 336 (1952), the Supreme Court remarked: "This court has recognized that forms of competition usual in the business world may be demoralizing to the ethical standards of a profession."

Industry group activity directed toward product standardization may affect price competition and thereby bring antitrust sanctions.

Joint industry action to develop a standard railroad coupler was upheld against government antitrust attack in *U.S.* v. *National Malleable & Steel Castings Co.,* 1957 Trade Cas. ¶68,890 (N.D. Ohio 1957), *aff'd per curiam,* 358 U.S. 38 (1958). The Court held that these efforts, which it called "a boon to our civilization" bringing "a type of human misery to its end," were neither illegal in themselves nor the foundation for subsequent activities alleged (but not found) to constitute price fixing and the exclusion of potential competitors.

The Government may get involved in the promulgation of product standards. Congress has provided for automobile safety standards in the National Traffic and Motor Vehicle Safety Act of 1966, 15 U.S.C. § 1391, and the Commerce Department regularly publishes product standards that have been accepted as the consensus of an industry. An industry member hurt by such standards was unsuccessful in a suit attacking the standards as a Section 1 Sherman Act conspiracy (*Structural Laminates, Inc.* v. *Douglas Fir Plywood Ass'n.,* 261 F.Supp. 154 (D. Ore. 1966), *aff'd,* 399 F.2d 155 (9th Cir. 1968), *cert. denied,* 393 U.S. 1024 (1969)). He lost his suit because he did not prove that the defendant trade association's failure to obtain a change in the standards was motivated by a desire to suppress competition. In *U.S.* v. *Johns Manville Corp.,* 259 F.Supp. 440 (E.D. Pa. 1966), industry product tests were upheld as "scientifically justified" even if they tended to eliminate some competition.

In *Radiant Burners, Inc.* v. *Peoples Gas Light & Coke Co.,* 364 U.S. 656 (1961), allegations of arbitrary and capricious denial of a seal of approval under trade association product standards were held to describe a violation of Section 1 of the Sherman Act. In *C-O-Two Fire Equipment Co.* v. *U.S.,* 197 F.2d 489 (9th Cir. 1952), product standardization was held illegal under the Sherman Act because it facilitated noncompetitive pricing.

The FTC saw a quality-competition-eliminating purpose or result in a macaroni manufacturers' rule reducing the percentage of durum-wheat flour used in their product (*National Macaroni Manufacturers Ass'n,* 65 F.T.C. 583 (1964), *aff'd,* 345 F.2d 421 (7th Cir. 1965)) but advised another trade association it had no objections to its publication of product standards "as industry goals" (FTC ADVISORY OPINION DIGEST 4 (1965)). See also *Fort Howard Paper Co.* v. *FTC,* 156 F.2d 899 (7th Cir. 1946), *cert. denied,* 329 U.S. 795 (1946) (Commission successfully enjoined crepe paper manufacturers from maintaining uniform product standards) and *Milk & Ice Cream Can Institute* v. *FTC,* 152 F.2d 478 (7th Cir. 1946) (Commission upheld on charge that product standards developed and adhered to for purpose of lessening competition).

The Commission refused to approve a trade association's product-standards program that made membership a condition of using the association's quality-certification mark (FTC ADVISORY OPINION DIGEST 152 (1967)). The Commission said nonmembers could be charged a higher fee for use of the mark, provided the differential merely insured that nonmembers "pay an equal share of the costs necessary to support the program."

In *U.S.* v. *Institute of Carpet Manufacturers,* 1942–43 Trade Cas. ¶56,097 (S.D.N.Y. 1941), the leading American carpet manufacturers, troubled by demands from large-volume purchasers for discriminatory quantity discounts which no one seller could afford to resist, voluntarily agreed with each other to discontinue this type of Robinson-Patman (Clayton Act) violation. The manufacturers' efforts were ended by a civil suit under the Sherman Act which resulted in a consent decree forbidding the manufacturers to agree "to refrain from giving volume allowances or rebates to purchasers of rugs and carpets." The manufacturers' unsuccessful attempt at self-regulation did not forestall a later direct government attack on the practices involved. The Federal Trade Commission concluded a series of individual Robinson-Patman Act proceedings in which the manufacturers were ordered to cease and desist from the very practices they had sought in concert to abandon some 25 years earlier, but a court of appeals reversed two of these cases and the situation is now about where it was before. See *Callaway Mills Co.,* (1963–1965 Transfer Binder) Trade Reg. Rep. ¶16,800 (F.T.C. 1964), *rev'd,* 362 F.2d 435 (5th Cir. 1966); *Bigelow-Sanford Carpet Co.* (1963–65 Transfer Binder) Trade Reg. Rep. ¶16,800 (F.T.C. 1964); *Philadelphia Carpet Co.,* (1963–65 Transfer Binder) Trade Reg. Rep. ¶16,801 (F.T.C. 1964); *aff'd,* 342 F.2d 994 (3rd Cir. 1965); *Cabin Crafts, Inc.* (1963–65 Transfer Binder) Trade Reg. Rep. ¶16,802 (F.T.C. 1964).

Among other trade association code sections that have been disapproved are provisions for one-year requirements contracts and uniform delivery and credit terms (FTC ADVISORY OPINION DIGEST 97 (1966)), prohibitions against advertising that one's service is better or faster (FTC ADVISORY OPINION DIGEST 80 (1966)), a construction contractors' rule requiring use of a bid depository and barring the submission of "split" bids—e.g., bids for only plumbing or only electrical work—(*Mechanical Contractors' Bid Depository* v. *Christiansen,* 352 F.2d 817 (10th Cir. 1965)), and a "no switching" rule for key employees (*Union Circulation Co.,* 51 F.T.C. 647 (1955), *aff'd,* 241 F.2d 652 (2d Cir. 1957)). The FTC has approved, though, a trade association's plan to require members to pledge compliance with trade practice rules (FTC ADVISORY OPINION DIGEST 64 (1966)).

There are precedents indicating that not only the substantive rules but also the enforcement provisions of an ethics code must be free of anticompetitive purpose or result. For example, one of the elements the Supreme Court stressed in reversing dismissal of the Sherman Act charge in the *Radiant Burners* case was the industry procedure for boycotting any product that wasn't awarded a seal of approval. Boycotts or "blacklists" have been major factors in many of the cases condemning industry procedures for self-regulation (*Standard Sanitary* v. *U.S.*, 226 U.S. 20 (1912); *Eastern States Retail Lumber Dealers* v. *U.S.*, 234 U.S. 600 (1914); *Fashion Originators' Guild* v. *FTC*, 312 U.S. 457 (1941)). The *Standard Sanitary* and *Fashion Originators* cases suggest that the good motives of the industry or its trade association are irrelevant. "The law is its own measure of right and wrong, of what it permits, or forbids" (226 U.S. at 49). In such situations, the trade association is "in reality an extra-governmental agency, which prescribes rules for the regulation and restraint of interstate commerce, and provides extra-judicial tribunals for determination and punishment of violations, and thus 'trenches upon the power of the national legislature and violates the statute' " (312 U.S. at 465). Cf. *Sugar Institute* v. *U.S.*, 297 U.S. 553, 598–599 (1936)).

Concern about creation of "an extra-governmental agency" was expressed by Federal Trade Commissioner Elman when he dissented from an advisory opinion clearing a provision in an industry code of ethics for the imposition of limited fines on violators (FTC ADVISORY OPINION DIGEST 128 (1967)). An organization of magazine publishers and subscription sales agencies formed to halt deceptive sales practices was told that the Commission had no objection to provisions authorizing the code's "administrator" to assess amounts of money to be paid by code violators "as liquidated damages, not as a penalty." The advisory opinion assumed "that there will be no coercion of any agency to subscribe to the plan, no coercion of any agency to remain in it after it has subscribed." The code obligated a participating agency to give six months' notice of withdrawal. Similar "liquidated damages" provisions were written into a cigarette advertising code the tobacco industry submitted to the Justice Department for clearance in 1964 (147 ATRR A-14 (5/5/64)). Because Congress and the FTC were considering advertising and labeling standards for the industry, the Antitrust Division declined to clear "permanent establishment" of the advertising controls but did agree "in the meantime" to bring no criminal prosecution based on adherence to the code (154 ATRR A-22, X-23 (6/23/64)).

In its advice to the subscription sales agencies, the FTC balked at sanctioning a plan to recommend that salesmen be suspended from their jobs for willful disobedience of the code. It did clear, though, provisions authorizing the code administrator to hold hearings and maintain a public list of willful violators. Later (FTC ADVISORY OPINION DIGEST 133 (1967)), the Commission advised a trade association that it could discuss an agreement to comply with a labeling ruling of a federal agency but could not take steps to enforce any such agreement. This ruling conforms to the approach the Commission takes in the administration of trade practice rules, (now called "guides"), which are often developed by the affected industry under FTC supervision. Each set of trade practice rules contains a standard provision that the industry "may, at its option, form a trade practice committee." That committee may publicize the trade practice rules and related FTC rules and may meet with the Commission to discuss administration and revision of the trade practice rules, but it may not "(1) interpret the rules; (2) attempt to correct alleged rule violations; (3) make determinations or express opinions as to whether practices are violative of the rules; (4) receive or screen complaints of violations of the rules; or (5) perform any other act or acts within the authority of the Federal Trade Commission or any other governmental agency or department."

In a bar association speech, Assistant Attorney General Donald F. Turner questioned both the adequacy and appropriateness of any joint industry efforts toward consumer protection as to quality or even safety (1967 New York State Bar Association Symposium 36). One of the points he made is that businessmen often act arbitrarily or discriminatorily when policing the activities of their competitors. The necessity for fair play among competitors in self-regulation situations was stressed by the Supreme Court in *Silver* v. *New York Stock Exchange,* 373 U.S. 341 (1963).

Most of the uncertainty concerning application of the antitrust laws to industry codes relates to enforcement provisions included in those codes. Language in some advisory opinions (such as FTC ADVISORY OPINION DIGEST 133) seems to indicate a reluctance on the part of the FTC to clear provisions for private sanctions against industry code violations, even when the conduct to be punished is forbidden by law. The Commission's reasoning in those opinions appears consistent with that of the *Standard Sanitary* and *Fashion Originators* cases. In the Commission's clearance of the subscription sales agencies' "liquidated damages" agreement many antitrust lawyers see a reversion to the approach taken by the Supreme Court in the *Sugar Institute* case in which the Court praised voluntary self-regulation by industry as sometimes "more effective than legal processes" and recognized that such self-regulation "may appropriately have wider objectives than merely the removal of evils which are infractions of positive law."

The key to the Commission's advice to the subscription sales agencies is probably to be found in its observation that its conclusion "is a tentative one since there is little recorded experience upon which to predicate such a judgment." The real test of an industry code is the manner of its operation. Since the subscription sales agencies' code does provide for the imposition of sanctions, anticompetitive consequences are clearly possible. If the trade association widely publicizes its activity, membership could become too important for a competitor to abandon in order to avoid discriminatory or anticompetitive penalties. It was only "in view of the magnitude of the problems which confront the industry" in the form of widespread deceptive selling practices that the Commission agreed to take the risk of industry self-regulation. Even then it gave only temporary three-year clearance, with instructions that the plan be resubmitted for new approval after three years, during which all enforcement proceedings must be reported to the Commission. No clearance was granted to any particular selling practices (*Hearst Corp.*, (1970–1973 Transfer Binder) Trade Reg. Rep. ¶19,841 (F.T.C. 1971)).

Actual anticompetitive "effects" led to the outlawing of industry self-regulation in the *Standard Sanitary, Eastern States Lumber, Fashion Originators, and Sugar Institute* cases. None of the court decisions finding Sherman Act violations have dealt with code provisions that merely could be anticompetitive if improperly used. Either they were anticompetitive on their face or they were in fact shown to have been used in an anticompetitive manner. The *Radiant Burner* and *Silver* complaints contained allegations of discriminatory or anticompetitive application.

The question remains whether an industry code that never inhibits competition is worth the trouble. The answer seems to be "yes" in industries plagued with Section 5 FTC Act violations that the Commission does not have the resources to deal with. There may exist industries in which a code of ethics that does nothing more than establish rules against clear violations of the law may prove valuable if it gives industry members confidence to adopt trade-policy changes they would not have the courage to initiate individually.

12. Labor Unions and the Antitrust Laws

Question: *To what extent are labor union activities exempt from the antitrust laws?*

Until the Clayton Act was passed in 1914, decisions like *U.S.* v. *Debs*, 64 F. 724 (N.D. Ill. 1894), and *Loewe* v. *Lawlor* (the "Dan-

bury Hatters" case), 208 U.S. 274 (1908), sustained contentions that
strikes, pickets, and boycotts are concerted activities that restrain
trade prohibited by the Sherman Act. Section 6 of the Clayton Act
provides: "the labor of a human being is not a commodity or
article of commerce. Nothing contained in the antitrust laws shall
be construed to forbid the existence and operation of labor organizations nor shall such organizations, or the members thereof, be
held or construed to be illegal combinations or conspiracies in
restraint of trade, under the antitrust laws." Section 20 provides
"that no restraining order or injunction shall be granted by any
court of the United States . . . in any case between an employer
and employees . . . involving, or growing out of, a dispute concerning terms or conditions of employment. . . ." In addition, Section 20 immunizes specific activities from injunction such as "ceasing
to perform any work or labor," picketing, or assembling "for the
purpose of peacefully . . . communicating information." The Section provides: "nor shall any of the acts specified in this paragraph
be considered . . . violations of any law of the United States."

   In *Duplex Printing Press Co.* v. *Deering,* 254 U.S. 443 (1921);
Coronado Coal Co. v. *United Mine Workers,* 268 U.S. 295 (1925);
and *Bedford Cut Stone Co.* v. *Journeymen Stone Cutters Ass'n,* 274
U.S. 37 (1927), the Supreme Court limited the immunity to disputes between an employer and his own employees and refused to
apply the exemption to "secondary" union activity. In 1932, with
the Norris-LaGuardia Act, Congress prohibited the application of
the antitrust laws to labor disputes. Section 1 states that no court
of the United States has jurisdiction to issue any restraining order
or injunction "in a case involving or growing out of a labor dispute." Section 4 immunizes, in much the same manner as does
Section 20 of the Clayton Act, specific acts of individuals and
unions.

   The Norris-LaGuardia Act was construed by the Supreme Court
in *U.S.* v. *Hutcheson,* 312 U.S. 219 (1941). The Court ruled that
Congress had legislatively overruled the *Duplex* case and its construction of Section 20 of the Clayton Act. The union's strike
activities were held to be among those enumerated in Section 4
of the Norris-LaGuardia Act and immunized from the Sherman
Act "where a union acts in its own self-interest and does not combine with non-labor groups."

   A labor union is not immune from an injunction based on a
Sherman Act violation if the controversy involved is not a "labor
dispute" within the meaning of the Norris-LaGuardia Act (*Columbia
River Packers Ass'n.,* v. *Hinton,* 315 U.S. 143 (1942)). In the
Columbia River case, some members of a union of fishermen owned
their own boats and were independent entrepreneurs rather than

employees. The union had combined with these businessmen to coerce the fish packers to buy only from union members. One packer refused and a boycott was set up against him. The Court upheld an injunction against the boycott, saying that the controversy was strictly between fish sellers and fish buyers.

In *Allen Bradley Co.* v. *Local 3, IBEW,* 325 U.S. 797 (1945), the Court found that a union-employer combination formed for the purpose of preventing manufacturers located in other cities from competing for local business would not be saved from the Sherman Act by the fact that one of the members of the combination was a union. The Court noted that a union's victory in a labor dispute might raise costs just as a monopoly does but added (at 809): "So far as the union might have achieved this result acting alone, it would have been the natural consequence of labor-union activities exempted by the Clayton Act from the coverage of the Sherman Act. But when the unions participated with a combination of businessmen who had complete power to eliminate all competition among themselves and to prevent all competition from others, a situation was created not included within the exemptions of the Clayton and Norris-LaGuardia Acts."

Summarizing the extent of labor's immunity, the Attorney General's National Committee to Study the Antitrust Laws reported in 1955 that union activities restraining commerce "may be vulnerable to antitrust proceedings: (1) Where the union engages in fraud or violence and intends or achieves some direct commercial restraint; (2) Where the union activity is not in the course of a labor dispute as defined in the Norris-LaGuardia Act. . . . and (3) Where a union combines with some nonlabor group to effect some direct commercial restraint" (Report at 299–300). The Committee went on to recommend some changes in the law. It denied any wish to change "labor's freedom under the antitrust laws to act in concert in order to promote union organization or bargain collectively over wages, hours, or other employment conditions." It was convinced, though, that some unions had worked for "commercial market restraints" that "run counter to our national antitrust policy." The Committee recommended that Congress pass "appropriate legislation to prohibit . . . union efforts at outright market control." Essential to this new legislation, the Committee insisted, is enforcement by action of the Government, rather than by private complaint, which is the technique adopted in the Taft-Hartley Act.

In the years following publication of the Committee's report, court cases have limited the types of competition-restricting activity in which unions will be permitted to engage. In *I.P.C. Distributors, Inc.* v. *Chicago Moving Picture Machine Operators,* 132 F.Supp. 294 (N.D. Ill. 1955), the union attempted a type of censorship;

it instructed its member projectionists not to handle a condemned motion picture. In an injunction suit brought by the distributor of the film, the district court held that censorship is not a legitimate and normal union objective and that the Union's concerted activity was outside the scope of the Norris-LaGuardia Act. In *U.S.* v. *Gasoline Retailers Ass'n.*, 285 F.2d 688 (7th Cir. 1961) a price-stabilization agreement between the retailers' association and a local of the teamsters union was condemned.

The policy of some unions in accepting as members workmen who are not actually employees but independent businessmen sometimes brings in conflict antitrust law and labor law principles. In *Los Angeles Meat & Provision Drivers Union* v. *U.S.*, 371 U.S. 94 (1962), independent entrepreneurs, as well as employees, were members of a union alleged to have engaged in activities prohibited by the Sherman Act. Independent grease peddlers in Los Angeles purchased waste grease from restaurants and other institutions and sold it to processors. In 1954 most of these peddlers became members of a special unit of the Los Angeles Meat & Provisions Drivers' Union. The grease-peddler members and their union then agreed upon fixed purchase and sale prices for the grease. These prices were forced upon restaurants and processors by threatening those who dealt with nonunion peddlers with strikes, boycotts, and other "union trouble." By 1959 the few peddlers who had not joined the union had been eliminated. The United States filed a complaint against the union, alleging a violation of Section 1 of the Sherman Act. The union admitted all the allegations of the complaint. The district court found that the grease peddlers were businessmen, not employees, and that their membership in the union did not bring the combination under labor's antitrust immunity. The court enjoined the activities and ordered the union to terminate the membership of the grease peddlers (*U.S.* v. *Los Angeles Meat & Provision Drivers Union*, 196 F.Supp. 12 (S.D. Calif. 1961)).

The Supreme Court affirmed this decree and found, as it had in *Columbia River Packers*, that the union was not insulated by the Clayton and Norris-LaGuardia Acts. The case was not one "involving or growing out of any labor dispute." The Court rejected the argument that the grease peddlers became a labor organization by "the simple expedient of calling themselves 'Local 626-B' of a labor union." In finding the peddlers independent entrepreneurs rather than employees, the Court relied on the lower court's finding that "there was no job or wage competition or economic inter-relationship of any kind between the grease peddlers and other members of the . . . union."

In a concurring opinion, Justice Goldberg, joined by Justice

Brennan, warned that the sanction of expulsion of the peddlers from the union was an extreme one sustained in this case only because of the stipulated facts. "Unless confined to use but rarely and then only in the most compelling circumstances," they cautioned, the expulsion order "may become a device for unfairly and improperly fractionalizing or decimating unions." Justice Douglas dissented on the ground that this was "a labor dispute within the meaning of the Norris-LaGuardia Act."

The labor exemption from antitrust may turn on a distinction between wage fixing and price fixing. In *St. Louis, Mo., Paper Carriers* v. *Pulitzer Publishing Co.*, 309 F.2d 716 (8th Cir. 1962), a proceeding was brought by a paper carriers union when the newspaper publishers refused to negotiate on the compensation the carrier should be allowed. The publishers contended that an agreement on that subject would be a price-fixing deal violating the Sherman Act. The court of appeals refused to settle the dispute, holding that it should be taken initially to the National Labor Relations Board.

In *American Federation of Musicians* v. *Carroll*, 391 U.S. 99 (1968), the Court concluded that a union's minimum price list for orchestra engagements was in substance a control of musicians' wages and therefore a proper subject of union interest. Several orchestra leaders sued the Federation for treble damages and an injunction. Orchestra leaders were pressured into becoming union members and were required to engage a minimum number of sidemen for club engagements and to charge prices set out in a price list booklet. The district court dismissed the complaint, finding all the union's practices within the definition of "labor dispute" in the Norris-LaGuardia Act. The Court of Appeals for the Second Circuit reversed on the ground that the fixing of minimum prices even by a union is illegal (310 F.2d 325 (1962)).

In reversing the court of appeals, the Supreme Court agreed with both lower courts that, even though the orchestra leaders are employers and independent contractors, they constitute not a "nonlabor" group but a "labor" group. The Court approved the criterion applied by the district court—the "presence of job or wage competition or some other economic interrelationship affecting legitimate union interests between the union members and the independent contractors." When that economic interrelationship exists, there is a labor dispute outside the reach of the Sherman Act; "the allowable area of union activity was not to be restricted to an immediate employer-employee relation."

Two possible qualifications of the rule stated by the Court may be inferred from footnote 10 of the opinion, which points out that "the 'price list' establishes only a minimum charge; there is no attempt to set a maximum. Nor does the union attempt by its minimum charge to assure the leader a profit above the fair value of his labor services." The footnote also quotes a statement by a dissenting judge in the court of appeals that "a different result might be warranted if the floor were set so high as to cover not merely compensation for the additional services rendered by a leader but entrepreneurial profit as well."

The price list was considered "indistinguishable in . . . [its] effect from the collective bargaining provisions" in *Local 24, International Brotherhood of Teamsters* v. *Oliver,* 358 U.S. 283 (1959). The *Oliver* opinion approved a negotiated requirement that rentals charged for use of owner-operated trucks be held up to a minimum level to preserve prevailing wage standards. The minimum-rental provision there was "narrowly restricted . . . to the times when the owner drives his leased vehicle for the carrier, and to the adverse effects upon the negotiated wage scale which might result when the rental for use of the leased vehicle was unregulated." In *Musicians* v. *Carroll,* the price list was similarly designed to protect sidemen and subleaders from job and wage competition of the leaders.

The distinction between union price-influencing activities legitimate as wage-boosting efforts and those that are nonlabor activities prohibited by the Sherman Act is not always easy to draw. If all members of the organization claiming union status are independent contractors or entrepreneurs rather than employees, apparently it is a Sherman Act violation for such an organization to maintain a standard of prices (*Columbia River Packers Ass'n* v. *Hinton,* 315 U.S. 143 (1942); *U.S.* v. *Women's Sportswear Mfrs. Ass'n,* 336 U.S. 460 (1949); *Taylor* v. *Local No. 7, International Union of Journeymen Horseshoers,* 353 F.2d 593 (4th Cir. 1965)). In *Musicians* v. *Carroll,* on the other hand, most of the union members were apparently mere sidemen whose economic interests were so closely tied to those of the orchestra leaders, who were also union members, that the union was permitted to set price minimums for the leaders. Likewise, in the *Oliver* case, employee truck drivers' wages were necessarily affected by the rentals collected by owner-operators of trucks.

Work-hour negotiations sometimes limit business hours, in some degree restraining trade. A retail marketing-hours restriction imposed by a butchers' union through multi-employer bargaining was approved by the Supreme Court in *Amalgamated Meat Cutters* v. *Jewel Tea Co.,* 381 U.S. 676 (1965). The only issue was "whether the marketing-hours restriction . . . is so intimately related to wages, hours and working conditions that the union's successful attempt to obtain that provision through bona fide, arms-length bargaining in pursuit of its own labor union policies . . . falls within the protection of the national labor policy." Justice White, writing for the Court, answered that the national labor policy "places beyond the reach of the Sherman Act union-employer agreements on when, as well as how long, employees must work."

Justices Douglas, Black, and Clark viewed the Chicago marketing-hours situation as union coercion of an employer into an agreement that prevents the employer from using convenient shopping hours as a means of competition. They regarded the union's collective agreement with the Chicago grocery stores as itself evidence of a conspiracy to impose the marketing-hours restriction on the complaining grocery chain by means of a strike threat. (For further discussion, see the following section).

13. Multi-Employer Collective Bargaining

Question: *Is industry-wide bargaining prohibited by the antitrust laws?*

At a meeting in February 1965 of the District of Columbia Bar Association's Antitrust Law Committee, Guy Farmer, former chairman of the National Labor Relations Board, suggested that labor-relations lawyers may have overlooked "one significant aspect" of the Supreme Court's decision in *Allen Bradley Co.* v. *Local 3, IBEW,* 325 U.S. 797 (1945). That opinion did more than curtail labor's antitrust exemption, he said. "*Allen Bradley* established a legal principal which made associations of employers potential co-conspirators with labor unions."

Mr. Farmer reported that between 80 and 100 percent of workers covered by union contracts in the coal-mining, clothing-manufacturing, building-construction, longshore, maintenance, hotel, and trucking and warehousing industries are covered by multi-employer contracts. In baking, book and job printing, textiles, glass and glassware, malt liquor, pottery, and the retail trades, the percentage is about 60 to 80 percent. Joint negotiations are conducted by the larger enterprises in other major industries, such as steel, although separate contracts are signed. Mr. Farmer said these employer associations or groupings seldom represent all the business components of the industry involved. Typically, the members of the association are the larger and more stable business units. Yet the labor agreement negotiated by the employer association generally sets the wage-rate and working-condition standards accepted "fairly uniformly" by the remainder of the industry. The employers participating in the joint negotiations frequently seek some sort of guarantee that nonparticipating competitors will not be permitted to negotiate more favorable terms with the union. Some contracts have included "most favored nation" clauses, assuring participating employers that the terms of their contract will be adjusted to match any more favorable terms negotiated by competing employers.

Mr. Farmer spoke one month after argument (186 ATRR A-1 (2/2/65)) had been held in the *Pennington* and *Jewel Tea Co.* cases (*UMW* v. *Pennington,* 381 U.S. 657 (1965); *Amalgamated Meat Cutters* v. *Jewel Tea Co.,* 381 U.S. 676 (1965)). In *Pennington,* the UMW was challenging a verdict against it in an antitrust damage suit brought by a small mine operator hurt by the National Bituminous Coal Wage Agreement of 1950. The UMW and the large mine operators had been charged with agreeing to eliminate overproduction in the coal industry by driving the smaller operators out of business. The union was said to have promised to go along with mechanization of the mines and to impose the terms of the Wage Agreement on all mine operators without regard to their ability to pay. The Wage Agreement forbade the mine operators to lease any of their coal lands to nonunion operators and to buy or sell coal mined by companies paying less favorable wage rates than those set out in the Agreement.

In support of antitrust exemption for arrangements of this sort, including the union promise to impose the same terms on the rest of the industry, the United Mine Workers pointed to the Supreme Court's statement in *Apex Hosiery Co.* v. *Leader,* 310 U.S. 469 (1940): "Since, in order to render a labor combination effective it must eliminate the competition from nonunion made goods . . . an elimination of price competition based on differences in labor standards is the objective of any national labor organization. But this effect on competition has not been considered to be the kind of curtailment of price competition prohibited by the Sherman Act."

The Supreme Court thought UMW counsel was reading too much into the *Apex* decision. The Court recognized that the labor exemption is available to collective-bargaining agreements on wages "not only between individual employers and a union but agreements between the union and employers in a multi-employer bargaining unit." The union is free "as a matter of its own policy" to seek the same wages from all other employers in the industry. Not every agreement resulting from union-employer negotiations is automatically exempt simply because it involves a compulsory subject of collective bargaining. "A union forfeits its exemption from the antitrust laws when it is clearly shown that it has agreed with one set of employers to impose a certain wage scale on other bargaining units." The Court could see nothing in national labor policy that conflicted with this restriction on union-employer agreements. "The union's obligation to its members would seem best served if the union retained the ability to respond to each bargaining situation as the individual circumstances might warrant."

In a footnote to his opinion for the Court, Justice White recognized the right of the union, acting unilaterally, to "adopt a uniform wage policy and seek vigorously to implement it even though it may suspect that some employers cannot effectively compete if they are required to pay the wage scale demanded by the union. . . . Such union conduct is not alone sufficient evidence to maintain a union-employer conspiracy charge under the Sherman Act. There must be additional direct or indirect evidence of the conspiracy. There was, of course, other evidence in this case, but we indicate no opinion as to its sufficiency."

In a concurring opinion joined by Justices Black and Clark, Justice Douglas read the opinion of the Court as saying (1) that a union may not agree on a wage scale that exceeds the financial ability of some employers to pay when that agreement is made for the purpose of forcing some employers out of business and (2) that "an industry-wide agreement containing those features is prima facie evidence of a violation." Those three justices dissented in the *Jewel Tea* case, when the Court split three ways in sustaining the Amalgamated Meat Cutters business hours limits for Chicago grocery stores. Justice White announced the decision of the Court, but his opinion was joined only by the Chief Justice and Justice Brennan. No claim was advanced in the Supreme Court that the Meat Cutters had conspired with some employers against others. The only issue was "whether the marketing-hours restriction . . . is so intimately related to wages, hours and working conditions that the union's successful attempt to obtain that provision through bona fide, arms-length bargaining in pursuit of its own labor union policies . . . falls within the protection of the national labor policy." White's answer was that national labor policy "places beyond the reach of the Sherman Act union-employer agreements on when, as well as how long, employees must work." A suggestion by Jewel Tea Co. that grocery stores could remain open in the evening without infringing the Meat Cutters' interests was rejected by Justice White. He was satisfied that there was evidence to support the district court's finding that meat could not be sold in the grocery stores after 6 p.m. unless the members of the meat cutters—or someone else doing their work—remained after that hour.

Justices Douglas, Black, and Clark viewed the Chicago marketing-hours situation as union coercion of an employer into an agreement that prevents the employer from using convenience of shopping hours as a means of competition, and they regarded the union's collective agreement with the Chicago grocery stores as evidence of a conspiracy to impose the marketing-hours restriction on the complaining grocery chain by means of a strike threat.

Justices Goldberg, Harlan, and Stewart dissented in *Pennington* but concurred in the Court's judgment extending antitrust exemption to the marketing-hours agreement. They viewed both these cases as "refusals by judges to give full effect to congressional action designed to prohibit judicial intervention via the antitrust route in legitimate collective bargaining." The Court's opinion in *Pennington* raised for them the possibility of judges and juries "making essentially economic judgments in antitrust actions by determining whether unions or employers had good or bad motives for their agreements on subjects of mandatory bargaining."

Counsel for the Industrial Union Department of the AFL-CIO told member unions that the decisions "reversed a universally held assumption as to the scope of the labor exemption, pointing to a conclusion in the 1955 report of the Attorney General's National Committee to Study the Antitrust Laws that the antitrust laws apply only to union activities involving "direct control of the market" (212 ATRR A-1 (8/3/65)). Among the consequences IUD counsel saw in the decisions, "one of the most alarming . . . is that they leave for determination by a trial judge or jury the question of whether a union (or an employer for that matter) should be held liable for treble damages under the Sherman Act." The question whether a union, in seeking to negotiate uniform contracts throughout an industry, is acting on its own or pursuant to an agreement with some of the employers is one that must be answered on the basis of all the circumstances of the case, "as interpreted in the light of the particular prejudices and economic philosophy of the fact finder." An inference was drawn from the *Jewel Tea* case that, had the trial court found no relationship between hours of work and marketing hours, antitrust exemption would have been denied the marketing-hours restriction. Convinced that the effects of the two decisions upon labor-union activities "will be adverse," IUD counsel held out hope that the rule applied by the court "may be narrowed in future litigation" on the sufficiency of the evidence to show an unlawful conspiracy and the type of collective-bargaining contract terms that can be said to violate the Sherman Act.

IUD counsel also found in the decisions significant consequences for employers; they saw the opinions as subjecting not only unions but also the collective-bargaining process to antitrust laws. Employers are liable equally with the union for any employer-union conspiracy in restraint of trade. While unions remain free to seek uniform labor standards throughout any particular industry, employers may not do so either by unilateral request to the union or by inter-employer agreement. If employers in an industry agree among themselves as to the union wage demands they will accede to, and thereby prevent the union from obtaining a satisfactory agreement, it may be that the union has an antitrust remedy, the IUD lawyers suggested. For example, if an association of employers initiates a lockout in response to a strike called against only one member employer, IUD counsel think there are "interesting possibilities for suits by the locked-out employees based on an antitrust theory rather than the unfair labor practice remedy which has previously been pursued."

In *Ramsey* v. *U.M.W.*, 401 U.S. 302 (1971), the Supreme Court adhered to its *Pennington* holding on a union's liability under the antitrust laws.

Supreme Court decisions on the scope of labor's antitrust exemption are resolutions of a conflict between two basic national policies. If the Sherman Act's goal of unfettered price competition were the only congressional policy to be implemented, some of the principal activities of labor unions would have to be outlawed because they reduce or eliminate price competition reflecting variations in labor costs. In a series of statutes including Section 6 of the Clayton Act, the Norris-LaGuardia Act, the National Labor Relations Act, the Fair Labor Standards Act, and the Davis-Bacon and Walsh-Healey Public Contracts Act, Congress has articulated a policy that this sort of price competition is to be sacrificed in the interest of industrial peace and a measure of economic security for the working man.

Until the decision in the *Pennington* case, labor lawyers thought the *Apex* and *Allen Bradley* opinions had established three clear principles: (1) that restraints relating to wages, hours, and working conditions are not subject to the Sherman Act even when accomplished by a combination of unions and employers; (2) that restraints on the marketing and pricing of goods do violate the Sherman Act when accomplished by a combination of unions and employers; and (3) that pricing and marketing restraints imposed by a union acting alone are within the exemption spelled out in Section 6 of the Clayton Act.

There seems to be little doubt that the opinion in the *Pennington* case revises the first of these principles. Some labor lawyers express concern about the impact the decision may have upon collective bargaining in industries where multi-employer negotiations prevail and unions have sought uniform standards with some success. Of particular significance, in their view, are the Court's statements suggesting that a union-employer conspiracy violating the Sherman Act can be proven, as in other antitrust cases, by indirect or circumstantial evidence. Alerted by the dissenting opinion of Justice Goldberg, they suggest that the Court's reasoning permits a jury to infer a conspiracy to drive out marginal producers merely from discussions at the bargaining table about the competitive effect wage rates may have on other employers in the industry.

There are both antitrust and labor lawyers who feel that these decisions upset a balance between labor law and antitrust law and create uncertainty and confusion for the future. They point to the three-way division among the justices as proof of the uncertainty and note also that antitrust law, which prevailed in these decisions, is less definite and clear, in general, than labor law. The uncertain state of the law is illustrated by a disagreement that prevails among lawyers over the present antitrust status of the "most favored nation" clauses negotiated in some industries. Although there are antitrust lawyers who do not think the court has condemned that type of arrangement, at least one expert in labor law has labeled them "clearly illegal." Counsel for the IUD was not sure where these clauses stand. They advised unions "to make no agreements with any employers as to what kind of agreements . . . the union will negotiate with other employers." They were sure that it would be illegal to place in an agreement with one group of employers a commitment by the union not to grant more favorable conditions to any competing employer.

The view has been expressed that unions may be ill-advised to campaign for uniform labor standards even on a unilateral basis. The hazard for unions seeking uniform labor standards and the employers they deal with would seem to lie in the threat of treble-damage suits by disgruntled marginal producers or recalcitrant employer-association members. That type of litigation can go to a jury on the issue of whether a conspiracy is to be inferred from the content of a multi-employer agreement and the history of negotiations leading up to it. Injunctions are issued by judges sitting without juries, operate only prospectively, and leave the union free to seek the same objectives by unilateral action, as did the injunction finally entered in the *Allen Bradley* case.

Another noteworthy aspect of the *Pennington* decision is its relationship to the development of automation. The Court has told the coal-mining industry that the marginal producers economically incapable of switching to automation cannot be foreclosed, by prior agreement in the rest of the industry, from at least trying to resist imposition of union wage scales and to offer, through use of cheaper labor, some price competition to the larger modernized mines.

The two decisions have been described as further manifestations of two trends in the Court's decisions: (1) a tendency to give broader application to the antitrust laws and (2) a reaction against the economic power that has been acquired by labor unions—a reaction seen in other decisions such as *American Ship Building Co.* v. *NLRB,* 380 U.S. 300 (1965), and *NLRB* v. *Brown,* 380 U.S. 278 (1965).

14. Petitioning the Government

Question: *Does the Sherman Act forbid cooperation between competitors to obtain government action which may lessen competition?*

People have a right to make their wishes known to their government, but the claim has sometimes been made that the Sherman Act outlaws combinations and conspiracies to influence public officials. In *Eastern Railroad Presidents Conference* v. *Noerr Motor Freight, Inc.,* 365 U.S. 127 (1961), the Supreme Court held that the Sherman Act "does not prohibit two or more persons from associating together in an attempt to persuade the legislature or the executive to take particular action with respect to a law that would produce a restraint or a monopoly."

In *Noerr,* the plaintiff trucking interests had alleged that the defendant railroad interests violated the antitrust laws with a publicity campaign that was designed not only "to foster the adoption and retention of laws and law enforcement practices restrictive of the trucking business" but also "to create an atmosphere of distaste for the truckers and their customers." Insofar as the railroads' activities "comprised mere solicitation of governmental action with respect to the passage and enforcement of laws," the Supreme Court explained, they bear little, if any, resemblance to the combinations normally held to violate the Sherman Act. Antitrust combinations, the Court said, "are ordinarily characterized by an express or implied agreement or understanding that the participants will jointly give up their trade freedom or help one another to take away the freedom of others through the use of such devices as price-fixing agreements, boycotts, market-division agreements, and other similar arrangements."

To hold that the Sherman Act forbids associations to influence the adoption or enforcement of laws, the Supreme Court reasoned, would impair the Government's power to restrict trade if it so chooses. Such a holding, in the Court's words, "would impute to the Sherman Act a purpose to regulate, not business activity, but political activity, a purpose which would have no basis whatever in the legislative history of that Act." It would also raise important constitutional questions because "the right of petition is one of the freedoms protected by the Bill of Rights, and we cannot, of course, lightly impute to Congress an intent to invade these freedoms."

The Supreme Court stressed in *Continental Ore Co.* v. *Union Carbide and Carbon Corp.,* 370 U.S. 690 (1962), that the *Noerr* decision dealt with "the passage and enforcement of laws." The Court reversed a lower court's refusal to admit evidence that a U.S. vanadium producer was eliminated from the Canadian market through action taken by Union Carbide's Canadian subsidiary while acting as a purchasing agent for the Canadian Government. Speaking for the Court, Justice White said there is no indication that Canadian law required the discriminatory action taken by its purchasing agency.

In *U.S.* v. *Sisal Sales Corp.,* 274 U.S. 268 (1926), a combination to monopolize an article of commerce produced abroad was held to violate the Sherman Act even though the conspirators' control of production was aided by persuading a foreign government to enact discriminatory legislation.

The Federal District Court for Eastern Tennessee considered a coal-mine operator's complaint that the UMW conspired with large mine operators to have Walsh-Healey Public Contracts Act prevailing-wage rates set so high that small coal companies would be driven out of business. The court's ruling, upheld by the court of appeals, 325 F.2d 804 (6th Cir. 1963), was that the *Noerr* doctrine is not so broad as to give an unlimited exemption from the Sherman Act to all concerted attempts to influence government officials. The district court instructed the jury that a concerted effort to influence prevailing-wage determinations by the Secretary of Labor would not be a violation of the antitrust laws, unless the effort "was part of the conspiracy to get the prevailing wages established in the coal industry so high as to drive the small operators out of business." A unanimous Supreme Court agreed with the UMW that both the court of appeals and the district court failed to take proper account of the *Noerr* case (*United Mine Workers of America* v. *Pennington,* 381 U.S. 657 (1965)). *Noerr,* the Court said, "shields from the Sherman Act a concerted effort to influence public officials regardless of intent or purpose." The Court stressed that "joint efforts to influence public officials do not violate the antitrust laws even though intended to eliminate competition."

The Court also struck down the district court's instructions to the jury with respect to the UMW's alleged efforts to induce the Tennessee Valley Authority to purchase coal only from mine operators who paid wages conforming to Walsh-Healey wage determinations. The jury was told that it is no violation of the antitrust laws for the union or the coal operators to urge TVA to abide by the spirit and letter of the Walsh-Healey Act or to modify its methods of buying coal, "unless the parties so urged the TVA to modify its policies in buying coal for the purpose of driving the small operators out of business." The fact is, the Supreme Court said in *Pennington,* that even when the conspirators' purpose is to destroy competition, "such conduct is not illegal, either standing alone or as part of a broader scheme itself violative of the Sherman Act. The jury should have been so instructed."

Another application of the *Noerr* doctrine is seen in a criminal action against Johns-Manville Corp. and Keasbey & Mattison Co. (*U.S.* v. *Johns-Manville Corp.,* 259 F.Supp. 440 (E.D. Pa 1966)). Defendants were charged with conspiring to influence the American Society for Testing Materials, municipalities, and public contracting authorities to adopt specifications aimed at excluding the products of foreign competitors. Over the Government's objection, the district court ruled that facts relating to the campaign to persuade governmental purchasing entities to exclude foreign products are inadmissible under the *Noerr* doctrine. Similar facts with respect to efforts to influence the adoption of product specifications by nongovernmental testing societies are inadmissible for the same reason, the court ruled in an unreported decision in the same case, "when it appears that the membership of such organizations is comprised in whole or in part of governmental agents and officials."

The Government argued unsuccessfully that the campaign to exclude the foreign products, whether directed at governmental or quasi-governmental agencies or at nongovernmental learned societies, regardless of the composition of their membership, is not "political" activity within the meaning of the *Noerr* decision. Rather, the Government argued, the campaign "is an integral part of an overall scheme in violation of a valid criminal statute" and is therefore not entitled to First Amendment protection. The Government attempted to distinguish the Johns-Manville campaign from that conducted by the railroads against the truckers on the ground that Johns-Manville sought to "influence the activities of the various governments solely as customers."

The *Pennington* opinion's statement that the *Noerr* doctrine protects a concerted effort "to influence public officials," gives that doctrine wide scope. Yet, there are indications that there may be limits to the protection. Some antitrust lawyers feel the Supreme Court's decisions in labor cases are not always safe precedents in other areas. For example, few are ready to believe that a conspiracy to rig bids on government contracts would be within the *Noerr* doctrine.

There is authority for excluding from the doctrine the use of fraud to influence public officials. When he wrote his concurring opinion in *U.S.* v. *Singer Mfg. Co.,* 374 U.S. 174 (1963), Justice

White apparently felt there is no constitutional right to deceive the Government in obtaining a patent. Stating that "collusion among applicants to prevent prior art from coming to or being drawn to the (Patent) Officer's attention is an inequitable imposition on the Office and the public," Justice White asserted that such collusion to secure a monopoly grant violates the Sherman Act. While the *Noerr* opinion stresses the constitutional right of a citizen to petition his Government, other Supreme Court opinions, like *Sisal* and *Continental Ore,* suggest that firms which join in concerted efforts to influence foreign governments to take action that restrains U.S. commerce do so at their peril.

On the other hand, Judge Van Dusen's action in the *Johns-Manville* case provides an answer, at least for the time being, to a question asked by many businessmen, lawyers, and government officials: Does the *Noerr* doctrine reach down to petty government officials? In the *Johns-Manville* case it did.

In *Trucking Unlimited* v. *California Motor Transport Co.,* 432 F.2d 755 (9th Cir. 1970), the court ruled that the *Noerr-Pennington* doctrine does not protect an agreement to employ judicial and administrative adjudicative processes as part of a scheme to restrain trade. According to the complaint, the defendant trucking companies, the largest highway common carriers in California and the Western States, undertook to reduce competition from the smaller companies which had relatively easy access to operating rights granted by the California Public Utilities Commission and the Interstate Commerce Commission. The policy of the California PUC was to encourage competition in the trucking industry by freely granting, and approving, the transfer of certificates of public convenience and necessity. Until 1963, it was the policy of the ICC to register automatically any certificate issued by the PUC without further hearing.

The defendants allegedly decided to destroy this access. According to the complaint, they established a joint trust fund, maintained by monthly contributions based upon each defendant's gross income, to finance opposition to all applications then pending or thereafter filed by their competitors with the PUC or the ICC. Each application was to be opposed with or without probable cause and regardless of its merits, and to be pursued through all stages of the administrative and judicial process. As a result, obtaining a certificate from either the PUC or ICC became an expensive and time-consuming process. The financial resources of the plaintiffs and other competitors were depleted; applications for operating rights were defeated, delayed, or restricted; and plaintiffs and other competitors were deterred from instituting and pursuing such applications.

The first ground for the decision of the court of appeals was its determination that the *Noerr-Pennington* doctrine immunizes concerted conduct to influence legislative and executive action but not judicial or administrative adjudicative action. As to the latter, the court said:

"The fundamental reason for the *Noerr-Pennington* exception does not apply. It is not the function of the courts to determine whether laws restraining trade will be enforced; nor is this the function of an administrative agency engaged in adjudication, as the PUC and the ICC are here.

"It would be pointless to limit the reach of the Sherman Act in order to protect the access of courts and agencies engaged in the adjudicative functions to information and opinion relevant to determinations which they have no power to make."

The second alternative ground was the court of appeals' determination that the alleged wrongful conduct came within the "sham" exception to the *Noerr-Pennington* doctrine. The "sham" exception is derived from the basic rationale of the *Noerr-Pennington* defense. The Act does not bar legislation or law enforcement restraining trade and therefore does not bar the solicitation of such action. Conversely, if joint action is for the purpose of imposing a direct restraint by the defendants' own conduct, the Sherman Act applies.

"There may be situations in which a publicity campaign, ostensibly directed toward influencing governmental action, is a mere sham to cover what is actually nothing more than an attempt to interfere directly with the business relationships of a competitor and the application of the Sherman Act would be justified" the court said.

The court of appeals noted that the defendant truckers allegedly tried to reduce competition from the smaller truckers "not by seeking to induce the PUC to change its [liberal] policy but rather by discouraging the filing of applications with the PUC and the ICC."

The Supreme Court affirmed the court of appeals' decision, finding the conduct within the "sham exception" (404 U.S. 508 (1972)). The majority opinion, written by Justice Douglas, first stated that, contrary to the first alternative ground of the court of appeals' decision, the *Noerr-Pennington* doctrine applies to joint efforts to influence courts and administrative agencies as well as legislative and executive officers, although protection may be less with regard to joint efforts before courts or agencies. After noting that the railroads in *Noerr* had employed various unethical tactics, Justice Douglas gave several instances in which unethical conduct during the adjudicatory process has resulted in sanctions, including antitrust sanctions. He went on to say that "a pattern of baseless, repetitive claims may emerge which leads the factfinder to conclude that the administrative and judicial processes have been abused. That may be a difficult line to discern and draw. But once it is drawn, the case is established that abuse of those processes produced an illegal result, viz., effectively barring respondents from access to the agencies and courts. Insofar as the administrative or judicial processes are involved, actions of that kind cannot acquire immunity by seeking refuge under the umbrella of 'political expression.' "

"A combination of entrepreneurs to harass and deter their competitors from having 'free and unlimited access' to the agencies and courts, to defeat that right by massive, concerted and purposeful activities of the group are ways of building up one empire and destroying another. As stated in the concurring opinion, that is the essence of those parts of the complaint to which we refer. If these facts are proved, a violation of the antitrust laws has been established. If the end result is unlawful, it matters not that the means used in violation may be lawful." He concluded by saying that the allegations, taken at face value, "come within the 'sham' exception in the Noerr case, as adapted to the adjudicatory process."

According to Justice Stewart, concurring, the majority "retreats from Noerr, and in the process tramples upon important First Amendment values." In his view, at least when there are no allegations of misrepresentations of fact or law to courts and agencies, and no claims of perjury, fraud, or bribery, there should "be no difference, so far as the antitrust laws and the First Amendment are concerned, between trying to influence executive and legislative bodies and trying to influence administrative and judicial bodies."

In the *Trucking Unlimited* case, the Supreme Court held that the *Noerr-Pennington* doctrine extends to joint efforts before courts and agencies. This was reaffirmed in *Otter Tail Power Co.* v. *U.S.*, 602 ATRR D-1 (1973). However, while the *Noerr-Pennington* doctrine affords some protection to such efforts, that protection is apparently more limited in the judicial and administrative setting than it is in regard to efforts to influence the legislative and executive branches.

According to the majority opinion in the *Trucking Unlimited* case, certain types of unethical conduct, which presumably are still immunized when efforts are made to influence the legislative and executive branches, are not immunized in connection with adjudicatory proceedings. As noted, even Justices Stewart and Brennan, the concurring Justices, acknowledge that "misrepresentations of fact or law" or "perjury or fraud or bribery" are not immunized if such conduct occurs in connection with adjudicatory proceedings. The concurring Justices would also agree that denial of access to courts and agencies can be within the "sham" exception. On this point, Justice Stewart seems to take the view that the appropriate test is whether "the real intent" of the defendants here was not to invoke the judicial and administrative processes but to deny to plaintiffs access to those processes. This seems similar to the test suggested in *Noerr,* that is, whether the direct injury is an "incidental result" of efforts aimed at influencing governmental bodies or is the result of "what is actually nothing more than an attempt to interfere directly" with the competitor's business.

The test adopted by the majority seems to have a different focus. Instead of concentrating on the "real intent," the majority's test seems to be whether there has been an abuse of judicial or administrative process and whether such abuse results in a foreclosure of a competitor from access to those processes. The scope of this test is not clear. It appears however, that the majority would find a showing of "a pattern of baseless, repetitive claims" resulting in foreclosure to be enough to bring the activity within the "sham" exception. Further evidence as to intent would seem unnecessary. Justice Douglas seems to suggest that the requisite purpose "may be implicit" in the very act of invoking the processes of the courts or agencies to oppose an application.

Can an abuse of process by a single large carrier be within the "sham" exception? Although the majority speaks of "concerted" activities of a "group," there are some indications from other language and from the rationale of the decision that a large carrier with enough power to block access may not be exempt. The loss of an exemption, however, means only loss of a defense; it would still be necessary to prove an antitrust violation (presumably, in the case of a single carrier, a violation of Section 2 of the Sherman Act).

The Supreme Court's decision means that there are risks attending opposition by groups of carriers (and possibly by large individual carriers) to applications by smaller competitors, when such opposition is without regard to the merits of each particular application. A claim of abuse of process, when it blocks a competitor's access to a court or agency, can now be raised in an antitrust court and could lead to treble-damage consequences.

The *Trucking Unlimited* decision has established that the *Noerr-Pennington* doctrine applies to some extent to conduct before courts and agencies. But consider that decision in connection with the Court's almost simultaneous rejection (with Justice Stewart dissenting) of a petition for certiorari in *Aluminum Company of America* v. *Woods Exploration and Producing Co.,* 438 F.2d 1286 (5th Cir. 1971) *cert. denied,* 404 U.S. 1047 (1972), in which the court of appeals held that alleged fraudulent conduct before an administrative agency was not protected by the *Noerr-Pennington* doctrine. These actions may indicate that the Court has a less expansive view of immunity of conduct before courts and agencies than it had, at the time of the *Noerr* and *Pennington* decisions, with regard to joint efforts to influence the legislative and executive branches.

15. Activities Under State Regulation

Question: *How far can state regulatory activity insulate business conduct which would otherwise violate the federal antitrust laws?*

The Supreme Court has held that state action can create immunity from the antitrust laws (*Parker* v. *Brown,* 317 U.S. 341 (1943)). The case involved an attempt by California to correlate the supply of raisins with market demand. The California legislature set up an agricultural prorate advisory commission to appoint a program committee. The committee would draw up a marketing plan that the commission would then approve or modify. The commission eventually adopted a plan that regulated the sale of all raisins grown in the state.

The Supreme Court held the program did not violate the Sherman Act. The Court viewed the program as state action under the authority of the state legislature and not covered by the Sherman Act. "We find nothing in the language of the Sherman Act or in its history which suggests that its purpose was to restrain a state or its officers or agents from activities directed by its legislature" (317 U.S. 350).

On the other hand, regulations adopted by private bodies operating under state law are not exempt from the antitrust statutes (*Asheville Tobacco Board of Trade, Inc.* v. *FTC,* 263 F.2d 502 (4th Cir. 1959)). Private contracts do not acquire immunity through state approval either. Immunity arises only where the legislature creates the entity and directs by statute the use of anticompetitive means to a governmental goal. Regulation of a private company is not the equivalent of delegation of governmental authority (*Travelers Insurance Co.* v. *Blue Cross of Western Penna.,* 298 F.Supp. 1109 (W.D. Pa. 1969)).

The Fourth and the Fifth Circuits, applying the doctrine of *Parker* v. *Brown,* have held that certain promotional practices of regulated electric utilities are immune from antitrust attack (*Washington Gas Light Co.* v. *Virginia Electric and Power Co.* (*VEPCO*), 438 F.2d 248 (4th Cir. 1971); *Gas Light Co. of Columbus* v. *Georgia Power Co.,* 440 F.2d 1135 (5th Cir. 1971)). In each case, the plaintiff gas company had charged that defendant's practices relating to the sale of electricity and the installation of electrical facilities were unlawful tie-ins to induce customers to install electric rather than gas facilities. The plantiff in the *Georgia Power* case had also alleged that defendant's practices were the product of "a nationwide conspiracy among electric utilities to eliminate natural gas as a competitive energy source." Each plaintiff sought treble damages and injunctive relief.

In *VEPCO,* the promotions were initiated in 1963 by the electric utility without the express approval or disapproval of the state regulatory commission. In 1966, the promotions were replaced by other promotions having about the same effect. In 1970, the commission issued an order prohibiting all such promotions, and the promotions were discontinued. The plaintiff had contended that, even though the commission was aware of VEPCO's promotional activities before 1966, it made no investigations and gave no approval (or disapproval) of the VEPCO plans, and that VEPCO's conduct was therefore "individual" and not "state action." Rejecting this contention, the court refused to equate "administrative silence with abandonment of administrative duty":

"It is just as sensible to infer that silence means consent, i.e., approval. Indeed, the latter inference seems the more likely one when we remember that even the gas company concedes that the SCC possessed adequate regulatory powers to stop VEPCO if it chose to do so, and that eventually SCC spoke affirmatively and first modified and finally ended the promotional practices upon which the suit was based. The antitrust laws are a poor substitute, we think, for plaintiff's failure to promptly protest to the SCC and to seek the administrative remedy ultimately shown to have been available and effective. We think VEPCO's promotional practices were at all times within the ambit of regulation and under the control of SCC, and we hold these practices exempt from the application of the laws of antitrust under the Parker doctrine."

(As an alternative ground for its decision, citing *Fortner Enterprises* v. *U.S. Steel Corp.,* 394 U.S. 495 (1969), the court held that the electric utility's sales practices involved only electricity, not two separate products, so that there was no tie-in cognizable under the antitrust laws.)

In *Georgia Power,* although the promotional practices were initiated by the electric utility, the court noted that "each of these acts and practices are rate schedules and each has been considered by the Georgia Public Service Commission in an adversary proceeding. Each is effective by order of the Commission."

On the basis of the "state's intimate involvement with the rate making powers," the court characterized the promotions as "products" of the state regulatory commission rather than of the electric utility. The court quoted approvingly from the *VEPCO* case, but expressly refused to go so far as to say that a regulatory agency's silence was tantamount to approval. "It is not necessary for us to extend the Parker exclusion to the point of its extension in [*VEPCO*] and we do not do so."

Some observers are doubtful about the reasoning in these cases, especially *VEPCO,* where silence was construed as approval of the promotions even though the regulatory commission ultimately prohibited such practices. These observers question whether such privately initiated practices are "state action" within the meaning of the *Parker* v. *Brown* doctrine. They suggest that where the state regulatory scheme contemplates some competition, as here, between gas companies and electric companies, the antitrust laws may be held to apply. There often is a fairly wide range of rates and practices which a regulatory commission can find to be reasonable and nondiscriminatory and, therefore, fairly broad discretion in choosing a particular rate or practice often lies with the regulated utility. Some suggest that where there is a conspiracy or an avowed monopolistic intention governing that choice, recourse to the antitrust laws will be available. *Georgia* v. *Pennsylvania R. Co.,* 324 U.S. 439 (1945), is cited. There, the Supreme Court held that a combination among carriers to set rates could be enjoined under the antitrust laws, even though the rates were subject to regulation by the Interstate Commerce Commission. Citing *Keogh* v. *Chicago & N.W. Ry. Co.,* 260 U.S. 156 (1922), the Court stated that "the fact that the rates which have been fixed may or may not be held unlawful by the Commission is immaterial to the issue before us." The Court explained:

"The reason is that the Interstate Commerce Act does not provide remedies for the correction of all the abuses of rate-making which might constitute violations of the antitrust laws. Thus a 'zone of reasonableness exists between maxima and minima within which a carrier is ordinarily free to adjust its charges for itself.' Within that zone the Commission lacks power to grant relief even though the rates are raised to the maxima by a conspiracy among carriers who employ unlawful tactics. If the rate-making function is freed from the unlawful restraints of the alleged conspiracy, the rates of the future will then be fixed in the manner envisioned by Congress when it enacted this legislation.

"Damage must be presumed to flow from a conspiracy to manipulate rates within that zone" ([Citation omitted.] 324 U.S. 460–461).

As previously noted, in *Georgia Power* (though not in *VEPCO*) one of the allegations was that the challenged practices were part of a nationwide conspiracy against gas companies.

Recent judicial development of the *Parker* doctrine by the lower courts is said by some to be inconsistent with the more recent pronouncements of the Supreme Court in the somewhat analogous line of cases construing antitrust exemptions created by federal regulatory statutes. In those cases, the exemptions have consistently been narrowly defined. See, for instance, *U.S.* v. *Philadelphia Nat'l Bank,* 374 U.S. 321 (1963), where the Court said: "repeals of the antitrust laws by implication from a regulatory statute are strongly disfavored, and have only been found in cases of plain repugnancy between the antitrust and regulatory provisions" ([Footnotes omitted.] 374 U.S. 350–351.)

It must be recognized, though, that where federal regulation is involved, the problem is one of reconciling federal regulatory and antitrust statues, as in *Thill Securities Corp.* v. *New York Stock Exchange,* 433 F.2d 264 (7th Cir. 1970), *cert. denied,* 401 U.S. 994 (1971), applying the Supreme Court's ruling in *Silver* v. *NYSE,* 373 U.S. 341 (1963), that repeal of the antitrust laws in the securities field "is to be regarded as implied only if necessary to make the Securities Exchange Act work, and even then only to the minimum extent necessary." This is quite different from the *Parker* doctrine which rests upon the Supreme Court's determination that Congress did not intend the antitrust laws to apply to state action at all. Some think that the notion of sovereign immunity is also involved in the *Parker* doctrine, and find support for their view in the recent decision of the court of appeals in *Hecht* v. *Pro-Football, Inc.,* 444 F.2d 931 (D.C. Cir. 1971).

In *Hecht,* the court of appeals held that a restrictive covenant in a lease of a publicly owned stadium to a professional football team, giving the team, in effect, a local monopoly, is not within the *Parker* v. *Brown* exclusion. Although the lessor, a District of Columbia agency (the Armory Board), is a federal agency, the parties had relied "most strongly" upon cases involving "state action;" and, "since the Armory Board here is somewhat similar to a state government agency," the court took those cases into account in reaching its decision. In considering the *Parker* v. *Brown* doctrine, the court took a narrow view of the Supreme Court's holding: "*Parker* v. *Brown* involves not just state government action; it involves regulatory action in the state's capacity as sovereign, and it involves sovereign state regulatory action which is consistent with federal national policy, i.e., the Agricultural Adjustment Act, enunciated by the national Congress, which is also the source of federal antitrust policy." The court also stated: "We think it significant that in those cases where the antitrust laws were held not to apply there was a national or state policy of importance approximately equal to the antitrust laws involved. For example, in *Parker*

v. *Brown* the state action was regulation of an important agricultural product, and a state regulation completely consistent with the federal Agricultural Adjustment Act."

It remains to be seen whether "state action" will be more narrowly defined and what role there may be for the antitrust laws to play where state regulation is involved. There are difficulties in defining that role. For instance, is the Justice Department to be a reviewing agency for the state regulatory commissions? It may be that the doctrine of primary jurisdiction will find some application here. In pointing out that the gas company in *VEPCO* had failed to complain promptly to the commission, the court may have had in mind the notion of primary jurisdiction or the related doctrine requiring the exhaustion of administrative remedies.

PART II

Problems in Distribution—Relations With Customers and Suppliers

A. MATTERS OF PRICE

1. Exchanging Price Information

Question: *What price information may competitors lawfully exchange?*

Agreements between competitors on prices were first declared to be Section 1 Sherman Act violations in *U.S.* v. *Trans-Missouri Freight Association,* 166 U.S. 290 (1897). Since then, a variety of price-monitoring and price-supervising programs, many run by trade associations, have been reviewed by the Supreme Court.

The collection and dissemination of price, sales, inventory, and customer data were enjoined in *American Column & Lumber Co.* v. *U.S.,* 257 U.S. 377 (1921). In that case there was evidence that the trade association had made a systematic effort, along with the distribution of the data, to have members cut production and raise prices. A more elaborate program of sales-data distribution, coupled with a penalty-backed agreement to adhere to announced price schedules, was outlawed in *U.S.* v. *American Linseed Oil Co.,* 262 U.S. 371 (1923). In *Sugar Institute* v. *U.S.,* 297 U.S. 553 (1936), and *U.S.* v. *Socony-Vacuum Oil Co.,* 310 U.S. 150 (1940), programs for the exchange of price information included commitments to adhere to announced price schedules.

In *Maple Flooring Mfrs. Assoc.* v. *U.S.,* 268 U.S. 563 (1925), the Court declared that ". . . trade associations or combinations of persons or corporations which openly and fairly gather and disseminate information as to the cost of their product, the volume of production, the actual price which the product has brought in past transactions, stocks of merchandise on hand, approximate cost of transporation from the principal point of shipment to the points of consumption as did these defendants and who, as they did, meet and discuss such information and statistics without however reaching or attempting to reach any agreement or any concerted action with respect to prices or production or restraining competition, do not thereby engage in unlawful restraint of commerce." The Maple Floor Manufacturers' Association did not, in its statistical reports to members, identify the parties to specific transactions. In *Cement Mfrs. Protective Ass'n.* v. *U.S.,* 268 U.S. 588 (1925), where prices to specific customers were exchanged, the Supreme Court upheld the exchange program after noting that its purpose was protection against fraudulent inducement to deliver more cement than needed for a specific job. Where "cement manufacturers, to protect themselves from delivering to contractors more cement than was needed for a specific job and thus receiving a lower price, exchanged price information as a means of protecting their legal rights from fradulent inducements to deliver more cement than needed for a specific job," the Court concluded there was no unlawful restraint of trade.

U.S. v. *Container Corp. of America,* 393 U.S. 333 (1969), "is unlike any of the other price decisions we have rendered," according to Justice Douglas, who wrote the majority opinion. The Supreme Court reinstated a Justice Department suit to enjoin a price-data exchange program that carried with it no systematic trade-association effort to boost prices nor any commitment to adhere to a price schedule. There was an exchange of information concerning specific sales to identified customers, not a statistical report on the average cost to all members.

The district judge dismissed the Government's complaint (273 F.Supp. 18 (M.D.N.C. 1967)) on the basis of findings that were left undisturbed on appeal. Competitive price information was sought by the sellers, manufacturers of corrugated paper containers, in order "to compete effectively for the business of a purchaser." Ordinarily, the prices most recently charged or quoted by competing suppliers were available from the purchasers themselves. Sometimes a seller found it necessary to obtain or verify the price information through direct contact with his competitor. While there was no express assurance that any seller who furnished such price information to a competitor was entitled to reciprocity when he needed similar information, the requested price information was "usually" furnished. These circumstances did not convince the district judge that the Government had proven a basis for inferring an agreement to exchange price information.

The trial court did not conclude that, assuming the existence of an agreement, its purpose or effect was to inhibit price competition. Among the market factors the judge cited as negating any impairment of price competition were: (1) a downward trend in price despite increasing manufacturing costs; (2) buyers' frequent changes of suppliers on the basis of price; (3) industry statistics showing an absence of price uniformity or price stability; (4) evidence that sellers' pricing decisions were based not only on price data ob-

tained from competitors but also upon plant production load, availability of needed materials, size of order, customer's credit rating,
and similar factors; and (5) failure of the Government to produce
any evidence from customers to show price stabilization.

Before the Supreme Court, the Government disclaimed any
attack on exchange of composite price information through a trade
association but charged "that defendants through a combination
have become too precise, and that precision inhibits competition."
The Supreme Court found both a "combination or conspiracy"
and an unlawful anticompetitive result. "Concerted action . . .
sufficient to establish the combination or conspiracy" was found in
evidence that "each defendant on receiving that request usually
furnished the data with the expectation that he would be furnished
reciprocal information when he wanted it."

The prohibited result was "to stabilize prices though at a downward level." To support its finding of price stabilization, the Supreme Court relied on findings of the trial judge that: (1) while
the containers vary as to dimensions, weight, and color, they are
substantially identical, no matter who produces them, when made
to the customer's specifications; (2) therefore, price was the medium
of competition; (3) knowledge of a competitor's price usually meant
that the seller matched that price or undercut it only slightly; (4)
despite the industry's excess plant capacity and the downward
trend of prices, it expanded during the year covered by the complaint from 30 manufacturers with 49 plants to 51 manufacturers
with 98 plants; and (5) the industry was dominated by relatively
few manufacturers; 18 defendants accounted for 90 percent of the
shipments.

From these facts "the inferences are irresistible," Justice Douglas
declared, "that the exchange of price information has had an
anticompetitive effect in the industry, chilling the vigor of price
competition." True, price competition was not eliminated entirely,
but "the limitation or reduction of price competition brings the
case within the ban, for as we held in *United States* v. *Socony-
Vacuum Oil Co.*, 310 U.S. 150, 224, n. 59 (1940), interference with
the setting of price by free market forces is unlawful per se."

There may be some markets, Justice Douglas acknowledged,
where such exchange of price information would have no effect
on a truly competitive price. However, when the market for a
fungible product is dominated by relatively few sellers, when "the
competition for sales is price, and when the demand is inelastic
(since the buyers placed orders for only immediate, short-run
needs), a lower price does not mean a larger share of the available
business but a sharing of the existing business at a lower return."
Therefore, the exchange of price data tends toward price uniformity, said Douglas.

In a separate concurring opinion, Justice Fortas stated his understanding that the majority opinion did not hold price-exchange arrangements illegal per se. In this instance, the exchange of prices did make it possible "for individual defendants confidently to name a price equal to that which their competitors were asking. The obvious effect was to 'stabilize' prices by joint arrangement."

In a dissenting opinion joined by Justices Harlan and Stewart, Justice Marshall stressed evidence that the defendants, while they account for 90 percent of the sales, are only 18 of 51 producers in their market, that market entry is easy, that the number of sellers increased from 30 to 51 during the eight-year period covered by the complaint, that increasing demand almost doubled the size of the market during the same period, and that there is some excess capacity in the industry. In such a market, he maintained, it is logical to assume that the smaller and newer sellers will cut prices to capture a larger market share. He found no evidence in the record to support the majority's "irresistible" inference of anticompetitive effect.

Antitrust lawyers find it useful to view from two separate standpoints the practice of exchanging price information among competitors. As counselors, they have long advised their clients to avoid price discussions, but they press the argument that exchange of price information is a Sherman Act violation only when it is shown to have a purpose or effect of curtailing competition.

The *Container Corporation* decision appears to vindicate both these conclusions. As Justice Fortas observed, the majority opinion did not find a per se Sherman Act violation in the exchange of specific information as to price to individual customers. Any such exchange is unlawful per se if, in Justice Douglas' terms, it interferes "with the setting of price by free market forces." In a market with declining prices, absence of price uniformity, and much switching of suppliers, the Court found that exchange of price quotations had a forbidden price-stabilizing effect, that "the inferences are irresistible that the exchange of price information has had an anticompetitive effect." If the inferences were irresistible in this industry, some lawyers suggest, every program among competitors for exchanging prices charged by identified sellers to identified buyers is a Sherman Act violation. The Court's per se rule of illegality for price-exchanging arrangements that "interfere" with free price competition probably means that justifications such as those asserted in the *Cement Manufacturers'* case will no longer save such arrangements.

In analyzing what price information exchange may be lawful it is probably useful to distinguish three different situations: (1) trade association statistical programs, (2) direct exchange of specific prices between business concerns where prices are not generally public or are difficult to obtain or calculate (as in *Container*), and (3) routine exchange of generally published price lists. The final judgment in the *Container* case permitted the third type over Department of Justice opposition (1970 Trade Cas. ¶73,091 (M.D. N.C. 1970)). The consent decree in the government civil case in the *Electrical Industry* cases prohibited exchange of pricing information not yet released to the trade generally but explicitly excepted exchange of price data after it had been generally released (1962 Trade Cas. ¶70,487 and ¶70,488). All three types may involve substantial antitrust risk since the exchange of prices is one leg of a circumstantial evidence case of price fixing or price tampering. Risk may be less if price data is obtained from "antiseptic" sources (dealers, trade journals, or services) rather than competitors since this minimizes circumstantial inferences.

As to Justice Douglas' opinion on the precedents sustaining trade-association programs for collecting and disseminating price statistics that do not identify specific transactions or parties, opinions are divided. Some experts feel that a good industry statistics-reporting program can have a greater stabilizing effect on prices than the occasional and irregular exchange of price quotes that occurred among the corrugated container manufacturers. Therefore, they believe, the curse of per se illegality falls on such programs as well. Other lawyers are just as convinced that a distinction must be made between trade-association reporting of pricing statistics and exchange of price quotes. They suggest that the *Maple Flooring Manufacturers'* case is still the law, at least for any industry that has not developed an "oligopolistic" structure.

Operating a trade-association statistical reporting program under the protection of the *Maple Flooring* decision is not a simple task. Even assuming an industry has a lawful and reasonable purpose for reporting its sales statistics and gets an FTC advisory opinion clearing its program, the program may by tainted by one or two instances of illegal exchanges of individual industry members. The trade association must be diligent in educating its members as to the importance of avoiding price discussions of any kind. Even if a seller's only motive in seeking his competitor's price is to avoid a Robinson-Patman Act violation, it may be that his only recourse is a look at the customer's invoice from the competing supplier. (See following section, II-A-2.)

2. Exchanging Price Information

Question: *May an exchange of current price information be justified as necessary to avoid violation of the Robinson-Patman Act?*

As discussed in the preceding section, the Supreme Court, in *U.S.* v. *Container Corp.,* 393 U.S. 333 (1969), ruled unlawful an arrangement that provided for "a request by each defendant of its competitors for information as to the most recent price charged or quoted, whenever it needed such information and whenever it was not available from another source." The Court found that the exchange of data had the effect of stabilizing prices in the industry, and that this was price fixing prohibited by the Sherman Act. The Court distinguished the case from *Cement Mfrs. Protective Ass'n.* v. *U.S.,* 268 U.S. 588 (1925), in which there was a similar exchange of price information but in which it found a controlling circumstance: "that cement manufacturers, to protect themselves from delivering to contractors more cement than was needed for a specific job and thus receiving a lower price, exchanged price information as a means of protecting their legal rights from fraudulent inducements to deliver more cement than needed for a specific job."

In *Wall Products* v. *National Gypsum Co.,* 326 F.Supp. 295 (N.D. Cal. 1971), six buyers of gypsum wallboard brought a treble-damage action against major producers alleging violations of Section 1 of the Sherman Act. Two claims were made: first, that before December 15, 1965, the defendants and other producers engaged in an arrangement, similar to the one in *Container,* to verify each other's deviations from list prices; and second, that after December 15, 1965, the major producers, each of which had more than a single plant, unlawfully conspired to refuse to deviate from their own list prices to meet deviations from the list price by single-plant producers. The district court upheld the latter claim, finding that the defendants' course of conduct in refusing to meet deviations by single-plant producers was more than mere "conscious parallelism" and amounted to a combination or conspiracy to maintain prices. (Damages were later assessed at more than $3 million (609 ATRR A-19 (4/17/73)).) Plaintiffs' claim relating to the price-verification arrangement was rejected by the court.

The court found that different brands of wallboard are interchangeable and that buyers generally choose from among competing sellers primarily on the basis of price. Prior to 1965, wallboard was theoretically sold according to list price. List prices of the major producers tended to be the same. As demand declined in relation to capacity prior to 1965, the practice of deviating from list prices became widespread. This was the situation when the sellers of wallboard entered into an arrangement with one another whereby a seller could verify with a competitor a customer's report of a deviation by that competitor from the list price.

The court found that this arrangement was the product of explicit agreements to exchange the information. It also found that the arrangement had a stabilizing effect upon prices. Nevertheless, it concluded that the arrangement, like the one in *Cement Mfrs.*, was rendered lawful by "controlling circumstances." According to the court, the "controlling circumstance" in the *Cement* case was the legitimate *purpose* of the verification arrangement. That purpose was to prevent abuse of the "specific job-contract" in the cement industry. The "specific job-contract" amounted to "an option to a contractor bidding on a particular job to purchase the quantity of cement which he required for that job at the price in effect when the contract was issued." Abuse could occur because the contractor, who was not obligated to buy under the "specific job-contracts," could enter into such contracts with several sellers and protect himself from future price increases.

The court upheld the verification arrangement in *Wall Products* upon finding that it served *two* legitimate purposes. First, noting that a seller must use "diligence to verify its customer's claim of a competitor's lower price in order to avail itself of the good faith defense under Section 2(b) of the Act" (citing *FTC* v. *A. E. Staley Mfg. Co.*, 324 U.S. 746 (1945)), and also noting that the seller can "meet but not beat" the competitor's lower price (citing *Standard Oil Co.* v. *FTC*, 340 U.S. 231 (1951)), the court concluded that the arrangement was designed for the purpose of facilitating compliance with the Robinson-Patman Act. The court found that wallboard buyers often had misrepresented competitive offers, and it stressed that the sellers verified with competitors only when other reliable means of verification were unavailable. The court observed that the U.S. Supreme Court did not deal with a Robinson-Patman justification in the *Container* case. (The *Wall Products* rationale was followed in *Belliston* v. *Texaco, Inc.*, 455 F.2d 175 (10th Cir. 1972). See also *Gray* v. *Shell Oil Co.*, 1972 Trade Cas. ¶74,247 (9th Cir. 1972); *Webster* v. *Sinclair Rfg. Co.*, 338 F.Supp. 248 (S.D. Ala. 1971)).

Second, aside from the Robinson-Patman justification, the court concluded that the arrangement served the purpose of enabling the sellers to protect themselves from the "fraudulent practices" of buyers. These practices included both the misrepresentation by the buyers of the offers they received and also, on occasion, the buyers' abuse of the wallboard industry's equivalent of the "specific job-contract."

Some antitrust experts expressed surprise at this conclusion of the court. In their view, the systematic exchange among competitors of current price information can potentially have such an effect of "chilling the vigor of price competition" (*Container, supra,* 393 U.S. at 337) that they question whether the district court has

succeeded in striking a balance between the competing claims of
the Robinson-Patman Act and the Sherman Act that would be
acceptable to the Supreme Court. They tend to doubt that the Supreme Court would share the district judge's overriding concern
about the fraudulent practices of buyers in view of the evident
concern in *Container* to prevent arrangements which stabilize
prices. As the district judge noted, however, the Court's treatment of
the *Cement* case in *Container* does suggest that the protection against
fraud be accorded some weight.

Experts also argue that verification arrangements in *Wall Products* go beyond anything that the FTC has required as "diligence"
in the meeting-competition defense. According to these observers,
the FTC has never yet insisted upon verification with a competitor.
In *Beatrice Foods Co.,* (1967–1970 Transfer Binder) Trade Reg. Rep.
¶19,045 (F.T.C. 1969), *aff'd sub nom. Kroger Co.* v. *FTC,* 438 F.2d
1372 (6th Cir. 1971), in exonerating a seller who was misled by the
buyer into "beating" competition, the Commission did not even discuss the fact that the seller knew the identity of competing sellers
and apparently made no effort to verify with the competing sellers
their reported offers. Since even occasional verification has never
been insisted upon by the FTC, these observers think that, a fortiori,
a *systematic* verification arrangement, like that in *Wall Products,*
would not be required. The Supreme Court's opinion in the *Staley*
case contains at least a strong intimation that the good faith requirement of the meeting-competition defense is lacking where the
matching of prices by sellers is part of an unlawful pricing system.

Observers also see similarities between *Wall Products* and *Container.* In each case, the product was said to be fungible; price was
the paramount sales factor; the industry was concentrated; and the
trend of prices was downward. In each case, there was an agreement to exchange price information, and the exchange of price information had a stabilizing effect on prices. After describing how
the defendants resorted to verification where necessary to avoid
violation of the Robinson-Patman Act, the court in *Wall Products*
described the competitive problem confronting them in these terms:
". . . defendants faced the ever present dilemma of going too low
and possibly causing further price deterioration or not going low
enough and losing the business." On the other hand, the Supreme
Court in *Container* observed: "Price is too critical, too sensitive a
control to allow it to be used even in an informal manner to restrain competition."

That the sellers in *Wall Products* verified with one another only
when accurate information was not otherwise available would not
appear to be a distinction, for in *Container* the Court noted that each
seller would request price information from a competitor "when-

ever it was not available from another source." The main distinction, aside from the occasional presence of the "specific job-contracts" in *Wall Products,* seems to have been the absence of the
Robinson-Patman justification in *Container.* A Robinson-Patman
justification almost always would be available in industries like
those in *Wall Products* and *Container.* If the reasoning of *Wall
Products* were to be generally adopted, what would be left of
Container?

In the *Wall Products* decision, both the plaintiffs and the defendants won something. The verification arrangement was upheld,
but the court did find a conspiracy in the later refusal of the larger
sellers to meet deviations by the single-plant sellers. The decision
was not appealed, so there has been no authoritative appellate determination of the scope of the "controlling circumstance" exception
to the *Container* rule. The validity of the court's reasoning on this
point in *Wall Products* is regarded by many as doubtful.

3. Cooperative Price Advertising

Question: *May competitors share the cost of advertisements
which include prices?*

In an advisory opinion of March 29, 1963, (91 ATRR X-1) the
Federal Trade Commission informed two inquiring Congressmen
and several groups of retail druggists that joint participation in
newspaper advertisements "which would contain any price or prices
or other terms or conditions of sale . . . would be open to challenge
as part and parcel of price fixing by agreement."

The Commission's advisory opinion was prepared in response to
inquiries "concerning the legality of various cooperative advertising
schemes proposed to groups of retail druggists by Marketing Programs, Inc., New York, New York," but the opinion spoke only
of a "proposed plan" providing "for the members of local associations to combine advertising allowances legally made available
to them by suppliers and to utilize such advertising allowances
in buying advertising space and in advertising through the utilization of that space names and addresses of the cooperating members and the items, including brand names of the items they are
offering for sale." If the proposed plans went no further than that,
if the advertising did not mention prices, the Commission could
see "no reason to challenge that aspect of the plan under the
laws entrusted to the Commission."

The Commission called attention to the fact that any understanding or agreement by members of the group fixing the price or
terms of sale of any item advertised "would contravene laws en-

trusted to the Commission for enforcement." The Commission went further: "The group publication of an advertisement containing any selling price raises a serious question whether the members of the group have agreed to and will sell at those prices. Consequently, the cooperative consideration of any advertisement which would contain any price or prices or other terms or conditions of sale . . . would be open to challenge as part and parcel of price fixing by agreement. Thus, the Commission is in no position to give its approval to any plan which would contain a basic flaw such as that."

Since the cooperative advertising was to be financed by advertising allowances made available by suppliers, the advisory opinion commented on the Robinson-Patman Act's application to the proposal. "If the agent for the members of the group should induce or knowingly receive advertising allowances which from the viewpoint of the supplier would contravene either subsection 2(a), 2(d), or 2(e) of the Clayton Act, as amended by the Robinson-Patman Act, then all members of the group, as well as their agent, would be liable to charges of violation of either Section 2(f) of the Clayton Act, as amended, or Section 5 of the Federal Trade Commission Act, or of violation of both."

Attached to the opinion were statements of four of the commissioners. Three of the statements were devoted primarily to answering a dissenting statement filed by Commissioner Elman. The theory of the dissent was that one of the purposes of the Robinson-Patman Act was to give small independent neighborhood retailers an opportunity to meet advertising competition from the large chain stores. For that reason, Commissioner Elman explained, a manufacturer who grants cooperative advertising allowances to some of his customers must make them available on proportionally equal terms to all other customers. However, he said, the "proportionally equal" allowance received by a small neighborhood retailer is not going to be enough to finance a large newspaper advertisement. Therefore, the only realistic way for him to compete with the chains is to join with other neighborhood retailers and pool his advertising allowances with theirs for the purchase of a large advertisement. To run such an advertisement without quoting prices, Commissioner Elman declared, "would be a waste of money."

Commissioner Elman did not view the retail druggists' plans as proposing an agreement among competing retailers to fix prices, which he recognized would be a per se violation of the antitrust laws. A restraint of trade is a per se violation of the antitrust laws, he went on, only when it has no function other than the stifling of competition. While an agreement to fix prices is unquestionably illegal per se, he reasoned, not every agreement or arrangement that has incidental effects on prices can be put in the same category.

What is involved in these proposals, as he saw them, is not an agreement among competitors to fix prices but an agreement among independent retailers, who are located in different neighborhoods and therefore do not compete with each other, to combine the advertising allowances to which they are legally entitled under the Robinson-Patman Act. "Plans for joint advertising by retailers are not necessarily, and in all circumstances, the equivalent of price-fixing conspiracies. Where, as is represented here, a plan has neither the purpose nor the effect of restraining competition, and involves no agreement by participating retailers to adhere to advertised prices, a per se test is inapplicable."

Commissioner Anderson expressed the "wish that I could dissent from what appears to be the majority in this case." He would have preferred to join Commissioner Elman, because, "it offends my sense of justice to find that the small industry members are unable to avail themselves of the same benefits as do their big brothers . . . but I believe that the law and the decisions as they now stand preclude such 'junction.' "

For Commissioners Everette MacIntyre and A. Leon Higginbotham, Jr, the question was whether the Commission should approve a proposed course of conduct that creates at least a substantial risk of civil or criminal prosecution. Commissioner Higginbotham dealt with Commissioner Elman's dissent point by point. First, he derived from *U.S.* v. *National Ass'n. of Real Estate Boards,* 339 U.S. 485, 489 (1950), a rule that unhampered discretion on the part of the businessmen involved to depart from the prices advertised "does not mitigate the offense." Second, even agreements only "incidentally" affecting price have been held illegal (*U.S.* v. *Socony-Vacuum Oil Co.,* 310 U.S. 150, 222 (1940)).

In answer to Commissioner Elman's suggestion that retail drug stores located in separate neighborhoods do not compete with each other, Commissioner Higginbotham cited the Supreme Court's finding in *Brown Shoe Co.* v. *U.S.,* 370 U.S. 294, 338 (1962), that "shoe stores in the outskirts of cities compete effectively with stores in central downtown areas." Finally, he said Commissioner Elman's statement that the proposals have neither the purpose nor effect of restraining competition and involve no agreement to adhere to advertised prices assumes the answer to the very issue presented by the proposals, whether in fact the purpose and effect of the plan could be construed to be a restraint on competition.

Three days after the Commission made its advisory opinion public, Lee Loevinger, then Assistant Attorney General in charge of the Antitrust Division, replied to an inquiry by Senator Hubert Humphrey (D-Minn). Mr. Loevinger expressed the opinion that "the action of a group of small retail business concerns in publishing cooperative advertising containing selling prices does not in and of itself constitute a violation of the Sherman Act." He also stated that the FTC had not submitted its advisory opinion to the Justice Department in advance, although the Commission's staff had submitted a memorandum to the Antitrust Division and had described a particular proposal for a joint advertising program. Because the proposal involved "explicit delegation of pricing authority and agreement to observe common prices by separate business concerns," the FTC staff was advised that "a grant of clearance for this specific program would be inconsistent with the antitrust laws."

The possibility of conflicting views at the FTC and the Antitrust Division, the present state of the applicable law, and the advisability of amending the Sherman Act and the FTC Act to permit cooperative price advertising by small businesses were explored in May 1963 at a meeting of the House Small Business Committee. At the hearing, the FTC Chairman and the head of the Antitrust Division showed no major disagreement, although the Assistant Attorney General did not seem ready to agree with the FTC statement that mere mention of prices would give a joint advertisement a "basic flaw." FTC Chairman Paul Rand Dixon described the specific plan denied clearance by the Commission. "The plan contemplated agreements between Marketing Programs, Inc., and various local and/or state retail druggist associations, under which said associations would assign to Marketing Programs, Inc., advertising and promotional allowances received by or available to each of the member druggists for the purpose of publishing joint advertisements featuring certain drugstore items and listing the names of the participating retailers.

"The basic selling point to be employed by Marketing Programs, Inc., for the purpose of inducing retail druggist associations and their members to engage in this program was that most independent drugstores were entitled to such small cooperative advertising allowances from their suppliers that such allowances were of no practical use to them individually, but that by pooling such allowances, participating drugstores could receive mention in a full-page advertisement featuring certain selected items. Under this plan, Marketing Programs, Inc., was to collect the allowances from suppliers, prepare the advertisements, place them in the appropriate advertising medium, and pay the costs thereof. . . . The proposal clearly indicated that the items to be featured and the prices to be advertised would be selected and/or established by a committee of retail druggists. Furthermore, it was even contemplated that such committee would select at least one item in each week's advertisement which would be featured as a 'loss leader.' "

Mr. Dixon acknowledged that the Commission's advice might have been "more clearly understood" if the Commission had spelled out the details of the cooperative-advertising proposal as thoroughly as they were explained to the Committee. Yet he reminded the Congressmen that the Commission thought it was writing only to those who had asked the question and were familiar with its factual basis.

With respect to the broad language in the advisory opinion applicable to "any advertisement which would contain any price or prices or other terms or conditions of sale," Mr. Dixon pointed out that the Commission's conclusion was that the advertisement "would be open to challenge as part and parcel of price fixing by agreement and would be subject to question under the laws administered by the Commission." There was no statement that all such cooperative advertising would be illegal per se; there would have to be evidence of a commitment to comply with the prices advertised (although Commissioner Higginbotham did state that "unhampered discretion to depart from the scheme involved does not mitigate the offense"). Even in instances where the FTC decides that the law has been violated, the Chairman went on, it has another decision to make, whether it would be in the public interest to issue a complaint. He informed the Congressmen that the FTC had never in its history seen fit to proceed against cooperative price advertising by small businesses. He said the unfair-methods-of-competition clause in the FTC Act is the only statute under which the Commission can move against price-fixing agreements. He expressed the view that the Commission cannot in good conscience advise businessmen to go ahead with a proposal that runs the risk of bringing on litigation by "one of my successors or someone else with responsibility."

Assistant Attorney General Lee Loevinger said that any disagreement between the Antitrust Division and the FTC "is more apparent than real." He agreed with the majority of the Commission that price fixing is illegal per se and that the specific plan the Commission's staff referred to his Division for its views should not have been granted clearance. Observing that the majority of the Commission chose to dwell on the things that small business cannot do, Mr. Loevinger suggested that a "different emphasis" should have been given. As he put it, "the mere fact that they have a cooperative advertisement with a mention of selling prices does not in my opinion in and of itself constitute a violation of the Sherman Act, nor is it conclusive evidence of violation of the Sherman Act. . . .

It would, as the FTC says, raise a question, but it would not necessarily make it illegal. . . . Situations do not arise in the neat manner that hypothetical questions do. They always come freighted with a whole complex set of background circumstances, and it is conceivable that cooperative advertising may be used as a device for price fixing. I would not want to be in a position of saying that cooperative advertising is immune to prosecution or cannot be used as evidence of price fixing."

Like the FTC, Mr. Loevinger testified, the Antitrust Division has brought no cases against cooperative advertising by small retailers. In fact, he said, the Division has explicitly refrained from bringing prosecutions in at least two instances.

In answer to a question about types of price advertising that might avoid the price-fixing tag, Mr. Loevinger referred to "a consent judgment in which there was a specific exception to an otherwise broad prohibition. This exception provided in substance that a number of small independent business enterprises, which manufactured the identical product, could engage in cooperative national advertising, stating suggested retail prices." Apparently Mr. Loevinger had reference to the consent judgment entered in *U.S.* v. *Spring-Air Co.,* 1962 Trade Cas. ¶70,402 (N.D. Ill. 1962). A few days after that consent judgment, the Federal District Court for Northern Illinois added a similar qualification to a 1960 judgment in *U.S.* v. *Restonic Corp.,* 1960 Trade Cas. ¶69,739 (N.D. Ill. 1960).

Earl W. Kintner, former FTC Chairman, appeared before the House Small Business Committee as special antitrust counsel for the National Association of Retail Druggists. Mr. Kintner related that he had been employed as NARD antitrust counsel at a time when there were three Justice Department suits charging state pharmaceutical associations with conspiring to fix prices on prescription drugs. The task assigned Mr. Kintner was the initiation of an educational program to bring the druggists in compliance with the law. Consequently, he went on, when the NARD in September 1962 passed a resolution to seek an advisory opinion from the FTC on cooperative advertising plans, there were "many of such proposals" already in Mr. Kintner's files, and requests for "railroad releases" and advisory opinions had already been made to the FTC and the Antitrust Division. Mr. Kintner said he submitted only one of the plans to the Commission's staff, feeling "quite confident once the air was cleared to rule myself on the other proposals."

During Mr. Kintner's testimony, references were made to two types of cooperative price advertising that everyone seemed to agree would not give rise to an inference of an illegal price-fixing agreement. The former FTC Chairman referred to weekly newspaper advertisements of a group of liquor stores in Washington, D.C. The members of the group were listed, but each item that was price advertised was shown as sponsored by only one of the group members. The second reference was to one of the NARD documents submitted to the FTC outlining a special type of program proposed to the Iowa Pharmaceutical Association. It was contemplated that only items for which manufacturers' suggested list prices were available would be advertised. Each advertisement would contain a disclaimer that "prices shown on this page are only manufacturers' suggested selling prices. In each store listed in the column at left, your pharmacist sets his own price—usually lower, never higher."

Even before the Commission had formally released its advisory opinion to the public, legislation had been proposed in the Senate by Senator Humphrey. S.1320 (92 ATRR A-1 (4/16/63)) would have added a new Section 11A to the FTC Act under which the Commission could have issued regulations authorizing "small business concerns" to engage in cooperative price advertising without violating "this Act or any antitrust act," except the Robinson-Patman Act. The new section would have taken its definition of "small business concerns" from Section 2 of the Small Business Act (15 U.S.C. §632).

Some antitrust lawyers find reassurance in the statements of Justice Department and FTC personnel that, as a matter of policy, legal action is not taken against cooperative price advertising by small businessmen. Some even see the possible curtailment of per se illegality and limited revival of the "rule of reason" approach in *Appalachian Coals, Inc.* v. *U.S.*, 288 U.S. 344 (1933), and *Chicago Board of Trade* v. *U.S.*, 246 U.S. 231 (1918).

In *U.S.* v. *Trenton Potteries Co.*, 273 U.S. 392 (1927) and *U.S.* v. *Socony-Vacuum Oil Co.*, 310 U.S. 150 (1940), the Supreme Court established a rule that all price-fixing agreements are forbidden by Section 1 of the Sherman Act, but even in those cases the Court emphasized the inevitable anticompetitive effect of the agreement in question. It could be argued that cooperative price advertising arrangements will often promote, rather than impair, price competition if they are limited to small businesses with chain-store competition, involve no coercion of, or undue restraints on, participating advertisers, and are reasonable as to duration and the number of items of merchandise covered. The *Socony-Vacuum* decision, it is often observed, must be evaluated in light of the fact that it involved major oil companies marketing 83 percent of the gasoline sold in the Midwest.

Does cooperative price advertising equal price fixing? It might be argued that cooperative price advertising without a commitment to comply with the advertised price would amount to fictitious pricing, a deceptive practice under Section 5 of the FTC Act.

The Supreme Court's statement in *Brown Shoe Co.* v. *U.S.*, 370

U.S. 294, 338 (1962), that suburban shoe stores "compete effectively with stores in central downtown areas," contradicts Commissioner Elman's theory that "independent retailers in different neighborhoods . . . do not compete with each other in any practical sense." The "rule of reason" approach would accept the proposition that cooperative price advertising by independent neighborhood retailers is a price-fixing arrangement among competitors but would excuse it as a reasonable means of preserving those retailers as a competitive force.

The advisory opinion to the druggists and the concern it produced discloses a basic weakness in any advisory opinion or "railroad release" procedure. When a contemplated business practice submitted for clearance is one whose legality depends upon the motive or purpose of the planners, it is probably impossible for the Government to give approval.

4. Advertising Plans

Question: *Does a manufacturer's cooperative merchandising plan for retailers violate the law if advertising benefits are available only for advertisements that either do not mention price or show a price no lower than the minimum established by the manufacturer?*

This question is dealt with in the initial decision filed by Federal Trade Commission Examiner Andrew C. Goodhope in the *General Electric* case, 88 ATRR A-10 (1963), *complaint dismissed,* 64 F.T.C. 1238 (1964). From 1952 until 1958, during which period it enforced a fair-trade program at the retail level, GE "had cultivated a broad spectrum of dealers including hardware, jewelry, drug, furniture, appliance and department stores." In February 1958, GE ended its fair-trade program after a series of adverse court decisions. Price wars broke out and the number of retail dealers handling GE products went from about 150,000 to about 75,000 or 80,000 within a year and a half. According to Examiner Goodhope's findings, the dealers lost were small retailers, who generally handle GE products only so long as they produce a profit.

Late in 1958 and early in 1959, GE announced a "cooperative merchandising plan" under which it provided assistance for a variety of promotional activities of distributors. The plan called for the accrual of separate cooperative advertising and promotion funds based, in Examiner Goodhope's words, "upon the distributor's purchases or sales of products within specified product lines." The distributors could use the accrued funds for cooperative advertising in local newspapers and other media, point-of-sale aids, salesmen's incentives, and demonstrators. The choice of any or all of these activities was left to the distributor.

Two restrictions were placed upon the content of any local retail-dealer advertising in which the distributor could participate and count on receiving partial reimbursement from GE. First, price comparisons were forbidden. Second, "in all states except Alaska, Missouri, Montana, Texas, Vermont, Nebraska, Utah, Virginia, West Virginia, and the District of Columbia," retailer advertising had to either mention no price at all or give prices no lower than minimums established by the Housewares Division. Examiner Good-hope described the second restriction as applicable "in 'fair trade' jurisdictions." The dealer was free to advertise GE products at lower prices, but he had to bear the entire cost of any such advertising. Even if GE bore part or all of the advertising costs, there was no restriction on the prices actually charged by a retail dealer.

In May 1962, the Federal Trade Commission attacked this advertising incentive plan under Section 5 of the FTC Act and Section 2(d) of the Robinson-Patman Act. The theory of the Section 5 count in the complaint was that the restrictions on retailer price advertising had the effect of inducing retail dealers to lessen or eliminate price competition and of depriving the public of knowledge of price competition. Under the Robinson-Patman Act's discriminatory-advertising-allowances ban, the charge was that the incentive payments were not proportionally available to those retailers who were forced by competition to advertise and sell GE products at prices lower than the minimum prices set by the manufacturer.

During hearings before the examiner and in its appeal to the FTC, GE took the position that the purpose of the restrictions on retailer price advertising was not to stabilize prices but merely to withhold GE financial support for "wholly unrealistic and unprofitable price advertising . . . detrimental to its own interests." GE insisted that the plan stemmed from a realization, developed from experience with fair trade, that the company could neither control retail prices nor stop the pricing and advertising practices that destroyed dealer profits. It simply did not want to aggravate matters by leading the remaining dealers to believe that it not only condoned but would subsidize such practices.

In applying Section 5 of the FTC Act, the examiner concluded that the plan was "an open invitation to distributors" to join GE in an attempt to stabilize the market. While he found the evidence on the actual effect of the plan on prices to be "in substantial conflict," he did find a shift of retailer price advertising from the products with minimum prices to those without minimums. In addition, according to the examiner, one GE official testified that the plan caused an increase in prices in the New York market. The exclusion of "non-fair trade states" from the plan's pricing restrictions was regarded by the examiner as "some proof that respondent . . . well understood that it was tampering with the retail prices of its products."

After argument, the Commission dismissed its complaint "without adjudicating any issue of fact or law contested on this appeal" (64 F.T.C. 1238 (1964)). The Commission "determined that the record is not adequate to enable an informed determination on the merits." Instead of remanding the case for the taking of further evidence, however, the Commission decided "the public interest would be better served by instructing its staff to maintain a close scrutiny of respondent's Cooperative Merchandising Plans to determine whether their purpose or effect is to bring about retailers' adherence to resale prices specified or suggested by respondent, or otherwise to constitute an unlawful price-fixing or price-stabilizing arrangement." Although Examiner Goodhope had found a violation of Section 2(d) of the Clayton Act as well, the Commission's dismissal order did not mention that aspect of the case.

Commissioner MacIntyre did not concur. According to the FTC decision, "It is [Commissioner MacIntyre's] view that the public interest would be better served by the Commission reaching and rendering a judgment in the disposition of this important case. It is his understanding that this case is a forerunner of other like important situations, the resolution of which will be required by the public interest."

At the 1964 spring meeting of the American Bar Association's Antitrust Section, members of a panel discussing "New Theories of Price Conspiracy" had difficulty reconciling the Commission's dismissal of the *GE* proceeding with the 1963 advisory opinion condemning retail druggists' cooperative advertising plans. (See section II-A-3, p. 83.) Memory of the furor produced in Congress by the cooperative-advertising opinion may have been one of the motivating factors in the dismissal of the *GE* proceeding.

Nonetheless, antitrust lawyers show little inclination to treat the Commission's action as in any way encouraging the adoption of advertising incentive plans with price advertising restrictions. (The Commission's Guides for Advertising Allowances and Other Merchandising Payments and Services, reissued in 1972, 4 Trade Reg. Rep. ¶39,035, state in Guide 7: "A seller should not refuse to participate in the cost of ads that feature prices other than the seller's suggested prices.") Even those lawyers who do not take the Commission's word that the order decides nothing "on the merits" attribute to it a very narrow scope. It is regarded by some as significant, for example, that GE's plan explicitly left the retailer free to omit prices entirely from his advertising and left its distributors free to spend their cooperative funds entirely for promotion at the wholesale level or, if used at the retail level, to use them all for promotional purposes other than advertising. It has been suggested that a plan for subsidizing only such advertising as omits any reference to price might not be regarded as price tampering in violation of Section 5 of the FTC Act. A plan for subsidizing only minimum-price advertising would seem clearly to fall within the advisory opinion on cooperative drug advertising, and many lawyers are still doubtful about a plan offering a choice between minimum-price advertising and no-price advertising. The Commission might have been prepared to decide the merits of the GE plan, it has been pointed out, if there had been evidence as to the percentage of retailers who used the plan; the percentages that advertised at, above, and below GE's minimum price; and the percentage that advertised without prices.

In spite of the examiner's treatment of the fair-trade aspects of the case, some lawyers feel that it may be significant that the price-advertising restrictions were effective only in fair-trade jurisdictions. In jurisdictions where public policy permits direct and absolute resale price maintenance, the reasoning goes, it would seem paradoxical to forbid the less restrictive price influencing attempted by plans like GE's. Some lawyers, however, insist that the tendency of the courts to restrict the application of the fair-trade exception would prevent this type of plan from qualifying as a sort of fair-trade arrangement. Court decisions that have dealt with the problem have not required a formal resale-price-maintenance contract (*U.S.* v. *Socony Mobil Oil Co.,* 150 F.Supp. 202 (D. Mass. 1957); *General Electric Co.* v. *Kimball Jewelers, Inc.,* 333 Mass. 665, 132 N.E. 2d 652).

In its dismissal order, the Commission said it would instruct its staff to maintain close scrutiny of the "purpose or effect" of GE's cooperative merchandising plan. This language seems to suggest that the Commission did not then regard the price-advertising restrictions as illegal per se. On the other hand, the Commission acted before the Supreme Court spoke so strongly in *Simpson* v. *Union Oil Co. of California,* 377 U.S. 13 (1964), against resale price maintenance through "clever draftsmanship." (See section II-A-6, p. 98.)

5. The Los Angeles Chevrolet Cases

Question: *May dealer associations regulate members' pricing and distribution methods?*

The practice of selling Chevrolets through discount houses and referral services apparently began in the Los Angeles area around 1953. Although the practice accounted for the sale of only a few hundred cars in 1953, by 1960 the number had increased to over 2,000 with a retail value of about $5 million. The discount houses, often located as far as 40 miles from the dealer with whom they cooperated, did not purchase the Chevrolets and resell them. They provided an established business location that served as a point of contact with potential Chevrolet customers; they referred potential customers to dealers; they took orders for new Chevrolets; they negotiated with potential customers on the prices, terms, and conditions of sale for new Chevrolet automobiles; they negotiated price allowances for trade-ins; and they delivered new Chevrolet automobiles to purchasers. They assumed no responsibility for servicing cars.

In response to some dealers' complaints, General Motors concluded that the use of discount houses and referral services by other dealers, if continued, would disrupt GM's dealer franchise system and adversely affect customer good will; that under these arrangements dealers were transferring their selling obligations under the selling agreements to unknown persons who had no obligation or interest in promoting Chevrolet good will; and that equivalents of dealer branch locations were being established without the GM approval required under the dealer selling agreement and without providing any facilities or personnel to service and repair Chevrolets. GM informed all of its automobile dealers throughout the country that, in light of the provisions of the dealer selling agreements, it opposed dealers' arrangements with discount houses and referral services.

Although some Los Angeles dealers complained about "cut-rate" or "discount" prices offered on sales by dealers through discount houses, GM insisted its only interest was in preserving the franchise system, not in maintaining a price level; that discounted prices were an accepted thing in the automobile business; and that there were enough Chevrolet dealers and dealers in other makes of automobiles in convenient proximity to any potential customer in the Los Angeles area to insure competition.

After GM's own investigation and announcement of its policy decision, three Chevrolet-dealer associations in the Los Angeles area themselves decided to investigate whether Chevrolet dealers in the area were still selling through discount houses and referral services.

In October of 1961, the Justice Department secured an indictment against GM and the three Chevrolet dealer associations in the Los Angeles area, accusing them of conspiring to stop Chevrolet dealers in the area from selling cars through discount houses and referral services. According to the indictment, the defendants, in violation of Section 1 of the Sherman Act, conspired to suppress and eliminate competition in the sale of Chevrolet automobiles. Less than a year later, the Government followed up with a civil suit to enjoin GM and the dealer associations from interfering with the sale of Chevrolet automobiles through the discount houses.

The complaint charged that GM and the associations, by undertaking some time in 1960 to halt sales through discount houses, conspired to eliminate competition in the sale and distribution of Chevrolet automobiles in the Southern California area, in violation of Section 1 of the Sherman Act. The complaint alleged that GM and the associations tried to persuade Chevrolet dealers to refrain from selling automobiles pursuant to agreements with discount houses; used "shoppers" to identify Chevrolet dealers who contined their business relationships with discount houses; and tried to persuade the Chevrolet dealers to repurchase Chevrolet automobiles purchased by the "shoppers." These practices, the complaint continued, denied Chevrolet dealers the right to sell their automobiles in accordance with free market conditions and deprived discount houses of the right to participate in the sale and distribution of Chevrolet automobiles.

In the criminal case, Judge Thurmond Clarke sustained GM's contention that the prosecution was an attack on the franchised-dealer method of selling automobiles (*U.S.* v. *General Motors Corp.,* 216 F.Supp. 362 (S.D. Calif. 1963)). In dismissing the indictment at the close of the Government's case, Judge Clarke stated that, if the Government were successful, General Motors would be forced to include discount houses in its distribution system and thereby adopt a method of merchandising not of its own choosing.

Judge Clarke observed that General Motors had chosen the franchised dealership as the most suitable outlet for merchandising Chevrolet automobiles. He indicated there was no real dispute that GM and the dealer associations had induced Chevrolet dealers to terminate selling arrangements with the discount houses and referral services. He disagreed with a Government contention that Chevrolet dealers were coerced into terminating their relations with the discount houses. He found the evidence consistent with the possibility that the dealers' decisions were precipitated by their own self-interest. "Indeed, termination of discount house operations was incumbent on the dealers under the provision of the franchise contract which prohibits a dealer from establishing a second location, without the consent of General Motors."

One Government contention, that GM and the associations engaged in a "boycott" that violated Section 1 of the Sherman Act even if there was no proof of its effect on competition, was given short shrift by Judge Clarke. He stated simply that "the government's argument is not well taken for the reasons stated in *Boro*

Hall Corp. v. *General Motors Corp.,* 37 F.Supp. 999 (S.D.N.Y. 1941), 124 F.2d 822 (2d Cir. 1942)."

In the district court the Government did not fare any better in its civil suit. Federal Judge Charles H. Carr said GM had the legal right, under its "dealer selling agreements," to bar Chevrolet dealers from selling through discount houses and that GM acted unilaterally, without conspiring with the Southern California dealer associations, in enforcing that contract right (*U.S.* v. *General Motors Corp.,* 234 F.Supp. 85 (S.D. Calif. 1964)). Considering all of the factors in the relationship between General Motors and its franchised dealers and the public, Judge Carr declared, "it must be concluded that the dealer contracts promote rather than suppress competition, and benefit the purchasing public."

Unlike Judge Clarke's decision in the criminal case, Judge Carr's judgment was appealable to the Supreme Court, where the Government won a unanimous reversal (384 U.S. 127 (1966)). The court held there was a conspiracy in restraint of trade by the joint action of dealers, dealers' associations, and General Motors to eliminate a class of competitors. The court found evidence of collaborative action in the dealers' joint efforts to obtain General Motors' help and to enforce the other dealers' promises to give up the discounting operation. The associations were found by the Court to have acted jointly to police the dealers' promises. The Court held that General Motors had collaborated in soliciting and accepting the assistance of the associations. The Court also noted that there was evidence that one of the purposes of eliminating the discounters was to protect the franchised dealers from price competition.

Although Judge Carr's specific findings of fact were not disturbed, the Supreme Court decided that his findings "include the essentials of a conspiracy within Section 1 of the Sherman Act" and therefore "cannot be squared with" his conclusion that there was no violation.

Writing for the Court, Justice Fortas pointed to findings (1) that the dealer associations had initiated a letter-writing campaign among their members to get General Motors to come to their aid against discount-house sales, (2) that GM personnel subsequently had discussed the matter with Los Angeles area dealers and elicited from each a promise not to do business with discounters, (3) that the associations had created a joint investigating committee and undertook to police compliance with those promises, and (4) that these collaborative efforts had induced several dealers to repurchase cars they had sold through discounters and to promise to make no further sales in that manner. In these findings, Justice Fortas saw "a classic conspiracy in restraint of trade: joint, collaborative action by dealers, the defendant associations, and General Motors to eliminate a class of competitors by terminating business dealings between them and a minority of Chevrolet dealers and to deprive franchised dealers of their freedom to deal through discounters if they so choose. . . . Elimination, by joint collaborative action, of discounters from access of the market is a per se violation of the Act."

The Government wanted the Court to hold the location clause unlawful and was willing to assume that this clause required GM approval of sales through discount houses. Because it found a conspiracy between General Motors and the dealer associations, however, the Supreme Court decided not to rule on the effect and validity of the location clause. "Whatever General Motors might or might not lawfully have done to enforce individual Dealer Selling Agreements by action within the borders of that agreement and the relationship which each defines, is beside the point."

Justice Harlan filed a concurring opinion. He called attention to the absence of anything in the Court's opinion to prevent General Motors from enforcing the sales-location clause by unilateral action.

On remand to the district court, final judgment was entered August 17, 1966. The district court enjoined General Motors for six months from conspiring with its dealers and from restricting sales through discount houses.

For the automobile industry and for franchising operations in general, the most significant aspect of the Supreme Court opinion in the *General Motors* case is the Court's refusal to pass on the legality of the "location clause" and its enforcement by GM through unilateral action. The "location clause" is one used in the dealer contracts of all four of the major automobile manufacturers. Justice Fortas' reliance on a "classic conspiracy" independent of the location clause or any other provision in the franchise agreement means that, at least for the time being, the automobile manufacturers can continue to control the location of their customers' places of business.

Some antitrust lawyers see in the decision a lesson for trade associations of retail dealers—that they simply cannot discipline their members on pricing and methods of distribution. Clearly, a manufacturer cannot lawfully assist them in policing members. On the other hand, the efforts of the three Los Angeles dealer associations to enforce the rule against dealing through discounters were not essential to the conclusion reached by the Supreme Court. Under the conspiracy theory applied by the Court, the Sherman Act violation occurred as soon as GM, at the urging of some of its dealers, induced other dealers to agree to stop dealing with discounters.

There seems to be general agreement, that, if conditions in the automobile industry are such as to encourage sales through discount houses or referral services—a matter on which the industry seems to be divided—the Supreme Court's reservation of judgment on unilateral action by the manufacturer leaves the car makers up in the air as to what they can and can't do.

6. Retail Price Control by Consignment

Question: *May consignment selling ever be used to control retail prices?*

In *U.S.* v. *General Electric Co.*, 272 U.S. 476 (1926), the Supreme Court allowed a manufacturer to retain control of the retail price of a patented product by making consignment agreements with retailers. While the decision dealt with the rights of patent owners, the language of the opinion was broader. The case involved arrangements GE had made with independent distributors and retailers of electric light bulbs after signing a Sherman Act consent decree requiring termination of resale-price maintenance agreements. The new contracts made the distributors and retailers GE's agents with responsibility to maintain a stock of light bulbs on consignment and sell them on GE's behalf under terms specified by GE. The Supreme Court found no violation of Section 1 of the Sherman Act, declaring that "the owner of an article patented or otherwise is not violating the common law or the antitrust law by seeking to dispose of his articles directly to the consumer and fixing the price by which his agents transfer the title from him directly to each consumer."

The *GE* opinion must be read in the light of the decision in *Simpson* v. *Union Oil Co. of Calif.*, 377 U.S. 949 (1964). Noting the *General Electric* opinion's reference to owners of articles "patented or otherwise," a 5–1 majority of the Supreme Court refused to apply the *General Electric* doctrine to consignment arrangements between a gasoline refiner and service-station operators with short-term leases. "The Court in that case particularly relied on the fact that patent rights have long included licenses 'to make, use, and vend' the patented article 'for any royalty or upon any condition the performance of which is reasonably within the reward which the patentee by the grant of the patent is entitled to secure.'
. . . The patent laws which give a 17 year monopoly on 'making, using, or selling the invention' are in pari materia with the antitrust laws and modify them pro tanto. That was the ratio decidendi of the General Electric case. See 272 U.S., at 485. We decline the invitation to extend it."

Union Oil Co. of California was sued by one of its former service-station operators, who, in order to obtain his first one-year lease on a station, was required to sign a "retail dealer consignment agreement." This agreement provided that gasoline delivered to the station would remain the property of Union as consignor and was to be sold only at the price specified by Union. The terms of the consignment agreement are the only facts stated by the Supreme Court. From the opinion of the court of appeals (311 F.2d 764 (9th Cir. 1963)), it appears that in March 1958 three competitive service stations close to the Union station lowered their prices on regular gasoline seven cents a gallon. After asking for and being denied permission to make a similar cut in price, Union's lessee did so anyway. As a result, his second one-year lease on the station was not renewed.

The operator's treble-damage complaint, alleging a violation of Sections 1 and 2 of the Sherman Act, was dismissed by the district court (162 F.Supp. 746 (S.D. Calif. 1958)) after both parties filed motions for summary judgment. The dismissal was affirmed by the court of appeals (311 F.2d 764 (9th Cir. 1963)), which held that Simpson, having a terminable lease, did not suffer any actionable damage.

Justice Douglas, author of the Supreme Court opinion, repeated the declaration in *U.S.* v. *Parke, Davis & Co.,* 362 U.S. 29 (1960), "that a supplier may not use coercion of its retail outlets to achieve resale price maintenance." He said there is nothing illegal about an owner's sending an article to a dealer who may in turn undertake to sell it only at a price set by the owner. "When, however, a 'consignment' device is used to cover a vast gasoline distribution system, fixing prices through many retail outlets, the antitrust laws prevent calling the 'consignment' an agency, for then the end result of *United States* v. *Socony-Vacuum Oil Co.* (310 U.S. 150 (1940)) would be avoided merely by clever manipulation of words, not by differences in substance." The *Socony-Vacuum* case was cited by Justice Douglas for the proposition that Section 1 of the Sherman Act does not permit agreements for resale price maintenance.

Consignments are useful, Justice Douglas acknowledged, in allocating risks between the parties involved and in determining their rights against each other. Yet they "do not necessarily control the rights of others, whether they be creditors or sovereigns. . . . Dealers, like Simpson, are independent businessmen; and they have all or most of the indicia of entrepreneurs, except for price fixing. The risk of loss of the gasoline is on them, apart from acts of God. Their return is affected by the rise and fall of the market price, their commissions declining as retail prices drop. Practically the only power they have to be wholly independent businessmen, whose service depends on their own initiative and enterprise, is taken from them by the proviso that they must sell their gasoline at prices fixed by Union Oil. By reason of the lease and 'consignment' agreement dealers are coercively laced into an arrangement under which their supplier is able to impose noncompetitive prices on thousands of persons who otherwise might be competitive."

The Court ordered that both sides be given "a hearing on all the other issues in the case, including those raised under the McGuire Act, 66 Stat. 631, 15 U.S.C. §45, and the damages, if any, suffered. We intimate no views on any other issue; we hold only that resale price maintenance through the present, coercive type of 'consignment' agreement is illegal under the antitrust laws, and that petitioner suffered actionable wrong or damage. We reserve the question whether, when all the facts are known, there may be any equities that would warrant only prospective application in damage suits of the rule governing price fixing by the 'consignment' device which we announce today."

Justice Stewart dissented. He maintained that, regardless of denials, the majority actually overruled the *General Electric* case. If a "decision of such impact and magnitude" is to be reached, he stated, it should be done only after reargument at which the Justice Department should be invited to express its views and only when the issue can be considered by a full court. Justice Stewart could not see how patent rights could have any bearing on the result in *GE* or the instant case. "Possession of patent rights on the article allegedly consigned has no legal significance to an inquiry directed to ascertaining whether the burden, risks, and rights of ownership actually remain with the principal or have passed to his agent. Nor is the power of a consignor to fix the prices at which his consignee sells augmented in any respect by the possession of a patent on the goods so consigned. It is not by virtue of a patent monopoly that a bona fide consignor may control the price at which his consignee sells; his control over price flows from the simple fact that the owner of goods, so long as he remains the owner, has the unquestioned right to determine the price at which he will sell them."

Justices Brennan and Goldberg filed a separate "memorandum" in which they said they "do not necessarily disagree" with the conclusion of the majority but felt that the court should first get the benefit of a district court trial on the question whether there is a "coercive type of consignment agreement." They also agreed with Justice Stewart that the Justice Department should have a chance to present views. "The decision may be expected to affect consignment agreements in many businesses, including outstanding agreements that may have been entered into in reliance upon *United States* v. *General Electric*."

As many as four doctrines might be sorted out of Justice Douglas' opinion in the *Simpson* case. First, statements such as the one that the dealers "are independent businessmen" who "have all or most of the indicia of entrepreneurs, except for price fixing," suggest the Court was saying that the "consignment" transaction is not what it purports to be on its face (*Straus* v. *Victor Talking Machine Co.*, 243 U.S. 490 (1917)). Second, the majority opinion might be read as saying that even a bona fide consignment agreement violates the Sherman Act when it is adopted as part of a deliberate plan to control the price at a lower distribution level. Third, the Court may be saying, as it did in *U.S.* v. *Parke, Davis & Co.*, 362 U.S. 29 (1960), that it is a Sherman Act violation to use coercion (here the "lacing together" of the short-term lease and consignment) to get an agreement whose effect is to control the price charged at a lower distribution level. Fourth, the Court may have singled out for condemnation consignment arrangements that have the effect of fixing price at a lower level and are used throughout "a vast . . . distribution system," in which realistically the retailer must handle one supplier's product exclusively.

Antitrust lawyers are in disagreement over which of these factors standing alone, or which combination of them falling short of all four, would produce the same result. Many experts feel that the one indispensable element in the *Simpson* case was the tie-in between the consignment arrangement and the one-year lease, the "coercion" element. They emphasize the court's statement that "by reason of the lease and 'consignment' agreement dealers are coercively laced into an [illegal] arrangement." Others make the point that, if Justice Douglas wanted to rely that much on the threat of lease termination, his opinion could have been shorter. The latter tend to stress the motive for the consignment arrangement and the type of marketing system in which it is used. They seem to assign little weight to the genuineness of the consignment agreement, that is, the degree to which it retains in the consignor all the true indicia of ownership and gives the consignee the attributes of an agent rather than a reseller.

A third group suggests that the decision may be limited to the special facts of the gasoline industry, noting that the Court said: "We hold only that retail price maintenance through the present, coercive type of consignment agreement is illegal under the antitrust laws." The separate opinion of Justices Brennan and Goldberg placed particular emphasis on that language from the majority opinion.

In his dissent, Justice Stewart read the majority opinion as "outlawing consignment selling if it includes a price limitation." Yet reservation by the consignor of the right to determine price is a characteristic of consignment agreements used extensively in other industries where the manufacturer does not participate so extensively in the advertising and marketing of his products, uses no coercion to initiate or perpetuate consignment arrangements, and uses that method of disposing of his products for reasons quite apart from control of prices. Sometimes the consignment agreement is a means of extending credit or of avoiding possible pricing problems under the Robinson-Patman Act. It may be doubtful that the Court intended its rationale to cover those situations.

The Federal Trade Commission issued orders outlawing consignment arrangements by Atlantic Refining Co. (63 F.T.C. 1409 (1963)) and Sun Oil Co. (63 F.T.C. 1371 (1963)). In those cases, the Commission made findings that permitted it to distinguish the consignment arrangements from the agency contract used by General Electric. Two distinguishing factors were stressed as to Atlantic's program. First, it was found that the retail dealers had not been made genuine agents of the refiner. "The change made was merely of form not of substance," since the dealers commingled all business receipts, continued to hold themselves out as full proprietors of their stations, and in effect had to pay for gasoline at delivery, not sale. They continued to operate their businesses in exactly the same manner, except that they could not determine their own gasoline prices. Second, emphasis was placed upon the temporary nature of Atlantic's program. General Electric's agency system was "permanently implemented and universally applied." What was said to set apart Sun's consignment arrangements was evidence that the agreements were worked out in group discussions with service station operators, giving the Commission a basis for finding horizontal as well as vertical price-fixing conspiracies.

The Sixth and Seventh Circuits upheld the Commission's orders (*Atlantic Refining Co.* v. *FTC,* 344 F.2d 599 (6th Cir. 1965); *Sun Oil Co.* v. *FTC,* 350 F.2d 624 (7th Cir. 1965)). In *Atlantic,* the court of appeals held there was no valid distinction between the coercion in *Simpson* and the "Hobson's choice" offered by Atlantic in the middle of a price war. As to Atlantic's argument that the Simpson system was permanent while this one was merely temporary, the court held that Atlantic's consignment agreements were a price-fixing mechanism and therefore illegal even if temporary.

In the *Sun Oil* case, the court of appeals recognized that the Supreme Court had not overruled *GE* but pointed out that the *GE* exception to the per se illegality of vertical price control was limited by *Simpson* v. *Union Oil Co.* to patented products. Nonetheless, the court of appeals was unwilling to rule that all consignment agreements are per se illegal. The FTC's order should be affirmed in this case, the court held, because the consignment plan, although not coercively induced, resulted in horizontal as well as vertical price control and was an illegal price-fixing device.

In May 1973, a district court held the General Electric system of consignment selling unlawful, despite the Supreme Court's 1926 decision upholding GE's system (*U.S.* v. *General Electric Co.,* 613 ATRR A-20 (S.D.N.Y. 1973)). Noting intervening court decisions, the district judge concluded that "a vast consignment agency system of distribution through independent businessmen, such as we have here, under which there was price fixing by the supplier, is a per se violation of the Sherman Act."

7. Resale Price Maintenance Through Refusal to Deal

Question: *May a manufacturer control retail prices by refusing to sell to retailers who do not adhere to prices suggested by the manufacturer?*

In 1911 the Supreme Court held that a manufacturer could not lawfully make contracts prohibiting his wholesalers and retailers from reselling to persons other than those designated, or at prices below those agreed upon. These contracts were held to be invalid both as restraints on trade against common law and as combinations in restraint of trade prohibited by the Sherman Act. In *Dr. Miles Medical Co.* v. *John D. Park & Sons Co.,* 220 U.S. 373 (1911), the manufacturer had sought to enjoin a wholesaler from interfering with these contracts. The wholesaler, who had not signed one of the contracts, was said to be procuring his supply by inducing other wholesalers to break their contracts with the manufacturer. The manufacturer argued that the contracts were valid because he was entitled to control the prices on all sales of his own product. The Court rejected this argument and noted that these contracts, by fixing the price the consumer pays, eliminated competition among retailers. (Justice Holmes dissented, stating, among other things, "I cannot believe that in the long run the public will profit by this Court permitting knaves to cut reasonable prices for some ulterior purpose of their own.")

In 1919 the question came to the Supreme Court again in a criminal prosecution under the Sherman Act (*U.S.* v. *Colgate & Co.,* 250 U.S. 300 (1919)). The Court held that no offense was charged by an indictment alleging only that a manufacturer specified resale prices to wholesalers and retailers and stated he would refuse to deal with those not adhering to such prices. The Court said:

"In the absence of any purpose to create or maintain a monopoly, the Act does not restrict the long recognized right of trader or manufacturer engaged in an entirely private business, freely to exercise his own independent discretion as to parties with whom he will deal; and, of course, he may announce in advance the circumstances under which he will refuse to sell" (250 U.S. at 307).

The first lower-court judge to attempt to reconcile the *Dr. Miles* and *Colgate* cases saw no distinction at all between a written resale-price-maintenance contract and an implied one backed by the sanction of refusal to deal. He concluded that the Supreme Court had intended to modify *Dr. Miles*. Although the indictment before him involved a written contract, he held that the *Colgate* doctrine controlled and no violation of the Sherman Act had been made out. In reversing, the Supreme Court said in *U.S.* v. *A. Schrader's Son,* 252 U.S. 85 (1920), that it had had no intention of overruling or modifying the *Dr. Miles* decision in its *Colgate* opinion. The Court distinguished between a manufacturer who indicated his price wishes and refused to deal with those who did not comply and a manufacturer who entered into agreements, "whether express or implied from a course of dealing or other circumstances" (252 U.S. at 99).

In *Frey & Son, Inc.* v. *Cudahy Packing Co.,* 243 F. 205 (D. Md. 1917), a trial judge instructed the jurors in a treble-damage action that, although there was no written agreement, they could infer an agreement in violation of the Sherman Act if they found that the defendant had indicated a resale price maintenance plan to his jobbers and they had cooperated in effectuating it. The jury returned a verdict for the plaintiff. On appeal, the court of appeals reversed, holding that there had been no written agreement between the defendant manufacturer and his wholesalers (261 F. 65 (4th Cir. 1919)). The Supreme Court reversed both lower courts (256 U.S. 208 (1921)). The court of appeals was wrong because under *Schrader* an express agreement is not necessary to a violation; an agreement can be inferred from a course of dealing. The trial court's charge was erroneous because an implied agreement could not be inferred from the facts, since the manufacturer's conduct went no further than that sanctioned by the *Colgate* case.

About the same time, in a case brought under the Federal Trade Commission Act, the FTC found that Beech-Nut Packing Company had violated Section 5's prohibition of "unfair methods of competition" by maintaing resale prices through its "Beech-Nut policy" (*Beech-Nut Packing Co.,* 1 F.T.C. 516 (1919)). The Supreme Court (*FTC* v. *Beech-Nut Packing Co.,* 257 U.S. 441 (1922)), following reversal by a court of appeals (264 F. 885 (2nd Cir. 1920)), upheld the Commission, holding that a manufacturer loses *Colgate's* protection if he goes beyond the exercise of the right of refusal to deal. The Court said the "Beech-Nut policy" went much further and embraced a "scheme" to restrain competition among retailers and was therefore an unfair method of competition. A similar system to control a distributor's resale prices was later held to go beyond *Colgate* and to violate Sections 1 and 3 of the Sherman Act (*U.S.* v. *Bausch & Lomb Optical Co.,* 321 U.S. 707 (1944)).

All these cases were discussed in *U.S.* v. *Parke, Davis & Co.,* 362 U.S. 29 (1960). There a manufacturer had told wholesalers he would refuse to sell to them if they supplied retailers who cut prices below the manufacturer's suggested retail prices. Because the wholesalers had withheld supplies from price-cutting retailers, the manufacturer was found to have joined in an illegal combination in violation of the Sherman Act.

There had been no written agreement between the parties, but the Court held that the manufacturer had, as in *Beech-Nut* and *Bausch & Lomb,* gone beyond a simple refusal to deal. By trying to bring retailers in line through pressure on wholesalers, the manufacturer had created an illegal combination. The Court acknowleged that by not overruling *Colgate* it created a possible inconsistency. "True, there results the same economic effect as is accomplished by a prohibited combination to suppress price competition if each customer, although induced to do so solely by a manufacturer's announced policy, independently decides to observe specified resale prices" (362 U.S. at 44).

Dissenting Justices Harlan, Frankfurter, and Whittaker said "that the Court has done no less than send to its demise the Colgate doctrine."

Klein v. *American Luggage Works, Inc.,* 206 F.Supp. 924 (D. Del. 1962), was a private action brought to recover treble damages. Klein was a retailer selling luggage manufactured, and sold directly to him, by American Luggage Works. American also supplied two other retail stores in the same trade area, Wanamaker and Strawbridge & Clothier. American attempted to maintain retail prices suggested to retailers in catalogues and preticketed on the luggage. American's sales representatives told retailers, including Klein, that full compliance with the suggested prices was mandatory and that retail sales below these prices would result in a refusal to deal with the price-cutter.

As a result of Klein's sales of American's luggage below the suggested prices, potential customers at the Wanamaker and Strawbridge stores told sales clerks that American luggage could be purchased for less elsewhere. These two retailers complained to American about sales to "discounters" and, after an investigation, American discontinued deliveries to Klein. Klein sued American, Wanamaker, and Strawbridge & Clothier, alleging an illegal conspiracy to fix resale prices in violation of Sections 1 and 3 of the Sherman Act.

The district court found that there was a conspiracy, that it was the proximate cause of damage to Klein, and that all the defendants were co-conspirators liable to Klein for treble damages. It said that the manufacturer had gone beyond the conduct "declared legally permissible by Colgate as definitively clarified in Parke, Davis." He had persuaded retailers to agree tacitly or otherwise to comply with suggested prices. Since the non-price-cutting retailers had actively volunteered assistance in discovering the price cutter, they were held to be co-conspirators. The court found no previous decisions as direct authority for this proposition but drew an analogy between the retailers' conduct and other price-fixing combinations such as *Interstate Circuit, Inc.* v. *U.S.*, 306 U.S. 208 (1939), and *U.S.* v. *Masonite Corp.*, 316 U.S. 265 (1942).

The district court opinion noted the inconsistency in *Parke, Davis* and expressed the court's own difficulty in paying lip service to the *Colgate* doctrine while finding an antitrust violation. After quoting the *Colgate* doctrine, it said: "The conceptual difficulty which inheres in this seemingly forthright line drawing process is the element of agreement which attends a seller's adherence to a manufacturer's schedule of resale prices. In the face of an advance announcement by the manufacturer that price cutters will be denied supply, a seller's compliance with prices suggested strongly infers a tacit or implied resale price maintenance agreement. The inference of agreement is no less present where the seller's acquiescence to prices suggested manifests a response to whatever inducements or coercive pressures result from the prior announcement and the consequent threatened deprivation of the line of goods in the event of non-compliance."

The findings of the district court in *Klein* were found by the court of appeals to be "without basis in the testimony" and "clearly erroneous" (323 F.2d 787 (3d Cir. 1963)). All that the evidence established, according to the court of appeals, was that retailers had been "advised" of American's policy and its expectation that its customers would not resell below preticketed prices. The finding that conforming retailers had assisted in the discovery of discounters was said to have been based on evidence that Wanamaker and Strawbridge sales clerks from time to time had passed on to American's sales representative complaints from potential customers that American Luggage was available elsewhere in Wilmington below preticketed prices. The court of appeals found the evidence did not establish that the sales representative ever reported these complaints to American and noted that the district judge had made no finding to that effect.

As described by the court of appeals, the district court's opinion adopted "the novel doctrine that retailers who adhere to suggested retail prices, knowing that compliance by competitors is expected by the manufacturer in consonance with his price maintenance policy, thereby, without more, become co-conspirators with the manufacturer." At the core of that doctrine, the court of appeals reasoned, must be a rule that "'conscious parallelism' in behavior is per se conspiratorial conduct." The court of appeals said that the Supreme Court precluded any such rule in *Theatre Enterprises, Inc.* v. *Paramount Film Distributing Corp.*, 346 U.S. 537 (1954). (Delaware is a "fair-trade" state; had American Luggage chosen to, it lawfully could have fixed the resale price of its products in Delaware. This may have affected the thinking of the reviewing court.)

In *Dart Drug Corp.* v. *Parke, Davis & Co.*, 221 F.Supp. 948 (D.D.C. 1963), *aff'd*, 344 F.2d 173 (D.C. Cir. 1965), the district court read the Supreme Court's *Parke, Davis* opinion as recognizing that the *Colgate* doctrine still applies "to a simple refusal to sell to a customer who will not resell at prices suggested by the seller." The first suspension by Parke, Davis of deliveries to Dart Drug, a discount chain, led to the filing by the Justice Department of a Section 1 civil injunction complaint. At that time Parke, Davis had also induced its wholesalers to stop selling to Dart. The subsequent refusal to deal, leading to the damage suit, was not accompanied by any attempt of Parke, Davis to induce its wholesalers or distributors not to sell to Dart, although Dart had to pay a higher price to the wholesalers than it would have had to pay Parke, Davis.

The district judge's opinion starts with the proposition that prior to enactment of the Sherman Act the common law gave any manufacturer or trader the right to deal or refuse to deal with anyone he chose, unless he was engaged in a "public calling." Although he did not explicitly adopt their view, the judge cited authorities "who have doubted whether the Sherman Act, in Section 1, has added anything to substantive law. It does provide additional remedies that did not exist at common law."

An argument that the second refusal of Parke, Davis to deal with Dart must be deemed to have been a product of the original combination between Parke, Davis and its wholesalers was rejected. "The mere fact that a person has violated the law on one occasion is no proof that some later action of his, which on its face is not a violation of law, must be tainted with the illegality of the prior act."

The court of appeals in *Quinn* v. *Mobil Oil Co.*, 375 F.2d 273 (1st Cir. 1967), affirmed dismissal of a treble-damage complaint for failure to allege an antitrust violation. A former operator of a Mobil gas station had alleged that, when his station lease came up for renewal in 1963, he was orally informed by Mobil that, unless he reduced the retail price of gasoline by one cent a gallon, his rent would be substantially increased.

Although his one-year lease was renewed at only a slight increase in rent, Mobil began pressuring him a few months later, he charged, to reduce his price. It delayed payments to him; attempted to unload consignments of tires, batteries, and accessories; and attempted to apply the money owed him to payment for this unwanted merchandise. The former station operator said he resisted these pressures and was then denied renewal of his lease in 1964.

"From these facts," it was clear to the court of appeals "that the only provision of the Federal antitrust laws that need be considered here is Section 1 of the Sherman Act." The court agreed that the complaint set out more than a simple refusal to deal but found the facts alleged to be distinguished from those in *U.S.* v. *Parke, Davis,* 362 U.S. 29 (1960); *Simpson* v. *Union Oil Co.,* 377 U.S. 13 (1964); *Broussard* v. *Socony Mobil Co.,* 350 F.2d 346 (5th Cir. 1965). In each of these cases, there was a combination or conspiracy either by virtue of the manufacturer's use of its wholesalers and other retailers to maintain resale prices or through the complaining retailer's temporary compliance with, or agreement to, the manufacturer's resale-price-fixing policy.

In a concurring opinion, Judge Coffin joined in the holding that allegation of conspiracy is essential, but said he would find no pleading of a Section 1 violation even if the complaint alleged a completed vertical price-fixing agreement. He distinguished between the anticompetitive effects of minimum resale price maintenance and the anticompetitive effects of maximum resale price maintenance, "as practiced by a single manufacturer or supplier."

Chief Judge Aldrich disagreed with both views. He found vertical price fixing illegal per se, whether maximum or minimum prices are set. And he saw "no difference in substance between pressure to induce the making of an unlawful agreement and pressure to reinstate one that has been broken. This would not only be an unfortunate distinction, since any future 'Quinn' could establish rights for himself simply by making the requested agreement one day and breaking it the next, but also, it seems to me, an illogical one."

The *Albrecht* case involved a price ceiling (*Albrecht* v. *Herald Co.,* 390 U.S. 145 (1968)). The St. Louis Globe Democrat advertised a suggested retail price for its papers. Carriers had exclusive territories subject to termination if their prices exceeded the suggested maximum. One carrier raised his delivery price. The Globe objected and advised the carrier that, because of the paper's reserved right to compete, it was informing his subscribers that the Globe itself would deliver at a lower price. In addition, the Globe hired a circulation company to solicit the carrier's subscribers. About 300 of the 1200 subscribers on the carrier's route switched to direct delivery by the Globe. Meanwhile, the Globe continued to sell papers to the carrier but warned him that he would be cut off if he continued selling at the higher price. Since the Globe did not want to deliver its own papers, it gave the 300 customers to another carrier who knew the Globe would not tolerate over-charging and understood he would have to return the route if the first carrier discontinued his pricing practice. The Globe then in-formed the first carrier he could have his customers back if he would charge the suggested price. When the carrier brought a treble-damage suit, the Globe stopped all deliveries to the carrier.

The jury returned a verdict for the Globe. The court of appeals affirmed the district judge's denial of the former carrier's motion for judgment notwithstanding the verdict (367 F.2d 517 (8th Cir. 1966)). The Supreme Court reversed. It held, citing *Parke, Davis,* there was a combination within the meaning of Section 1 of the Sherman Act among the Globe, the circulation company, and the carrier who took over part of the treble-damage claimant's route. The finding of combination was based on the circulation company's knowledge that the purpose of the solicitation campaign was to force the damage claimant to lower his price and on the replace-ment carrier's knowledge that he was getting the route as part of a program to obtain conformance to advertised prices. From its *Parke, Davis* opinion, the Court derived the proposition that a "combina-tion," as that term is used in the Sherman Act, is a concept "in addition to contracts and conspiracies express or implied."

In footnote 6, the Court elaborated: "Under Parke, Davis peti-tioner could have claimed a combination between respondent and himself, at least of the day he unwillingly complied with respon-dent's advertised price. Likewise, he might successfully have claimed that respondent had combined with other carriers because the firm-ly enforced price policy applied to all carriers, most of whom acquiesced in it. . . . Petitioner's amended complaint did allege a combination between respondent and petitioner's customers. Be-cause of our disposition of this case it is unnecessary to pass on this claim. It was not, however, a frivolous contention. See *FTC* v. *Beechnut Packing Co.,* 257 U.S. 441 (1922)."

The Court quoted from *Kiefer-Stewart Co.* v. *Seagram & Sons, Inc.,* 340 U.S. 211 (1951), that agreements to fix maximum prices "no less than those to fix minimum prices, cripple the freedom of traders and thereby restrain their ability to sell in accordance with their own judgment." "Unpersuasive" was the Court's characteriza-tion of the court of appeals' suggestion that the maximum resale price was necessary to protect the public from the anticompetitive impact of the carrier's exclusive territories. If the court of appeals were correct, "the entire scheme must fall under Section 1 of the Sherman Act."

Some say the *Colgate* doctrine is dead, but the holding of the case may be as sound as it ever was. In the *Colgate* case, the Court decided only that it is not a crime for a manufacturer to announce that he will refuse to deal with those who do not adhere to specified resale prices. In sustaining defendant's demurrer to an indictment, the Court accepted the trial court's restrictive interpretation of the terms of the indictment as not charging Colgate "with selling its products to dealers under agreements which obligated the latter not to sell except at prices fixed by the company." In the unlikely event the same question is ever again presented to the Supreme Court, the Court might very well decide it the same way. The mere announcement is still not a crime; it is the implementing conduct that may be.

As a practical matter, it is diffcult, if not impossible, to make use of the *Colgate* doctrine without running substantial risk of treble-damage actions or Government action. (But see *U.S.* v. *O. M. Scott Co.,* 303 F. Supp. 141 (D.D.C. 1969)). There is a danger that tacit understandings may be inferred from the manufacturer's unilateral announcement of, and some resellers' adherence to, specified resale prices. In the *Parke, Davis* case, the Supreme Court found something more: "When the manufacturer's actions . . . go beyond mere announcement of his policy and the simple refusal to deal, and he employs other means which effect adherence to his resale prices . . . he has put together a combination in violation of the Sherman Act" (362 U.S. at 44).

A decision by top management to announce a Colgate-type policy may result in action by subordinates beyond monitoring or control which can later be characterized by a treble-damage plaintiff as evidence of a conspiracy. Once a policy of refusing to deal with price cutters has been announced, a process of investigation, checking on customers, and setting customer-informers in motion may result in an inference of unlawful combination. Having announced a Colgate-type policy, getting rid of any customers for whatever the reason may present a sticky situation. Even where the manufacturer has a valid business reason for his refusal to deal, sales personnel may be strongly motivated to inform other accounts that the termination was prompted in part by price cutting.

(A manufacturer who pretickets prices on his products may face a dilemma. He may find he is squeezed from two directions. If he comes too close to fixing the resale price of his products, his action may be unlawful. On the other hand, if retailers do not substantially adhere to the preticketed prices, he may be in trouble for fictitious pricing.)

In *Osborn* v. *Sinclair Refining Co.*, 286 F.2d 832 (4th Cir. 1960), the court stated that a seller goes beyond the simple refusal-to-deal policy permitted by *Colgate* if he "pressures his customers or dealers into adhering to resale price maintenance or exclusive dealing or tie-ins." The court did not define the word "pressures," nor did it indicate whether extensive publication of a refusal-to-deal-with-discounters policy might not itself be considered "pressure."

In a related area, the courts have disagreed over whether a supplier can stop dealing with one of its customers in response to the customer's initiation of antitrust treble-damage litigation. In *House of Materials Inc.* v. *Simplicity Pattern Co.*, 298 F.2d 867 (2d Cir. 1962), the court refused to allow entry of an injunction requiring continuation of dealings with the customer. In *Bergen Drug Co.* v. *Parke, Davis & Co.*, 307 F.2d 725 (3rd Cir. 1962), on the other hand, the court ordered entry of such an injunction. (See section IX-E, p. 649.)

8. Fair Trade

Question: *Why don't all manufacturers who wish their dealers to maintain a suggested retail price adopt a "fair trade" program?*

The fixing of prices at retail specifically permitted by statute in most states is commonly called "fair trade." Under specified circumstances, manufacturers are permitted to establish by contract with wholesalers and retailers minimum resale prices. Model contracts and charts showing the rules in each state are published in 2 Trade Reg. Rep. ¶6041–52.

Since vertical, as well as horizontal, price-fixing agreements violate Section 1 of the Sherman Act (*Dr. Miles Medical Co.* v. *Park & Sons*, 220 U.S. 373 (1911)), special federal legislation was necessary to permit fair trading in interstate commerce. The McGuire Act, 15 U.S.C. § 45 (a)(2), amended Section 5(a) of the Federal Trade Commission Act to provide that nothing in the antitrust laws is to be regarded as invalidating any contracts prescribing "minumum or stipulated prices" for the resale of trademarked or brand-name commodities that are "in free and open competition" with other "commodities of the same general class," when such contracts are made lawful for intrastate transactions by "any statute, law, or public policy" of the state involved.

Some state laws authorizing fair-trade contracts make sales below the established minimum price illegal for every merchant with knowledge of such contracts even if he has not signed one. Beginning with the Florida Supreme Court's 1949 decision in *Liquor Store, Inc.* v. *Continental Distilling Co.*, 40 So. 2d 371 (Fla. 1949), the courts of some two dozen states have struck down this "nonsigner clause" as either a violation of state constitutional due process requirements or as an unlawful delegation of legislative power. Without the nonsigner clause, a fair-trade program is not very effective. Court decisions against the "nonsigner clause," repeated failure of efforts to obtain a federal fair-trade law, and general disillusionment with the effectiveness of resale-price maintenance programs under any circumstances have caused some manufacturers previously attracted to fair trade to abandon it, but fair trade has not yet died out completely.

In litigation attempts to enforce fair-trade contracts, manufacturers frequently meet the claim that they have not been diligent or even handed in their enforcement programs. The courts seem to agree that a manufacturer cannot require one retailer or class of retailers to comply with a price minimum if others are allowed to get away with price cutting.

In an antitrust treble-damage suit against his manufacturer-supplier, one retailer claimed that the manufacturer's failure to enforce fair-trade contracts against some retailers constituted a discrimination in "services" within the meaning of Section 2(e) of the Clayton Act, as amended by the Robinson-Patman Act. By finding that there was no factual basis for the claim of discrimination, the Federal District Court for Northern Illinois avoided a decision on the validity of that theory (*Maltis Drug Co.* v. *Shulton, Inc.,* 168 ATRR A-12 (1964)).

The decision in *General Electric Co.* v. *R.H. Macy Co.,* 103 N.Y.S. 440 (N.Y. Sup. Ct. 1951), is generally regarded as an authoritative exposition of the manufacturer's enforcement responsibility. The court said that a manufacturer who seeks to enjoin price cutting by a particular retailer must be able to prove that the manufacturer's price structure is realistic, has a reasonable chance of enforcement, and is, in fact, effectively enforced. It was also said that a manufacturer must be prepared to show that it has not picked out only large retailers to keep in line but must also watch small retail outlets, no matter how costly the chore may be. As five "basic essentials" of a satisfactory enforcement program, the opinion said, the manufacturer should (1) keep itself informed of price-cutting activities and other trends generally known in the industry, (2) keep a close watch over violaters and take appropriate action where indicated, (3) investigate and follow up complaints vigorously, (4) enforce fair-trade prices by repeated legal action if necessary, and (5) make its enforcement program "a continuing and sustained one."

In its report on the fair-trade bill introduced in the 88th Congress (called the "Quality Stabilization Bill"), the House Commerce Committee adopted the criteria set out in the *Macy* case as the appropriate ones to be applied under paragraph (11) of that bill (Report of House Interstate and Foreign Commerce Committee on Quality Stabilization, H.R. Rep. No. 566, 88th Cong., 1st Sess. (1965)). Paragraph (11) would have made it a defense to a fair-trade injunction suit "for the defendant to establish that the plaintiff has not used due diligence to effectuate observance or enforcement of plaintiff's rights" under the bill "against other persons who are in substantial competition with the defendant."

Although references in the *Macy* opinion to effective enforcement and to industry situations where fair-trade enforcement is not feasible would seem to give the manufacturer the responsibility of being successful in his enforcement efforts, subsequent decisions, even under New York's fair-trade law, have merely required "reasonable," "diligent," and "nondiscriminatory" enforcement efforts. An example is *Parke Davis & Co.* v. *Jarvis Drug Co.,* 208 F.Supp. 350 (S.D.N.Y. 1962). In that case the district court granted a preliminary injunction against a price-cutting retailer on the basis of evidence that the complaining drug manufacturer had engaged in extensive enforcement efforts. The court was convinced that evidence of "a regular and diligent enforcement program . . . not discriminating as between the small and the large retailer" was enough to outweigh professional-shopper testimony that had induced the judge to deny a preliminary injunction five months earlier (1962 Trade Cas. ¶70,318). The professional shoppers had filed affidavits that in three instances they had been able to buy the drug manufacturer's fair-traded product at about a 25-percent discount.

Similarly, in *Bulova Watch Co.* v. *Klein,* 1965 Trade Cas. ¶71,407 (N.Y. Sup. Ct. 1965), a retailer was unable to block a New York state court injunction with price-cutting evidence his shoppers had collected at competitor's stores. For cases in other states applying the "reasonable and diligent" test, see *Revere Copper and Brass, Inc.* v. *Economy Sales Co.,* 127 F.Supp. 739 (D. Conn. 1954); *Lionel Corp.* v. *Klein,* 114 A.2d 652 (Del. 1955); and *Hutzler Bros.* v. *Remington-Putnam Book Co.,* 46 A.2d 101 (Md. 1946).

The New York courts have held that a manufacturer has no affirmative duty to develop an actual enforcement plan or program. In *National Distillers and Chemical Corp.* v. *R.H. Macy & Co., Inc.* 1965 Trade Cas. ¶71,423 (N.Y. App. Div. 1965), the court concluded that the judge below had "misplaced the emphasis of the decisions" when he denied a temporary fair-trade injunction because the manufacturer had failed to develop a satisfactory enforcement program. In the Appellate Division's view, "the only bar to enforcement . . . is where it can be shown that the manufacturer deliberately abandoned the contract . . . or where he is using it inequitably to favor some retailers against others." Otherwise, the manufacturer may reasonably expect "that retailers will abide by the law and infractions can be dealt with without the necessity for litigation. . . . And if need be, he can proceed against whatever violater he chooses (*Seagram-Distillers Corp.* v. *Ackerman,* 263 App. Div. 1016)." On the subject of the retailer's "professional shopper" evidence, the Appellate Division said: "It is only where such price cutting by others is with the connivance or consent of the producer that the fact takes on significance, because it is only then the attempt to enforce an agreement would become inequitable."

One enforcement technique that apparently is frequently used but produces little litigation is the cessation of dealing with price-cutting resellers. Although there do not seem to be any court decisions on the legality of a refusal to deal as a fair-trade enforcement technique, approval can be inferred from the district court's holding in *Upjohn Co.* v. *Ace Prescription,* 1964 Trade Cas. ¶71,142 (S.D.N.Y. 1964), that a manufacturer did not lose his right to enforce fair trade merely because he had not discontinued selling to a price-cutting retailer who had ignored enforcement threats.

Special enforcement dilemmas are encountered where fair-trade and non-fair-trade jurisdictions adjoin in a single market area. Aside from the customer-relations problem encountered when a reseller has to fair-trade in competition with someone a few miles away who cannot be required to maintain prices, there does not seem to be any bar to sectional enforcement in this kind of market area.

In *General Electric Co.* v. *American Buyers Coop. Inc.,* 1956 Trade Cas. ¶68,341 (Cir. Ky. 1956), the court permitted enforcement of fair trade against a northern Kentucky retailer despite his evidence that his southern Indiana competitors were cutting prices. In addition to noting that an Indiana court had held that state's nonsigner clause unconstitutional, the court decided the manufacturer owed Kentucky retailers no duty to engage in enforcement activity in another state. In *Gadol* v. *Dart Drug Corp.,* 161 A.2d 122 (Md. 1963), the court went further and regarded the proximity of non-fair-trade areas as a factor justifying the manufacturer's failure to engage in more aggressive enforcement efforts within the fair-trade jurisdiction. Interstate transactions present problems to enforcement of a fair-trade program on many products. See *Bissell Carpet Sweeper Co.* v. *Masters Mail Order Co.,* 240 F.2d 684 (4th Cir. 1957); *General Electric Co.* v. *Masters Mail Order Co.,* 244 F.2d 681 (2d Cir. 1957), *cert. denied,* 355 U.S. 824 (1957); *Corning Glass Works,* F.T.C. D.8874, 618 ATRR A-1, E-1 (6/19/73).

A manufacturer's enforcement task may be complicated by the fact that violations are not always apparent in a retailer's posted or advertised prices. Cases in various states have established that the manufacturer must police the retailer's distribution of trading stamps with sales of the fair-traded product. Manufacturers have been held to have abandoned their fair-trade programs when they allowed retailers to set the type and value of the trading stamps to be given (*Jantzen, Inc.,* v. *E. J. Korvette, Inc.* 219 F.Supp. 604 (S.D.N.Y. 1963)); when they allowed retailers to give "bonus" stamps (*Gillette Co.* v. *White Cross Discount Centers,* 1962 Trade Cas. ¶70,481 (Pa. Ct. Com. Pls. 1962)); and when they allowed the retailer to hold "double stamp" days (*Rubbermaid, Inc.* v. *Claber Distributing Co.,* 1965 Trade Cas. ¶71,393 (Ohio Ct. Com. Pls. 1965)). In at least one case, *Colgate-Palmolive Co.* v. *Max Dichter & Sons,* 142 F.Supp. 545 (D. Mass. 1956), the toleration of trading stamps issued at the regular rate was held to represent acquiesence in price cutting and a bar to injunctive relief.

Care must be taken by the manufacturer not to promote or cause deviations from its fair-trade program through its own marketing techniques. Some producers have created problems for themselves by marketing combination packages with components that are fair-traded separately. If the package deal calls for a price lower than the aggregate of the components' prices, the manufacturer might be found to have abandoned his fair-trade program (*Gillette Co.* v. *Two Guys From Harrison, Inc.,* 177 A.2d 555 (N.J. Sup. Ct. 1962); *Upjohn Co.* v. *Vineland Discount Health & Vitamin Center, Inc.,* 235 F.Supp. 191 (D.N.J. 1964)).

It has been held that a manufacturer cannot enforce a fair-trade program under which he has established, for various classifications of customers, price differentials that are not justified by differences in the costs of serving those customer groups (*Champion Spark Plug Co.* v. *T. G. Stores, Inc.,* 239 F.Supp. 941 (D. Md. 1965)).

When state fair-trade laws were enacted, it was contemplated that fair-trading manufacturers' enforcement efforts would be supplemented by litigation initiated by retailers who favor fair trade. The statutes authorized fair-trading retailers to bring unfair competition suits against price-cutting competitors. Among the court decisions that have allowed damage or injunction suits by retailers are *Winfield Drug Stores, Inc.* v. *Warshaw,* 1956 Trade Cas. ¶68,447 (N.Y. Sup. Ct. 1956); *Iowa Pharmaceutical Assn.* v. *Mays Drug Products Co.,* 294 N.W. 756 (Iowa Sup. Ct. 1940); *Schenley Products Co.* v. *Franklin Stores Co.,* 199 A. 402 (N.J. Ct. Err. & App. 1938). However, in *Shuman* v. *Bernie's Drug Concessions,* 1961 Trade Cas. ¶70,155 (Pa. Ct. Com. Pls. 1961), a court refused to give fair-trading retailers an injunction against a discounting competitor. The theory was that, under the U.S. Supreme Court's 1936 decision in *Old Dearborn Distributing Co.* v. *Seagram-Distillers Corp.,* 299 U.S. 183 (1936), the sole legitimate purpose of the fair-trade laws is to protect the manufacturer's good will. Subsequently, though, in *Olin Mathieson Chemical Corp.* v. *Red Cross Stores,* 414 Pa. 94 (Pa. Sup. Ct. 1964), the Pennsylvania Supreme Court declared the Pennsylvania act's nonsigner clause unconstitutional.

When fair-trading retailers band together to enforce resale-price maintenance among their competitors, they are on more uncertain legal ground. In the *Winfield Drug Stores* case, cited above, a New York judge granted a temporary injunction against price cutting by the plaintiff's competitors despite a suggestion that the plaintiff was carrying out the policy of a trade association to which it belonged. In *DeCandido* v. *Wagonfeld,* 190 N.Y. S.2d 858 (N.Y. Sup. Ct. 1959), on the other hand, a retail druggist was denied an injunction when the court found out that his suit was sponsored by an association of pharmacists who competed with each other. In the *Iowa Pharmaceutical Association* case, cited in the preceding paragraph, 23 drugstore operators were permitted to join in a single action to restrain a competitor from discounting fair-traded products. It has held that the complaining retailers had a right to sue as representatives of other drug retailers interested in enforcing fair trade.

A manufacturer who initiates a fair-trade program has no legal duty to enforce it except in so far as Section 5 of the Federal Trade Commission Act discourages the furnishing of retailers with unrealistic price-lists that permit false "bargain" claims. Decisions requiring a manufacturer to enforce diligently and generally if he wants to enjoin any particular retailer's price cutting simply mean that the manufacturer must be prepared for a vigorous enforcement campaign if he wants his fair-trade program to work. Many who have tried fair-trading in large-scale merchandising operations have found it to be expensive and almost impossible to maintain on a universal basis. Some experts in this area are convinced that *no* manufacturer can expect a fair-trade program to be effective unless he is prepared to carry through vigorously with extensive and expensive enforcement efforts. Constant policing activity must be engaged in, and prompt and uniform action must be taken when deviations from minimum price schedules are found. When legal action becomes necessary, one way that has been used to show that diligent and nondiscriminating efforts are being made is the filing of simultaneous suits against all known violators.

A few manufacturers have found it possible to maintain resale prices through selective distribution systems limiting sales of their products in fair-trade states to actual signers of fair-trade agreements and in non-fair-trade states to resellers who faithfully follow list prices. Yet such a method may place the manufacturer at competitive disadvantages, since rival manufacturers are able to sell through more extensive distributions and service networks of distributors. Moreover, retailers expected to comply with list prices may also be willing to transship to discounters.

Although states that now permit enforcement of fair-trade prices against nonsigners recognize the right of retailers to bring suit under the fair-trade acts, the conflict of authority over the role that may be played by associations of retailers suggests that manufacturers cannot count on much assistance from their customers, except possibly in the reporting of cut-rate sales. The situation may vary from state to state, depending on the attitude of local judges. In some states, judges tend to look upon fair trade as a form of price fixing and bar retailer enforcement. Since the statutes explicitly provide for retailer suits, most of the states that have not declared fair-trade or the nonsigner clause unconstitutional are thought likely to continue permitting retailer suits.

B. RESTRICTIONS ON RESALE

1. Territories for Distributors and Dealers

Question: *Are any arrangements between a manufacturer and his dealers to protect dealers' territories permitted?*

Early lower court decisions upheld territorial restrictions in agreements between manufacturers and their dealers, but the Justice Department campaigned persistently against them as unreasonable restraints of trade. The Supreme Court first declined to declare such restrictions automatically unlawful but has now done so.

In *Phillips* v. *Iola Portland Cement Co.,* 125 F.593 (8th Cir. 1903), the court of appeals refused to outlaw a cement manufacturer's sales contract that prevented the buyer from selling outside Texas. The court emphasized the existence of competing manufacturers and concluded that the restraint did not have any substantially adverse effect on competition. In 1915, the Court of Appeals for the Fifth Circuit found nothing illegal in an automobile manufacturer's requirement that its exclusive agent for certain counties in Texas restrict his sales to those counties (*Cole Motor Car Co.* v. *Hurst,* 228 F.280 (5th Cir. 1915)). On the other hand, a district court, in instructions to a jury, said it would be illegal under the Sherman Act for a manufacturer, in appointing dealers, to exact from each of them an obligation not to sell outside his territory (*Lowe Motor Supplies Co.* v. *Weed Chain Tire Grip Co.,* Supp. Vol. V, Trade Reg. Rep. ¶5506 (S.D.N.Y. 1917)).

In 1949 the Justice Department began a campaign against territorial restraints. Its expressions of disapproval, apparently based on dicta in *U.S.* v. *Bausch & Lomb Co.,* 321 U.S. 707, 721 (1944), induced automobile manufacturers to delete from their dealer-franchise agreements a clause prohibiting dealers from operating outside their prescribed territories. Over the next decade, at least 16 manufacturers in other industries accepted consent judgments prohibiting territorial restrictions on dealers and distributors.

On October 31, 1963, the Justice Department filed suit for an injunction against Studebaker for allocating to each distributor of its "STP" oil additive "an exclusive territory within which no other co-conspirator distributor is to sell oil additives." Studebaker agreed to a consent order enjoining price fixing and allocation of territories (*U.S.* v. *Studebaker,* 1965 Trade Cas. ¶71,410 (D. Nebraska 1965)).

The Justice Department attacked the territorial-allocation feature of licensing arrangements by filing Section 1 Sherman Act injunction complaints against two organizations of bedding manufacturers. They both signed consent judgments (*U.S.* v. *Restonic Corp.,* 1960 Trade Cas. ¶69,739 (N.D. Ill. 1960); *U.S.* v. *Spring-Air Co.,* 1962 Trade Cas. ¶70,402 (N.D. Ill. 1962)).

Spring-Air Company owned the trademarks of 34 small bedding manufacturers attempting to compete with large nation-wide firms by advertising the "Spring-Air" name on a nation-wide basis and standardizing the products sold under that name. Each manufacturer-licensee agreed not to manufacture, sell, ship, or deliver Spring-Air trademarked products outside its assigned territory or to sell Spring-Air products for resale outside the territory. Consent judgments prohibited any agreements "to limit or restrict the persons to whom or the territories within which products may be sold." The defendants also agreed not to reach any understanding "to fix, determine, maintain, or adhere to price or other terms or conditions of sale." On the other hand, they were specifically permitted to "agree upon and use suggested retail prices for the purpose of national advertising of any products."

Less than two months later, in the *Denison Mattress Factory* case, a court of appeals told Spring-Air its territorial restrictions did not necessarily violate the antitrust laws after all (*Denison Mattress Factory* v. *Spring-Air Co.,* 308 F.2d 403 (5th Cir. 1962)). The Denison Mattress Factory, a Texas partnership, decided to withdraw from the group and terminated its contract without paying assessments owed Spring-Air for advertising and other services. Spring-Air won a judgment in the district court, and Denison appealed. The manufacturer contended, among other things, that its contract with Spring-Air violated the antitrust laws in that it provided that Denison would not manufacture or sell Spring-Air products outside its assigned sales area or make "any sale of Spring-Air products if it knows that the purchaser intends to resell, deliver, or ship the same for resale out of said assigned sales area." Other provisions of the contract authorized Spring-Air to designate a supplier for all material going into Spring-Air products. Denison was free to sell its own non-Spring-Air products, which actually accounted for the bulk of its business, outside its exclusive Spring-Air sales area, but products were not permitted to bear a label referring to the supplier chosen by Spring-Air. The contract also provided that Denison would not manufacture or sell any other nationally advertised bedding products in competition with Spring-Air products.

After reviewing prior court decisions on ancillary covenants in restraint of trade, the court of appeals observed that "the cases seem to follow the principle that if the primary purpose of the contract is lawful, e.g., to protect one in the fruits of his labor, and if the arrangement was actuated by or could be explained on the basis of legitimate business justification as opposed to the desire to increase market control through economic leverage, then the court will generally hold any individual restraint of trade, not harmful to competition or the public, to be lawful." As the court saw it, Spring-Air had not only a right to license its trade-mark to exclusive dealers, "but also had an affirmative duty to itself and to the public to invoke some kind of control and restraint upon its various licensees to prevent losing its property rights thereunder." Consequently, the court said, the contract provision dividing trade territories, "in the circumstances of this case is not offensive to the antitrust laws. The division of territory was not the central purpose of the contract."

The matter was dealt with by the U.S. Supreme Court in *White Motor* v. *U.S.*, 372 U.S. 253 (1963), in which a 6–3 majority of the Justices reversed a district court holding, 194 F.Supp. 562 (N.D. Ohio 1961), that territory and customer restrictions on a truck manufacturer's franchised distributors and dealers were illegal per se, enjoinable without the necessity of a trial to prove actual or potential effect on competition or to look for underlying economic facts that might make the business practice a reasonable one.

The case left the legal status of customer and territory restrictions unsettled. The district judge had granted a pretrial government motion for summary judgment. Because this was its "first case involving a territorial restriction in a vertical arrangement," the Supreme Court concluded that "we know too little of the actual impact both of that restriction and the one respecting customers to reach a conclusion on the bare bones of the documentary evidence before us." In the majority opinion, Justice Douglas stated that the Court was intimating "no view one way or the other on the legality of such an arrangement, for we believe that the applicable rule of law should be designed after a trial."

The Court concluded that "horizontal" agreements among manu-

facturers, or among dealers, to establish territorial limitations would
be "naked restraints of trade with no purpose except stifling of
competition." On the other hand, a territorial limitation imposed
"vertically" by agreement between a manufacturer and his dealers
or distributors "may or may not have this purpose or effect. We
do not know enough of the economic and business stuff out of
which these arrangements emerged to be certain. They may be too
dangerous to sanction or they may be allowable protections against
aggressive competitors or the only practicable means a small company has for breaking into or staying in business . . . and within
the 'rule of reason.' We need to know more than we do about the
actual impact of these arrangements on competition to decide
whether they have such a 'pernicious effect on competition and lack
any redeeming virtue' . . . and therefore should be classified as per
se violations of the Sherman Act."

In *Snap-On Tools Corp.* v. *FTC,* 321 F.2d 825 (7th Cir. 1963), a
divided court of appeals read Justice Douglas' opinion as holding
"that vertical allocations of dealer territory are not per se violations
of the Sherman Act." The court of appeals set aside a Federal
Trade Commission cease-and-desist order issued under Section 5 of
the FTC Act enjoining Snap-On from (1) fixing the resale price of
its tools, (2) setting geographical or territorial limits within which
dealers might sell Snap-On tools, (3) forbidding its dealers to sell
to certain firms specified by Snap-On, and (4) forbidding dealers
to engage in any business similar to Snap-On's for at least one
year after termination of their dealerships. The Commission had
refused to consider each of these restrictions separately; it had
considered each as part of an integrated distribution system, "the
purpose and effect of which are to prevent competition in the resale
of Snap-On products at the dealer level."

An examination of Snap-On's distribution methods persuaded
the court that the exclusive-territory arrangements tend to promote
rather than suppress competition in the distribution of tools. The
court of appeals quoted with approval the FTC examiner's finding
that "there is merit in [Snap-On's] contention that the maintenance
of exclusive territories is indispensable to the successful operation
of its business; that 'confusion and chaos' would result if it were
forced to abandon the policy." The opinion stated that customers
are free to sell to any customer who wishes to purchase from them
within their assigned territories. In addition, while Snap-On sells
directly to industrial accounts, the court apparently accepted Snap-
On's contention that dealers are free to solicit this business as well.

The court noted the existence of over 80 competing manufacturers
in the hand-tool industry, the "bitter and bloody" competitive conditions that prevail, and Snap-On's relatively small size in the in-

dustry. "Noncompetitive activity on Snap-On's part in interbrand competition, price-wise or territory-wise, could cause it to be submerged by the other companies in the field, both large and small. Sound business judgment would not overlook this fact when assessing reasons for limiting 'bitter and bloody' competition among intrabrand competitors."

Chief Judge John S. Hastings dissented. He objected to the majority's rejection of the Commission's findings and adoption of the hearing examiner's. Declaring that the real controversy in this case involved the legal conclusions to be drawn from the evidence in the record, Judge Hastings insisted that the Commission's judgment should control, not its examiner's. He distinguished the Commission's position from that of the Antitrust Division in the *White Motor* case. "The Commission here chose not to contend for a per se rule but elected to prove its charges. . . . The voluminous record of the Commission hearing indicates compliance in that respect with the mandate in White Motor. The Commission has evaluated the record and made its own findings and conclusions based thereon. I would credit the Commission's action in this regard rather than substitute for it the findings of its hearing examiner, which the Commission rejected." The Commission asked the Solicitor General to file a Supreme Court petition for review of the decision, but none was ever filed.

Issues similar to those in *Denison* were involved in the Government's case against Sealy (*U.S.* v. *Sealy, Inc.,* 1964 Trade Cas. ¶71,258 (N.D. Ill. 1964), *rev'd,* 388 U.S. 350 (1967)). The Sealy license agreements with mattress producers contained provisions assigning an exclusive territory to each licensee. Sealy agreed not to license any other person to manufacture or sell products within that area, and the licensee agreed not to manufacture or sell Sealy products outside the area. The Justice Department contended that the territorial trademark licenses were entered into for the purpose of dividing the market and eliminating competition among the licensees. The Government's evidence was wholly documentary, consisting almost entirely of Sealy's corporate documents and correspondence. The Government argued that the division of territories was illegal per se; consequently, it presented no evidence on the competitive effect of the arrangements.

In the district court, Judge Austin regarded the history of Sealy's operations as demonstrating "that there has never been a central conspiratorial purpose on the part of Sealy and its licensees to divide the United States into territories in which competitors would not compete. Their main purpose has been the proper exploitation of the Sealy name and trademarks by licensing bedding manufacturers to manufacture and sell Sealy products in exchange for royalties to Sealy." The territorial restrictions were "secondary, or ancillary, to the main purpose of Sealy's license contracts. . . . It is obvious that an essential inducement to prospective licensees, to get them to undertake the obligations of a Sealy license, was the grant of exclusive rights in the territories in which Sealy asked them to manufacture, distribute, and pay royalties." There were no restrictions upon the areas in which licensees would manufacture and sell their own private-brand products, as long as they were not passed off as Sealy products. The only portion of the complaint that was sustained by Judge Austin was the charge that Sealy and the licensees had conspired to set minimum retail prices on Sealy products and to induce retailers to adhere to those prices. An injunction against that conspiracy was granted.

The case went to the Supreme Court (*U.S.* v. *Sealy*, 388 U.S. 350 (1967)). The Court found a horizontal market-splitting agreement. Having done so, the Court did not take the next step and declare the arrangement illegal per se. Rather, the Court looked for further factual support for finding a Section 1 Sherman Act violation and found it in Sealy's fixing, and the licensee-manufacturers' policing, of retail prices. At that point, according to Justice Fortas' opinion, the court was faced with an "aggregation of trade restraints" like that involved in *Timken Roller Bearing Co.* v. *U.S.*, 341 U.S. 593 (1951). "This unlawful resale price-fixing activity refutes Sealy's claim that the territorial restraints were mere incidents of a lawful program of trademark licensing." Justice Fortas applied a rule of per se illegality to this "aggregation of trade restraints."

In *U.S.* v. *Serta Associates, Inc.*, 296 F.Supp. 1121 (N.D. Ill. 1968), the Government attacked an organization of bedding manufacturers at the same time as Sealy. Because the facts and issues were similar, the district court held the *Serta* case in abeyance until the Supreme Court had decided *Sealy*. Once the Supreme Court had rendered its decision, the district court held that because the actions of the association were the result of horizontal cooperation among the members, because it assigned exclusive territories, and because the members fixed prices, there was an aggregation of trade restraints and a violation of Section 1 of the Sherman Act. The district court was affirmed by the Supreme Court (393 U.S. 534 (1969)).

The relative size of the company involved was said to be a factor when the court of appeals decided *Sandura Co.* v. *FTC*, 339 F.2d 847 (6th Cir. 1964), although the court explicitly stated it was not of the view "that small competitors should be allowed the use of illegal tools to meet the competition of the so-called giants." Only the assignment of closed, exclusive territories to franchised distributors was in question. The court concluded that the closed territories were essential if Sandura, a producer of floor coverings, was to maintain a devoted distributor system. The court was impressed by testimony of distributors that they would not have been willing to invest in warehouse facilities and inventory in the absence of the grant of closed territories. Sandura has never accounted for more than 4.8 percent of the floorcovering industry's sales and must compete with a big three owning about 91 percent of the industry's assets, as well as several large diversified firms. The court's holding was that closed distributor territories increased "interbrand competition without any . . . detriment to intrabrand competition" (339 F.2d at 858).

When the Federal Trade Commission decided the case, it concluded that the closed territories must be prohibited because they were part of an over-all scheme for fixing prices at the retail level. The court of appeals did not think the Commission's findings on that point were supported by substantial evidence. The retailer-franchising plan, the method through which retail price maintenance was accomplished, was instituted two years before the imposition of territorial restrictions on distributors and had already proved successful. The FTC took the position in its decision against Sandura that the policy of franchising retail dealers and forbidding distributors to sell to nonfranchised dealers imposed another illegal restriction on the distributors. Yet the court of appeals does not mention the Commission's findings on retailer franchising and treats the closed-distributor-territories issue as the only one raised on appeal. There was some evidence that the closed distributor territories had a "horizontal" origin. The court of appeals did not consider the Commission's evidence on that point, a single letter from Sandura's general sales manager to a distributor, as enough to overcome "the overwhelming evidence that the restrictions were adopted because they were necessary to Sandura's survival."

In *U.S.* v. *Arnold, Schwinn & Co.,* 237 F.Supp. 323 (N.D. Ill. 1965), the Government in a civil injunction suit charged that the Chicago bicycle manufacturer had (1) engaged in retail price maintenance in states that have no fair-trade laws, (2) conspired with its distributors to create an exclusive sales territory for each, and (3) extracted from its distributors a commitment that resales would be made only to franchised retailers. As for retail price maintenance, the court found that the Government had not proven its case, that Schwinn retailers in non-fair-trade states have at all times been free to establish their own retail prices. Territorial restrictions on the distributors' choice of customers, on the other hand, were enjoined as illegal per se because some of them had acquired a "horizontal" flavor. While territorial assignments were handled "vertically" by Schwinn, the court found that beginning in 1952, "territorialization was discussed with approval at most of the meetings of the Schwinn Cycle Distributors Association and that Association had knowledge of and agreed to the territorialization carried on by certain distributors who were members of the Association. . . . Such division of territory by agreement between the distributors is horizontal in nature, and whether agreed upon after being imposed or even merely suggested from above in a vertical manner by the manufacturer does not alter its illegality."

The district court applied the rule of reason to the charge that Schwinn's franchising of retailers placed an illegal restriction upon its distributors' choice of customers. In dealing with this charge, the opinion begins with an observation that Schwinn is "a pigmy, compared with its giant bicycle competitors, Sears, Roebuck & Co., and Montgomery Ward & Co." As viewed by the court, the Government's position in this case leaves the "giants" free to exercise full control over the marketing and pricing of their bicycles through vice presidents in charge of retailing and through their own retail outlets. The district judge refused to penalize Schwinn for "being a pigmy" and distributing its products through distributors who buy and resell.

The court found that from 1952 to 1962 well over half of the bicycles sold by Schwinn were sold directly to retailers on direct orders from those retailers. Although the distributor in whose territory the direct-buying retailer is located was paid the regular commission on such a direct sale, Schwinn shipped directly to the retailer, billed the retailer, extended him credit, and collected from him. Even in those instances where a distributor bought bicycles for inventory and resold to retailers, however, the district court found that Schwinn's relationship with its distributors was that of agency. "The sale is not made to the distributors for use but as an intermediate step to the retailer who sells to the public." Applicable here, the court reasoned, "is the rule of common law that generally what one may do himself he may likewise do by or through an agent." Schwinn "has made agents of its distributors, in the same manner that it would make an agent of a corporate official, say its president or vice president, or other officer." Moreover, valid business reasons were found to exist for this retailer-franchising policy. Bicycles need frequent service that hardware stores, department stores, and most other sales outlets do not furnish. Schwinn turned to franchised retail cycle outlets because the more specialized type of retailer was able to furnish the necessary service. The opinion makes the point that neither the distributors nor the franchised retailers are required to deal exclusively in Schwinn bicycles. Distributors usually handle the lines of several bicycle manufacturers, and almost all of the retail dealers who appeared as witnesses carried several brands of bicycles.

The Supreme Court concluded that Schwinn enforced the challenged restrictions by threats of termination and that an "agreement" existed (*U.S.* v. *Arnold, Schwinn & Co.,* 388 U.S. 365 (1967)). With respect to the legality of the "agreement," the Court distinguished between the "sale" and "agency" transactions. Justice Fortas stated as to restrictions on resale: "As the District Court held, where a manufacturer *sells* products to his distributor subject to territorial restrictions upon resale, a per se violation of the Sherman Act results. And, as we have held, the same principle applies to restrictions of outlets with which the distributors may deal and to restraints upon retailers to whom the goods are sold. Under the Sherman Act, it is unreasonable without more for a manufacturer to seek to restrict and confine areas or persons with which an article may be traded after the manufacturer has parted with dominion over it. . . . Such restraints are so obviously destructive of competition that their mere existence is enough."

In a sweeping concluding statement of his opinion, Justice Fortas condemned as criminal conduct previously adopted by many as a commonly accepted method of doing business. The opinion read "Once the manufacturer has parted with title and risk, he has parted with dominion over the product, and his effort thereafter to restrict territory or persons to whom the product may be transferred—whether by explicit agreement or by silent combination or understanding with his vendee—is a per se violation of § 1 of the Sherman Act."

In *Tripoli Co.* v. *Wella Corp.,* 286 F.Supp. 264 (E.D. Pa. 1968), *aff'd,* 425 F.2d 932 (3rd Cir. 1970), *cert. denied,* 400 U.S. 831 (1970), Tripoli, a distributor of beauty supplies to professional beauticians and barbers, had distributed for 30 years a line of cosmetics, including hair dyes and tints, manufactured by defendant Wella. When defendant discovered that plaintiff was also selling directly to the consuming public, defendant refused to deal further with plaintiff. Plaintiff brought suit, alleging violation of the Clayton and Robinson-Patman Acts, seeking treble damages and an injunction. In a motion for summary judgment, Wella claimed that its termination of Tripoli was intended to prevent Tripoli from selling at retail potentially dangerous products designed for professional use only. Although Tripoli opposed the summary judgment motion on the ground that this customer restriction was unlawful per se under the Sherman Act, the district court granted defendant's motion, and the plaintiff appealed. The court of appeals affirmed the district court's decision rejecting a per se rule. The court was convinced that "not all restraints in a system of distribution fall into the per se category." Rather, the court found, "Schwinn has to be read . . . in its factual context [as] . . . a restraint on the territories in which and retailers to whom a purchaser may resell a bicycle, a product so simple in use that most ultimate consumers are children." The court noted the statement in the *Schwinn* opinion that "under the Sherman Act it is unreasonable without more for a manufacturer to seek to restrict and confine areas or persons with whom an article may be traded." However, said the court, "here there is more and the restraints are of a different order." Defendant's restriction of resales to professional users must be tested by a "standard of reasonableness." The court rejected the decision in *U.S.* v. *Glaxo Group, Ltd.,* 302 F.Supp. 1 (D.D.C. 1969). In that case the district court had interpreted *Schwinn* to impose a per se rule on all post-sale restraints regardless of purpose. The court of appeals stated: "We do not believe that in the 'age of consumerism' the Supreme Court intended so drastic a reduction of the areas in which a manufacturer may exercise responsibility to the consumer as is suggested in Glaxo."

Applying a "rule of reason" to defendant's restraints, the court found the restraints "not only reasonable but appropriate in the public interest." The court noted that all but two of the restricted products involved were specially packaged for the professional trade; that the misuse of Wella's products created the danger of blindness and burning of the scalp; that such danger was communicated by means of cautionary labels affixed to the product containers; and that no danger to competition between Wella wholesalers existed as a result of the restrictions. Whether Wella was interested in protecting the public from injury or protecting itself from product liability, its customer limitations, according to the court, had a "lawful main purpose, to which the restriction on resale of potentially dangerous products is reasonably ancillary."

Three of seven judges dissented from the *Tripoli* decision. They felt that the case should not be disposed of on summary judgment, that a genuine factual issue remained as to whether plaintiff was terminated because it failed to follow Wella's price-fixing policy. The dissenters concluded that the determination of whether Wella's customer-class restrictions violated the Sherman Act, either under a per se rule or a "rule of reason," could not be made without further facts (such as the true extent of the danger posed by improper use of the products). The dissenters also noted that the "inadequately drawn complaint" and "loosely conducted" pretrial proceedings, as well as certain "self-serving statements," made the case particularly inappropriate for summary judgment.

The *Glaxo* decision (*U.S.* v. *Glaxo Group, Ltd.,* 302 F.Supp. 1 (D. D.C. 1969)) involved a Sherman Act challenge to an allegedly restrictive patent-licensing agreement whereby Glaxo and its licensees agreed that the patented product, griseofulvin, would not be resold to any independent third party in bulk form without Glaxo's consent. The Government moved for partial summary judgment, arguing that under *Schwinn,* this was a per se Sherman Act violation. The district court found that an "agreement" existed and rejected defendant's argument that the doctrine of ancillary restraints should apply. The court refused to limit *Schwinn* to its facts, since "the language of the [Schwinn] majority opinion . . . and the complaint of the dissent presage no such narrow application" (302 F.Supp. at 8 (citing key *Schwinn* language at 388 U.S. 365, 379)). The court considered but rejected arguments that a per se view of *Schwinn* could destroy a developing franchising system. The district court said that "it would be presumptuous . . . for this court to read the rule of reason back into a sale situation; that possibility has been foreclosed [by the Supreme Court]."

One can find support in the *Schwinn* opinion for the contention that customer-class restrictions are not per se unlawful. Justice Fortas noted that the Government never contended for a per se rule but spoke of the "specifics of the challenged practices and their impact upon the marketplace." In considering whether the vertical restraint was "sheltered by the rule of reason" and rejecting the possibility, since Schwinn was not a new market entrant nor a "failing company," the Court used language which did not have the ring of the per se rule. Furthermore, in adopting a "rule-of-reason" approach as to "agency" sales, the Court tended to undercut its own per se rule for outright sales.

A cautious counsellor will probably not wish to advise on the basis of *Tripoli* that customer-class restrictions are no longer per se unlawful. Experts point out that the *Tripoli* case involved questionable pleading, confusing pretrial procedures, and summary judgment upon affidavits only. Also, the decision fails to account for the key *Schwinn* language which seems to state the per se rule. Some would regard *Tripoli* as establishing an "almost per se rule," despite *Schwinn.* These commentators point to *U.S.* v. *Jerrold Electronics,* 187 F.Supp. 545 (E.D. Pa. 1960), *aff'd,* 365 U.S. 567 (1961), and *Dehydrating Process Co.* v. *A.O. Smith Corp.,* 292 F.2d 653 (1st Cir.), *cert. denied,* 368 U.S. 931 (1961), which defined limited exceptions to the allegedly per se tying-agreement rule. They urge that even *Schwinn's* per se rule creates nothing more than a strong rebuttable presumption of illegality, and note that the common law restraint on alienation cases cited by Justice Fortas in *Schwinn* has several exceptions engrafted by the courts.

Still, some urge that the efforts of the Court of Appeals for the Third Circuit to find a relationship to the public interest in restrictions on resale of hazardous products cannot be disregarded completely, although such considerations were rejected years ago as any possible justification for patent-license restrictions otherwise unlawful (*Ethyl Gasoline Corp.* v. *U.S.,* 309 U.S. 436 (1940)). Where the facts as to the extent of a product hazard are set forth in more substance than they were in *Tripoli,* perhaps a pure customer-class restriction will be upheld under the Sherman Act. There appears to be support for this position in the decision of the Illinois Court of Appeals in *Clairol, Inc.* v. *Bender,* 467 ATRR A-7 (Ill. Ct. of Appeals 1970).

Some suggest that a more workable test, the one really intended by Justice Fortas in *Schwinn,* is one of "presumptive illegality." This was the test urged by the Government in *Schwinn.* Under this test a customer-class restriction would not be held unlawful per se, but would be considered unlawful unless there is persuasive proof of justification for it. This test could take substantial and provable consumer protection interests into consideration. Perhaps enforcement officials will be moved by the same policy considerations as those which the court in the *Tripoli* case found persuasive without accepting the legal rationale that *Schwinn* must be limited to its facts. The Justice Department or Federal Trade Commission can, within their discretion, decline to proceed against otherwise unlawful customer restrictions where the public health may be jeopardized. Alternatively, negotiated consent decrees can provide for exceptions in Tripoli-type circumstances. This has already been done by the Justice Department in decrees such as *Bayer-Chemagro,* 1969 Trade Cas. ¶72,918 (D.D.C. 1969). There, customer class restrictions were enjoined except where a refusal to sell to a purchaser marketing to a restricted class is based upon a belief that use by members of the class "endangers the health or safety of human beings or plant or animal life."

One element in the *Tripoli* case that tends to detract from its impact is the resale price fixing by Wella, although the claim was not proved and was eventually abandoned by the plaintiff. Absent price fixing, Wella might have refused to deal unilaterally with customers reselling to restricted purchaser classes, and the *Colgate* doctrine might have protected such conduct. Wella's announced price-fixing policy, coupled with a threat of termination, might have provided the *Tripoli* court with sufficient ammunition to find a Sherman Act "combination" like that in *U.S.* v. *Parke, Davis & Co.,* 362 U.S. 29 (1960), although this is not specifically set out in the opinion.

The *Topco* case involved a question left unanswered by Justice Fortas in *Sealy,* that is, whether an agreement among small grocers like the Sealy agreement, would be a per se violation of the Sherman Act. In *U.S.* v. *Topco Associates,* 319 F.Supp. 1031 (N.D. Ill. 1970), the district court upheld an arrangement whereby Topco, a cooperative buying organization whose members are small and medium-sized supermarket chains, limits the territory within which each of its members may resell Topco-owned brands. The Government had urged that this arrangement eliminated competition in Topco and other brands and that it constituted a per se violation of Section 1 of the Sherman Act. In upholding Topco's territorial restraints, the district court indicated that virtually all the national chains have private brands, and that they are almost essential in supermarket competition. The court noted that in *Sandura Co.* v. *FTC,* 339 F.2d 847 (6th Cir. 1964), the court of appeals "concluded that a system of exclusive territorial distributorships promoted interbrand competition without any demonstrated detriment to intrabrand competition, since the record indicated that the bulk of the expense and effort necessary to develop consumer acceptance had to be borne by the distributors who testified that they would not be interested in Sandura distributorships if they were not exclusive." Comparing *Sandura* to the case at hand, the court said: "Except for the fact that the Sandura distributorships were conferred by the manufacturer and not, as in Topco, by a board controlled by existing franchisees, the record here is virtually identical." The court concluded:

"Whatever anti-competitive effect these practices may have on competition in the sale of Topco private label brands is far outweighed by the increased ability of Topco members to compete both with the national chains and other supermarkets operating in their respective territories. Moreover, if the testimony of all the live witnesses at the trial is correct, the elimination of the Topco territorial limitations in the franchises would result in the demise of the Topco organization and its private label program with no benefit to competition in those private label brands and with a substantial reduction in the competition between its members and both the national chains and other supermarkets. Expressed another way, the relief which the government here seeks would not increase competition in Topco private label brands but would substantially diminish competition in the supermarket field."

The Supreme Court held that the Topco territorial arrangement is per se unlawful (*U.S.* v. *Topco Associates,* 405 U.S. 596 (1972)). Justice Marshall wrote the opinion. Justice Blackmun wrote a concurring opinion. Chief Justice Berger dissented. Justices Powell and Rehnquist did not participate. "One of the classic examples of a per se violation of § 1 is an agreement among competitors at the same level of the market structure to allocate territories in order to minimize competition." The Court supported this statement with a string of citations, beginning with *U.S.* v. *Addyston Pipe & Steel Co.,* 175 U.S. 211 (1899), and ending with *U.S.* v. *Arnold, Schwinn & Co.,* 388 U.S. 365 (1967), and *Serta Associates* v. *U.S.,* 393 U.S. 534 (1969). One of those cases, *United States* v. *Sealy,* 388 U.S. 350 (1967), the Court went on to say, is "on all fours with this case." Noting that in *Sealy* price fixing as well as territorial restrictions were involved, the Court added: "To the extent that Sealy casts doubt on whether horizontal territorial limitations, unaccompanied by price fixing, are per se violations, we remove that doubt today."

In further explanation of the application of the per se rule, the Court remarked that "courts are of limited utility in examining difficult economic problems." Noting that per se rules have the virtue of certainty, it said: "Should Congress ultimately determine that predictability is unimportant in this area of the law, it can, of course, make per se rules inapplicable in some or all cases, and leave courts free to ramble through the wilds of economic theory in order to maintain a flexible approach."

After citing *U.S.* v. *Philadelphia National Bank,* 374 U.S. 321 (1963), the Court dealt specifically with the reasoning of the lower court:

"The District Court determined that by limiting the freedom of its individual members to compete with each other, Topco was doing a greater good by fostering competition between members and other large supermarket chains. But, the fallacy in this is that Topco has no authority under the Sherman Act to determine the respective values of competition in various sectors of the economy. On the contrary, the Sherman Act gives to each Topco member and to each prospective member the right to ascertain for itself whether or not competition with other supermarket chains is more desirable than competition in the sale of Topco brand products. Without territorial restrictions, Topco members may indeed '[cut] each other's throat.' . . . But, we have never found this possibility sufficient to warrant condoning horizontal restraints of trade."

Chief Justice Burger filed a lengthy dissenting opinion. He characterized the territorial arrangement in Topco as reasonably ancillary to a cooperative endeavor, and, after reviewing the cases cited by the majority, expressed his view that a per se rule had not previously been established by the Court. He concluded by suggesting that, in the absence of new legislation, "grocery staples marketed under private label brands with their lower consumer prices will soon be available only to those who patronize the large national chains."

Before this decision there had been some doubt that all horizontal territorial arrangements, regardless of the competitive situation, were per se unlawful. There had been some feeling that the Court might find some way to accommodate the "little fellow" trying to compete on more equal terms with his larger competitors. According to some observers, there is now little doubt that, so far as horizontal territorial restrictions are concerned, the "little fellow" will get no special treatment from the Supreme Court.

Still, it may be argued, the *Topco* rule, like the *Schwinn* rule, may be subject to exceptions in unusual circumstances, and a territorial arrangement may be upheld, possibly as incidental to a joint activity, e.g. a joint sales agency, if supported by a really persuasive economic analysis showing the arrangement is necessary for the survival of small firms competing with larger. Some say Topco Associates was not really small and the economic analysis relied upon was not really persuasive. The Court distinguished between vertical arrangements and horizontal arrangements. Despite the Court's expressed reluctance "to ramble through the wilds of economic theory," it is still possible that the Court would be more receptive to economic analysis offered in support of a challenged vertical arrangement. In any event, the Court declared unequivocally that procompetitive effects in one market cannot be used to justify anticompetitive effects in another.

The district's court's final judgment in the *Topco* case enjoined any restriction of the territories within which or the persons to whom members may sell Topco brand products, but also provided that notwithstanding these restrictions, the association could, with limitations, do the following: (1) create or eliminate areas of prime responsibility; (2) designate the location of the place of business for which a trademark license would be issued; (3) determine warehouse locations; (4) terminate members who did not adequately promote the sale of the association's products; (5) formulate passovers to compensate for good will developed for the association's products in an area in which another member began to sell; and (6) engage in any activity subsequently made lawful by act of Congress (1973 Trade Cas. ¶74,391 (N.D. Ill. 1973)). The Government appealed from this decree, contending that its practical effect would be to overrule the Supreme Court decision. The Court affirmed the district court order without opinion (1973 Trade Cas. ¶74,728 (10/9/73)).

2. Resale Restrictions

Question: *May a manufacturer offer a product at one price for unrestricted use and at a lower price for restricted use only?*

Distinguishing *U.S.* v. *Arnold, Schwinn & Co.,* 388 U.S. 365 (1967), the Court of Claims ruled that a resale restriction imposed by a manufacturer is not a per se violation of the antitrust laws so long as the product is otherwise available to the purchaser without the resale restriction and at a reasonable price (*Carter-Wallace* v. *U.S.* 449 F.2d 1374 (Ct. Cl. 1971)).

Carter-Wallace sued to recover for the Government's alleged infringement of Carter-Wallace's patent for meprobamate, a tranquilizer drug. The Government in its answer raised the defense that Carter-Wallace, which manufactured meprobamate and sold it to licensees, misused its patent by imposing a resale restriction upon two of its licensee-purchasers. One of the Government's contentions as to the resale restriction was that it was per se unlawful under the *Schwinn* doctrine. The court's ruling on this contention came on plaintiff's motion to strike certain defenses or for summary judgment as to those defenses.

The Government had previously sued Carter-Wallace under the antitrust laws in connection with an earlier licensing arrangement under the meprobamate patent. That case ended with a consent decree (*U.S.* v. *Carter Products, Inc.,* 211 F.Supp. 144 (S.D.N.Y. 1962)), which required Carter-Wallace "to sell meprobamate to any qualified pharmaceutical manufacturer at no more than a specified maximum price [$20 per pound, subject to a certain adjustment] for unrestricted use and sale by such manufacturers." At the time of the decree, Carter-Wallace had outstanding license agreements with American Cyanamid and Merck. Those agreements provided that Carter-Wallace would sell meprobamate, at a price lower than the $20 per pound decree price, to the two licensees and that the licensees in turn would resell the drug only as part of certain combination drugs. Those two license agreements were not invalidated by the decree so long as the two licensees were free to buy meprobamate, like any other qualified pharmaceutical manufacturer under the decree, at the decree price and without any resale restriction.

As Court of Claims Judge Davis summed it up, the effect of the decree was that "(1) American Cyanamid and Merck, as well as other qualified pharmaceutical houses, were free after the consent judgment to buy meprobamate from plaintiff on nondiscriminatory terms for unrestricted use, except that (2) American Cyanamid and Merck were bound by the terms of the earlier licenses to sell only combination drugs insofar as they bought meprobamate at the price agreed to in the license, which was considerably lower than $20 per pound. If, however, American Cyanamid or Merck bought meprobamate at the price set out in the consent judgment (i.e., no more than $20 per pound), rather than that agreed to in the license, then they were free to make unrestricted use and sale of it." The court further noted that this arrangement had continued since 1962 and that the $20 per pound decree price was presumptively fair.

The court determined that the proper way to consider the challenged practice was to view it "in the round." So viewed, "it is plain that it imposes no absolute restriction on the use of meprobamate by American Cyanamid and Merck since those two companies, as all other qualified pharmaceutical houses, can purchase the drug at the decree's nondiscriminatory (and fair) price for unrestricted use and disposition. What Carter-Wallace does is to set a lower price at which American Cyanamid and Merck can buy the meprobamate if they wish to use it in particular combinations. However, the vendee firms if one looks at their business as a whole, are not prohibited or deterred from making any use they wish of the meprobamate. Nor is any disadvantage (as compared to their competitors) placed upon them if they do. [Footnote omitted.]"

In choosing to consider the practice "in the round" the court acknowledged that "there are perhaps some individual sentences in *U.S.* v. *Univis Lens Co.,* 316 U.S. 241 (1942), and *U.S.* v. *Arnold, Schwinn & Co.,* 388 U.S. 365 (1967), which, taken in isolation, can be read as saying that each unit of the meprobamate must be considered by itself and independently—without regard to American Cyanamid's and Merck's business as a whole, or the whole of its dealings with Carter-Wallace. On that view, there is, per se, an unlawful restriction on the disposition of those particular units of the drug which are sold by plaintiff at the lower price."

The court distinguished the *Univis* and *Schwinn* cases on the ground that in each of those cases the vendor had exercised an absolute right to control the vendee's use or disposition of the purchased product. Here, by contrast, American Cyanamid and Merck "can sell or dispose of the drug as they will, provided they pay the decree price everyone else pays."

The court cited *Tripoli Co.* v. *Wella Corp.* 425 F.2d 932 (3d Cir. 1970), *cert. denied,* 400 U.S. 831 (1970), as support for its ruling that the practice was not per se unlawful. Although safety considerations supported the resale restriction in *Tripoli,* the court found it most significant that the court in *Tripoli,* "embarking on a 'rule of reason' analysis after and cognizant of Schwinn, thought that the Supreme Court opinion did not automatically outlaw any and all post-sale restrictions. Indeed, the restrictions in Tripoli were much stronger and more burdensome than the readily avoidable limitation here."

The court said that it found plausible Carter-Wallace's explanation for the differential between the decree price and the lower price available under the Merck and American Cyanamid agreements: "Carter-Wallace says that the licenses impose obligations on Cyanamid and Merck, in addition to the initial payment for the drug, which inure to plaintiff's benefit—it receives royalties based on sales of the combination drugs and is given new-drug-applications, thereby avoiding the effort and expense of developing them itself. The licensees are also required to make specified expenditures for pro-

motion of the drugs. What Carter-Wallace seems to be arguing in
this connection is that it lowers the initial price of meprobamate
purchased for use in combination drugs because of these other
obligations placed on the licensees, and that those obligations are
part of its compensation for the drug; the initial charge would be a
type of down payment rather than the entire purchase price. Of
course, all these propositions are still hypotheses, and they may
not be accurate in actual fact, but there is enough of a possibility
that plaintiff's actions could be justified (or shown to be noninjuri-
ous) to counsel against a conclusive presumption of anticompetitive
taint which would warrant the automatic and unqualified rule defendant proposes. [Footnote omitted.]" (The Government did not
ask for trial or any further inquiry as to its Schwinn defense.)

The court made it clear that in reaching its conclusion that there
was no per se violation, it had considered the drug as if it were
unpatented, and so it had "no occasion, therefore, to consider the
mooted issue of whether there are exceptions for patented goods
from the coverage of the doctrine relating to post-sale restrictions
as enumerated in Schwinn (and Univis), and if so what those qualifications are."

In justifying its arrangements with American Cyanamid and
Merck, Carter-Wallace pointed to obligations which the latter two
companies incurred when they purchased meprobamate at the lower
price for use in combination drugs. These obligations to pay to
Carter-Wallace royalties based on the sale of combination drugs,
to provide new-drug-applications, and to promote the drugs were
said to be part of the compensation which Carter-Wallace received
from the two companies.

A resale restriction can possibly be justified when it is reasonably
ancillary to a price differential in such circumstances. If promotional expense, for instance, is to be borne by the vendee in reselling a product for a particular use, a lower price might be justifiable, as a use restriction upon resale might be to facilitate the
arrangement. Similarly, it could be argued that if a lower than
normal price is necessary for the vendee's introduction of a product
into a new geographic area, a territorial restriction might be justified
in conjunction with the lower price.

Along these same lines, some would argue that in order to avoid
Robinson-Patman trouble, a manufacturer should be able to impose
customer limitations upon its wholesaler customers, when the manufacturer sells to the wholesalers at one price and to direct-buying
retailers at a higher price.

The availability of the product without restrictions would also
seem to be an important consideration. However, the mere availability of the product at a higher price would be insufficient to
immunize a resale restriction even if the higher price is held to be

"fair," as it was here. Even if the product were readily available at the higher price, the price differential itself could be coercive, and a coercive differential would make the resale restriction suspect. See *Carter Carburetor* v. *FTC,* 112 F.2d 722 (8th Cir. 1940).

Some think that in order to minimize the risk of a resale restriction, the price differential associated with it either should be directly and provably commensurate with the extra expenses incurred by the vendee in providing the additional services deemed part of the compensation or should be clearly necessary to market the product effectively within the areas to which resale is restricted.

Although the court expressly stated that it made the ruling without regard to the existence of the patent, it may still be questioned whether, without the patent, the same result would have been reached. It could be argued that from the public's point of view there may be a significant incentive in allowing a patent-owning manufacturer to charge a lower-than-normal price (and impose along with it the facilitating resale restriction) for low-value uses because of the risk that, if the lower price and resale restriction were not permitted, the patent owner might decide not to sell the product at all for those uses. If the product were not patented, the risk would be less significant because there would be others who might be willing to manufacture and sell the product for those uses. Regardless of whether a product is patented, there might be situations in which the uses of a product have such low value that no manufacturer would sell for such uses without resort to a price differential facilitated by a resale restriction.

What would the Government's position have been had Carter-Wallace itself not manufactured and sold the drug to American Cyanamid and Merck but had licensed them to manufacture it and to sell it? The Government has tended to take the position that the patent rights end with the sale of the product. Cf. *U.S.* v. *General Electric Co.,* 272 U.S. 476, 489 (1926); *Ethyl Gasoline Corp.* v. *U.S.,* 309 U.S. 436, 455–456 (1940). If Carter-Wallace had made no sales, would the Government have reasoned that the patent rights had not yet come to an end? Even should the patent rights be deemed not to have ended, the effects of the restriction would still have to be analyzed for determination of lawfulness. As to these questions, the law is unsettled.

C. DUAL DISTRIBUTION

Question: *Do any provisions of the antitrust laws prohibit a seller from competing with his customers?*

In 1958 the Senate Small Business Committee's Subcommittee on Monopoly conducted hearings on "dual distribution" for the flat-glass industry (S. Rep. No. 1015, 86th Cong. 1st Sess. (1959)). In 1959, the Subcommittee on Retailing, Distribution, and Marketing Practices examined dual distribution in the automotive tire industry. In 1963 Subcommittee No. 4 of the House Committee on Small Business held hearings on complaints aimed at manufacturers who retail through factory-owned outlets, bypass intermediary channels of distribution to sell directly to large accounts, or market their regular products at reduced prices under special labels. See DUAL DISTRIBUTION AND RELATED VERTICAL INTEGRATION, Hearings of House Small Business Committee's Subcommittee No. 4, 88th Congress, Vols 1–3, U.S. Government Printing Office.

Complaining small businessmen generally assume that a retailer cannot compete on equal terms with his suppliers. They argue that a manufacturer can subsidize its retail outlets from profits obtained in other operations and can favor its own outlets by supplying them with scarce goods, repair parts, or technical information not available to other retailers.

Complainants have suggested various remedies. One proposal would require all sellers to give functional discounts and thereby enable independent retailers or wholesalers to compete with factory-owned outlets. Another would authorize government-sanctioned industry conferences at which agreements on distribution methods could be formulated with FTC approval. One witness, representing the Paint & Wallpaper Association of America, suggested the enactment of legislation that would prohibit a manufacturer from giving functional, advertising, or other competitive discounts, services, or facilities to its own company-owned stores if similar advantages are not conferred on its independent customers. An official of the National Candy Wholesalers Association, on the other hand, did not think it would be sufficient to plug "loopholes" in the Robinson-Patman Act or to require functional discounts. He favored an outright ban on dual distribution by manufacturers. He recommended legislation that would permit the manufacturer to sell directly to retailers only in areas where the manufacturer was not selling to wholesalers and to consumers only in areas where it was not selling to wholesalers or retailers.

Another witness wanted not only to outlaw dual distribution but to make dual distributors subject to private treble-damage actions under the Clayton Act. After tracing the problems of independent refiners and service-station operators, a spokesman for the Independent Refiners Association of America said the thrust of his proposal is to provide the independent refiner with a cause of action for damages when its integrated competitors price products at a level that "involves a sacrifice of necessary costs and profits related to any particular functional aspect of their integrated operation and where the effect of that sacrifice may be substantially to lessen, injure, destroy or prevent competition." One other proposal, made by independent dealers in several industries, calls for enactment of legislation similar to the Automobile Dealers Act (15 U.S.C. §§ 1221–1225) to give the dealer his "day in court" in the event of cancellation of a franchise. (See section VI-E, p. 445.) Cancellations, the House Subcommittee was told, occur frequently when a manufacturer sets up his own outlet.

It was suggested that publication of compliance reports furnished the Federal Trade Commission by firms placed under cease-and-desist orders would go a long way toward eliminating the distributional "jungle" that has grown up in some industries. A witness for the Automotive Service Industry Association testified that the FTC has failed "to resolve the antitrust problems of the Robinson-Patman Act." Scores of complaints have been filed against manufacturers and wholesalers of automotive parts, he said, and most have resulted in cease-and-desist orders. "One would ordinarily think that, as a result, our industry would be the most enlightened group of businessmen as to what pricing conduct does and what does not violate the Robinson-Patman Act. . . . On the contrary, there is utter confusion as to what is lawful and unlawful and the Commission does not help to clarify this situation." Much of the confusion, he contended, resulted from the Commission's refusal to publish compliance reports. The Commission now makes such reports available to the public.

Opinions expressed at dual distribution hearings were far from unanimous that dual distribution is an evil. Many witnesses said that it is but a natural outgrowth of a profit-motivated economy and might, in fact, lead to increased economic efficiency. A Department of Commerce official observed that the rate of increase in productivity per man-hour in distribution has been only about half the rate of increase in manufacturing. "If we are to set public policy in order to permit maximum increases in productivity per man-hour, it is important that we not retard improvements in the efficiency in the distribution of the economy."

A university professor testified that, from an economic point of view, dual distribution can have either of two general consequences: "It can be a vehicle for the enhancement of the market power of those firms already in possession of at least some quantum of such power, and in the process work to a serious disadvantage of unintegrated small business competitors; or it may simply develop in response to the pressure of market forces on producing firms to reduce costs. . . . These two consequences, while either may work to the temporary or enduring disadvantages of small unintegrated competitors, have totally different public-policy implications." He concluded that only when dual distribution results in furthering market power without any corresponding increases in efficiency in distribution can the practice be characterized as an evil.

Sometimes manufacturers feel that existing distribution facilities lack the necessary adjustment and growth potential to serve the market. Witnesses testified that they often establish company-owned outlets as experimental stores to develop new sales techniques and merchandising improvements that can be passed on to independent distributors to improve their profit positions. Other manufacturers say that it is often necessary to demonstrate market possibilities before existing distribution channels will risk the investment in additional inventories or take on additional installation or servicing functions.

Bills have been introduced in Congress that would compel firms selling in competition with their customers to separate the cost data on each of their establishments that compete with independent customers in the sale or industrial use of their products. S. 1108 and H.R. 3559, 88th Cong., 1st Sess. (1963) would have required firms engaged in dual distribution to publish annual statistical data disclosing, for each product produced and distributed by dual distribution, "(1) the aggregate dollar amount of the company's net sales for that product during the year to all independent establishments and (2) the dollar amount or value of net sales or transfers of that product from the producer thereof to each related establishment, identifying the establishments separately by name or other designation or location, and the respective amounts of sales or transfers of that product to each." In addition, each "related establishment" of a company engaged in dual distribution would have had to publish an annual operating statement showing its total sales; a breakdown of its direct and indirect costs, labor costs, and profits or losses; and a statement of capital additions with identification of their source.

S. 1107 and H.R. 3562, 88th Cong., 1st Sess. (1963) would have amended Section 2 of the Clayton Act, as amended by Robinson-Patman, to apply to "all transfers between related establishments" whenever the purposes and policy of the Robinson-Patman amendments of Section 2 would be served. Discrimination in prices, in advertising allowances, or in services and facilities would have been forbidden in dealings between dual-distributing manufacturers and their marketing divisions or affiliates "in those situations in which related establishments compete horizontally or directly with independent establishments, with respect to the same product or products of a producer, and with the effect or results proscribed by Section 2." For transfers between related establishments, "price" was defined as the transfer price entered on the

books for accounting purposes. Transfers between related establishments were characterized as constructive sales, so that the dual-
distributing manufacturer would become the "seller" and its marketing division or affiliate would become the "purchaser" for
Robinson-Patman Act purposes.

There seems to be fairly general agreement among antitrust lawyers that most of the remedies suggested as to dual distribution are
too extreme, even assuming there is a social evil or an antitrust
"loophole" to be corrected, which most of them doubt. The feeling
is that dual-distribution practices differ so greatly among the various industries that any attempt to develop a generalized solution is
futile. There is also considerable doubt among antitrust experts that
the bills proposed would ever have any actual inhibiting effect on
the dual-distribution practices they are designed to discourage. The
record-keeping and report-filing requirements of the one set of bills
would not actually require any changes in business practices. The
attempt in the other pair of proposals to extend the Robinson-Patman Act's discrimination ban to the invoicing of merchandise to a marketing division or affiliate seems to make no real
change. As a practical matter, whether an integrated manufacturer
"sells" its merchandise to marketing outlets organized as separate
subsidiary corporations or "transfers" the merchandise to stores
operated by its own marketing division, the "price" at which the
marketing outlet is billed for the merchandise is a mere accounting
figure. The price can always be set at a level equivalent to the
price charged an independent wholesaler or retailer. Likewise, the
affiliated outlet can often be billed for services or facilities at prices
unattractive to independents. For reasons inherent in the status of
the independent, some services rendered for the affiliate, such as
management services, could never be provided.

In one sense, dual distribution might be regarded as having nothing to do with discrimination in prices or services and hence as
being foreign to the scope and purpose of the Robinson-Patman
Act. Viewed that way, dual distribution is simply a phenomenon of
vertical integration, which in turn is a Sherman Act monopolization
problem, if any. If Congress determines that the Sherman Act is
inadequate to deal with abuses in dual-distribution practices, it can
amend the statute. It has been suggested that any changes should
be aimed clearly and solely at vertical integration that results in
monopoly power.

The goal of some witnesses and legislators suggesting dual-
distribution legislation seemed to be the creation of a class of
businessmen who would be insulated from economic change in
much the same way brokers are protected by Section 2(c) of the
amended Clayton Act. Their thinking seemed to follow what some

Robinson-Patman Act critics have labeled the "soft competition" line, which may account for their tendency to turn to the Robinson-Patman Act for relief.

Some dual-distribution practices could be treated as unfair methods of competition under the existing provisions in Section 5 of the Federal Trade Commission Act. In *Roux Distributing Co., Inc.,* 55 F.T.C. 1386 (1959), the Commission's complaint, which was dismissed for failure of proof, attacked a dual distribution system only on the theory that it was an unfair method of competition to restrict the customer classifications open to resellers at various levels of distribution. The manufacturer was charged with doing more than merely underselling some of his customers at a lower distribution level; he was said to have in effect forbidden them to compete with him. Substantially the same charges were involved in *U.S.* v. *Revlon,* 1964 Trade Cas. ¶71,040 (S.D.N.Y. 1964), a Justice Department injunction suit based on Section 1 of the Sherman Act. In *Rea* v. *Ford Motor Co.,* 1972 Trade Cas. ¶74,015 (W.D.Pa. 1972), it was held that the jury could find an antitrust violation from a showing that an auto manufacturer, in competition with independent dealers, subsidized factory stores with the intent to drive out the independents. See also *Belliston* v. *Texaco, Inc.,* 455 F.2d 175 (10th Cir.) *cert. denied,* 408 U.S. 928 (1972).

D. TYING PRODUCTS TOGETHER

1. Tying Arrangements

Question: *May a seller restrict sales of his product to those willing to buy another of his products?*

"Tying arrangements" have long been thought to be in conflict with the antitrust laws. The classic theory of their unacceptability was expressed by the Supreme Court in *Northern Pacific Ry. Co.,* v. *U.S.,* 356 U.S. 1, 506 (1958): "Indeed, tying arrangements serve hardly any purpose beyond the suppression of competition. . . . They are unreasonable in and of themselves whenever a party has sufficient economic power with respect to the tying product to appreciably restrain free competition in the market for the tied product and a not insubstantial amount of interstate commerce is affected."

Prohibitions against certain tying arrangements were made by Section 3 of the Clayton Act, but in *Northern Pacific* the Court extended them to Section 1 of the Sherman Act, since the tying product there, land, was not covered by the Clayton Act, which applies only to "goods, wares, merchandise, machinery, supplies or other commodities" (5 U.S.C. § 14). The courts now apply similar standards under both statutes. Both before and since the decision in *Northern Pacific,* the requirements for proof of per se illegality under Section 3 of the Clayton Act have been progressively relaxed. In *International Salt Co.* v. *U.S.,* 332 U.S. 392 (1947), the tying product was patented; the requisite economic power was presumed. In *U.S.* v. *Loew's, Inc.,* 371 U.S. 38 (1962), a "blockbooking" case, the tying product, motion picture film, was copyrighted. As in *International Salt,* monopoly power was presumed.

In *Northern Pacific* the Court found "sufficient economic power" with respect to the tying product in the preferred location of land along the route of the railroad; the desirability of the land was used to require purchasers or lessees to consent to "preferential routing" of their goods by the defendant railroad. In the early tie-in cases (*International Business Machines Corp.* v. *United States,* 298 U.S. 131 (1936) (tie-in of tabulating machine punch cards unlawful under Section 3 of the Clayton Act); *Morton Salt Co.* v. *G. S. Suppiger Co.,* 314 U.S. 488 (1942) (tie-in of unpatented salt tablets by manufacturer of patented dispenser)) the tie-in was found unlawful on the theory that the defendant had attempted to extend into unrelated products or services the economic power implicit in the ownership or control of a patent, a copyright, or a regulated monopoly such as the Northern Pacific Railroad.

Alleged tie-ins have been justified where strong countervailing considerations could be shown. For example, in *United States* v. *Jerrold Electronics Corp.,* 187 F.Supp. 545 (E.D. Pa. 1960), *aff'd per curiam,* 365 U.S. 567 (1961), a tie-in of CATV equipment and service was justified during the development period of a new industry, although the arrangement became unreasonable once the need for the manufacturer's own services had passed. Similarly, in *Dehydrating Process Co.* v. *A. O. Smith Corp.,* 292 F.2d 653 (1st Cir. 1961), *cert. denied,* 361 U.S. 931 (1961), a tie-in of a patented silo and a patented unloading device was upheld, where there had been substantial customer dissatisfaction with the unloaders when purchased alone. In these cases, it could be said that only a "single product" was being sold, since in practical effect, the "tying" products could not adequately perform their functions without the use of the "tied" product. In *Jerrold Electronics,* the justification for the manufacturer's insistence on the use of its own service organization expired once the market could support an adequate alternative. See also *Baker* v. *Simmons Co.,* 307 F.2d 458 (1st Cir. 1962) (tie-in of leased motel advertising signs to manufacturers' mattresses justified where brand name and goodwill would suffer by lessees' use of inferior mattresses) and *FTC* v. *Gratz,* 253 U.S. 421 (1920).

Can a seller's mere grant of credit, even at terms most favorable for the borrower, to induce a purchase ever be deemed a per se illegal tying arrangement in which the credit is the tying product and the item sold is the tied product? The Supreme Court's answer to this question has yet to be given, but a tying arrangement may be found "where the credit is provided by one corporation on condition that a product be purchased from a separate corporation, and where the borrower contracts to obtain a large sum of money over and above that needed to pay the seller for the physical products purchased." That seems to be the teaching of *Fortner Enterprises, Inc.* v. *U.S. Steel Corp.,* 293 F.Supp. 762 (W.D. Ky. 1966), *aff'd,* 404 F.2d 936 (6th Cir. 1968), *rev'd,* 394 U.S. 495 (1969). The case has been much discussed. Citations are collected at 452 F.2d 1095, 1096 fn. 2. Other cases since have involved loans as tie-ins (*Cities Service Oil Co.* v. *Coleman Oil Co.,* 1973 Trade Cas. ¶74,424 (1st Cir. 1972); *Atlantic Richfield Co.* v. *Malco Petroleum, Inc.,* 471 F.2d 1258 (6th Cir. 1972)). In the *Fortner* case, petitioner Fortner, a real estate developer, financed the purchase of land and the construction of prefabricated homes by borrowing money from U.S. Steel Credit Corporation (Credit Corporation), a subsidiary of U.S. Steel Corporation. Under the loan agreement Fortner was required to erect homes manufactured by U.S. Steel on the land purchased with the proceeds of the loan. The Credit Corporation provided 100 percent financing, which terms were unavailable elsewhere in the area. After entering into the loan agreement, Fortner claimed that the materials supplied by U.S. Steel were priced unreasonably high and were defective and unusable, requiring additional expenditures and delaying the project. Fortner sued U.S. Steel and the Credit Corporation, alleging violations of Sections 1 and 2 of the Sherman Act and seeking treble damages for lost profits and a decree enjoining the enforcement of the tie-in provisions. After pretrial proceedings, the district court entered summary judgment against Fortner, holding that Fortner had failed to establish sufficient economic power over the tying product, credit, and foreclosure of a substantial amount of commerce with respect to the tied product, prefabricated houses. The court of appeals affirmed. The Supreme Court, dividing 5–4, reversed and ordered the case to trial.

Writing for the majority, Justice Black said that the lower courts had misconstrued the *Northern Pacific* standard: ". . . these standards are necessary only to bring into play the doctrine of per se illegality. Where the standards were found satisfied, in *Northern Pacific* and *International Salt* . . . the Court approved summary judgment *against* the defendants but by no means implied that inability to satisfy these standards would be fatal to a plaintiff's case." Black stressed that summary judgments should be used sparingly in antitrust litigation and were particularly inappropriate when applied against a plaintiff. (Two weeks later, in *Norfolk Monument Co.* v. *Woodlawn Memorial Gardens, Inc.,* 394 U.S. 700 (1969), the Court summarily reversed the dismissal of a private treble-damage suit on the same grounds.)

Justice Black said that "petitioner has raised questions which, if proved at trial, would bring this tying arrangement within the scope of the *per se* doctrine." It was unquestioned that Fortner had borrowed the money and had been required to use U.S. Steel's houses on the land purchased with the borrowed funds. Even if the *Northern Pacific* standards were not met, the Court said, the case could go off on general Sherman Act conspiracy theories, citing *Perma-Life Mufflers* v. *International Parts Corp.,* 392 U.S. 134, 138–139 (1968); *Timken Co.* v. *U.S.,* 341 U.S. 593, 598 (1951); *Kiefer Stewart Co.* v. *Jos. Seagram & Sons,* 340 U.S. 211, 215 (1951); and *U.S.* v. *Yellow Cab Co.,* 332 U.S. 218, 227 (1947).

As to the market foreclosure necessary to support the per se rule, in a footnote the Court said that the significant figure with respect to market foreclosure was the percentage of annual sales of homes, or prefabricated homes, in the area foreclosed by the tie, but later in the text, referred to the national total of tied sales of U.S. Steel houses, and called that figure "not insubstantial" (*Standard Oil Co. of Calif.* (Standard Stations) v. *U.S.,* 337 U.S. 293 (1949)). Having found that the market foreclosure was "not insubstantial," the Court found that the Credit Corporation may have had "sufficient economic power" over the credit, stating that "the proper focus of concern is whether the seller has the power to raise price, or impose other burdensome terms such as a tie-in, with respect to any appreciable number of buyers within the market." Apparently if a tie-in *is* a tie-in, that is, if customers purchase the tied product, there is said to be "sufficient economic power" over the tying product to make the transaction unlawful per se. Only U.S. Steel offered 100 percent financing, and its houses were the least expensive of their type in the local market, but in the Court's view, "uniquely and unusually advantageous" terms might themselves reflect a lender's power in the credit market; it said that it would read any such claims of uniqueness in the light most favorable to a treble-damage plaintiff.

Over two vigorous dissents, by Justice White (joined by Justice Harlan) and Justice Fortas (joined by Justice Stewart), the Court found that the "sale" of credit by the Credit Corporation was separable from the sale of houses by U.S. Steel; the Court distinguished "the usual sale on credit," where "a single individual or corporation simply makes an agreement determining when and how much he will be paid for his product." Justice Black also noted that Fortner had contracted "to obtain a large sum of money over and above that needed to pay the seller for the physical products purchased" and concluded that "we cannot see how an arrangement such as that present in this case could ever be said to involve only a single product."

In his dissent, Justice Fortas argued that the credit arrangements were not distinguishable from the sale of the houses. "This is a sale of a single product with the incidental provision of financing." Justice White thought that there might be a tie-in but that the Credit Corporation lacked "sufficient economic power" over the supply of credit. He said that credit financing is extremely common in the American economy, and that often a seller's credit is available only to the purchaser of his goods: "The logic of the majority opinion, then, casts great doubt on credit financing by sellers." (Justice Black said that "it will be time enough to pass upon the issues of ['usual'] credit sales when a case involving it actually arises.")

Justice Black's opinion for the majority contains broad language, but many antitrust specialists read the decision narrowly. It has been suggested that *Fortner* may well prove to be no more than a "sport." Many believe that the concept of tie-ins between separate corporations is central to an understanding of the case, and that credit financing by a single business entity may be distinguished, as Justice Black's own opinion distinguished it, from the facts in *Fortner*.

Viewed narrowly, the following factors make Fortner distinguishable from garden-variety financing transactions. Two separate corporations, the seller and its subsidiary financing company, were responsible for the tying arrangement. The amount of the loan exceeded the cost of the product sold. The issue arose against a background of U.S. Steel's economic power and an allegation that a relatively small buyer was forced to accept inferior, unreasonably priced goods. Although no monopolization issue was presented for decision, an attempt to understand the majority's opinion, or at least the result, may be aided by a consideration of the Sherman Act Section 2 overtones in the case.

The Court's mandate, remanding "with directions to let this suit proceed to trial," left the question of whether anything, other than damages, remained to be tried. Justice Black said: "It may turn out that the arrangement involved here serves legitimate business purposes and that U.S. Steel's subsidiary does not have a competitive advantage in the credit market." Justice Fortas responded that the majority, in an earlier part of the opinion, explicitly found it clear that *Fortner* raised questions of fact which, if proved at trial, would bring the tying arrangement within the scope of the per se doctrine. According to Justice Fortas, if it is the earlier sentence that determines the range of issues open on remand, there will be no examination at the trial of the economic background of the credit arrangements nor of the effects, if any, of the arrangement on competition in the prefabricated-house market. All that need be shown by *Fortner,* Justice Fortas claimed, is that U.S. Steel conditioned the extension of its subsidiary's credit on agreement to purchase U.S. Steel prefabricated houses; that would be sufficient to demonstrate the automatic illegality of the credit arrangement. Upon remand, the district court directed a verdict for plaintiff. The court of appeals reversed, holding that the question of violation of the Sherman Act as well as the question of damages should go to the jury (452 F.2d 1095 (6th Cir. 1971), *cert. denied* 406 U.S. 919 (1972)). The court said (at 1103): "As we read the majority opinion in *Fortner,* the holding was that a tying arrangement achieves an unlawful restraint when 'the seller can exert some power over some of the buyers in the market.' The majority opinion did not hold that the acceptance of the tie-in by customers without more is proof of economic power. If the majority had intended to indicate that acceptance of a tie-in by an appreciable number of customers is sufficient proof of the requisite economic power, it would have been sufficient for Mr. Justice Black to have said so and thus to avoid the exhaustive treatment which he gave to the question of economic power in the tying product set forth in other portions of his opinion."

Justice Black's references to "legitimate business purposes" and "competitive advantage" may lend some support to the view that, despite the variety of factors cited, the Court was actually moved by an unstated belief that U.S. Steel was "competing too hard." The "legitimate business purposes" language also could make pertinent other unique factors in the *Fortner* situation. First, would it matter if, under state law, a seller cannot avoid separating its sales and financing functions? Second, would the limiting of credit to the amount necessary to finance the purchase of prefabricated houses undermine a seller's security for such purchase once the houses were placed on land financed by someone else?

Some experts view *Fortner* as an attack upon the horizontal assumption of a banking function by industrial companies. Others see it as throwing a cloud over the *vertical* integration of sales and financing functions. It could be that the sale of the houses and the credit really was the sale of a "single product," as Justice Fortas insisted, but the Supreme Court in *Fortner* has removed the "single" product defense when a large corporation sells one product and its financing subsidiary "sells" credit where the amount and the terms of the credit may, as a practical matter, allow undue leverage over the borrower's freedom of choice. It also may be that *Fortner* could be distinguished in those cases where the financing is done at the instigation of the buyer, where a large agricultural corporation or user of raw materials finances the equipment used by small farmers, lumbermen, and the like. Section 3 of the Clayton Act applies only to sellers, who are more likely to be in a position to impose anticompetitive restraints. Some specialists point out that it is rare for land and buildings on it to be financed separately and that it may have been that once U.S. Steel took a mortgage on the land purchased with the proceeds of its loan, Fortner could not have turned elsewhere for financing of the buildings. On this analysis, it may be questioned whether U.S. Steel would have lent the money for land acquisition in the first place.

2. Tying Arrangements and Section 5 of the FTC Act

Question: *Does the FTC Act's prohibition of "unfair methods of competition" go further than the Clayton and Sherman Acts against tying arrangements?*

In 1956, the Federal Trade Commission issued three complaints attacking "sales commission" arrangements between oil refiners and tire manufacturers covering the tire companies' sales of tires, batteries, and accessories (TBA) to wholesalers and retailers of the refiners' gasoline. Under the "sales commission" plan, it was alleged, the refiner sponsored the tire manufacturer's line of TBA in return for a percentage commission from the tire company. After hearings, the Commission declared these arrangements unfair methods of competition prohibited by Section 5 of the FTC Act and ordered all six of the respondents to terminate their relationships with each other and to forego similar arrangements with any other tire producer or oil company.

While the Commission was proceeding on these complaints, *Osborn* v. *Sinclair Refining Co.,* 286 F.2d 832 (4th Cir. 1960), was decided. Sinclair's refusal to continue selling oil and gas to a dealer who would not buy satisfactory quantities of a "sponsored" line of TBA was held to show that Sinclair had illegal tying arrangements with its customers in violation of Section 1 of the Sherman Act. It made no difference to the court that there was no express written tie-in contract with the dealers or that Sinclair did not require the dealers to carry the sponsored line of TBA exclusively.

The Commission's orders got a mixed reception in the courts of appeals. The order against Atlantic and Goodyear (Docket 6487) was sustained (*Atlantic Refining Co.* v. *FTC*, 331 F.2d 394 (7th Cir. 1964)). That court agreed with the Commission that, while the Atlantic-Goodyear agreement itself had no tying provisions, its effect, when combined with the refiner's economic power over its retailers, was that of a tying arrangement and an unfair method of competition in violation of Section 5. The order against Texaco and Goodrich (Docket 6485), on the other hand, was set aside (*Texaco Inc.* v. *FTC,* 336 F.2d 754 (D.C. Cir. 1964)). The D.C. court objected to the outright ban on all TBA commission arrangements, seeing no reason for condemning one that does not "result in unfair competition," and to the sufficiency of the evidence on which the Commission based its coercion and competitive-effect findings. The third order, against Shell and Firestone (Docket 6486), was enforced in part (*Shell Oil Co.* v. *FTC,* 360 F.2d 470 (5th Cir. 1966), *cert. denied,* 385 U.S. 1002 (1967)). That court affirmed the sections of the Commission's order that dealt with the sales-commission system but found the record did not support the Commission's finding that Shell coerced dealers.

In the *Atlantic-Goodyear* case, the decisions of the FTC and the court of appeals were affirmed by a divided Supreme Court (381 U.S. 357 (1965)). The Court's six-justice majority found substantial evidence to support the Commission's conclusion that Atlantic had "leverage" over its dealers by reason of its short-term station leases and equipment-loan contracts and its control of the dealers' supply of gasoline and oil. The Court was satisfied with the Commission's finding that Atlantic, sometimes with the help of Goodyear, "not only exerted the persuasion that is a natural incident of its economic power, but coupled with it direct and overt threats of reprisal . . . Indeed, the Commission could properly have concluded that it was for this bundle of persuasion that Goodyear paid Atlantic its commission" (381 U.S. at 368).

In reviewing the Commission's conclusion that the sales-commission plan was an unfair method of competition, the Court began with a recognition that the Goodyear-Atlantic contract was not a tying arrangement, although it had the same "competitive characteristic . . . [i.e.] the utilization of economic power in one market to curtail competition in another." The Court cited FTC findings that wholesalers and manufacturers of competing brands of TBA, and even Goodyear wholesalers who were not authorized supply points, had been foreclosed for the Atlantic-dealer market. In addition, Goodyear itself was excluded from selling to Atlantic wholesalers in territories where Atlantic had an arrangement with Firestone, and Atlantic wholesalers and retailers had to compete with other wholesalers and retailers who were free to stock several brands of TBA. "Thus the Commission was warranted in finding that the effect of the plan was as though Atlantic had agreed with Goodyear to require its dealers to buy Goodyear products and had done so."

In the Supreme Court Atlantic and Goodyear did not challenge provisions in the Commission's order designed to insure Atlantic dealers freedom of choice in the purchase of TBA. They objected only to the order's ban on TBA sales-commission arrangements in general. On this, the Supreme Court divided. Justices Stewart and Harlan could see "no reason to assume that the sales-commission plan of distribution gave to Atlantic any distinctive capacity to effect the arrangement which is the gravamen of the violation proved. The core of that violation is Atlantic's coercion of its dealers." Justice Goldberg, of the view the Commission may have concluded that the sales-commission plan was inherently unfair, would have sent the case back to the Commission for more explicit findings on inherent unfairness.

The majority, in an opinion by Justice Clark, found the Commission justified in concluding that it was not enough to prohibit merely the use of coercive tactics. "The long existence of the plan itself, coupled with the coervice acts practiced by Atlantic pursuant to it, warranted a decision to require more. The Commission could have decided that to uproot the practice required its complete prohibition; otherwise dealers would not have enjoyed complete freedom from unfair practices which the Act condemns. These are matters well within the ambit of the Commission's authority."

The Court was not impressed by Goodyear's complaint that the Commission had no evidence of the economic power of any of the other oil companies with which it had sales-commission arrangements. "This order does not necessarily prohibit Goodyear from making contracts with companies not possessed of economic power over their dealers. The evidence in this particular record, however, does involve relationships such as it has enjoyed with Atlantic and its propensity to use those relationships for an unfair competitive advantage. Goodyear offered no evidence that it has arrangements differing from those mentioned in the instant case. In these circumstances it is sufficient to point out that in the event it has such a contract with such a company it may seek a reopening of the order approved today." The Court pointed to "substantial evidence" before the Commission of Goodyear's "propensity to use the power structure of Atlantic and at least four other oil companies to further its own distribution program."

The Court was not convinced that the Commission was obliged to consider the possibility of economic justification for the TBA marketing program or to make a more extensive economic analysis of the competitive effect of the program. "Upon considering the destructive effect on commerce that would result from the widespread use of these contracts by major oil companies and suppliers, we conclude that the Commission was clearly justified in refusing the participants an opportunity to offset these evils by showing of economic benefit to themselves." As for economic analysis, the Court declared it "enough that the Commission found that a not insubstantial portion of commerce is affected," since the effect of the marketing plan was found to be "similar to that of a tie-in."

A week later the Court followed up with an order directing remand of the *Texaco-Goodrich* case to the FTC for a new hearing without the participation of Chairman Paul Rand Dixon (381 U.S. 739 (1965)). In addition to disagreeing with the Commission on the merits, the D.C. Court of Appeals had decided that the Chairman had expressed a disqualifying predisposition in a speech made before the Commission ruled on the matter. The Solicitor General did not request Supreme Court review of the ruling on disqualification.

When the case finally reached the Supreme Court again (*FTC* v. *Texaco,* 393 U.S. 223 (1968)), the Court rejected a court of appeals' suggestion that proof of overt coercion was essential to the result reached in the *Atlantic* case (381 U.S. 357 (1965)). In upholding the Commission in the *Texaco* case, despite the lack of evidence of overt coercion, the Court found "dominant economic power" of an oil company over its retail dealers to be "inherent in the structure and economics of the petroleum distribution system," of which the crucial elements were said to be (1) one-year service station leases terminable on 10 days notice; (2) the oil company's right to terminate without advance notice if "housekeeping" provisions in the lease are not fulfilled; and (3) one-year gasoline-supply contracts terminable on 30 days' notice. In such a market, the opinion notes, "the sales commission system for marketing TBA is inherently coercive. A service station dealer whose very livelihood depends upon the continuing good favor of a major oil company is constantly aware of the oil company's desire that he stock and sell the recommended brand of TBA" (393 U.S. at 229). While the *Texaco* opinion does not discuss the issue in terms of per se illegality, Justice Marshall, a member of the *Texaco* majority, has since described the opinion as adding the TBA commission arrangements to the list of per se antitrust violations (*U.S.* v. *Container Corp. of America,* 393 U.S. 333 (1969)). A "per se rule of 'inherent' coercion" was also detected in *Texaco* by Justice Stewart, who dissented.

The Supreme Court's decisions in the *Atlantic* and *Texaco* cases, like that in *Simpson* v. *Union Oil Co. of California,* 377 U.S. 13 (1964), are examples of the Court's feeling of the 60's that oil companies have too much power over their retail dealers. In the TBA cases the Court saw a powerful alliance of the major oil companies and the major tire manufacturers to the detriment of competition. One may question whether the result of these cases will actually make much difference in gasoline marketing. The same could be said of *Standard Oil of California* (Standard Stations) v. *U.S.*, 337 U.S. 293 (1949), in which the Court ruled illegal contracts requiring retail dealers to fill all their petroleum needs from one refiner. The gloomy predictions of Justice Douglas in his dissent in that case as to a hastening of the trend to integration do not appear to have come true.

3. Purchase Requirements in Trademark Licenses

Question: *May a trademark licensor require his licensee to purchase supplies from the licensor?*

In *Timken Roller Bearing Co.* v. *U.S.*, 341 U.S. 593 (1951), the Supreme Court declared that restraints of trade cannot be justified "as reasonable steps taken to implement a valid trademark licensing system. . . . A trademark cannot be legally used as a device for Sherman Act violation. Indeed, the Trademark Act of 1946 itself penalizes use of a mark 'to violate the antitrust laws of the United States.' " The Supreme Court was referring to Section 33(b) (7) of the Lanham Trademark Act, 15 U.S.C. § 1115(b) (7), which provides only that, when a mark has become incontestable under Section 15 of the Act, its registration shall be conclusive evidence of the registrant's ownership and exclusive right to use the mark except when "the mark has been or is being used to violate the antitrust laws." Since the enactment of that provision in 1946, trademark infringers have tried to use it as a vehicle for transferring the doctrine of patent misuse to the trademark field and for establishing the defense of misuse in trademark-infringement suits, but the courts have generally refused to apply the misuse doctrine to trademarks (*Waco-Porter Corp.* v. *Tubular Structures Corp.*, 222 F.Supp. 332 (S.D. Calif. 1963)).

One of the obligations imposed upon a trademark owner, at the risk of losing his trademark rights, is to insure that any licensee maintains quality standards (*Dawn Donut Co.* v. *Hart's Food Stores,* 267 F.2d 358 (2d Cir. 1959); *duPont* v. *Celanese Corp.*, 167 F.2d 484 (CCPA 1948); *Arthur Murray, Inc.* v. *Horst,* 110 F.Supp. 678 (D. Mass. 1953); *Morse-Starrette Products* v. *Steccone,* 86 F.Supp. 796 (N.D. Calif. 1949)).

Licensees often contract to buy from the licensor or suppliers designated by the licensor all products that are to be resold or used in connection with the main product or service marketed under the trademark. When reasonably ancillary to the protection of a trademark or trade name, exclusive-dealing and supplier-selection licensing restrictions, that might otherwise be unlawful, have been upheld (*Carvel Corp.* 68 F.T.C. 128 (1965); *Susser* v. *Carvel Corp.*, 332 F.2d

505 (2d Cir. 1964); *Purity Cheese Co.* v. *Ryser,* 153 F.2d 88 (7th Cir. 1946). Cf *Arthur Murray, Inc.* v. *Reserve Plan, Inc.,* 406 F.2d 1138 (8th Cir. 1969)).

Licensors have various ways of obtaining compensation for the use of their trademarks and the know-how they pass along to licensees. Some collect a lump-sum franchise fee when the contract is signed; others collect royalties based on sales. In addition, almost all franchised retail and service operations sell or use supplementary, nontrademarked lines of products, accessories, or equipment, and it is often to the licensor's advantage to take on the task of supplying his licensees with these requirements.

There are various commercial motives for the licensing of trademarks. In cases like *Engbrecht* v. *Dairy Queen Co.,* 203 F.Supp. 714 (D. Kansas 1962), and *Susser* v. *Carvel Corp.,* 332 F.2d 505 (2d Cir. 1964), the trademark owner licensed use of the mark in geographical areas to which he was financially unable to expand his manufacturing and marketing operations. The trademarks involved in *Denison Mattress Factory* v. *Spring-Air Co.,* 308 F.2d 403 (5th Cir. 1962), and *U.S.* v. *Sealy, Inc.,* 1964 Trade Cas. ¶71,258 (N.D. Ill. 1964), belonged to groups of established manufacturers who pooled their financial resources to organize companies to develop product specifications, promote trademarks, and make possible marketing on a national scale. Sometimes the trademark licensor neither manufactures goods nor performs services but develops a product for which he selects a trademark, establishes quality standards, plans national promotional campaigns, and then authorizes his licensees to make the product and sell it under the trademark within defined areas.

Another type of trademark-licensing arrangement is illustrated by *Wyatt Earp Enterprises, Inc.* v. *Sackman, Inc.,* 157 F.Supp. 621 (S.D.N.Y. 1958), and *Lone Ranger, Inc.* v. *Currey,* 79 F.Supp. 190 (M.D. Pa. 1948). In these cases the primary motivation appears to have been the use of a "celebrity" mark, rather than the development and identification of a particular product or quality of product. Section 45 of the Lanham Act contemplates the development of "collective marks" by marketing cooperatives and trade associations, as well as "certification marks" of persons other than the owner of the mark.

In *Denison Mattress Factory* v. *Spring-Air Co.,* the court of appeals found restrictions on the licensee's source of materials to be reasonably ancillary to the primary purpose of the license, to protect trademark rights. In *Baker* v. *Simmons Co.,* 307 F.2d 458 (1st Cir. 1962), the court reached a similar result with respect to a "tying arrangement" that required hotels and motels displaying a mattress company's trademark to use that brand of mattresses exclusively. Such a requirement was viewed as reasonably ancillary to legitimate advertising purposes.

In *Susser* v. *Carvel Corp.,* the court foresaw situations in which "tying" the purchase of supplies to a trademark license would constitute "a per se violation" of the Sherman Act, when the trademark "has acquired such prominence" that it "would satisfy the market dominance test of Times Picayune [345 U.S. 594 (1953)] and Northern Pacific [356 U.S. 1 (1958)]." The Carvel trademark before the court was displayed by only 250 out of a total of 125,000 retail outlets for ice cream cones in Carvel's market area. Not only does the owner of such a trademark lack market dominance, the court reasoned, but his marketing practices affect an insubstantial amount of commerce.

Those court decisions that have sustained tying clauses in trademark licenses as reasonable and necessary to maintain quality and protect the trademark seem to have assumed they are "tying arrangements." The Federal Trade Commission has disagreed. In dismissing a Section 5 FTC complaint against Carvel Corp., the soft-ice-cream franchisor who won the case in the Court of Appeals for the Second Circuit, the Commission decided "Carvel's franchise agreements cannot be regarded as tie-in arrangements because the trademark license conceptually cannot constitute a 'tying' product and, even if it could, it could never be regarded as a separable 'product' apart from the mix and commissary items to which it is attached within the meaning of the typical tie-in arrangement" (68 F.T.C. 128 (1965)). The Commission pointed to court decisions that the property right in a trademark exists only as an adjunct to the product it identifies and that trademarks may be licensed only on condition that the trademark owner retain control over the licensee's use of the mark.

Having put aside the "tying arrangement" label, the Commission determined that Carvel's requirement that its franchisees buy all their ice cream ingredients from Carvel-approved sources is "a valid and reasonable exercise of the legitimate business interests of the trademark owner in protecting his mark and insuring the quality and uniformity of his product." The purpose of these restrictions was not to restrain interstate commerce, the FTC concluded; they were merely ancillary to the principal purpose of a lawful contract.

The Commission's hearing examiner had found that the restrictions on the Carvel dealers' sources of supply of ice cream ingredients were unreasonable, since Carvel could have prescribed specifications for the manufacture of the ice cream mix. He had relied on the Supreme Court's statement in *Standard Oil* v. *U.S.,* 337 U.S. 293 (1949), that "tying arrangements serve hardly any purpose beyond the suppression of competition. . . . Specification of the type and quality of the product to be used in connection with the tying device is protection enough." The Commission pointed out that the Supreme Court was dealing with the legality of requirements contracts. The FTC refused to read into that decision a broad rule affecting trademark licenses. While quality might be achieved by specifications, the Commission reasoned, uniformity of product probably could not be. Consequently, the Supreme Court's language "would not necessarily be applicable to the present case where a trademarked product as distinctive as a food is involved." Counsel supporting the complaint did not present enough evidence to persuade the Commission to find that mere specifications would have produced the requisite quality and uniformity control. Specifications were found inadequate in *Susser* v. *Carvel* and in *Engbrecht* v. *Dairy Queen Co.*

The Commission could not see the same problems of uniformity of quality and ease of administration in connection with other items that become part of the finished product sold to the consumer, such as toppings, nuts, flavors, and cones. The portion of the complaint attacking restrictions of the sources of those ingredients was dismissed for lack of evidence that a substantial amount of commerce was affected. Carvel's ban against its dealers' handling of other foods, such as hamburgers, hot dogs, and coffee, was found to be reasonably ancillary to the purpose of protecting the "trademark image" of a particular type of retail outlet. Because Carvel is not in competition with manufacturers or distributors of these other products, the Commission saw no violation of Section 3 of the Clayton Act.

Commissioner Jones' opinion in the *Carvel* case can be read as implying (1) that a licensor will not be permitted to designate suppliers when product specifications are adequate to maintain quality and uniformity, (2) that a different rule might determine reasonableness when a product "as distinctive as a food" is involved, (3) that an overall purpose to restrain trade will produce a different result, and (4) that similar restrictions might not be acceptable in a market more difficult to enter than the soft-ice-cream market. Cf. *Standard Oil Co. of Calif.* v. *U.S.*, 337 U.S. 293 (1949); *International Salt Co.* v. *U.S.*, 332 U.S. 392 (1947); and *U.S.* v. *Loew's, Inc.*, 371 U.S. 38 (1962).

Some lawyers see in *Carvel* four circumstances that, although not mentioned, contributed to the result and therefore limit the scope of the Commission's decision: the relative size of the trademark owner, the inability of his trademark to dominate the particular market, the absence of any suggestion of a "horizontal" effort among the franchised outlets to have the restrictions imposed, and the widespread acceptance of franchising as an efficient marketing method.

Commissioner Jones' opinion is regarded by some as significant for its discussion of what the Commission would have done with the Carvel contracts if they had been treated as tying arrangements. First of all, the Commission declared that a trademark, unlike a patent or a copyright, does not confer monopoly power on its owner in the conventional sense and therefore does not automatically give him the power to compel purchase of undesired products from the trademark owner or his designated supplier. Second, the absence of any evidence of barriers to entry into the soft-ice-cream business deterred the Commission from concluding the Carvel trademark had acquired such pre-eminence that Carvel possessed enough dominance of the market to render its tying requirements illegal per se. Here the Commission's thinking seemed to parallel the Supreme Court's dictum in *White Motor Co.* v. *U.S.*, 372 U.S. 253 (1963), that tying arrangements may fall in the category of per se violations, "though not necessarily so."

Regardless of any other bases for the decision, the Commission's opinion does contain the flat statement that a trademark license cannot constitute a tying product. Since the Commission does not appeal from dismissal of one of its own complaints, there was no further review, but the Supreme Court's decision in *Fortner Enterprises, Inc.* v. *U.S. Steel Corp.*, 394 U.S. 495 (1969), may have effectively reversed the Commission. (See section II-D-1, p. 140.)

4. Franchising—the Chicken Delight Case

Question: *Did* Chicken Delight *change the rule of* Susser v. Carvel?

In a treble-damage action alleging violation of Section 1 of the Sherman Act several franchisees challenged Chicken Delight's contracts, which required franchisees to purchase specified cookers, packaging items, and food preparation mixes. Apparently the prices the franchisees were required to pay for the specified products were higher than those generally available from alternate sources. The agreements were challenged as unlawful tying arrangements. After all evidence was in, the franchisees moved for a directed verdict. The district court found that the tie with respect to packaging products violated Section 1, but sent to the jury the question whether defendant's requirements on its dips, cookers, and mixes fell within the "quality control" justification for otherwise unlawful tie-ins. The jury found for the franchisees (*Siegel* v. *Chicken Delight Inc.,* 311 F.Supp. 847 (N.D. Calif. 1970)).

District Judge Harris first dealt with and rejected Chicken Delight's argument that, since the franchise contract related to only one product, the Chicken Delight system, no tie-in arrangement was involved. The court observed that "a trademark license which is granted on the condition that the licensee purchase other products can clearly be a 'tying item' " and that "the tied items were the . . . paper packaging products, . . . cookers . . . and the food preparation mixes" (citing *Susser* v. *Carvel Corp.,* 332 F.2d 505 (2d Cir. 1964)).

The court found that the unique tying product, the trademark, had the requisite market power to bring the case within the Sherman Act and saw no need to examine in detail the relevant market for the Chicken Delight trademark, concluding from *Northern Pacific Railway Co.* v. *U.S.,* 356 U.S. 1 (1957), and *Fortner Enterprises* v. *U.S. Steel,* 394 U.S. 495 (1969), that "market power can be inferred from the existence of the tie-in," particularly where the seller successfully imposes the tying arrangement "on a substantial amount of commerce" (*Advanced Business Systems and Supply Co.* v. *SCM Corp.,* 415 F.2d 55, 62 (4th Cir. 1969)). Judge Harris rejected as "artificial" any distinction, for purposes of analyzing market power, between tying arrangements under Sherman Act, Section 1, and Clayton Act, Section 3.

Defendant advanced four justifications for the tying agreements: (a) reimbursement, in lieu of royalties, for the valuable trademark; (b) assurance to the franchisee of initial equipment and a continuous source of supply; (c) new business entry; and (d) quality control trademark goodwill protection. The first three defenses were rejected summarily by the court. An anticompetitive tie-in is not a "convenient accounting method," the court wrote, particularly where a defendant could specify a percentage-of-gross royalty for the use of the Chicken Delight trademark. (In fact, the defendant, Chicken Delight, charged no royalty fee.) The court also rejected defendant's argument that any damages to its franchisees were offset by the royalty value of the Chicken Delight trademark. In the court's view, any assurance of proper equipment and a continuous supply source could, without the imposition of a tie-in, easily have been provided by the defendant's designation of substitute manufacturers or distributors. As to "the new business" justification, the court pointed out that the permissible use of tie-in was limited in *U.S.* v. *Jerrold Electronics Corp.,* 187 F.Supp. 545 (E.D. Pa. 1960), *aff'd per curiam,* 365 U.S. 567 (1961), to the early stages of a business whose technology was complex and unproven. In contrast, defendant's tie-in agreements had been used since 1963, remaining unchanged from that time.

The court also rejected the quality-control defense as applied to the packaging products, reasoning that any competent packaging manufacturer could have supplied satisfactory packaging upon proper specification of printing type and color. As to the tied dips, spices, and cookers, which allegedly imparted a secret, unique flavor to the Chicken Delight product, the district court recognized that, under *Susser*, "the quality control defense is relevant." The court sent this issue to the jury with instructions that it accept the defense only if "specifications for a substitute would be so detailed that they could not practically be supplied" (citing *Standard Oil Co. v. U.S.*, 337 U.S. 293, 305–306 (1949)). The jury, by special verdict, determined that quality control could have been effected by means other than a tie-in.

On review, the court of appeals affirmed the district court's holding that defendant's contracts constituted a tying agreement but remanded for a determination of whether damages had resulted (448 F.2d 43 (9th Cir. 1971)).

There seems to be general agreement that Judge Harris made no new law in holding that a trademark may be a "tying product." The *Susser* case, which he cited, had concluded that "it is the lease of the trademark itself . . . to which are tied the other products." Similarly, the *Susser* court extended the "presumption of economic power" to the Carvel trademark. Some would still argue that, since a trademark is not a "disparate product" that can be tied, a tying theory in cases of franchises such as Chicken Delight is strained. Yet, other courts have expanded the concept of tying product to other intangibles. In *Washington Gas Light Co.* v. *VEPCO*, 309 F.Supp. 1119 (E.D. Va. 1970), *rev'd*, 438 F.2d 248 (4th Cir. 1971) the district court held that the provision of underground electrical installations was a "tying product" used to induce builders to purchase and install only electric appliances in their homes. (The court of appeals held there was only one product.) In *Gas Light Co. of Columbus* v. *Georgia Power Co.* 313 F.Supp. 860 (M.D. Ga. 1970), the court, commenting directly on the *Vepco* district court opinion, rejected the characterization of the arrangement as a tie-in. Others point out that it is not the nature of the "product" involved in a tie-in that is relevant; it is the fact that a trademark is used to force the purchase of another product that is the essence of "tying," and metaphysical distinctions between "product" and trademark are irrelevant.

If the district court had applied an exclusive-dealing principle to the *Chicken Delight* facts instead of a tying theory, a less stringent test of legality would have faced the Chicken Delight franchisors. Some experts suggest that, if the franchisor had not reached quite so far in terms of the restrictions imposed, the court could easily have gone the other way, regardless of the technicalities. Perhaps Judge Harris was applying a patent-misuse principle, holding, in effect, that under the Sherman Act franchisors cannot license their trademarks in a manner to coerce franchisees to give up alternate supply sources. On this theory, though, the court could probably have relied upon the per se concept or acceptable inferences available under a tie-in theory, although there are those who regard any patent misuse as a per se violation of the Sherman Act.

Are the Sherman and Clayton Act tests of market power as to tie-ins different? Some say the *Chicken Delight* case settles the issue and that there is no difference. They point out that if the tie-in is successful, the requisite market power will be inferred, regardless of whether the challenge is brought under the Clayton or the Sherman Act. Others suggest that the imposition of a tie-in on an insubstantial amount of commerce might not violate the Sherman Act, even though it could constitute a Clayton Act violation.

Experts differ on the proper test to be used in determining whether the restrictions on purchases of cookers and mixes in *Chicken Delight* were justified by the necessity of quality control. Judge Harris instructed the jury that the tie-in could not be justified unless it was "impractical for the franchisor to specify in detail a substitute" for the tied products that would protect the trademark goodwill. Some contend that such instructions place too great a burden upon the franchisor and urge a broader test: Was the tie-in (or other restrictive practice) reasonably ancillary to the protection of the trademark? Under such a test, the *Chicken Delight* case might have resulted in the same verdict. If the franchisor not only restricted specified sources for mixes and cookers, but also restricted use of packaging products, that combination of limitations might have taxed even a concept of "reasonableness." Had some of the limitations been absent perhaps the jury would have found for defendant under a test of reasonableness.

Some advocates of franchising see a necessary distinction between a normal tie-in of two products and a *Chicken Delight* type tie-in. They would not apply per se tying clause concepts across the board, as the court in this case seems to do. They argue that there is a basis for a distinction in that a franchise such as Chicken Delight exploits a trademark whose worth depends solely upon its public impact. In contrast, the tying of two or more actual products in the sale or franchising of a discrete product (e.g. Schwinn bicycles) may have little or no economic justification. Furthermore, since the Lanham Act requires trademark owners to protect the goodwill of their marks by policing licensees, it is argued that reasonable tie-in restrictions are permissible there, though tie-ins in other circumstances would be per se unlawful. This distinction between franchise tie-ins and other product tie-ins may have been granted limited recognition in *McDonald's Corp.* v. *Moore,* 363 F.2d 435 (5th Cir. 1966), in which the court ruled that the quality control defense does not apply to the tied sale of durables, but does apply to franchised trademarks. The FTC staff report by the "Ad Hoc Committee on Franchising" submitted to the Commission on June 2, 1969, rejected the existence of any "special franchise case law," yet its case review seems limited to the franchising of discrete products such as TBA, *Atlantic Refining Co.* v. *FTC* 331 F.2d 394 (7th Cir. 1964), *aff'd* 381 U.S. 357 (1965); mufflers, *Perma-Life Mufflers, Inc.,* v. *International Parts Corp.,* 376 F.2d 692 (7th Cir. 1966), *rev'd,* 392 U.S. 134 (1968); and shoes, *FTC* v. *Brown Shoe Co.,* 384 U.S. 316 (1966).

If, as Judge Harris appears to believe, the quality control defense does not apply unless franchisors cannot practically specify substitutes for their mixes or ingredients in detail, there may be a problem for franchisors who wish to preserve the secrecy of their recipes. Some experts take the position that quality control does not require supplier restrictions and that only the need to preserve secrecy will justify a tie-in restricting sources of ingredients. Thus, in the FTC *Carvel* case, discussed in the previous chapter, evidence of the need to maintain secrecy was introduced (*Carvel Corp.* 68 F.T.C. 128 (1965)). The Chicken Delight jury may have reflected a belief that all fried chicken is the same, and that no truly secret recipe exists.

The FTC's *Carvel* decision may not square with Judge Harris' narrow application of the quality control defense. In dismissing a Section 5 FTC Act proceeding against Carvel, franchisor of a trademark, despite Carvel's requirement that its ice cream mix was to be purchased only from Carvel-designated sources, the Commission chose not to define the restriction as a tie-in but to examine whether the supply restrictions were reasonably ancillary to the protection of the trademark. In *Susser* v. *Carvel,* the court found that a tie-in did exist, but concluded that ingredient supply restrictions were justified by the need for quality control connected with the problem of ingredient secrecy. Perhaps the results of the Carvel cases were the same, although based on different considerations. In both, a rule of "reasonable ancillarity" was employed in dealing with the buying restrictions.

In discussing the *Carvel* cases and the "rule of reason", the FTC's Ad Hoc Franchising Committee noted that underlying the Commission's dismissal was its belief that Carvel was "legitimate" because franchisees obtained real economic benefits and were not captives of the system, coerced to pay higher prices for supplies. In contrast, Chicken Delight franchisees had to pay higher than normal prices for the tied products. Furthermore, the Commission did not find evidence of extensive injury to competition resulting from the supply restrictions. In *Chicken Delight,* a treble-damage action, the court may have been concerned with the fact of injury. This may help to explain why the *Chicken Delight* court took a narrow view of the quality-control defense.

In *Warriner Hermetics, Inc.* v. *Copeland Refrigeration Corp.,* 1972 Trade Cas. ¶74,062 (5th Cir. 1972), limitation of the franchisor's freedom may have been carried a step further. In that case the court held that plaintiff-franchisee was entitled to have the jury instructed that defendant's policies of barring franchised wholesalers from dealing in compressors rebuilt by nonauthorized rebuilders and of barring franchised rebuilders from obtaining parts from non-Copeland sources constituted per se violations of the Sherman Act.

E. RECIPROCITY

Question: *Is it unlawful for two companies to agree to buy from each other?*

"Reciprocity" was defined in the Federal Trade Commission's opinion in the *Consolidated Foods* case, 62 F.T.C. 929 (1963), as "a practice whereby firms, overtly or tacitly, make concessions to one another in order to promote their business interests." The FTC noted that the most common form of reciprocity is "reciprocal buying"—a concept regarded as "nothing more than the simple idea that 'I will buy from you if you will buy from me,' or the unspoken 'If I buy from him, he will buy from me.' "

The antitrust enforcement agencies regard mutual accommodation, friendly or otherwise, with suspicion. As early as the 1930's, the FTC held that the use of buying power to encourage suppliers to purchase was an unfair method of competition, in violation of Section 5 of the Federal Trade Commission Act (*Waugh Equipment Co.,* 15 F.T.C. 232 (1931); *Mechanical Manufacturing Co.,* 16 F.T.C. 67 (1932); and *California Packing Corp.,* 25 F.T.C. 379 (1937)). The first two of these cases were brought against large meat packers who controlled smaller companies manufacturing railroad equipment. The meat packers were major rail shippers and induced the railroad companies to buy equipment manufactured by the packers' subsidiaries through threats to withdraw large shipments of freight. Similarly, in *California Packing Corp.,* a large

diversified processor and distributor of food products owned a subsidiary operating a waterfront transportation terminal. The distributor threatened to shift its purchases of raw and manufactured materials from suppliers who did not use this terminal to those who did.

An indictment in 1961 charged General Motors Corporation with
violating Section 2 of the Sherman Act by misusing its economic
power as the nation's largest shipper of freight to force most of the
nation's railroads to buy GM locomotives. One of the alleged mis-
uses was the routing of rail shipments to purchasers of GM locomotives while withholding shipments from lines that purchased other
locomotives. The court granted the Government's motion to dismiss
for lack of evidence to sustain the burden of proof ((1961–70 Transfer Binder) Trade Reg. Rep. ¶45,061 Cas. No. 1005). A civil action
against General Motors alleging the same misuse of power and
praying that General Motors be required to divest itself of its Diesel
Locomotive Manufacturing Division was dismissed without prejudice by the District Court for the Northern District of Illinois on
June 6, 1967 ((1961–70 Transfer Binder) Trade Reg. Rep. ¶45,063,
Cas. No. 1733).

The Supreme Court's *Consolidated Foods* decision sustained an
FTC order condemning a corporate acquisition that the Commission found had brought about a change in the structure of an industry, giving the acquiring company reciprocal buying power
(*FTC* v. *Consolidated Foods Corp.,* 380 U.S. 592 (1965)). The acquisition of Gentry, Inc., one of two dominant producers of dehydrated onion and garlic, by Consolidated Foods Corp., a large
diversified producer and seller of food products, was labeled a Section 7 Clayton Act violation. Consolidated bought large quantities from food processors who use dehydrated onion and garlic in
their products. The Commission found that a reciprocal buying policy had a great chance of success and posed a "most serious threat
to competition." In the Commission's view, the acquisition presented Consolidated "with an opportunity, previously unavailable,
to reap a profit from sales in one product area, dehydrated onion
and garlic, on the sheer strength of its buying power in other markets." The mere "opportunity" was regarded as enough to render
the merger unlawful.

The Commission's divestiture order was set aside (*Consolidated
Foods Corp.* v. *FTC,* 329 F.2d 623 (7th Cir. 1964)). When the case
was argued in the Supreme Court, counsel for Consolidated did not
attempt to dispute the FTC's proposition that a probability of substantial reciprocal buying represents a threat to competition cognizable under Section 7 of the Clayton Act. He conceded that "either
getting reciprocal agreements or coercive reciprocity" is a violation
of Section 1 of the Sherman Act and Section 5 of the FTC Act. The

Solicitor General agreed that Section 5 of the FTC Act might be applied. His brief noted that the Commission had issued Section 5 orders against reciprocity in the 1930's and suggested that companies practicing reciprocity might also violate the monopolization ban in Section 2 of the Sherman Act "if they got big enough." Yet he could not see a violation of Section 1 of the Sherman Act. In response to a series of questions from Justice White, he did agree, though, that two companies like Consolidated and Gentry could violate Section 2 if, instead of merging, they got together and agreed to use reciprocal buying power in the way the FTC found became probable when Consolidated acquired Gentry.

The Supreme Court reversed the court of appeals and upheld the commission (380 U.S. 592 (1965)). The Court declared that "the 'reciprocity' made possible by such an acquisition is one of the congeries of anticompetitive practices at which the antitrust laws are aimed, if the probable consequence of the acquisition is to obtain leverage in one field or another. The practice results in 'an irrelevant alien factor,' . . . intruding into the choice among competing products, creating at the least 'a priority on the business at equal prices.' . . . Reciprocal trading may ensue not from bludgeoning or coercion but from more subtle arrangements. A threatened withdrawal of orders if products of an affiliate cease being bought, or a conditioning of future purchases on the receipt of orders for products of that affiliate is an anticompetitive practice. Section 7 of the Clayton Act is concerned 'with probabilities, not certainties.' . . . Reciprocity in trading as a result of an acquisition violates Section 7, if the probability of a lessening of competition is shown" (380 U.S. at 595).

"We do not go so far as to say that any acquisition no matter how small, violates Section 7 if there is a probability of reciprocal buying. . . . But where, as here, the acquisition is of a company that commands a substantial share of a market, a finding of probability of reciprocal buying by the Commission, whose expertise the Congress trusts, should be honored, if there is substantial evidence to support it" (380 U.S. at 600).

In assessing the probable competitive effect of the merger, the Supreme Court focused upon the standing of Gentry in the dehydrated onion and garlic market, without considering Consolidated's relative standing or leverage vis-a-vis its suppliers, customers, or competitors in its own market. Prior to its acquisition by Consolidated, Gentry had about 32 percent of total sales and, together with its principal competitor, accounted for almost 90 percent of industry sales. Seven years after the merger the combined share of the two largest firms remained at about 90 percent, but Gentry's had risen to 35 percent.

Two factors seem to stand out in the Court's reasons for sustaining the FTC's conclusion that the merger would probably have an anticompetitive effect. First, the Court pointed to direct evidence that after the acquisition Consolidated undertook to assist Gentry in selling, sometimes successfully. "Reciprocity was tried over and again and it sometimes worked." Second, the Court stressed the fact that following the merger Gentry was able to increase its share of dried-onion sales by 7 percent and hold its losses on garlic sales to 12 percent, even though its product was inferior, implying that these figures evidence the presence of reciprocity as a market factor.

In *U.S.* v. *Ingersoll-Rand Co.,* the district court granted a preliminary injunction against Ingersoll-Rand's acquisition of three producers of coal-mining equipment (218 F.Supp. 530 (W.D. Pa. 1963), *aff'd,* 320 F.2d 509 (3d Cir. 1963)). The court observed that the acquisition would increase Ingersoll-Rand's steel purchases to such an extent that the coal mines' purchase of mining equipment could be influenced by their desire to retain the good will of the steel industry, one of their largest customers. The district judge was fearful of "secondary" or "round-robin" reciprocity. There was no proof of an attempt or intent to engage in reciprocal buying, but "the mere existence of this purchasing power might make its conscious employment toward this end unnecessary; the possession of the power is frequently sufficient, as sophisticated businessmen are quick to see the advantages in securing the good will of the possessor."

One of the questions left unsettled in *Consolidated Foods* was the extent to which noncoercive but "overt" reciprocity might be treated as a Section 5 FTC Act violation or, if the companies "got big enough," a Section 2 Sherman Act violation, if it did not appear to be a violation of Section 1 of the Sherman Act.

In *U.S.* v. *General Dynamics,* the district court refused to make a distinction between reciprocal dealing arrangements effected through coercion and "a mutual patronage agreement wholly without such overtones. . . . While the former practice certainly is more offensive, the latter arrangements are equally disruptive of the competitive processes" (258 F.Supp. 36 (S.D.N.Y. 1966)). In the *General Dynamics* case the Government attacked under Section 1 of the Sherman Act and Section 7 of the Clayton Act the 1957 merger of General Dynamics Corp. and Liquid Carbonic Corp. In the year of the merger General Dynamics made purchases from all its suppliers totaling about 1½ billion dollars. With the acquisition of Liquid Carbonic, General Dynamics' suppliers became, for the first time in any significant degree, customers for a product manufactured by General Dynamics, Liquid Carbonic's industrial gases.

General Dynamics had a "Special Sales Program" to develop reciprocal relations with its suppliers who purchased industrial gases.
The Government also charged that General Dynamics violated Section 1 of the Sherman Act after the merger by actually promoting
Liquid Carbonic Division sales through the use of its purchasing
power.

To determine whether either coercive reciprocity or mutual patronage violated Section 1, the court applied "the standards of decision delineated by the Supreme Court in [tying arrangement]
cases." Both reciprocity and tying arrangements deny competitors
access to one market because of the seller's power or leverage in
another and not because the seller has a better product or a lower
price. The court measured reciprocal dealing by the test adopted in
the *International Salt* case, 332 U.S. 392 (1947): a tying arrangement is per se illegal if a "not insubstantial" amount of commerce
is affected.

There seems to be an inconsistency between the court's holding
that the merger violated Section 1 and that the reciprocal dealing
actually resulting from the merger did not. The court, in outlawing
the merger, found "that a 'not insubstantial' amount of commerce
was affected as a result of the merger agreement." It then went on
to find that the actual resulting reciprocity did not involve a substantial amount of commerce. The key to the distinction lies in the
court's insistence on proof of specific reciprocal-dealing contracts
between identified parties. Each of those contracts, as the judge
viewed them, "affected" only the industrial gas purchases of a single manufacturer. The merger agreement, on the other hand, was a
combination specifically intended, he found, to put the Liquid Carbonic Division in a position to control a major part of the entire
industrial gas market.

One could argue that in determining the amount of commerce
affected, reciprocity contracts are not analogous to tying arrangements. In a tie-in arrangement the leverage linked with the tying
product is created by the purchaser's desire for that particular
product; he has made a unilateral decision based on price, quality,
services, or unavailability of the product from other sources. On the
other hand, his purchase of the tied product is not the result of a
unilateral decision, but is forced upon him by the need for the
tying product. In a reciprocity arrangement there are two purchasers, and neither's decision is unilateral. Both purchasers make their
decisions at least partly for the purpose of making a sale, so that
there are two "foreclosures" of competition.

What this means, in terms of the *General Dynamics* case, is that
not only did General Dynamics select its suppliers with a view to
making industrial gas sales, but industrial gas users picked their

supplier with a view to selling to General Dynamics. Yet the court did not include in "commerce affected" the amount of General Dynamics' purchases that were involved in the proven reciprocity contracts yielding $177,225 in General Dynamics sales.

The Government relied on evidence that reciprocity was systematically interjected into sales presentations and on statistics showing that the reciprocity program was effective. The court refused to infer the existence of Section 1 contracts or combinations from that evidence and insisted upon proof of "particular contracts with identifiable parties." The Government was able to prove only $177,225 in industrial gas sales with reciprocal buying terms. In the *International Salt* case, the "commerce affected" was tie-in sales of the "tied" product that totaled $500,000 and were found "not insubstantial." While that figure had "no magical significance" for the district court, it was the lowest figure so far designated by the Supreme Court as "not insubstantial." Since the Government had already proven that the merger enabling General Dynamics to engage in reciprocity was a Sherman Act violation, the Court considered the case "an inappropriate vehicle for finding an amount considerably less than $500,000 as 'not insubstantial.' "

The *Consolidated Foods* decision was distinguished in *United States* v. *Penick & Ford, Ltd.*, 242 F.Supp. 518 (D.N.J. 1965). The court denied a preliminary injunction against the acquisition by R. J. Reynolds Tobacco Co. of Penick & Ford, the country's fourth largest corn-products manufacturer. The Government argued that the acquisition would place Reynolds, a major purchaser of paper packaging products, in a position actively to persuade its paper suppliers to use P & F's starch. Cornstarch producers, it was alleged, are also major purchasers of paper packaging containers and generally practice reciprocity. Thus, the Government argued, the combined purchasing power of Reynolds and P & F would of itself induce purchases by paper product producers. In denying the motion for a preliminary injunction, the district court relied on evidence of Reynolds' past buying policies and on testimony that P & F's reciprocal system would be dismantled. Unlike Consolidated Foods, Reynolds made a showing that it did not intend to exercise its reciprocal buying power, and the district court doubted its extent in any event. The *Reynolds* case was later terminated by a consent decree (*U.S.* v. *R. J. Reynolds Tobacco Co.*, 1969 Trade Cas. ¶72,886 (D.N.J. 1969)).

The Federal Trade Commission and the Justice Department have challenged reciprocal practices in and out of the merger context. In *Allis-Chalmers Mfg. Co.* v. *White Consolidated Industries, Inc.*, 414 F.2d 506 (3rd Cir. 1969), *cert. denied*, 396 U.S. 1009 (1970), the court of appeals ordered a preliminary injunction against White Industries' takeover of Allis-Chalmers, where a White-Allis combination would have been a major purchaser of steel and the Blaw-Knox Company, a White subsidiary, was one of the leading manufacturers of metal rolling mills for the steel. Although other grounds were asserted for issuance of the injunction, the court of appeals split 2–1, and Judge Seitz, who made the majority, limited his concurrence to the reciprocity issue.

The Federal Trade Commission has moved against reciprocal practices, including "consensual" or "noncoercive" reciprocity. The Commission has obtained affidavits of discontinuance from manufacturers allegedly violating Section 5 of the FTC Act by reciprocity. In one such case, *U.S.* v. *Union Bag-Camp Paper Corp.,* 1966 Trade Cas. ¶71,698 (S.D.N.Y. 1965), Union Camp Corporation agreed to make future purchases and sales on the basis of price, quality, and service, and volunteered to withdraw from membership in a "trade relations" association. Chase Bag Co. agreed to similar provisions.

The district court entered a final consent decree prohibiting for 10 years reciprocal arrangements between the United States Steel Corp. and its suppliers (*United States* v. *United States Steel Corp.,* 1969 Trade Cas. ¶72,826 (W.D. Pa. 1969)). The Justice Department had alleged that the reciprocal practices amounted to attempts to monopolize the steel purchases of actual and potential suppliers. U.S. Steel also agreed to abolish its Customer Relations Section, and to take steps to prevent its sales personnel from using its purchases to leverage sales.

The Antitrust Division has pressed the view that reciprocal relationships may violate Section 1 of the Sherman Act. In *United States* v. *General Tire & Rubber Co.,* 1970 Trade Cas. ¶73,303 (N.D. Ohio 1970), the Division contended that General Tire & Rubber and its subsidiaries violated Sections 1 and 2 of the Sherman Act by using their combined purchasing power to increase their sales of tires, advertising time, and other products and services. This is the first case in which the Section 1 issue was presented in a nonmerger context. The parties signed a consent decree barring General Tire from making purchases based on its sales to the supplier.

Reciprocity counts have become commonplace in Justice Department complaints attacking conglomerate mergers. Though the Government failed to obtain immediate relief against Northwest Industries' acquisition of B. F. Goodrich, the district court took precautions against the possibility of reciprocal dealing (*U.S.* v. *Northwest Industries,* 301 F.Supp. 1066 (N.D. Ill. 1969)). The court prohibited Northwest from taking any action that might inhibit its ability to comply with a future divestiture order and specifically required it to refrain from reciprocal dealing in the products of either company.

Similarly, Judge Timbers, refusing to preliminarily enjoin the ITT-Hartford and ITT-Grinnell mergers, suggested hold-separate provisions that would preclude all reciprocal dealing (*U.S.* v. *International Telephone and Telegraph Corp.,* 324 F.Supp. 19 (D. Conn. 1970)).

In public addresses, senior officials of the Antitrust Division have stated enforcement objectives in the reciprocity area. In a speech before the Antitrust Committee of the Federal Bar Association, September 1969, Baddia J. Rashid, the Antitrust Division's Director of Operations, citing the *General Dynamics* decision, concluded that "elaborate proof of particular contracts should not be required" to support a finding of a Section 1 violation, particularly where there is a "conscious pursuit of a systematic reciprocity program, which includes the maintenance of trade balance records comparing sale and purchase information, which favors one's own customers when purchasing, and which is communicated to customers and suppliers in the expectation that they will act upon it . . ." (426 ATRR X-1 (9/9/69)). In this view, such a program, especially where a company has "substantial leverage," may amount not only to a Section 1 combination or conspiracy, but also to an attempt to monopolize in violation of Section 2 of the Sherman Act. He cited the General Tire and Rubber complaint as an illustration of that approach. He also cited the U.S. Steel consent judgement as an example of relief "aimed at the system itself, and not just at the resulting agreements."

As for "coercive reciprocity" and "mutual patronage reciprocity," Rashid said that the real issue is "whether and to what extent there is in practice a difference between a systematic trade relations program, on the one hand, and reciprocal dealing arrangements on the other." He concluded that "antitrust policy is anti-reciprocity." Similar views were expressed by Roland W. Donnem, the Antitrust Division's Director of Planning, in a speech on August 12, 1969, before the American Bar Association in Dallas (423 ATRR A-16 (8/19/69)).

Some antitrust specialists do not believe the Justice Department intends to draw a distinction between "coercive" and "noncoercive" reciprocity. Some think that the type of reciprocity may merely affect the particular statute under which it is attacked. For example, they believe that "coercive" reciprocity will continue to be viewed as a violation of Section 5 of the FTC Act and perhaps of Section 2 of the Sherman Act as well, and that overt or tacit consensual reciprocity, along the lines suggested in the Rashid speech, may be a

combination or conspiracy forbidden by Section 1 of the Sherman
Act. As for the mere power to engage in reciprocity, the Government will probably continue to challenge mergers under Section 7
of the Clayton Act where the result would be the existence (even if
unexercised) of reciprocity power.

With respect to "intra-enterprise reciprocity," some specialists
point out that many parents require reciprocity with and between
their subsidiaries, and that this practice is legal. Others, however,
warn that the mere prospect of post-acquisition "legal" reciprocity
"within the corporate family" may trigger Justice Department action, not on Section 1 combination and conspiracy grounds, but on
Clayton Act Section 7 grounds that such practices might tend to
lessen competition.

Some practitioners would emphasize that most of the decided
cases, especially *FTC* v. *Consolidated Foods,* 380 U.S. 592 (1965),
involved systematic reciprocity programs. Others point to the *Penick & Ford* decision, which they read as involving only an "appre-
hension of reciprocity." The *Allis-Chalmers* case, some think, takes
potential reciprocity close to the outer limits. In its petition seeking
Supreme Court review, White Industries said that the court of appeals ruling means that any company with the status of a "larger
purchaser" than its competitors possesses inherent, illegal reciprocity
"potential," the mere possession or acquisition of which is tantamount to a per se violation of the antitrust laws. The court of appeals cited the "present preliminary stage of the proceedings" as
reason enough for not expressly dealing with the matter of each
party's share of the market in the lines of commerce under consideration. Judge Timbers in the *ITT* case distinguished *Allis-Chalmers*
on the ground that ITT, unlike White Industries, presented "substantial, credible and persuasive" evidence of a company policy
against reciprocal dealing. For that reason, Judge Timbers found
it necessary to reach the legal basis of the Government's claim,
i.e. "that the mere showing that a merger will create a market
structure conducive to reciprocal dealing . . . is sufficient to halt a
merger under Section 7."

Open contractual reciprocal dealing is now difficult to defend.
The areas of concern today involve the less visible "potential" reciprocity and its likely post-merger alteration of market structure.
Penick & Ford, Northwest Industries, and the *ITT* cases, support the
conclusion that, at least in the lower courts, a Government attack
based solely on "potential reciprocity" or "reciprocity effect" can be
countered. The success of the defense would seem to rest primarily
on the careful marshaling of facts necessary to show a strong and
effective past policy against reciprocal dealing and corporate procedures and structure that would make such dealing economically

unlikely in the future. The *ITT* cases exemplify this type of evidence. Judge Timbers noted that ITT has a written policy against reciprocity, does not collect sales and purchasing data necessary to identify reciprocal dealing opportunities, and is organized around a "profit center" concept that is not conducive to reciprocity.

While the future of reciprocity as an antitrust violation is still cloudy, most antitrust experts generally agree that reciprocity serves no legitimate economic or social purpose. If there is a "not insubstantial" amount of commerce involved, the courts may infer an agreement, particularly when a concentrated industry is involved. If a company's salesmen have access to purchasing information, coordinate the purchasing information with their sales, and use it in sales talk, a court might construct an agreement from those factors. In view of the broad administrative powers the Supreme Court has recognized under Section 5 of the FTC Act, the Commission's attitude toward reciprocity may be more significant than that of the lower federal courts. Perhaps the best advice that antitrust counsel can give a company is: Don't give purchasing data to your salesmen.

Some antitrust experts doubt that a per se test can be justified for reciprocal arrangements. If the arrangement is a result of "back scratching" or is simply bartering, then they say there should be no violation. These experts might agree, though, that if one party has leverage, coercion can be inferred.

PART III

Mergers

A. WHICH MERGERS ARE PROHIBITED?

1. Mergers Under the Sherman Act

Question: *Does the Sherman Act prohibit any corporate mergers?*

"In 1890 the primary target of the Sherman Act's general language—'combinations or conspiracies in restraint of trade'—was the corporate consolidation rather than the price fixing or market-allocation agreement. . . . This being so, it is a curious fact of history that for over 40 years . . . horizontal mergers have been practically immune from prosecution under the Sherman Act, while absolute prohibitions have been judicially erected and vigorously enforced against price fixing and other practices." So said the chief of the Antitrust Division (William Orrick) to the Association for Corporate Growth (149 ATRR A-1 (5/19/64)). He noted that in the early part of this century the Justice Department had had a brief period of success in antimerger litigation under the Sherman Act. In the four "railroad cases" decided between 1904 and 1912, the Supreme Court had sustained application of the Sherman Act to mergers and given it a scope that seemed to bar any merger of substantial competitors (*Northern Securities Co.* v. *U.S.*, 193 U.S. 197 (1904); *U.S.* v. *Union Pacific R.R.*, 226 U.S. 61 (1912); *U.S.* v. *Reading Co.*, 253 U.S. 26 (1920); *U.S.* v. *Southern Pacific Co.*, 259 U.S. 214 (1922)). But there had been no other important antimerger litigation under the Sherman Act until the late 1940's, when the Justice Department brought a Section 1 Sherman Act suit to challenge an asset acquisition by Columbia Steel Company. The Supreme Court's 1948 decision sustaining denial of an injunction in that case was generally read as meaning that Section 1 of the Sherman Act would not be an effective bar to mergers of competitors (*U.S.* v. *Columbia Steel Co.*, 334 U.S. 495 (1948)).

Mr. Orrick's review of this history preceded his evaluation, from the Antitrust Division's point of view, of another Supreme Court decision released only a month before he spoke, *U.S.* v. *First National Bank and Trust Co. of Lexington*, 376 U.S. 665 (1964). In an opinion striking down the consolidation of the first and fourth largest banks in Lexington, Ky., a 5–4 majority of the Court reinstated the doctrine of the railroad cases. Justice Douglas' opinion for the Court adopted the rule that "where merging companies are major competitive factors in a relevant market, the elimination of significant competition between them, by merger, itself constitutes a violation of Section 1 of the Sherman Act." The Court found that the two banks had no "predatory" purpose when they made their agreement to consolidate. Nevertheless "significant competition will be eliminated by the merger"—the test of illegality derived from the railroad cases. The record contained testimony from presidents of three of the four remaining banks that the consolidation would seriously affect their ability to compete effectively, that the "image of bigness" is a powerful attraction to customers, and that the multiplicity of extra services the consolidated bank could offer in the trust field tends to foreclose competition there.

In relying on the railroad cases, the Supreme Court based its decision primarily on the elimination of competition between the two merging companies, "without reference to the strength or weakness of whatever competition remained." In his commentary, Justice Douglas pointed out that the bank established by the consolidation was slightly larger, in-assets, deposits, and loans, than all the remaining banks of the area combined. Prior to the consolidation, the two banks had held almost 95 percent of all trust assets in the area and had accounted for over 92 percent of all trust-department earnings.

The *Columbia Steel* case was not overruled; it was "confined to its special facts." Justice Douglas noted that the Columbia Steel acquisition was declared lawful "after the Court observed, inter alia, that because of rate structures and the location of United States Steel's fabricating subsidiaries, the latter were unable to compete effectively in Consolidated's market." Justice Brennan and Justice White joined in a concurring opinion based "solely on the conclusion that the factors relied on in *United States* v. *Columbia Steel Co.* . . . as applied to the facts of this case, clearly compel the reversal." While their concurring opinion did not indicate disagreement with the railroad cases, they did not find it necessary in deciding the case to go beyond the test laid down in *Columbia Steel.*

In a dissenting opinion in which Justice Stewart joined, Justice Harlan argued that the *Columbia Steel* opinion had overturned the reasoning of the railroad cases and established that elimination of competition alone is not enough to turn a merger into a combination or a conspiracy violating Section 1 of the Sherman Act. "Stripped of embellishments, the Court's opinion amounts to an invocation of formulas of antitrust numerology and a presumption that in the antitrust field good things come usually, if not always, in small packages." Justice Harlan insisted that none of the findings of the district court or of the Supreme Court majority relate to any of the factors listed in the *Columbia Steel* case except "bigness."

Mr. Orrick found it impossible to "overestimate the importance" of the *Lexington Bank* decision. "Thus history has returned to the Antitrust Division the antimerger weapon in Section 1 of the Sherman Act which it once had and which may well be easier to deal with than the weapon Congress fashioned in Section 7 of the Clayton Act." With its requirement that the Government satisfy three statutory conditions—"line of commerce," "section of the country," and anticompetitive effect, he explained, Section 7 calls for "the most complex and protracted kinds of litigation known in the law. . . . In the future, however, it may be that we no more need to examine the market impact of horizontal mergers than we need to examine the market impact of price-fixing agreements."

As if to prove that he meant what he said, the Assistant Attorney General two weeks later signed an injunction complaint attacking a newspaper publisher's stock and asset acquisitions as violations of Sections 1 and 2 of the Sherman Act as well as of Section 7 of the Clayton Act. The complaint, filed against E. W. Scripps Co., Cincinnati, went back to challenge acquisitions beginning in 1956. Scripps signed a consent order in 1968 requiring complete divestiture of its interest in the Cincinnati Enquirer, Inc., (*U.S.* v. *E. W. Scripps Co.,* 1968 Trade Cas. ¶72,586 (S.D. Ohio 1968)).

The "future" in which Mr. Orrick suggested that horizontal mergers may be assigned the same per se illegality as price fixing has in fact arrived, according to two Supreme Court justices. In *U.S.* v. *Continental Can Co.,* 378 U.S. 441 (1964), the same two Justices who dissented in the *Lexington Bank* case accused the majority of "laying down a 'per se' rule that mergers between two large companies in related industries are presumptively unlawful under Section 7 of the Clayton Act." And there are lawyers who feel that the only difference between the Section 7 test of competitive injury and Justice Douglas' standard in the *Lexington Bank* case—"the elimination of significant competition between" merging companies that "are major competitive factors in a relevant market"—is his use of the word "major."

The *Lexington Bank* case gives the Justice Department the possibility of two counts in horizontal merger case complaints, one under the Sherman Act and one under the Clayton Act. While it may be, as Mr. Orrick said, that the three elements of proof in a Section 7 case make Clayton Act litigation complicated, that statute's competitive-injury test is still regarded by some attorneys as easier to satisfy than the Sherman Act's. The question remains: Is there any difference or only an abstract, theoretical distinction between proving actual restraint of trade under the Sherman Act and showing a probability that the merger will "tend substantially to lessen competition," as the Clayton Act requires?

The resurrection of Sherman Act merger proceedings could have some impact in areas where there are technical obstacles to applying Section 7 of the Clayton Act. At least three such areas exist: (1) asset acquisitions that are made in industries, such as banking, not subject to FTC regulation and therefore not covered by Section 7; (2) asset consolidations that involve FTC-regulated industries but were accomplished before 1950, when the Clayton Act was amended to cover asset purchases; and (3) stock acquisitions predating enactment of the Clayton Act in 1914. In fact, the Antitrust Division left a Clayton Act count out of the *Lexington Bank* complaint for the purpose of getting a Supreme Court ruling that would permit use of the Sherman Act against bank asset acquisitions.

Insofar as the injunction complaint filed against the Scripps newspaper chain represents an attempt to restore newspapers to an earlier competitive status, it demonstrates the Justice Department's willingness at that time to go into the past and bring Sherman Act proceedings against industries with histories of increased concentration through mergers. A more definite expression of that intention may have been given by Assistant Attorney General Orrick in his April, 1964, speech before the American Bar Association's Antitrust Section (24 ABA ANTRITRUST L.J. 44 (1964)). Referring to "the new time dimension given to Section 7" by the Supreme Court's decision in *U.S.* v. *E. I. duPont de Nemours & Co.,* 353 U.S. 586 (1957), Mr. Orrick declared that action "against previously accomplished mergers . . . even in the absence of a current merger" is "certainly an important part of our current thought." And he termed "greatly exaggerated" the difficulties involved in "unscrambling the corporate omelet." "A court need not unscramble the corporate omelet; it need only divide it into two or more servings" (145 ATRR A-2 (4/21/64)).

2. Corporate Acquisitions and Section 7 of the Clayton Act

Question: *What are the basic antitrust rules concerning corporate acquisitions?*

In 1914, Congress, in Section 7 of the Clayton Act, prohibited corporate acquisitions where the effect "may be to substantially lessen competition between the corporation whose stock is so acquired and the corporation making the acquisition or to restrain . . . commerce in any section or community, or tend to create a monopoly of any line of commerce." For many years before the Second World War, the Federal Trade Commission, in its annual reports to the Congress, suggested amendments to this statute. The final report of the Temporary National Economic Committee also recommended changes. After the war, in response to a fear by some of what they regarded as a rising tide of economic concentration in American industry, and bolstered by the FTC's 1948 report on corporate mergers, a thorough examination of the purposes and provisions of Section 7 of the Clayton Act was undertaken in the 80th and 81st Congress. As a result, Section 7 was amended in 1950. The amendment added language to include within the coverage of the statute the acquisition of assets as well as the acquisition of stock. By various additions and deletions, the effects clause was changed to prohibit acquisitions where "in any line of commerce in any section of the country, the effect of such acquisition may be substantially to lessen competition or to tend to create a monopoly."

The decade following the 1950 amendment of Section 7 brought many Justice Department and FTC actions against corporate acquisitions alleged to be in violation of Section 7. During the Eisenhower Administration, the Department of Justice filed 45 suits under Section 7. The first was filed in 1955. The Federal Trade Commission began one proceeding in 1952, and from 1954 through March 1961 brought an additional 43 proceedings. Although at the FTC the pace in the initiation of such proceedings slackened in the '60's, the Antitrust Division continued its barrage of Section 7 suits. In 1961, 18 cases were begun, exceeding the record of any previous year.

In November, 1955, as one of five suits attacking corporate mergers filed during that first year of Justice's amended Section 7 activity, the Government sought an injunction against the contemplated merger of G. R. Kinney Co., Inc., and Brown Shoe Co., Inc., through an exchange of Kinney stock for that of Brown. The Government's motion for a preliminary order restraining the merger during the course of the litigation was denied by the U.S. district court in the following year (*U.S.* v. *Brown Shoe Co.,* 1956 Trade Cas. ¶68,244 (E.D. Mo. 1956)). The companies were permitted to merge on the condition that their business be operated separately and assets be kept separately identifiable. On this basis, the merger was carried out on May 1, 1956. In November 1959, the district court held the merger illegal (179 F.Supp. 721 (E.D. Mo. 1959)). The Supreme Court upheld the district court's conclusion (370 U.S. 294 (1962)). Twelve years after passage of the amendment, and six years after consummation of the merger in question, the Supreme Court stated authoritatively for the first time its interpretation of the 1950 amendment.

Two previous cases in which the Government's complaints were based in part on amended Section 7 had come to the Court (*Md. and Va. Milk Producers Ass'n.* v. *U.S.*, 362 U.S. 458 (1960), and *Jerrold Electronics Corp.* v. *U.S.*, 365 U.S. 567 (1961)), but a resolution of the issues presented in those cases did not, in the Court's view, require review of the 1950 amendment.

Of the more than 40 proceedings brought by the Federal Trade Commission since the 1950 amendment, none had been reviewed by the Supreme Court at the time of the *Brown Shoe* decision. Neither *Crown-Zellerbach* v. *FTC*, 296 F.2d 800 (9th Cir. 1961), *cert. denied*, 370 U.S. 937 (1962), nor *Erie Sand and Gravel* v. *FTC*, 291 F.2d 279 (3rd Cir. 1961), had reached the Court. In *Crown-Zellerbach*, the Supreme Court has since denied review of the court of appeals' decision which upheld the Commission's conclusion that the acquisition in question violated amended Section 7 (370 U.S. 937 (1962)).

The Court's opinion in *Brown*, written by the Chief Justice, provided a lengthly catalog of Section 7 literature. Five distinct sections of the opinion discuss (1) history of the litigation and industry background; (2) jurisdiction of the Court to review the district court's decision under Section 2 of the Expediting Act, 15 U.S.C. § 29; (3) legislative history of amended Section 7, with a statement of eight "factors" as "background" against which the case is measured; (4) vertical aspects of the merger; and (5) horizontal aspects of the merger. The Court emphasized that Brown was the third largest seller of shoes by dollar volume in the United States, the fourth largest shoe manufacturer, and a retailer with over 1,230 outlets. Kinney was described as eighth largest in the country by dollar volume among those primarily selling shoes, a large manufacturer of shoes, and a retailer with over 350 retail outlets. The Court concluded that in both the vertical and horizontal aspects the relevant lines of commerce were men's, women's, and children's shoes. As to the relevant geographic markets, the Court agreed with the parties that the entire nation was the appropriate market for evaluation of the vertical aspects of the merger and for its horizontal aspect so far as shoe manufacturing was concerned. With respect to shoe retailing the Court concluded that cities and their environs with populations exceeding 10,000 and with both Brown and Kinney retail shoe outlets were the appropriate geographic markets for analysis of the horizontal aspects of the merger. As to both vertical and horizontal aspects, the Court's majority concluded that the merger would have effects prohibited by Section 7.

Justices Harlan and Clark filed separate opinions. Justice Harlan dissented on the question of jurisdiction, finding the district court's action not a final judgment ripe for review by the Supreme Court, but stating on the merits his opinion that an examination of the vertical aspects of the merger was sufficient to show its violation of Section 7. Justice Clark concurred with the Court on the question of jurisdiction and on the conclusion that the merger violated Section 7. He concluded that "it would be more reasonable to define the line of commerce as shoes . . . and the market as the entire country."

The Court's opinion, because of its length and encyclopedic discussion, was thought to provide antitrust lawyers with many pegs upon which to hang future arguments in defense of corporate mergers, but such pegs were loosely anchored. Instead of establishing firm guidelines, the opinion of the Court indicated the broad scope of various considerations to be taken into account in gauging the effect of a given merger. According to the Court, "Congress indicated plainly that a merger had to be functionally viewed in the context of its particular industry. That is, whether the consolidation was to take place in an industry that was fragmented rather than concentrated, that had seen a recent trend toward domination by a few leaders or had remained fairly consistent in its distribution of market shares among the participating companies, that had experienced easy access to market by suppliers and easy access to suppliers by buyers or had witnessed foreclosure of business, that had witnessed the ready entry of new competition or the erection of barriers to prospective entrants, all were aspects, varying in importance with the merger under consideration which would properly be taken into account" (370 U.S. at 321). Some commented at the time that in the Brown-Kinney merger such factors as concentration, domination, and foreclosure of markets were notable by their absence.

As in many cases, the meaning of the Court's decision was probably found in what the Court actually did and not what it said it was doing. The Court declared the Brown-Kinney merger illegal on two grounds, as a forward vertical integration and as a horizontal merger on the retail level. With Justices Frankfurter and White not participating, the remaining seven Justices were unanimous in concluding that the merger violated amended Section 7. The separate opinions concurring on the merits required less, rather than more, discussion in reaching this conclusion. The message of the Court's unanimous conclusion of illegality could perhaps be even better appreciated with the realization that, despite the Court's description of Brown and Kinney as "large" and "leading," market shares of each were small in a fragmented industry compared with those of large or leading firms in such concentrated industries as steel and automobiles. Brown produced only 4 percent of the nation's footwear and Kinney manufactured less than ½ percent and retailed less than 2 percent of the nation's shoes.

3. Foreign Acquisitions

Question: *To what extent do the antitrust laws apply to foreign acquisitions by U.S. corporations?*

Until recent years, foreign acquisitions had been attacked by the U.S. Government only incidentally in litigation aimed at broad conspiratorial or monopolistic patterns of conduct of which the acquisitions constituted only parts (*U.S.* v. *National Lead Co.,* 63 F.Supp. 513 (S.D.N.Y. 1945), *aff'd,* 332 U.S. 319 (1947); *U.S.* v. *Imperial Chemical Industries,* 105 F.Supp. 215 (S.D.N.Y. 1952)). A foreign acquisition, standing alone, was attacked in *U.S.* v. *Jos. Schlitz Brewing Co.,* 253 F.Supp. 129 (N.D. Calif. 1966), *aff'd,* 385 U.S. 37 (1966), but the Government's real object was to prevent Schlitz control of a California brewery operated by a subsidiary of the acquired foreign company.

In 1968, the Justice Department filed an injunction suit under Section 7 of the Clayton Act attacking the stock acquisition by The Gillette Company of a German manufacturer of electric razors. The purpose of the suit was not to protect or promote the export trade of the United States but to preserve a potential competitor for the domestic shaving instrument market ((1961–70 Transfer Binder) Trade Reg. Rep. ¶45,068 Cas. No. 1988). Similarly, the FTC has ordered divestiture of a German typewriter manufacturer because of the effects of the acquisition on the domestic U.S. market (*Litton Industries, Inc.,* (1970–73 Transfer Binder) Trade Reg. Rep. ¶20,267 and ¶20,333 (F.T.C. 1973)).

The Federal Trade Commission attacked the acquisition of the third largest domestic producer of chocolate by an organization, W. R. Grace & Co., that had no other chocolate production facilities in the United States but whose South American factories made it one of the world's six largest producers. The Commission's Section 7 complaint attacked the tendency "to create a monopoly throughout the United States, or in portions thereof." Grace was described as "a leading exporter to the United States." Grace agreed to a consent order providing that for 10 years it would not acquire the stock or assets of any corporation engaged in the manufacturing of chocolate or cocoa products without prior FTC approval (*W. R. Grace & Co.,* 71 F.T.C. 312 (1967)).

The legislative history of the antimerger provisions in Section 7 of the Clayton Act says nothing as to the intent of Congress regarding foreign acquisitions. Yet acquisition of a foreign competitor is a transaction to which the antitrust laws have been applied (*U.S.* v. *Jos. Schlitz Brewing Co.,* 253 F. Supp. 129 (N.D. Calif. 1966); *Dresser Industries, Inc.,* 63 F.T.C. 250 (1963)). The "commerce" protected by the antitrust laws is defined as including "trade or commerce . . . with foreign nations."

The *Schlitz* decision is the only reported court opinion exploring the impact of the antitrust laws specifically on a foreign acquisition unrelated to other anticompetitive conduct. There no longer seems to be any doubt about the power of U.S. courts to apply the antitrust laws to foreign mergers. Contracts made and transactions consummated outside the boundaries of the United States and lawful where made or consummated have been held subject to the antitrust laws if they have an impact on the foreign or domestic commerce of the United States (*U.S.* v. *American Tobacco Co.,* 221 U.S. 106 (1911); *U.S.* v. *Aluminum Co. of America,* 148 F.2d 416, 444 (2d Cir. 1945)). The federal courts ordered termination of joint foreign interests in the *National Lead* and *Imperial Chemical Industries* cases.

The antitrust curb most frequently applied against mergers is Section 7 of the Clayton Act. In addition, an agreement by one corporation to acquire another or the actual acquisition itself is a "contract, combination . . . or conspiracy" that can be "in restraint of trade" and hence a violation of Section 1 of the Sherman Act (*U.S.* v. *First National Bank & Trust Co. of Lexington,* 376 U.S. 665 (1964)). In recent years the Federal Trade Commission has intensified efforts to subject consolidations, mergers, and acquisitions of businesses to the "unfair methods of competition" ban in Section 5 of the FTC Act. (See, e.g., *Beatrice Foods Co.,* 67 F.T.C. 473 (1965)).

The Clayton, Sherman, and FTC Acts differ significantly in the jurisdictional language that determines their applicability to foreign acquisitions. Section 7 of the Clayton Act applies only to the acquisition by one corporation "engaged in commerce" of "another corporation engaged also in commerce," if the acquisition may substantially lessen competition "in any line of commerce in any section of the country." Section 1 of the Clayton Act defines "commerce" as including "trade or commerce with foreign nations." Acquisition of a foreign company falls within Section 7, therefore, only if the acquired firm is actually "engaged" in the foreign commerce of the United States and if its acquisition may lessen competition "in any line of commerce in any section of the country."

A foreign company has been treated as "engaged in commerce" for Clayton Act purposes because it produces and sells a product that flows continuously into the United States (*U.S.* v. *Jos. Schlitz*

Brewing Co., 253 F.Supp. 129 (N.D. Calif. 1966)). By analogy, a foreign business would seem to be "engaged in commerce" if it buys products flowing continuously from the United States, for "commerce" has been held to include the whole sequence of purchase, transportation, and sale (*U.S.* v. *Sanders,* 99 F.Supp. 113 (W.D. Okla. 1951), *aff'd,* 196 F.2d 895 (10th Cir. 1952)). However, there do not seem to be any decisions on the issue whether acquisition of such a foreign buyer could ever be regarded as affecting competition "in any section of the country," that is, whether competition among U.S. exporters occurs in this country or in their foreign markets.

Section 1 of the Sherman Act, on the other hand, prohibits "every contract, combination . . . or conspiracy" in restraint of "commerce among the several states, or with foreign nations," and adds no requirement that the conspirators be themselves "engaged in commerce." A U.S. corporation might be found in violation of the Sherman Act, though not of the Clayton Act, if, in order to increase its power over a foreign market, it should acquire a foreign competitor that never produces for the U.S. market or buys U.S. exports. The Sherman Act's phrase "commerce . . . with foreign nations" has been given broad scope. In *Pacific Seafarers, Inc.* v. *Pacific Far East Line, Inc.,* 404 F.2d 804 (D.C. Cir. 1968), *cert. denied,* 393 U.S. 1093 (1969), it was read as including U.S. flagship transport service between foreign ports.

An acquisition of a foreign company, such as that described in the above paragraph, having no direct connection with U.S. commerce, may be subject to Sherman Act challenge for the acquisition's impact on U.S. export trade. One federal court has based a Sherman Act order requiring dissolution of foreign joint ventures upon a finding that American-owned foreign factories precluded "American competitors from receiving business they might otherwise have received from the markets served by these jointly owned foreign factories. . . . Nor is it any excuse that the use of foreign factories has increased the movement of raw materials from American to foreign shores. We may disregard the point that the books are not in balance when raw materials actually transported are set off against finished products potentially transported. It is more significant that Congress has not said you may choke commerce here if you nourish it there" (*U.S.* v. *Minnesota Mining & Mfg. Co.,* 92 F.Supp. 947, 961–962 (D. Mass. 1950)).

The Sherman Act's impact is not limited to corporations; acquisitions of or by partnerships or associations are also subject to its ban on combinations in restraint of trade.

Section 5 of the FTC Act could be used as a supplement to Section 7 of the Clayton Act; the FTC Act does not require that both the merging companies be "engaged in commerce." Like the Clayton Act, the FTC Act defines "commerce" as including "commerce . . . with foreign nations." Furthermore, its substantive and enforcement provisions are explicitly made applicable, in Section 4 of the Webb-Pomerene Act, 15 U.S.C. § 64, to "unfair methods of competition used in export trade against competitors engaged in export trade, even though the acts . . . are done without the territorial jurisdiction of the United States." Unlike the Sherman Act, the FTC Act can apparently be used against acquisitions that merely threaten to harm competition or to eliminate potential competition. The Supreme Court has given the Commission broad discretion in implementing the language of Section 5. Like the Sherman Act, though, the FTC Act is not limited to corporations.

Government civil proceedings to enforce any one of these statutes may be subject to no time limit. Under Section 7, the legality of a merger is tested by its anticompetitive potentiality at the time of litigation, regardless of how much time has passed and how much the market has changed since the merger was consummated (*U.S. v. duPont,* 353 U.S. 586 (1957)). But see "The Backward Sweep Theory and the Oligopoly Problem," 32 ABA ANTITRUST L. J. 306 (1966). A corporate merger that constitutes a restraint of trade or an unfair method of competition is likely to remain so and thus remain subject to attack under the Sherman or FTC Act.

All the foregoing principles are equally applicable to the second major device by which U.S. companies enter foreign markets, the joint venture. Any doubt that Section 7 of the Clayton Act applies to the transaction whereby a joint venturer obtains his stock ownership in the joint venture was eliminated by the Supreme Court's 1964 decision in *U.S.* v. *Penn-Olin Chemical Co.,* 378 U.S. 158 (1964). In *U.S.* v. *Monsanto Co.,* 1967 Trade Cas. ¶72,001 (W.D. Pa. 1967), the Government obtained a consent order forcing a domestic corporation to drop out of a joint venture with a foreign competitor. The complaint was based on both Section 1 of the Sherman Act and Section 7 of the Clayton Act.

While theoretically there is much that could be done under the antitrust laws to stop foreign acquisitions, they have apparently not yet been selected by enforcement officials as an appropriate area for pioneering on a large scale. Despite the ruling in the *Schlitz* case, foreign acquisitions as such have been attacked by the Government only incidentally in litigation aimed primarily at consolidations affecting domestic commerce. In the Government's view, the *Gillette* case involves a foreign acquisition that would eliminate a strong future competitor for the domestic shaving equipment industry and one that, assuming it to be a product-extension or conglomerate merger, clearly falls within either paragraph 18(a)(i) or paragraph 18(a)(iv) of its Merger Guidelines, 1 Trade Reg. Rep. ¶4510 (1968).

Any extensive antitrust enforcement program in foreign commerce would probably be coordinated, through action of higher executive authority, with other Government programs affecting foreign trade, including those related to the balance of payments, national defense, foreign aid, and tariffs. In the present climate of antitrust enforcement, it seems probable that the threat of antitrust enforcement action hangs over the acquisition of a foreign company only if that acquisition is part of a larger anticompetitive scheme, or if the acquired company is a competitor of the buyer that does business in the United States or is a likely potential competitor in the United States market.

Use of the antitrust laws to eliminate American ownership and support of foreign competition reducing the export trade of the United States would not be easy. Application of the Clayton Act's relatively broad antimerger provisions would raise jurisdictional problems. See Interview with Donald Turner, 37 ABA ANTITRUST L. J. 290, 304 (April 4, 1968). Efforts to coordinate strong antitrust enforcement with such other unrelated policies as balance of payments might result in distortions of antitrust law. As now written, the antitrust laws are designed to "yield the best allocation of our economic resources" (*Northern Pacific Ry. Co.* v. *U.S.*, 356 U.S. 1, 4 (1958)). Protection of one area of the business community from competitive encroachments by another, e.g., U.S. exporters from U.S.-owned foreign factories, has always been regarded as inconsistent with that purpose.

The recent increase in private antitrust litigation is also unlikely to raise any threat to foreign acquisitions by U.S. business enterprises. Antitrust litigation tends to be lengthy, costly, and uncertain in outcome. If the suit complains of conduct affecting foreign enterprises and foreign commerce, the complexities, costs, length, and uncertainty of the litigation would probably increase. Discovery programs could become unmanageable when access to foreign document files becomes necessary. Problems of market definition and proof of anticompetitive impact take on new dimensions. It is not surprising, therefore, that private antitrust litigation has concentrated on domestic commerce.

4. Supreme Court Section 7 Opinions

Question: *Following the* Brown Shoe *decision, what clarification has the Supreme Court given to the Clayton Act's prohibition of anticompetitive corporate mergers of competitors or suppliers and customers?*

In *U.S.* v. *Brown Shoe Co., Inc.,* 370 U.S. 294 (1962), the Supreme Court affirmed a district court judgment that Section 7 prohibits the merger of two vertically integrated shoe manufacturer-retailers. The court noted that the four largest shoe manufacturers (including Brown) were found to have 23 percent of the market; the 24 largest manufacturers, about 35 percent. Brown, the acquiring company, was the fourth largest shoe manufacturer. Kinney, the acquired company, was the twelfth largest manufacturer and operated the nation's biggest independent chain of family shoe stores. The Court found a trend in the industry toward vertical integration increasing foreclosure of retail shoe outlets from independent manufacturers, as well as a continuing increase in concentration in manufacturing. The Court concluded that since the merger involved the largest vertical foreclosure possible in the industry, and since the merged company would hold from 5 percent to 57 percent of at least one retail line of commerce in 118 geographic markets, the merger violated Section 7.

In *U.S.* v. *Bliss & Laughlin, Inc.,* 202 F.Supp. 334 (S.D. Calif. 1962), *rev'd,* 371 U.S. 70 (1962), *dismissed,* 1963 Trade Cas. ¶70,734 (S.D. Calif. 1963), the district court had dismissed the complaint after trial but before the decision in *Brown Shoe.* As if to underscore the landmark character of that decision, the Supreme Court, at the suggestion of the Government, vacated the judgment of dismissal and remanded the case for reconsideration in light of *Brown Shoe.*

The Court reversed a district court's dismissal after trial of a complaint challenging under Section 1 of the Sherman Act and Section 7 of the Clayton Act the merger of two commercial banks (*U.S.* v. *Phila. Nat'l. Bank,* 374 U.S. 321 (1963)). The merging banks were the second and third largest of the 42 commercial banks in the relevant geographic market. The Court found a substantial trend toward commercial-banking concentration in the market, which was reflected in the prominence of mergers in the prior growth of the merging banks. The merged bank would have held at least 30 percent of the relevant market, raising the share of the two largest banks from 45 percent to 60 percent. The Court characterized the case as "only a straightforward problem of application to particular facts" of the test stated in *Brown Shoe,* and emphasized the factual character of both product and geographic market definition issues. It went on to hold, though, that "a merger which produces a firm controlling an undue percentage share of the relevant market, and [which] results in a significant increase in the concentration of firms in that market is so inherently likely to lessen competition substantially that it must be enjoined in the absence of evidence clearly showing that the merger is not likely to have such anti-competitive effects." This refinement of the *Brown Shoe* standard is to be applied "only with respect to mergers whose size makes them inherently suspect in light of Congress' design in Section 7 to prevent undue concentration." Since a market share of 30 percent was held to threaten undue concentration, the district court's judgment of dismissal was reversed.

In *U.S.* v. *El Paso Natural Gas Co.,* 376 U.S. 651 (1964), *consent judgment,* 1965 Trade Cas. ¶71,453 (D. Utah 1965); 291 F.Supp. 3 (D. Utah 1968), *remanded,* 395 U.S 464 (1969), *pet. for rehearing denied,* 399 U.S. 937 (1970), *motion for modification of mandate denied,* 405 U.S. 1061 (1972), the Court reversed a district court judgment of dismissal after trial. The Justice Department's Section 7 complaint attacked the acquisition, by the sole supplier of out-of-state natural gas in California, of "the only other important interstate pipeline west of the Rocky Mountains." The fact that the acquired pipeline had never succeeded in its efforts to break into the California market did not, the Court held, disprove its position as a competitive factor in California. "Unsuccessful bidders are no less competitors than the successful one. The presence of two or more suppliers gives buyers a choice." In the natural gas industry, "the competition . . . is for the new increments of demand that may emerge with an expanding population and with an expanding industrial or household use of gas." The Court repeated a declaration of the *Brown Shoe* opinion that the concern of Congress when it enacted Section 7 of the Clayton Act was with "the probabilities, not certainties."

In *U.S.* v. *Continental Oil Co.,* 377 U.S. 161 (1964), *dismissed,* 1965 Trade Cas. ¶71, 557 (D.N.M. 1965), *remanded,* 387 U.S. 424 (1967); *summary judgment for the Government,* 1967 Trade Cas. ¶72,292 (D.N.M. 1967), *final judgment,* 1968 Trade Cas. ¶72,374 (D.N.M. 1968), *aff'd,* 393 U.S. 79 (1968), there was an appeal from a summary judgment for the defendants on the pleadings, depositions, and exhibits. Without briefs, oral argument, or opinion, the Court vacated the judgment and remanded for trial a complaint seeking separation of the largest of New Mexico's seven oil refineries from Continental Oil Co. Continental is described in the complaint as the ninth largest crude oil producer in the country and the 14th largest refiner. In its jurisdictional statement to the Supreme Court, the Justice Department had asserted that triable disputes existed in the case as to "(1) whether the State of New Mexico constituted a relevant submarket; (2) whether the two companies were in competition prior to the acquisition; (3) whether the acquiring company had engaged in anticompetitive conduct following the acquisition; and (4) whether there were mitigating circumstances which justified the acquisition."

In *U.S.* v. *Aluminum Co. of America,* 377 U.S. 271 (1964), *judgment entered,* 1967 Trade Cas. ¶71,980 (N.D.N.Y. 1966), *judgment modified,* 1967 Trade Cas. ¶71,973 (N.D.N.Y. 1966), *vacated as moot,* 389 U.S. 49 (1967), the Court reversed a district judge who had dismissed after trial a complaint attacking Alcoa's acquisition of the fourth largest "independent" aluminum electric cable manufacturer. In defining the product market in which the competitive effect of the merger was to be measured, the Court ruled that any combination of submarkets that in the aggregate constitute a product market is also a line of commerce under Section 7. The opinion separated insulated aluminum conductor from insulated copper conductor, although they compete with each other, and combined it with bare aluminum conductor into one relevant market or line of commerce.

Although the acquired cable producer accounted for only about 1.3 percent of the nation's output of aluminum conductor, the Court decided that conditions in the industry were such that an acquisition of this size was "unreasonably likely to produce a substantial lessening of competition." Just prior to the merger, Alcoa, the leading producer of aluminum conductor, controlled 27.8 percent of the market; and, with its three leading competitors, it controlled more than 76 percent of the market. As the Court read Section 7, its basic premise is "that competition will be most vital 'when there are many sellers, none of which has any significant market.' *United States* v. *Philadelphia National Bank,* 374 U.S. at 363. It would seem that the situation in the aluminum industry may be oligopolistic."

In *U.S.* v. *Penn-Olin Chemical Co.,* 378 U.S. 158 (1964), *dismissed,* 246 F.Supp. 917 (D. Del. 1965), *aff'd,* 389 U.S. 308 (1967), the Court applied Section 7 to a joint venture. The district court had dismissed after trial a complaint against two companies' formation of a joint venture to erect and operate a manufacturing plant in a geographical area in which neither company had previously done any significant amount of business. The opinion placed its emphasis upon the importance of potential competition to the maintenance of competitive market conditions. The Court held a joint venture may violate Section 7 if one of the partners might with reasonable probability have entered the market while the other "remained at the edge of the market, continually threatening to enter." Directing a determination whether this standard was met, the Court remanded the case to the district court, which had based its dismissal of the complaint on a finding that there was no reasonable probability that both joint venturers would have built a plant in the geographic area involved had there been no joint venture.

Potential competition also played a part in *U.S.* v. *Continental*

Can Co., 378 U.S. 441 (1964). There, a district judge had dismissed, at the close of the Government's case, a complaint attacking the acquisition of the nation's third largest glass-container producer by the second largest metal-container manufacturer. In the Supreme Court, glass and metal containers were recognized as two separate lines of commerce, "But given the area of effective competition between these lines, there is necessarily implied one or more other lines of commerce embracing both industries." The Court found "a rather general confrontation between metal and glass containers and competition between them for the same end uses which is insistent, continuous, effective and quantitywise very substantial." The Court cited uses for which metal has replaced glass and for which glass has replaced metal as the leading container. "Though the interchangeability of use may not be so complete and the cross-elasticity of demand not so immediate as in the case of most intra-industry mergers, there is over the long run the kind of customer response to innovation and other competitive stimuli that brings the competition between these two industries within Section 7's competition-reserving proscriptions." The inappropriateness of rigid rules in product-market definition was emphasized, as well as the lack of necessity for accurate delineation of the product market's scope or accurate measurement of market shares.

The Court's previous Section 7 decisions were read as establishing that "market shares are the primary indicia of market power but a judgment under Section 7 is not to be made by any single qualitative or quantitative test. The merger must be viewed functionally in the context of the particular market involved, its structure, history and probable future. Where a merger is of such size as to be inherently suspect, elaborate proof of market structure, market behavior and probable anti-competitive effects may be dispensed with in view of Section 7's design to prevent undue concentration. Moreover, the competition with which Section 7 deals includes not only existing competition but that which is sufficiently probable and imminent." The Court decided that, since the market share of the acquiring company in the market for glass and metal containers was increased by the merger from 21.9 percent to 25 percent and the number of firms holding 70 percent of the market was reduced from 6 to 5, a prima facie showing of unlawfulness under Section 7 had been made. The judgment was reversed and the case remanded for presentation of a defense. On remand, the court approved divestiture of nine of Continental's plants and permitted the corporation to retain two others (*U.S.* v. *Continental Can Co., Inc.,* 1964 Trade Cas. ¶71,264 (S.D.N.Y. 1964)).

Shortly after this string of successes in the Supreme Court, the Justice Department won a litigated merger case at the district court level—the first such victory in nine decisions handed down after the

Brown Shoe case. The Federal District Court for Southern New York enjoined the acquisition by the world's largest copper producer of the country's second largest insulated wire and cable fabricator (*U.S.* v. *Kennecott Copper Corp.,* 231 F.Supp. 95 (S.D.N.Y. 1964), *aff'd,* 381 U.S. 414 (1965)). The competitive effect of the merger was measured in two product markets. With respect to paper-insulated power cable, the acquisition was a horizontal merger of competitors, one holding 19.6 percent of the market and the other holding 2.1 percent. Noting that the Supreme Court's Alcoa decision outlawed a 1.3 percent acquisition, the district judge declared these percentages high enough to suggest a probable substantial lessening of competition. Much of the opinion was devoted to the vertical aspects of the case, the combination of a copper producer and a copper fabricator. The district judge found that the main purpose of the acquisition of the fabricator was to assure the acquiring company a future market for the sale of its refined copper, the other product market considered. With repeated references to the vertical-integration discussed in the *Brown Shoe* case, the district court stressed the trend toward vertical integration in the copper industry. Recognizing that the acquisition was motivated in large part by a fear that the independent fabricators might cease to exist, the court reasoned that the acquiring company "has made the problem even worse by removing an independent from the market and then competing with the remaining independents."

The Justice Department's Supreme Court victories in merger cases eliminated much of the previous uncertainty in this area. Experts generally agree that any consolidation of two healthy competitors with any substantial share of a significant market will be said by the Supreme Court to violate Section 7. It may also be that the rule is similar for vertical mergers. Justices Harlan and Stewart, dissenting in the *Continental Can* case, flatly stated that the Court was "laying down a 'per se' rule that mergers between two large companies in related industries are presumptively unlawful."

There may still be industries with interstate enterprises so small that combination of two of them would be regarded as no substantial threat to competition. But there is a feeling among many antitrust lawyers that the rules now established give Section 7 such a broad scope that the extent of its application to conventional horizontal and vertical mergers will in large part depend upon work-allocation and policy decisions in the Antitrust Division and the Federal Trade Commission. The Supreme Court, in cases like *Continental Can* and *Penn-Olin,* has given the Justice Department much latitude in constructing a relevant market.

There remains some uncertainty about how post-acquisition evidence is to be used in measuring the anticompetitive effect of a merger. The enforcement agencies and the courts are in agreement that such evidence can be used to show adverse competitive effect, but the FTC indicated in *FTC* v. *Procter and Gamble Co.,* 386 U.S. 568 (1967), that, unless there are special circumstances, the rule does not work in converse to let the merging companies present post-acquisition figures showing lack of competitive effect. While the Supreme Court refused to give any weight to post-acquisition conduct in the *Continental Can* case, it was dealing only with a situation where the merged companies' conduct may have been influenced by the pressure of the pending Section 7 suit.

Another area in which some antitrust lawyers see issues still to be resolved is that of possible defenses. In the last paragraph of his *Brown Shoe* opinion, Chief Justice Warren left open to merging companies the privilege of showing "mitigating factors, such as the business failure or the inadequate resources of one of the parties that may have prevented it from maintaining its competitive position" or "a demonstrated need for combination to enable small companies to enter into a more meaningful competition with those dominating the relevant markets," but in *U.S.* v. *Bethlehem Steel Corp.,* 168 F.Supp. 576 (S.D.N.Y. 1958), the second and sixth ranking steel producers were denied the right to combine for the purpose of competing more vigorously with the leading producer.

5. Horizontal Mergers

(a) Question: *Are all mergers of competitors prohibited?*

The Justice Department challenged the 1960 acquisition by Von's Grocery Co., Los Angeles' third ranking grocery chain, of Shopping Bag Stores, the area's sixth largest grocery chain, as a violation of Section 7 of the Clayton Act. Not satisfied with the evidence on probable anticompetitive effect, the district court dismissed the case (*U.S.* v. *Von's Grocery Co.,* 233 F.Supp. 976 (S.D. Calif. 1964)).

In its appeal to the Supreme Court, the Justice Department anticipated that the case would "largely determine the structure of the market for retail groceries in the important Los Angeles metropolitan area. Even more important, it will provide a significant guideline for similar retail sectors of the economy throughout the Nation." In its brief, the Government proposed for markets where economic power is relatively dispersed a rule of "presumptive illegality" for a merger between direct competitors (1) when there is a significant tendency in the direction of undue concentration in the market and (2) when the merger appreciably increases the existing level of concentration.

While the Supreme Court did not expressly adopt that proposed rule it did find a Section 7 violation (384 U.S. 270 (1966)). The purpose of the 1950 amendment to Section 7, Justice Black's opinion pointed out, "was to prevent economic concentration in the American economy by keeping a large number of small competitors in business." In the Los Angeles retail grocery market, the Court saw "exactly the threatening trend toward concentration which Congress wanted to halt." The number of small grocers had been declining and continued to decline after the merger. This change in the number of grocery companies was accompanied "by a large number of significant absorptions of the small companies by the larger companies." A Government expert witness testified that between 1949 and 1958 nine of the top 20 chains acquired 126 stores from their smaller competitors. In that period, Von's increased the number of its stores from 14 to 27 and Shopping Bag increased its stores from 15 to 34. Combined, they became the second largest grocery chain in the Los Angeles area, with 7.5 percent of the market. "What we have . . . is simply the case of two already powerful companies merging in a way which makes them even more powerful than they were before. If ever such a merger would not violate Section 7, certainly it does when it takes place in a market characterized by a long and continuous trend toward fewer and fewer owner-competitors which is exactly the sort of trend which Congress, with power to do so, declared must be arrested."

In a concurring opinion, Justice White explained that he did not read the Court's opinion as saying "that in any industry exhibiting a decided trend toward concentration, any merger between competing firms violates Section 7, absent some special proof to the contrary."

Two weeks later, evidence of a concentration trend in the beer industry caused the Court to reinstate a suit to undo the 1958 acquisition of Blatz Brewing Co., the nation's eighteenth largest brewer, by Pabst Brewing Co., then the tenth largest (*U.S.* v. *Pabst Brewing Co.,* 384 U.S. 546 (1966)). Again Justice Black wrote the Court's opinion. He described evidence to the effect that the merger made Pabst the nation's fifth largest brewer with 4.9 percent of the industry's total sales and Wisconsin's largest brewer, with 23.95 percent of all the sales made in that state. By 1961, Pabst had increased its share of the national beer market to 5.83 percent and its share of the state market to 27.41 percent. Between 1934 and 1961, the number of breweries operating in the United States declined from 714 to 229, the opinion reported. During the last four years of that period, the total number of competitors selling beer in the United States dropped from 206 to 162, and the number of companies selling beer in Wisconsin declined from 77 to 54. At the same time, the nation's ten largest brewers increased their combined shares of sales from 45.06 percent in 1957 to 52.6 percent in 1961. In the state of Wisconsin, the four leading sellers accounted for 47.74 percent of the state's sales in 1957 and increased their share to 58.62 percent by 1961. In the three-state area of Wisconsin, Illinois, and Michigan, the number of major brewers selling beer dropped from 104 to 86 between 1957 and 1961, and the eight leading sellers increased their combined shares of the market from 58.93 percent to 67.65 percent.

Pabst contended that this concentration trend is irrelevant because the Government failed to show that the trend is the result of mergers. Justice Black found no burden on the Government to supply such proof. "Congress, in passing Section 7 and in amending it with the Celler-Kefauver Anti-Merger Amendment, was concerned with arresting concentration in the American economy, whatever its cause, in its incipiency." In the district court, the suit had been dismissed at the close of the Government's case (233 F.Supp. 475 (E.D. Wisc. 1964)). The district court had ruled, first, that the Government had not shown any probability of anticompetitive effects in the nationwide market, and, second, that the evidence was inadequate to show that either Wisconsin or the three-state area was a "relevant geographic market within which the probable effect of the acquisition of Blatz by Pabst should be tested." In holding that the Government had proven a Section 7 violation, subject to any defense Pabst might present, Justice Black objected to the geographic-market proof requirements imposed by the district judge. Section 7 "requires merely that the government prove the merger has a substantial anticompetitive effect somewhere in the United States—'in any section' of the United States. This phrase does not call for the delineation of 'section of the country' by metes and bounds as a surveyor would lay off a plot of ground. . . . Congress did not seem to be troubled about the exact spot competition might be lessened; it simply intended to outlaw mergers which threatened competition in any or all parts of the country. Proof of the section of the country where the anticompetitive effect exists is entirely subsidiary to the crucial question in this and every Section 7 case which is whether a merger may substantially lessen competition anywhere in the United States."

In the *Von's Grocery* case, Justices Stewart and Harlan dissented, maintaining there is only one thread of consistency in the Court's Section 7 decisions: "the government always wins." They concurred in reinstatement of the action against the Pabst-Blatz merger but only on the ground that the Government's evidence is in fact sufficient to establish, subject to rebuttal, that Wisconsin and the three-state area are both proper sections of the country in which to measure competitive effect. They did not subscribe to Justice Black's doctrine limiting the Government's obligation to prove a geographic market. They would require the evidence to include a definition of "an area in which the parties to the merger or acquisition compete, and around which there exists economic barriers that significantly impede the entry of new competitors."

Justice Black's views on proving geographic market had the support of only five justices. Justice Fortas filed a concurring statement arguing that "unless both the product and the geographical market are carefully defined, neither analysis nor result in antitrust is likely to be of acceptable quality"—a position in line with the views he later expressed for a majority of the Court in *U.S.* v. *Grinnell Corp.,* 384 U.S. 563 (1966). Justice White joined the majority only "in so far as it holds the merger of Pabst and Blatz may substantially lessen competition in the beer industry in the nation as a whole."

In its first opinion interpreting the 1950 Celler-Kefauver amendments (*Brown Shoe Co.* v. *U.S.,* 370 U.S. 294 (1962)), the Court found a Section 7 violation in the merger of two competing manufacturers controlling only 4 percent and .5 percent of their market, but the opinion used language that district judges later relied upon to reject a series of government attacks on mergers. Those district court decisions were reversed by the Supreme Court, and in *U.S.* v. *Alcoa,* 377 U.S. 271 (1964), the Court outlawed the acquisition of a producer who accounted for only about 1.3 percent of sales in the relevant market. The Supreme Court opinions in the grocery and beer cases further strengthen the prohibition against horizontal mergers. Some lawyers think the holding in *Von's Grocery* limits the impact of the Court's suggestion in the *Brown Shoe* case that it might be possible to demonstrate a "need for combination to enable small companies to enter into a more meaningful competition with those dominating the relevant markets." Justice Black made reference to that part of the *Brown Shoe* opinion but refused to apply it to consolidation of "two of the most successful and largest companies in the area."

In addition, the *Pabst* opinion's rejection of any necessity for showing a causal relationship between a concentration trend and mergers indicates that the law may inhibit consolidations of competitors even in those industries where they produce more efficient methods. The majority in the *Pabst* case eased the Government's burden of proving relevant geographic market. It is important to note, however, that the Court did not eliminate the necessity for identifying a relevant "section of the country" but merely said it need not be marked off "by metes and bounds as a surveyor would lay off a plot of ground." (It may be difficult to see how the Government would go about compiling market-share and other market statistics without first marking off geographical boundaries for the market.)

The Justice Department has not brought criminal prosecutions against companies for merging illegally, although, as discussed above, Section 1 of the Sherman Act has been applied to mergers, but, if a competitor is acquired, it may be that about the only thing the Government must prove to get a Clayton Act divestiture order is that there is a trend toward concentration in the industry involved. FTC statistics plus other testimony collected at Senate Antitrust Subcommittee hearings on economic concentration suggest there are few industries without a trend toward concentration. Application of Section 7 to mergers between competitors may be limited only by manpower shortages in the two enforcement agencies and their sometimes divergent views as to proper enforcement policy.

(b) Question: *Is any increase in market share ever permitted?*

In *Stanley Works* v. *FTC,* 469 F.2d 498 (2nd Cir. 1972), the court of appeals, over the vigorous dissent of Judge Mansfield, upheld an FTC determination that Stanley's acquisition of Amerock was unlawful under Section 7 of the Clayton Act. The parties to the FTC proceeding stipulated that sales of cabinet hardware products in the nation constituted the appropriate product and geographic markets and that there were no relevant submarkets. Sales in that market amounted to $76–80 million in 1965. The market was concentrated, with the top four firms accounting for 49–51 percent of the sales. Amerock, the acquired firm, was the largest firm in the market, with sales approximating $18 million, or about 22–24 percent of the market. Stanley was the 10th largest, with sales of about $800,000, or a market share of only 1 percent. On the other hand, Stanley was much the larger of the merging firms in terms of assets; its assets amounted to $125 million, compared with $25 million for Amerock.

Section 7 of the Clayton Act does not apply unless the effect of a merger "may be substantially to lessen competition." Although the basis of the Commission's decision was in dispute, two appellate court judges agreed with what they determined to be the Commission's conclusion, that the acquisition eliminated significant actual and potential competition. Analyzing the "effects" in the instant case, the court held that in the already concentrated cabinet hardware industry, in which there were few sellers and in which the four leading sellers dominated approximately 50 percent of the market, a merger involving the leading firm, controlling 22–24 percent of the market, with a firm like Stanley, would seriously threaten substantial anticompetitive consequences. This conclusion presumed that the 1 percent increase in market share brought about by the Stanley-Amerock merger was not so slight as to avoid being a threat to competition.

What factors may one refer to in attempting to predict whether an increase in market share is so small as to avoid the proscription of Section 7? The *Stanley-Amerock* court seemed swayed by the cumulative effect of several factors: 1) the degree of market concentration prior to the merger and 2) the relative position of the merged parties in that market thereafter. The Commission's determination that the relevant market was already concentrated at the time of merger required the court to treat Stanley's acquisition of Amerock with suspicion. Quoting from the decision of the Supreme Court in *U.S.* v. *Continental Can,* 378 U.S. 441 (1964), the court said: "[W]here there has been a 'history of tendency toward concentration in the industry' tendencies toward further concentration 'are to be curbed in their incipiency.' . . . Where 'concentration is already great, the importance of preventing even slight increases in concentration and so preserving the possibility of eventual deconcentration is correspondingly great.' " The court concluded that where the four leading firms have 49–51 percent of the market, the market is concentrated for antitrust purposes.

The court in *Stanley* agreed with a Commission determination that the merger of the tenth ranking firm (1 percent of the market) with the top firm (22–24 percent of the market) would increase concentration at the top of the market, the so-called market position factor, and "might have a 'tipping effect' . . . turning a concentrated market manifesting limited signs of price competition into a rigid, lifeless market tending toward even greater concentration and economic enervation." This conclusion of anticompetitiveness was further supported by statements of Stanley personnel that "a *de novo* entry might contribute to an on-going, industry-wide decline in prices and profits, but that an entry by way of an acquisition might lead to a reversal of the decline." Finding that the relevant market was already concentrated and that the merger would increase concentration at the top of the market, the court concluded that the combined market share of the merging parties was increased above a *de minimis* amount. In support of its decision proscribing the merger, the court cited several Supreme Court opinions condemning acquisitions of firms possessing 1.47 and 1.3 percent of the market, respectively.

It may be that acceptable increases in market power are inversely proportional to the level of market concentration and to the resulting position of the merged parties in the market. That is, what might be acceptable for a nonranking firm in a nonconcentrated market might not be for the same firm operating within a more concentrated market, and would not be for a ranking firm doing business in a concentrated industry.

In Judge Mansfield's view, the parties' stipulation of the relevant market did not foreclose further inquiry as to the actual impact of the acquisition upon competition:

"Product markets and market percentages, whether or not stipulated, are of significance in determining the probable effect of a merger on competition where they reflect actual competition between the parties. But to determine whether a merger forecloses *actual* competition, one looks to the *actual* competitive facts (the competitive overlap between the parties) within the given product market rather than halt at overall market percentages and look no further. This process does not, as the majority suggests, change the parties' stipulation as to the overall market, or create distinct lines of commerce or sub-markets. It merely judges actual competitive effects according to economic realities within the stipulated market rather than ignore undisputed competitive facts of record."

Noting that there were two kinds of cabinet hardware, residential and institutional, and that there were six different channels of distribution, Judge Mansfield calculated that the actual competitive overlap between Stanley and Amerock amounted to only 0.35 percent of the market. Having also questioned firm size in that market as a significant factor, since "small companies thrive and have increased in number," he concluded that the anticompetitive effect of the acquisition was insignificant.

Stanley Works presents a classic confrontation between differing points of view as to proper method of assessing the anticompetitive effects of an acquisition. On the one hand, there is Judge Mansfield's detailed market analysis; on the other, there is the majority's reliance on bare market figures. The latter approach is best exemplified, perhaps, by the Department of Justice's own guidelines (1 Trade Reg. Rep. ¶4510 (1968)), which are consistent with the court's decision. Although Judge Mansfield's approach may be the more sophisticated, the majority's is more in keeping with the Supreme Court trend toward simpler rules in merger cases. (Compare the majority opinion in *U.S.* v. *Von's Grocery Co.,* 384 U.S. 270 (1966), with Justice Stewart's dissenting opinion, 384 U.S. at 281.) The majority in *Stanley Works* evidently felt constrained from further inquiry into the competitive situation by the stipulation that there were no relevant submarkets, and by Stanley's own memoranda indicating its belief that the acquisition might have a stabilizing effect on prices in the industry. It appears that the stipulation as to the relevant market was most critical to the final outcome.

This case may stand for the proposition that a merger becomes increasingly precarious as concentration increases toward the top of the market. This means that increased concentration at the low end of the market is more likely to be tolerated than at the top, even though the gain on the bottom side is the greater of the two. Therefore, the *de minimis* line is drawn, according to the *Stanley* court, at the point where an acquisition begins to have a "tipping effect," bringing to an already concentrated market substantial anticompetitive consequences.

6. "Product Extension" Mergers

Question: *What has the Supreme Court said about mergers of companies not directly competing but having products in related markets?*

In 1957, the Federal Trade Commission filed a Section 7 Clayton Act complaint attacking the acquisition, 60 days previously, of the assets of Clorox Chemical Co., the nation's leading producer of household liquid bleach, by Procter & Gamble Co., the leading manufacturer of household cleansing agents other than bleach. This combination was unlike most mergers to which Section 7 of the Clayton Act had previously been applied. The merger was not "horizontal"—between companies that produce or sell the same product or interchangeable products—nor was it "vertical"— between companies that, prior to consolidation, had a supplier-customer relationship.

The Commission decided that the merger was illegal, reasoning (in an opinion by Commissioner Elman) primarily in terms of the standards applicable to "conglomerate" mergers, that is, those mergers "involving firms which deal in unrelated products"; but the transaction was called "a product-extension merger"—"the merger of sellers of functionally closely related products which are not, however, close substitutes." The product-extension merger was said to be "another variant of the conventional horizontal merger" (*Procter & Gamble Co.*, 63 F.T.C. 1465, 1543 (1963)).

In upholding the FTC order, the Supreme Court stated: "All mergers are within the reach of Section 7 and all must be tested by the same standard, whether they are classified as horizontal, vertical, conglomerate or other" (*FTC* v. *Procter & Gamble Co.*, 386 U.S. 568 (1967)). The need for the words "or other" became apparent when the Court, like the FTC, labeled the P&G-Clorox combine a "product-extension" merger. "The products of the acquired company are complementary to those of the acquiring company and may be produced with similar facilities, marketed through the same channels and in the same manner, and advertised

by the same media." Justice Douglas, writing for the Court, found
the anticompetitive effects of the merger as follows: "(1) The substitution of the powerful acquiring firm for the smaller, but already
dominant, firm may substantially reduce the competitive structure
of the industry by raising entry barriers and by dissuading the
smaller firms from aggressively competing; (2) The acquisition eliminates the potential competition of the acquiring firm."

It was not disputed that household liquid bleach was the relevant
product market, and the relevant geographic markets were the entire
country and a number of separate regional markets. According to
the Court, the household liquid bleach industry was heavily concentrated, and bleach was a distinctive product with no close substitutes.
High shipping costs, combined with low sales prices, made it
unprofitable to ship bleach more than 300 miles from the point of
manufacture. Most manufacturers were limited to a single region
because they had only one plant.

Clorox was described by the Court as the only manufacturer of
household liquid bleach that sells nationally. At the time of the
merger Clorox was making approximately 50 percent of national
sales. Its nearest rival accounted for just under 16 percent of total
industry sales and limited its distribution to areas west of the Mis-
sissippi. The six largest manufacturers of bleach controlled almost
80 percent of the market, and the remaining 20 percent was divided
among more than 200 small producers. Territorial limitations on
distribution were said to give Clorox greater dominance than was
shown by figures for national sales. Clorox's seven principal competitors did no business in New England, the Middle Atlantic States,
or metropolitan New York. In those areas its market share was 56
percent, 72 percent, and 64 percent respectively.

The Court stated that, since all liquid bleaches are chemically
identical, advertising and sales promotion are vital. In 1957 Clorox
spent almost $3.7 million on advertising. Another $1.7 million was
spent for other promotional activities. The FTC found these heavy
expenditures went far to explain why Clorox had secured so high a
market share even though the retail price for its bleach was equal
to or sometimes higher than those of its competitors.

P&G was characterized by the Court as a large, diversified manufacturer of low-price, high-turnover household products. At the
time of the acquisition, P&G accounted for 54.4 percent of all
packaged detergent sales. The three leading manufacturers in this
market accounted for 80 percent of total sales. In 1957 P&G was
the nation's largest advertiser, spending more than $80 million on
advertising and $47 million on sales promotion. According to the
Court, P&G enjoyed substantial advantages in advertising and sales
promotion as a result of its large sales volume and its ability to
advertise its products jointly.

The Supreme Court was satisfied that the interjection of P&G into the liquid bleach industry would lessen price competition, which was not regarded as vigorous. The Court said: "there is every reason to assume that the smaller firms would become more cautious in competing due to their fear of retaliation by Procter. It is probable that Procter would become the price leader and that oligopoly would become more rigid." The relatively limited resources available to Clorox and its resulting inability to obtain discounts restricted the amount it could spend on advertising. Even though P&G could not devote its entire budget to advertising Clorox, it could divert a large portion to meet the short term threat of a new entrant. The Court dismissed the argument that possible economies, including advertising economies, can be used as a defense to illegality. Also dismissed as a consideration in determining the legality of the acquisition was evidence that Procter had not engaged in predatory practices and that other producers, subsequent to the merger, were selling more bleach for more money than ever before. The Court noted that the Commission had placed no reliance on the post-acquisition activities of Procter in holding that the acquisition was unlawful. The Court stated: "If the enforcement of Section 7 turned on the existence of actual anti-competitive practices, the congressional policy of thwarting such practices in their incipiency would be frustrated."

The Court agreed with the FTC's conclusion that the Clorox acquisition eliminated P&G as a potential additional competitor—in fact, as the most likely new entrant in the liquid bleach industry. P&G had recently launched a new abrasive cleaner in an industry similar to the liquid bleach industry, and it had wrested leadership from a brand that had in that market an even larger share than Clorox had in its market. Liquid bleach is a natural avenue of diversification, the Court reasoned, since it is complementary to P&G's products, is sold to the same customers through the same channels, and is advertised and merchandised in the same manner.

Much of the interest of the antitrust bar and the business community in the P&G case both before and after the decision was based on a belief that the case had an important bearing on the extent to which Section 7 of the Clayton Act would be applied to conglomerate mergers, but the FTC and the Supreme Court took the P&G-Clorox combination out the the "conglomerate" classification, characterizing the merger as one of "product extension." Nevertheless, some antitrust experts read the opinion as establishing broad principles that could be relied upon by the enforcement agencies in Clayton Act proceedings against conglomerate mergers. The first aspect of the Supreme Court's opinion that one might point to in support of a complaint against a purely "conglomerate" merger is the emphasis it places on the elimination of

P&G as a potential additional producer and marketer of household liquid bleach. It could be argued that any time a company acquires a going business in a new industry it has demonstrated the existence of a desire to enter that industry, even if its only purpose was to obtain a broader, more diversified, and therefore more stable base of operations. (See section III-A-7(b), p. 202, discussing the *Kennecott* case.)

The anticompetitive dangers that the Supreme Court saw for the household bleach market should P&G enter with its "deep pocket" for advertising and promotion are matters that could also arise as the result of a purely conglomerate merger. There must be many industries in which the substitition of a huge, powerful outsider for one of the major competitors already in the industry could be said to "reduce the competitive structure of the industry by raising entry barriers and by dissuading the smaller firms from aggressively competing."

The opinion relied on the close relationship between household bleach and the products already marketed by P&G. In effect, the Court saw in the merger a quasi-horizontal element that will not be present in a purely conglomerate merger. The Court was dealing not only with related products or markets but also with the largest firms in each of those two markets. Clorox was the largest producer of liquid household bleach, described by the Court as the "dominant" firm in that market. There are few industries that can be said to have a single "dominant" firm, so most purely conglomerate acquisitions might be distinguished from P&G-Clorox on that ground. The product made and sold by Clorox had the same chemical formula as the product marketed by its competitors, a factor of some significance in the Supreme Court's and the FTC's unfriendly attitude toward the deep pocket advertising P&G might engage in. Therefore, the *Clorox* opinion could be distinguished by counsel defending an acquisition of a leader in an industry whose members sold products that varied in style, quality, and usefulness.

Each of these three factors was stressed by the FTC majority when it struck down General Foods' acquisition of SOS (*General Foods Corp.,* 69 F.T.C. 380 (1966), *aff'd,* 386 F.2d 936 (3rd Cir. 1967)). The Commission's 4–1 majority stressed the structural similarity between the household steel-wool market and the liquid bleach market and rested its holding squarely on its P&G-Clorox decision. (Commissioner Elman dissented, emphasizing the absence of any suggestion that General Foods could be considered a potential competitor in the steel-wool soap-pad market.) Like P&G, General Foods is engaged in the sale of a broad range of low-cost, high-turnover household consumer goods sold in grocery stores and supermarkets through massive advertising and sales promotion.

Also, household steel wool, like liquid bleach, can be marketed by the same techniques and through the same distributional outlets and is purchased by the housewife at the same time as other products sold by General Foods. Advertising is a central factor in the marketing of steel-wool pads, and the various brands of pads are virtually indistinguishable from each other.

The reliance the Supreme Court placed on the evidence that the Clorox acquisition eliminated P&G as a potential additional competitor in the household bleach market could be an important means of distinguishing that combination from most purely conglomerate mergers. The evidence cited by Justice Douglas for his finding that Procter was a likely entrant dealt with the close economic relationship between P&G's past activities and the production and marketing of household liquid bleach, with the ready availability of raw materials and equipment for bleach production, and with other similar economic factors.

Some experts see in the Supreme Court's decision another manifestation of the Court's conviction that any hardening of a market situation with few sellers is bad per se. They feel that the Court would have reached the same result if the Clorox acquisition had been accomplished by U.S. Steel, for example, instead of P&G. This line of thinking minimizes the importance of many of the elements specifically mentioned by Justice Douglas—the lack of quality differences in the industry's products, the close relationship between household bleach and P&G's regular line of products, and the elimination of a possible new competitor. Such discussion may be purely academic, for it seems doubtful that the enforcement agencies have either the time or the inclination to mount an antimerger attack of the scope that the Court might allow. Despite the result in P&G-Clorox, the FTC agreed to a consent order that let P&G keep most of the assets of the largest independent coffee company in the country, a firm about four times as big as Clorox (*Procter & Gamble Co.*, 71 F.T.C. 135 (1967)).

The Commission was breaking new ground in its proceeding against the Clorox acquisition. In early litigation against conventional horizontal and vertical mergers, the FTC and the Antitrust Division started with the combinations they regarded as the most clear-cut violations of Section 7. Then the *Phila. Nat'l. Bank* and the *Brown Shoe* opinions of the Supreme Court made it clear that Section 7's restrictions extend far beyond combinations of the giants in an industry. While the size and economic power of the companies involved in the Procter-Clorox merger gave this case an economic magnitude, the Commission denied adopting a "view that bigness per se is anti-competitive or undesirable." The opinion emphasized "disparity of size, not absolute size" and said that size disparity may have little or no competitive significance in other industries. What makes size disparity an important factor in the Clorox acquisition was said to be Procter's control of overpowering marketing machinery. Procter's power to out-advertise and out-promote the rest of the liquid bleach industry is related to four of the five major factors cited by the Commission as showing the illegality of the merger.

It is disputed whether the Commission's reliance upon Procter's advertising strength should be considered a general attack on the use of advertising to maintain or enlarge one's share of a market. The Commission anticipated criticism and gave assurance of the Commission's belief that "advertising performs a socially and economically useful function" and that it "should stimulate competition, and, by increasing the sale of the advertised product, lower the unit cost of that product." The circumstances said to make the Procter-Clorox combination different are that (1) it involves a homogeneous product (2) "produced under conditions of oligopoly."

7. Potential Competition Theory and "Toehold" Acquisitions—the FTC Views

(a) Question: *May a potential market entrant make an acquisition for the purpose of market entry?*

The Supreme Court has said that the elimination of potential competition can be a significant factor in the assessment of competitive effects in merger cases (*U.S.* v. *El Paso Natural Gas Co.*, 376 U.S 651 (1964)). In several cases, the "elimination of potential competition" test has been applied to challenged acquisitions, primarily where the acquiring firm was or could have been a potential competitor of the acquired firm by expanding internally into the acquired company's market.

The FTC has refined the potential competition concept, holding in the *Bendix* case that a major potential entrant able to enter a given market by the acquisition and development of a small company (a "toehold" acquisition) violates Section 7 when it acquires instead a leading company in that market. (*Bendix Corp.*, 3 Trade Reg. Rep. ¶19,288 (FTC 1970), *rev'd*, 450 F.2d 534 (6th Cir. 1971)). The court of appeals reversed on the ground that the Commission violated the Administrative Procedure Act by deciding the case on a theory not previously raised during the proceeding.

Bendix, one of the nation's largest manufacturers of a diverse line of products, including automotive parts and accessories, acquired the Fram Corporation in 1967. Fram was at the time the

third largest producer of automotive filters with 12.4 percent of the
overall market and 17.2 percent of the passenger car filter aftermarket. The total automotive filter market was said to be concentrated.
The top three producers (G.M., Purolator, and Fram) had 62.9 percent, and the top six had 79.6 percent of the market. In the aftermarket, the same top three had 71.3 percent and the top six had
88.6 percent. The automotive filter market was said to be characterized by (a) unsophisticated technology, (b) stable prices and lethar-
gic competition, and (c) entry barriers due to the presence of Ford
and G.M. and the necessity for heavy advertising outlays and complex distributional systems.

Bendix had its own automotive filter division with $1.1 million in
1966 sales, primarily to the original equipment market for heavier
vehicles. There may have been some actual competition between
Bendix and Fram, depending upon the definition of the line of
commerce. Complaint counsel did not urge this as a ground of illegality, and the FTC relegated discussion of this point to a footnote.

For several years Bendix was shown to have considered entry,
through acquisition, into the automotive filter market, particularly
the passenger car aftermarket, and to have negotiated for possible
acquisition of companies smaller than Fram, such as Wix, Hastings,
and Walker. No acquisition had been made, however, prior to the
purchase of Fram. The Commission found this history of negotiation for other acquisitions of significance in its treatment of the
potential competition issue. The hearing examiner dismissed the
complaint against Bendix, finding that Bendix was unlikely to enter
the automobile filter aftermarket by internal expansion and hence
was not eliminated as a "potential competitor." The Commission
accepted the fact that Bendix would not expand internally, but rejected the examiner's definition of potential competition as "unduly
narrow." Had Bendix chosen to acquire a smaller company, capable of growth and development, it might have made a "procompetitive toehold entry." According to the FTC, Fram would then have
remained a viable competitive entity and the presence of Bendix in
the market as a new factor would have enhanced competition.
When Bendix acquired Fram, a leading company, it foreclosed forever its own potential for competing via the toehold route.

The crucial determination, in the Commission's view, was not
whether the acquiring company could enter a concentrated market
by internal growth; rather, it was "(1) the actual elimination of the
additional decision-making, the added capacity, and the other market stimuli which would have resulted had entry taken a procompetitive form, such as internal expansion; and (2) the anticompetitive consequences of the removal of the disciplining effect
of a potential competitor from the market's edge. We believe that

these adverse effects on competition may result from the elimination of a potential entrant who might have entered by internal expansion or who might have entered by a toehold acquisition."

In the opinion of the Commission, written by Commissioner Elman, several factors were pointed to as compelling the conclusion that Bendix was a likely potential entrant by means of a toehold acquisition, and that the elimination of such potentiality by the merger was a substantial loss to competition. First, Bendix had canvassed the market carefully for the proper acquisition, negotiating with firms smaller than Fram; hence, its intent to enter by acquisition was clear. Secondly, Bendix was peculiarly suited to make a success of any smaller company it acquired. Its marketing and distribution organization was particularly adapted to the automotive field where it had an overall strong presence. It already supplied and manufactured original equipment automotive filters. Its overall financial resources available for heavy advertising and other forms of nonprice competition put it in a strong position to advance a smaller company. Finally, few if any other firms of the Bendix dimension were likely or capable of making a similar toehold entry. Thus, the Commission held: ". . . a merger with a leading firm, especially in a concentrated industry, which eliminated the likelihood of such a desirable entry through a toehold acquisition is embraced within the prohibitions of the statute" (at 21,446).

In overturning the hearing examiner's dismissal of the complaint, the Commission was faced with an established key finding of fact by the examiner—that Bendix positively would not enter by internal expansion. Rather than overturning this finding, Commissioner Elman's opinion imported the notion of a toehold acquisition. The Commission held that a large company entering a concentrated market must enter either by internal expansion or by acquiring a smaller firm already in the market; it may not acquire an industry leader. The FTC rationale seems to have been that a toehold acquisition would maintain existing competition between industry leaders while adding a new competitive force to the market.

Under the theory of the *Bendix* opinion, it may be that, where internal expansion is not seriously contemplated, even some nontoehold acquisitions may be permissible. The size and particular know-how of Bendix and the concentration in the automotive filter aftermarket may have moved the Commission to adopt the toehold theory. If Bendix had been operating farther from the Fram product market, perhaps the FTC would have held differently. Some would argue, for example, that an acquisition by a firm which in no way operates in the acquired company's market (a "pure" conglomerate merger) would avoid the *Bendix* result.

Moreover, the Commission in *Bendix* considered as significant certain entry barriers to the passenger car filter aftermarket, including (a) the sheer size and resources of General Motors and Ford, present in this market, and (b) the importance of substantial and experienced distributional and promotional programs to success in sales.

The Commission does not seem to be saying that all acquisitions by large firms of industry leaders in concentrated markets are per se violations of Section 7 of the Clayton Act. FTC Chairman Weinberger discounted such a notion in a statement of May 15, 1970, before the House Antitrust Subcommittee, although he warned that such transactions would be carefully scrutinized by the FTC. Also it should not be forgotten that in 1969 the Attorney General stated that the Department of Justice "will probably oppose any merger by one of the top 200 manufacturing firms of any leading producer in any concentrated industry" (413 ATRR X-11 (6/10/69)). The factors outlined above buttress the notion that *Bendix* is not a per se case; the key issues continue to be the likelihood of potential entry and its competitive significance.

Some experts caution that it would be unsafe to counsel that all toehold acquisitions will necessarily be blessed by the FTC or Justice Department. If it can be shown that internal expansion by the acquiring company is practical and has been given careful attention, entry by toehold acquisition into a concentrated market might also be challenged under the elimination-of-potential-competition doctrine. Moreover, in *Bendix,* Commissioner Elman indicated that a toehold acquisition would be "pro-competitive," and, thus, meet the test of *Brown Shoe* (370 U.S. 294 (1962)) for *any* merger in a concentrated market. Some urge that the toehold acquisition by an industrial giant of a small company which is a technological leader in the relevant market could violate Section 7. A contrary indication is that of the FTC acceptance of a consent order from Textron, permitting the acquisition of Fafnir Bearing, an industry leader in a concentrated market, but requiring divestiture of Parkersburg-Aetna, a smaller company in the same market whose purchase could be defined as a toehold acquisition by Textron ((1970–73 Transfer Binder) Trade Reg. Rep. ¶19,783 (FTC 1971)).

The FTC opinion in the *Bendix* case contained no statement of the size or market share limitation to qualify an acquired firm for the title "toehold." Fram was the third largest firm (17.2 percent), and its acquisition was held unlawful by the Commission. Yet the FTC discussed the Bendix interest in the fourth and fifth largest firms (with respective market shares of 9.5 percent and 3.9 percent) as if these might have been acceptable acquisitions. The concept of toehold acquisitions was adopted in the Justice Department's Merger Guidelines, argued by the Department in the *ITT-ABC* case, and expounded by Assistant Attorney General McLaren in several speeches.

In the FTC's *General Foods/SOS* merger case, 69 F.T.C. 380 (1966), *aff'd,* 386 F.2d 936 (3rd Cir. 1967), the FTC found a violation of Section 7 when GF, a large, diversified home-products firm, acquired SOS, the second largest producer of steel scouring pads in a highly concentrated market headed by Brillo (with a market share of over 40 percent). Commissioner Elman found in *General Foods,* as he had found in *Bendix,* that a large firm had acquired a leading firm in a concentrated industry. However, based upon his analysis of potential competition, Mr. Elman, in dissent, argued that the SOS acquisition did not violate Section 7 for two reasons: (a) there was no evidence that GF intended or was able to enter by internal expansion, and (b) there was evidence that emerging competition of non-steel-wool scouring devices would tend to counter any adverse effect upon competition ensuing from the substitution of GF for SOS in the steel-wool market. He also argued that, given the elimination of SOS as a separate competitive entry, Brillo remained the market leader and a formidable foe for GF. He concluded that, in contrast to the *P&G* case (where P&G was the most likely potential entrant by internal expansion), "the Commission takes a long step toward ruling that a 'big' firm may grow only by internal expansion." Neither the dissent nor the majority opinion in the *General Foods* case considered the possibility of a toehold acquisition by GF.

(b) Question: *Will the elimination of a potential entrant in an unconcentrated market be regarded as significantly anticompetitive?*

In *Kennecott Copper Corp.* v. *FTC,* 467 F.2d 67 (10th Cir. 1972), the court upheld an FTC divestiture order upsetting, as a violation of Section 7 of the Clayton Act, the 1968 acquisition by Kennecott, the nation's largest copper producer, of Peabody Coal Company, one of the nation's two leading coal producers. The court found that there was sufficient evidence to sustain the Commission's determination that the acquisition eliminated Kennecott as a significant potential competitor in the coal industry and that because of Kennecott's deep pocket, the acquisition probably would accelerate a trend toward concentration in that industry.

The Commission made several findings for which the court of appeals found support in the record. The Commission found that coal rather than a broader energy market was the relevant product market and the nation as a whole was the relevant geographical market. Although the coal industry is not now concentrated, the Commission concluded that it was "trending toward concentration" with the top four firms increasing their combined market share from 15.8 percent to 29.2 percent between 1954 and 1967, and accounting for nearly two thirds of industry growth during the same period. From the evidence presented, the Commission determined that Peabody had experienced remarkable growth, accounting for 45 percent of the industry growth between 1955 and 1965 and over 90 percent of industry growth in 1965. The coal industry was found to have high barriers to entry, and Kennecott, whose "entry into the coal business one way or another was almost certain," was "not only a likely entrant but also the most likely entrant into the coal business" by way of either a de novo entry or a toehold entry through the acquisition of a small coal company; "no other likely entrants were shown to exist." In the Commission's view, Kennecott, as a potential competitor waiting in the wings, exerted an influence on the market. Finally, the Commission found that according to the deep pocket theory, the addition of the "immense resources" of Kennecott to Peabody would lead to a larger share of the market for Peabody and to an increase in industry concentration.

Probably the most significant aspect of the court's decision was the application of the potential-competition theory in an industry that was not concentrated but was only "trending toward concentration." As the court of appeals noted, "ordinarily the potential competition concept comes into play where the industry is regarded as an oligopoly." It might be argued that where there is no concentration, the mere existence of a potential competitor, "waiting anxiously" in the wings, can have little effect on the behavior of firms already in the market. On the other hand, the elimination of potential competition can be anticompetitive also in eliminating the possibility that, but for the acquisition, the potential competitor would actually enter the market. The court found that Kennecott was "almost certain" to enter the market, presumably on a large scale. Thus, it could be argued that the acquisition was significantly anticompetitive regardless of the existence of any waiting-in-the-wings effect.

Critics of the decision might reply that it would be too speculative to say that such eventual entry, if it indeed were to take place, would have a significant impact on the market. According to the critics, the effect on competition would depend on the state of the market at the time of the eventual entry. Critics also question some of the court's other findings. Although Kennecott had plausibly urged that certain organizations (oil and gas companies with their experience in a closely related field, railroads with large coal land holdings, and utilities which are large coal users) by their very nature are potential entrants into the coal market, the court found that "no other likely entrants were shown to exist." It could be argued that better proof that other companies were potential entrants would be very difficult for a defendant to produce (at least where the entry barriers are high), regardless of the true state of affairs.

The court's application of the deep pocket theory might also be questioned in view of the evidence showing that the second largest coal company was owned by Continental Oil Company and that other large firms outside the coal industry had acquired coal properties. Those critical of the decision would argue that since the industry was not concentrated, the effect of this acquisition on competition was too slight to justify divestiture. According to this point of view, despite the court's application of the potential-competition and deep pocket theories, the critical factor in this case was simply that the largest firm in one industry acquired one of the two leading firms in a related industry and that such an acquisition was not necessarily anticompetitive in the traditional sense, but had become presumptively unlawful by virtue of this decision. This unlawfulness was implicit in the remarks of the Assistant Attorney General in charge of the Antitrust Division, Thomas K. Kauper, speaking at Northwestern University. Mr. Kauper reaffirmed the statement of Attorney General Mitchell in June 1969: "The Department of Justice will probably oppose any merger by one of the top 200 manufacturing firms with any leading producer in any concentrated industry" (413 ATRR X-11 (6/10/69)).

In support of the court's decision, it could be argued that, in view of Peabody's spectacular growth, the combination of the resources of these two large firms in a market "trending toward concentration" might well accelerate the coming of concentration and, hence, that the decision is consistent with the case law and with the congressional intent behind the Clayton Act to stop concentration in its incipiency.

Kennecott might be compared with the FTC decision in *Beatrice Foods* (1970–73 Transfer Binder) Trade Reg. Rep. ¶20,121 (FTC 1972). According to the Commission, in *Beatrice,* the administrative law judge, in finding the acquisition unlawful, was apparently of the view that an acquisition of a leading firm in the market by a likely entrant or potential entrant in the market is unlawful despite a finding that the market was "substantially fragmented." Overruling the administrative law judge, the Commission held that the record failed to support a finding in this instance that the elimination of the potential entrant was significantly anticompetitive because there were low barriers to entry and a sufficiently large number of other potential entrants. Construing its own decision in *Kennecott,*

the Commission said, "the Commission [in *Kennecott*] determined
that in the [coal] industry . . . high barriers to entry existed and
this was cited as a factor co-equal with the rapid trend toward concentration found in that case. . . ." Thus, *Beatrice* might be distinguished from *Kennecott* because of the difference in the number
of potential competitors.

Also of interest in the *Kennecott* case is the determination that
coal was the relevant market for testing the anticompetitive effect of
the acquisition. This is different from the determination in *U.S.* v.
General Dynamics Corp., 341 F.Supp. 534 (N.D. Ill. 1972), where a
wider energy market, including oil, gas, and nuclear fuel, was held
to be the relevant market for testing an acquisition of one coal producer by another. The determination in *Kennecott* is also, arguably,
inconsistent with the recommendation to the Commission from its
own Bureau of Economics, in the first of a four-part study of the
energy sector of the economy, that acquisition by firms in one field
of firms in other energy fields should generally be considered horizontal acquisitions in a wider energy market.

(In its petition for certiorari, filed October 25, 1972, Kennecott
claimed a conflict between the Tenth Circuit's decision and *General
Dynamics, supra* (in which review has been granted, 41 U.S.L.W.
3323 (U.S. Dec. 11, 1972)), and raised several of the issues mentioned above. Should the Supreme Court take the case, some of
these issues may be resolved. See also *U.S.* v. *Falstaff Brewing
Corp.*, 603 ATRR D-1 (Sup. Ct. 1973), in which the Court held that
the district court erred in assuming that because Falstaff would not
have entered the market other than by an acquisition, it could not
be considered a potential competitor.)

8. Conglomerate Mergers

Question: *Do the antitrust laws prohibit conglomerate mergers?*

A conglomerate merger may be defined as one of companies that
are neither competitors (horizontal) nor supplier and customer
(vertical). At the Senate Judiciary Committee's hearing on
confirmation of his appointment in 1969, Assistant Attorney General Richard M. McLaren announced that the Antitrust Division
would give "high priority" to antitrust action against conglomerate
mergers. He took the position that court actions against conglomerate acquisitions should be attempted under Section 7 of the Clayton Act before new legislation was sought. The views Mr. McLaren
expressed seemed to bring a change of policy at the Justice Department. An earlier Assistant Attorney General, Donald F. Turner,
had remarked a number of times that he thought new legislation

was needed to deal with conglomerate mergers. "For example . . .
Congress should pass a statute that would say to the top 50 or 100
companies 'any time you make an acquisition in excess of a certain
size you must peel off assets of comparable magnitude' " (Hearings
Before the Senate Small Business Committee, 90th Cong., 1st Sess.
(1967)). Mr. Turner's view won support from the staff of the Cabinet Committee on Price Stability, which, in a report calling for vigorous antitrust enforcement to curb concentration, said the Clayton Act appears inadequate to cope with conglomerate mergers
(Study Paper Number 2, Studies by the Staff of the Cabinet Committee on Price Stability, January 1969).

Early in 1968, the Joint Economic Committee of Congress expressed concern about the trend revealed in the Commission's statistics and questioned whether the FTC and the Justice Department
were being as vigorous and imaginative as they might be in applying the antitrust laws to conglomerate mergers. The Committee
described the enforcement agencies as "well equipped with legal
authority" to investigate and challenge such mergers. Four months
later, citing the "growing concern on the part of . . . congressional
committees," the FTC directed its staff to begin an investigation of
conglomerate mergers (FTC Resolution Directing Investigation of
Acquisitions and Mergers, July 2, 1968). Staff inquiry was "to cover
not only the short-run anti-competitive aspects of such mergers, but
also broader issues, including the relationship between conglomerate mergers and technical or business efficiencies, the economic performance of conglomerate firms in the market place, and the effect
of conglomerate mergers on the competitive vigor of enterprises by
their change in status from independent firms to subsidiaries or divisions of conglomerates, and the impact of such structural changes
on long-run competitive activity." Upon completion of the staff
investigation, the Commission announced, it would hold a public
hearing. Two staff reports have been publicly released; the latest
one, released on January 2, 1973, contains few conclusions on the
effects of conglomerate mergers. The staff's principal point seems to
be that there is an "information loss" when diverse companies are
reported on publicly only in consolidated fashion.

There were also expressions of concern in 1969 about the entry
of conglomerates into regulated industries. On February 7, 1969,
the Federal Communications Commission announced its intention
to investigate conglomerate ownership of broadcasting stations, and
Chairman Wright Patman of the House Banking Committee introduced a bill to regulate "one-bank holding companies."

Mr. McLaren kept his word to the Senate Judiciary Committee.
Upon his recommendation, many Department of Justice complaints
were filed against conglomerate mergers, but district court decisions

have been inconclusive or the cases have been settled by consent. In *U.S.* v. *Northwest Industries, Inc.,* 301 F.Supp. 1066 (N.D. Ill. 1969), a preliminary injunction was denied; in *U.S.* v. *White Consolidated Industries, Inc.,* 323 F.Supp. 1397 (N.D. Ohio 1971), a preliminary injunction was granted and the merger abandoned. *U.S.* v. *Ling-Temco-Vought, Inc.* was settled by a consent decree, 315 F.Supp. 1301 (W.D.Pa. 1970), requiring LTV to divest either Jones & Laughlin or both Braniff Airways and Okonite Company (1970 Trade Cas. ¶73,228 (W.D. Pa. 1970); 1971 Trade Cas. ¶73,607 (W.D. Pa. 1971)). Three acquisitions by ITT were attacked without success in the district courts. ITT's acquisition of Grinnell Corp. was found not to violate Section 7 (234 F.Supp. 19 (D. Conn. 1970), *appeal dismissed,* 404 U.S. 801 (1971)). A preliminary injunction against ITT's acquisition of Hartford Fire Insurance Co. was denied (306 F.Supp. 766 (D. Conn. 1969), *appeal dismissed,* 404 U.S. 801 (1971)). The acquisition of Canteen Corp. was held not to violate Section 7 (1971 Trade Cas. ¶73,619 (N.D. Ill. 1971)). These cases were settled by decrees providing for divestiture by ITT of (a) a division of Grinnell (1971 Trade Cas. ¶73,655, (D. Conn. 1971)); (b) either Hartford Fire Ins. Co. or ITT Avis, ITT Levitt & Sons, and Hamilton Life Ins. Co. (1971 Trade Cas. ¶73,666 (D. Conn. 1971)); and (c) ITT Canteen (1971 Trade Cas. ¶73,667 (N.D. Ill. 1971)).

Justice Department opposition before the FCC caused International Telephone & Telegraph Corp. to call off its agreement to acquire American Broadcasting Companies, Inc.; Bethlehem Steel Corp. was induced to abandon plans to acquire Cerro Corp. (WALL STREET JOURNAL, March 21, 1968); and Justice Department and FTC investigations may have been instrumental in persuading Gulf and Western, one of the largest conglomerates, to drop attempts to acquire Allis-Chalmers Co. and Armour & Co.

The Supreme Court's only decision on conglomerate mergers is *FTC* v. *Procter & Gamble Co.,* 386 U.S. 568 (1967). "All mergers are within the reach of Section 7 and all must be tested by the same standard whether they are classified as horizontal, vertical, conglomerate or other." The relationship between the products of P&G, the acquiring firm, and Clorox, the acquired company, gave that merger a quasi-horizontal element, but the Court stressed three competitive factors that appear relevant to mergers that are more conglomerate than the product-extension type: (1) the relative disparity in size and strength between P&G and the largest firms in the liquid bleach industry; (2) excessive concentration in the liquid bleach industry and Clorox's dominant position in the industry; and (3) the elimination of P&G as a potential competitor in the liquid bleach industry.

In *General Foods Co.* v. *FTC,* 386 F.2d 936 (3rd Cir. 1967), *cert. denied,* 391 U.S. 919 (1968), a court of appeals held that proof of elimination of a potential competitor is not essential to establishing the illegality of a product-extension type of conglomerate merger. The anticompetitive effects attributed there to the entry of a giant parent into a market of smaller firms were deterrence of new entrants from the market and inducement of existing sellers to compete less vigorously for fear of retaliation.

Resulting opportunity for reciprocal dealing was a principal basis for the Supreme Court's finding of forbidden anticompetitive effect in *FTC* v. *Consolidated Foods Corp.,* 380 U.S. 592 (1965). The Justice Department has filed Section 7 complaints grounded on the reciprocal-dealing theory of competitive effect. In *U.S.* v. *General Dynamics Corp.,* 258 F.Supp. 36 (S.D.N.Y. 1966), the Government obtained a decree requiring General Dynamics, a major government contractor, to divest itself of an industrial gas producer whose products it had promoted through use of its purchasing power. A consent order entered in May 1964 forced Ingersoll-Rand Co., a big steel purchaser, to give up plans to buy three producers of coal-mining equipment (*U.S.* v. *Ingersoll-Rand Co.,* 1964 Trade Cas. ¶71,074 (W.D. Pa. 1964)). Earlier, in granting a preliminary injunction against the acquisitions (218 F.Supp. 530 (W.D. Pa. 1963)), the district court observed that the acquisitions would increase Ingersoll-Rand's steel purchases to such an extent that the coal mines' purchase of mining equipment could be influenced by the mines' desire to retain the goodwill of the steel industry, one of their largest customers.

In a suit challenging the acquisition of Penick & Ford, a large corn-products manufacturer, by R.J. Reynolds Tobacco Co., an important user of paper packaging products in which corn starch is an ingredient, the New Jersey Federal District Court denied a preliminary injunction (*U.S.* v. *Penick & Ford, Ltd.,* 242 F.Supp. 518 (D.N.J.1965)) for lack of evidence that Reynolds would go along with the corn starch industry's reciprocity practices. (A consent decree was later entered (1969 Trade Cas. ¶72,886 (D.N.J.1969).)

The Justice Department listed in its Merger Guidelines only two types of conglomerate mergers "as having sufficiently identifiable anticompetitive effects to be the subject of relatively specific structural guidelines": (1) those eliminating potential entrants to an industry and (2) those creating a danger of reciprocal buying. But "the Department will ordinarily investigate the possibility of anticompetitive consequences, and may in particular circumstances bring suit, where an acquisition of a leading firm in a relatively concentrated or rapidly concentrating market may serve to entrench or increase the market power of that firm or raise barriers to entry in that market."

In his article, "Conglomerate Mergers and Section 7 of the Clayton Act," 78 HARV. L.REV. 1313 (1965), Donald Turner discussed four other possible anticompetitive results of conglomerate mergers. (1) Economics of scale in production, distribution, research, selling, management, or capital acquisition may reduce the conglomerate's costs to a point that it can drive smaller competitors out of a business. (2) A diversified firm may be able to drop its prices in one of its markets so low that competitors are wiped out in that market. (3) Substitution of a large, wealthy conglomerate as owner of one of many small competitors may frighten the others into competing less vigorously for fear of provoking retaliation. (4) Entry of the large conglomerate may discourage entry of new competitors. Yet he did not rate the threat of these results as sufficiently serious to outweigh the advantages of encouraging economies of scale. His view that promotional economies should not be an affirmative ground for invalidating a merger under existing antitrust law was apparently rejected by the Supreme Court in the *P&G-Clorox* case.

Conglomerate acquisitions may be made without a thought to acquiring market leverage through reciprocity or a deep pocket. Some may be nothing more than empire building, either out of a desire for power and publicity or a compulsion to compete with other expanding conglomerates. Sometimes the acquiring company has idle cash it must invest and intends to choose the best investment, or it may want to diversify to smooth out seasonal peaks and valleys in its income or to reduce its dependence upon a line of business that has become more competitive, is losing out to technological advance in related product lines, or is becoming subject to increasing governmental regulation.

Other acquisitions are prompted by securities-market factors— e.g., the acquired firm's capitalization, profit ratio, or rate of growth is such that amalgamation produces a stock-earnings ratio higher than the acquiring company's and therefore pushes up the price of the stock once the merger is consummated. Sometimes tax considerations are paramount; one company may have losses that can be set off against the other's taxable earnings. The acquired company may have plant sites, raw materials, cash, management or technical know-how, or personnel that the acquiring company needs.

The impetus for the merger may come from the acquired company. It may seek to sell out to forestall a takeover by a company that is interested only in short-term capital gains or would make an undesirable parent for some other reason. Small one-man or family corporations may be forced to sell out because cash is needed to settle the leading stockholder's estate or pay estate taxes or because the decedent was the guiding force whose loss crippled the management of the business. The most common motive for the acquired company is probably the premium offered for its stock. Take-over prices rose to an all-time peak in 1968, according to a study released by W. T. Grimm & Co., Chicago, financial consultants specializing in corporate mergers. The average price paid under successful tender offers in 1968 was 24.6 times earnings, a 40 percent increase over the 17.6 ratio that prevailed in 1967. An average premium of 25 percent over market price was paid for take-over stock in 1968.

The first step in assessing the status of conglomerate mergers under existing law is to segregate out those that have clear anticompetitive potentialities. Product-extension and market-extension mergers are said to fall within that category, for they may have a horizontal aspect. In addition, court proceedings seem to establish a firm basis for attacking conglomerate acquisitions that eliminate potential competitors, for the presence of this element likewise gives a merger a quasi-horizontal character.

Even a "pure" conglomerate merger, one uniting companies in businesses so unrelated that neither would have moved into the second field on its own, is not necessarily untouchable. If the merger gives either company great economic power or leverage in its market, there may be a basis for attacking it.

9. FTC Merger-Policy Statements

Question: *Aside from formal proceedings, what has the FTC done to clarify the antitrust rules concerning corporate mergers?*

In 1964, Federal Trade Commissioner Philip Elman proposed at a Federal Bar Association briefing conference in Washington, D.C., that the Commission study merger economics in particular industries and prepare rules or guidelines defining the type or size of merger it would proceed against in each industry. Merger standards were high on the list of guidelines Assistant Attorney General Donald F. Turner decided to issue soon after he took charge of the Antitrust Division in mid-1965. At the American Bar Association Antitrust Section's spring meeting of 1966, Mr. Turner virtually promised to issue merger guidelines before October 1 of that year.

The FTC took action first. On January 17, 1967, the Commission released statements of its enforcement policies regarding mergers in the food-distribution industries and acquisitions of ready-mixed concrete companies by cement manufacturers.

In the food-distribution industries, the Commission promised to "focus particular attention on mergers or acquisitions by food retailing and wholesaling corporations with combined annual sales in excess of $100 million" (1 Trade Reg. Rep. ¶4525). The greatest diligence, the Commission announced, would be exercised when mergers resulted in combined annual food sales of more than $500 million. As background for its establishment of these standards, the Commission told of its observation of "very significant changes during the past decade and a half" in the structure of food retailing. Increasing concentration in both national and local markets and the growing importance of grocery chains have forced the Commission to devote "much of the . . . merger enforcement activity . . . to this sector of the economy." The Commission described briefly each of its complaint proceedings in this area, including pending litigation against Kroger Co. (Docket 7464) for five acquisitions made in the late 1950's.

With regard to vertical cement-industry mergers, the Commission stressed both the size of the acquired ready-mixed-concrete producer and its relative position in its local metropolitan market (1 Trade Reg. Rep. ¶4520). The Commission promised to investigate any acquisition of a ready-mixed concrete firm in a market to which the acquiring cement producer was either an actual or potential supplier. Whenever such an investigation revealed an "acquisition of any ready-mixed-concrete firm ranking among the leading four nonintegrated producers in any metropolitan market, or the acquisition of any ready-mixed-concrete company or other cement consumer which regularly purchases 50,000 barrels of cement or more annually," the Commission indicated that it would issue a Section 7 complaint, "unless unusual circumstances in a particular case dictate the contrary."

The Commission's policy statement as to the cement industry echoed some of the allegations made in its cement-industry complaints—for example, that vertical mergers "may set off a 'chain' reaction of acquisitions" and "may" inhibit new entrants. While the background information set out in the statement did not relate to any specific complaint proceedings, it did list several specific metropolitan markets in which the ready-mixed-concrete industry was regarded as "quite concentrated." The Commission concluded "that vertical mergers and acquisitions involving cement manufacturers and consumers of cement, particularly ready-mixed-concrete companies, can have sustantial adverse effects on competition in the particular market areas where they occur." The Commission relied heavily on a report filed by its economics staff in April 1966, on "Mergers and Vertical Integration in the Cement Industry" and on the results of public hearings held by the Commission following publication of that report.

Having established guides to indicate when it would move against food and cement mergers, the Commission adopted a novel device for insuring that the guides would be applied in the two industries involved. It announced that each year it would serve every food retailer and wholesaler making annual sales in excess of $100 million and every portland cement producer, regardless of size, with a Section 6(b) FTC Act order requiring each to give the Commission at least 60 days' advance notice of any proposed acquisition covered by the policy statements. In this particular aspect of the Commission's action, Chairman Dixon and Commissioner MacIntyre did not concur. (See discussion in section III-C-2, p. 237, on problems of enforcement of this requirement.)

Respondents in both industries have demanded dismissal of complaint proceedings against them because of the issuance of these policy statements. The Commission denied the dismissal motion of three cement producers (*Lehigh Portland Cement Co.,* 71 F.T.C. 1618 (1967)), as well as Lehigh's motion to transfer its case to the Antitrust Division (71 F.T.C. 1656 (1967)). The cement producers objected to the Commission's conduct of industry-wide public hearings investigating the cement industry and its release of an economic report while it was litigating complaint proceedings against them. These actions by the Commission were attacked as infringements of administrative due process of law in the pending complaint proceedings. The Commission rejected these contentions, holding that the policy statements merely set forth criteria for identifying acquisitions that warrant the Commission's immediate attention (71 F.T.C. 1690 (1967)). In any specific proceeding, the Commission said, the issues would still be decided on the basis of the record in that particular case. "Respondents are entitled to have their cases adjudicated by commissioners with open minds, not empty ones" (71 F.T.C. 1622). A similar motion by Kroger Co., based on the policy statement with respect to food-distribution mergers, was denied by the Commission as moot in 1968 (*Kroger Co.* (1967–1970 Transfer Binder) Trade Reg. Rep. ¶18,582 (FTC 1968)). (See also discussion in section VIII-B-2, p. 491.)

There has been no court challenge to the Commission's authority to issue these guidelines, which are simply announcements in advance of the circumstances under which the Commission will initiate an investigation or deem the issuance of a Section 7 Clayton Act complaint to be in the public interest. The Commission's declarations are not binding on anyone and apparently do not constitute "rules" or "regulations" needing a base in a statutory grant of authority.

Some antitrust experts have suggested that the policy statements contain no information a businessman cannot get from any competent lawyer. In *U.S.* v. *Von's Grocery Co.,* 384 U.S. 270 (1966), the Supreme Court struck down a food-distribution merger that created a regional supermarket chain with annual sales of less than $175 million. The Commission's proceedings against vertical cement-industry acquisitions have made it clear that it regards as suspect any cement-producer acquisition of a substantial ready-mix firm.

As indicated by the *Lehigh* and *Kroger* cases, the Commission is satisfied that the consideration and issuance of statements of this sort do not result in improper prejudgement of matters in litigation. This is consistent with the view taken by the Commission, and indeed required for its continued existence in its present form, that it does not improperly prejudge a case when it reviews, as required by Section 11 of the Clayton Act, a proposed Section 7 complaint and concludes that there is reason to believe a violation has occurred.

10. Department of Justice Merger Guidelines

Question: *Has the Government stated clearly which mergers it will oppose?*

Unlike the FTC, the Justice Department has made no attempt to establish guidelines for particular industries, but has spelled out general standards said to be "the standards currently being applied by the Department of Justice in determining whether to challenge corporate acquisitions and mergers under Section 7" (1 Trade Reg. Rep. ¶4510 (Released May 30, 1968)).

In a press release announcing the guidelines, Attorney General Ramsey Clark expressed hope that they would "provide a basis for a continuing dialogue between government and business concerning the role and scope of anti-merger enforcement in the maintenance of a free competitive economy." The Department anticipated "that it will amend the guidelines from time to time . . . to reflect changes in enforcement policy that might result from subsequent court decisions, comments of interested parties, or Department reevaluations. Because changes in enforcement policy will be made as the occasion demands and will usually precede the issuance of amended guidelines . . . the existence of unamended guidelines should not be regarded as barring [the Department] from taking any action it deems necessary to achieve the purposes of Section 7." At a press conference held in conjunction with announcement of the guidelines, a Justice Department spokesman reported that the guidelines were not cleared with the FTC and that the Commission's policy statements were not presented to the Justice Department in advance of publication.

The Antitrust Division's guidelines focus on market structure, according to the Department, "chiefly because the conduct of the individual firms in a market tends to be controlled by the structure of that market, i.e., by those market conditions which are fairly permanent or subject only to slow change (such as, principally, the number of substantial firms selling in the market, the relative sizes of their respective market shares, and the substantiality of barriers to the entry of new firms into the market)."

In the guidelines the first step in making an assessment of market structure is ascertainment of the relevant market. "A market is any grouping of sales (or other commercial transactions) in which each of the firms whose sales are included enjoy some advantage in competing with those firms whose sales are not included. The advantage need not be great, for so long as it is significant it defines an area of effective competition among the included sellers in which the competition of the excluded sellers is, ex hypothesi, less effective." This test of significant competitive advantage is observed by the guidelines in describing the product dimension of the relevant market ("line of commerce") and its geographic dimension ("section of the country"). Acknowledging that precise delineation of geographic markets is often impossible, the Antitrust Division says it will "challenge any merger which appears to be illegal in any reasonable geographic market, even though in another reasonable market it would not appear to be illegal."

Ordinarily, the Division's judgment on whether to attack a horizontal merger will be based on market shares. In a "market highly concentrated," one in which the four largest firms control "approximately 75 percent or more" of the business, acquisition of a company with only 1 percent of the sales will be challenged if the acquiring firm has 15 percent or more; acquisition of a company with 2 percent of the sales will be challenged if the acquirer has 10 percent; and acquisition of a 4-percent element in the market will be challenged if the acquirer also has as much as 4 percent. In a market that is less highly concentrated, acquisition of a company making 1 percent of the sales will be attacked if the acquiring company has at least 25 percent of the market; acquisition of a company with 2 percent of the sales will be attacked if the acquirer has as much as 20 percent; acquisition of a company with 3 percent of the market will be challenged if the acquirer has 15 percent; acquisition of a company with 4 percent will not be allowed if the acquirer has 10 percent; and a company controlling 5 percent of the market will not be permitted to acquire one that has 5 percent or more of the sales.

The guidelines say that the Department will apply stricter standards in a market showing a trend toward concentration. A concentration trend exists, according to the guidelines, when the aggregate market share of any grouping of the largest firms in the market from the two largest to the eight largest has increased by 7 percent or more of the market since any base year five to 10 years prior to the merger. In these circumstances, the Division will challenge the acquisition by any of these largest firms of any company with a market share of 2 percent or more.

In addition, the guidelines set out two non-market share standards that will cause the Justice Department to sue: (1) "acquisition of a competitor which is a particularly 'disturbing,' 'disruptive,' or otherwise unusually competitive factor in the market;" and (2) a merger involving a substantial company that, while it has an insubstantial market share, "possesses an unusual competitive potential or has an asset that confers an unusual competitive advantage."

"With all vertical mergers it is necessary to consider the probable competitive consequences of the merger in both the market in which the supplying firm sells and the market in which the purchasing firm sells, although a significant adverse effect in either market will ordinarily result in a challenge by the Department." A vertical merger will be regarded as having an objectionable competitive impact on the supplying firm's market when a supplying firm with 10 percent or more of the sales in that market acquires one or more purchasing firms accounting in the aggregate for 6 percent or more of the total purchases in that market, "unless it clearly appears that there are no significant barriers to entry into the business of the purchasing firm or firms."

The guidelines express a view that this test with regard to effect on the supplying firm's market will normally result in challenges against most of the vertical mergers that may have adverse effect in the purchasing firm's market. Additional situations are set forth in which vertical mergers will be regarded as raising entry barriers in the purchasing firm's market or as creating disadvantages for the purchasing firm's competitors and therefore will be found objectionable. The most common of these situations arises when the supplying firm and its competitors sell a complex changing product or a scarce raw material or other product whose supply cannot be readily expanded to meet increased demand. The merged firm may have the power to use any temporary superiority, or any shortage, in the product of the supplying firm to put competitors of the purchasing firm at a disadvantage. Where such a product is a significant feature or ingredient of the end product manufactured by the purchasing firm and its competitors, the Antitrust Division says it will ordinarily challenge a merger or series of mergers between a supplying firm accounting for 20 percent or more of the market sales and a purchasing firm or firms accounting in the aggregate for 10 percent or more of the sales in its market.

Even when those market-share figures are not involved, the Department will ordinarily challenge "acquisitions of suppliers or customers by major firms in an industry in which (i) there has been, or is developing, a significant trend toward vertical integration by merger such that the trend, if unchallenged, would probably raise barriers to entry or impose a competitive disadvantage on unintegrated or partly integrated firms, and (ii) it does not clearly appear that the particular acquisition will result in significant economies of production or distribution unrelated to advertising and other promotional economies." See *U.S.* v. *Mead Corp.,* 1970 Trade Cas. ¶73,137 (S.D. Ohio 1970).

Action will also be taken to stop acquisition of a customer or supplier for the purpose of increasing the difficulty of entry by potential competitors or putting competitors "at an unwarranted disadvantage."

In the category of "conglomerate mergers," the guidelines put all "mergers that are neither horizontal nor vertical," so that the term includes market-extension mergers, that is, consolidation of companies selling the same product in different geographic markets, and product-extension mergers, or, in the words of the FTC's P&G-Clorox opinion, 63 F.T.C. 1465 (1963), consolidations of "sellers of functionally closely related products which are not, however, close substitutes." The guidelines deal with three categories of conglomerate mergers: (1) those eliminating potential entrants, (2) those creating a danger of reciprocal buying, and (3) those that threaten to entrench or enhance the market power of the acquired firm.

Assuming that potential competition may often be the most significant competitive limitation on the exercise of market power by leading firms, the guidelines predict action against "any merger between one of the most likely entrants into the market" and (1) any firm with "approximately 25 percent or more" of the market; (2) one of the two largest firms in a market if their share therein amounts to "approximately 50 percent or more"; (3) one of the four largest firms in a market if the eight largest have "approximately 75 percent or more" of the market and the merging firm has "approximately 10 percent or more"; or (4) one of the eight largest firms in a market if their total share amounts to "approximately 75 percent or more" and either (a) the merging firm's share is "not insubstantial" and there are no more than one or two "likely entrants" or (b) the merging firm is a rapidly growing firm.

"Any merger which creates a significant danger of reciprocal buying" will "ordinarily" be challenged. And a "significant danger of reciprocal buying is present whenever approximately 15 percent or more of the total purchases in a market in which one of the merging firms ('the selling firm') sells are accounted for by firms which also make substantial sales in markets where the other merging firm ('the buying firm') is both a substantial buyer and a more substantial buyer than all or most of the competitors of the selling firm." The Department will ordinarily challenge any merger undertaken to facilitate the creation of reciprocal-buying arrangements, as well as any merger creating the possibility of substantial reciprocal buying by a company with a record of reciprocal buying. Except in "exceptional circumstances," the guidelines do not accept resulting economies as justification for a merger creating a significant danger of reciprocal buying.

Mergers involving potential competition and reciprocal buying are the only two types of conglomerates that the guidelines regard "as having sufficiently identifiable anticompetitive effects to be the subject of relatively specific structural guidelines." Yet "the Department will ordinarily investigate the possibility of anticompetitive consequences, and may in particular circumstances bring suit, where an acquisition of a leading firm in a relatively concentrated or rapidly concentrating market may serve to entrench or increase the market power of that firm or raise barriers to entry in that market."

At the time of issuance of the guidelines, antitrust experts saw little, if anything, new in them as to the general factors the Justice Department said it would take into account in enforcing Section 7 of the Clayton Act, but the guidelines were thought by some to make a significant contribution to "the numbers game", the use of market-share figures to show a merger's anticompetitive possibilities. The definition, for example, of a "concentration trend" in terms of a specific percentage increase in the shares of a definite number of firms was novel. The guidelines do not appear to have been meant to tighten antimerger enforcement; in fact, market-share figures given by the guidelines appear higher in some instances than the Supreme Court's decisions would require them to be.

It has been suggested that reliance in the guidelines entirely upon sales figures leaves a gap, though it may be a small one. Anticompetitive results can follow from the merger of two important buyers in a market even when they use the purchased material in the production of two different products and therefore do not themselves sell in the same market or in competition with each other. Their merger might have no impact at all in either of the two markets in which they sell and yet give them domination of the market in which they buy their common raw material.

While publication of the guidelines may have simplified prediction of Government actions against some mergers, there is still some room for uncertainty. Guidelines on acceptable market share figures do not answer all questions. In many situations, they move the discussion more promptly to market definition, over which there may be differences. Much extended litigation in the merger field has involved market definition (*U.S.* v. *Pabst Brewing Co.,* 384 U.S. 546 (1966); *U.S.* v. *Continental Can Co.,* 378 U.S. 441 (1964); *U.S.* v. *Aluminum Co. of America,* 377 U.S. 271 (1964); *U.S.* v. *Phila. Nat'l Bank,* 374 U.S. 321 (1963)). The Government often contends for a narrow market definition that will give the merging companies the most impressive market shares; defendants may argue that the market includes a broader range, stressing substitutes.

B. THE FAILING-COMPANY DOCTRINE

Question: *When is the acquisition of a "failing" company permitted?*

"In the light of the case thus disclosed of a corporation with resources so depleted and the prospect of rehabilitation so remote that it faced the grave probability of a business failure with resulting loss to its stockholders and injury to the communities where its plants were operated, we hold that the purchase of its capital stock by a competitor (there being no other prospective purchaser), not with a purpose to lessen competition, but to facilitate the accumulated business of the purchaser and with the effect of mitigating seriously injurious consequences otherwise probable, is not in contemplation of law prejudicial to the public and does not substantially lessen competition or restrain commerce within the intent of the Clayton Act" (*International Shoe Co.* v. *FTC.,* 280 U.S. 291 (1930)). This language in the *International Shoe* case has come to be known as the failing-company defense in antimerger proceedings under Section 7 of the Clayton Act. The defense, which was noted in the legislative history of the 1950 amendments to Section 7 (H. Rep. No. 1191, 81st Cong., 1st Sess. 6 (1949); S. Rep. No. 1775, 81st Cong., 2d Sess. 7 (1950)), has been recognized as valid in at least nine merger cases but has been sustained in only two. The defense succeeded in *U.S.* v. *Md. and Va. Milk Producers Ass'n.,* which involved acquisition of two dairies "hopelessly insolvent and . . . deeply in debt" (167 F. Supp. at 808 (D. D.C. 1958), *aff'd,* 362 U.S. 458 (1960)), and in *Granader* v. *Public Bank,* 417 F.2d 75 (6th Cir. 1969), *cert. denied,* 397 U.S. 1065 (1970), which involved acquisition of a bank, found by a state court to be "on the brink of bankruptcy with no possibility of recovery," by the competitor that made "the best offer" at a sale conducted by the Federal Deposit Insurance Corporation as court-appointed receiver. In the *Granader* case, the court acknowledged that application of the failing-company defense involved a determination of who else would or could purchase the failing business, but its opinion does not indicate that it made such a determination. The court granted summary judgment sustaining the failing-company defense on the basis of the evidence that the successful bidder "provided the best offer in light of the circumstances."

Mere evidence that the former owners of the acquired business enterprise had made a firm and unqualified decision to liquidate it will not suffice (*Erie Sand and Gravel Co.* v. *FTC*, 291 F.2d 279 (3rd Cir. 1961)). In the horizontal-merger case of *Erie Sand and Gravel,* there were other potential purchasers who would have guaranteed continuation of the acquired firm's business under new proprietorship, but they were outbid by the acquired firm's major competitor. The court of appeals limited the *International Shoe* doctrine "to the acquisition of a competitor which is in such straits that the termination of the enterprise and the dispersal of its assets seems inevitable unless a rival proprietor shall acquire and continue the business." Another court took a similar attitude toward evidence that, upon the death of a key official in the midst of difficult rehabilitation efforts, the directors of a company decided to give up (*Crown-Zellerbach Corp.* v. *FTC*, 296 F.2d 800 (9th Cir. 1961)).

In *U.S.* v. *Diebold, Inc.,* 369 U.S. 654 (1962), the Supreme Court reversed summary judgment against the Government after finding a genuine factual controversy on the issue of whether "Diebold was the only bona fide prospective purchaser" of the failing business. (The litigation eventually ended in a consent order, 1963 Trade Cas. ¶70,738 (S.D. Ohio 1963).) In *U.S.* v. *Phila. Nat'l Bank,* 374 U.S. 321, 372, n. 46 (1963), the Supreme Court suggested that the failing-company defense "might have somewhat larger contours as applied to bank mergers because of the greater public impact of a bank failure." Also, in *U.S.* v. *Third Nat'l Bank in Nashville,* 390 U.S. 171 (1968), the Court seemed to read the 1966 Bank Merger Act's concern for "the convenience and needs of the community" as permitting a competitor's acquisition of a bank that is in a "stagnant and floundering" condition. The Supreme Court stressed the need for eliminating other less anticompetitive methods of saving the "floundering" bank and satisfying the community's "convenience and needs." The district judge was instructed on remand to ascertain whether the bank's ownership had made "concrete efforts to recruit new management" and to assess the possibility of a sale of the bank to other owners who might be willing to face up to the management difficulties over a more extended period.

Continental Oil Company's (Conoco) acquisition of Malco Refineries was held to have violated Section 7 and divestiture was ordered over Conoco's contentions that at the time it acquired Malco, neither it nor Malco alone could have afforded the substantial modernization needed to compete in the New Mexico market, that Malco's sales and profits had been declining, and that its own refinery would have been closed had the merger not taken place. The Government argued that Malco's profitable history (its earnings decline notwithstanding) showed that it was not "failing," and that its profits had actually increased after the merger. The district court found for the Government (1968 Trade Cas. ¶72,374 (D.N.M. 1968), and the Supreme Court affirmed *per curiam,* (393 U.S. 79 (1968)), citing *U.S.* v. *Third Nat'l. Bank* (Nashville) and *International Shoe.*

The Justice Department gave its view of the defense in its merger guidelines as follows:

"A merger which the Department would otherwise challenge will ordinarily not be challenged if (i) the resources of one of the merging firms are so depleted and its prospects for rehabilitation so remote that the firm faces the clear probability of a business failure, and (ii) good faith efforts by the failing firm have failed to elicit a reasonable offer of acquisition more consistent with the purposes of Section 7 by a firm which intends to keep the failing firm in the market. The Department regards as failing only those firms with no reasonable prospect of remaining viable; it does not regard a firm as failing merely because the firm has been unprofitable for a period of time, has lost market position or failed to maintain its competitive position in some other respect, has poor management, or has not fully explored the possibility of overcoming its difficulties through self-help.

"In determining the applicability of the above standard to the acquisition of a failing division of a multi-market company, such factors as the difficulty in assessing the viability of a portion of a company, the possibility of arbitrary accounting practices, and the likelihood that an otherwise healthy company can rehabilitate one of its parts, will lead the Department to apply this standard only in the clearest of circumstances" (1 Trade Reg. Rep. ¶4510 (1968)).

The FTC has defined the defense as "the notion that the challenged acquisition could not under any circumstances be regarded as having the probability of substantially lessening competition because the acquired company was in such financial condition that it could no longer be regarded as a competitor in any sense of the word, actual or potential" (*Dean Foods Co.,* 70 F.T.C. 1146 (1966)). In the *Dean Foods* case, the Commission reversed its hearing examiner's acceptance of the defense, citing his failure to take into account the "overall profit picture" of all operations of the company said to be failing, including profitable operations of its subsidiaries in other markets not affected by the merger and its nonoperating income from securities and real estate holdings.

This theory that the defense might be applicable to a financially healthy company's sale of a "failing" division or subsidiary was also rejected by the Commission earlier in *Farm Journal, Inc.,* 53 F.T.C. 26 (1956). On the other hand, a district judge said, in *U.S.* v. *Reed Roller Bit Co.,* 274 F.Supp. 573 (W.D. Okla. 1967) that the doctrine "would seem" to extend to the sale of an unprofitable subsidiary by a prosperous parent.

In its litigated cases, the Federal Trade Commission has been slow to accept the failing-company defense, but in 14 of the 26 merger-clearance advisory opinions released February 13, 1968, the Commission gave the acquired companies' usually "failing," but sometimes "unprofitable," "poor," or "distressed" condition as a major reason for its failure to oppose the transaction (FTC ADVISORY OPINION DIGESTS 165–170, 176–180, 182, 184–185, 189 (FTC 1968)). Generally, the Commission also relied on indications that reasonable efforts had been made to find other buyers. Often, too, an additional factor was cited as minimizing probable anticompetitive effects: ease of entry into the industry involved, declining state of the industry as a whole, or limited geographical or product scope of existing competition between the merging firms. In six instances, the acquiring company was seeking clearance under an outstanding FTC order prohibiting further acquisitions without advance Commission approval.

The failing-company defense was originally adopted in a decision that permitted the largest company in an industry to acquire another of the giants in its industry, whose next financial statements would have disclosed "a condition of insolvency" under state law. The *International Shoe* opinion dismissed as "speculation" suggestions that the acquired manufacturer might have obtained "further help from the banks" or "might have availed itself of a receivership." The company's officers, stockholders, and creditors were deemed "more able than commission or court to foresee future contingencies" and choose the best course of action.

This line of thinking seems far removed from the current attitude reflected in the more recent decisions, with the possible exception of the *Granader* case. The Supreme Court may expect more today in the way of exhaustion of alternative remedies than it did in 1930. In *Citizen Publishing Co.* v. *U.S.,* 394 U.S. 131 (1969), the Court said the defense is not available "unless it is established that the company that acquires the failing company . . . is the only available purchaser." In a 7-0 decision (Justice Harlan concurring and Justice Fortas not participating), the Court affirmed the district court's findings that a joint-operating agreement between two Tucson newspapers, THE STAR and THE CITIZEN, served to fix prices, pool profits, and control the Tucson daily newspaper market.

The agreement took effect in 1940. At that time THE STAR was operating at a modest profit, while THE CITIZEN had sustained losses from 1932 to 1940. Despite its losses, THE CITIZEN'S owners had made no effort to sell the paper, and one of its owners had indicated a willingness to contribute further resources to its operation. The district court found that it was not in imminent danger of dissolution (280 F.Supp. 978 (D. Ariz. 1968)). The agreement ended all commercial competition between the two papers, although they continued to compete editorially. Originally entered into for a 25-year term, the agreement was extended in 1953 until 1990. From its inception, the agreement proved increasingly profitable for each party.

Justice Douglas' opinion for the Court held it "plain beyond peradventure of doubt" that the agreement violated Section 1 of the Sherman Act (the Court did not reach the question of alleged monopolization in violation of Section 2 of the Act), and concluded that only "the failing company defense, a judicially created doctrine," could save the agreement. The Court found that the defendants had failed to carry their burden of establishing the defense:

"[I]f we assume *arguendo* that in 1940 the then owners of the Citizen could not long keep the enterprise afloat, no effort was made to sell the Citizen; its properties and franchise were not put in the hands of a broker; and the record is silent on what the market, if any, for the Citizen might have been. Cf. *United States* v. *Diebold, Inc.,* 369 U.S. 654, 655.

"Moreover, we know from the broad experience of the business community since 1930, the year when the International Shoe case was decided, that companies reorganized through receivership, or through Chapter 10 or Chapter 11 of the Bankruptcy Act often emerged as strong competitive companies. The prospects of reorganization of the Citizen in 1940 would have to be dim or nonexistent to make the failing company doctrine applicable to this case."

The Supreme Court said, "[w]e confine the failing company defense to its present narrow scope." Yet, it also added new requirements of proof, such as a showing that the "failing" company had actively attempted (by use of a broker's services) to find an alternative purchaser, and that reorganization under the Bankruptcy Act would not have saved it. Once those burdens are met, and the classic test of *International Shoe* is complied with, it seems that, under *Citizen Publishing,* the defense would still be of assistance to an antitrust defendant. Indeed, it appears that in *Citizen Publishing,* the defense, although limited, was read into Section 1 of the Sherman Act.

In *Bowl America, Inc.* v. *Fair Lanes, Inc.,* 299 F.Supp. 1080 (D. Md. 1969), the district court refused to apply the defense in a Section 1 case, where the defendants were found to have acquired a chain of competitive bowling alleys in order to restrain competition. The court pointed out that the defense could not be applied in any event, since the defendants had acted with an anticompetitive purpose, but it regarded the defense as "doubtful" in a Section 1 case, and refused to read *Citizen Publishing* as actually authorizing the use of the failing-company defense in that context. In *Citizen Publishing* the defense failed because of a lack of proof; but if the *Bowl America* example is followed, *Citizen Publishing* may be read even more narrowly than Justice Douglas' opinion would indicate.

The Federal Trade Commission has stated an even more restrictive view of the defense than did the Supreme Court in *Citizen Publishing.* Under *Citizen Publishing,* a merger or other combination whose effect may be anticompetitive may be saved on a proper showing. Yet in *United States Steel Corp.* (74 F.T.C. 1270 (1968), *remanded,* 426 F.2d 592 (6th Cir. 1970)), decided 2–1 shortly before the *Citizen Publishing* decision (with Commissioner Elman dissenting and Commissioner McIntyre not participating), the FTC held that under *International Shoe* and the amended Section 7, there was no automatic failing-company defense.

In the majority opinion for himself and Commissioner Jones, Chairman Dixon found that Certified Industries, Inc., was "failing" when acquired by the Universal Atlas Cement Division (UAC) of U.S. Steel, but also found that UAC, at the time of the acquisition, was one of the four largest producers of portland cement in the United States and that Certified was one of the four largest producers of ready-mix concrete in the New York City area. Having found the merger anticompetitive, he reviewed the legislative history of the 1950 amendment to Section 7 and concluded that neither it nor *International Shoe* created an automatic exemption from antitrust liability merely because a company is failing:

"We are of the opinion, however, that the failing company doctrine does provide a true exception to Section 7, an exception which may immunize an acquisition having the prescribed effect on competition. But we agree with counsel supporting the complaint that this defense is not created automatically by the mere showing that the acquired company was in a failing condition.

". . . to be consistent with *International Shoe* and with the legislative intent expressed in the amendment of Section 7, in any case involving the acquisition of a failing company we must determine whether the acquisition may result in a substantial lessening of competition and, if so, the acquisition must be declared illegal in the absence of probable harm to innocent individuals so serious and substantial that the public interest requires that the acquisition nevertheless be permitted."

Commissioner Elman dissented, suggesting that the failing-company doctrine may be supported by a "due process" principle of public policy, that small businessmen and investors not be forced to dispose of failing firms at distress prices or suffer bankruptcy, for the sake of antitrust policy. In his view, "[t]he failing company defense is just that, a defense to the charge that a particular merger—otherwise anticompetitive—offends Section 7."

Antitrust experts are unable to reconcile *United States Steel* and *Citizen Publishing*, except on the view that the Commission may be a step ahead of the courts in reading the defense out of the law. The Justice Department's Merger Guidelines appear consistent with the restrictive view of the Supreme Court in *Citizen Publishing*. Yet the FTC's majority's view has found favor with the Justice Department in the past. See the Government's brief in *U.S.* v. *Richfield Oil Corp.*, 1967 Trade Cas. ¶72,066 (S.D. Calif. 1966) (dismissed as moot), where it was argued that the failing-company doctrine was not a defense, but was only one factor to be considered in determining the competitive effect of a merger.

One reason for possible change may be the 1950 revision of Section 7's competitive-injury test. It is no longer necessary to show that the effect of the acquisition "may be to substantially lessen competition between the corporation whose stock is so acquired and the corporation making the acquisition." As now written, Section 7 merely requires a showing that "the effect of such acquisition may be substantially to lessen competition." Whatever the technical niceties, it can probably still be assumed that no anticompetitive consequences will flow from the acquisition of a company that is out of the market anyway.

It may be that the defense succeeds in saving more mergers than the public record indicates. Antitrust lawyers report that the enforcement staffs at both the Antitrust Division and the FTC may sometimes accept failing-company defenses that might not be sustained by the Commission or the courts.

Availability of the defense to a failing division or subsidiary of an otherwise thriving company is the subject of disagreement among members of the antitrust bar. While some have no doubt that "failing" status depends on the condition of the entire business organization, others reject the suggestion that a company must either continue a failing operation or scrap it without salvaging its value as an operating enterprise. Perhaps the FTC and the Antitrust Division do not agree on this matter either, for the Merger Guidelines seem to take a more lenient attitude toward sales of failing divisions than have the FTC decisions. In *U.S.* v. *Lever Bros. Co.,* 216 F.Supp. 887 (S.D.N.Y. 1963), the district court may be said to have accepted a "failing brand" defense. In that case the court held that acquisition by Lever from Monsanto of the trademarks, copyrights, patents, and inventory of "All," a detergent, did not substantially lessen competition.

In *Crown Cork & Seal Co.,* Docket 8687, the hearing examiner rejected a failing-company defense based on evidence that the acquired company was in financial trouble because of losses in divisional operations that were not related to the industry in which the Commission's complaint alleged anticompetitive efforts resulting from the merger. The Commission dismissed the complaint in a brief statement that there were "special circumstances surrounding the acquisition" (74 F.T.C. 251, 297 (1968)).

There could be some question about whether the failing-company doctrine applies to vertical acquisitions. The Merger Guidelines indicate the Antitrust Division has no doubt about it. The FTC, however, may have entertained a different view at one time. See *U.S. Steel Corporation,* 74 F.T.C. 1270, 1290 (1968). An argument can be made that the doctrine has greater merit for vertical than horizontal mergers. Acquisition of a financially troubled company by a supplier or by a customer may revive the failing business as a factor in the market, whereas a horizontal merger always assures elimination of the "failing" company as a competitor.

Will the doctrine save an acquisition when other purchasers of the failing business are available but in each instance acquisiton by the other purchaser would have greater anticompetitive effects? Some of the FTC's advisory opinions indicate that the Commission would answer yes.

C. CONSEQUENCES

1. Restraining Orders and Preliminary Injunctions Against Mergers

Question: *When will the Department of Justice or FTC sue to prevent a merger before it occurs?*

By Section 15 of the Clayton Act (15 U.S.C. § 25), the U.S. attorneys in the various federal districts, under the direction of the Attorney General, are assigned the duty to bring injunction suits to "prevent and restrain" violations of Section 7. Once a petition is filed, Section 15 provides "the court may at any time make such temporary restraining order or prohibition as shall be deemed just in the premises."

In applying Section 15, the district courts have looked to traditional equitable principles. Rule 65 of the Federal Rules of Civil Procedure states the procedure and the standards to be satisfied in the procurement of temporary restraining orders and preliminary injunctions. The motion for such an order is addressed to the discretion of the court. A temporary restraining order may be entered without notice and upon a summary showing that it is needed to prevent immediate and irreparable injury to the applicant. It may be made effective for no longer than 10 days, although the period of its effectiveness may be extended "for good cause shown."

The applicant for a preliminary injunction, the purpose of which is to preserve the status quo until a final determination of the action can be made after a full hearing, has the burden of showing that he will probably prevail in the main action. Among the factors the court may examine before it issues a preliminary injunction are: certainty of injury to the moving party if the motion is denied and the final decision is in his favor, lack of any means of repairing any injury caused the moving party by a denial of the motion, absence of disproportionate inconvenience or loss to the opposing party, and unlikelihood of an adverse effect on the public interest.

There is a cautious attitude on the part of the federal judiciary toward granting motions for preliminary injunctions and temporary restraining orders, but the Government has been able to obtain both in antimerger actions (*U.S.* v. *Chrysler Corp.*, 232 F.Supp. 651 (D.N.J. 1964); *U.S.* v. *Allied Chemical Corp.*, 1964 Trade Cas. ¶71,311 (S.D.N.Y. 1965); *U.S.* v. *Ingersoll-Rand Co.*, 218 F.Supp. 530 (W.D. Pa. 1963) *aff'd*, 320 F.2d 509 (3rd Cir. 1963); *U.S.* v. *Standard Oil Co. of N.J.*, 1965 Trade Cas. ¶71,503 (D.N.J. 1965); 253 F.Supp. 196 (D.N.J. 1966); *U.S.* v. *Joseph Schlitz Brewing Co.*, 253 F.Supp. 129 (N.D. Calif. 1966); *aff'd*, 385 U.S. 37 (1966), *pet. for rehearing denied*, 385 U.S. 1021 (1967)). In the *Chrysler, Ingersoll,* and *Allied Chemical* cases, the temporary prohibitions led to abandonment of the proposed acquisitions. In the *New Jersey Standard* and *Schlitz* proceedings, temporary restraining orders were, by stipulation, allowed to continue in effect pending the outcome of the litigation.

The Government did not always win the first round. Once its inability to get a preliminary injunction caused it to discontinue the action (*U.S.* v. *FMC Corp.*, 218 F.Supp. 817 (N.D. Calif. 1963), *appeal dismissed*, 321 F.2d 534 (9th Cir. 1963), *application for temporary injunction denied*, 84 S.Ct. 4 (1963)). Two lengthy cases involved bank mergers (*U.S.* v. *Third National Bank in Nashville*, 1964 Trade Cas. ¶71,209 (M.D. Tenn. 1964); 260 F.Supp. 869

(M.D. Tenn. 1966), *rev'd,* 390 U.S. 171 (1968); *consent decree,* 1968 Trade Cas. ¶72,556 (M.D. Tenn. 1968); *U.S.* v. *Crocker-Anglo National Bank,* 223 F.Supp. 849 (N.D. Calif. 1963); 263 F.Supp. 125 (N.D. Calif. 1966); 277 F.Supp. 133 (N.D. Calif. 1967)). Sometimes the filing of a Section 7 complaint caused the companies to abandon merger plans (*U.S.* v. *Standard Oil Co., New Jersey,* 147 ATRR A-19 (S.D. Calif. 1964); *U.S.* v. *America Corp.,* 1963 Trade Cas. ¶70,923 (S.D. Calif. 1963)).

Two of the federal district judges who entered preliminary injunctions published opinions. In the *Chrysler* case, Judge Wortendyke of the New Jersey Federal District Court stressed the "reasonable probability" that the Government could show that Chrysler's proposed acquisition of Mack Trucks, Inc., would violate Section 7. He cited evidence that the four largest truck manufacturers, of which Chrysler was one, controlled almost 90 percent of the industry and noted that Chrysler had already announced plans for a substantial investment in expansion of its heavy-truck marketing facilities, an investment that "would be unnecessary should it acquire Mack and thus secure the elimination of Mack's substantial competition in this field."

Judge Wortendyke dismissed as irrelevant the truck manufacturers' argument that there had been no showing of irreparable injury to warrant issuance of a preliminary injunction. Since Section 7 of the Clayton Act proscribes mergers and acquisitions that "may" substantially lessen competition, he explained, the Government need not show that it will prevail upon a trial of the merits. At the same time, according to the court, the only harm the two firms could experience from a preliminary injunction "would be such as the parties fully anticipated and provided for" in the merger agreement. Yet, if consummation of the acquisition were permitted, "Mack's position as a profitable, independent manufacturer and effective competitor in the relevant markets would completely vanish."

An opinion by Western Pennsylvania Federal District Judge Rosenberg in the *Ingersoll-Rand* case described a preliminary-injunction hearing that had the appearance of a full dress rehearsal of a trial. The hearing took five full days and produced 800 pages of testimony, as well as much documentary evidence. After examining that evidence, Judge Rosenberg made tentative findings as to "line of commerce," "section of the country," and "probable competitive impact." He concluded "as of now, that the effect of the proposed acquisitions may be substantially to lessen competition, or to tend to create a monopoly." He found it "difficult to understand" why Ingersoll-Rand opposed a preliminary injunction, "considering the hardships of divestiture."

In this particular case, Judge Rosenberg stated, allowing even temporary acquisition of the companies would "undoubtedly result in the passing of records, trade secrets and other confidential matters into the possession and control of Ingersoll-Rand prior to the court's final adjudication," so that divestiture would leave "a residue with possible concomitant injury. . . . Displacement and dislocation of management personnel, assets and records of the acquired companies, together with all other matters which concern the preservation of competitive vigor should be delayed until a decision is rendered at a final hearing." Any inconvenience to the companies involved could not outweigh "the public interest in preserving a free-competitive economy." For the Government's showing of irreparable harm, Judge Rosenberg looked to "the history of mergers and the efforts by the government to limit them or to neutralize certain destructive effects to the nation's economy." Citing the congressional findings prior to the 1950 amendments of the Clayton Act as "an expression of the public policy of the nation," he concluded: "the threatened violation of the law here is itself sufficient public injury to justify the requested relief."

Another sort of preliminary relief is available in some situations. In the *Brown Shoe* case, 370 U.S. 294 (1962), in which the Supreme Court affirmed a divestiture order, the district judge had denied a motion for a preliminary injunction against consummation of the acquisition, but he did order that the merged companies be operated separately pending the outcome of the case (*U.S.* v. *Brown Shoe Co.,* 179 F.Supp. 721 (E.D. Mo. 1959)). Title to the acquired assets had to be vested in a subsidiary of Brown Shoe, and the subsidiary had to have independent management under a board containing no Brown Shoe directors. The order prohibited commingling of the assets or net earnings of the subsidiary with those of the parent, any hypothecation or incumbrance on the shares of the subsidiary, and the closing of retail outlets or factories of the subsidiary because of competition with the parent.

Generally, the Government has sought an outright prohibition of the merger while the suit is pending, but it did sign a stipulation permitting completion of a stock acquisition, providing the acquired companies were operated as separate entities (*U.S.* v. *General Telephone and Electronics Corp.,* 156 ATRR A-5 (S.D.N.Y. 1964)).

Under Section 11 of the Clayton Act (15 U.S.C. § 21), authority to enforce Section 7 is also "vested in the Interstate Commerce Commission where applicable to common carriers subject to the Interstate Commerce Act, as amended; in the Federal Communications Commission where applicable to common carriers engaged in wire radio communication or radio transmission of energy; in the Civil Aeronautics Board where applicable to air carriers and foreign air carriers subject to the Civil Aeronautics Act of 1938; in the Federal Reserve Board where applicable to banks, banking associations, and trust companies; and in the Federal Trade Commission where applicable to all other character of commerce."

Section 11 provides for the issuance of a complaint by the agency designated for intervention in the proceeding by the Attorney General, and for review or enforcement of the agency's order by the court of appeals for the circuit in which the violation occurred. But nothing is said about temporary orders to maintain the status quo while an administrative hearing is held, and there is no provision in the Federal Rules for the issuance of preliminary injunctions by courts of appeals. In *Federal Reserve Board* v. *Transamerica Corp.,* 184 F.2d 311 (9th Cir. 1950), under the All-Writs Act, 28 U.S.C. §1651 (a), the court of appeals held that the Board could obtain a preliminary injunction against an acquisition, consummation of which would thwart both the Board's regulatory jurisdiction over such mergers and the court of appeals' jurisdiction to review the Board's action. Under the All-Writs Act, the federal courts are authorized to "issue all writs necessary or appropriate in aid of their respective jurisdictions."

Two attempts by the Federal Trade Commission to use the All-Writs Act in similar fashion were rejected. In 1955, a court of appeals, without opinion, turned down an FTC request for an order holding up the acquisition later outlawed in *A.G. Spalding & Bros., Inc.,* v. *FTC,* 301 F.2d 585 (3rd Cir. 1962). In *FTC* v. *International Paper Co.,* 241 F.2d 372 (2nd Cir. 1956), the court decided the Commission had no authority to seek injunctive relief under the All-Writs Act. In both those cases, the FTC sought a court order in advance of administrative proceedings. The court's action in the *Transamerica* case was taken in somewhat different circumstances. The stock acquisition attacked there had been consummated, and hearings on possible divestiture were in progress when arrangements were made for transfer of the assets of the acquired banks. The Board wanted an injunction to prevent that transaction, which would prevent appropriate divestiture. In this context the court made its determination that the Board's regulatory jurisdiction and the court's appellate jurisdiction would be defeated if a writ were not issued.

The Commission did not accept these court of appeals decisions as settling the issue (Footnote 10, *Ekco Products Co.,* 65 F.T.C. 1163, 1215 (1964)). The FTC threatened to relitigate the issue during investigation of the merger plans of department-store chains, but the companies assured the FTC staff that the two enterprises would be operated independently after the acquisition was consummated.

In *FTC* v. *Dean Foods Co.,* 384 U.S. 597 (1966), a five-four majority of the Supreme Court sustained the Commission's contentions that it had standing to sue for temporary antimerger injunctions under the All-Writs Act and that the courts of appeals had jurisdiction to grant such injunctions. Speaking through Justice Clark, the majority found "ample precedent to support jurisdiction of the court of appeals to issue a preliminary injunction . . . upon showing that an effective remedial order, once the merger was implemented, would be virtually impossible, thus rendering the enforcement of any final decree of divestiture futile." Section 11 (c) of the Clayton Act, Justice Clark noted, gives the courts of appeals exclusive jurisdiction to review FTC orders against illegal mergers. This grant of authority "includes the traditional power to issue injunctions to preserve the status quo while administrative proceedings are in progress and prevent impairment of the effective exercise of appellate jurisdiction."

Justice Fortas wrote a dissent, in which he was joined by Justices Harlan, Stewart, and White. They saw the majority opinion as "radical surgery upon the administration of Section 7 of the Clayton Act." It burdens the courts of appeals with "original jurisdiction which they cannot properly exercise and a fact-finding function in elaborate, complex situations, which they should not be asked to take."

The dissenters were convinced that there was no basis in law or precedent for what the majority did. The FTC was not intended to be a litigation arm of the United States except as its own final orders might be involved, they maintained. Rather, the Commission is supposed to act deliberately as an expert and bring to bear upon the complex economic problems of a merger "that judgment and experience which can emerge only from a careful factual inquiry, taking evidence, and the formulation of a report. The Federal Trade Commission was not intended to be a gun, a carbon copy of the Department of Justice."

On remand from the Supreme Court, the Court of Appeals for the Seventh Circuit granted the Commission a temporary injunction effective for a period of four months. The decree enjoined Dean and Bowfund Corp., formerly Bowman, "from making any material changes, directly or indirectly, with respect to the capital stock or corporate structure of Bowfund Corp., or with respect to the assets purchased by Dean from Bowman . . . including the operation and policies affecting those assets (other than changes made in the ordinary course of business) pending an entry of a final order . . . in respect to the proceeding presently before the Federal Trade Commission." If the purchaser of one of the Bowman delivery routes should seek to procure milk supplies from Dean, Dean is directed to "attempt to persuade them to purchase such milk or products under the Bowman label and to supply such milk or products from a processing plant or plants formerly operated by Bowman." In no event is Dean to sell milk to the route purchasers under the Dean label.

The court of appeals filed no opinion with its temporary injunction. Its order merely recited that the court "considered affidavits, materials, and briefs filed by both parties . . . their arguments in open court, and . . . the opinion of the United States Supreme Court." The FTC later issued a divestiture order (70 F.T.C. 1146 (1966)) that was modified by the court of appeals (1967 Trade Cas. ¶72,086 (7th Cir. 1967)), and reissued in the modified form (71 F.T.C. 731 (1967)).

The Commission has made little use of its authority to seek preliminary injunctions since the *Dean Foods* case. The principal value to the Commission of the decision has been a stronger hand in negotiating agreements that acquired firms will be run separately and not scrambled into the acquiring firm pending final decision on lawfulness of the acquisition.

At the time of the *Dean Foods* decision, some lawyers thought the possibility of the FTC's obtaining preliminary relief would create more enforcement problems than it could solve. Until the court of appeals issued the preliminary injunction, they were convinced, and many still are, that the courts of appeals would be unreceptive to FTC pleas for preliminary injunctions. Relying on the Justice Department's experiences in attempting to get preliminary injunctions from federal district judges, they insisted that courts were ordinarily willing to block an imminent merger only when persuaded that the Government had a prima facie case worth hearing and only when the Government was prepared for early hearing. It would be more difficult to satisfy a court of appeals on these two points, the reasoning goes, since appeals courts have no control over the docket in which the case would be tried and because the FTC has a record of long, drawn-out merger proceedings. As Justice Fortas pointed out in his dissenting opinion, there are factors in merger cases that encourage the development of a substantial record even on a motion for preliminary relief, and the courts of appeals are said to be ill-equipped or not inclined to try complex antitrust litigation in the first instance. An adverse reaction on the part of the courts of appeals, it was anticipated, might serve to prejudice the FTC's case from the outset.

The Commission's success in its first attempt raises doubt about the accuracy of that assessment, and the *Pepsico* case does not really dispel the doubt. In that case, *FTC* v. *Pepsico., Inc.,* 1973 Trade Cas. ¶74,450 (2d Cir. 1973), the court of appeals, although satisfied of the reasonable probability that the FTC could prove a violation, refused an injunction, but ordered continued separate operation of certain assets so that divestiture might later be ordered. Some suggest that courts of appeals are more likely than district judges to grant interlocutory relief. If the action of the court of appeals in the *Dean Foods* case is any test, a court of appeals apparently can grant a temporary decree without making the formal findings of fact required of a district judge. At one time, at least, there were attorneys in the Antitrust Division who felt the Government's odds were better before a three-judge court than before a single judge. They preferred a two-out-of-three series to a sudden-death playoff. District judges, especially those who are unfamiliar with antitrust or not convinced of its worth, sometimes don't like to take the sole responsibility of issuing a preliminary injunction.

Some antitrust experts feel the *Dean Foods* decision will add to the competitive spirit between the two enforcement agencies and may thereby produce more enforcement activity under Section 7.

If the standard mentioned by the Court of Appeals for the Seventh Circuit in its order is to be taken at face value, the test to be applied in determining whether a temporary injunction will issue could also increase the flow of temporary injunctions. Apparently in reliance on the Supreme Court's statement that temporary injunctions will be entered to "prevent impairment of the effective exercise of appellate jurisdiction," the court of appeals spoke only in terms of the probability of the issuance of an FTC order, not the probability of eventual success by the Commission in having its order upheld by the courts. The language of the court's order might be read as meaning there will be no such balancing of the equities as occurs in the federal district courts, since the only purpose of the order is to protect appellate jurisdiction.

The Supreme Court opinion uses language suggesting that, when the Court speaks of protecting appellate jurisdiction, it has in mind assurance that an effective, not a futile, divestiture order will be possible at the close of the litigation. That language indicates it is the final, court-reviewed result that must be looked to, not merely the FTC order. In a motion for a preliminary injunction under the All-Writs Act, the Commission is acting as a prosecutor, and, according to the court of appeals, the Commission must prove it will probably find a Section 7 violation and issue a divestiture order. This could lead to difficulty. On one occasion a member of the Commission suggested publicly that the Commission had strong evidence against a respondent. He was later told he had disqualified himself from acting in the proceeding (*Texaco, Inc.* v. *FTC,* 336 F.2d 754 (D.C. Cir. 1964)).

When the Commission's power to seek temporary injunctions was argued before the court of appeals, counsel for Dean Foods charged that such powers would eventually be extended to other FTC enforcement proceedings, not just those in merger cases. FTC counsel denied that the Commission had any intention to seek temporary injunctions under the FTC Act or the Robinson-Patman Act. In other than merger cases, a showing could probably seldom be made that a change in the status quo would make any FTC order later issued futile. Yet it might be shown, for example, that an advertising program attacked under Section 5 of the FTC Act will do its harm to the public interest and end before the Commission can issue an order. In addition, some lawyers think a Section 3 Clayton Act exclusive-dealing case might present circumstances outrageous enough to induce the commissioners to seek preliminary relief.

The lower federal courts have produced conflicting decisions on the appealability of orders granting or denying preliminary injunctions. In the *Ingersoll-Rand* case, 320 F.2d 509 (3rd Cir. 1963), the court of appeals accepted Ingersoll-Rand's argument that preliminary injunctions are appealable. On the other hand, in the *FMC* case the court refused to let the Government appeal from a denial of a preliminary injunction (321 F.2d 534 (9th Cir. 1963), *application for temporary injunction denied,* 84 S. Ct.4 (1963)). Justice Goldberg agreed the order was not appealable. He refused to delay matters in that case to give the Government a chance to seek Supreme Court review.

The issue has its roots in Section 1292 (a) (1) of the Federal Judicial Code and in Section 2 of the Expediting Act of 1903, 15 U.S.C. § 29 (1903). Section 1292 (a) (1) of the Judicial Code provides that "interlocutory orders of the district courts granting, continuing, modifying, refusing or dissolving injunctions or refusing to dissolve or modify injunctions" are appealable to the courts of appeals "except where a direct review may be had in the Supreme Court." The Expediting Act makes final judgments in the Government's civil antitrust suits appealable directly to the Supreme Court, but says nothing about interlocutory orders. In *U.S.* v. *California Cooperative Canneries,* 279 U.S. 553 (1929), the Supreme Court interpreted the Expediting Act as precluding "the possibility of an appeal to either court from an interlocutory decree."

The court of appeals in *Ingersoll-Rand* pointed out that the language "except where a direct review may be had in the Supreme Court" was added to Section 1292 of the Judicial Code in 1948, after the *California Canneries* decision. Reading Section 1292 in conjunction with Section 1291, which provides for court of appeals review of final district court decisions "except where a direct review may be had in the Supreme Court," the court saw a congressional intent "that interlocutory orders, such as the one at bar, are reviewable by a court of appeals excepting and only excepting those types of cases in which an interlocutory order is directly reviewable by the Supreme Court." The Expediting Act does not make interlocutory or preliminary orders appealable directly to the Supreme Court.

When the Government argued that line of reasoning in the *FMC* case, Justice Goldberg replied that such a contention "in effect requires an implied overruling and revocation of the established construction of the Expediting Act." He said it would "do violence to decisions of this Court now to open the floodgates by permitting appeals of interlocutory orders in antitrust cases decided by single-judge district courts."

By a vote of 6 to 3 (Douglas, Stewart, and Rehnquist, JJ., dissenting) the Supreme Court held that there can be no interlocutory review, under 28 U.S.C. §1292 (b), of orders in actions brought by the Government for injunctive relief (*Tidewater Oil Co.* v. *U.S.,* 41 U.S.L.W. 4053 (U.S. Dec. 6, 1972)). Section 1292(b) provides for interlocutory review in the court of appeals of orders certified by the trial judges as involving a controlling question of law. According to the Supreme Court, such review is barred in Government antitrust actions by Section 2 of the Expediting Act. The Court noted that with the passage of the Expediting Act in 1903, Congress deliberately withdrew from courts of appeals a pre-existing jurisdiction for interlocutory appeals from orders granting or continuing an injunction in Government antitrust actions. Though it conceded that the issue was not free from doubt, it also noted that the exclusivity of the Supreme Court's jurisdiction over appeals in such cases had since become well established and that there was no indication that, with the enactment of Section 1292(b) in 1958, Congress intended to change this situation. In reaching its determination that courts of appeals have no jurisdiction under Section 1292(b), the Court also made it clear that it has no jurisdiction under Section 1292(a), which provides for interlocutory review of preliminary injunctive orders by courts of appeals.

Although the Expediting Act has been construed to bar interlocutory review by courts of appeals in government antitrust actions, the Court noted that interlocutory review is possible under the All Writs Act, 28 U.S.C. § 1651(a), "but application for the extraordinary writ must be made to this Court where 'sole appellate jurisdiction lies' in such cases," citing *United States Alkali Export Associa-*

tion, Inc. v. *United States,* 325 U.S. 196, 201–203 (1945), and *De-Beers Consolidated Mines, Ltd.* v. *United States,* 325 U.S. 212, 217 (1945). The Court's opinion concludes with the statement that "[t]he exclusive nature of the jurisdiction created in Sec. 2 of the Expediting Act has consistently been recognized by this Court, and we hold today that that exclusivity remains unimpaired."

Although *Tidewater* appears, at first glance, to make it clear that courts of appeals have no jurisdiction to review any sort of order in government antitrust actions, the U.S. Court of Appeals for the Second Circuit (Moore and Timbers, JJ., with Mulligan dissenting) subsequently held that it has jurisdiction to hear an appeal from an "ancillary" order in such an action (*International Business Machines Corp.* v. *U.S.,* 1973 Trade Cas. ¶74,293 (2d Cir. 1972)). The court order in *IBM* required the defendant to produce in discovery 1,200 documents that the defendant claimed were privileged. Viewing this order as one threatening irreparable injury to IBM, the majority deemed it a "final" order under the rule of *Cohen* v. *Beneficial Industrial Loan Corp.,* 337 U.S. 541 (1949), and therefore subject to review under 28 U.S.C. § 1291, which provides for review of final orders by the courts of appeals. According to the majority, the Expediting Act left room for review of such ancillary orders. It relied primarily upon *Shenandoah Valley Broadcasting, Inc.* v. *ASCAP,* 375 U.S. 39 (1963), *modified,* 375 U.S. 994 (1964), in which the Supreme Court held that an appeal from an order construing a consent decree issued in a government antitrust suit was properly before the court of appeals since it was an "ancillary" order and since the controversy was one "entirely between private parties and . . . outside the mainstream of the litigation in which the government [was] directly concerned."

The majority distinguished *Tidewater* on the ground that the primary consideration underlying that decision was to limit "review of important questions of antitrust law to [the Supreme] Court." In *IBM,* by contrast, the relief sought was "entirely collateral to the issues in the main case. It is even further removed from the principal action than the situation presented in *Cohen* was from the main case there. It is for this reason that we say the Expediting Act by language and intent does not bear upon the specific problem now before us. To hold otherwise would be to say that no appellate review is ever available to restrain threatened court action no matter how irreparable the damage flowing therefrom. This we are not prepared to say." Because of the threatened irreparable injury, the majority also found jurisdiction under the All-Writs Act.

Dissenting, Judge Mulligan gave his view that the appeal was barred by the Expediting Act. The Court in *Tidewater,* he stated, "plainly indicates that the Act was intended to preserve to the Supreme Court alone the right to review all interlocutory orders and then only when there is an appeal from the final judgment. Piecemeal appeal was sought to be eliminated and there is no suggestion that our Court act to screen appeals on the basis of our determination as to their trade regulatory significance." As for the All-Writs Act, Judge Mulligan noted the Supreme Court's apparent assertion of the exclusivity of its own jurisdiction under that Act.

Although the Court in *Tidewater* did not specifically deal with the question of the reviewability of ancillary orders, the opinion could reasonably be read, as Judge Mulligan has read it, as stating that the Supreme Court has exclusive jurisdiction to review all orders arising out of antitrust actions brought by the Government for injunctive relief. The worst fear of the majority in *IBM,* that there would be no recourse from a lower court order "no matter how irreparable the damage flowing therefrom," does not seem well placed in view of the Supreme Court's own observation that interlocutory review is possible under the All-Writs Act (but only, it would seem, in the Supreme Court). It should be emphasized, however, that the All-Writs Act is apparently rarely applied and is not available except in extraordinary situations.

The majority of the Supreme Court is now on record favoring amendment of the Expediting Act, which "unjustifiably burdens this Court with inadequately sifted records and with cases which could be disposed of by review in the courts of appeals." Justice White, who concurred with *Tidewater,* disavowed "the advisory to Congress reflecting one view of the relative merits of the Expediting Act." Justice Douglas, who dissented, disagreed with "the intimations in both the majority and minority opinions that because of our overwork the antitrust cases should first be routed to the courts of appeals and only then brought here." "The case for our 'overwork' is a myth," and the Justices, he declared, have "vast leisure time."

Motions for temporary restraining orders and preliminary injunctions have also been litigated in private suits to enjoin alleged violations of Section 7 of the Clayton Act. For examples, see *Hamilton Watch Co.* v. *Benrus Watch Co.,* 206 F.2d 738 (2d Cir. 1953); *E. L. Bruce Co.* v. *Empire Millwork Corp.,* 164 F.Supp. 446 (S.D.N.Y. 1958); and *American Crystal Sugar Co.* v. *Cuban-American Sugar Co.,* 143 F.Supp. 100 (S.D.N.Y. 1956). The elements balanced by the courts in those cases may have been somewhat different; for one thing, the plaintiff may have had a greater burden in proving that consummation of the merger would cause irreparable injury to the public interest.

The lawyer may be asked the following about a prospective merger: (1) What is the likelihood that a preliminary injunction will be granted; (2) will the Federal Trade Commission or the Department of Justice conduct the investigation?

The two agencies have never announced any set plan for dividing merger investigations. When one learns of a merger it wants to investigate, it checks with the other before proceeding. Some industries are recognized by both agencies as "belonging" to one or the other, generally because that agency has accumulated market-share statistics and general familiarity with the industry. A department store, cement company, or food processor acquisition is more likely to be reviewed by the FTC. Banks, oil refiners, motion-picture producers, distillers, and heavy-machinery producers are more likely to be looked at by the Antitrust Division. In some areas, such as chemicals and basic metals, the two agencies compete with each other for the choice cases. Jurisdictional disputes are negotiated on a case-by-case basis. Sometimes the Justice Department's capacity to seek preliminary relief in a district court is the deciding factor.

2. FTC Premerger Notification

Question: *By what authority does the FTC require premerger notification?*

In January 1967 the Federal Trade Commission publicly stated its enforcement policy with respect to mergers in the food distribution industries (1 Trade Reg. Rep. ¶4525) and to vertical mergers in the cement industry (1 Trade Reg. Rep. ¶4520). (Section III-A-8, p. 205.) Over the dissents of Chairman Dixon and Commissioner MacIntyre, the Commission ordered every Portland cement producer and every food retailer or wholesaler whose annual sales were $100 million or more to file a Special Report under Section 6(b) of the FTC Act at least 60 days in advance of any proposed merger or acquisition. In a press release issued at the time, the Commission said, ". . . in order to implement its enforcement program expeditiously and uniformly, it must know of prospective acquisitions [in the food distribution industry] in advance of their consummation" (FTC release dated January 17, 1967). No litigation over failure to file has been reported.

Both the Commission and the Justice Department have sought congressional approval for premerger notification programs, but Congress has not acted on their requests. See, for example, H.R. 2511 (Celler), 90th Congress, and predecessor bills in earlier Congresses. An apparent attempt by the Antitrust Division to seek pre-acquisition information by a Civil Investigative Demand under 15 U.S.C. § 1312 was struck down by a district court. *In re Union Oil Co. of Calif.,* 225 F.Supp. 486 (S.D.Calif. 1963), the court held that the statute did not empower the Antitrust Division to inquire into possible future, as opposed to past or existing, antitrust violations.

In April 1969, the Commission announced it would require corporations contemplating certain mergers to notify it of their intentions and to file a special report within 10 days after reaching agreement in principle, and at least 60 days before the merger or acquisition is consummated. The Commission acted pursuant to a resolution. The resolution applied to "any merger or acquisition of firms which (1) are subject to the Commission's jurisdiction, (2) have assets of $10 million or more, and (3) have combined assets of $250 million or more." For such mergers or acquisitions, each party is required to notify the Commission no less than 60 days prior to consummation. Any party with assets of $250 million or more will have to file a special report in response to an order of the Commission. Parties with assets of at least $10 million but less than $250 million may be required to notify the Commission within 10 days after reaching agreement, and to file a special report upon direction of the Commission.

Similar requirements apply to stock acquisitions. Within 10 days after amassing 10 percent or more of the voting stock of any corporation with assets of at least $10 million, a corporation with assets of $250 million or more will be required to notify the FTC and to file a special report in response to an FTC order. Where the combined assets total $250 million or more, the notice requirements apply to the acquiring corporation, which may have to file a special report upon demand. If the acquiring corporation is to hold 50 percent or more of the stock, one with assets of $250 million or more has to notify the FTC of the proposed acquisition and file a special report in response to a Commission order at least 60 days in advance. Where the combined assets would total $250 million, 60 days' notice is required of the acquiring corporation, which may have to file a special report upon demand. Special reports also may be required of corporations whose voting stock had been or was about to be acquired, as indicated.

On May 10, 1969, special report forms, cleared by the Bureau of the Budget, were sent to 265 manufacturing and mining corporations, 23 merchandising corporations, 9 consumer loan companies, 31 property and liability insurers, 74 life insurance companies, 33 one-bank holding companies, and 40 "miscellaneous" corporations (in transportation, entertainment, financial, and other fields) with assets of $250 million or more. Other potential respondents were informed of the notice requirements through the FEDERAL REGISTER, in which the FTC's official announcement appeared on May 10, 1969. According to the FTC's Press Release and the Federal Register notice, the special reports will be treated confidentially by the FTC, but the premerger notification data will be made public. Under the resolution adopted in April 1972, and re-affirmed in February 1973 (1 Trade Reg. Rep. ¶4540), the form now required is not substantially different from that provided for in the 1969 resolution.

The Commission rests its authority to require premerger notification on Sections 3, 6, 9, and 10 of the Federal Trade Commission Act, 15 U.S.C. §§ 43, 46, 49, and 50. If the power to require premerger notification exists, it would be found in Section 6(b). In *United States* v. *Morton Salt Co.*, 338 U.S. 632 (1950), the Supreme Court read the Commission's Section 6(b) investigative authority broadly, stating, "we find nothing that would deny its use for any purpose within the duties of the Commission" (338 U.S. at 649). Although the Court suggested that there might be limits to the scope of inquiry under the statute, it gave no intimation that the Commission was restricted to existing or past matters.

In *Morton Salt* the Commission sought special reports to check on compliance with a court decree, while here the rationale would seem to be that offered at the time the food and cement merger guides were issued, the Commission's need to know of prospective mergers in advance. The Commission's press release of April 13, 1969, gave no reason for its notification and special report requirement other than its "statutory responsibilities to enforce Section 7" of the Clayton Act and the acceleration in the pace of merger activity. Nonetheless, the FTC's authority under Section 6(b) to require notification and special reports is not generally disputed. A narrower approach was suggested in *U.S.* v. *St. Regis Paper Co.*, 181 F.Supp. 862 (S.D.N.Y. 1960), in which it was held that Section 6(b) was adopted as a convenience not only to the Government but to the business community, and that only information compiled in the ordinary course of business would be required.

Some antitrust experts question the legal support for the FTC's notification requirement, particularly if interpreted as creating a 60-day preliminary injunction against all mergers involving large corporations, arguing that the requirements of notice and a 60-day waiting period constitute "an agency statement of general or particular applicability and future effect" and thus constitute rule-making under the Administrative Procedure Act, 5 U.S.C. § 551(5). See *NLRB* v. *Wyman Gordon Co.*, 394 U.S. 759 (1969). In a letter to a bar association committee, released July 16, 1969, the FTC Chairman disclaimed for the Commission any intention of creating a waiting period (1 Trade Reg. Rep. ¶4540.20). Others suggest that since the Commission may seek a temporary injunction in any event, under *FTC* v. *Dean Foods*, 384 U.S. 597 (1966), the principal sanction behind the 60-day notice requirement may be a proceeding on the merits against a corporation that fails to wait. In *Dean Foods* a complaint already had been issued, and the FTC was able to allege that it was probable that it ultimately would enter an order finding a violation of the law. On the assumption that a corporation notifies the Commission of merger or acquisition plans and files the required special report, the FTC might possess sufficient information to seek a temporary injunction under *Dean Foods,* and then move into a full-blown Section 7 proceeding.

In requiring general premerger notification, the Commission apparently acted unanimously, as it did not do in its food and cement industry policy statements. While some experts, on the theory that a subpoena calls only for existing material, question whether the Commission has the legal authority to require advance notice of developments that may later occur, others consider that the *Morton Salt* decision established the sweeping breadth of Section 6(b) and that the courts are not likely to require the Commission repeatedly to require corporations to give notice.

Assuming that a corporation does not give notice or file a special report, what then? Under Section 10 of the Act, a corporation failing to file a required report is subject to a civil forfeiture action to recover $100 per day of noncompliance. The Commission must first serve a notice of default and 30 days must elapse after notice. Some lawyers suggest that upon receipt of a default notice, the corporation could purge itself of any default by filing within 30 days. Others point out that the failure to notify by a certain time can never be cured once the time has passed. Still others suggest that, in addition to possibly inviting an antitrust action, such a procedure might be a willful disregard of the FTC's lawful process, which could result in criminal penalties under Section 10.

3. Divestiture

Question: *What remedies are available to restore competition if a merger is declared unlawful?*

The Clayton Act provides alternative civil remedies. Section 15 gives the federal district courts "jurisdiction to prevent and restrain violations" and gives the Attorney General "the duty . . . to institute proceedings in equity to prevent and restrain such violations." Section 11 authorizes remedial action by the Federal Trade Commission, the Federal Communications Commission, the Interstate Commerce Commission, the Civil Aeronautics Board, or the Federal Reserve Board in the industry in which they have jurisdiction. The agency may issue "an order requiring such person to cease and

desist from such violations, and divest itself of the stock, or other
share capital, or assets, held . . . contrary to the provisions of Section 7."

Whatever the problems, the federal courts' willingness to attempt
divestiture in the form of separation of a going business into two
independent enterprises is illustrated by the "egg unscrambling"
ordered in the *Lexington Bank* case, *U.S.* v. *First Nat'l. Bank and
Trust Co. of Lexington,* 193 ATRR A-10 (E.D. Ky. 1965). In the
first order to require separation of merged banking operations, the
court ordered that the merged bank "without delay take all necessary steps to create a separate, competitive and independent commercial bank which shall be the equivalent of the former Security
Trust Company at the time of its consolidation with the former
First National Bank and Trust Company of Lexington." Security
Trust had to be given back "its name, its directors, its officers and
personnel, its offices, furniture and equipment, its capital surplus
and undivided profits, and loans, savings, checking and trust accounts, plus its proportionate share of any increments and improvements since that date."

When divestiture is ordered, it may be difficult to find a suitable
buyer of the stock or assets to be divested when the acquired company cannot be reestablished as a separate concern. Sometimes the
Government agrees to a sale that itself might be a horizontal or
vertical merger with possible impact on competition. An example is
the sequel to the Supreme Court's opinion in the *Brown Shoe* case,
370 U.S. 294 (1962), which outlawed the acquisition of a family
shoe-store chain by a major shoe manufacturer with some retailing
activities. The Justice Department agreed to transfer of the
shoe-store chain to F.W. Woolworth Co., another retailing chain.
The divestiture resulting from *U.S.* v. *Continental Can Co.,* 378
U.S. 441 (1964), was Continental's sale of the Hazel-Atlas
glass-container-producing plants to Brockway Glass Co., a competitor of Hazel-Atlas. The end result of *Crown Zellerbach Corp.,* 54
F.T.C. 769 (1957), *aff'd,* 296 F.2d 800 (9th Cir. 1961), was the sale of
the stock and assets of St. Helen's Pulp and Paper Co. to another
West Coast paper producer smaller in size than Crown Zellerbach.

In the *Crown Zellerbach* case, the FTC staff prepared a plan for
a "spin-off" reorganization whereby the company's stock in St.
Helen's would have been "passed through" to Crown Zellerbach's
stockholders. In the *Consolidated Foods* case, the Commission entered an order giving Consolidated a choice between (1) selling the
acquired company to strangers and (2) organizing a new corporation and distributing the new firm's stock to Consolidated's stockholders in proportion to their holdings of Consolidated Foods Corporation stock (62 F.T.C. 929 (1963), *order set aside,* 329 F.2d 623

(7th Cir. 1964), *rev'd*, 380 U.S. 592 (1965)). Consolidated's officers, directors, and executive employees, as well as anyone owning more than 1 percent of Consolidated's stock, were disqualified from holding any post in the new company and were required to sell their shares of the new firm's stock within six months.

The spin-off device is said to have three shortcomings: (1) it can be used only when willing and able management personnel are available for the "spun-off" enterprise; (2) it will work only if adequate working capital or credit can be made available; and (3) it will not be effective if the stock of the divesting company is closely held. There may also be a problem of finding management and working capital or credit for the new enterprise when the divestiture device is the organization of a new corporation to buy and operate the enterprise to be divested. Such a procedure was used successfully in *A.G. Spalding & Bros., Inc.,* 56 F.T.C. 1125 (1960), *aff'd,* 301 F.2d 585 (3rd Cir. 1962).

Another divestiture problem may occur when the enterprise to be disposed of has disappeared as a separate enterprise. This is illustrated by the acquisition of Blatz Brewing Co. by Pabst Brewing Co. Pabst absorbed Blatz's management and equipment into its own operations and completely dismantled the Blatz brewery, so that there was no identifiable or separable operation (*U.S.* v. *Pabst Brewing Co.,* 233 F.Supp. 475 (E.D. Wisc. 1964), *rev'd,* 384 U.S. 546 (1966), 296 F.Supp. 994 (E.D. Wisc. 1969), *plan accepted,* 303 F.Supp. 1400 (E.D. Wisc. 1969)). In *Ekco Products Co.,* the acquired company was engaged in an identifiably different line of business, so the Commission could deal with the problem by ordering the acquiring company to dispose of all assets "peculiar" to the industry it had entered by means of the Section 7 violations. In its opinion declaring the acquisition illegal, the Commission explored the scope of its remedial powers under the Clayton Act and claimed broad discretionary jurisdiction of the type exercised by the courts (65 F.T.C. 1163 (1964)). In *Diamond Alkali Co.,* it was the acquiring company, rather than the acquired, that closed down its plant. The FTC staff's brief on appeal from the examiner's initial decision in that case suggested that Diamond Alkali be given three years to divest itself of the acquired plant. According to one lawyer in the Merger Division, the staff's purpose was to give Diamond Alkali time to re-enter the market on its own through the construction of a new plant. While the suggestion was made, the brief did not ask that the order require Diamond Alkali to build a plant. The FTC issued a divestiture order (72 F.T.C. 700 (1967)).

To insure viability of the new or divested enterprise, a variety of ancillary restraints and affirmative obligations have been imposed by Section 7 orders, particularly consent orders. In a speech on

January 27, 1965, to the Antitrust Section of the New York State
Bar Association, Assistant Attorney General William H. Orrick, Jr.,
expressed the view "that any divestiture order . . . should require
divestiture of sufficient cash to insure adequate working capital for
the divested company plus such cash or assets as may be required
to finance any needed capital improvements, or other modernization of the plant to be divested." (A somewhat analagous provision,
although phrased in more general terms, appears in the consent
judgment in *U.S.* v. *Owens-Illinois Glass Co.,* 1963 Trade Cas.
¶70,808 (N.D. Ohio 1963). Owens-Illinois was directed to "use its
best efforts to maintain each of such properties at not less than the
standards of operational performance in effect on the date of this
final judgment." The company also agreed to "reasonably cooperate with the purchaser in the employment of personnel associated
with the operation and management of the properties . . . and
shall release from any employment contract any persons who . . .
notify Owens-Illinois of their desire to accept such employment. In
U.S. v. *Ryder System, Inc.,* 1961 Trade Cas. ¶70,056 (S.D. Fla.
1961), a consent judgment required a truck-leasing firm to provide
purchasers of equipment to be divested "reasonable assistance . . .
in the selection and acquisition of an appropriate location or locations."

The FTC's consent orders have gone further in imposing obligations on the divesting company. In *Hooker Chemical Corp.,* 59
F.T.C. 254 (1961), it was agreed (1) to "provide the purchaser of
the divested assets with engineering assistance in the setting up of
test equipment and methods of testing," (2) to give the purchaser a
list of all customers who made any purchases of the divested enterprise's products during the previous four and a half years, and (3)
to make available to the purchaser a supply of the raw materials
needed in the operation of a divested business. In the *Ekco* case,
too, the order required divestiture of "all other assets as may be
necessary to reconstitute" the divested enterprise "as a going concern and effective competitor." Also, Ekco was directed to "furnish
such technical and marketing information . . . as may be reasonably requested by the purchaser."

In 1961, Ford acquired from Electric Autolite Company the assets constituting Electrolite's domestic spark plug business. At the
time of the acquisition, three major competitors (General Motors
[AC], Champion, and Autolite) accounted for nearly all of the original equipment ("OE") business. They competed in a market in
which the "OE tie" was said to be a dominant factor; sales of a
brand in the replacement market, or "aftermarket," might depend in
great degree upon sales of the brand in the OE market, because
mechanics might follow the practice of replacing OE spark plugs

with spark plugs of the same brand. Despite the OE tie, the trial court found that there was a trend toward private brands: "There are findings that the private brand sector of the spark plug market will grow substantially in the next decade because mass merchandisers are entering this market in force. They not only sell all brands over the counter but have service bays where many carry only spark plugs of their own proprietary brand. It is anticipated that by 1980 the total private brand portion of the spark plug market may then represent 17% of the total aftermarket." The trial court ruled that the acquisition violated Section 7 of the Clayton Act, and ordered divestiture and relief ancillary to divestiture (*U.S.* v. *Ford Motor Co.,* 1971 Trade Cas. ¶73,445 (E.D. Mich. 1970)).

The Supreme Court sustained the trial court's holding that the acquisition was unlawful on two grounds: First, the acquisition eliminated Ford as potential competitor, which had "a moderating influence on Champion and on other companies derivatively"; second, the acquisition foreclosed Ford as a major purchaser of spark plugs (*Ford Motor Co.* v. *U.S.,* 405 U.S. 562 (1972)). In holding the acquisition unlawful, the Court refused to consider the allegation that the acquisition made Autolite a more effective competitor with GM and Champion. Quoting from *U.S.* v. *Phila. Nat'l. Bank,* 374 U.S. 321 (1963), it said that Congress had proscribed "anticompetitive mergers, the benign and the malignant alike, fully aware, we must assume, that some price might have to be paid."

The main issue in the case concerned the propriety of the relief ancillary to divestiture. The lower court had ordered Ford to divest itself of the trade name "Autolite" and the spark plug plant it had acquired. In addition to divestiture, the decree provided that Ford was prohibited for 10 years from manufacturing spark plugs, that Ford was required for five years to purchase one half of its spark plug requirements from Autolite under the "Autolite" trade name, and that Ford was prohibited for five years from using its own trade name on spark plugs. In short, for a substantial period of time, Ford was prohibited from entering the spark plug business on its own.

The Court upheld this ancillary relief on the ground that it was "designed to give the divested plant an opportunity to establish its competitive position." Quoting from *U.S.* v. *E.I. du Pont de Nemours & Co.,* 366 U.S. 316 (1961), the Court added: "it is well settled that once the Government has successfully borne the considerable burden of establishing a violation of law, all doubts as to remedy are to be resolved in its favor." The Court noted that Ford conceded that if the divested plant "is to survive it must for the foreseeable future become and remain the OE supplier to Ford and secure and retain the benefits of such OE status in sales of replacement plugs."

Although the Chief Justice concurred on the merits and also apparently on divestiture, he found the ancillary relief to be "Draconian" and without justification. He gave three reasons for his view that it was error for the trial court to require Ford "to support Autolite." First, he read the trial court's findings as indicating that an independent Autolite would be weak, not because of the acquisition, but because of a condition existing before the acquisition, namely, that Autolite's sales in the aftermarket depended upon its continued status as a supplier of OE plugs to one of the big three automakers. Such status, the Chief Justice pointed out, could have been terminated by an automaker at any time. Second, he noted that the relief, for a substantial period of time, would eliminate Ford as a potential competitor and would foreclose Ford as a large purchaser of spark plugs. These were the anticompetitive effects that led to the finding of a violation. Third, it was doubtful, according to the Chief Justice, that the new Autolite would be able to survive beyond the time the relief was effective. If Ford should later enter the spark plug business, then the new Autolite would probably have to get a large share of the private label business, and there would be other companies competing for it.

This case might well be taken as a warning to companies considering an acquisition. An acquiring company cannot count on a simple, painless divestiture should its acquisition later be held unlawful. A court might well decide that additional relief would be necessary to ensure the viability of the divested company. The Supreme Court has made it clear that once a violation of Section 7 is established the courts and enforcement agencies have a broad warrant in fashioning effective relief.

FTC Chairman Kirkpatrick gave a broad construction to the *Ford* holding. In remarks before the Antitrust Section of the ABA on April 14, 1972, Mr. Kirkpatrick said that the Ford decision "goes well beyond traditional antitrust enforcement and gives both the Commission and the Antitrust Division the authority, indeed the mandate, not merely to challenge anticompetitive practices, but to create conditions in which competition may be resumed." He went on to say: "The decree affirmed by the Supreme Court encompassed a remedy which, while going well beyond the specific violation of law alleged, recognized the absence of competitive conditions and set about to restore competition where none had existed for many years and where, prior to the illegal acquisition, future competition was a dim hope at best." Contrary to Mr. Kirkpatrick's views as well as those of the Chief Justice, that the new

Autolite's weakness was the result of pre-existing conditions and not of the acquisition, the majority in *Ford* did seem to stress that the ancillary relief was necessary simply to correct the unlawful effects of Ford's acquisition.

There is often a long delay between the date a challenged acquisition takes place and the date an order, if any, is issued. This delay is often to the advantage of the acquiring company, which can enjoy the benefits of the acquisition during the delay. The *Ford* case suggests that the relief finally ordered might be more severe, because of a change in competitive conditions or otherwise, than anyone imagined at the outset. One wonders if anyone in 1961, when Ford evidently had the option of de novo entry, could have foreseen that Ford would later be prohibited for a substantial period of time from entering the spark plug business at all upon losing this case.

As to the merits, it may be that the Court made new law in refusing even to consider Ford's argument that the acquisition actually enhanced competition by making Autolite a better competitor with the larger General Motors and Champion firms. In his concurring opinion, Justice Stewart remarked that "the Court obviously provides no answer to the argument when it quotes Philadelphia National Bank for the proposition that arguments unrelated to the merger's effect upon competition are irrelevant in a § 7 case." It should perhaps be noted, however, that in *Phila. Nat'l. Bank* the Court also ruled out procompetitive consequences of a merger in one market as justification for anticompetitive effects in another (374 U.S. at 370).

What about the selling company where the acquisition is later declared unlawful? In a speech while serving as Assistant Attorney General in charge of the Antitrust Division, William Orrick warned selling companies that they are not "home free" when they succeed in consummating a merger over Justice Department opposition. It is the Antitrust Division's view, he stated, that the selling company can be ordered to re-acquire the assets or stocks illegally sold. In *U.S.* v. *Anheuser-Busch,* 1960 Trade Cas. ¶69,599 (S.D. Fla. 1960), which ended in a consent judgment, the Division did indeed make that argument, although another satisfactory purchaser appeared before the issue could be resolved. In *Tidewater Oil Co.* v. *U.S.,* 596 ATRR E-1 (Sup. Ct. 1972), the Government has successfully insisted on retaining the seller as a party in a Section 7 suit.

When the merger to be dissolved is a "vertical" merger (a supplier-customer merger), restoration of the divested enterprise as an effective factor in the market may require special measures to fit the company back into the flow of business and to make customers and suppliers once more available to it. For example, in *Lone*

Star Cement Corp., 67 F.T.C. 67 (1965), Lone Star signed a consent order requiring it to see that the ready-mixed concrete plants it was to dispose of received an adequate supply of sand and gravel for the three years following divestiture.

In *U.S.* v. *Times Mirror Co.,* 274 F.Supp. 606 (C.D. Calif. 1967), *aff'd,* 390 U.S. 712 (1968), the district court, having found a newspaper acquisition to be a violation of Section 7 of the Clayton Act, was asked by the Justice Department not only to require divestiture of the acquired enterprise, but also to forbid the defendant to acquire any other daily newspaper in its metropolitan area. The court refused to issue "a perpetual injunction" against mergers in a market whose future it "cannot prejudge with sufficient certainty." The district court cited the Supreme Court's statement in *Brown Shoe Co.* v. *U.S.,* 370 U.S. 294, 319–20 (1962), that "legislative history illuminates congressional concern with the protection of competition not competitors, and its desire to restrain mergers only to the extent that such combinations may tend to lessen competition." The district court denied a motion for a 12-year requirement of advance Justice Department approval of any Times Mirror acquisition, subject to the court's review of any denial of approval.

The FTC's power to issue orders against future mergers, at least when the complaint is based entirely on Section 7 of the Clayton Act, was questioned in an appeal from the initial decision by American Brake Shoe Co. American contended that the only remedy the Commission had authority to grant in a Section 7 case was divestiture of the illegally acquired stock or assets. Since the Commission did not add a Section 5 FTC Act count to its complaint, counsel agreed that court decisions recognizing broad Section 5 remedial powers were "not in point." Despite respondent's argument, the Commission issued a cease-and-desist order (*American Brake Shoe Co.,* (1967–1970 Transfer Binder) Trade Reg. Rep. ¶18,339 (FTC 1968)) ordering Brake Shoe not to acquire any producer or seller of sintered metal friction material for the subsequent 10 years without the prior approval of the Commission. A court of appeals modified the order, limiting it to the acquisition of any producer, and affirmed the Commission's power to issue such an order (*Abex Corp.* v. *FTC.,* 420 F.2d 928 (6th Cir.), *cert. denied,* 400 U.S. 865 (1970)).

Merger-decree clauses restricting defendants' future acquisitions are common, although some orders fail to deal with future mergers. Several FTC orders that lack provisions restricting future mergers are consent orders involving the cement industry, for which the Commission issued antimerger guidelines. (See section III-A-9, p. 210.) Among Justice Department decrees ignoring future mergers are two involving industries in which there are relatively few competitors (*U.S.* v. *Eversharp, Inc.,* 1967 Trade Cas. ¶72,221 (E.D. Pa. 1967); *U.S.* v. *Alcoa,* 1967 Trade Cas. ¶71,980 (N.D.N.Y. 1966)); one enjoining an acquisition that was abandoned after it was delayed by preliminary injunction (*U.S.* v. *Pennzoil Co.,* 1966 Trade Cas. ¶71,675 (W.D. Pa. 1966)); one outlawing a conglomerate merger only because of its "reciprocity" opportunities (*U.S.* v. *General Dynamics Corp.,* 1966 Trade Cas. ¶71,952 (S.D.N.Y. 1966)); two containing no divestiture requirements (*U.S.* v. *World Journal Tribune Corp.,* 1966 Trade Cas. ¶71,925 (S.D.N.Y. 1966); *U.S.* v. *West Va. Pulp & Paper Co.,* 1966 Trade Cas. ¶71,652 (S.D.N.Y. 1966)); and another containing only a conditional divestiture requirement (*U.S.* v. *Aluminium, Ltd.,* 1966 Trade Cas. ¶71,895 (D.N.J. 1966)). All but the *Alcoa* and *General Dynamics* decrees were entered by consent.

Most FTC future-merger clauses are effective for a specified number of years, usually 10, although in either consent orders or settlements of court-review proceedings the term has varied. In *Reynolds Metals Co.,* 69 F.T.C. 772 (1966) and *Broadway-Hale Stores, Inc.,* 69 F.T.C. 601 (1966), the ban was for five years. In *Foremost Dairies, Inc.,* 71 F.T.C. 56 (1967), Foremost was forbidden to make any future acquisitions of pharmaceutical manufacturers, without a time limitation. In a joint-venture case (*Phillips Petroleum Co.,* 70 F.T.C. 456 (1966)), the Commission's consent order adds a 15-year prohibition against joint ventures. The consent order allowing Procter & Gamble Co. to retain J.A. Folger Co., a coffee processor, added a seven-year ban on acquisition of "any household product company" to its 10-year prohibition for coffee manufacturers or sellers (71 F.T.C. 135 (1967)).

Ten years is the common time limit in the future-merger bans negotiated by the Antitrust Division. Of the 17 future-merger clauses obtained by the Division in 1966 and 1967, only four set other time periods. In *U.S.* v. *Hat Corp.,* 1967 Trade Cas. ¶72,056 (D. Conn. 1967) and for one defendant in *U.S.* v. *Valley Nat'l. Bank of Ariz.,* 1966 Trade Cas. ¶71,901 (D. Ariz. 1966), the term is 15 years. For two other defendants in *Valley Nat'l. Bank,* and in *U.S.* v. *Nat'l. Cleaning Contractors, Inc.,* 1966 Trade Cas. ¶71,814 (S.D.N.Y. 1966); *U.S.* v. *Pittsburgh Brewing Co.,* 1966 Trade Cas. ¶71,751 (W.D. Pa. 1966); and *U.S.* v. *Von's Grocery Co.,* 384 U.S. 270 (1966), the term is cut to five years. In *U.S.* v. *American Smelting & Refining Co.,* 1967 Trade Cas. ¶72,003 (S.D.N.Y. 1967), the ban is to be effective only so long as the defendant continues to hold stock in the company it was charged with acquiring unlawfully. All of these deviations, except that of the *Von's* case, are in consent decrees.

Future-merger bans are usually limited to the particular industry involved, but only in exceptional circumstances are they limited to specified geographical areas. None of the FTC's future-merger orders reviewed above set geographical limits. Area boundaries have been written into decrees ending eight Justice Department suits (*U.S. v. Peabody Coal Co.,* 1967 Trade Cas. ¶72,213 (N.D. Ill. 1967); *U.S. v. First Nat'l. Bank of Lexington,* 1967 Trade Cas. ¶72,180 (E.D. Ky. 1967); *U.S. v. Gulf & Western Industries Inc.,* 1967 Trade Cas. ¶72,166 (C.D. Calif. 1967); *U.S. v. Chicago Title and Trust Co.,* 1966 Trade Cas. ¶71,745 (N.D. Ill. 1966); *U.S. v. Schlitz Brewing Co.,* 253 F.Supp. 129 (N.D. Calif. 1966); *U.S. v. Valley Nat'l. Bank, U.S. v. Pittsburgh Brewing Co.,* and *U.S. v. Von's Grocery Co.* (cited above)). In the two bank-merger cases the defendant banks lacked authority to do business anywhere except in the areas covered by the future-merger restrictions.

All of the FTC antimerger orders entered in 1966 and 1967 required that advance Commission approval be obtained for any merger consummated during the time period set by the order. Uniformity did not prevail in the court decrees obtained by the Antitrust Division. In the *Pittsburgh Brewing case,* the decree required nothing more than advance notice of any merger consummated during the next five years. Defendants in four cases (*U.S. v. Herff Jones Co.,* 1967 Trade Cas. ¶72,099 (S.D. Ind. 1967); *U.S. v. Monsanto Co.,* 1967 Trade Cas. ¶72,001 (W.D. Pa. 1967); *U.S. v. Kimberly-Clark Corp.,* 264 F.Supp. 439 (N.D. Calif. 1967); *U.S. v. Schlitz Brewing Co.*) were required to get advance consent from the Justice Department and, if denied it, were specifically accorded a right to seek relief from the court. Peabody Coal and Von's Grocery also need the Attorney General's consent before proceeding with a merger, but no provision is made for court review of a denial of consent. Five of the Antitrust Division's decrees (*U.S. v. National Steel Corp.,* 1967 Trade Cas. ¶72,036 (S.D. Texas 1967); *U.S. v. Newmont Mining Corp.,* 1966 Trade Cas. ¶71,709 (S.D.N.Y. 1966); *U.S. v. First Nat'l. Bank of Lexington, U.S. v. American Smelting,* and *U.S. v. Gulf & Western Industries, Inc.*) say nothing about consent from anyone; they simply prohibit acquisitions for the designated period of time. The *Hat Corp., Valley National Bank, National Cleaning,* and *Chicago Title* decrees impose what appear to be absolute prohibitions for some defendants or for a portion of the time period covered but only consent requirements for other defendants or time periods.

In *U.S. v. duPont,* 366 U.S. 316 (1961), the Supreme Court declined to rule on a contention that Section 11 requires the appropriate administrative agency to issue a divestiture order whenever a Section 7 violation is found. The Court explicitly held that federal district judges asked in a Section 15 suit to adjudge the legality of a merger retain the "broad remedial powers" traditionally possessed by courts of equity. The "discretion" the Supreme Court was willing to allow the lower courts is limited by its definition of "the key to the whole question of an antitrust remedy" as "the discovery of measures effective to restore competition." Recognizing that there may be "economic hardship" in forcing the separation of two entities that have already combined their operations into a single business enterprise, the Court proclaimed that "economic hardship can influence choice only as among two or more effective remedies." In merger cases, divestiture, though the "most drastic," is also the "most effective of antitrust remedies." The Court declared "complete divestiture . . . peculiarly appropriate in cases of stock acquisitions which violate Section 7. . . . It should always be in the forefront of a court's mind when a violation of Section 7 has been found." When a district judge concludes "that complete divestiture is a necessary element of effective relief, the government cannot be denied the latter remedy because economic hardship, however severe, may result." However, the "economic hardship" often involved in splitting up a business will frequently have a direct bearing on the effectiveness of divestiture as a remedy. As the Supreme Court pointed out in the *duPont* case, an "effective" remedy in a Section 7 case is one that restores the competition destroyed by the merger or eliminates the "tendency towards monopoly" created by the merger. This restorative purpose is not accomplished unless the enterprise to be divested survives the "economic hardship" occasioned by the divestiture and again becomes a significant competitive factor in the market.

Some FTC orders (most by consent) and some court consent decrees rely entirely upon future-merger prohibitions to remedy the alleged antitrust violation and require no divestiture of the companies said to have been unlawfully acquired. In *National Tea Co.*, 69 F.T.C. 226 (1966), one commissioner questioned the Commission's power to restrict future mergers in a Section 7 Clayton Act case without ordering divestiture. He argued (1) that the Commission must find a violation before it can issue any order at all and (2) that, if it finds a violation, it must order divestiture. The Commission's majority did find Section 7 violations by National Tea but concluded that "dynamic features of the industry" would dissipate their effects if no further acquisitions were permitted. There was a similar order in *U.S.* v. *Jerrold Electronics, Corp.*, 187 F.Supp. 545 (E.D. Pa. 1960). The Section 7 portions of that decree, though, were based on different findings. The district judge found that none of the acquisitions raised a sufficient anticompetitive threat to violate Section 7, but he imposed a three-year ban on future mergers because the defendant's acquisitions "are approaching, if not beyond, the point where it can be said that it is a reasonable probability that they will have the prohibited effect." The *Jerrold Electronics* order was the first of the litigated judgments to restrict future mergers. The inclusion of future-merger provisions in consent decrees began as early as *U.S.* v. *Nat'l Food Products Corp.,* 2 Trade Reg. Rep. ¶8834.50 (S.D.N.Y. 1926).

Except for the *Times Mirror* opinion of the Federal District Court for Central California, there do not seem to be any precedents specifically exploring the power of a federal district court to enjoin a class of future mergers. There are decisions, though, that a federal court has all its traditional equity powers in an antitrust injunction suit and that it can prohibit otherwise lawful conduct when such a prohibition is necessary to remedy an antitrust violation (*U.S.* v. *Ward Baking Co.,* 376 U.S. 327 (1964); *U.S.* v. *Loew's, Inc.,* 371 U.S. 38 (1962); *U.S.* v. *Bausch & Lomb Optical Co.,* 321 U.S. 707 (1944)).

In 1957 an FTC order first prohibited a class of future mergers (*Internat'l. Paper Co.,* 53 F.T.C. 1192 (1957)). A year earlier, in *Farm Journal, Inc.,* 53 F.T.C. 26 (1956), an initial decision that became the Commission's decision without formal review deplored the Commission's lack of "general equity power." Without it, the examiner reasoned, the Commission cannot do anything in a Section 7 Clayton Act case except order divestiture. Apparently the examiner was influenced by the declaration of the Supreme Court in *Arrow-Hart* that "the Commission is an administrative body possessing only such powers as are granted by statute. It . . . has not the additional power of a court of equity to grant other and further relief" (*Arrow-Hart & Hegeman Electric Co.* v. *FTC.,* 291 U.S. 587 (1934)). Yet in *Ekco Products Co.,* 65 F.T.C. 1163 (1964), the Commission imposed a 20-year prohibition on future mergers that a court of appeals found "rather harsh" but "within the broad scope allowed the Commission in such cases" (*Ekco Products Co.* v. *FTC,* 347 F.2d 745 (7th Cir. 1965)).

In a dissenting opinion in *Foremost Dairies, Inc.,* 60 F.T.C. 944, 1093 (1962), Commissioner Elman concluded that the Commission can issue a Section 7 order against a class of future acquisitions. Two of the three cases he relied on were Section 5 FTC Act cases (*Jacob Siegel Co.* v. *FTC,* 327 U.S. 608 (1946); *FTC* v. *Nat'l. Lead Co.,* 352 U.S. 419 (1957)), and the third was a Section 2 Clayton Act case (*FTC* v. *Ruberoid Co.,* 343 U.S. 470 (1952)). The *Siegel* opinion recognized the Commission's "wide discretion in its choice of remedy" under Section 5. Earlier, in *FTC* v. *Eastman Kodak Co.,* 274 U.S. 619 (1927), the Supreme Court had denied that the Commission, even under Section 5, had been "delegated the authority of a court of equity," but that reasoning seems to have been abandoned in view of the Court's statement in *Pan American World Airways* v. *U.S.,* 371 U.S. 296, 312, n. 17 (1963), that "authority to mold administrative decrees is indeed like the authority of courts to frame injunctive decrees." That footnote cited *FTC* v. *Mandel Bros.,* 359 U.S. 385 (1959), which allowed the Commission "wide discretion" in choosing a remedy under the Fur Products Labeling Act. Section 8(a)(2) of the Fur Products Act says the Commission shall have "the same jurisdiction, powers and duties as though all applicable terms and powers of the Federal Trade Commission Act were . . . made a part of this Act."

In *FTC* v. *Ruberoid Co.,* 343 U.S. 470 (1952), the Supreme Court, rejecting objections to a general prohibition of future price discrimination, reasoned that a Clayton Act order prohibiting future transactions must be read as prohibiting only those that are actually violations of the Act. The meeting-competition and cost-justification defenses must be read into a Section 2 order. The same inherent limit was attributed to Section 5 FTC Act orders in *FTC* v. *Nat'l. Lead Co.* If that reasoning is applicable to Section 7 of the Clayton Act, which is tied to the same enforcement language as Section 2, a future-merger ban adds nothing to the statutory prohibition. If only illegal future mergers are prohibited by such a decree, moreover, there was no need for the court in the *Times Mirror* case to "prejudge" the future of the newspaper market with "certainty." The Times Mirror could defend any subsequent merger covered by the decree on the same grounds as it could use in the absence of a decree.

The authority of the courts and the Commission to prohibit a designated category of future acquisitions may be of less than vital importance to antitrust enforcement. Most future-merger prohibitions come into existence by consent, not as a result of litigation. The consenting party seems precluded from denying that the court had power to enter the judgment he consented to (*Swift & Co.* v. *U.S.,* 276 U.S. 311, 327 (1928)). There are merger cases in which the defendants appear to be delighted to give up something they may never want, or may never get a chance to buy, in order to keep some of what they now have and want. Also, there are situations in which the enforcement agencies feel they can afford to drop divestiture demands in return for consent to orders barring future acquisitions. Prohibitions against future mergers in an industry are thought by some to be powerful devices for preserving competition and halting a trend toward concentration. Some suggest that solid blocks of these decrees in some industries might prove more significant than piecemeal divestiture.

Power in the courts or the FTC to forbid acquisitions may be most significant for situations in which the enforcement agency wants to add such a prohibition to full divestiture. If it were to become established that blanket prohibitions against future mergers are outside the powers of a court or of the FTC, then the Government would no longer be in a strong position to negotiate decrees containing such prohibitions when it is willing to give up its goal of divestiture.

Litigation of more cases may put an end to much of the uniformity that appears in the future-merger clauses described above, since litigation adds another variable factor: a court. One provision likely to stay is that requiring the defendant or respondent to seek clearance before making another acquisition. An area of future dispute regarding future merger clauses, suggested by the Supreme Court's opinion in *California* v. *El Paso Natural Gas Co.*, 386 U.S. 129 (1967), may be expanded when members of an industry intervene to demand relief from future acquisitions even when the Government does not.

In some situations divestiture leaves the acquiring firm with "know how" or special trade information whose procurement was a principal motive of the acquisition and whose retention poses a threat to competition. In *U.S.* v. *Allied Chemical Corp.*, 1964 Trade Cas. ¶71,311 (S.D.N.Y. 1965), the Antitrust Division was able to persuade the district court to retain a suit against abandoned merger plans on the theory that the Government might be able to prove that the companies' exchange of records, processes, and know-how amounted to an acquisition of "intangible assets" violating Section 7. Farm Journal did not even bother taking an appeal from an FTC hearing examiner's 1956 order requiring it to dispose of trade names and subscriber and advertiser lists obtained when it bought, and stopped publication of, the Country Gentleman (53 F.T.C. 26 (1956)). The Journal had already completed its initial solicitation of the subscribers and advertisers on the Country Gentleman lists.

There are antitrust lawyers who feel that partial divestiture will become a common relief measure. In the *Brown Shoe* case, 370 U.S. 294 (1962), the Supreme Court, in footnote 56, seemed to suggest the use of partial divestiture in some situations. After stating that the relatively limited scope of merging companies' former competition with each other would be no bar to a finding of a violation of Section 7, the Court declared: "That fact would, of course, be properly considered in determining the equitable relief to be decreed." The FTC settled for only partial divestiture in the *Lone Star* case, as did the Antitrust Division in the *Continental Can* case. In *U.S.* v. *Western Electric Co.*, 1956 Trade Cas. ¶68,246 (D. N.J. 1956), the Antitrust Division settled for an order that did not carry through on the suit's original divestiture purpose but merely required, at least partly in lieu of complete divestiture, that the companies grant nonexclusive licensing under their existing and future patents on telephone equipment.

In consent orders such as those entered in the *Hooker Chemical* and *Owens-Illinois* cases, some experts see the development of increased sophistication and flexibility on the part of the enforcement agencies in the settlement of merger suits. There will probably remain situations, assuming there is a violation of Section 7, in which effective relief will be possible only when the Government is able to get a temporary restraining order or preliminary injunction against the merger before consummation. In this situation, effective action may depend on an interim injunction (or an agreement between the parties) requiring the acquiring company to maintain the competitive vigor of the acquired company pending the outcome of the litigation.

PART IV

Discrimination

A. TYPES OF VIOLATION

1. Proving Competitive Injury

Question: *Are all price discriminations unlawful?*

The purpose of the Clayton Act's curb on discriminations in price has been said to be to forbid the practice by "great and powerful combinations . . . to lower prices of their commodities, often times below the cost of production in certain communities and sections where they had competition, with the intent to destroy and make unprofitable the business of their competitors, and with the ultimate purpose in view of thereby acquiring a monopoly in the particular locality or section in which the discriminating price is made" (H.R. 627, 63rd Cong., 2d Sess., pp. 8 and 9 (1914)). Section 2 of the Clayton Act, which declared unlawful price discriminations whose effect "may be to substantially lessen competition or tend to create a monopoly in any line of commerce," was first applied primarily when the seller's discrimination in price could be shown to have an adverse effect on competition between the seller and his competitors. However, in *Van Camp & Sons Co.* v. *American Can Co.,* 278 U.S. 245 (1929), the U.S. Supreme Court made it clear that Section 2 could be applied to price discriminations adversely affecting competition among the customers of the seller; and in 1936, the Robinson-Patman amendments made the *Van Camp* doctrine an explicit part of the statute. Section 2(a) of the Clayton Act now bans price discrimination "where the effect of such discrimination may be substantially to lessen competition or tend to create a monopoly in any line of commerce, or to injure, destroy, or prevent competition with any person who either grants or knowingly receives the benefit of such discrimination, or with customers of either of them."

The cases under Section 2(a) distinguish between the type of competitive-injury evidence required when the competition affected is "primary-line" competition, competition among sellers, and when it is "secondary-line" competition, competition among customers.

The distinction was recognized by the Supreme Court in *FTC* v. *Anheuser-Busch, Inc.,* 363 U.S. 536, 552 (1960). The Court indicated that in a primary-line-competition case it would require an explicit demonstration of adverse competitive effect; yet the Court denied that it was departing from its statement in *FTC* v. *Morton Salt Co.,* 334 U.S. 37 (1948), a secondary-line-competition case, that it is "self evident . . . there is a 'reasonable possibility', that competition may be adversely affected by a practice under which manufacturers and producers sell their goods to some customers substantially cheaper than they sell like goods to the competitors of these customers."

As in *Anheuser-Busch,* most of the Federal Trade Commission's Section 2(a) cease-and-desist orders based on injury to primary-line competition have been issued against territorial price discrimination, the charging of different prices by a multimarket seller in different geographical areas. Two issues have been at the core of many of these cases: (1) whether proof of predatory intent on the seller's part is necessary and (2) whether mere diversion of competitors' business is proof of injury to competition.

The competitive-injury issue may be an important one, for not all territorial price variations are anticompetitive. It is said that few national or even regional marketers are in a position to establish the same competitive price for their products in every community or marketing area. Price levels may be generally lower in one area than in another; the seller's product may enjoy greater consumer acceptance in one market than another; the seller may wish to reduce his price to dispose of surplus inventories. Some say that requiring a seller under pressure from one of those factors to lower his price in every geographical area might inhibit competition by destroying price flexibility.

The Federal Trade Commission's decision in the *Anheuser-Busch* case, 54 F.T.C. 227 (1957), shows its approach to the competitive injury requirement when it relies on injury to competition at the seller's level. The Commission resorted to the diversion-of-business approach; it based its cease-and-desist order on a finding that *Anheuser-Busch's* territorial pricing "resulted in a substantial diversion of sales from competitors to itself." Distinguishing cases involving "predatory," "vindictive," or "punitive" price cuts, the court of appeals decided it is not enough to show that Anheuser-Busch "more than tripled its sales" and caused "serious declines" in the market shares of its competitors (*Anheuser-Busch, Inc.* v. *FTC,* 289 F.2d 835 (7th Cir. 1961)). Reading Section 2(a) of the Clayton Act as "not concerned with mere shifts of business between competitors," the court saw at least two additional competitive-injury elements the Commission had failed to satisfy. First, the court wanted proof of "substantial impairment of the vigor or health of the contest for business," which would establish injury to "competition," as distinguished from mere injury to a competitor. Second, the court stressed the absence of evidence that Anheuser-Busch "had aid from its other markets" to finance its reduction of prices in one metropolitan area.

In the *Borden Company* case, 64 F.T.C. 534 (1964), the Commission insisted that there are circumstances "from which it can be reasonably concluded that sporadic price discriminations of short duration would be likely to lessen competition." Borden's "sporadic price discriminations" caused its competitors losses of business that "took place over an extended period of time." Rejecting Borden's suggestion that a market-share loss must be permanent to establish the anticompetitive effects contemplated by the statute, the Commission found that "a continuation of the price discrimination here present, involving sales below cost, most assuredly would effect a permanent decrease in the market shares of [Borden's] competitors." The court of appeals declared the *Morton Salt* test inapplicable in a primary-line case and reversed the Commission for following the diversion-of-business test rejected in *Anheuser-Busch* (*Borden Co.* v. *FTC,* 339 F.2d 953 (7th Cir. 1964)). The FTC wanted to seek Supreme Court review; the Solicitor General refused.

The "aid from other markets" requirement was spelled out in greater detail in *Shore Gas & Oil Co.* v. *Humble Oil & Refining Co.,* 224 F.Supp. 922 (D.N.J. 1963), a private treble-damage action. The district judge did not think it sufficient to show that competitive injury resulted from a price concession made to one customer by a seller who did not cut prices elsewhere. Injury to competition at the seller's level, he reasoned, cannot be considered the "effect" of the discrimination in price, rather than merely of the lower price, unless it can be shown that the price cut was made possible or "subsidized" by the higher prices received on other sales. The "subsidy" element can be inferred from evidence that the cut price was below cost. In the judge's view, a requirement that the treble-damage claimant prove lateral support for the low price that cost him a sale "gives the discriminating seller a yardstick by which he can measure the legality of a price before he institutes it. It is not beyond practicality to require him to examine the price he is about to charge and determine whether it will be self-sufficient. If he finds the price independent of other prices, he can charge it without fear of primary-line injury and resulting treble-damage suits. If on the other hand he finds that the price will be supported and subsidized by other prices, he knows that he may be held responsible for consequent injury to competition. If a mere low price causing injury is held within the Act, however, a discriminating seller is unable to predict whether a low individual price he is about to charge will subject him to legal sanctions. Though the Statute requires that any resulting injury must be anticompetitive, this does not present the seller with a meaningful gauge of legality of a price until it is too late; until the price has or has not in fact resulted in the prohibited consequences."

The judge sought "to reconcile the administration of the Robinson-Patman Act with the broader central aim of the antitrust laws: to instill and maintain in the business community active competition among its members." The treble-damage claim arose out of competitive bidding by two gasoline distributors for the account of a cab company. Competitive bidding is a common way distributors serving Monmouth and Ocean Counties, N.J., compete for contracts to supply large industrial consumers. "In the instant case the only competitive effect of sustaining Shore's case without proof of causation would be to render impractical the only meaningful price competition in which Shore, Humble and their rivals are presently engaged. The spirit of the antitrust laws dictates otherwise."

On the other hand, a competitive-bidding custom failed to deter a Federal Trade Commission hearing examiner from finding a Section 2(a) violation in *Quaker Oats Co.,* Docket 8112 (1963). He found "probable injury" to primary-line competition on the basis of a "sharp drop" in a competitor's sales to the customer. The Commission dismissed the complaint (63 F.T.C. 2017 (1963)).

In the *Dean Milk* case, the Commission, divided 3–2, restated its diversion-of-business doctrine in an apparent effort to strengthen it and again seek Supreme Court resolution of the problem (68 F.T.C. 710 (1965)). Chairman Dixon's opinion recognized that the courts have been reluctant to find possible competitive injury when the actual effects have been limited to temporary diversion of business and there is no indication of a predatory intent. He said, "it is the Commission's opinion that a finding of possible substantial competitive injury on the seller level is warranted in the absence of predation where the evidence shows significant diversion of business from the discriminator's competitors to the discriminator or diminishing profits to competitors resulting either from the diversion of business or from the necessity of meeting the discriminator's lower prices, provided that these immediate actual effects portend either a financial crippling of those competitors, a possibility of an anticompetitive concentration of business in larger sellers, or a significant reduction in the number of sellers in the market." This rule, the opinion goes on, does not base the finding of possible competitive injury solely upon diversion of business or lost profits. Rather, "the emphasis is placed upon the reasonably foreseeable results of the diversion or loss of profits. If the diversion of business and loss of profits herald a trend toward further losses of business and profits and the increased concentration of business in fewer sellers, or there is a reasonable possibility that some sellers will be driven out of business, there is sufficient cause to conclude that the effect of the price discrimination may be to substantially lessen competition or tend toward creation of a monopoly . . . or that competition with the discriminator may be lessened or injured."

A court of appeals denied enforcement to part of the Commission's order and enforced another portion only after modifying it (*Dean Milk Co.* v. *FTC,* 395 F.2d 696 (7th Cir. 1968)). The court found there was not sufficient evidence of injury to primary-level competition. It did find evidence of injury at the buyer level but said it was limited to two market areas; so the Commission's order, covering every community in which respondent did business, was too broad. The court limited the order to the two affected areas.

The statute makes no reference to predatory intent. Nevertheless, when the FTC and the courts find drastic local price cuts designed to take business from a smaller, weaker competitor, they have found the proscribed threat to competition (*Porto Rico American Tobacco Co.* v. *American Tobacco Co.,* 30 F.2d 234 (2nd Cir. 1929); *E.B. Muller & Co.* v. *FTC,* 142 F.2d 511 (6th Cir. 1944); *Moore* v. *Mead's Fine Bread Co.,* 348 U.S. 115 (1954); *Maryland Baking Co.,* 52 F.T.C. 1679 (1956), *aff'd,* 243 F.2d 716 (4th Cir. 1957)). The predatory intent in a Section 2(a) geographical pricing case was discussed by the Commission in its decision against *Lloyd A. Fry Roofing Co.,* 68 F.T.C. 217 (1965). After finding that the evidence established predatory intent, the Commission denied that it had to rely on such a finding. "The Act speaks of the effect of the discrimination, not the intent of the discriminator." The Commission noted that in *Balian Ice Cream* v. *Arden Farms Co.,* 231 F.2d 356 (9th Cir. 1955), the court said, "if the intent to destroy were found to exist, it might tend to render the injury probable." The Supreme Court's opinion in the *Anheuser-Busch* case commented that predatory intent "bears upon the likelihood of injury to competition."

In its *Utah Pie* decision, which two dissenting Justices read "as protecting competitors, instead of competition," the Supreme Court found sufficient proof of competitive injury to sustain a jury determination that three frozen-pie makers selling nationwide had violated the Robinson-Patman Act when they cut prices in only the Salt Lake City market (*Utah Pie Co.* v. *Continental Baking Co.,* 386 U.S. 685 (1967)). When Utah Pie Co. entered the frozen-pie market, it entered at a price below the prices for pies sold by the three defendant companies, Pet Milk Co., Continental Baking Co., and Carnation Co. During most of the period involved in the suit,

1958–1961, Utah's prices were the lowest in the Salt Lake City market. It began selling at a price of $4.15 per dozen, and at the time the suit was filed its price was $2.75 per dozen. Pet, which was offering pies at $4.92 at the beginning of the period, was offering pies at $3.56 in March and April of 1961. Carnation's price in early 1958 was $4.82, but it was selling at $3.56 at the conclusion of the period; and in the interval its price was as low as $3.30. The price range of Continental during the period covered by the suit ran from a 1958 high of more than $5 per dozen to a 1961 low of $2.85.

During seven of the 44 months involved in the suit, Pet, which shipped to Salt Lake City from its California plant, sold at prices lower than it charged in the California market, even though selling in Salt Lake City involved a $.30–$.35 freight cost per dozen pies. Continental made two two-week offers in Salt Lake City at a price less than its direct cost plus an allocation for overhead. At the same time, Continental sold the pies at a higher price outside Salt Lake City. Carnation, in order to get new business, reduced its prices in Salt Lake City to a price below its cost level.

During 1958, the year before the price cuts, Utah Pie had 66.5 percent of the Salt Lake City sales, Carnation had 10.3, Continental 1.3, and Pet 16.4. In 1959, Utah's market share dropped to 34.3; Carnation had 8.6; Continental's share was 2.9; and Pet had 35.5. Utah Pie increased its market share in 1960 to 45.5 percent; Carnation had 12.1; Continental had 1.8; and Pet dropped to 27.9. In 1961 the market share of Utah Pie was 45.3 percent; Carnation's was 8.8; Continental's was 8.3; and Pet had 29.4 percent.

Impressed by evidence of predatory intent and below-cost sales, the Supreme Court rejected suggestions that a competitive-injury finding is foreclosed by the complaining competitor's increasing sales volume, continued profits, and ability to make responsive price cuts. Justice White, who wrote the majority opinion, found unconvincing the notion that "there is no reasonably possible injury to competition as long as the volume of sales in a particular market is expanding and at least some of the competitors in the market continue to operate at a profit. Nor do we think that the Act only comes into play to regulate the conduct of price discriminators when their discriminatory prices consistently undercut other competitors." He recognized that many of the "primary-line cases" that have been litigated in the courts involved "blatant predatory price discriminations employed with the hope of immediate destruction of a particular competitor." In such a case, Justice White went on, it is easy to find injury to competition. However, he said, "we believe that the Act reaches price discrimination that erodes competition as much as it does price discrimination that is intended to have immediate destructive impact. In this case, the evidence shows a drastically declining price structure which the jury could rationally attribute to continued or sporadic price discrimination."

One of the factors relied upon by the court of appeals (349 F.2d 122 (10th Cir. 1965)) in setting aside the jury's award of damages was evidence that Utah Pie had responded to a competitor's price cut by reducing its own price to 10 cents below the competitor's. In Justice White's view, the jury could "reasonably conclude that a competitor who is forced to reduce his price to a new all-time low in a market of declining prices will in time feel the financial pinch and will be a less effective competitive force." He also insisted that consideration be given to the consequences of this price cutting on other producers who might want to enter the market.

The Court distinguished "fierce competitive instincts" from illegal anticompetitive behavior. "Actual intent to injure another competitor does not, however, fall into [the fierce-competitive-instincts] category, and neither, when viewed in the context of the Robinson-Patman Act, do persistent sales below cost and radical price cuts themselves discriminatory. Nor does the fact that a local competitor has a major share of the market make him fair game for the discriminatory price cutting free of Robinson-Patman Act proscriptions."

The three defendant pie companies argued that prior court and FTC decisions in which no primary-line injury to competition was found established a standard that compelled affirmance of the court of appeals' holding. The Supreme Court disagreed. In *Anheuser-Busch, Inc.* v. *FTC*, 289 F.2d 835 (7th Cir. 1961), there was no general decline in price structure attributable to the defendant's price discrimination. Nor was there any evidence that price discriminations were "a single lethal weapon aimed at a victim for predatory purposes." In *Borden Co.* v. *FTC*, 339 F.2d 953 (7th Cir. 1964), the court reversed the Commission's decision on price discrimination in one market for want of sufficient interstate connection, and the Commission's charge regarding another market failed to show any lasting impact upon prices caused by the single, isolated incident of price discrimination.

The *Utah Pie* decision deals only with the question of injury to competition; it does not involve the question of impact of an antitrust violation upon Utah Pie itself. The decision is further evidence of the Supreme Court's belief that jury trials are the best method for handling antitrust disputes. There is little doubt of the esteem in which the Supreme Court of the '60's held treble-damage suits as an antitrust enforcement tool or of its dislike of summary judgments. See *Radiant Burners Co., Inc.* v. *Peoples Gas, Light & Coke Co.*, 364 U.S. 656 (1961); *Continental Ore* v. *Union Carbide & Carbon Corp.*, 370 U.S. 690 (1962); *Poller* v. *CBS*, 368 U.S. 464 (1962).

The dissenters' assertion that the majority is "protecting competitors, instead of competition" seems to emphasize once again what some critics consider to be a dichotomy between the Sherman and Robinson-Patman Acts. Assuming the discrimination "had any effect," Justice Stewart stated, "that effect must have been beneficient. . . . Lower prices are the hallmark of intensified competition." Both the legislative history and the language—"injure, destroy, or prevent competition with any person"—of the Robinson-Patman Act demonstrate that it is aimed at the protection of smaller competitors. On the other hand, the Sherman Act, as it is interpreted today, may be consumer-oriented. Its policy is said to be to protect competition by channeling business into the hands of the most efficient, and thereby to give consumers the best possible product at the lowest possible price. Those who view "deteriorating" or "drastically declining" price structures as a good thing may be thinking in Sherman Act terms. Yet, it can be argued that Utah Pie, by having its plant in Salt Lake City, is more efficient than the three defendants whose plants are distant from the Salt Lake City market. There are those who believe that the two statutory policies cannot be reconciled. A national company may be confronted with a problem when it seeks to enter a new market. If entry is attempted by temporarily setting a lower price than the company is charging elsewhere, local competitors may complain, particularly if that lower price is below cost. All three defendants in the *Utah Pie* case sold below cost. The Court's opinion stressed "persistent sales below cost and radical price cuts themselves discriminatory." In *Dean Milk Co.* v. *FTC,* 395 F.2d 696 (7th Cir. 1968), both the Commission and the court of appeals acknowledged that a new entrant may not be able to avoid prices below full costs on first entering. The court of appeals gave more leeway than the FTC for the new entrant.

The FTC has read the Supreme Court's language in the *Morton Salt* case as setting a less stringent standard for proceedings involving injury to secondary-line competition. Often the Commission is satisfied with evidence of a price difference plus proof of low mark-ups or low profit margins at the customer's level of the industry. In *Sun Oil Co.,* 55 F.T.C. 955, 962 (1959), the Commission stated: "It seems self-evident that where a producer is selling a homogeneous product, such as salt, automotive parts, or gasoline, where competition is extremely keen among retailers, and where margins of profit or mark-ups are small, a lower price to one or some of the competing retailers not only 'may' but must have the effect of substantially lessening competition." When the Commission followed that line of reasoning in *American Oil Co.,* 60 F.T.C. 1786 (1962), its decision was reversed (*American Oil Co.* v. *FTC,* 325 F.2d 101

(7th Cir. 1963), *cert. denied,* 377 U.S. 954 (1964)). The Commission found that it was not necessary to place "complete reliance" on *Morton Salt's* language. "The record in this case contains evidence of a positive character fully justifying a finding of probable injury to competition." There was evidence "that competition did exist between the favored and non-favored customers . . . and that the price difference . . . was sufficient to give the former a significant competitive advantage."

In a complaint against American Oil issued in November 1960, the Commission charged that during a 1958 price war American gave its independent dealers in Smyrna, Georgia, larger discounts on gasoline purchases than were granted to competing dealers in the adjacent town of Marietta. Ranging from 3½ to 11½ cents a gallon, the discrimination in favor of Smyrna dealers developed as a result of a price war started when Shell Oil Co. posted a pump price meeting that of a "Paraland" station located in Smyrna. The other major brands joined in the price cutting, and American, before each grant of a "competitive price allowance," first verified that the dealer's nearby major-brand competitors were receiving price assistance from their suppliers. The price discriminations lasted only about two weeks, but the Commission was able to cite testimony of some of the nonfavored dealers that their business "slackened up each day" during that period. This testimony, plus the fact that the normal gross profit realized by a gasoline dealer was only 5 cents per gallon, convinced the Commission majority that American's Marietta dealers "were undoubtedly at a disadvantage insofar as competition with other major-brand dealers is concerned."

The court of appeals noted that in *FTC* v. *Sun Oil Co.,* 371 U.S. 505 (1963), the Supreme Court stated that the FTC (and the courts) "must make realistic appraisals of competitive impact" and not rely on "mechanical word formulas." Citing its *Anheuser-Busch* opinion on injury to primary-line competition, the court of appeals insisted on proof of "such an injury as will with reasonable probability substantially lessen the ability of the unfavored dealers to continue to compete." All it could find in the Commission's record was evidence of "relatively minor and temporary loss of business" by the Amoco dealers operating in areas adjacent to the area of the price war. The court of appeals was not convinced that several dealers' loss of business was in fact an "effect" of the American Oil Company's reduction of prices for dealers located in the price-war area. Rather, the court considered it just as likely that the loss of business was "for the most part attributable to the fact that the major brands of gasoline were being sold in the [price-war] area for substantially less than in the [adjacent] area."

The court's application of the "ability to compete" test to buyer-competition cases was part of a drift away from the competitive-injury rule originally distilled from the Supreme Court's *Morton Salt* opinion. (Some antitrust lawyers take the Robinson-Patman Act decisions of the Seventh Circuit with a grain of salt, feeling that the Supreme Court does not give the Act as limited a scope as does the Seventh Circuit.) In the years since the *Morton Salt* decision, there have been many FTC opinions in buyer-competition cases that gave no evidence of the type of analysis called for by the *American Oil* case. The Commission has often seemed to assume competitive injury once it is shown that competing customers have been charged different prices, and even the Seventh Circuit may have moved in this direction where the differential is "substantial and sustained" (*Bargain Car Wash., Inc.,* v. *Standard Oil Co. (Ind),* 1972 Trade Cas. ¶74,121 (7th Cir. 1972)). The standard set by the *American Oil* case, if accepted by the Supreme Court, would fore-stall the assumption of the existence of competitive injury and require the Commission to come up with more than proof of a mere diversion of business from the customers discriminated against. As some antitrust experts have put it, the Commission would have to show injury to competition, rather than merely injury to a competitor or competitors.

The *Morton Salt* doctrine is regarded by some as still having a place in trade regulation law but, they say, should be limited to the type of situation it dealt with: systematic, substantial, and continuing price differentials. On the other hand, there is some support for the proposition that the good-faith-meeting-of-competition defense in Section 2(b) was added to the Clayton Act by the Robinson-Patman Act for the purpose of taking care of defensive and temporary price cuts. Supporters of that view point to legislative history as showing that Congress did intend to protect competitors rather than competition.

With respect to price discrimination affecting competition among sellers, the Commission never acquiesced in the competitive-injury test adopted by the Court of Appeals for the Seventh Circuit. Nevertheless, since the *Anheuser-Busch* opinion, the Commission probably has made, at the investigative stage and before issuance of a formal complaint, a significant distinction between buyer-competition and seller-competition cases. Except for a few proceedings involving elements of predatory pricing, seller-competition cases have been scarce.

The court's cause-and-effect reasoning in *Shore-Humble, supra,* has been both criticized and praised for the very same reason: it creates an almost impossible burden of proof in seller-competition cases not involving below-cost sales. If given general acceptance, that opinion's theory could be a big obstacle in private treble-damage suits under Section 2(a) and to FTC enforcement activity.

The difference between the FTC and the courts over the nature of competitive-injury evidence needed in Robinson-Patman Act cases may be a reflection of the intent of the agency to carry out the purposes it perceives in the legislative history of the statute and the efforts of the courts to give the Act a reading they deem to be consistent with what the New Jersey district court called "the spirit of the antitrust laws," the "hard-competition" basis of the Sherman Act.

The scope of the prohibition in the Commission's cease-and-desist orders in geographical-pricing cases has been a subject of dispute. The type of order used by the Commission began in *Maryland Baking Company* 52 F.T.C. 1679 (1956), *aff'd,* 243 F.2d 716 (1st Cir. 1957). The approval of the court of appeals was obtained only after the Commission agreed to modify its order. As originally worded, the order prohibited the Maryland Baking Company from "selling ice cream cones to any purchaser at higher prices than the prices charged any other purchaser engaged in the same line of commerce where, in the sale of said cones to such purchaser charged the lower price, . . . the Maryland Baking Company is in competition with another seller." In response to a complaint that such a prohibition would put the company's prices "in a strait jacket throughout the country," the Commission agreed to amend its order to prohibit selling "at a price which is lower than the price charged any other purchaser engaged in the same line of commerce, where such lower price undercuts the price at which the purchaser charged the lower price may purchase . . . from another seller."

In similar fashion, the Commission was persuaded to modify a geographical-pricing order against Forster Mfg. Co. That order required Forster to stop "selling woodenware products to any purchaser at a price which is higher than the price charged any other purchaser where respondents, at the time, are selling in two or more trading areas and in the trading area in which such products are sold at the lower price are in competition with any other seller who then and thereafter enjoyed a substantially smaller volume of sales" (62 F.T.C. 852 (1963)). On review, the court of appeals suggested that the Commission's order "might well be clarified and perhaps somewhat modified" (*Forster Mfg. Co. v. FTC.,* 335 F.2d 47 (4th Cir. 1964)). The Commission then issued a new order directing Forster to stop "selling such products to any purchaser at a price which is lower than the price charged any other purchaser at the same level of distribution, where such lower price undercuts the lowest price offered to that purchaser by any other seller having a substantially smaller annual volume of sales" (68 F.T.C. 191 (1965)). In his opinion explaining the new order, Chairman Dixon pointed out that the Commission was not prohibiting all future price discriminations but only "those we believe are virtually certain to have the adverse competitive effects described by the statute—those directed against competitors who are substantially smaller than respondents and thus are unable, no matter how efficient they might be, to withstand a discriminatory price attack."

Although the FTC seems committed to the rule that predatory intent need not be proven, the courts have generally found a Section 2(a) violation in geographical pricing only when they have had proof of such intent. They also look for competitive results other than mere temporary diversion of business, such as a substantial disparity in size between the price cutter and his competitors (*Atlas Building Products Co.* v. *Diamond Block and Gravel Co.*, 269 F.2d 950 (10th Cir. 1959)); persistent sales below cost (*Moore* v. *Mead's Fine Bread Co.*, 348 U.S. 115 (1954)); or actual or impending elimination of the seller's sole rival from a particular market (*Moore* v. *Mead's Fine Bread Co.*)).

Some experts have seen in the geographical-pricing cases a gradual enlargement of the type of conduct that will be regarded as showing predatory intent. The evidence on predatory intent in most of the cases is viewed by these experts as showing nothing more than that the respondent seller was out to get additional business for himself. That intent was translated by the Commission, and sometimes by the courts, into an intent to eliminate competitors.

2. Private-Label Price Differentials

Question: *May a manufacturer discriminate in price between products sold under his own brand name and those sold under private labels?*

Manufacturers may produce and pack their products under their own brands and also under the brands of their customers, sometimes to the customer's own unique specifications. Sometimes the manufacturer uses the same raw materials and processes; he simply stamps a different label on the can or package. Even when the only difference between the products as they leave the factory is their label, the manufacturer may wish to sell the customer-brand item at a lower price. For that item, he does not have to spend money on brand advertising or other promotional expense.

Whether a price differential allowed to customers who buy and resell under their own private brands is a violation of the Clayton Act's Section 2 proscription against anticompetitive price discrimination depends first on whether a different label makes a difference in "grade and quality." Section 2(a) of the Clayton Act, as amended by the Robinson-Patman Act, makes it illegal "to discriminate in price between different purchasers of commodities of like grade, and quality." If the private-brand product is made to the buyer's unique specifications, the manufacturer may not be obligated to maintain any price relationship between that product and those he makes and markets under his own brand. Over the years the FTC has ruled several times that brand names and labels alone do not create "grade and quality" differences. It so held in *Borden Co.,* 62 F.T.C. 130 (1963).

Borden was found to have injured competition both among its customers and between itself and its competitors when it charged less for evaporated milk packed under its customers' private brands than it charged for the chemically identical Borden-brand evaporated milk, although it was unable to prove justifying cost differences. Relying on statements in the 1955 Report of the Attorney General's National Committee to Study the Antitrust Laws (pp. 157–159), the Commission decided that the economic factors inherent in brand names and national advertising should not be considered in applying the "like grade and quality" test. Rather, "market factors which may dictate that there will be different prices . . . can then be considered in connection with the provisions of Section 2."

A 2–1 Commission majority issued an order that Borden "cease and desist from discriminating in the price of such products of like grade and quality by selling to any purchaser at net prices higher than the net prices charged any other purchaser who, in fact, competes with the purchaser paying the higher prices." This language, the Commission declared, would eliminate the effects of the discrimination upon both primary-line and secondary-line competition, but when it had to defend its order in the court of appeals, the Commission stated in its brief that insofar as any secondary-line competition is concerned, the order requires Borden merely to make private-brand packing "available to all customers who want it." The court of appeals never reached that problem. It accepted Borden's argument that customer preference for "Borden" evaporated milk makes that milk a "premium" product of higher "grade and quality" than the private-label milk. Without reaching any other issues in the case, the court set aside the Commission's order (*Borden Co.* v. *FTC,* 339 F.2d 133 (5th Cir. 1964)).

In the Supreme Court, the Commission won a 7–2 decision reinstating its interpretation of the "grade and quality" test and directing the court of appeals to move on to the rest of the issues raised in the appeal from the Commission's order (*FTC* v. *Borden Co.* 383

U.S. 637 (1966)). The Supreme Court endorsed the view of the Attorney General's Committee "that tangible consumer preferences as between branded and unbranded commodities should receive due recognition in the more flexible 'injury' and 'cost justification' provisions of the statute."

Justice White, who wrote the Supreme Court opinion, could find nothing in the language of the statute to indicate that the grade of a product is not to be determined simply by the product's own physical or chemical characteristics. During congressional committee hearings on the proposed 1936 amendments to the Clayton Act, an amendment was offered to have the statute refer to sales of commodities of "like grade, quality and brand." The refusal of the House Judiciary Committee to adopt that change at a time when the private-brand issue was before the FTC in *Goodyear Tire and Rubber Co.,* 22 F.T.C. 232 (1936), was considered significant. The Commission's construction of the statute was regarded by the Court as more in line with the purposes of the Robinson-Patman Act. "Subject to specified exceptions and defenses, Section 2(a) proscribes unequal treatment of different customers in comparable transactions, but only if there is the requisite effect upon competition, actual or potential. But if the transactions are deemed to involve goods of disparate grade or quality, the section has no application at all and the Commission never reaches either the issue of discrimination or that of anticompetitive impact. We doubt that Congress intended to foreclose these inquiries in situations where a single seller markets the identical product under several different brands, whether his own, his customers or both. Such transactions are too laden with potential discrimination and adverse competitive effect to be excluded from the reach of Section 2(a) by permitting a difference in grade to be established by the label alone or by the label and its consumer appeal.

"If two products, physically identical but differently branded, are to be deemed of different grade because the seller regularly and successfully markets some quantity of both at different prices, the seller could, as far as Section 2(a) is concerned, make either product available to some customers and deny it to others, however discriminatory this might be and however damaging to competition. Those who were offered only one of the two products would, be barred from competing for those customers who want or might buy the other. The retailer who was permitted to buy and sell only the more expensive brand would have no chance to sell to those who always buy the cheaper product or to convince others, by experience or otherwise, of the fact which he and all other dealers already know—that the cheaper product is actually identical with that carrying the more expensive label."

Like the Attorney General's Committee, the Supreme Court was divided in its interpretation of the statute. In the view of Justices Stewart and Harlan, "there is nothing intrinsic to the concepts of grade and quality that requires exclusion of the commercial attributes of a product from their definition. The product purchased by the consumer includes . . . a host of commercial intangibles that distinguish the product in the market place. The premium paid for Borden brand milk reflects the consumer's awareness, promoted through advertising, that these commercial attributes are part and parcel of the premium product."

Responding to the dissent in a footnote to his opinion, Justice White observed that the dissenters' test would immunize from the Act not only a price differential between a proprietary label and a private label but also a price differential between two different producer-owned labels when one has less market acceptability than the other. If "consumer preferences" create a difference in grade or quality, he said, Borden would be able to discriminate between two purchasers of private-label milk, as long as one's label commands a higher price than the other's.

Another point made by the dissent was that in cases like *Universal-Rundle Corp.*, 65 F.T.C. 924 (1964), and *Quaker Oats Co.*, 66 F.T.C. 1131 (1964), "the Commission has itself explicitly resorted to consumer preference or marketability to resolve the issue of 'like grade and quality' in cases where minor physical variations accompany a difference in product brand. The caprice of the Commission's present distinction thus invites Borden to incorporate slight tangible variations in its private label products, in order to bring itself within the Commission's current practice of considering market preferences in such cases."

Slight variations in the product were considered by the court of appeals in *Fred Meyer, Inc.* v. *FTC*, 359 F.2d 351 (9th Cir. 1966), in outlawing a private-brand price differential on hosiery. It was asserted there that the favored buyer's additional specifications on its purchase orders compelled a conclusion that the buyer bought hosiery of a different grade and quality from that purchased by a competitor who paid a higher price. The court of appeals wanted evidence that the changes called for by the specifications produced some "difference in the marketability, appearance, durability, cost or manner of manufacture, or other indicia of 'grade and quality' of the goods."

In *Borden Co.* v. *FTC.*, 381 F.2d 175 (5th Cir. 1967), the court did not have to deal with the cost-justification issue of the *Borden* case in carrying out the Supreme Court's mandate that it conduct "further proceedings consistent with this opinion." Before it reached that problem, the court discovered a lack of evidence to support either the FTC's finding that Borden's lower price for evaporated milk packed under private labels caused injury to competition between Borden and other milk processors or its finding that that the price difference injured competition among Borden's customers.

The Commission's finding of injury to primary-line competition was based on the testimony of officials of several of Borden's competitors that they were unsuccessful in competing for business with Borden since Borden was able to sell private-label milk for a lower price than they could. Nonethless, the court of appeals pointed out that this testimony relates to the price difference between Borden's private-label milk and its competitor's private-label milk; it does not relate to the price difference between the brands of milk marketed by Borden, which is the precise price discrimination alleged in the complaint. "Therefore, injury proved in the primary line, if any, is not the effect of the price difference in issue."

In rejecting FTC findings that secondary-line competition was hurt, the court of appeals reasoned that, if a private-brand price differential "reflects no more than a consumer preference for the premium brand, the price difference creates no competitive advantage to the recipient of the cheaper private brand product on which injury could be predicated. '[R]ather it represents merely a rough equivalent of the benefit by way of the seller's national advertising and promotion which the purchaser of the more expensive branded product enjoys.' (Report on the Antitrust Laws, 159.) The record discloses no evidence tending to show that Borden's price differential exceeds the recognized consumer appeal of the Borden label. Nor has it been suggested that the prices are unreasonably high for Borden-brand milk on the one hand, or unrealistically low for the private-label milk on the other. . . . No customer has been favored over another."

Although the court of appeals once again set aside the Commission's cease-and-desist order, this time the Commission could not persuade the Solicitor General to seek Supreme Court review.

Assessment of the court of appeals' ruling must begin with recognition that the court has granted Robinson-Patman Act clearance to any bona fide private-brand price differential, one that truly reflects a difference in market value attributable to a difference in consumer brand preference. The court's "no competitive advantage" rationale eliminates only the possibility of injury to secondary-line competition and is not relevant in determining whether a private-brand differential has hurt the manufacturer-sellers' own competition. (It makes no difference to the competing manufacturers being undersold that they are losing the market to a rival who is favoring "no customer . . . over another.") In addition, the no-causation reasoning with respect to proof of injury to primary-line competition would seem to make that route as well a difficult one for the Commission to follow. The Commission's evidence of injury to primary-line competition in Robinson-Patman Act cases has generally consisted of sales losses and customer alienations attributable to the difference between the injured competitors' prices and the lower price the respondent seller charged on some sales. The Fifth Circuit now has said it is "immaterial" that the respondent seller's prices on other sales were higher. Apparently the Commission can no longer leave to inference the proposition that the customer-diverting price cuts were possible only because the seller was able to charge more elsewhere. At least one other federal court has seen a need for separate proof in a primary-line case that the lower prices were financed by higher prices on other sales (*Shore Gas & Oil Co., Inc.* v. *Humble Oil & Refining Co.*, 224 F.Supp. 922 (D. N.J. 1963)).

There are a few considerations, though, that may limit the impact of the court of appeal's decision on private-brand pricing. First of all, while the court assigns the FTC the burden of proving that a private-brand differential exceeds the name brand's consumer appeal, the issue arises only when there is a "recognized" consumer preference for this brand over the customer's private label. If that is the standard, the retail chain that promotes its "private" brand into national prominence loses its right to negotiate for a private-brand discount.

Some antitrust lawyers think the court of appeals' reasoning on secondary-line competition is likely to gain acceptance only for those situations in which the manufacturer makes private-brand manufacture and pricing available to all his customers. Yet uniform availability may wipe out actionable discrimination in any case based on injury to secondary-line competition. When the first Borden appeal was argued, the FTC indicated it would settle for uniform availability in a secondary-line situation. In addition, such a requirement would give most manufacturers problems and would foreclose private-brand pricing to many. Manufacture under private labels at reduced prices is economically feasible for many manufacturers only if the number of brands to be handled is relatively few and the volume of production under each brand is relatively large. Otherwise, the administrative and management detail become sufficiently burdensome to wipe out the cost savings attributable to the absence of a need for advertising.

In the food industry, the National Commision on Food Marketing found private brands to be available in a wide range of products. While the greatest volume of private-label business is in the hands of the big grocery chains, the Commission discovered that all categories of retailers sell private-brand foods. Yet the concept of "uniform availability" may not even exist in the processing of natural products such as fruits, vegetables, and fish. In those product lines, a packer first appropriates the quality and quantity he wants for his own advertised brand and then offers only the excess for private-brand sale.

General acceptance of the court of appeals' principles might magnify the Commission's task in private-label cases based on injury to secondary-line competition. Proving that the price differential exceeds recognized consumer preference will be complicated by such factors as price changes, special prices, cents-off labels, local and temporary prices cuts, and even price-marking errors. The Commission is not likely to acquiesce in the court of appeals' ruling that the difference between the price of Borden-brand milk and the price of private-brand milk is "immaterial" to a finding of injury to primary-line competition. The principle embodied in that ruling is broad enough to take in all the Commission's primary-line Robinson-Patman Act cases. There may be no reason for supposing that a geographical price difference, for example, is more "material" than a private-brand differential to the issue of whether injury to competition for the trade of customers offered the lower price was caused by the price differential.

At least some of the antitrust bar expects the FTC to go on attempting to apply Robinson-Patman to private-brand pricing but to exercise restraint in its choice of cases. Some lawyers are prepared to advise their clients to go ahead with deals for private-brand discounts but to make sure they are kept within limits reasonably related to consumer brand preference. That advice may have no meaning for the client. Some in the food industry insist that the court of appeals' key phrase, "recognized consumer brand preference," is meaningless because housewives shop for prices in the grocery store; brand preference, they say, is ordinarily manifested only when there is no price differential. Note, though, that the court was talking about a price differential charged wholesalers and retail chains, not a retail price differential. If brand is considered by the housewife when prices are equal, it has a value which may support a price differential.

3. "Fourth-Line" Injury to Competition

Question: *How far down the chain of customers must one look in deciding whether a discrimination is unlawful?*

Section 2(a) of the Clayton Act does not prohibit all price discriminations, but only those having the proscribed adverse effect on competition. For a plaintiff to recover for competitive injury as a result of price discrimination, there must be a showing that the effect of the discrimination may be substantially to injure, destroy, or prevent competition with any person (i) who either grants or (ii) knowingly receives the benefit of the discrimination, or (iii) with customers of either of them. The language of the statute has long been read to include within the scope of its coverage three levels of competitive injury: (1) primary line, or injury to competitors of the seller; (2) secondary line, or competitors of a favored purchaser; and (3) tertiary line, or competitors of the customer of a favored purchaser. In *Perkins* v. *Standard Oil Co. of Calif.*, 395 U.S. 642 (1969), the Supreme Court for the first time recognized a fourth level of competitive injury, a level previously considered too remote to be considered a "customer" of the beneficiary of the favored sale.

Plaintiff Perkins had been a large independent oil and gasoline dealer at both wholesale and retail levels. Defendant Standard had supplied Perkins with substantially all of its gasoline, but during the period in question, had charged Perkins a higher price than it charged (1) its own branded dealers in competition with Perkins, and (2) Signal Oil and Gas Co., a competing wholesaler. The purchasers in the chain from Signal were majority-owned subsidiaries: Signal sold to Western Hyway, its 60-percent-owned subsidiary; and Western sold to Regal Stations Co., its 55-percent-owned subsidiary. Regal competed with Perkins at the retail level. According to Perkins, the competitive harm done by the price discrimination enjoyed by Regal eventually forced Perkins to sell what remained of his business.

At trial, Perkins proved injury at both the secondary and fourth levels. On appeal the court of appeals refused to recognize the fourth-level injury (*Standard Oil* v. *Perkins,* 396 F.2d 809 (9th Cir. 1967)). The Supreme Court, however, recognized the extension of the scope of Section 2(a) to the "fourth-level" of competition, at least as presented by the facts in Perkins. Justice Black's opinion held that a limitation of Section 2(a) to third-level injury was "wholly an artificial one and . . . completely unwarranted by the language or purpose of the Act." The court relied on the *Fred Meyer* decision to support its broad reading of the meaning of "customer." "In *FTC* v. *Fred Meyer, Inc.,* 390 U.S. 341 (1968), we held that a retailer who buys through a wholesaler could be considered a 'customer' of the original supplier within the meaning of § 2(d) of the Robinson-Patman Act, a section dealing with discrimination in promotional allowances which is closely analogous to § 2(a) involved in this case. In Meyer, the Court stated that to read 'customer' narrowly would be wholly untenable when viewed in light of the purposes of the Robinson-Patman Act. Similarly, to read 'customer' more narrowly in this section than we did in the section involved in Meyer would allow price discriminators to avoid the sanctions of the Act by the simple expedient of adding an additional link to the distribution chain."

Because of the corporate relationship of the companies in the favored line of distribution, i.e. Signal, Western Hyway, and Regal, Justice Black added: "We find no basis in the language or purpose of the Act for immunizing Standard's price discriminations simply because the product in question passed through an additional formal exchange before reaching the level of Perkins' actual competitor." The Court nevertheless recognized the necessity for a showing of a causal connection between the discrimination and the injury complained of. Yet it declined to exclude it as a matter of law, saying, "[i]f there is sufficient evidence in the record to support an inference of causation, the ultimate conclusion as to what that evidence proves is for the jury."

Justice Marshall (joined by Justice Stewart) concurred in part and dissented in part. He concurred in the decision insofar as it was based upon the passing on of the discriminatory price through a chain of majority-owned subsidiaries, but he considered that the real injury was at the "buyer" or secondary-line level, with Signal itself in competition with Perkins through the subsidiaries. He dissented from any intimation that the jury might properly have found a causal connection had independent firms intervened in the distribution chain.

Some antitrust experts caution against overestimating the effect of the *Perkins* case, stressing that there is no new law in it. A few view the holding as bringing *Fred Meyer's* expanded definition of "customer" to all appropriate Section 2(a) cases. Under this view, any retailer who buys a manufacturer's goods in a chain of distribution stemming from a disfavored customer of the manufacturer may maintain a Section 2(a) treble-damage action against the manufacturer provided the requisite allegation of competitive injury is made. Yet it is questionable whether the "floodgates of litigation" will be opened by the *Perkins* case. To recover, the plaintiff retailer must prove that the defendant manufacturer's discrimination was the cause of his injury. Perkins did so, but he was virtually a single-product retailer. The multiproduct retailer may face a more difficult burden of attributing substantial injury to discriminatory sales made by a single manufacturer.

If the discriminatory sale is made by the manufacturer, the retailer's competition may have only received part, if any, of the benefits of the favored sale. Compared with the primary- or secondary-line case, intervening causes of injury are more likely to be present. It has also been suggested that the high cost of treble-damage litigation will effectively preclude most businesses in the fourth-line context from availing themselves of the *Perkins* case.

Vertically integrated companies with dual distribution systems may be faced with increasing exposure to liability as a result of *Perkins*. This exposure is probably eliminated by a seller's charging all purchasers, regardless of their functional level, the same price, and selling to whomever he chooses. (Section 2(a) provides "that nothing herein contained shall prevent persons engaged in selling goods, wares, or merchandise in commerce from selecting their own customers in bona fide transactions not in restraint of trade.") Traditionally, this pricing policy, in one sense an economic discrimination, has not been viewed as violative of Section 2(a). See, e.g., *Santo Petroleum Corp.* v. *American Oil Co.,* 187 F.Supp. 345, 353–354 (E.D.N.Y. 1960).

4. Functional Discounts

Question: *Does the Robinson-Patman Act prohibit functional discounts?*

Manufacturers may market through more than one type of distribution outlet. They may sell at one price to all customers, whether consumers, retailers, wholesalers, or customers who purchase for use in further manufacturing or processing. Or they may find it advantageous to price the product differently for each type of purchaser. Where sales are made at different prices to different types of purchasers, assertedly performing different distributional "functions," these prices have come to be known as "functional" prices and the differences as "functional discounts."

In an early version of the bill that later became the Robinson-Patman Act, there appeared a provision "that nothing herein contained shall prevent differentials in prices as between purchasers depending solely upon whether they purchase for resale to wholesalers, to retailers, or to consumers, or for use in further manufacture." Before final passage this provision was eliminated. The price-discrimination ban in Section 2 of the Clayton Act, as amended by the Robinson-Patman Act, contains no reference to functional discounts or functional prices. The law provides that only those discriminations in price that may adversely affect competition are prohibited.

Properly administered, the traditional "functional discount" accords each customer the same price advantage as every one of his competitors, that is, every other customer at his "functional" level. If the schedule of differentials does not result in different prices to competing purchasers, usually there can be no adverse effect on competition between buyers. On this theory the Federal Trade Commission and the courts have generally permitted functional pricing. Legality or illegality has turned on the question of adverse competitive effect, actual or potential. In the Sparkplug Cases (*General Motors,* 50 F.T.C. 54 (1953); *Champion Spark Plug,* 50 F.T.C. 30 (1953); *Electric Auto-Lite,* 50 F.T.C. 73 (1953)), the Commission recognized the commercial practice of granting graduated prices to different functional categories, but issued orders against the unequal treatment of those who were in fact competing with each other. Complications have come with the development of distributional enterprises that do not fit neatly into the traditional manufacturer, wholesaler, and retailer categories but resell at several levels. The situation is further confused by some sellers' practice of justifying discounts to some buyers by pointing to the performance of certain services (sometimes called "functions") and ignoring the buyer's rung in the distribution ladder. The legality of this practice is sometimes tested under Section 2(d) of the Act, which prohibits discriminatory allowances, rather than under the terms of Section 2(a), which forbids certain price discriminations.

In the *Mueller* case, 60 F.T.C. 120 (1962), the Federal Trade Commission found unlawful, as price discrimination, an alleged "functional discount." Implicitly the Commission reaffirmed its allegiance to the theory that functional pricing is not prohibited by the Robinson-Patman Act unless the price differences result in an adverse effect on competition. The Commission's opinion left unanswered several interesting questions.

Mueller, a manufacturer of equipment used in water and gas distribution systems, sold water-works products to jobbers, which it classified as either "limit" or "regular" jobbers. On some products "limit" jobbers received a 25-percent discount and "regular" jobbers received a 15-percent discount. The hearing examiner found that the "limit" jobber maintained an adequate inventory of the items on which it received a 25-percent discount, whereas the "regular" jobber maintained little or no inventory, making almost all of its purchases for drop shipment by Mueller to the jobber's customers. The hearing examiner concluded that the additional 10-percent discount received by the "limit" jobber was a functional discount granted as compensation for the services performed by the jobber in maintaining an adequate inventory. Finding that the cost of warehousing equalled or exceeded the difference in discounts, the examiner decided that there was no reasonable possibility of substantial injury to Mueller's "regular" jobbers. He relied upon *Doubleday & Co.,* 52 F.T.C. 169 (1955).

According to the Commission, the examiner interpreted the *Doubleday* case to mean either (1) that a price differential granted as compensation for services will not result in injury to competition or (2) that a differential granted for this purpose is permissible regardless of injury to competition. The Commission held that there is no support in law for either proposition. If he meant that no competitive injury will result from a functional discount reasonably related to expenses assumed by the buyer, the Commission explained, his reasoning "ignores the fact that the favored buyer can derive substantial benefit to his own business in performing the distributional function paid for by the seller." The alternative interpretation, that even though there might be competitive injury the price differential is lawful, would, in the Commission's view, add "a defense to a prima facie violation of Section 2(a) which is not included in either Section 2(a) or Section 2(b)." The Commission quoted with approval its opinion in *General Foods Corp.*, 52 F.T.C. 798 (1956): "The law permits the seller to pay for services or facilities furnished in the resale of goods. If he elects to do so, the payments must be in accordance with the terms or conditions laid down in Section 2(d). To hold that the rendering of special services ipso facto gives him a separate functional classification would be to read Section 2(d) out of the Act."

Mueller had argued that its payments to customers for furnishing certain services and facilities were nondiscriminatory allowances, benefits available to all jobbers "on proportionally equal terms" within the meaning of Section 2(d) and therefore should not be held to violate Section 2(a). The Commission found that the additional 10 percent discount granted to "limit" jobbers was not in fact made available on proportionally equal terms to all competing customers. It declined to state any conclusion on (1) whether Section 2(d) actually applies in this situation or (2) whether the 10-percent discount granted "limit" jobbers could be regarded as "an allowance for services furnished by said jobbers in connection with the processing, handling, sale, or offering for sale of certain products." The Commission felt that the added discount to warehousing jobbers actually subsidized their existing competitive advantage.

A discount compensating a buyer for a clearly identifiable distribution expense without adding to his competitive advantage, if such a thing is possible, might be legal. The Commission did not say so. Nor did the Commission speculate as to what the result might have been if Mueller had permitted all the jobbers to choose which type of jobber they wished to be. Even then, the question would arise whether the alternative was within the practical reach of all jobbers.

Some trade-regulation lawyers insist that the term "functional discount" should properly be applied only to a price differential granted for a particular status in the distribution system and that a service discount, the Mueller type, should not be described as a functional discount. They suggest that a payment for services that are available on proportionally equal terms to competing customers would have no adverse effect on competition and therefore violates neither Section 2(d) nor Section 2(a).

The *Mueller* case suggests but does not answer a number of questions concerning the relationship or lack of relationship between the various subsections of Section 2 of the amended Clayton Act. Is compliance with Section 2(d) ("proportionally equal" allowances) a defense to a price-discrimination charge under 2(a)? How can one objectively tell a price difference from an allowance for services? What is a "service" anyway? Is brokerage a service? How can one tell a price difference or an allowance for services from "anything of value as a commission, brokerage, or other compensation, or any allowance or discount in lieu thereof" referred to in Subsection 2(c)? Anyone contemplating the grant of a discount to buyers who perform a specific service might be well advised to make sure that it is both legal under Section 2(d), available to all customers on proportionally equal terms, and defensible under Section 2(a) on some basis such as cost justification or lack of injury to competition.

5. Jobber-Owned Warehouse Distributors and the Price Discrimination Ban

Question: *How do the functional discount decisions apply to jobber-owned distributors?*

The Federal Trade Commission brought many Robinson-Patman Act cases in the automobile-parts industry. It began in December 1949 with the filing of five complaints, four of them against parts manufacturers for giving discriminatory discounts in violation of Section 2(a) of the Clayton Act, as amended, and one against a jobbers' buying organization for receiving discriminatory discounts in violation of Section 2(f). By the end of 1962, Section 2(a) complaints had been filed against about two dozen parts manufacturers and Section 2(f) complaints against 13 jobber groups.

Automobiles are repaired by car dealers with parts departments and also by gas stations and garages. The necessity of providing quick availability of the many thousands of parts needed by a gas station or garage has produced a complex pattern of distribution and pricing. A warehouse distributor maintains a large inventory of parts and usually sells solely or primarily to jobbers. A jobber carries a smaller inventory of fast moving parts and resells primarily to gas stations, garages, and car dealers. The picture is complicated by the fact that warehouse distributors sometimes sell directly to gas stations and garages and thus compete with their jobber customers. Also, jobbers sometimes sell to other jobbers. There is, then, no clear-cut distinction between a "warehouse distributor" and "jobber."

Parts manufacturers may invoice parts to both warehouse distributors and to jobbers at the same price, which is sometimes called a "jobber price." Since the warehouse distributors resell primarily at the jobber level and usually at the suggested jobber price, most manufacturers grant warehouse distributors a discount off the face of the invoice. Some suppliers, however, require them to report jobber sales at the end of the month, and they are then credited with the warehouse discount on the succeeding month's purchases. The redistributing jobber pays the full jobber price but each month reports his sales to other jobbers and is then similarly credited with the warehouse discount. The warehouse discount is substantial, usually ranging from 15 percent to 25 percent off the jobber's price.

In the early jobber-group cases, the Commission encountered operations characterized by its examiners as pure "bookkeeping devices." The only function they performed was to combine the separate purchase orders of jobber members for goods "drop-shipped" directly from the manufacturer to the jobber. Combining the orders enabled them to qualify for the maximum volume rebates offered by suppliers. In cases like *American Motor Specialties Co.* v. *FTC*, 278 F.2d 225 (2d Cir. 1960), and *Mid-South Distributors* v. *FTC*, 287 F.2d 512 (5th Cir. 1961), the courts of appeals upheld Commission orders against jobber organizations of that type. Warehouse distribution in the current sense did not then exist, and volume rebate schedules were in vogue. Warehouse and redistribution discounts were given their impetus by the early supplier cases, which substantially eliminated the volume-rebate schedules of most manufacturers, the only inducement suppliers could then offer a jobber to purchase in large quantities and thereby insure availability of their products in the field.

As more warehouse distributors came into being, ready, willing, and able to carry the large inventories required to provide immediate availability, many manufacturers turned from volume rebates to warehousing discounts to induce warehousing of substantial inventories and redistribution at the jobber level. Some of the group jobbers responded by reorganizing their operations and investing in buildings and substantial inventories to perform the warehousing function. The Commission proceeded against one such reorganized operation in *Alhambra Motor Parts* v. *FTC,* 309 F.2d 213 (9th Cir. 1962), but the court of appeals drew a distinction between the "bookkeeping device" type of operation and jobber organizations that perform a warehousing operation to qualify for the warehousing or redistribution discounts. Without disturbing the Commission's order insofar as it prohibited the jobber organization from inducing or receiving volume or cash discounts for "so-called brokerage" services, the court of appeals directed the Commission to reconsider its prohibition against a "warehouse redistribution" or "functional" discount the parts manufacturers were giving the jobber organization. The Commission was ordered to evaluate the "economic and legal significance of the facts: (1) that the group buying organization performed substantially the same economic function as other warehouse distributors who received the same functional discount; (2) that the performance of this function resulted in cost savings to the sellers; and (3) that the distribution to the jobber-members of the net gain from the functional discounts in accordance with the volume of their purchases was within the aegis of Section 4 of the Act." Section 4 provides that "nothing in this act shall prevent a cooperative association from returning its members . . . the net earnings or surplus resulting from its trading operations, in proportion to their purchases or sales." The Commission issued a second cease-and-desist order (68 F.T.C. 1039 (1965)).

The Commission encountered another jobber-group warehousing operation in *National Parts Warehouse,* 63 F.T.C. 1692 (1963). (The Commission's order was affirmed (*General Auto Supplies* v. *FTC,* 346 F.2d 311 (7th Cir. 1965)). A petition for certiorari was dismissed (382 U.S. 923 (1965)).) NPW was a limited partnership with 55 "limited partners" who were parts jobbers operating in the southeastern quarter of the United States and in Indiana. The Commission found that NPW engaged in a warehousing operation with about 65,000 sq. ft. of modern warehouse space, employed over 50 persons, and maintained an inventory in excess of $800,000. For the first time, the Commission was proceeding against a jobber-owned warehouse that sold to jobbers generally as well as to members.

The Commission found that NPW, which was managed by the only general partner of the firm, "performs many of the functions that a warehouse distributor normally performs, purchasing for its own account, warehousing merchandise, billing its jobber customers at the manufacturer's suggested jobber prices, and settling its accounts with suppliers on a monthly basis, receiving discounts and allowances from the suppliers in accordance with its arrangements with them. It employs only one salesman, however, and his duties are restricted to sales to nonpartners." There was also a finding that the general partner spent two days a week selling to limited partners. As to about 20 percent of NPW's sales, the Commission found that the merchandise does not go through its warehouse but is drop-shipped to its jobber partners. There was no finding as to whether or not similar drop-shipments were made by suppliers for "independent" warehouses, although evidence to that effect was presented by NPW.

According to the Commission's opinion, written by Chairman Dixon, NPW cited its warehousing operation as a basis for distinguishing its situation from earlier cases involving mere "bookkeeping devices." The warehousing service was said to justify a conclusion that, for the purpose of applying Section 2(a), NPW, rather than its jobber partners, is in fact the "purchaser" of automobile parts from the manufacturers. Therefore, the members could not have "received" discriminatory discounts.

Chairman Dixon disposed of the contention in one paragraph. "As to the remaining 80 percent of NPW's 'sales,' it may be true that NPW actually performs the same warehousing function that 'other' warehouse distributors perform. But we do not see how that affects the question of whether NPW is a 'purchaser' in its own right, or a mere agent of its owner jobbers. The mere ownership and operation of physical facilities cannot convert an agent into a principal. It is the fact that these jobber partners of NPW own it outright, and 'control' the flow of its income from the partnership coffers to their own pockets, that establishes the principal-agent relationship, and makes them responsible for its acts. The clothing of their creature with the trappings of a 'warehouse distributor' does not cause the parties to cease being principal and agent, and become, instead, 'seller' and 'buyer' " (63 F.T.C. at 1722).

"Ingenious but unsound" (at 1719) is the characterization Chairman Dixon gave NPW's attempt to distinguish itself from the other jobber organizations by reason of its status as a limited partnership rather than a corporation. NPW's theory was that a limited partner does not have the same "control" over the limited partnership as stockholders have over a corporation through their power to elect the board of directors. The Commission did not think "management" control is the type of "control" with which the statute is concerned and concluded (at 1722) that NPW's " 'control' over the prices it 'charges' its own jobber partners, is, figuratively speaking, roughly comparable to that exercised by a sieve over water being poured through it. The jobber partners, in reserving to themselves the absolute legal right to receive all of their creature's profits, have made themselves responsible for the acts by which it 'earns' those profits. Everything that NPW does is done not for itself, but for those who receive its profits. It is, therefore, their agent."

With regard to competitive injury and the jobbers' knowledge thereof, Chairman Dixon was satisfied with proof of "a price advantage of 11.43 percent in an industry where net profit margins rarely exceed 3 percent." Evidence that few competing nonmember jobbers had gone out of business and affirmative denials by some of them that they had been injured failed to deter the Commission from applying the Supreme Court's 1948 statement in *FTC* v. *Morton Salt Co.,* 334 U.S. 37 (1948). "[It is] obvious that the competitive opportunities of certain merchants were injured when they had to pay." The Commission was likewise unimpressed by lack of evidence that member jobbers had used their price advantage to cut resale prices. The favored jobbers can use their price concessions in many different ways, the Commission reasoned, and the Clayton Act, unlike the Sherman Act, is interested not merely in results that have already come to pass but also in those that "can be reasonably anticipated in the future."

The Commission rejected a suggestion that NPW members had no way of knowing their warehousing service did not effect savings for the manufacturers to "cost justify" the discounts received by NPW. The Commission found that the manufacturers' salesmen continued to call on, and take orders from, NPW's jobber partners just as they did in dealings with nonmember jobbers. In fact, NPW's operations were found to have increased in two respects the manufacturers' costs of selling to the member jobbers. First, NPW was able to aggregate its orders into large enough quantities to transfer the freight cost from its members to the manufacturers. Second, NPW ran an annual "trade show" at which the manufacturers felt obligated to present exhibits, making promotional expenditures that were not incurred in selling to nonmember jobbers.

In a separate opinion, Commissioner Elman objected that the Commission had not evaluated the economic and legal significance of NPW's warehousing operation. He could find nothing in the Robinson-Patman Act to compel "such a rigid and unbending test of illegality" as the majority's "control" criterion. To hold that the jobber partners' "control" over the terms on which they obtain parts through NPW is the deciding factor, Commissioner Elman went on, means that there is no opportunity for lawful operation of this type of buying organization. He wanted the Commission to determine "whether the advantage accruing to NPW's jobber-partners constitutes the kind of competitive advantage which the Robinson-Patman Act intended to forbid." If NPW performs substantially the same economic function as other warehouse distributors who are permitted to receive the functional discount, Commissioner Elman concluded, "the problem is one of vertical integration, not price discrimination, and although its competitive implications may deserve attention, the solution is not to be found in the Robinson-Patman Act." Commissioner Higginbotham, concurring separately, thought the drop-shipped portion of NPW's business was enough to justify entry of a Section 2(f) order.

Some think that the *NPW* decision has little value as a precedent, that it merely disposes of a set of complicated and almost unique facts in a clouded area of the law. The case has been described as another example of the confusion created by the failure of Congress to make a clear policy decision on functional discounts. Another school of thought, however, reads the Robinson-Patman Act as in fact establishing a clear policy on functional discounts. The test of legality is the presence or absence of competitive injury. In *General Foods Corp.,* 52 F.T.C. 798 (1956), the Commission held that a "functional discount" given to a large buyer for providing services may injure competition and therefore is illegal. Now the Commission has held that such a discount may also injure competition and violate the act when it is given to an organization of small buyers. This analysis of the *NPW* decision seems to be buttressed by the Commission's action in *Hruby Distributing Co.,* 61 F.T.C. 1437 (1962). That was a Section 2(c) "brokerage" case in which the Commission allowed an independent food distributor to accept a "functional" discount. The touchstone of the case was the absence of any likelihood of injury to competition.

The Commission's rationale seems to be that discounts given for services must either (1) be cost justified under Section 2(a) of the Act, or (2) be offered all customers on proportionally equal terms within the meaning of Section 2(d). The Commission is judging discounts from the viewpoint of the seller's method of doing business, not the buyer's. The suggestion that the *NPW* opinion has no legal significance outside the automobile-parts industry has validity, if any, only because the merchandising practices involved are in some respects peculiar to the industry. An "order-desk" wholesaler of the type known in other lines of products such as clothing might have to be prepared, if it were a cooperative buying enterprise organized by retailers, to justify any "functional" allowance under the same test as was applied to NPW.

6. Advertising Allowances in Dual Distribution Systems

Question: *What are the consequences of the FTC's ruling that wholesalers and retailers are competing customers entitled to proportionally equal promotional allowances?*

Some manufacturers sell directly to selected retailers but distribute through wholesalers as well, leaving to the wholesalers the trade of retailers whom the manufacturer cannot conveniently deal with directly. A basic purpose of the Robinson-Patman Act is frequently said to be to prohibit large buyers from using their market power to obtain discriminatory prices and other indirect favoritism. The Act does not prohibit sellers from choosing wholesalers, retailers, and consumers as their customers and charging all of them the same price.

Favoritism for direct-buying retailers may result from a manufacturer's offering to such retailers promotional allowances that are denied to wholesalers or to the wholesaler's retail customers. Until the Supreme Court's decision in *FTC* v. *Fred Meyer, Inc.,* 390 U.S. 341 (1968), the theory generally prevailed that allowances could properly be offered to direct-buying retailers alone, since wholesalers do not compete with such retailers in the resale of the products and since retailers purchasing from wholesalers, although they compete with direct-buying retailers, were not "customers" of the manufacturer, and Section 2(d) of the Clayton Act, as amended by Robinson-Patman, requires that promotional allowances be made available on proportionally equal terms to "customers competing in the distribution" of the products promoted.

In the *Fred Meyer* decision, a proceeding against a direct-buying retailer, not a manufacturer, the Commission announced a doctrine that would apparently require manufacturers to grant proportionally equal allowances to wholesalers whenever allowances are granted to direct-buying retailers of the same product (63 F.T.C. 1 (1963)). The Commission's order prohibited Fred Meyer from inducing or receiving promotional allowances when Fred Meyer knew or should have known that such allowances are not made available by the supplier on proportionally equal terms to all customers competing in the sale or distribution of the supplier's products. "Customers competing" was explicitly defined to include "other customers who resell to purchasers who compete with respondents in the resale of such supplier's products."

The Commission acknowledged in the *Fred Meyer* case that it was reversing its earlier decision in *Liggett & Myers Tobacco Co., Inc.,* 56 F.T.C. 221, 250–252 (1959), and accepting the dissenting opinion of Commissioner Kern (56 F.T.C. at 253) in concluding that wholesalers are "competing" with direct-buying retailers in the "distribution" of the products in question. The basis of the dissent in *Liggett & Myers* was evidence that the placement of vending machines in retail stores diverted the trade of such stores from their wholesale suppliers. The Commission pointed to the decision in *Krug* v. *International Telephone & Telegraph Corp.,* 142 F.Supp.

230–236 (D. N.J. 1956), in which it was held that a wholesaler can maintain a treble-damage suit against his manufacturer-supplier for granting advertising allowances only to direct-buying retailers.

In a separate opinion, without suggesting that the "indirect customer" doctrine had been satisfied, Commissioner Elman maintained that the manufacturer should be required to offer the allowances, not to the wholesaler, but to the retailer customers of the wholesaler. In proceedings under Section 2 (e), which forbids discrimination in the furnishing of "services or facilities," he observed that the Commission had required services "to competing retailers on proportionally equal terms" (*Elizabeth Arden,* 39 F.T.C. 288, 305 (1944)). He denied that Section 2(d) was to be interpreted differently merely because it forbade discrimination among "customers" instead of among "purchasers," as does Section 2(e).

The Commission's order was set aside by a court of appeals (*Fred Meyer, Inc.* v. *FTC,* 359 F.2d 351 (9th Cir. 1966)) for lack of evidence (1) that Meyer's manufacturer-suppliers had in some way dealt directly with retailers competing with Meyer and (2) that products sold by the manufacturer-suppliers could be traced through wholesalers to the shelves of the competing retailers. These two requirements were imposed by the court of appeals as elements of the "indirect customer" doctrine.

The Supreme Court parted company with both the FTC and the court of appeals and held that the indirect-buying retailers competing with Meyer, and not their wholesaler-suppliers, were the disfavored buyers entitled to receive the manufacturers' promotional allowances on proportionally equal terms with Meyer (*FTC* v. *Fred Meyer, Inc.,* 390 U.S. 341 (1968)). The Supreme Court did not question the validity of the "indirect customer" doctrine. The key element leading the Supreme Court to conclude that the Commission did not need to resort to the "indirect customer" doctrine was the FTC finding, unchallenged by the court of appeals, that Meyer competed in the resale of these manufacturers' products with retailers who purchased through wholesaler customers of the manufacturers. "Whether suppliers deal directly with disfavored competitors or not, they can, and here did, afford a direct buyer the kind of competitive advantage which Section 2(d) was intended to eliminate."

As for Meyer's contention that the indirect-buying retailers were not "customers" of the discriminating manufacturers within the meaning of Section 2(d), "it rests on a narrow definition of 'customer' which becomes wholly untenable when viewed in light of the central purpose of Section 2(d) and the economic realities with which its framers were concerned." That purpose is "to curb and prohibit all devices by which large buyers gained preferences over smaller ones by virtue of their greater purchasing power.' *FTC* v. *Henry Broch and Co.,* 363 U.S. 166, 168 (1960)."

To an FTC suggestion that it will often not be feasible for suppliers to bypass their wholesalers and grant promotional allowances directly to their many retail outlets, the Supreme Court replied that "our decision does not necessitate such bypassing. . . . Nothing we have said bars a supplier, consistently with other provisions of the antitrust laws, from utilizing his wholesalers to distribute payments or administer a promotional program, so long as the supplier takes responsibility, under rules and guides promulgated by the Commission for the regulation of such practices, for seeing that the allowances are made available to all who compete in the resale of his product."

As it did in other opinions such as *FTC* v. *Sun Oil Co.,* 371 U.S. 505 (1963), and *FTC* v. *Henry Broch & Co.,* 363 U.S. 166 (1960), the Supreme Court found in the Robinson-Patman Act a general "requirement of proportional equality" in the treatment of competitors. The exent to which the *Meyer* decision will in fact assist wholesaler-supplied retailers depends on how manufacturers and independent wholesalers react to the problems the decision is likely to create for them. The number, scope, and severity of the manufacturer's problem in maintaining equality in advertising assistance to retailers depends on the perishability, unit value, service requirements, and other features of the product he markets; the number of retailers involved; the geographical scope of his market; retailer and wholesaler inventory-turnover rates; and other characteristics of his market, such as relative importance of advertising as opposed to price competition. Some dual-distributing manufacturers may find the administration of an advertising program that complies with the "proportional equality" standard so burdensome that they will terminate all such programs. A few may even simply stop selling to wholesalers, confident that direct-buying retail chains offer ample markets for many lines of products. That solution may have limited value, though, for a manufacturer willing to sell directly to anyone may have to market his product through wholesalers because some retailers need the wholesalers' full-line service.

The typical manufacturer weighing the continuation or initiation of retailer-advertising assistance has no way of knowing what he must do to avoid Robinson-Patman Act litigation, for the ruling in the *Meyer* case raises more questions than it answers. How does a manufacturer find out which direct-buying retailers have competitors who obtain the manufacturer's product through wholesalers and therefore must be given notice of any available advertising assistance? If he finds a direct-buying retailer who has no such competition, how can he be sure that competition will not develop, after the advertising program starts, by reason of a delayed sale from a wholesaler's inventory? How can he give indirect-buying retailers adequate notice without prohibitive expense? One producer thinks he has solved that difficulty by printing the notice prominently on his shipping carton. What formula for computing the advertising allowance will assure "proportional equality" among retailers of greatly disparate sizes and purchase volumes? A percentage of purchase volume won't do; the manufacturer wouldn't have a uniform or accurate price base for evaluating the purchases of wholesaler-supplied retailers.

Perhaps anticipating these problems for manufacturers, the Supreme Court made it clear that it was not barring a supplier "from utilizing his wholesalers to distribute payments or administer a promotional program." Yet how much supervision of the wholesaler then becomes necessary? Could a manufacturer's careful supervision of his wholesaler to assure equality reach a point of refinement such that it might be considered a vertical conspiracy in restraint of trade and a Section 1 Sherman Act violation? Could the policing of the wholesaler's activity reach the point where the wholesaler's customers would become the manufacturer's "indirect customers" entitled to buy at the same price as direct-buying retailers? Can a manufacturer who gives wholesalers a functional discount require them to use part of the discount? More significantly, perhaps, is the wholesaler going to get something for his greater effort? Even if manufacturers decide generally to continue using wholesalers, it may be difficult for wholesalers to survive in a distribution system depending on manufacturer-retailer cooperation in advertising. Some manufacturers consider their independent wholesalers too apathetic about retailer-advertising assistance to be counted on for a vital role in administration of a cooperative-advertising program. The *Fred Meyer* opinion made it clear that the manufacturer who uses independent wholesalers retains "responsibility, under rules and guides promulgated by the Commission," for the proportional equality of the program.

The Commission has attempted to supply answers to some of these questions in the so-called Fred Meyer guides, an updating of its Guides for Compliance with Section 2(d) first published in 1960 (Guides for Advertising Allowances and other Merchandising Payments and Services, as amended August 4, 1972). Robinson-Patman Act enforcement by the Commission has been practically nonexistent in recent years. It may be that the most substantial hazard for manufacturers who fail to comply with the rules on "proportional equality" is treble-damage liability in private actions. In this connection, the possibility of retailer class actions under Rule 23 of the Federal Rules of Civil Procedure should be kept in mind.

7. Late Delivery

Question: *Is the consistent late delivery of goods a Robinson-Patman violation?*

In *Centex-Winston Corp.* v. *Edward Hines Lumber Company,* 447 F.2d 585 (7th Cir. 1971), *cert. denied,* 405 U.S. 921 (1971), the plaintiff, a Chicago area builder, charged that defendant's consistent delivery of lumber behind schedule, in preference to plaintiff's competitors, constituted a violation of Section 2(e) of the amended Clayton Act, for which he sought treble damages. Section 2(e) of the amended Clayton Act provides, "It shall be unlawful for any person to discriminate in favor of one purchaser . . . of a commodity bought for resale . . . by furnishing . . . any services or facilities connected with the processing, handling, sale, or offering for sale . . . upon terms not accorded to all purchasers on proportionally equal terms."

The district court, ruling that Section 2(e) does not apply to this practice, granted defendant's motion to dismiss, and plaintiff appealed. Defendant contended that consistent, preferential differences in the timeliness of delivery services are not within Section 2(e) because (a) they are not "promotional services" and (b) they are not "connected with the . . . sale of lumber." The court of appeals rejected both contentions. The court held that continuous and consistent variance in delivery terms could impede the resale of the commodity, citing *FTC* v. *Simplicity Pattern Co.,* 360 U.S. 55 (1959), where preferential absorption of transportation costs by the seller was held to violate Section 2(e). The court stated that Section 2(e) was directed broadly against special favors to one purchaser where goods are sold or resold and that the section should not be confined to conventional promotional practices if evasion of the Robinson-Patman Act is to be prevented.

Despite the court's holding, plaintiff will not necessarily prevail. The complaint would fail if defendant establishes (a) that a "meeting competition" defense exists, (b) that there was no "discrimination" in delivery service or that such discrimination was "de minimis," or (c) that the preference in delivery service was made only "in proportion to the capacity of each customer to participate in the advantage."

There have been decisions prior to *Centex* which have applied Section 2(e) (and its counterpart, Section 2(d), which covers payments for these services) to other types of services not clearly "promotional." For example, in *Joseph Kaplan & Sons, Inc.* v. *FTC,* 347 F.2d 785 (D.C. Cir. 1965), Section 2(e) was applied to merchandise return privileges. *K. S. Corp.* v. *Chemstrand Corp.,* 198 F.Supp. 310

(S.D.N.Y. 1961), also suggests the possibility that the discriminatory withholding of trademarked products may be in violation of Section 2(e). In *General Foods Corp.,* 52 F.T.C. 798 (1956), the FTC held that the provision of special institutional-size packaging was within the ambit of Section 2(e). In *FTC* v. *Borden Co.,* 383 U.S. 637, 644 (1966), the Supreme Court implied that withholding private labels from some customers while making private-label products available to others may constitute a Robinson-Patman violation.

The Commission's "Guides for Advertising Allowances and Other Merchandising Payments and Services," as amended August 4, 1972, cite as "some examples" the following "services" covered by Section 2(e): any kind of advertising, catalogs, demonstrators, display and storage cabinets, display materials, special packaging or package sizes, accepting returns for credit, and prizes or merchandise for conducting promotional contests.

While many believe that the holding of *Centex* will stick, some antitrust lawyers suggest that preferential delivery services should instead be treated under Section 2(a) of the amended Clayton Act (price discrimination). Section 2(a) requires a showing that the effect of discrimination in price "may be to lessen competition or tend to create a monopoly," whereas Section 2(e) is regarded as a per se statute, requiring no showing of competitive injury. Consequently, it is argued, decisions such as *Centex* incorrectly place discriminatory terms of sale under Section 2(e), where the plaintiff's evidentiary burden is much lighter than under 2(a), and will encourage too much litigation. These experts suggest that delivery service should be analyzed under Section 2(a), where tighter control can be effected through the injury requirement. Legislative history of the Robinson-Patman Act, it is argued, supports this deference to Section 2(a) where close questions arise as to the nature of a "service." Otherwise, it is contended, every price discrimination may be thought to come within Section 2(e) as a valuable type of "service" to a customer.

Other practitioners point out that the language of Section 2(e) contains no reference to "promotional" activities in connection with the word "services" and argue that it is just as logical to include delivery service in 2(e) as it would be to confine the service to 2(a). It can be said that Section 2(a)'s injury requirement has been so diluted by the Commission and the courts as to make it indistinguishable from per se Section 2(e), in view of secondary-line (customer injury) cases such as *FTC* v. *Morton Salt Co.,* 334 U.S. 37 (1948).

As to treble-damage actions, some observers believe that since the plaintiff cannot recover without first proving the fact of injury, it may make little difference whether a discriminatory practice is placed within Section 2(a) or Section 2(e). There is some disagreement between commentators as to the latter point, because some courts have been willing to use any reasonable method of computing damages without a detailed consideration of competitive injury. In *Fowler Manufacturing Co.* v. *Gorlick,* 415 F.2d 1248 (9th Cir. 1969), for example, the court required only proof of the amount of price difference as the measure of damages, without specific proof of competitive injury. Yet compare holdings such as *Enterprise Indust., Inc.* v. *Texas Co.,* 240 F.2d 457 (2d Cir. 1957), *cert. denied,* 353 U.S. 965 (1957). In any event, under Section 2(e) the problem of damage measurement may be more complex than under 2(a), since it requires the placing of a dollar value on services given to customers.

While the Court of Appeals for the Seventh Circuit held 2(e) applicable to preferential delivery service, it indicated that the defendant could prevail if the discrimination was "de minimis," or spasmodic, or if the delivery plan was proportional to "the capacity of each customer to participate." Some observers suggest that the concepts of continuity and substantiality of discrimination have not been applied before by the FTC to Section 2(e) cases. In this sense, the Court of Appeals in *Centex,* while expanding the concept of "services" under 2(e) for the benefit of offended purchasers, may have given the seller more protection by requiring a consistent and substantial discrimination; this may modify the traditional view that Section 2(e) is a per se statute.

On the concept of "proportionalization" of services, the Commission in its *Guides* noted that there is "no single way [to proportionalize] prescribed by law," but that the "best" way would be to base payments or services on the customer's dollar volume or quantity of purchases. The *Centex* court's test of "capacity to participate" may be unique but not necessarily beyond the scope of the *Guides*. However, it may be an entirely different matter to quantify this standard. Also, in discussing proportionalization, the Court of Appeals for the Fifth Circuit, in *Colonial Stores, Inc.* v. *FTC,* 450 F.2d 733 (5th Cir. 1971) commented that while the value of service to *the supplier* (another test used as an alternative to volume of purchases) can enter into the equation, the basic factor is one of proportionality between offers to *the customer*. The Fifth Circuit seems to rely on the purchase volume test in judging this proportionality.

The Court of Appeals for the Seventh Circuit failed to consider whether the offending seller had offered alternatives to the plaintiff in lieu of fast delivery; perhaps this would be sufficient to meet the "availability" test of 2(e). Another unanswered question is whether the plaintiff's opportunity to get better delivery service from competitors of the defendant would constitute a defense. This argument appears to have been given only limited weight by the courts in price discrimination cases under Section 2(a).

Are there other types of services, not traditionally "promotional," which may be held within 2(e) in view of *Centex?* Perhaps favorable treatment by a seller in turning over orders obtained by its salesmen to intermediary customers on a discriminatory basis may, as suggested in *General Foods,* some day be held to violate Section 2(e). Also, notwithstanding two prior court determinations that favorable credit terms do not violate section 2(e), *Skinner* v. *United States Steel Corp.,* 233 F.2d 762 (5th Cir. 1956), and *Secatore's Inc.* v. *Esso Standard Oil Co.,* 171 F.Supp. 665 (D. Mass. 1959), an FTC consent order indicates the Commission's belief that the grant of preferential credit terms may violate section 2(e) (*American Candle Co.,* (1970–73 Transfer Binder) Trade Reg. Rep. ¶ 19,598 (FTC 1971)). The FTC has also indicated that the discriminatory furnishing of in-store services, such as stocking shelves, checking inventory, and building displays, is covered under Section 2(e) (FTC Guide 14, example 5). May the offer of free storage space also be included under Section 2(e)?

The question also remains whether the quality of "services" provided plays a role under Section 2(e). *Centex* is read by some observers as being a case on service quality. Aside from the application of *Centex* to other types of services, its application to a dual distribution system should also be considered. The Supreme Court's decision in *FTC* v. *Fred Meyer, Inc.,* 390 U.S. 341 (1968), has been considered by many observers as applying to Section 2(e) as well. If this is so, and a seller is responsible for providing proportionally equal treatment to its "customers" who purchase from wholesalers, how can the seller insure equally prompt delivery from wholesalers? It may be that any application of the *Fred Meyer* doctrine to Section 2(e) will have to vary depending upon the nature of the service provided.

Is the Robinson-Patman Act to be interpreted as a "fairness in dealing" statute which will not be strictly construed? Some lawyers argue, in light of *Kroger Co.* v. *FTC,* 438 F.2d 1372 (6th Cir. 1971), *cert. denied,* 404 U.S. 871 (1971), that such will be the Commission's approach in the future to all shabby dealings involving some form of discrmination, whether or not covered by the precise language of the Act.

If there is a trend towards the application of the per se Section 2(e) of the Robinson-Patman Act to a variety of services not clearly "promotional," should sellers quite simply refuse to deal rather than submit themselves to the risk of a treble-damage action? Most attorneys would counsel no differently after *Centex:* counselors would tend to advise against discrimination in general, without regard to whether 2(a) or 2(e) should be applied. On the other hand, those who choose for economic reasons to treat customers differently may be asking for trouble in light of *Centex*. Of course, treble-damage actions are not the only means of Robinson-Patman enforcement. While Robinson-Patman enforcement actions by the Commission in recent years have been few, a change could come at any time.

B. THE "BROKERAGE" PROVISION

Question: *How have court decisions affected the FTC's doctrines that discrimination is not an element of and cost-justification not a defense to a charge of paying illegal brokerage?*

Section 2(c) of the Clayton Act is said to have been designed to end "dummy brokerage" arrangements. The stimuli for its enactment came from the FTC's chain-store investigation in the 1930's and demands from organized food brokers threatened by the direct-buying practices of the large grocery chains. The broker served as a middleman between the producer organizations and retail grocers or small wholesalers. Ordinarily he served as the seller's agent and received a commission from him. To secure a competitive advantage from the elimination of the broker, direct-buying chains sometimes arranged to have the usual brokerage paid to "dummy" brokers controlled by the chains.

Section 2(c) was aimed directly at this practice. It provides "that it shall be unlawful for any person engaged in commerce, in the course of such commerce, to pay or grant, or to receive or accept, anything of value as a commission, brokerage, or other compensation, or any allowance or discount in lieu thereof, except for services rendered in connection with the sale or purchase of goods, wares, or merchandise, either to the other party to such transaction or to an agent, representative, or other intermediary therein where such intermediary is acting in fact for or in behalf, or is subject to the direct or indirect control, of any party to such transaction other than the person by whom such compensation is so granted or paid."

In *FTC* v. *Henry Broch & Co.,* 363 U.S. 166 (1960), a 5–4 majority of the Supreme Court outlawed an agreement between a seller and his broker to split a price cut demanded by a buyer. The respondent, Henry Broch & Co., was a food broker that generally received a 5-percent commission on sales made for Canada Foods, Ltd., a processor of apple concentrate. Although Canada Foods' price was $1.30 per gallon, one buyer, in the market for an unusually large amount of the apple concentrate, was willing to pay only $1.25. Canada Foods would not accept the offer unless Broch would agree to take a 3-percent brokerage fee instead of the usual 5 percent. Broch accepted that condition without making it known to the buyer. The Supreme Court majority's analysis of this sequence of events was that the broker, Broch, had passed on to the buyer an indirect allowance "in lieu of" the brokerage payment the broker had foregone.

The Court did not want its decision to be read as outlawing every price reduction based upon savings in brokerage fees. "Whether such a reduction is tantamount to a discriminatory payment of brokerage depends on the circumstances of each case." For example, if Broch had agreed to accept a 3-percent commission on all sales made on Canada Foods' behalf, the opinion elaborated, "there plainly would be no room for finding that the price reductions were violations of Section 2(c). Neither the legislative history nor the purpose of the Act would require such an absurd result, and neither the Commission nor the courts have ever suggested it." The price reduction worked out by Broch and Canada Foods was illegal because it was "made to obtain this order and this order only"; it was "discriminatory."

Justice Whittaker wrote a dissenting opinion, in which Justices Frankfurter, Harlan, and Stewart joined. In their view, this was a Section 2(a) price discrimination case, not a Section 2(c) brokerage case. They were convinced that Broch had not paid anything to the buyer "as a commission, brokerage, or other compensation" within the meaning of Section 2(c). Declaring that the majority's real concern in the Broch case was the fact that a buyer had obtained a discriminatory price advantage, they maintained that all complaints of that type should be brought under Section 2(a).

The *Broch* opinion's insistence that legality turned on the "clearly discriminatory" nature of the brokerage reduction was implemented by the Court of Appeals for the Fifth Circuit when it decided *Thomasville Chair Co.* v. *FTC,* 306 F.2d 541 (5th Cir. 1962), *dismissed on remand,* 63 F.T.C. 1048 (1963). Thomasville Chair had been selling its furniture products to 200 "jobber" accounts at prices about 5 percent under the prices charged "carload" customers. At the same time, Thomasville had paid its salesmen 6 percent sales commission on sales to carload customers and only 3 percent on sales to jobbers, who generally had bought in much larger quantities. Before the FTC, Thomasville had attempted to show that the price differential favoring jobbers reflected savings in production, sales, and delivery costs. The Commission found that Thomasville's savings in servicing the jobber accounts were not large enough to cover the price difference unless the 3-percent

differential in salesmen's commissions was included. When a seller
passes a saving in salesmen's commissions along to its customers in
this fashion, the Commission concluded, it is giving "an allowance
or discount in lieu" of "a commission, brokerage, or other compensation."

The court of appeals agreed with the Commission that the phrase
"commission, brokerage, or other compensation," as interpreted in
the *Broch* opinion, is broad enough to cover commissions paid the
seller's own salesmen. Turning to the Supreme Court's use of the
word "discriminatory" with reference to the Broch-Canada Foods
price concession, the court of appeals read that word as meaning
"without justification based on actual bona fide differences in the
costs of sales resulting from the differing methods or quantities in
which such commodities are sold or delivered." Since the Supreme
Court specifically disclaimed any intention to outlaw "every reduction in price, coupled with a reduction in brokerage," the court of
appeals reasoned, the FTC must make "a full scale inquiry" into
the propriety of Thomasville's maintenance of a list of preferred
"jobber" accounts and into the legality of Thomasville's contract
for compensating its salesmen at a lower commission rate for sales
to those accounts. The holding of the *Broch* opinion was limited to
savings in brokerage that were "passed on to a single buyer who
was not shown in any way to have deserved favored treatment." In
its proceeding against Thomasville, the court of appeals declared,
the FTC should have given consideration to the possibility that the
"jobber" accounts "deserved favored treatment" by virtue of
"differentials permitted under Section 2(a) of the Act." The Commission's argument that Section 2(a)'s cost-justification defense is
not available in a Section 2(c) case was rejected. On remand, the
Commission dismissed the complaint, issuing a brief memorandum
opinion indicating that "the Commission does not, however, acquiesce in the opinion of the Court of Appeals as such, which contains dicta with which the Commission does not necessarily agree"
(63 F.T.C. 1049).

Some lawyers find clear distinctions between the cost-justification
type of reasoning in *Thomasville* and the *Broch* opinion's reliance
on discrimination. They draw a distinction between the fees paid
independent brokers and the commissions paid one's own em-
ployee-salesmen. They are reluctant to give much weight to the
Thomasville Chair case until the legal status of the jobber discounts
is cleared up either on Supreme Court review or through new action by the FTC.

There is widespread feeling, probably based on thinking like that
of the *Broch* dissenting opinion, that Thomasville Chair's conduct
should have been tested by the FTC under Section 2(a), not Sec-

tion 2(c). This line of thought attributes to the court of appeals an attempt to read all of Section 2 of the Clayton Act as a single entity and to make sense out of the use of Section 2(c) here by giving that subsection some of the same limitations written into Section 2(a). Still, there is fairly general agreement that a direct application of the cost-justification defense to Section 2(c) would not be sustained by the Supreme Court. In *FTC* v. *Simplicity Pattern Co.,* 360 U.S. 55 (1959), the Court explicitly limited the cost-justification defense to Section 2(a) proceedings.

Some of the teachings of the *Broch* majority opinion are clear. Section 2(c) does not require a uniform rate of commission on sales to all customers, nor does it absolutely prohibit the passing on of savings in brokerage commissions. Whether a reduction in price is tantamount to a "discriminatory payment of brokerage" depends on the circumstances of each case. Among these circumstances are any services rendered by the buyer to the seller or broker, or anything in the buyers' method of dealing that justifies its getting a discriminatory price. A determination whether those circumstances are present in a particular case necessarily entails the kind of evidentiary analysis contemplated by the court of appeals' remand order in the *Thomasville Chair* case. If the seller's customer classification is a permissible one and its commission schedule is reasonable, it would appear that savings in commissions may be "passed on" to the buyer.

The court of appeals' cost-justification approach in *Thomasville Chair* raises a fundamental question that is not treated expressly in either the *Broch* or *Thomasville* opinions. Can a seller who uses brokers in selling to one group of customers, but not to another, give the latter group a lower price reflecting the full amount of the normal brokerage fee? If a seller were given the right to "pass on" such savings in legitimate brokers' fees, Section 2(c) would be removed entirely from the path of the food chains whose direct-buying practices were so instrumental in producing the "brokerage" clause.

There is another element in the *Broch* case that attracted little attention in the court of appeals' opinion but should not be overlooked. Broch granted its discount in response to pressure from a big buyer. Logically, a customer powerful enough to induce a seller to talk an independent broker into a commission reduction that can be passed along as a price cut might be able to get the same concession from his seller on salesmen's commissions when brokers are not used. In the *Thomasville Chair* case, however, both the court of appeals and the FTC hearing examiner cited uncontroverted evidence to the effect that the salesmen considered the reduced commission rates on jobber accounts to be justified by a difference in the sales effort and expense involved in serving the jobber accounts. If the salesmen were hired with notice of the differential in commissions and if the differential was not a result of demands from the jobbers, it could certainly be argued that the Thomasville discounts fall outside the scope of Section 2(c)'s legislative purpose as disclosed by the history of the provision in Congress. H.R. Rep. 2287, 74th Cong., 2d Sess., p. 17 (1936), declares that, "when free of the course of influence of mass buying power, discounts in lieu of brokerage are not usually afforded to buyers who deal with the seller direct since such sales must bear instead their appropriate share of the seller's own selling costs."

In view of the Supreme Court's 1959 decision in the *Simplicity Pattern* case, it seems safe to assume that the Court will continue to give at least token recognition to the rule that the brokerage provision of Section 2(c) is independent of Section 2(a)'s price-discrimination provisions. At the same time, however, there will be situations in which both the FTC and the Supreme Court will use what the *Broch* minority called "adroit foot work" to strengthen a Section 2(c) case with references to "discrimination" and lack of cost-justification.

One of the criticisms leveled at the Robinson-Patman Act is that enforcement efforts have been aimed more often at small merchants than at the chains it was intended to inhibit. Even the brokerage provisions in Section 2(c) of the Clayton Act, as amended by Robinson-Patman, have been turned against the buying practices of small businesses. Soon after the statute went into effect, it was established that the "except for services rendered" clause could not be applied to an agent purchasing on behalf of a group of small buyers. In cases such as *Oliver Bros., Inc.* v. *FTC*, 102 F.2d 763 (4th Cir. 1939), and *Biddle Purchasing Co.* v. *FTC*, 96 F.2d 687 (2nd Cir. 1938), it was held (1) that a purchasing agent retained and compensated by buyers cannot lawfully receive compensation from sellers even for services ordinarily performed by sellers' brokers and (2) that the brokerage commissions were in any event passed along to the buyers, who admittedly had rendered no service to earn them. To the suggestion that the Robinson-Patman Act was directed at chain-store buying practices based on buying power, the *Oliver* opinion replied: "The Act makes no distinction as to size and shows no intention to give the small any more than the great the right to receive brokerage commissions on their purchases."

Under Section 4 of the Robinson-Patman Act, a cooperative association may distribute its earnings among its members without violating Section 2 of the Clayton Act. In *Quality Bakers of America* v. *FTC*, 114 F.2d 393 (1st Cir. 1940), the court sustained the

Federal Trade Commission's position that paragraph (c) of Section 2 is a "distinct and complete provision in itself," not touched by the exemption that Section 4 offers cooperatives. In this climate, buying groups concentrated their efforts on obtaining "discounts" and "advertising allowances" from suppliers, instead of asking for "brokerage" or "brokerage commissions." Consequently, most of the Commission's Robinson-Patman Act complaints against buyer groups have been based on Section 2(f), which makes it unlawful "knowingly to induce or receive a discrimination in price." The Commission's power to move against a cooperative in this fashion has been upheld in the courts of appeals. In *American Motor Specialties Co.* v. *FTC,* 278 F.2d 225 (2nd Cir. 1960), and *Mid-South Distributors* v. *FTC,* 287 F.2d 512 (5th Cir. 1961), the courts held that the exemption granted cooperatives by Section 4 does not insulate them from prosecution for illegal activity, but merely allows them to distribute earnings, even if they result from illegal activity. The Supreme Court, in *U.S.* v. *Md. and Va. Milk Producers Assn.,* 362 U.S. 458 (1960), further limited the antitrust exemption accorded cooperatives.

In its proceeding against Central Retailer-Owned Grocers, Inc., (CROG) and its membership, consisting of 35 retailer-owned wholesale grocers, the Commission returned to reliance on the brokerage provisions in Section 2(c) (60 F.T.C. 1208 (1962)). CROG was a corporation owned by its members. It bought food products packed under private labels and resold them only to its member-owners. At the beginning of each buying season, the members submitted estimates of their needs to CROG, and these estimates furnished the quantity basis for CROG's negotiations with its suppliers. Once a discount price was set, each member submitted to CROG orders of its needs for private-label merchandise. CROG then prepared a confirmation order, a copy of which went to the supplier of the product ordered. The supplier shipped the products directly to the member-owner, but billed CROG. Then CROG paid the supplier and in turn billed the member-owner at a price higher than CROG's cost. After paying its operating cost, CROG distributed anything that was left to its members in accordance with the amount of business each had done with CROG during the year.

At the FTC hearings, CROG's officials testified that brokerage was never discussed at negotiations between CROG and its suppliers, but the Commission found that the amount of the price concessions, discounts, or allowances could be correlated mathematically with the normal brokerage commissions paid by the suppliers on other sales. "The fact that the parties to the sales do not openly employ the terminology of brokers' dealings does not pre-

clude the inference that payments had been made in lieu of brokerage. . . . The nature of such payments must be determined from all
circumstances surrounding the transactions in issue."

The Commission did not consider it necessary to document or
detail the "mathematical correlation" between the discounts
granted CROG and the normal brokerage rates paid by CROG's
suppliers. This correlation was called "additional support" for an
inference, drawn from the way CROG did business, that the discounts were paid "in lieu of brokerage." The services performed by
CROG in securing sources of private-label merchandise for its
members were declared "equivalent to the functions of brokers."
The Commission cited testimony of officials of CROG's suppliers to
the effect that the discounts granted CROG reflected savings attributable to elimination of the need for dealing with each of CROG's
member-owners individually and elimination of the work of soliciting and taking orders from CROG. "Compensation for such service
is in lieu of brokerage," the Commission declared.

CROG's argument that it bought the food products on its own account and did not act as intermediary, agent, or broker for its
members was rejected by the Commission. From CROG's articles
of incorporation, the Commission determined that CROG's only
purpose in making the purchases was to secure savings for its members. Indeed, the corporation could make no purchases from suppliers until it received an order from one of its members. Since
CROG's negotiations with suppliers were geared solely to the needs
of its members, the FTC reasoned, it "would confuse form with
substance" to hold that CROG bought in an independent capacity.

Commissioner Elman dissented, arguing that the Commission
was improperly applying Section 2(c) to "discrimination" rather
than "unearned brokerage." For him, it was entirely consistent with
the evidence to assume that CROG was "simply attempting to conduct its business in accordance with the requirements of Section
2(c) . . . and that it therefore accepted price concessions from its
suppliers only when they were not made in compensation for brokerage functions . . . or for savings in seller's brokerage." As he
viewed it, the majority decision failed to recognize "the value of
cooperative buying groups in achieving the competitive strength
which the Robinson-Patman Act was also intended to safeguard."

On appeal, the court of appeals saw the case much as did Commissioner Elman (*Central Retailer-Owned Grocers, Inc.* v. *FTC,* 319
F.2d 410 (7th Cir. 1963)). "It is apparent to us that an inference of
the Commission to the effect that Central [CROG] received commissions, brokerage, or other compensation, or allowances or discounts in lieu thereof, from its suppliers, was improperly drawn
from comparisons of brokerage paid by such suppliers on sales
which they made through brokers, with the price reductions

granted to Central. The inference upon which the Commission's finding and order are based has no substantial evidence in the record to support it. Instead, the record convincingly shows that the payments made by Central to its suppliers were for merchandise which it bought upon its own credit and not on orders of its members transmitted by it to the suppliers.

"The fact that Central, because of its strong purchasing power was able to buy at favorable prices, or on discounts and allowances by its suppliers, is not proof that Central was rendering a broker service. It bought on its own order and on its own credit. It was billed by the suppliers and it paid the bills. A broker does not purchase for his own account, is not billed by the seller, and does not make payment to the seller. Central was able to secure favorable prices from its suppliers, because of (1) their assured volume of business, (2) their lack of any credit risk, (3) a reduction in their billing work, and (4) Central's advance commitments for later re quirements. The result was that the suppliers knew that, in selling to Central, they were for these reasons realizing savings in their business operations, which enabled Central's members, in turn to benefit when they purchased from Central. Reason does not permit our ignoring these facts in order to declare illegal a worthy effort by a number of wholesale grocers, owned by retailers, to reduce the ultimate sale prices to the consumer, by entering into the arrangement with Central, which made them stronger in their competition with large chain stores."

The disagreement between the majority of the Federal Trade Commissioners on one side and the Seventh Circuit and Commissioner Elman on the other over whether the price reductions negotiated by CROG were to be called "discounts" or "brokerage" was more than an exercise in semantics. The "brokerage" provisions in Section 2(c) of the Clayton Act as amended by Robinson-Patman adopt the concept antitrust lawyers like to call "per se illegality." If the price concessions can properly be called genuine "discounts" not given in lieu of brokerage, the FTC could proceed against them only under Section 2(f) of the Act. Section 2(f) requires proof (1) that the price concessions are discriminatory and (2) that their effect "may be substantially to lessen competition or tend to create a monopoly in any line of commerce."

The attitude that prevailed in the *CROG* case was related to the nature of CROG's membership. The court saw "a worthy effort by a number of wholesale grocers, owned by retailers, to reduce the ultimate sale prices," and Commissioner Elman recognized "the value of cooperative buying groups in achieving the competitive strength which the Robinson-Patman Act was also intended to safeguard." As some experts see it, however, the court of appeals, in its concern for small business, cut a big loophole in Section 2(c). If a buyers' cooperative can get price concessions by using the procedures described, they reason, there is nothing in Section 2(c) to prevent the big chains from using the same procedures. They see no basis in Section 2(c) for a distinction between small business and big business, although they recognize that a buying agent for chain stores would be subject to the receipt-of-discriminatory-prices restriction in Section 2(f) of the Act and could also be proceeded against under the restraint-of-trade and monopolization provisions of the Sherman Act. *U.S.* v. *New York Atlantic & Pacific Tea Co.,* 173 F.2d 79 (7th Cir. 1949), was such a Sherman Act case.

There is general agreement, though, that the basic issue before the court of appeals and the FTC was one of fact. Did CROG receive what amounted to a discount or allowance in lieu of brokerage or did it receive price concessions that could realistically be distinguished from brokerage? It has been suggested that while the court of appeals seems to have substituted its judgment for the Commission's, the Commission's decision and its examiner's findings furnished at best a very sketchy factual basis for the Commission's conclusion that the discounts were in fact given "in lieu of brokerage." The Commission's reference to a "mathematical correlation" between the discounts and normal brokerage fees may not deserve much weight. Legitimate discounts based, for example, on quantities purchased could work out to the same percentages as brokerage fees. It is the broker's function to eliminate the solicitation and service of a multitude of small accounts by the seller. If the FTC wants to apply per se rules, it could be said it should at least make adequate findings.

For buyer organizations, the *CROG* case does make it clear that the words or labels used in negotiating price concessions may have some significance. Commissioner Elman, for one, regarded it as entirely natural that CROG's executives should avoid use of the word "brokerage" and negotiate only for "discounts" or "promotional allowances." "Surely the parties' failure to call these concessions 'brokerage' is not evidence that they were brokerage. Why is it not consistent with the facts to assume that CROG was simply attempting to conduct its business in accordance with the requirements of Section 2(c)."

C. BUYERS' LIABILITY FOR INDUCING PREFERENTIAL TREATMENT

Question: *What are the legal consequences of a buyer's inducement of preferential prices, services, or allowances?*

The Robinson-Patman Act, passed in 1936, amended Section 2 of the Clayton Act's prohibitions against discriminatory pricing of commodities. The amendments were said to be aimed at the prevention of misuse by large buyers of their purchasing power to extract from suppliers favorable prices, allowances, and services not available to small competitors. Notwithstanding the legislative objective, most of the language in amended Section 2 spells out prohibitions against sellers, and most enforcement proceedings have been directed against sellers or brokers. Viewing the FTC enforcement record up to 1957, Corwin D. Edwards, in his book entitled THE PRICE DISCRIMINATION LAW, stated that a "striking feature of the distribution of emphasis is the fewness of cases in which the Commission has proceeded against buyers of goods for inducing or receiving illegal discriminations. Twelve orders out of 311 were issued against such buyers, less than 4 percent of the total. Although the amended statute was intended primarily to cope with the problem of the powerful buyer, its use for direct attack on buyers has been negligible. Presumably, the neglect of this part of the law is to be attributed to the fact that the statute is so drawn as to emphasize law violations by sellers and to create unusual difficulties in proceedings against buyers based on any other charge than receipt of unlawful brokerage."

Section 2 contains two direct references to buyer responsibility. Section 2(f) provides that "it shall be unlawful for any person engaged in commerce, in the course of such commerce, knowingly to induce or receive a discrimination in price which is prohibited in this Section." The FTC has seemed to regard this subsection as only the inverse of Subsection 2(a), which prohibits the granting by a seller of certain discriminations in price, and has attacked the inducement of discriminatory allowances on services under Section 5 of the FTC Act. There are no court decisions eliminating the possibility that Subsection 2(f) prohibits the inducement of discriminatory allowances and services, the granting of which is prohibited by Subsections 2(d) and 2(e). In the only 2(f) case ever to reach the Supreme Court, the Court expressly declined to pass upon the question, stating, "We of course do not . . . purport to pass on the question whether a 'discrimination in price' includes the prohibitions in such other sections of the Act as Sections 2(d) and 2(e)" (*Automatic Canteen Co.* v. *FTC,* 346 U.S. 61, 73, n. 14 (1953)).

The other direct reference to buyer responsibility is contained in Section 2(c), which makes it unlawful, among other things, "to receive or accept anything of value as a commission, brokerage, or other compensation, or any allowance or discount in lieu thereof, except for services rendered." Soon after the statute's enactment, the FTC proceeded against A & P (*Great Atlantic & Pacific Tea Co.* v. *FTC,* 106 F.2d 667 (3rd Cir. 1939)), but the bulk of subsequent proceedings have been directed mostly at what have been called "puny respondents from the backwaters of business."

FTC efforts to proceed directly against buyers were discouraged by the Supreme Court's decision in *Automatic Canteen Co.* v. *FTC,* 346 U.S. 61 (1953). The Court held that proof of violation requires a showing that the buyer knew or should have known that the seller had no defense, such as cost justification, for the lower price "knowingly" induced. Under a "balance of convenience" rule, the burden of coming forward with evidence about a lack-of-cost justification was said to be on the Commission. The Court set aside an order against a large buyer of candy for resale where the evidence showed that the respondent received, and in some instances solicited, prices it knew were as much as 33 percent lower than those quoted other purchasers. The Court said that Section 2(f) "does not reach all cases of buyer receipt of a prohibited discrimination in prices"; a buyer "is not liable under Section 2(f) if the lower prices he induces are either within one of the seller's defenses such as cost-justification or not known by him not to be within one of those defenses"; and "the burden of coming forward with evidence as to costs and the buyer's knowledge thereof" does not shift "to the buyer as soon as it is shown that the buyer knew the prices differed."

Subsequent Section 2(f) litigation has involved buying groups formed for the purpose of receiving favorable discounts on automotive parts. Two of these cases have been fully litigated with orders being upheld by the courts (*American Motor Specialties Co.* v. *FTC,* 278 F.2d 225 (2nd Cir. 1960), *cert. denied,* 364 U.S. 884 (1960); *Mid-South Distributors* v. *FTC,* 287 F.2d 512 (5th Cir. 1961), *cert. denied,* 368 U.S. 838 (1961)).

In upholding the Commission's order in the *American Motor Specialties* case against an auto-parts buying group and its members, the court of appeals stated that respondents "of course knew, that they, as individual firms, were receiving goods in the same quantities and were served by sellers in the same manner as their competitors, and hence organized themselves into a buying group in order to obtain lower prices than their unorganized competitors. Hence, by the very fact of having combined into a group and having obtained thereby a favorable price differential, they each, under *Automatic Canteen,* were charged with notice that this price differential they each enjoyed could not be justified. And this knowledge of each of the 17 individual firms is imputable to the organization of which they were all members. Thus, irrespective of whether the buying groups' efforts to bargain with the various manufacturers constituted an improper inducement under Section 2(f), we hold that the Commission introduced sufficient evidence to fulfill the requirements of *Automatic Canteen* when it showed that petitioners knowingly *received* preferential price treatment of such a nature as to violate Section 2" (278 F.2d at 228–229).

Ironically, these successful FTC proceedings have been directed against *small* buyers who banded together to receive preferential discounts available to large buyers. In the *Mid-South* case, the Court of Appeals for the Fifth Circuit conceded that the buying groups were formed defensively to meet the competition of larger rivals. The court stated: "If this is to entrench further the large chain-store automobile-gasoline-dealer competitors and aggravate, not lessen, the competitive disadvantage which these Member-Jobbers must bear, the result, if bad economics or bad social policy, is for Congress to change. Until that is done, one caught in the middle cannot, to ward off his huge and overpowering rival, injure, even unwittingly, a smaller one. When David slays Goliath, no one else may be hurt." When the Commission later ordered a larger buyer to cease and desist from inducing or receiving discriminatory prices, its order was upheld by a court of appeals even though the Commission found that the seller's price cut was defensible (*Kroger Co.* v. *FTC,* 438 F.2d 1372 (6th Cir. 1971)).

Using its authority under Section 5 of the FTC Act to prevent "unfair methods of competition" and "unfair or deceptive acts or practices," the Commission has proceeded against the inducement of discriminatory allowances. In *Grand Union Co.,* 57 F.T.C. 382 (1960), *modified and affirmed,* 300 F.2d 92 (2d Cir. 1962), the Commission issued an order against the knowing inducement of discriminatory advertising allowances, holding that such action was "counter to the policy" of the amended Clayton Act and "as such is an unfair trade practice." In *Union News Co.,* 58 F.T.C. 10 (1961), *modified and aff'd,* 300 F.2d 104 (2d Cir. 1962), *cert. denied,* 371 U.S. 824 (1962), and *Giant Food Inc.,* 58 F.T.C. 977 (1961), *modified and aff'd,* 307 F.2d 184 (D.C. Cir. 1962), *cert. denied,* 372 U.S. 910 (1963), the Commission also condemned under Section 5 of the FTC Act the knowing inducement of discriminatory promotional payments and allowances. In *R. H. Macy & Co., Inc.,* 60 F.T.C. 1249 (1962), *modified and aff'd,* 326 F.2d 445 (2d Cir. 1964), the complaint seemed to attack buyer inducement of payments even when the seller was not in violation of the law by making the payments.

Violations of the FTC Act not covered by the Sherman or Clayton Act may not be subject to private treble-damage action, since the FTC Act is not an "antitrust law," as defined in Section 1 of the Clayton Act. (See section IX-A-5(e), p. 583.)

D. THE "COMMERCE" REQUIREMENT

Question: *Is it essential to proof of a Section 2(a) Clayton Act violation that at least one of the two sales be shown to have crossed a state line?*

Section 2(a) of the Clayton Act, as amended by the Robin-son-Patman Act, makes it "unlawful for any person engaged in commerce, in the course of such commerce . . . to discriminate in price between different purchasers of commodities of like grade and quality, where either or any of the purchases involved in such discrimination are in commerce," and where the potential effect may be adverse to competition. As originally passed by the House of Representatives, the bill that became the Robinson-Patman Act contained additional language: "It shall also be unlawful for any person, whether in commerce or not . . . to discriminate in price between different purchasers of commodities of like grade and quality where in any section or community and in any line of commerce such discrimination may substantially lessen competition in commerce among either sellers or buyers or their competitors." According to the conference committee report on the bill finally enacted, this additional language was omitted because "the preced-ing language already covers all discriminations, both interstate and intrastate, that lie within the limits of federal authority" (H.R. Rep. No. 2951, 74th Cong., 2d Sess. 6 (1936)).

There has been litigation over the significance of the requirement that "either or any of the purchases involved" be "in commerce." It has been suggested that this language is the only one of the three jurisdictional "commerce" requirements in Section 2(a) that has any real importance. If one of the two sales alleged to have been made at discriminatory prices was "in commerce," that is, actually crossed a state line, it would appear that the seller must be "en-gaged in commerce" and the discrimination occurred "in the course of such commerce" (Rowe, PRICE DISCRIMINATION UNDER THE ROBINSON-PATMAN ACT, 78 (Little, Brown & Co. 1962)).

In *Willard Dairy Corp.* v. *National Dairy Products Corp.,* 309 F.2d 943 (6th Cir. 1962), *cert. denied,* 373 U.S. 934 (1963), the court of appeals upheld dismissal of a treble-damage suit brought by a local competitor complaining about discrimination in the prices charged by the local plant of a large multistate dairy company. The court of appeals required evidence that the local plant had made interstate shipments and declared immaterial the fact that the mul-tistate dairy made interstate shipments from plants other than the one involved in this particular litigation. When the Supreme Court refused review, Justice Black dissented. He regarded the court of appeals' decision as irreconcilable with *Moore* v. *Mead's Fine Bread Co.,* 348 U.S. 115 (1954). In that case, the Court sustained a Section 2(a) treble-damage suit against a New Mexico bakery for a discrim-inatory reduction of its wholesale bread prices in a single New Mexico town where it had competition from the treble-damage claimant. The defendant bakery had not reduced its prices elsewhere, including a Texas community it served with a bread truck operating out of New Mexico. Because the price cut complained of was supported by an interstate "treasury," the Supreme Court reinstated a treble-damage judgment the court of appeals had set aside (208 F.2d 777 (10th Cir. 1954)). The court of appeals had reasoned that the territorial price cut had caused injury to only a local competitor whose business was unrelated to interstate commerce. While the *Moore* opinion did refer to interstate sales at prices higher than those charged in the complaining competitor's territory, Justice Black insisted that it had condemned "the monopolistic practice under which profits made in nondiscriminatory interstate transactions are used to offset losses arising from discriminatory price cutting at the local level."

The Federal Trade Commission has never really made clear its position on the need for proof that at least one sale crossed a state line. In *Foremost Dairies, Inc.,* 62 F.T.C. 1344 (1963), the Commission ruled that a large multistate dairy violated Section 2(a) when it charged different prices on sales in New Mexico of milk processed at a New Mexico dairy. The Commission relied on evidence that much of the milk processed in the New Mexico plant originated on out-of-state farms, and it rejected a suggestion that the brief processing at the New Mexico plant "negatives the interstate character of these transactions." The fact was stressed that "Foremost is a large interstate corporation with major offices in Florida and California."

In *Borden Co.,* 64 F.T.C. 534 (1964), the Commission declared that local sales by a multistate dairy corporation are sales "in commerce" and therefore subject to Section 2(a). Only three commissioners participated in the decision; one of them concurred only in the result; one dissented, taking the position that the rule the majority wanted to use applies only to territorial price discrimination threatening injury to the discriminating seller's competitors, and not to price discriminations said to injure competition among the seller's customers.

When the issue came up again in *National Dairy Products Corp.,* 70 F.T.C. 79 (1966), the Commission dropped a Section 2(a) count based on local sales by a multistate dairy, even though its hearing examiner had found illegal price discrimination. The Commission reversed the examiner for lack of detailed evidence of the Dairy's internal operations to show the relationship and interdependence of the dairy's various branches, zones, and divisions.

In the *Borden* case, the Commission was reversed (*Borden Co.* v. *FTC,* 339 F.2d 953 (7th Cir. 1964)). The reversing court followed the lead of the Sixth Circuit's decision in the *Willard Dairy* case and also pointed out that in *Standard Oil Co.* v. *FTC,* 340 U.S. 231

(1951), the Supreme Court said that in order for sales to come under the Robinson-Patman Act, "they must have been made in interstate commerce." In the *Foremost* case, on the other hand, the Commission's order was upheld (*Foremost Dairies, Inc.* v. *FTC,* 348 F.2d 674 (5th Cir. 1965), *cert. denied,* 382 U.S. 959 (1965)). That court did not rely, though, on the theory that the seller's general involvement in interstate commerce can eliminate the need for proof that one of the two sales at discriminatory prices was made across state lines. Rather it agreed with the Commission's reasoning that milk obtained from out-of-state farms and processed in a local dairy for local sale remained in commerce until the final retail sale was made and therefore that the discrimination did directly involve sales made in commerce.

Previously the Court of Appeals for the Fifth Circuit had played down the importance of interstate sales in *Shreveport Macaroni Mfg. Co., Inc.* v. *FTC,* 321 F.2d 404, (5th Cir. 1963), *cert. denied,* 375 U.S. 971 (1964). In applying Section 2(d)'s ban on discriminatory promotional allowances, the court of appeals recognized the existence of text authorities supporting the need for proof that one of the two sales evidencing discrimination crossed a state boundary. Nonetheless it refused to read the statute "so narrowly." Although the court did have evidence of the involvement of interstate sales, it said it was enough that the manufacturer paying the discriminatory allowances and the two favored customers all did an interstate business in the products on which the discriminatory allowances were paid, and that the allowances were made or used in interstate commerce. Section 2(d) makes it unlawful "for any person engaged in commerce" to pay discriminatory allowances "in the course of said commerce," but it does not contain the language, "where either or any of the purchases involved in such discrimination are in commerce."

The issue has also come up in the application of the "brokerage" ban in Section 2(c) of the Clayton Act. The brokerage provision does not contain the language "where either or any of the purchases involved in such discrimination are in commerce." It does not speak at all in terms of discrimination in two or more separate sales or in dealings with two or more separate customers. In *Rangen, Inc.* v. *Sterling, Nelson & Sons,* 351 F.2d 851 (9th Cir. 1965), the court applied Section 2(c) to what it recognized as being a purely intrastate sale. As the court read the *Borden* and *Willard Dairy* cases, they "tend to support the view that transactions of the character involved in our case are not 'in the course' of interstate commerce." However, it was decided that the rationale of *Moore* v. *Mead's Fine Bread* was controlling. "In Moore, defendant was able to reduce local prices because of the financial resources provided by its interstate business. In our case, Rangen was better able to compete in his interstate business because he was receiving an unfair preference in his local Idaho business. . . . The concept to which we refer is something more than the broader test of 'affecting interstate commerce,' which is applied under the Sherman Act. Critical here is the fact that Rangen's payments . . . gave it a definite advantage in its own interstate dealings—the 'beneficiary' was its interstate business—and therefore the payments must be regarded as having been made in the course of its own interstate commerce."

At first glance, the statement in the conference committee report on the Robinson-Patman Act that the intent of Section 2(a) was to cover "all discriminations, both interestate and intrastate, that lie within the limits of federal authority" might seem to support an argument that it is not necessary to show a sale actually crossing a state line. In 1936 when the Act was passed, however, the requirement of a sale "in commerce" may have meant a sale crossing state boundaries. Probably "the limits of federal authority" over commerce have expanded since 1936, and it may be contended that Congress intended to make full use of any subsequent extensions of those limits. In applying other statutes, e.g., the Fair Labor Standards Act and the Sherman Act, the courts have tended to allow the statutorily covered area to expand with changes of constitutional interpretation. Under those statutes, jurisdiction has been asserted over intrastate activities that have a direct, substantial, and intended impact on interstate commerce. The precedents seem to require that, in a Section 2(a) case, one of the sales at discriminatory prices must have crossed a state line, although one court of appeals seems to have taken a different view (*Littlejohn* v. *Shell Oil Co.,* 1972 Trade Cas. ¶73,897 (5th Cir. 1972)). That court held that a complaint need not allege that one of the sales was interstate "as long as it charges that interstate sales were used to underwrite allegedly discriminatory intrastate price-cutting tactics." Despite some wavering by the FTC, most of its decisions have made a point of finding that one or more of the sales involved did cross a state line. Also, no matter what language the Supreme Court used in its opinion in *Moore* v. *Mead's Fine Bread,* that case involved a seller who sold across state lines at unreduced prices.

Some suggest that it seems incongruous to apply a different rule under Subsections (c) and (d), as was done in the *Shreveport Macaroni* and *Rangen* cases. Despite the variations in jurisdictiional language concerning "commerce," the courts have tended to look at these subsections as means of preventing circumvention of Section 2(a)'s ban on discriminatory pricing and to adjust their scope to that of Section 2(a) (*FTC* v. *Henry Broch & Co.,* 363 U.S. 166

(1960); *Thomasville Chair Co.* v. *FTC*, 306 F.2d 541 (5th Cir. 1962)). Compare *FTC* v. *Simplicity Pattern Co.*, 360 U.S. 55 (1959). Possibly, the *Rangen* and *Shreveport Macaroni* decisions reflect a thrust similar to that of the dissent in *Borden* and of the interstate commerce cases under other statutes. Where price discrimination by a multistate business injures one of its interstate competitors, as in *Rangen,* or when the discrimination is among buyers operating interstate, as in *Shreveport,* it can be contended that the discrimination has a direct, substantial, and intended effect on interstate commerce and is thus within the expanded interstate commerce power. Where, however, the only alleged impact of an intrastate transaction is on intrastate commerce, the Robinson-Patman Act and the commerce power simply do not cover the situation. One point the decisions do make clear is that once there is a sale across state lines, it is unlawful to discriminate in favor of or against the purchaser even if the entire anticompetitive effect is felt by purely local commerce.

E. DEFENSES

1. Meeting Competition

Question: *When will a discriminatory price, allowance, or service be excused as meeting that of a competitor?*

"Nothing contained herein shall prevent a seller rebutting the prima-facie case thus made by showing that his lower price or the furnishing of services or facilities to any purchaser or purchasers was made in good faith to meet an equally low price of a competitor, or the services or facilities furnished by a competitor." With these words, Section 2(b) of the Clayton Act, as amended by the Robinson-Patman Act, attempts to preserve price competition among sellers who are forbidden, by the other subsections of Section 2, to discriminate among their customers in the setting of prices, the payment of allowances, or the furnishing of services or facilities.

In *Standard Oil Co. of Indiana,* 41 F.T.C. 263 (1945), *order enforced,* 173 F.2d 210 (7th Cir. 1949), *rev'd,* 340 U.S. 231 (1951); 49 F.T.C. 923 (1953), *order vacated,* 233 F.2d 649 (7th Cir. 1956), *aff'd,* 355 U.S. 396 (1958), the FTC outlined its interpretation of Section 2(b). It held that mere proof of "a difference in prices charged competing customers" is a "prima-facie case" as that term is used in the Section 2(b) proviso. Such a case could be rebutted by showing that the price difference represented a good-faith attempt to meet competition. If the Commission's evidence went further and demonstrated "by additional and affirmative evidence" that the price difference "may . . . substantially . . . lessen competition" within the meaning of Section 2(a), then meeting competition would not serve as justification for the price difference.

The Commission was reversed by the Supreme Court (*Standard Oil Co.* v. *FTC,* 340 U.S. 231 (1951)). Finding the legislative history "inconclusive," the Court held that the Section 2(b) proviso "is readily understandable as simply continuing in effect a defense which is equally absolute, but more limited in scope than that which existed under Section 2 of the original Clayton Act." Forced by that decision to consider Standard's defense on its merits, the FTC rejected the defense a second time, finding evidence of a discriminatory pricing "system" instead of "good faith" departures from a nondiscriminatory price scale. The Supreme Court (355 U.S. 396 (1958)) affirmed a court of appeals holding (233 F.2d 649 (7th Cir. 1956)) that the evidence supported Standard's view, not the Commission's.

A dozen years passed before the FTC encountered a litigated case in which it accepted the defense. Continental Baking Co., the first respondent to raise the defense successfully before the Commission, had been charged with violating both Section 2(a)'s ban on price discrimination and Section 2(d)'s ban on nonproportional advertising allowances. The Commission affirmed a hearing examiner's finding that both the price and the advertising-allowance concessions were made in good faith to meet competition (63 F.T.C. 2071 (1963)). The Commission found first, that Continental had for years refused to follow its major competitors in the granting of discriminatory discounts, until its forebearance so impaired its market position that its officers decided the granting of discounts was essential to prevent further drastic loss of business. Second, Continental adopted "a highly selective" discount policy, permitting discounts to a particular customer only when he had been offered an equal or larger price cut on a competing product line and that price cut was large enough to induce the customer to stop buying Continental's products. Third, Continental took care to insure the genuineness of the competitive necessity for discounts, giving a concession only after a customer's claim of discounts from competitors had been adequately verified by Continental's sales representatives. Fourth, none of the discounts granted ever produced a Continental price lower than the competitor's net price.

Speaking of the Section 2(b) defense in general, the Commissioner explained that the concept of good faith is essential. "This is a flexible and pragmatic, not technical or doctrinaire, concept. The standard of good faith is simply the standard of the prudent businessman responding fairly to what he reasonably believes is a situation of competitive necessity. *FTC* v. *A. E. Staley Mfg. Co.,* 324

U.S. 746, 759–60 (1944); see *Standard Oil Co.* v. *FTC,* 340 U.S. 231, 249–50 (1951)). Such a standard, whether it be considered 'subjective' or 'objective' is inherently ad hoc. Rigid rules and inflexible absolutes are especially inappropriate in dealing with the 2(b) defense; the facts and circumstances of the particular case, not abstract theories or remote conjectures, should govern its interpretation and application. Thus, the same method of meeting competition may be consistent with an inference of good faith in some circumstances, inconsistent with such an inference in others" (63 F.T.C. 2163).

Two months later, the Commission again encountered the defense. The meeting-competition defense was applied to discriminatory price cuts made by Ponca Wholesale Mercantile Co. in New Mexico to match offers from manufacturers selling directly to retailers (64 F.T.C. 937 (1964)). Under New Mexico law, state tax stamps had to be affixed to cigarette packages and cartons by the cigarette distributor or retailer and had to be affixed within the boundaries of the State. As a result, chain retailers had a choice of either buying directly from the tobacco companies and setting up their own stamping facilities within the state or purchasing from wholesalers such as Ponca, who could perform the stamping service. The FTC staff argued that Ponca's sale of stamped cigarettes removed it from competition with the manufacturers, who could sell only unstamped cigarettes. The Commission accepted the examiner's finding that, had the chains not been able to buy at a discount from Ponca, they would have bought from the manufacturers and stamped the cigarettes themselves, and he dismissed the staff argument as flying "in the face of economic reality." Ponca's efforts to compete with the manufacturers in sales of cigarettes to chain stores "should not be subject to handicaps over and above those inherent in this situation by a strained and hypertechnical definition of competition not consonant with the realities of the market place."

In *Beatrice Foods Co., Inc.,* 67 F.T.C. 473 (1965), a hearing examiner sustained the good-faith defense with the fact findings closely paralleling those of the *Continental Baking* case.

Before its *Continental Baking* decision, the Commission had attempted to limit the scope of the meeting-competition defense in at least five ways. In the Supreme Court's *Standard Oil* opinion, the Court referred to price differentials made in good faith "to meet a lawful and equally low price of a competitor." In *Tri-Valley Packing Assn.,* 60 F.T.C. 1134 (1962), the Commission read the *Standard Oil* opinion as meaning that a seller meets the "good faith" requirement of Section 2(b) only when his competitor's lower price is also a "lawful" price. From there, a 4–1 Commission majority moved on to the conclusion "that as a part of the good faith requirement of this defense, respondent must at least show the existence of circumstances which would lead a reasonable person to believe that the lower prices it was meeting were lawful prices." In presenting its good-faith defense, Tri-Valley had shown that a number of its competitors (in the Commission's words) "had engaged in pricing practices whereby they had usually sold goods to certain favored customers at a 'market price' which respondent admits was set by the buyer." Yet this evidence did not indicate to the majority whether the competitors' prices could be justified on the basis of cost differences or otherwise excused under any of the Robinson-Patman Act's exceptions "or that respondent had reason to believe that they could be justified." (Earlier, in *Standard Oil Co.* v. *Brown,* 238 F.2d 54 (5th Cir. 1956), a private treble-damage action, the court of appeals had read the Supreme Court's term "lawful" as meaning nothing more than that the seller cannot meet lower prices "that he knows to be illegal or that are of such a nature as are inherently illegal.")

The Commission's cease-and-desist order in *Tri-Valley* was set aside (329 F.2d 694 (9th Cir. 1964)). The court did not pass on the Commission's ruling that the seller, to establish the meeting-competition defense, must show circumstances that would lead a reasonable person to believe the lower prices he was meeting were "lawful." The court of appeals' opinion indicates that, in argument of the appeal, counsel for the Commission seemed to prefer a different basis for rejecting the meeting-competition defense—that the discriminatory price cuts were made, not in response to individual competitive situations, but as part of a pricing system. Because it felt the Commission had not dealt adequately with the factual and legal questions presented by this "pricing system" argument, the court of appeals sent the case back to the FTC for further proceedings. The Commission reinstated its order (70 F.T.C. 79 (1966)). This time the Commission decided that Tri-Valley's meeting-competition defense should not be rejected on any theory that the company's prices were adopted to meet a pricing system employed by its competitors. "We believe that respondent could as a matter of law reduce its prices in individual transactions to meet lower prices of its competitors on California Street even if the latter were using a formal pricing system. *Federal Trade Commission* v. *National Lead Co.,* 352 U.S. 419 (1949)."

The Commission held in *Forster Mfg. Co., Inc.,* 62 F.T.C. 852 (1963), that discriminatory price cuts made to meet competition must be made on a customer-by-customer basis. The meeting-competition defense was rejected because Forster had made its price cut effective throughout the metropolitan area in which it had encountered the price competition. The Commission based its ruling on the Supreme Court's statement in *FTC* v. *A. E. Staley Mfg. Co.*, 324 U.S. 746 (1945), that the Robinson-Patman Act "places emphasis on individual competitive situations rather than upon a general system of competition." In the *Staley* decision the Court refused to allow application of the defense to discriminatory price cuts given as part of a pricing system or in accordance with a general formula. The Court reasoned that Section 2(b)'s proviso "presupposes that the person charged with violating the Act would, by his normal, nondiscriminatory pricing methods, have reached a price so high that he could reduce it in order to meet the competitor's equally low price. . . . Respondents have never attempted to establish their own nondiscriminatory price system, and then reduced their price when necessary to meet competition. Instead they have slavishly followed in the first instance a pricing policy which, in their case resulted in systematic discriminations. . . . Moreover, there is no showing that if respondents had charged nondiscriminatory prices, they would be higher in all cases than those now prevailing under their basing point system. Hence it cannot be said that respondents' price discriminations have resulted in 'lower' prices to meet equally low prices of a competitor" (324 U.S. at 754–755). Under these circumstances, the Court concluded that the meeting-competition defense offered rested "upon the assumption that the statute permits a seller to maintain an otherwise unlawful system of discriminatory prices, merely because he has adopted it in its entirety, as a means of securing the benefits of a like unlawful system maintained by his competitors." The Supreme Court rejected that assumption.

The Commission's decision against Forster Mfg. Co. was reversed (335 F.2d 47 (1st Cir. 1964), *cert. denied*, 380 U.S. 906 (1965)). The court of appeals objected to requiring a seller to show that he knew in advance the amount of his competitor's offers and the identity of each competitor who made them. The Commission was instructed, on reconsideration of the case, to require a showing only of facts that would lead a "reasonable and prudent" person to believe he was meeting competition. This "reasonable and prudent person" rule was taken from the Supreme Court's *Staley* decision. According to the *Staley* opinion, the "good faith" requirement means that "the statute at least requires the seller, who has knowingly discriminated in price, to show the existence of facts which would lead a reasonable and prudent person to believe that the granting of a lower price would in fact meet the equally low price of a competitor."

The court of appeals was more impressed than the Commission with the seller's contention that specific information about the amounts of competitive offers and their sources would be difficult to obtain. "We may not be in as intimate touch with the ways of commerce as the Commission, but we would be naive indeed if we believed that buyers would have any great solicitude for the welfare of their commercial antagonists, sellers. The seller wants the highest price he can get and the buyer wants to buy as cheaply as he can, and to achieve their antagonistic ends neither expects the other, or can be expected, to lay all his cards face up on the table. Battle of wits is the rule. Haggling has ever been the way of the market place. The Commission's requirement is unrealistic."

When the FTC reconsidered the *Forster* case on remand, it denied any intention to require "proof positive" that the seller knew in advance either the amount of the competitive offers or the identity of the competitors who made them (68 F.T.C. 191 (1965)). Noting that only full access to a buyer's books and records could furnish such proof, the Commission declared that it "intended no more than that respondents, in failing to demand a statement of those particulars from its favored buyer, that is, in guessing blindly at an alleged 'competitive offer in an unknown amount made by an unnamed competitor,' as they argued it to the court, had shown . . . an 'entire lack . . . of diligence on the part of the respondents to verify the reports' of lower competitive prices."

The Commission's reasoning was that the buyer's report of lower price offers, "like a witness' testimony in court," takes on increased credibility as detail is added. The only evidence Forster presented, the Commission explained, was that the favored buyer had received "more interesting offers." What was needed was evidence that Forster took steps to investigate competitive prices it claimed to have met and thus "to learn of the existence of facts which would lead a reasonable and prudent person to believe that the granting of a lower price in effect would be meeting the lower price of a competitor" within the meaning of the Supreme Court's opinion in the *Staley* case. Forster's second review petition was dismissed (361 F.2d 340 (1st Cir. 1966), *cert. denied,* 385 U.S. 1003 (1967)).

In *C. E. Niehoff & Co.,* 51 F.T.C. 1114 (1955), the Commission disapproved a hearing examiner's theory that a "showing that a seller's discriminations were temporary and localized in area is an indispensable prerequisite to establish a defense" under Section 2(b). In addition, several of the courts of appeals have indicated they would apply the defense to area-wide price cuts. In the *Forster* case, the Commission refused to follow a ruling to that effect in *General Gas Corp.* v. *National Utilities of Gainesville,* 271 F.2d 820 (5th Cir. 1959). See also *Balian Ice Cream Co.* v. *Arden Farms Co.,* 231 F.2d 356 (9th Cir. 1955) and *Ludwig* v. *American Greetings Corp.* 282 F.2d 917 (6th Cir. 1960).

In *Rabiner & Jontow, Inc.,* 70 F.T.C. 638 (1966), the Commission rejected the meeting-competition defense of a garment manufacturer charged with granting disproportionate advertising allowances. In the words of the Commission majority, the manufacturer failed to show that "any particular payment was made to meet a specific competitive offer." What the majority would require is proof that after "a comprehensive, nondiscriminatory program" of cooperative advertising had been established, deviations occurred in "individual instances shown to be good faith attempts to meet promotional allowances furnished by competitors." On appeal the seller challenged only the propriety of enforcing an order against it while its competitors remained free to follow the same practices. The court of appeals upheld the Commission's order (386 F.2d 667 (2nd Cir. 1967), *cert. denied,* 390 U.S. 1004 (1968)), pointing out that the meeting-competition defense is "implicit in every order issued under" the Robinson-Patman Act. A suggestion that the order should leave the seller free "to meet competition generally without showing that any particular payment was made to meet a specific competitor's offer" was rejected.

In *Beatrice Foods Co.,* 67 F.T.C. 973 (1965), a quantity discount granted to one favored customer was exonerated on the basis of a carefully documented showing that the respondent could have lost that customer's business if it had failed to match a competitive offer. Similarly, in *National Dairy,* 70 F.T.C. 79 (1966), *aff'd,* 395 F.2d 517 (7th Cir. 1968), *cert. denied,* 393 U.S. 977 (1968), the Commission validated the meeting-competition defense in some instances where respondent's officers testified "that they personally contacted the store owners whom they named, and they gave the time and place of the conversation, the amount of the competitor's offer, and, in most instances the name of the competitor."

Discrimination in advertising allowances was the context of another FTC definition of its Section 2(b) proof requirements in *Surprise Brassiere Co., Inc.,* 71 F.T.C. 868 (1967). "Respondent must prove that its discriminatory allowances were responsive to offers by other sellers in specific competitive situations and that it had reason to believe it was meeting such offers." Relying on *Callaway Mills Co.,* 64 F.T.C. 732 (1964), *order vacated,* 362 F.2d 435 (5th Cir. 1966), Surprise Brassiere asked the reviewing court to hold that it could meet competition generally through meeting a plan or system of its competitors. The court took the position that Surprise Brassiere's argument had no factual support in the record of the FTC proceeding (406 F.2d 711 (5th Cir. 1969)). Unlike Callaway Mills, the court of appeals explained, "Surprise was not confronted with the problem of trying to match its prices with the prices of competitors that varied according to the cumulative annual purchases of each customer. It was faced with specific competitive situations but its proof did not show that it limited its variances to specific competitive situations." In the court's view the FTC "required no more than is taught in *Staley*. The Supreme Court in Staley, did not think it an impossible burden to require . . . a showing of diligence on the part of respondents to verify the reports which they received, or to learn of the existence of facts which would lead a reasonable and prudent person to believe that the granting of a lower price would in fact be meeting the equally low price of a competitor.' 324 U.S. at p. 759." More applicable to Surprise's pricing practices, the court said, are the *Rabiner & Jontow* case and *Exquisite Form Brassiere Inc.* v. *FTC*, 360 F.2d 492 (D.C. Cir. 1965), *cert. denied,* 384 U.S. 959 (1966), where "the courts upheld the view that a seller cannot deviate from promotional advertising programs in order to meet competition generally as opposed to meeting competition in individual competitive situations." In *Exquisite Form,* the Court of Appeals for the D.C. Circuit explicitly held that the *Staley* rule against adoption of a discriminatory system to meet a discriminatory system is as applicable to advertising allowances as it is to prices and discounts therefrom.

Each of the Commission's other three holdings restricting the scope of the Section 2(b) defense has been reversed. One, that a seller cannot give one buyer a special price cut in order to help the buyer meet his competition, was reinstated by the Supreme Court in *FTC* v. *Sun Oil Co.,* 371 U.S. 505 (1963). Sun Oil had granted a lower price to a retail gasoline dealer in Jacksonville, Fla., in order to enable the dealer to match the price cuts of another retailer selling a nonmajor brand of gasoline just across the street. The Commission found that Sun's lower price to the selected dealer illegally discriminated against other Sun dealers in the Jacksonville area. The court of appeals reversed (294 F.2d 465 (5th Cir. 1961)), holding that the Commission's rule would force Sun either to expand into the retailing field, putting the whole burden of competing on the individual dealer, or, by reducing its price to all area dealers, "set off price wars throughout Florida and Southeast United States."

Without dissent, the Supreme Court reversed the court of appeals and agreed with the Commission that the Section 2(b) defense is available only to a seller who cuts prices to meet his own competition (371 U.S. 505 (1963)). As the justices saw it, this was the "normal and customary meaning" of the statute's words "showing that his lower price . . . was made in good faith to meet an equally low price of a competitor." The phrase "equally low price of a competitor" was read as referring to the price of a competitor of the seller, not a competitor of the buyer. "Were something more intended by Congress, we would have expected a more explicit recitation as, for example, in the case of Section 2(a) in which the intent to give broader scope was expressly effected by the prohibition of price discrimination which, inter alia, adversely affected competition not only with the seller . . . who grants the favored price, but with the knowing recipient thereof . . . and 'with customers of either of them.' "

The Court seemed to place more emphasis on economic considerations than on the wording of the statute. "To allow a supplier to intervene and grant discriminatory price concessions designed to enable its customer to meet the lower price of a retail competitor who is unaided by his supplier would discourage rather than promote competition. So long as the price-cutter does not receive a price 'break' from his own supplier, his lawful reductions in price are presumably a function of his own superior merit and efficiency. To permit a competitor's supplier to bring his often superior economic power to bear narrowly and discriminatorily to deprive the otherwise resourceful retailer of the very fruits of his efficiency and convert the normal competitive struggle between retailers into an unequal contest between one retailer and the combination of another retailer and his supplier is hardly an element of reasonable and fair competition.

"We see no justification for such a result in Section 2(b). Restriction of the defense to those situations in which a supplier responds to the price concessions of its own competitor—another supplier—maintains general competitive equities. Fairness demands neither more nor less. We discern in Section 2 neither a purpose to insulate retailers from lawful and normal competitive pressures generated by other retailers, nor an intent to authorize suppliers, in response to such pressures created solely at the retail level, to protect, discriminatorily, sales to one customer at the expense of other customers."

The Court did not completely bar the door to Sun. In a footnote to its opinion, the Court observed that the result might have been different if the record had shown that the nonmajor brand gasoline retailer whose price cuts initiated the price war was an integrated supplier-retailer. The Court said it "would be presented with a different case" if it appeared that the gasoline retailer whose price cuts started the price war was "an integrated supplier-retailer, or . . . had received a price cut from its own supplier—presumably a competitor of Sun." That reservation, when coupled with the Court's assumption that the price cuts of the retailer who started the price war were "a function of his own superior merit and efficiency," is taken by some antitrust lawyers to mean that the Court would apply the meeting-competition defense in the "different case." In other words, it would allow a price reduction made in response to the price cut of an integrated wholesaler-retailer or of a retailer aided by a price "break" from his supplier.

The opinion also left unresolved the question of whether a wholesaler, for example, is to be permitted to lower his price to the level at which the manufacturer sells to direct-buying retailers and whether a manufacturer can discriminate in prices charged direct-buying retailers in order to meet the price offered by a wholesaler.

In *Ponca Wholesale Mercantile Co.,* 64 F.T.C. 937 (1964), an FTC hearing examiner allowed a wholesaler to meet the price charged by a manufacturer selling directly to retailers. In *Sunshine Biscuits, Inc.,* 59 F.T.C. 674 (1961), the Commission declared that the defense applies only to discriminatory price cuts made to keep old customers, not those made to win new ones. Under such a doctrine, the Court of Appeals for the Seventh Circuit reasoned, "competition for new customers would be stifled and monopoly would be fostered. In such situations an established seller would have a monopoly of his customers and a seller entering the market would not be permitted to reduce his prices to compete with his established rivals unless he could do so on a basis such as cost justification" (*Sunshine Biscuits, Inc.* v. *FTC* 306 F.2d 48 (7th Cir. 1962)).

Although the FTC was persuaded by the Solicitor General not to seek Supreme Court review of the court of appeals' holding, the Commission announced that it would continue to adhere to its ban on "aggressive" price cuts that are discriminatory. At least two hearing examiners, without citing the *Sunshine Biscuits* case, subsequently handed down initial decisions that the meeting-competition defense is available even when special treatment is offered a new customer (*Continental Baking Co.,* 63 F.T.C. 2071 (1963); *Ponca Wholesale Mercantile Co.,* 64 F.T.C. 937 (1964)).

Two courts of appeals took the Commission to task for refusing to apply the meeting-competition defense in discriminatory-advertising-allowance cases under Section 2(d) of the Act. The first court to consider the problem was the Court of Appeals for the District of Columbia Circuit in *Exquisite Form Brassiere, Inc.,* 301 F.2d 499 (D.C. Cir. 1961), *cert. denied,* 369 U.S. 888 (1962); 360 F.2d 492 (D.C. Cir. 1965), *cert. denied,* 384 U.S. 959 (1966). Literally, the court conceded, Section 2(b) of the Act merely permits a seller "in good faith to meet an equally low price of a competitor or the services or facilities furnished by a competitor." It does not use the words of Section 2(d), which makes it unlawful for a seller to pay ". . . a customer . . . compensation . . . for any services or facilities furnished by . . . such customer . . . unless such payment . . . is available on proportionally equal terms to all other customers." The court of appeals refused to "quibble about the reality that services or facilities are furnished by a vendor whether they are supplied

in kind or are acquired by the customer with subsequent reimbursement by the vendor." Moreover, the opinion continued, the economic evil sought to be outlawed by the statute is the same whether
the services and facilities are furnished by the customer or by the
customer with reimbursement. The same line of reasoning was subsequently followed, with the same results, by the Seventh Circuit
in *Shulton, Inc.* v. *FTC,* 305 F.2d 36 (7th Cir. 1962).

Without the participation of the Solicitor General, the Commission sought Supreme Court review of the *Exquisite Form* case, but
review was denied (369 U.S. 888 (1962)). Subsequently. in *J. A.
Folger & Co.,* 61 F.T.C. 1166 (1962), the Commission indicated that
it had capitulated on this point and would apply the defense to
discriminatory promotional allowances. Then, in *Max Factor & Co.,*
66 F.T.C., 184 (1964), the Commission remanded a discriminatory-
allowance proceeding to the hearing examiner for the admission of
evidence that the advertising payments were made in good faith to
meet competition. In the *Exquisite Form* proceeding, a hearing
examiner held, on remand, that the evidence offered by the company did not establish the defense. Nonetheless, the Commission
reinstated its cease and desist order (64 F.T.C. 271 (1964)), and it
was affirmed on appeal (360 F.2d 492 (D.C. Cir. 1965), *cert. denied,*
384 U.S. 959 (1966)).

Despite its frequent rebuffs in the court of appeals, the Commission has attempted to add one more requirement the seller's
"good faith" evidence must meet. In the *Callaway Mills* case, a
two-commissioner majority adopted the rule that the seller must
prove that the competitor's price was charged for merchandise "comparable in materials and construction" to the seller's merchandise
(64 F.T.C. 732 (1964)). The Commission's opinion was written by
Chairman Paul Rand Dixon for himself and Commissioner Everette
MacIntyre. Commissioner Sigurd Anderson concurred "in the result"; Commissioner Philip Elman dissented; and Commissioner
John R. Reilly, not having heard oral argument, did not participate.
The Chairman's opinion began with a review of the Supreme
Court's 1951 rejection of the Commission's early rule that the meeting-competition defense is not available to a seller when his price
discriminations may cause serious injury to unfavored customers.
While the Commission acknowledged its obligation to follow the
Supreme Court's interpretation, it said, "it is our view that the
proponent of a statutory defense which, when successfully inter-
posed, permits systematic price discriminations injurious to smaller
retailers should be held to a strict showing that its lower prices
were, in fact, set to meet the equally low prices of competitors."
Applying the defense in this case would have had the effect of
permitting "the indefinite continuation of substantial injury to

smaller rug retailers" in their competition with favored chain stores, according to the majority. "Such a result should be reached only with caution after due deliberation."

When the FTC staff attempts to prove unlawful price discrimination, Chairman Dixon continued, it is required to identify with exactness the particular goods involved and to show that goods alike in grade and quality were sold at different prices. "It is equally incumbent upon the proponent of a meeting-competition defense to identify with particularity both his goods and the competing goods whose price was met so that the fact finder can determine the validity of the defensive claims." If the discriminatory price cut was made to "meet" the price of inferior goods, the Commission reasoned, then the price cutter has in effect undercut his competitor's price and has not really taken "defensive" action. Commissioner Elman, on the other hand, could not agree that Section 2(b) should be given "a narrow, grudging interpretation," since one of its main purposes is to alleviate price rigidity. According to Elman, ". . . even if 2(b) is construed narrowly, it cannot reasonably be interpreted to require proof that a respondent's products are of 'like grade and quality' compared with its competitors' products. The 'like grade and quality' provision of 2(a) qualifies the requirement of that section that the seller maintain in price uniformity among competing purchasers. Transposed to a 2(b) context, the provision is meaningless, since 2(b) is solely concerned with permitting the respondent to meet a competitive situation. A seller is permitted by 2(b) to meet a competitive price, that is, a price on competing products, irrespective of whether those products are of 'like grade and quality', for 2(a) purposes, to his own. This is the holding of *Balian Ice Cream Co.* v. *Arden Farms Co.*, 231 F.2d 356 (9th Cir. 1955), and, until today, was, I think, considered a well-settled proposition."

Relying on the *Staley* decision, the Court of Appeals for the Fifth Circuit held in *Callaway* that a respondent relying on the meeting-competition defense "must only show facts which would lead a 'reasonable and prudent person' to believe that the granting of lower prices would in fact meet the equally low price of a competitor." In the court's view, "in the totality of the circumstances" revealed by its analysis of competition in the carpet industry, "the discount system, thoughtfully tailored by both petitioners to meet their individual problems in the market, was a mature and reasoned approach to a very real and difficult competitive program, and petitioners carried their burden of showing 'good faith' " (362 F.2d 435 (5th Cir. 1966)). The court of appeals ruled that a meeting-competition defense need not include proof that the products on which discrimination occurred are of the same grade and quality as the products on which the competitors cut prices. What the Commission should look for, the court ruled, is evidence indicating that the price discriminator's products have "salability" qualities comparable to those of its competitors' products.

In view of the difficulty members of the FTC have had in reaching agreement on the approach to be taken in evaluating meeting-competition evidence, the language used in the various opinions may have less significance than the evidentiary records on which the decisions are based. Even the reviewing court's *Callaway* ruling may be regarded as a factual judgment that in the circumstances the respondents had acted in "good faith" in adopting their quantity discount systems.

As another example, the "lawful price" requirement voiced again in the *National Dairy* case may really have little doctrinal significance; it is regarded by some lawyers as a phrase thrown in by Chairman Dixon on behalf of a majority whose ruling is in fact attributable to dissatisfaction with the meeting-competition evidence presented to the Commission. The majority's willingness in the *Tri-Valley* case to allow the meeting of a competitor's formal pricing system cannot be regarded as a significant relaxation of the majority's restrictions on the meeting-competition defense, since a respondent is still required to make his own price adjustments "in individual transactions." Looking at the facts in these proceedings, experts view the decisions as putting a premium on documentation of competitive situations. In informal discussions with businessmen and their lawyers, the FTC staff advises careful documentation. Both the Commission and its staff are more impressed with current documentation than with documentation produced once the Commission has begun an investigation or prepared a proposed complaint. Even when documentation is maintained concurrently with cut-rate sales, the proof requirements in the Commission's factual determinations in these cases are tough to meet, notwithstanding the Commission's apparent acquiescence in the courts' "reasonable person" standard. The strictness of the Commission's proof requirements is apparent not only in its opinions supporting cease-and-desist orders but also in its decisions dismissing complaints, such as *Beatrice Foods Co.,* 67 F.T.C. 473 (1965). It helps if the seller is a small company trying to survive against larger competitors. In *Continental Baking Co.,* the first contested case in which the Commission ever sustained the meeting-competition defense, a controlling element was proof that Continental had "bled" for a few years before it gave in to the pressure of the discriminatory discount systems prevalent in its market. In other words, apparently what must be documented is a truly defensive action taken in an harsh competitive situation. The pricing decisions for most enterprises must be made by subordinate sales personnel operating in the field at the point of sale, where a lawyer is not readily available. Some sellers find it essential, therefore, that a well thought out and carefully worded company-policy statement be circulated among all sales personnel with authority to make pricing decisions. What is emphasized in such a policy statement is the importance of the good faith behind the decision to give one customer or a few customers a special price cut on the theory that one is meeting competition. It does no good to have the transaction and its background well documented if the documents are going to help the FTC staff prove a Section 2 violation, rather than help the company prove it was meeting competition in good faith.

2. Cost Justification

(a) **Question:** *How may price differences be justified by cost differences?*

Section 2(a) of the Clayton Act, as amended by the Robinson-Patman Act, provides that "nothing herein contained shall prevent differentials which make only due allowance for differences in the cost of manufacture, sale, or delivery resulting from the differing methods or quantities in which such commodities are to such purchasers sold or delivered."

In April 1937, only 10 months after the Robinson-Patman Act was passed, the JOURNAL OF ACCOUNTANCY carried an enthusiastic article by an accountant convinced that the new law had opened new vistas of opportunity for his profession. Recognizing that most cost-justification defenses would be based on differences in distribution costs, he predicted: "This should lead to a wholesome development of cost accounting technique in the rather neglected field that lies beyond the factory door." He visualized a wholesale transfer of manufacturing cost accounting techniques to distribution costs but he could see a big difference between the two fields, since "factory costs relate to items or lines of products, whereas distribution costs relate also to channels of distribution, classes of customers, methods of sale and delivery, and various quantity and service characteristics." He anticipated eventual development of "a series of unit service costs . . . , from which it will be possible to compute the cost of selling and delivery for any method of distribution, any class of trade, any group of customers, for any customer individually and finally for any particular order."

Two years later the Federal Trade Commission, in a report to the House Commerce Committee on case studies and distribution-cost accounting, held out a similar hope, describing distribution cost accounting as "still a developing field and becoming increasingly important." The Commission hailed the preparation of accounting manuals by the National Electrical Manufacturers Association, the Rubber Manufacturers Association, and the National Wholesale Druggists Association.

In 1955 the Report of the Attorney General's National Committee to Study the Antitrust Laws included the observation (at 174) that the distribution cost breakdowns needed for a Robinson-Patman cost defense "are obviously not suitable for periodic entry into a seller's regular books of account."

The Federal Trade Commission appointed, in 1954, an Advisory Committee on Cost Justification, which was expected by the Commission's Chairman to "make a significant contribution to improve cost accounting methods and techniques" so that "sellers who wish to facilitate a determination of compliance would be able to organize their records accordingly." However, the Committee's report, filed in 1956, was forced to recognize that "it has not been customary for business enterprises to calculate and record the costs of commodities and distribution services in the detail required for a Robinson-Patman Act determination. An approximate knowledge of costs by products and by customers may well be of value for management purposes, but the requirements of good management do not demand the extent of detail, or continuity of records, needed for an instantaneous solution of the problems presented under the Act."

In none of the reported price-discrimination cases has a cost-justification defense been attempted with cost records prepared in advance as a matter of business routine. The "cost studies" used in those cases were reviews of past operations for which only "average" cost figures for a few types of transactions were available. This characteristic of cost justification was recognized by the Supreme Court when it first encountered the proviso in *Automatic Canteen Co.* v. *FTC,* 346 U.S. 61 (1953).

To cost-justify price differences said to violate the price-discrimination ban in Section 2(a) of the Clayton Act, as amended by the Robinson-Patman Act, a businessman must prove "differences in the cost of manufacture, sale, or delivery resulting from the differing methods or quantities in which such commodities are to such purchasers sold or delivered." Logically Section 2(a)'s use of the words "manufacture, sale, or delivery" indicates that every sort of cost actually incurred is cognizable under the cost-justification proviso if the differences shown result from "differing methods or quantities" of sale or delivery. On the other hand, the statutory language also indicates that a respondent or defendant is not called upon or even permitted to produce evidence of every kind of cost in his operations.

(b) Question: *What kinds of costs may be considered?*

The costs used should have three general characteristics. First, to represent any actual "justification" for a price difference, the cost of the item must be larger per unit sold for the customers paying the higher price. Second, the cost difference must result from "differing methods or quantities" of sale or delivery. Third, the differences in methods or quantities must be differences as between customers paying lower prices and those paying the higher price. In at least one FTC case (*Standard Oil Co.* 41 F.T.C. 263 (1945), *order enforced,* 173 F.2d 210 (7th Cir. 1949), *rev'd,* 340 U.S. 231 (1951); 49 F.T.C. 923 (1953), *ordered vacated,* 233 F.2d 649 (7th Cir. 1956), *aff'd,* 355 U.S. 396 (1958)), a respondent contended that it had a right to include and exclude such cost categories as it chose. Transportation costs were left out. The FTC staff insisted that Standard produce the transportation costs. Since the respondent eventually acceded to the demand, the issue never reached the Commission itself. Later, in *International Salt Co.,* 49 F.T.C. 138 (1952), one of the arguments made by the Commission's accountants against the validity of a cost study (which was rejected by the FTC without reference to this point) was based on the "suspicious" omission of certain cost items, such as warehousing, whose inclusion might "have an effect injurious to cost justification." Yet in *Morton Salt Co.,* 39 F.T.C. 35 (1944), *remanded,* 1944–45 Trade Cas. ¶57,365 (7th Cir. 1945), 40 F.T.C. 388 (1945), *order set aside,* 162 F.2d 949 (7th Cir. 1947), *rev'd,* 334 U.S. 37 (1948), the staff had made no objection to the omission of many items of cost. The successful cost-justification defense in *Minneapolis Honeywell Regulator Co.,* 44 F.T.C. 351 (1948), *rev'd in part,* 191 F.2d 786 (7th Cir. 1951), *cert. denied,* 344 U.S. 206 (1952), consisted of evidence covering only about 7 percent of the company's selling and administrative costs.

The obvious requirement that the costs used to justify price differences must differ in amount per unit between the favored and unfavored classes of customers has presented many FTC respondents with difficult problems of proof. Development of such proof can be particularly difficult for a manufacturer who wants to show differences in manufacturing costs but who produces a uniform line of products for inventory and then makes sales from inventory. As the 1956 report of the FTC's Advisory Committee on Cost Justification said, "manufacturing costs . . . are likely to be segregated to show cost differences resulting from differing methods or quantities of sale only where goods are made upon customer order." The made-to-order situation is illustrated by the successful cost-justification defense offered in *B.F. Goodrich Co.,* 50 F.T.C. 622 (1954). By stipulation, the FTC staff agreed that price differences in some discount brackets were justified by variations in cost attributable to manufacturing specifications and styles for rubber footwear.

Apparently it is of no help to the manufacturer to be able to show that the groups of customers paying different prices are served from different manufacturing plants and that the plants' locations cause different production costs. For example, a plant located further from the source of raw materials will have higher material costs because of higher freight; a plant located in or near a large metropolitan area may have higher labor costs than one located in a less industrialized area. While there are no reported decisions on the allowability of cost differences of that type, attorneys dealing with the Commission have reported that during pre-complaint investigations the Commission's staff has rejected such cost differences, arguing that they are not attributable to "differing methods or quantities" of sale or delivery. The staff has refused to recognize a right in the seller to assign some customers to its high-cost plant and others to low-cost plants.

Even when goods are produced for warehouse stock in accordance with production schedules based on prospective aggregate sales to all customers, however, there is one type of business situation that may produce cognizable cost differences. In presenting the Conference Report on the Robinson-Patman Bill to the House of Representatives, one of the conferees said: "Where one customer orders from hand to mouth during the rush of the season, compelling the employment of more expensive overtime labor . . . while another orders far in advance, permitting the manufacturer to use cheaper off-season labor, with elimination of overtime, or perhaps to buy his raw materials at cheaper off-season prices, such savings as between the two customers may . . . be expressed in price differentials" (80 Cong. Rec. 9417 (1936)). A manufacturer whose production schedules are prepared on the basis of individual customer orders will normally have an easier time collecting evidence of production cost differences.

Some manufacturing expenses will be the same for all orders, regardless of their size, and others may increase in amounts that are not proportional to the size of the order. In each instance, the cost per unit of product will decrease as the size of the order increases. Examples of such expenses are machine "set up," employee training, tooling, development of production methods and standards, product development and design, and sometimes even raw materials or parts. Manufacturing cost differences were shown in *U.S. Rubber Co.,* 46 F.T.C. 998 (1950), and *Thompson Products,* 55 F.T.C. 1252 (1959).

It may be that cost elements such as product development and design and materials will rarely be major factors in cost-justification defenses. Once differences in cost elements of that sort become substantial, they may tend to establish that the products sold at different prices were not "of like grade and quality" within the meaning of Section 2(a) of the Act. In the *Thompson Products* case, for example, some of the automobile parts sold to original equipment manufacturers were more complete and more costly to manufacture than those sold to distributors, and with other parts the reverse was true. To settle the problem of what would be considered parts "of like grade and quality," the Commission's staff and Thompson Products agreed that the parts to be considered within the prohibition of Section 2(a) and therefore to be dealt with in the cost-justification evidence were those for which manufacturing costs did not differ by more than 10 percent. In *Universal-Rundle Corp.,* 65 F.T.C. 924 (1964), *order set aside,* 352 F.2d 831 (7th Cir. 1965), *rev'd,* 387 U.S. 244 (1967), *order set aside,* 382 F.2d 285 (7th Cir. 1967), the Commission upheld a hearing examiner's determination that bathroom fixtures made with the same raw materials and the same manufacturing operations were not of "like grade and quality" because the favored customer's specifications called for smaller dimensions and a different design.

The seller may prefer reliance on the "like grade and quality" test, since it might be less expensive to litigate. While lower costs ordinarily suggest lower quality, a difference in "grade or quality" apparently immunizes any price differential, no matter how unrelated to quality or cost. In *Borden Co.* v. *FTC,* 339 F.2d 133 (5th Cir. 1964), *rev'd,* 383 U.S. 637 (1966), *petition to set aside cease and desist order granted,* 381 F.2d 175 (5th Cir. 1967), the court of appeals considered it unnecessary to pass on matters of cost justification once it had determined that the seller's customers were buying products of a different grade and quality.

The requirement that the cost differences result from "differing methods or quantities" of sale or delivery was added to Section 2(a) of the Clayton Act by the Robinson-Patman Act in 1936. There is evidence in the legislative history of the Robinson-Patman Act that the new language was intended to prevent sellers from justifying a price differential on the basis of "incremental" costs, the mere out-of-pocket cost of the increment of activity occasioned by a sale in quantity. As the House Judiciary Committee put it, the new proviso "precludes differentials based on the imputation of overhead to particular customers, or the exemption of others from it, where such overhead represents facilities or activities inseparable from the seller's business as a whole and not attributable to the business of particular customers or of the particular customers concerned in the discrimination" (2287 74th Cong., 2d Sess. 10 (1936)). In its 1956 report, which the Commission never approved or disapproved, the FTC's Advisory Committee on Cost Justification accepted that interpretation.

Cost-justification defenses presented to the FTC have usually been based on differences in distribution costs. Unit costs of sale and delivery can often be shown to vary with the number of units per order, the timing of orders, the selection of delivery methods, the degree of selling effort necessary, the customer's demands for guarantees and service, and, sometimes, the total volume of purchases over a period of time. Examples of unit costs of sale and delivery that frequently vary with the size of order are transportation, warehousing, sales promotion, sales accounting, sales management, sales administration, salesmen's salaries and expenses, and special selling services for the customer. Although "sales promotion" costs are often listed separately from advertising, the only difference lies in the medium used to create demand for the seller's product. Advertising uses such mass communication media as newspapers, magazines, television, and catalogues, whereas the item "sales promotion" covers the cost of display of the product, the use of point-of-sale materials, demonstrations, and premiums. The "sales administration" item includes the cost of clerical work in the sales department and administration of the physical aspects of the distribution operations. "Sales accounting" includes such items as the cost of billing, accumulating sales statistics, accounting for inventory, and recording credit transactions, and the office costs of handling orders.

Whether the absence or reduction of broker's fees can be cited as a basis for a price difference was the subject of apparent disagreement among the Supreme Court justices in *FTC* v. *Henry Broch and Co.*, 363 U.S. 166 (1960), *order modified,* 285 F.2d 764 (7th Cir. 1960), *rev'd,* 368 U.S. 360 (1962). Noting that the Senate had considered but deleted from Section 2(a) a provision that would have excepted brokerage savings from the cost-justification proviso, the Court found the legislative history "barren of any indication that a change in substance was intended by this deletion." The deletion was seen as showing "both an intention that 'legitimacy' of brokerage be governed entirely by Section 2(c) and an understanding that the language of Section 2(c) was sufficiently broad to cover allowances to buyers in the form of price concessions which reflect a differential in brokerage costs" (363 U.S. at 171 n. 8). The dissenting justices, on the other hand, found an "evident intention of Congress in Section 2(a) to permit sellers to pass through to buyers, in the form of reduced prices, any true savings in the cost of distribution of their goods," including savings in brokerage costs (363 U.S. at 185).

One of the co-authors of the Robinson-Patman Act has listed the "elimination of . . . brokers" as a factor to be taken into consideration in determining whether a special price cut has merely made "due allowances for differences in costs" (Wright Patman, COMPLETE GUIDE TO THE ROBINSON-PATMAN ACT (Prentice Hall, 1963)). In addition the Court of Appeals for the Fifth Circuit in *Thomasville Chair Co.* v. *FTC,* 306 F.2d 541 (1962), accepted differences in salesmen's commissions as cost justification for a price 'difference in a proceeding based on the brokerage provisions in Section 2(c) of the Act. At least two FTC hearing examiners have allowed the inclusion in cost studies of savings on brokers' commissions (*American Metal Products Co.,* 60 F.T.C. 1667 (1962); *Borden Co.,* 62 F.T.C. 130 (1963)). In subsequently reversing its examiner in the *Borden* case, the Commission declared explicitly that "savings in costs resulting from the elimination of brokers' commissions are not allowable cost savings under Section 2(a)."

Whether cost differences can be derived from direct costs that vary with sales price such as sales commissions, excise taxes, and percentage royalties, was recognized as a problem in the report of the FTC's Advisory Committee on Cost Justification. The Committee found "nothing inherently unacceptable in such cost differences," but "there may be exceptions." As an example of the "exceptions," it cited the possibility that percentage sales commissions might not properly reflect the time and effort expended in selling to different classes of customers. Under those circumstances, "such cost differences would not be acceptable, and a more precise method of allocating sales commissions should be utilized."

Because the discriminatorily lower price automatically produces a smaller commission, tax, or royalty, the FTC's staff has taken the position that the cost saving is not one "resulting from the differing methods or quantities" of sale or delivery. An example occurred in *American Motors Corp.,* 68 F.T.C. 87 (1965), *remanded,* 384 F.2d 247 (6th Cir. 1967), *cert. denied,* 390 U.S. 1012 (1968), where the hearing examiner's initial decision rejected the staff's argument. In *International Salt Co.,* 49 F.T.C. 138 (1952), the staff called the use of such cost differences a "bootstrap method" of cost justification, since the cost difference resulted directly from the grant of a discriminatory price cut. The Commission rejected the cost study without discussing the "bootstrap" objection.

Occasionally, cash discounts have been listed in cost-justification defenses, but in *Curtiss Candy Co.,* 44 F.T.C. 237 (1947), and *Sylvania Electric Products, Inc.,* 51 F.T.C. 282 (1954), the Commission's staff objected that a cash discount "represents no cost of manufacture and no cost of sale and no cost of delivery." If the same percentage cash discount is available to all customers, it was argued, then there is no cost differential. On the other hand, if the discount varies from customer to customer, then the discount itself constitutes a price differential that must be justified. Subsequently, the Advisory Committee on Cost Justification recommended that cash discounts always be considered in determining price rather than cost, a procedure the Commission's staff endorsed in *Thompson Products.*

Many of the cost items traditionally presented in cost-justification defenses represent expenses of performing functions other than those of a mere seller or supplier. The seller often functions as a financing institution, advertising agency, management consultant, or landlord to his customer. While these types of expenses have in general been accepted as normal distribution costs, in *Standard Oil of Indiana* the FTC staff argued, and the Commission agreed, that "landlord" costs cannot properly be regarded as costs of sale and delivery. The figure presented by Standard and disallowed by the Commission as an added cost of selling to leased-station operators was the amount by which "rent revenue" was exceeded by combined plant-maintenance costs, building depreciation, equipment depreciation, real estate taxes, and a share of the salaries and other expenses of the company's real estate and tax department.

In the litigated cases, the requirement that the cost differences result "from differing methods or quantities" has been applied to prevent the use of two categories of distribution costs. In *Thompson Products Co.,* 55 F.T.C. 1252 (1959), the Federal Trade Commission cited that requirement as its reason for rejecting an attempt to use "return on investment" as an element of cost. It seems that Thompson had almost $9 million invested in buildings, inventory, organization, and credit facilities that were used only in servicing wholesale customers and not in servicing original-equipment manufacturers who purchased Thompson's parts in bulk from the production lines. In refusing to let Thompson add, as a cost of doing business with the wholesalers, a "profit" on the $9 million investment comparable to its overall ratio of profit to capital, the Commission quoted from the legislative history regarding adoption of the "differing methods or quantities" phrase and declared "this whole concept of return on investment is contrary to the legislative intent of the Congress." *Thompson Products* was cited by the Commission in *Borden Co.,* when it disallowed an "investment cost" item based on the investment Borden maintained in larger inventories needed to serve the customers paying the higher price. The cost item claimed was an 8-percent return on the average additional investment in inventory. The Commission stressed the absence of "an actual, incurred cost."

In *Shell Oil Co.*, 66 F.T.C. 1336, 1477 (1964), a hearing examiner applied the same requirement to prevent a refiner from showing that constant turnover among its lessee dealers necessitated expenditure of substantially more money in training those dealers than was spent in training dealers who own their own stations. The vital fact, in the eyes of the examiner, was that the same training methods were used for both types of dealers. The only difference in the service provided the two types of station operators was that Shell representatives had spent more time doing the same thing in the leased stations than in the dealer-owned stations. "Such differences in the cost of selling which have been shown are not shown to have resulted from differing methods of selling or quantities sold to two distinct classes of purchasers. Insofar as the cost of making the original sales contract is concerned, there is nothing to show that the method of making such contracts differed or that the costs of making sales contracts differed between different classes of customers."

In *Champion Spark Plug Co.*, 50 F.T.C. 30 (1953), the seller introduced evidence that favored customers assumed many merchandising functions that otherwise would have had to be performed by the seller. Two favored customers whose discounts were sought to be cost justified were major oil refiners that not only redistributed Champion Spark Plugs to their service stations but also engaged in sales promotion, furnished sales training, and prepared posters, displays, catalogs, and training manuals. The FTC staff questioned the pertinence of this testimony to a cost-justification defense, suggesting that its effect is to show a violation of the discriminatory-allowances ban in Section 2(d) of the Act. The hearing examiner agreed that these promotional allowances, "being unlawful, could not be availed of by Champion in justification of its price discriminations." Although the issue never reached the Commission in the *Champion* case, earlier in *Standard Oil of Indiana*, the Commission refused to consider advertising costs incurred by favored jobbers as producing a "reciprocal benefit" justifying a special discount. The buyer's costs may be relevant in determining whether there has been any injury to competition. See *Doubleday & Co.*, 52 F.T.C. 169, 209, n. 7 (1955). Cf. *Mueller Co.*, 60 F.T.C. 120 (1962), *aff'd*, 323 F.2d 44 (7th Cir. 1963), *cert. denied*, 377 U.S. 923 (1964).

Because there are almost as many different methods of classifying and recording costs as there are business enterprises, compilation of an exhaustive list of cognizable costs is impracticable. On the other hand, it would appear that only one category of costs can be regarded as clearly not includible in a price-justifying cost analysis: "incremental" costs. While the Federal Trade Commission and its examiners have on various occasions ruled against a number of other categories of costs, Robinson-Patman Act experts are not all ready to concede that the law is settled with respect to those items. First of all, they are not sure the Commission's rule against inclusion of a return on investment would stand up in court, especially since the *Borden* opinion hints that the Commission would allow "actual incurred" interest and financing charges. Second, since the costs of other activities "collateral" to ordinary sales functions have been allowed, the Commission's *Standard Oil* ruling against "landlord" costs is not accepted by all. Third, while the Federal Trade Commission, in refusing to consider savings in brokerage, may point to the Supreme Court's opinion in the *Broch* case, the Court of Appeals for the Fifth Circuit, in the *Thomasville Chair* case, did not go along with that interpretation of the Supreme Court's opinion. Fourth, the absence of any explicit FTC decision on its staff's "bootstrap" argument leaves undetermined the status of cost differences derived from costs that vary with sales price, such as sales commissions, excise taxes, and percentage royalties. The Commission's Advisory Committee thought such costs were acceptable, as did the hearing examiner in the *American Motors* case Finally, the examiner's refusal in the *Shell Oil* case to recognize an added expense of training lessee gasoline dealers (because there was more frequent turnover than among dealers who owned their own stations) never received the endorsement of the FTC itself, for the complaint was dismissed for administrative reasons.

The relative scarcity of cost-justification litigation, as well as the infrequency, even in that type of litigation, of opinions dealing directly with types of cognizable costs and cost concepts, make it unlikely that any of these questions will be definitely settled in the near future.

(c) Question: *What customer groupings are permitted?*

The 1956 report of the FTC Advisory Committee on Cost Justification commented: "Classification or grouping of customers, orders, commodities, and transactions has repeatedly been recognized by the Federal Trade Commission as a valid business practice. What this means is that it is not necessary to cost-justify each sale transaction or sales to each individual customer. . . . At the same time, the privilege of classification is not a license to disregard sound business and accounting concepts. In order to become the basis for cost justification of price differentials, the classification should be logical and should reflect actual differences in the manner or cost of dealing. Great care should be taken in establishing price classes to make sure that all members of the class are enough alike to make the averaging of their costs a sound procedure. Customer groupings may properly be based not only on quantities sold but also according to the way customers place their orders: whether for immediate delivery or later shipment on a fixed schedule in large or small orders; placed directly at the factory or through a sales branch; for on-peak or off-peak manufacture, etc. These trade factors may all be reflected in cost and as criteria for customer classification."

The FTC decisions referred to by the Advisory Committee are probably *Minneapolis-Honeywell Regulator Co.*, 44 F.T.C. 351 (1948), *rev'd in part*, 191 F.2d 786 (7th Cir. 1951), *cert. denied*, 344 U.S. 206 (1952), and *Champion Sparkplug Co.*, 50 F.T.C. 30 (1953). In the *Minneapolis-Honeywell* case, which involved graduated volume discounts based on annual purchases, the FTC's staff asked for a rule barring cost justification of price differentials between competing customers whose annual purchases, while in different discount brackets, were near the dividing line between brackets and therefore were not significantly different in amount. The Commission sustained the customer groupings, finding no "competitive importance" in this occasional discrimination between customers with similar purchase volumes. In the *Champion Sparkplug* case, on the other hand, the Commission made it clear that customer groupings may not be so broad that they lose meaning in cost comparisons. "A cost justification based on the difference between an estimated average cost of selling to one or two large customers and an average cost of selling to all other customers cannot be accepted as a defense to a charge of price discrimination."

In *Thompson Products, Inc.*, 55 F.T.C. 1252 (1959), a manufacturer of automotive parts had tried to use "average" costs and "average" price quotations in an effort to cost-justify diverse price cuts negotiated with automobile manufacturers. The Commission rejected this attempt to put all automobile manufacturers in a single category, pointing out that competing parts distributors and jobbers "must compete in as many areas of competition with vehicle manufacturers as there are manufacturers buying the common parts and not with a single hypothetical original-equipment manufacturer."

Two private treble-damage actions under Section 2(a) of the Clayton Act have produced four court opinions discussing this problem of customer classification (*Russellville Canning Co.* v. *American Can Co.*, 87 F.Supp. 484 (W. D. Ark., 1949), *rev'd*, 191 F.2d 38, (8th Cir. 1951); *Bruce's Juices* v. *American Can Co.*, 87 F.Supp. 985 (S.D. Fla. 1949), *aff'd*, 187 F.2d 919 (5th Cir. 1951), *petition for cert. dismissed on motion of petitioner's counsel*, 342 U.S. 875 (1951)). Both district courts seemed to think quantity-discount systems can be justified only by proof of corresponding differences in the cost of selling to individual customers. Both judges rejected cost justifications based on the allocation of average sales costs to various purchase-volume brackets, and the *Bruce's Juices* damage judgment was upheld on appeal. The Court of Appeals for the Eighth Circuit, with one judge dissenting, reversed the district court determination that customers had been improperly grouped. The court indicated doubt that a "district court has the same power as the Federal Trade Commission to disapprove . . . a system of quantity discounts." The district court's function was limited to "deciding whether the quantity discounts granted by the defendant did not exceed a due allowance for the difference in the cost of selling cans to the different classes into which its customers were divided." The discounts had to be upheld if "the system was adopted in good faith and the cost study during the test period . . . was honestly maintained, and reflected with substantial accuracy the differences in selling costs as between the customers in Class C and those in Classes A and B."

Customer groupings were dealt with by the Supreme Court in *U.S.* v. *Borden Co.,* 370 U.S. 460 (1962), reinstating two civil injunction suits filed by the Justice Department. The Court's opinion, written by Justice Clark, considered cost studies introduced by two Chicago dairies to justify their charging two large chain stores lower prices than independent grocery stores charged for the same products. One dairy's cost study compared the average selling cost per $100 of sales to the chains with the average costs of a similar volume of sales to each of four of the independent stores, which were subdivided by volume of purchases. The other dairy's cost study compared the "standard" cost per unit of product delivered to the chains with the corresponding "standard" cost of serving the independents.

Justice Clark started with a recognition that the language of the proviso "is literally susceptible of a construction which would require any discrepancy in price between any two purchasers to be individually justified." Yet "the proviso has not been so construed by those charged with its enforcement. . . . To completely renounce class pricing as justified by class accounting would be to eliminate in practical effect the cost justification proviso as to sellers having a large number of purchasers, thereby preventing such sellers from passing on economies to their customers. . . . But this is not to say that price differentials can be justified on the basis of arbitrary classifications or even classifications which are representative of a numerical majority of the individual members. At some point practical considerations shade into a circumvention of the proviso. A balance is struck by the use of classes for cost justification which are composed of members of such self-sameness as to make the averaging of the cost of dealing with the group a valid and reasonable indicium of the cost of dealing with any specific group member. High on the list of 'musts' in the use of the average cost of customer groupings under the proviso of Section 2(a) is a close resemblance of the individual members of each group on the essential point or points which determine the costs considered."

Applying those standards to the dairies' cost studies, the Court found that the "independent stores" classification used in the cost study included some large independents having volumes comparable to, and sometimes larger than, those of the chain stores. Therefore, the cost figures contained "artificial disparities between the larger independents and the chain stores." Moreover, the grouping together of the two chains had the effect of raising the average volume of the stores of the smaller of the two grocery chains in relation to that of the larger independents. In addition, many independents were assigned cost factors that did not reflect actual costs of serving them. For example, one dairy assigned to each independent a portion of the total expenses involved in making daily cash collections, but it was not shown that all independents paid cash; only a "large majority" did so. The other dairy allocated only to the independents costs for "optional customer service" and daily cash collection. Here there was no evidence that all the independents received these services daily or even on a less frequent basis. Such a cost analysis, the court concluded, "possibly allocates costs to some independents whose mode of purchasing does not give rise to them."

Justice Harlan dissented, taking the position that the district court had assessed the overall adequacy of the cost studies "in accordance with accepted principles of law in this field." Justice Douglas filed a special concurring opinion advocating the use of "store-by-store costs." He would permit the use of average costs for even a single chain only when there is "centralized purchasing" by the chain. In this case, deliveries were made to individual stores, not to the chains' central warehouses.

Justice Douglas' "store-by-store" standard for cost justification was later applied by an FTC hearing examiner in *National Dairy Products Corp.*, 70 F.T.C. 79 (1963), *aff'd*, 395 F.2d 517 (7th Cir. 1968), *cert. denied*, 393 U.S. 977 (1968). In opposing the "store-by-store" approach, National Dairy pointed out that the cost-justification proviso refers to differences in costs of selling or delivering to "purchasers," not "stores." The "point of competition" contemplated by Congress, it was argued, is between "purchasers," rather than between their individual stores. The examiner was impressed by testimony of independent grocers that they compete with the specific chain-store outlets in their immediate localities. He also thought it significant that the products involved were dairy products, which do not lend themselves to the warehousing and central-distribution techniques of grocery chains.

The FTC stated its views on average prices and costs for an extensive line of products in *Sylvania Electric Products Inc.*, 51 F.T.C. 282 (1954). Sylvania, which sold almost 600 types of replacement radio tubes, had given a special price concession to another radio manufacturer buying for resale through its marketing organization. The cost studies presented by Sylvania did not attempt a separate justification for the price differential on each of the many types of tubes it marketed. A "weighted average" was used. The average price per tube paid by parts distributors was compared with the amount they would have paid if given the discounts allowed the manufacturer. Evidence was presented of greater distribution costs incurred in selling to the distributors, and the aggregate of these additional distribution costs was put forth as sufficient to justify the aggregate price difference arrived at by use of the "weighted average."

The Commission found it significant that Sylvania distributed its entire line of products through each of the two channels of distribution. Because dealers were generally repairmen, every distributor and each one of its dealer-customers needed a complete line of Sylvania tubes. In these circumstances, the Commission apparently expected its staff to prove that the lack of uniformity in the price difference on the various types of tubes had competitive significance. "There is no showing that the tubes which are in the greatest demand are the ones on which the price spread is the greater. To the contrary it appears that the types of tubes on which the price differentials are larger are in the least demand." The defense was sustained. Subsequently, in the *Thompson Products* case, the Commission's staff acquiesced in comparable cost averaging by product.

In the *Borden* case, 62 F.T.C. 130 (1963), *order set aside,* 339 F.2d 133 (5th Cir. 1964), *rev'd,* 383 U.S. 637 (1966), *order set aside,* 381 F.2d 175 (5th Cir. 1967), the Commission refused to extend the reasoning of the *Sylvania* case to a seller charged with price discrimination in the marketing of a single product, evaporated milk. "Broad averages" were used in computing the comparative costs of selling the condensed milk under the Borden brand and of selling it at a lower price in cans bearing the customer's private labels. The Commission fell back on reasoning similar to that used by the Supreme Court in *U.S.* v. *Borden Co.,* 370 U.S. 460 (1962). Listing several market areas in which Borden's product was available to private label purchasers at prices significantly below the "average private label price," the Commission declared: "The price competition which the Borden brand customers faced was not the average private label price . . . but rather the lower actual prices, above mentioned. The use of broad averages [here, price averages] . . . levels the extremes and ignores specific markets or transactions where the greater differences may result in the lessening of competition." Furthermore, the FTC declared, the average cost figures used for Borden-brand and private-brand customers ignored the fact that the customers actually fell into different types of groupings if classified by the extent of service required. For example, sales department expenses would more accurately have been allocated among three customer groups: customers on whom no salesman called, those in whose stores salesmen's activities were restricted, and those where the salesmen performed the full range of in-store service activities such as building floor displays and arranging stock.

There has been one court decision dealing with the propriety of averaging cost savings over a multitude of transactions. In *Reid* v. *Harper & Bros.,* 235 F.2d 420 (2d Cir. 1956), the court of appeals refused to set aside a jury verdict that apparently accepted comparative costs computed by averaging total shipments for an entire year. The complaining buyer objected that this procedure used savings on large sales to the three favored customers to justify discriminations on sales of smaller quantities that did not yield any cost savings when compared to the complaining buyer's purchasers. "To require a seller in these circumstances," the court reasoned, "to justify the cost differential in each and every transaction with his buyers, rather than on the aggregate basis of their dealings, would prove unduly onerous. The impact of such a requirement might be to discourage all price differentials, even those actually justified by cost distinctions."

(d) Question: *How should cost studies be prepared?*

Robinson-Patman Act lawyers and accountants have had to develop their cost-justification evidence in "cost studies," elaborate and detailed allocations of costs incurred during a representative time period and, sometimes, within a typical market area. These studies have been the source of every cost-justification defense presented to the Commission in its reported cases. The cases are almost worthless as precedents. The FTC's Advisory Committee on Cost Justification attributed the failure of the cases to develop costing standards or principles to "the infinite variations of internal organization, methods of doing business, availability of accounting and statistical data, and other important factors." The Committee felt that "any attempt to lay down detailed procedures for all business enterprises or otherwise to strait-jacket cost justification would be self-defeating."

Accountants who have worked on Robinson-Patman cost studies have often complained of the absence of FTC guidelines or even instructions to its staff defining acceptable methods of allocating costs among customers, products, or transactions. Each case seems to be litigated as an isolated problem for which costing procedures and principles must be developed anew. Even in such seemingly similar situations as *International Salt Co.,* 49 F.T.C 138 (1952), and *Morton Salt,* 39 F.T.C. 35 (1944), *remanded,* 1944–45 Trade Cas. ¶57,365 (7th Cir. 1945), *modified order,* 40 F.T.C. 388 (1945), *order set aside,* 162 F.2d 949 (7th Cir. 1947), *rev'd,* 334 U.S. 37 (1948), there were significant differences in methods of cost analysis used by the companies. The Commission's staff does not usually prepare any cost study of its own to counter the respondent's, but ordinarily confines itself to checking the respondent's figures, securing supplemental data, and reallocating costs in accordance with accounting theories the FTC attorneys or accountants consider equally or more appropriate in the circumstances.

Although less expensive than the detailed segregation of distributing costs in regular books of account, even a one-shot cost study can involve the expenditure of substantial sums of money and substantial amounts of executive time. To design a cost study that will produce, at the lowest possible expense, the evidence needed for a cost-justification defense is something that cannot be done by either an attorney or an accountant working alone. To be successful a cost defense should be prepared under the joint supervision of a team of attorneys, accountants, and company executives. There is substantial agreement that the executives' role is to furnish the details on their company's methods of operation and on the workings of the market involved, details that the lawyers and accountants will use in ascertaining which cost categories are likely to differ substantially from customer group to customer group and how costs can be reasonably allocated among those groups. There has been disagreement over the relative roles of attorneys and accountants in the preparation of cost studies. Despite the stress placed by the FTC's Advisory Committee on Cost Justification upon the use of accountants and accepted accounting procedures, some accountants seem to have the impression that lawyers, both in and outside the FTC, have little desire to rely on accountants in resolving problems encountered in cost studies.

It may be a mistake for lawyers to reserve to themselves all decisions about methods of identifying and allocating cost and classifying customers or transactions. The initial decision in *Admiral Corp.,* 67 F.T.C. 379 (1963), suggests that such an approach on the part of an attorney may create an unfavorable impression. Rejecting the cost-justification defense before him, the examiner made the comment that "the averaging concept used in this case was one determined upon by the chief defense counsel and not by the accountants." Respondent's counsel had objected to the FTC staff's questioning of the respondent's accountant regarding the validity of the cost-averaging techniques used in the cost study. Counsel insisted that "this is a legal question" and "not really an accounting question," but the questioning was allowed. The accountant then testified that his work had "consisted solely of checking counsel's mathematics." The FTC later dismissed the complaint (67 F.T.C. 375 (1965)).

In the litigated cases, the FTC hearing examiners (now administrative law judges) and the FTC itself have placed so much stress on accounting considerations and relied so often on the FTC accounting staff that the practice has developed of having cost studies prepared by public accounting firms. Even if the study is prepared by a company's own accountants, it is generally reviewed by an outside accountant. Some large accounting firms have developed staffs of experts in Robinson-Patman cost justification. Nevertheless, the attorney is generally regarded as the key member of the team. If he is to present the cost-justification defense effectively at the investigative stage or during formal hearings, he must be the one who guides the study. Of course, the actual figures that make up the cost study will be the direct results of the efforts of the respondent's accounting department, and it is the accountant's expertise that is ordinarily given the most weight in identifying, grouping, and allocating costs. Because the accountant will usually be the witness who explains the cost analysis, his views must be given added weight by the attorney guiding the defense, for he cannot be expected to testify effectively, especially on cross-examination, in support of a cost analysis that deviates from his own theories of cost determination.

The first step in the preparation of a cost study is the elimination of cost items that are not likely to produce any substantial differences among the group of customers receiving different prices. Minneapolis-Honeywell persuaded the FTC to accept a cost-justification defense based on an analysis of only 7 percent of distribution costs. While a cost study of that scope will rarely succeed, skilled judgments in this area can not only cut down the expense but in some instances may actually make the study more useful for cost-justification purposes. A cost study that is too broad may be as worthless as one that is too narrow. In *Standard Brands,* 29 F.T.C. 121 (1939), *aff'd,* 189 F.2d 510 (2d Cir. 1951), for example, one of the objections raised by the FTC staff to the respondent's cost data was that the figures represented costs incurred throughout the United States, whereas the price schedule being attacked as discriminatory was in effect in only part of the country.

The next step in preparing the cost study, setting the time, territory, and product limits on the scope of the study, is one in which the accountant and the company executive will play major roles. Through consultation with the appropriate executive, the accountant must determine which company locations and which accounting periods of the year, or which particular years, are most representative of the company's operations in general. If the study is prepared in answer to an FTC complaint, its scope will necessarily be determined in large part by the scope of the charges.

Objections to the scope of a cost study will in most instances take the form of complaints that not enough data has been selected, that the seller has gone too far in the use of sampling techniques. The FTC's Advisory Committee on Cost Justification recognized that the use of sampling techniques "is essential if the cost analysis is to be kept within reason. . . . The type of sampling most likely to be used in Robinson-Patman Act cost studies is the so-called 'judgmental' sampling, in which the data are carefully selected for their known representative character. The competence of the judgment must be established. The random, or statistical, sample should be used where feasible, however, because of its demonstrable lack of bias." Both types of samples are often used. Judgmental sampling might be used, for example, in picking a representative geographical area or accounting period. Random or statistical sampling would be more appropriate, on the other hand, in selecting particular cost items for detailed analysis.

The committee report expressed the view that a cost study based upon a full quarterly, semi-annual, or annual accounting period should ordinarily be acceptable as fairly representative. Use of a full accounting period, the committee pointed out, has the advantage of making it easy to record accurate inventory adjustments and to obtain other "closing" data. Any time period selected should be free "from seasonal, cyclical, or accidental variance in volume of business, characteristics of sales transactions, or incidence of expenses." In some types of businesses, it may be difficult or impossible to select a time period that can be shown to be truly representative of overall cost experience. To cope with that problem, some cost studies have taken cost samples from each accounting period of the years covered by the FTC complaint.

Similar difficulties commonly arise in selecting a geographical market for cost-study purposes. For many industries there is no such thing as one "typical market area." Costs, prices, competitive situations, or customer groupings may differ so greatly between types of areas that separate cost studies must be made for urban, rural, and "mixed" areas. Sometimes every metropolitan area differs from every other metropolitan area to such a degree that the only feasible alternative to a complete study of all costs is an analysis of a random cost sample lifted from each of the areas.

One of the reasons commonly cited by the Commission and its examiners for rejecting cost-justification defenses is the use of improper methods of allocating costs among various products, customer groups, and transactions. Some cost factors can be divided by the use of such simple techniques as counting, weighing, measuring, and timing. The portion of salesmen's compensation and expenses to be assigned a particular customer or transaction, for example, can often be ascertained by conducting studies of the amount of time a salesman spends on a single call. An FTC examiner has ruled that time-study allocation of salesmen's compensation can be proper even when the salesmen are paid entirely by percentage commissions (*American Motors Corporation*, 68 F.T.C. 87 (1965), *remanded for dismissal*, 384 F.2d 247 (6th Cir. 1967), *cert. denied*, 390 U.S. 1012 (1968)). A study of the time a warehouseman spends loading a truck will provide a basis for allocating his compensation, and the time it takes a truck driver to make a delivery to a particular customer can furnish a basis for assigning delivery costs to that customer. The cost of billing a particular customer might be ascertainable simply by counting the number of lines on his billing statement and determining from total billing costs the unit cost of inserting one line. The costs of processing a customer's order are, on the other hand, more likely to be determined by computing the cost per order.

These so-called "direct costs" comprise only a part of the total costs to be analyzed. The bulk of the expenditures to be allocated may be general administrative and selling functions that cannot be identified directly with a particular customer, product, or transaction. Frequently, the seller's books will reflect these "indirect" costs in broad accounts that encompass a variety of distribution functions. For example, an account reflecting the expenses of a regional warehouse accounting department will, for cost-analysis purposes, ordinarily have to be separated into the costs of preparing warehouse payrolls, of keeping inventory records, of preparing shipping documents, of maintaining accounts receivable records, and of handling credit approvals and collections. A basis for allocating the total cost to each of these functions and then reallocating it to units of product, groups of customers, or types of transactions might be determined in a number of ways, such as statistical analysis of the company's past experiences, a sample test of performance during a current accounting period, or establishment of an estimated standard cost allowance for a particular product, customer group, or type of transaction. Presumably, an allocation or apportionment method historically used by the seller in keeping its accounts or evaluating its performance in particular areas would, if available, be the best method of allocation. If, however, the historical method is arbitrary or illogical, it may be necessary to choose a new method of cost analysis. In *Standard Brands,* the use of predetermined percentage factors for allocating costs was the fatal flaw in a cost study. The Commission found them objectionable because they were not based on a detailed cost study. Use of those percentage factors was supported by the testimony of three accountants, and the percentages were based on "earning statements" kept by Standard Brands for several years to develop operating profits by product. The accountants testified that these predetermined percentage factors had always produced results close to actual costs.

There are so many judgments to be made in the preparation of a Robinson-Patman Act cost study that, when it is prepared for use in answer to an FTC complaint, it would appear that consultation with the Commission's accounting staff during preparation might be as important as assistance from a public accountant. Professor Taggart's book on cost justification (Herbert F. Taggart, COST JUSTIFICATION, U. of Mich. Business Studies, Vol. 14, No. 3 (Supplement 1964)) reports that the cost study used in *U.S. Rubber Co.,* 46 F.T.C. 998 (1950), was prepared under "almost . . . direct supervision" of the FTC accounting staff.

Most writings about the Robinson-Patman Act take the position that the cost proviso's use of the phrase "due allowance" indicates a congressional intent that the proviso is to be applied flexibly, so as to require only a "reasonable allowance" for cost differences. In cases like *U.S. Rubber Co.* and *B. F. Goodrich Co.,* 50 F.T.C. 622 (1954), the Commission established a "de minimis" doctrine that a competitively insignificant residue of price differential left unjustified by cost differences would be disregarded. In *U.S. Rubber,* the "de minimis" doctrine was applied to permit unjustified price differences of $.0047, $.0064, and $.0092 per dollar of gross sales. In *Goodrich,* too, the unjustified differences that were ignored in the stipulation signed by the FTC staff were less than one cent per gross sales dollar.

Although the cost studies presented as defenses in all the FTC's reported cases were prepared during litigation, lawyers and accountants active in Robinson-Patman Act matters now recommend the preparation of cost studies in advance, either for the purpose of ascertaining whether existing price schedules can be defended or for the purpose of planning future pricing policies. FTC field office staffs may be more willing to go along with cost studies prepared in advance of a formal investigation. Federal district judges and FTC examiners have repeatedly raised the question of whether a cost study prepared after the fact represents a "good faith" attempt to comply with the law. Counsel supporting the FTC complaint against Minneapolis-Honeywell suggested that any cost study offered to justify price differences must be one that was prepared contemporaneously and used in settling prices; the FTC accountant assigned to the case disagreed. Should investigation or litigation later occur, cost studies prepared in advance can be the subject of conferences between the Commission's accounting staff and the seller's accountants, with the result that the seller often has a chance to submit additional cost data or revise certain aspects of the study.

The preparation of a pre-investigation cost study cannot be regarded as the end of the seller's task, if he is to remain ready for an FTC investigation. As market conditions and pricing policies change, the study must be renewed. Even if there are no changes, customer groupings, cost-averaging methods, and cost-allocation procedures must be checked periodically to make sure they retain their validity. Lawyers on the Commission's staff have insisted that customer groupings must be checked at least annually. A possible substitute for constant rechecking of a cost study may be suggested by *Thompson Products, Inc.*, 55 F.T.C. 1252 (1959). The allocation of selling expenses in that case was regarded as accurate by the FTC's staff only because of a "cost budget control plan" the company used to control the number and the length of sales calls.

Attorneys and accountants dealing with the Commission's investigators in the field find them flexible and willing to accept reasonable cost studies, particularly if the studies are prepared in advance of any investigation and for use in fixing pricing policy. There have apparently been instances when the investigators have based recommendations against the filing of a complaint upon cost studies that justified only the greater part of the price differences but were supplemented by a showing that the remainder was attributable to a good-faith meeting of competition.

From the litigated cases can be gleaned a list of obvious pitfalls that must be avoided in the preparation of a Robinson-Patman Act cost study. First, the *Standard Brands* case makes it clear that the use of arbitrary predetermined percentage factors in allocating costs must be avoided, even if those percentage factors are used in the seller's regular accounting procedure. The *Standard Brands* case also suggests that it will be difficult to justify price differences in one geographical area by presenting a cost study from another, particularly if the other area is more or less urbanized or industrialized. Third, although it would not seem to be necessary to include all cost items in the study, the FTC's staff can be expected to ferret out any cost factor that, properly allocated, shows a greater cost of serving favored customers and offsets the cost differences shown to justify price differences. Therefore, an effective cost study will consider all material cost differences, whether they further or retard cost justification. Fourth, broad averaging of costs and classifications of customers must be avoided. Fifth, as demonstrated by the decision in *H.C. Brill Co., Inc.,* 26 F.T.C. 666 (1938), the seller and his counsel cannot assume, but must be prepared to prove, that customers qualifying for cumulative volume discounts place individual orders and accept individual shipments that do in fact produce lower unit distribution costs.

Perhaps some confusion in this area of cost justification and the scarcity of successful defenses in litigated cases may be attributable to the fact that in our economic system short-run costs actually do not carry as much weight in the determination of prices as the Act seems to assume. Only a monopolist can price solely by cost. Most of a businessman's reasons for wanting large orders from the type of volume purchaser who will qualify for a discount are unrelated to immediate cost reductions. Whether he is preparing an offer to such a prospective customer or is considering an offer from a prospect, the seller must consider (1) the prestige and, in effect, free advertising he will gain in the industry once his product is bought and used or resold by a major customer; (2) the eventual reduction in the general level of costs and therefore in prices, with further concomitant boosts in sales volume, as a result of the increased volume of business; and (3) the immediate contribution the new business will make towards meeting fixed expenses, a cost factor not allowable in a cost-justification defense.

In effect, the Robinson-Patman Act may require a businessman to ignore all these factors and consider only short-run cost differences, unless he can show he had reason to believe that the price cut was necessary to keep the customer from accepting an equally low offer from another supplier. The FTC has taken the position, despite the contrary view of a court of appeals, that even competition must be ignored when the prospective buyer is a new customer (*Sunshine Biscuits, Inc.,* 59 F.T.C. 674 (1961), *rev'd,* 306 F.2d 48 (7th Cir. 1962), FTC Release, 11/23/62). It is this unrecognized lack of relationship between costs and prices that puts the strain on respondent's accountants in cost-justification defenses and makes necessary the preparation of a special cost study that really is not "accounting" at all but a highly specialized and synthetic game.

F. WITHHOLDING CEASE-AND-DESIST ORDERS IN ROBINSON-PATMAN ACT CASES

Question: *Will the Commission issue an order in every case in which a violation is found?*

In the *Atlantic Products* case, 63 F.T.C. 2237 (1963), the Federal Trade Commission withheld a Robinson-Patman Act cease-and-desist order and instead announced plans to prepare a trade regulation rule covering discriminatory advertising allowances in the luggage industry. Those familiar with the agency's activities could recall no earlier instance when the Commission had failed to issue a cease-and-desist order once it had found a violation of Section 2 of the Clayton Act. Three times since that decision the Commission has found it "in the public interest" to withhold a prohibitory order after either finding a violation or refusing to rule on whether a violation has occurred. By these actions, the Commission appeared to qualify the Robinson-Patman Act's prohibitions with a "public interest" concept such as that specifically set out in Section 5 of the FTC Act.

Although the Commission had never previously claimed or exercised any discretion to withhold orders against Robinson-Patman violations, its authority to do so seems to have been established in the Supreme Court's opinion in *Moog Industries* v. *FTC*, 355 U.S. 411 (1958). That decision resolved a dispute among the courts of appeals over whether a court of appeals could suspend the effectiveness of a Commission order until proceedings could be completed against similar practices of the respondent's competitors. In denying the courts' power to make that decision, the Supreme Court stated: "The decision as to whether or not an order against one firm to cease and desist from engaging in illegal price discrimination should go into effect before others are similarly prohibited depends on a variety of factors peculiarly within the expert understanding of the Commission. . . . It is clearly within the special competence of the Commission to appraise the adverse effect on competition that might result from postponing a particular order prohibiting continued violations of the law. Furthermore, the Commission alone is empowered to develop that enforcement policy best calculated to achieve the ends contemplated by Congress and to allocate its available funds and personnel in such a way as to execute its policy efficiently and economically."

The Commission's explanation for withholding entry of a final order in the *Atlantic Products* case was that it had reason to believe that "the practice of granting unlawful advertising allowances may be widespread among luggage manufacturers, including major competitors of the instant respondents." The Commission pointed to the language used in *Moog Industries* that "responsible exercise of the Commission's discretion in determining whether, and when, not to enter an immediate cease and desist order . . . may involve consideration of circumstances going beyond those reflected in the particular record." Here, apparently, the circumstances outside the record were indications of widespread discrimination throughout the industry. Also, Atlantic had discontinued the practice found to be discriminatory and had given the Commission sworn assurances that it would not resume the practice.

Similar factors may have been operative in the *Chesebrough-Pond's* decision, 66 F.T.C. 252 (1964), in which the promotional payments of 17 drug producers were found to be illegally discriminatory. The complaints were concerned with the manufacturers' payments for advertising in customer-owned publications. The hearing examiner had concluded that the manufacturers' payments violated Section 2(d) of the Clayton Act, and the Commission agreed. The Commission was convinced that the manufacturers had voluntarily discontinued the illegal payments, and the Commission had assurances from the companies that the illegal practices would not be resumed. This time, though, the Commission's alternative was not the initiation of a trade-regulation rule proceeding, but the promulgation of "declaratory findings," which the manufacturers promised would "be looked upon by them as a binding guide to future conduct." To make sure that there is no misunderstanding on either side," the Commission directed each of the manufacturers to file a report within 30 days describing the manner and form of their compliance with the requirements of Section 2(d) of the Clayton Act. With that, the Commission dismissed the complaints.

Considerations quite different from those mentioned in *Atlantic Products* and *Chesebrough-Pond's* apparently motivated the Commission in the *Sperry Rand* proceeding (64 F.T.C. 842 (1964)). The Commission decided it would not be in the public interest to issue a Section 2(a) price-discrimination order on the basis of proof of one "isolated, nonrecurring transaction" in which a special discount was granted. Shortly after its announcement of a new-model typewriter and discontinuance of production of an earlier model, Sperry Rand had sold a quantity of the earlier-model typewriters to Sears at prices about $15 below those generally charged Sears' competitors. The Commission's hearing examiner had found that the sale had inflicted injury on Sears' competitors, was not cost justified, and had not been made in good faith to meet competitive offers from Sperry Rand's competitors.

Another defense rejected by the hearing examiner was based on the fourth proviso in Section 2(a) of the Act, "that nothing herein contained shall prevent price changes from time to time where in response to changing conditions affecting the market for or the marketability of the goods concerned, such as but not limited to actual or imminent deterioration of perishable goods, obsolescence of seasonal goods, distress sales under court process, or sales in good faith in discontinuance of business in the goods concerned." In the examiner's view, the "Quiet-Riter" typewriter that Sperry Rand had discontinued for the "Quiet-Riter Eleven" was not, despite the new model's "numerous improvements," "obsolescent." He regarded the new typewriter as "a mere modification of respondent's basic QR portable typewriter product."

Noting that the purpose of its cease-and-desist orders was not to punish violators but to prevent the recurrence of unlawful conduct, the Commission decided that the probability of recurrences "is remote and insubstantial. . . . It appears that the special sale to Sears Roebuck which is the basis of the complaint was an isolated, non-recurring transaction, which occurred as the result of abnormal conditions in the industry and in respondent's business that are very unlikely to be repeated. The effects on competition of this single incident appear too insubstantial to require formal action." The result was dismissal of the complaint. Commissioner McIntyre did not concur. He was unable to "locate in the record of this proceeding the evidence apparently relied upon by the majority" in its finding that the likelihood of recurrence of the discriminatory conduct was remote and insubstantial.

An explicit change of policy was announced by the Commission in *Max Factor,* 66 F.T.C. 184 (1964). The Commission declared its intent to deal with discriminatory promotional payments solicited for special-event advertising by proceeding against the buyer under Section 5 of the FTC Act rather than against the suppliers under the Robinson-Patman Act. Without adjudicating the merits of the case, the Commission dismissed charges that two cosmetic manufacturers had violated Section 2(d) of the Robinson-Patman Act by paying discriminatory promotional allowances to a large supermarket chain in connection with "anniversary sales" and "beauty carnivals."

Each of these cases contains special operative facts that limit its scope as a precedent. The *Sperry Rand* decision, for example, dealt with an "isolated, nonrecurring transaction." It should not be read as standing for the proposition that every business enterprise, like the dog belonging to a tort-suit defendant, is entitled to one bite before any responsibility is incurred under the law. It has, in fact, been suggested that this decision belongs in a class by itself, that it is simply a product of the Commission's reluctance to grapple with the problem of determining the scope of the Robinson-Patman Act's "obsolescence" exception.

The Commission's action in *Chesebrough-Pond's* should be compared with FTC activity against similar conduct in the apparel industry. Enforcement efforts against clothing manufacturers paying discriminatory promotional allowances were pressed with continued vigor. Nothing was said about relying instead upon complaints against the buyers, and the Commission showed no willingness to allow time for voluntary compliance by the industry. The moral would seem to be that the Commission regarded the 17 complaints in the *Chesebrough-Pond's* case as presenting a special situation, and that their dismissal is not to be viewed as a broad precedent.

A later development in a companion case to *Max Factor* suggests that the issuance of an order may be the point of no return for the Commission exercise of discretion. In *Shreveport Macaroni Mfg. Co.,* 66 F.T.C. 1546 (1964), the Commission refused to modify or vacate a cease-and-desist order already outstanding against another supplier who participated in the same buyer's special sales events. The case was distinguished from *Max Factor* because a violation had already been found and an order issued.

These cases, particularly *Atlantic Products,* could represent a recognition of a mandate in the Supreme Court's *Moog Industries* opinion that Robinson-Patman Act enforcement follow a policy of pragmatic discretion, rather than dogmatic reaction. While members of the bar who view the Commission's actions in that light do not agree with everything the Commission said or did in these cases, they generally approve of this sort of experimentation. The "per se" or automatic nature often attributed to the Robinson-Patman Act's prohibitions accounts for many of the criticisms that have been voiced regarding the statute and for many of the efforts to have it amended. A more flexible use of its prohibitions by the Commission might eliminate some of the opposition to the Act and its purpose.

It appears that the Commission is likely to require the concurrence of four factors before it will exercise its discretion to withhold a cease-and-desist order. First, the Commission must be convinced that withholding an order will not cause harm to the "public interest." Second, the respondent will be a member of a larger group, some of whom have not been, or perhaps cannot be, proceeded against. Third, the Commission may want some assurance that the conduct found to be a violation of the Act is not likely to be repeated. Fourth, there must be an alternative way of terminating the unlawful conduct and protecting the public interest.

G. CRIMINAL PROCEEDINGS

Question: *What enforcement has there been of the criminal provision in the Robinson-Patman Act?*

Section 3 of the Robinson-Patman Act (15 U.S.C. § 13a) provides criminal penalties for three types of conduct. First, it is a crime for anyone to participate or assist in a sale that "discriminates to his knowledge against competitors of the purchaser." Second, it is criminal "to sell goods in any part of the United States at prices lower than those exacted by said person elsewhere in the United States for the purpose of destroying competition, or eliminating a competitor." The final clause makes it a crime "to sell . . . goods at unreasonably low prices for the purpose of destroying competition or eliminating a competitor."

Section 3 has been much criticized since its passage in 1936. In 1955 the Attorney General's National Committee to Study the Antitrust Laws recommended repeal of Section 3 "as dangerous surplusage." Up to that time, only five cases had ever been filed under Section 3, and in four of them the Section 3 charge was supplemental to Sherman Act charges.

For years there was a lively debate whether private treble-damage suits could be founded on violations of Section 3. In 1958 the Supreme Court settled this question, concluding that Section 3 is not one of the "antitrust laws" mentioned in Section 4 of the Clayton Act, which authorizes private damage relief (*Nashville Milk Co.* v. *Carnation Co.,* 355 U.S. 373 (1958)). In subsequent Congresses, bills have been introduced that would reverse that decision.

In *U.S.* v. *National Dairy Products Corp.,* 372 U.S. 29 (1963), the Supreme Court, presented with its first opportunity to interpret any part of Section 3, made it clear that the repeal advised by the Attorney General's Committee would have to be done by Congress, if at all. National Dairy and one of its executives were indicted under Section 3's third clause on charges of selling milk at unreasonably low prices for the purpose of destroying competition. The indictment alleged that National Dairy had used advantages attributable to the multi-state scope of its operations "to finance and subsidize a price war against small dairies . . . by intentionally selling milk below National's cost." The district court dismissed the indictment, declaring the statute unconstitutionally vague. The Supreme Court read the statute and the indictment together and concluded that defendants were adequately "informed of the nature and cause of the accusation," as required by the Federal Constitution's Sixth Amendment.

Justices Black, Stewart, and Goldberg dissented. Quoting the Attorney General's Committee that "doubts besetting Section 3's constitutionality seem well founded," they charged the majority with usurping the functions of Congress by drastically rewriting the statute. For Justice Clark and the majority for which he spoke, the missing link supplied by the indictment is the charge of "selling . . . below . . . cost." In the history behind Section 3's "unreasonably low prices" ban, Justice Clark perceived an intent of Congress to prohibit "selling below cost, unless mitigated by some acceptable business exigency." A suggestion that the phrase "below cost" might itself be as vague and indefinite as "unreasonably low" posed a question that the majority did not think it was required to answer. "It may well be that the issue will be rendered academic by a showing that National Dairy sold below" any conceivable cost figure. In addition, the majority felt that the indictment's allegation of the additional element of predatory intent "provides further definition of the prohibited conduct." In rejecting a suggestion that it should ascertain the constitutional clarity of Section 3 "on its face," the Court asserted that it has held "many times that statutes are not automatically invalidated as vague simply because difficulty is found in determining whether certain marginal offenses fall wthin their language."

On remand, the district court fined the corporation and one of its officers (1964 Trade Cas. ¶71,163 (W.D. Mo. 1964)). This decision was affirmed by a court of appeals (350 F.2d 321 (8th Cir. 1965)). This decision was later vacated on procedural grounds (384 U.S. 883 (1966)), then reversed and remanded (384 F.2d 457 (8th Cir. 1967), *cert. denied,* 390 U.S. 957 (1968)), then dismissed by the Government on May 9, 1968, and the conviction of the individual defendant was vacated (313 F.Supp. 534 (W.D. Mo. 1970)). Thus, there was no successful prosecution despite the preliminary rounds the Government won. The court of appeals opinion, 350 F.2d 321, is significant in its holding that sales below "fully distributed costs," including not just production costs but also delivery, selling, and administrative costs, are at "unreasonably low prices."

The vagueness of Section 3's "unreasonably low prices" ban may be no more striking than the vagueness of Section 1 of the Sherman Act, which is also a criminal statute. For the ordinary businessman, or indeed even for the antitrust expert, "every unreasonable contract in restraint of trade" may contain no more adequate forewarning of conduct prohibited than does the phrase "unreasonably low prices for the purpose of destroying competition or eliminating a competitor." Yet antitrust lawyers at least are accustomed to the vagueness of the Sherman Act. So few prosecutions have been brought under Section 3 of the Robinson-Patman Act that there has been little opportunity to become similarly accustomed to the scope of its prohibitions.

In a predatory-pricing prosecution under Section 2 of the Sherman Act, the Government's case must include proof of intent to monopolize and definitions of markets and market shares. It has been suggested that the Government might sometimes find it easier to prove "the purpose of destroying competition or eliminating a competitor" required by Section 3. On the other hand, the fine Section 3 authorizes can go no higher than $5,000, whereas a Sherman Act fine can reach $50,000.

H. P. Hood & Sons, Inc., a New England dairy, was indicted for both discriminating in price and selling below cost (*U.S.* v. *H.P. Hood & Sons, Inc.,* 215 F.Supp. 656 (D. Mass. 1963), *rev'd sub nom., U.S.* v. *Welden,* 377 U.S. 95 (1964); *guilty plea entered by H. P. Hood, Inc.* (1961–70 Transfer Binder) Trade Reg. Rep. ¶45,062 Cas No. 1658). Only the price-discrimination count was based on Section 3 of the Robinson-Patman Act. The sales-below-cost allegation was part of a Section 2 Sherman Act count.

PART V

Patents and Antitrust

A. ANTITRUST AND PATENT LAW—SOME BASIC CONSIDERATIONS

Question: *What inventions do patents cover?*

A patent may be characterized as creating a protected and absolute, though temporary, monopoly. Practices of patent owners in the use, exploitation, and transfer of patent rights raise questions regarding the proper limits of that monopoly. Where those limits are breached, application of the antitrust law begins. The 1955 Report of the Attorney General's National Committee to Study the Antitrust Laws (at 226) speaks of "the sound rule that monopoly power individually acquired solely through a basic patent, or aggregation of patent grants should not by itself constitute monopolization in violation of Section 2 [of the Sherman Act]. It would be paradox to encourage individual invention by grant of a patent and then penalize that temporary monopoly by deeming it 'monopolization.'" Moreover, "the mere accumulation of patents, no matter how many, is not in and of itself illegal" (*Automatic Radio Mfg. Co.* v. *Hazeltine Research, Inc.*, 339 U.S. 827 (1950)). These statements refer to an accumulation of patents obtained by original grant from the Patent Office, not by assignment or license from an outside inventor.

Explicitly authorized by constitutional provision and defined by statute since 1790, the patent system is said to have been adopted not primarily to enrich the inventor, but to promote technological progress by (1) encouraging investment in research and development, (2) encouraging the early disclosure of patentable inventions so they will ultimately become available to the public, and (3) affording some protection to risk capital invested in the exploitation of patentable inventions.

Section 154 of the Patent Code specifies that every patent shall contain a grant "for the term of 17 years, of the right to exclude others from making, using, or selling the invention throughout the United States."

The courts speak of "combination patents," which include machine patents and cover the relation or connection of a group of elements in a particular way. Combination patents do not cover the elements independent of their combination. In *American Lecithin Co.* v. *Warfield,* 105 F.2d 207 (7th Cir. 1939), for example, the combination patent covered the inclusion of a small amount of lecithin in a chocolate mass to prevent graying, but the patent did not give the patent owner the right to control either chocolate or lecithin alone.

A "process patent" covers specified acts or a series of acts or treatments to produce a result. Since a patented process, like a patented combination, is distinct from the machine that performs it and from the product, a process patent gives the owner merely the right to exclude others from doing the acts. In *Leitch Mfg. Co.* v. *Barber Co.,* 302 U.S. 458 (1939), a process patent for spraying wet concrete with a bituminous emulsion to retard curing was held to give the patent owner no right to control the unpatented emulsion.

The courts also talk of "product patents" or, more frequently, "patented products." A patented product is, in the statutory language, either a "manufacture" or a "combination of matter." "Combinations of matter" is a phrase used to describe new and useful compounds or mixtures. Today it most frequently refers to new chemicals, which represent the fastest growing area of patent-procurement activity.

The usual way for a patent owner to enforce his patent, or "to exclude others from making, using or selling the invention throughout the United States," is by infringement suit for an injunction against the infringing practice or for damages, or both. The suit is brought in a court of equity; the damages in theory represent an accounting for the infringer's profits. Yet Section 284 of the Patent Code (35 U.S.C. § 284) now states that the patent owner is to recover "damages adequate to compensate for the infringement but in no event less than a reasonable royalty for the use made of the invention by the infringer, together with interest and costs." Moreover, "the court may increase the damages up to three times the amount found and assessed." In practice, treble damages are awarded sparingly and usually only where there is a clear showing of deliberate and willful infringement.

Sometimes patented inventions are thought of as self-contained, complete articles that are exploited by the inventor himself and may be the basis for development of a new industry. Most patents now are narrow improvements on existing devices. Many are owned by corporations and are the inventions of scientists working in corporate research laboratories. The inventor of a self-contained, complete product will often not be able to get the full economic benefit from his discovery by exploiting it himself but must license to others the practice of his invention.

Although it would appear to thwart temporarily the purposes of the patent system, a patent owner is ordinarily free not only to keep his invention to himself but also to refrain from using it at all. On the other hand, as pointed out by the Attorney General's Committee, "nonuse may be part of a scheme to foreclose competitors or may evidence intent to monopolize through suppression. . . . We believe that an improper purpose unduly to restrain trade, to monopolize or attempt to monopolize through individual nonuse should give rise to antitrust liability. On the other hand where there is no affirmative showing that the purpose or effect of nonuse is unreasonably to restrain trade, to monopolize or attempt to monopolize, the patentee's conduct does not transgress the antitrust laws. Clearly, however, contracts, combination or conspiracy among patentees to refrain from using or to refuse to license others to use patented inventions should be deemed unreasonable per se" (Report of the Attorney General's National Committee to Study Antitrust Laws, at 223).

Many of the court decisions regarded as precedents for what is lawful exploitation of a patent were made not in antitrust cases, but in patent-infringement actions in which the defense of "misuse" was raised. The defense is an appeal for application of the maxim of the law of equity that "he who comes into equity must come with clean hands." The term "misuse" "usually refers to an important class of cases in which the patentee is denied relief because he has employed his patent in an effort to extend the monopoly of his patent" (ENCYCLOPEDIA OF PATENT PRACTICE AND INVENTION MANAGEMENT, p. 155 (Reinhold Publishing Corp. 1964)).

The misuse defense is an extension of the "clean hands" doctrine; the patent owner is denied relief even if his misuse has not injured the infringer and even if his patent is valid, was properly obtained, and was plainly infringed. The patent misused must be the patent alleged to have been infringed (*Sperry Products, Inc.* v. *Alcoa,* 171 F.Supp. 901 (N.D. Ohio 1959), *aff'd,* 285 F.2d 911 (6th Cir. 1960), *cert. denied,* 368 U.S. 890 (1961).

Successful invocation of the defense leaves the patent owner without any equitable relief, either by way of an injunction or by way of an accounting for profits. In order for the defense to be successful, the alleged infringer need not prove a misuse serious enough to be a violation of the antitrust laws (*Baldwin-Lima-Hamilton Corp.* v. *Tatnall Measuring Systems Co.,* 169 F.Supp. 1 (E.D. Pa. 1958), *aff'd,* 268 F.2d 395 (3rd Cir. 1959), *cert. denied,* 361 U.S. 894 (1959)). While not every misuse of a patent rises to the dignity of an antitrust violation, any use of a patent in violation of the Sherman, Clayton, or FTC Acts is probably a misuse of the patent. The advantage of proving an antitrust violation is that the alleged infringer may then be in a position to counter-claim for treble damages.

B. PROBLEMS IN ACQUIRING THE PATENT

1. Patent Procurement and Accumulation

Question: *What types of patent-procurement activities are likely to expose patent owners to antitrust difficulty?*

When an inventor applies to the Patent Office for a patent, one hurdle he must clear is "prior art." He must describe a "process, machine, manufacture, or composition of matter" that was not previously "known or used by others" or in public use or on sale in this country more than a year prior to the date of his application (Patent Code, 35 U.S.C. §§ 101–102). In *Walker Process Equipment, Inc.* v. *Food Machinery & Chemical Corp.*, 382 U.S. 172 (1965), the Supreme Court saw a possible Section 2 violation in enforcement of a patent obtained by a false sworn statement to the Patent Office that the applicant had no knowledge or belief that his invention had been in public use more than a year prior to the filing of the application. Enforcement of a patent so obtained, it was ruled, violates Section 2 of the Sherman Act when "the other elements necessary to a Section 2 case are present." The court limited its holding to "a special class of patents, those procured by intentional fraud." Good faith on the part of the patent owner, including "an honest mistake as to the effect of prior installation upon patentability," would be a complete defense to any antitrust suit. In addition, the party who brings suit has the burden of proving "the exclusionary power of the illegal patent claim in terms of the relevant market for the product involved." When the *Walker Process Equipment* case was argued, the Government appeared as amicus curiae to argue that sound antitrust enforcement policy calls for a campaign against some patent-procurement and patent-licensing practices. The Justice Department asked that patents obtained by fraud be declared per se violations of Section 2. The Supreme Court's opinion termed that suggestion "premature." The Court declined to extend the "carefully limited" area of per se illegality "on the bare pleadings and absent examination of market effect and economic consequences."

Some years earlier in *Hazel-Atlas Glass Co.* v. *Hartford-Empire Co.*, 322 U.S. 238 (1944), the Supreme Court had recognized fraud on the Patent Office as a basis for invalidating a patent in an infringement suit. Some of the language of that opinion has been cited for the proposition that knowing misrepresentations to the Patent Office invalidate the patent even if it is not shown that the Patent Office was influenced by the false statement. Nevertheless, lower federal courts (see, for example, *Corning Glass Works* v. *Anchor Hocking Glass Corp.*, 253 F.Supp. 461 (D. Del. 1966), *rev'd in part*, 374 F.2d 473 (3rd Cir. 1967); 300 F.Supp. 1299 (D. Del. 1969)) have insisted that the misrepresentation to the Patent Office must be "material," that is, a statement without which the patent would not have been issued. See also *Edward Valves, Inc.* v. *Cameron Iron Works, Inc.*, 286 F.2d 933 (5th Cir. 1961), *cert. denied,* 368 U.S. 833 (1961), and *Foundry Equipment Co.* v. *Carl-Mayer Corp.*, 128 F.Supp. 640, (N.D. Ohio 1955), *aff'd*, 233 F.2d 179 (6th Cir. 1956).

In *American Cyanamid Co.*, 63 F.T.C. 1747 (1963), the FTC claimed jurisdiction under Section 5 of the FTC Act to prevent enforcement of a patent obtained by misrepresenting and concealing prior art in a Patent Office proceeding. The court of appeals first remanded the case for consideration without the participation of the Chairman (363 F.2d 757 (6th Cir. 1966); 72 F.T.C. 623 (1967), *aff'd*, 401 F.2d 574 (6th Cir. 1968).

Another hurdle sometimes in the path of a patent application is a competing inventor. To determine which of the two or more inventors was the first, the Patent Office conducts an "interference" or an "interference proceeding," pitting the inventors against each other as adversaries. Like adversary proceedings in the courts, interferences can be terminated by settlement. In 1963, the Supreme Court came across an interference settlement that it found to have been executed for the purpose of facilitating the issuance of a patent with broad coverage and strengthening the two inventors' efforts to stifle competition from other manufacturers (*U.S.* v. *Singer Mfg. Co.*, 374 U.S. 174 (1963)). While the Court's opinion treated the interference settlement simply as one aspect of a conspiracy to exclude competition, Justice White, in a special concurring opinion, concluded that the purpose of the settlement was to prevent prior art from coming to the Patent Office's attention. "Such collusion to secure a monopoly grant runs afoul of the Sherman Act's prohibitions against conspiracies in restraint of trade—if not bad per se, then such agreements are at least presumptively bad." Justice White said he had no objection to unilateral attempts to secure broad claims in a patent or to interference settlements involving only the interests of the adversaries. Yet here "there is a public interest . . . which the parties have subordinated to their private ends—the public interest in granting patent monopolies only when the progress of the public is given a novel and useful invention."

One of the cases cited by Justice White as authority for his view is *Precision Instrument Mfg. Co.* v. *Automotive Maintenance Machinery Co.*, 324 U.S. 806 (1945). The interference proceeding in that case was settled by an applicant who believed his opponent had committed perjury in the proceeding. The applicant did not disclose that belief to the Patent Office, but in the settlement he took a concession of priority from his opponent and an assignment of the opponent's application. Then, after making some changes, he obtained patents under both applications. The Court held that a patent owner who got his patent that way could not sue for infringement.

In 1962, Congress recognized the possibility that interference-settlement agreements could be used to violate the antitrust laws and added to Section 135 of the Patent Code (35 U.S.C. § 135) a new subsection (c) making interference settlements and any patents obtained as a result of such settlements unenforceable unless the settlement agreement was in writing and filed in the Patent Office before termination of the interference.

The mere purchase of a patent in and of itself is not an antitrust violation. According to the Attorney General's Committee, "Impropriety will arise only where such acquisition is part of an illegal purpose or plan. To make such a determination, any questioned acquisition should be weighed in its entire context. Important considerations include: (a) the nature, number and value of the patents acquired, in relation to the market for competing patented or unpatented processes or products; (b) whether the inventor is using the patent, or has the ability and plans to use it, as against evidence of the purchaser's actual or intended use, (c) whether the purchase had the purpose and probable effect of resolving patent conflict; (d) the purpose and effect of the purchase on the market position of the purchaser and the increase or decrease in competition in the relevant geographic and product market."

For antitrust purposes, accumulation of patents by a single owner may be more serious if he is a purchaser than if he is an inventor. In *U.S.* v. *United Shoe Machinery Corp.,* 110 F.Supp. 295 (D. Mass. 1953), *aff'd,* 347 U.S. 521 (1954), the fact that United Shoe had purchased only about 5 percent of its many patents was noted with approval by the court. It was also pointed out that United Shoe had derived no greater benefits from purchase of the patents than it would have derived from nonexclusive licenses. Similarly, in *Dollac Corp.* v. *Margon Corp.,* 164 F.Supp. 41 (D.N.J. 1958), *affirmed on non-antitrust issues,* 275 F.2d 202 (3rd Cir. 1960), after recognizing that the mere accumulation of patents is not a violation of the antitrust laws, the court said: "The principle is particularly applicable where, as here, most of the unexpired patents cover inventions conceived and developed by the employees of the defendant under an established research program."

In *U.S.* v. *Columbia Pictures Corp.,* 189 F.Supp. 153 (S.D.N.Y. 1960), a case involving acquisition of copyright licenses, the court refused to treat Section 7's terms "acquire" and "assets" as "terms of art or technical legal language. . . . They are generic, imprecise terms encompassing a broad spectrum of transactions whereby the acquiring person may accomplish the acquisition by means of purchase, assignment, lease, license, or otherwise." In *U.S.* v. *Lever Bros. Co.,* 216 F.Supp. 887 (S.D.N.Y. 1963), it was held that a trademark is an "asset" whose acquisition can violate Section 7.

One of the FTC's Section 7 consent orders, *Vendo Co.,* 54 F.T.C. 253 (1957), requires a company to make purchased patents available to its competitors for licensing at a "reasonable royalty." The Commission's complaint was based on the patent owner's acquisition of a competitor to terminate that competitor's alleged infringement of patents. In accepting a consent settlement, the Commission's hearing examiner found that the only important assets involved in the acquisition were patents held by the alleged infringer.

A third method of acquiring patents from others is the inclusion of grant-back covenants in patent licenses. A "grant-back" requires the patent licensee to assign or license back to the licensor any patent on an improvement in the products or the processes of the licensed patent. A covenant to give back exclusive licenses under any future improvement patents was held not to be illegal per se in *Transparent-Wrap Machine Corp.* v. *Stokes & Smith Co.,* 329 U.S. 637 (1947). Justice Douglas, writing for a 5-4 majority, pointed out that the Patent Code explicitly makes all patents assignable. "One who uses one patent to acquire another is not extending his patent monopoly to articles covered by the general law" but is "using one legalized monopoly to acquire another legalized monopoly." At the close of his opinion, however, Justice Douglas stated that grant-back covenants "could be employed with the purpose or effect of violating the antitrust laws" and denied any intention to give those covenants antitrust immunity. "Indeed, the recent case of *Hartford-Empire Co.* v. *U.S.,* 323 U.S. 386 (1945), 324 U.S. 570 (1945), dramatically illustrates how the use of a condition or covenant in a patent license that the licensee will assign improvements patents may give rise to violations of the antitrust laws."

Several district courts have considered grant-back arrangements antitrust violations when combined with other anticompetitive activity. In *U.S.* v. *General Electric Co.* (Carboloy), 80 F.Supp. 989 (S.D.N.Y. 1948), grant-back arrangements were held illegal when combined with price-fixing agreements. In *U.S.* v. *General Electric Co.* (lamps), 82 F.Supp. 753 (D.N.J. 1949), a patent owner's requirement that his licensee grant back nonexclusive licenses on any improvement patents was struck down because the specific intent of his licensing policy was to perpetuate domination over the industry. In *U.S.* v. *Alcoa,* 91 F.Supp. 333 (S.D.N.Y. 1950), it was held illegal for the owner of process patents basic to an entire industry to license them to its only two competitors on grant-back terms. In that "peculiar context," the court reasoned, the licensor achieved a marked advantage over its competitors by having exclusive control over its own improvements and free use of any improvements of each of its licensees, whereas each of the licensees would have the benefit of only its improvements. One court of appeals has declared grant-back arrangements illegal when they "effect a restraint of trade or create monopolies, if designed for that purpose" (*Kobe, Inc.* v. *Dempsey Pump Co.,* 198 F.2d 416 (10th Cir.), *cert. denied,* 344 U.S. 837 (1952)).

The *Trans-Wrap* decision is still followed. The order issued in the *General Electric Lamp* case, 115 F.Supp. 835, 848 (D. N.J. 1953), allowed GE to require the grant-back of nonexclusive, reasonable royalty licenses when it licensed "future patents." *Binks Mfg. Co.* v. *Ransburg Electro-Coating Corp.,* 281 F.2d 252 (7th Cir. 1960), *cert. dismissed,* 366 U.S. 211 (1961), followed the rule that an arrangement for nonexclusive royalty-free licensing back of improvement patents is not illegal when not a part of "a widespread network . . . affecting an entire industry." In *Swofford* v. *B & W, Inc.,* 251 F.Supp. 811 (S.D. Texas 1966), *aff'd,* 395 F.2d 362 (5th Cir. 1968), *cert. denied,* 393 U.S. 935 (1968), *rehearing denied,* 393 U.S. 1060 (1969), the district court followed *Trans-Wrap* in permitting a patent owner to condition settlement of a patent infringement suit on the alleged infringer's assignment back of a related patent.

The Antitrust Division has questioned the *Trans-Wrap* decision's continued vitality. In a speech in August 1965 at the meeting of the ABA Antitrust Section, Assistant Attorney General Donald F. Turner declared his intention to "seek to establish, contrary to Trans-Wrap, that a clause in a patent license requiring the licensee to grant back to the patentee all future improvement patents should be unlawful per se for the simple reason that it is much more restrictive than necessary to protect the patentee's legitimate interests" 29 ABA ANTITRUST L. J. 188 (1965). In a question-and-answer period following his prepared remarks, Mr. Turner explained that he intended his "per se" rule only for "the grant back of the patent itself and the grant back of an exclusive license. . . . We will certainly not oppose as per se illegal a grant back of a nonexclusive license. Of course I cannot say that we would never oppose the grant back of a nonexclusive license. I think that prima facie such a grant would be all right, but you can get some rather complex cases involving patent licensing, cross licensing, and a general pattern of unlawful restraint of which this grant might be a part." In his use of the phrase "exclusive license," Mr. Turner did not indicate whether he was including a "sole" license, under which the patent owner merely promises that no one else will be licensed, or was referring only to the grant of an exclusive license to make, use, and sell, which excludes the licensor himself from competing. In 1969, the Department of Justice filed a suit attacking grant-back clauses as violations of Section 1 of the Sherman Act. The suit was settled by consent (*U.S.* v. *Wisc. Alumni Research Foundation,* 1970 Trade Cas. ¶73,015 (W.D. Wisc. 1970)).

Supreme Court decisions like *Singer, Walker Process,* and *Brulotte* v. *Thys Co.,* 379 U.S. 29 (1964), suggest that the trend may be toward stricter application of the antitrust laws to patent owners. It may be that the Clayton Act's antimerger provisions will be applied to the purchase of patents. Some experts think the purchase of additional patents by a dominant manufacturer holding a position like United Shoe's, for example, would be held a Section 7 violation today, even though United Shoe's patent purchases were held not to violate Section 2 of the Sherman Act. The language used by the district court in the *Columbia Pictures* case could create problems in Section 7 cases involving patents. Could the taking of a non-exclusive patent license be treated as an "acquisition" that threatens injury to competition and hence violates Section 7? While it is difficult to think of situations in which the taking of a nonexclusive license would raise such a threat, it is conceivable that the dominant manufacturer in a market might, by taking such a license on an important discovery of a minor competitor, greatly increase its power to wipe out the last vestiges of competition. A firm in such a position might be able to make an offer the small competitor could not afford to turn down even if he knows the license will lead to his retirement. On the other hand, the question arises: what will happen to the invention in such a market if the dominant company is not to use it? If one producer is so powerful that it would gain ground merely by having the use of the same improvement its competitors have, then there may be no way to put the invention to effective use except by making it available to that producer. In any event, it may be that many markets reflect a type of competition that will be facilitated, not inhibited, by nonexclusive patent licenses.

In some industries, grant-back arrangements are not considered important commercially. Unless the patent owner is in an industry where technological change is so much the rule of the day that he has to have grant-back covenants to make sure he isn't driven out of business by his competitors' new discoveries, some say it is not worth the antitrust risks to take a grant-back clause. If the patent owner does need such a covenant, he may be well advised to limit himself to a guarantee of nonexclusive licenses.

2. Fraud on the Patent Office

Question: *What are the elements of a finding of antitrust violation in fraudulent patent procurement?*

The defense of fraud on the Patent Office has been available to defendants accused of patent infringement since the 1945 Supreme Court decision in *Precision Instrument Mfg. Co.* v. *Automotive Maintenance Machinery Mfg. Co.*, 324 U.S. 806 (1945). The Supreme Court went further in *U.S.* v. *Singer Mfg. Co.*, 374 U.S. 174 (1963), and suggested for the first time that fraudulent conduct before the Patent Office could be an antitrust violation. In that case Singer had agreed with another defendant to terminate interference proceedings and to enter into a cross-licensing agreement in order to keep information from reaching the Patent Office that would have prevented the issue of a patent. The Court found that the agreement was "in restraint of trade" in violation of Section 1 of the Sherman Act.

Two years later, in *Walker Process Equipment, Inc.* v. *Food Machinery & Chemical Corp.*, 382 U.S. 172 (1965), the Court decided that the assertion of a patent procured by fraud could constitute illegal "monopolization" under Section 2 of the Sherman Act if the other elements (including relevant market) of a Section 2 violation were present. In that case the defendant alleged that the patentee had fraudulently procured the patent by knowingly concealing the fact that the invention had been in public use for more than one year before the filing date of the application. Since *Walker,* the issue of fraudulent procurement has been raised with increasing frequency in patent and antitrust litigation.

Most fraud cases involve a misrepresentation or omission of some fact by the applicant during the prosecution of his case before the Patent Office. The two types of situations that have generated the most litigation are: (1) the *Walker* situation, in which the applicant knowingly conceals the fact that his invention has been in public use for more than one year before the filing date of the applicant, and (2) the situation in which applicant submits a fraudulent affidavit to the Patent Office to convince the examiner that his invention is patentable. The best known example of the latter is *American Cyanamid Co.* v. *Federal Trade Commission*, 363 F.2d 757 (6th Cir. 1966), *aff'd after remand,* 401 F.2d 574 (6th Cir. 1968). There Pfizer Co., with the knowledge of its licensee, American Cyanamid, made affidavits to the Patent Office during the prosecution of the application on its drug tetracycline, falsely swearing that tetracycline was not a by-product of the known process of producing aureomycin. The misrepresentation in the affidavit has cost

Pfizer and American Cyanamid millions of dollars in private antitrust claims.

Since the *Precision Instrument* case, it has generally been held
that to be considered fraudulent, a misrepresentation must: (1) be
submitted with knowledge of its falsity, (2) be submitted with the
intent to deceive, (3) relate to a material fact, and (4) have been
relied on by the Patent Office in granting the patent. The last two
requirements have often been referred to as the "but for" rule,
meaning that no patent would have issued "but for" the misrepresentation. These requirements have been very broadly applied by
the courts in fraud cases. See *Waterman—Bic Pen Corp.* v. *Sheaffer
Pen Co.*, 267 F.Supp. 849 (D.Del. 1967), and *Tractor Supply Co.* v.
International Harvester Co., 155 U.S.P.Q. 420 (N.D. Ill. 1967).

Some courts have questioned the requirement that the misrepresentation must have been material or that the patent would not
have issued "but for" the misrepresentation. Why, these courts ask,
should an applicant whose misrepresentation later turns out to be
immaterial be exonerated from his wrongdoing and be permitted
to enforce his patent? In *Ritter* v. *Rohm and Haas,* 271 F.Supp.
313, 342 & n. 73 (S.D.N.Y. 1967), the court adopted this reasoning
and held that an intentional misrepresentation is ground for holding a patent unenforceable despite the fact that the misrepresentation may not have been material. In *Diamond International Corp.*
v. *Walterhoefer,* 289 F.Supp. 550 (D. Md. 1968), the court said that
intentional misstatements of facts concerning the most relevant
prior art may bar enforcement of a patent regardless of whether
the patent would have issued "but for" the misrepresentation.

In *Corning Glass Works* v. *Anchor Hocking Glass Corp.,* 253
F.Supp. 461 (D.Del. 1966), *modified,* 374 F.2d 423 (3rd Cir. 1967);
300 F.Supp. 1299 (D.Del. 1969), the district court suggested two
different standards of materiality. One would be applied in affirmative actions under the antitrust laws; and the other, where fraud
is used as an equitable defense to a claim of patent infringement.
To sustain a claim under the antitrust laws, the court said, the misrepresentation would have to be material; to form the basis of an
equitable defense that would merely result in holding the patent
unenforceable, the fraud would not have to be material. Some
courts have not found the existence of fraud even in the presence
of a material misrepresentation. In *Indiana General Corp.* v. *Krystinel Corp.,* 421 F.2d 1023 (2d Cir. 1970), the court said that even
though the patent would not have issued "but for" the misrepresentation, it would not grant attorneys' fees because the trial court
had "balked" at finding the patentee's misrepresentations a deliberate fraud. Likewise, in *Blonder-Tongue Laboratories, Inc.* v. *Univ.
of Ill. Foundation,* 422 F.2d 769 (7th Cir. 1970), *rev'd on other*

grounds, 402 U.S. 313 (1971), the court of appeals held that a patent was not unenforceable because of fraud even though the patentee had antedated a publication with a Rule 131 affidavit knowing that a similar earlier article, which he could not swear behind, had been published. Because the existence of the earlier article was disclosed on the face of the article which was used as a reference by the examiner, the court held that the examiner should have been aware of the earlier article and therefore refused to find the patentee guilty of fraud. On this reasoning, fraud will prevent the enforcement of a patent except where the examiner should have been alert enough to be aware of the fraud, even though in fact he was not. However, the Seventh Circuit, in *Blonder-Tongue,* did use the apparent existence of fraud to lessen the presumption of validity of the patent.

The second part of the "but for" requirement, that the examiner must have relied on the misrepresentation in issuing the patent, may be difficult to prove. In cases involving a statutory bar, reliance on a misinterpretation by the Patent Office is presumed, because the examiner would not have had authority to issue the patent had he known of the statutory bar. In cases involving misrepresentations in affidavits, however, the court must either look to the file history, as in *SCM Corp.* v. *RCA,* 318 F.Supp. 433 (S.D.N.Y. 1970), where it is often difficult to determine what the examiner would have done if he had known that a particular statement was false, or hear the examiner's testimony on the matter of whether or not he relied on a misrepresentation. In the *American Cyanamid* case the court held that the examiner's testimony about his reliance on the patentee's misrepresentations that tetracycline was not a by-product of the known process of producing aureomycin was admissible despite the fact that the examiner admitted that he did not specifically recall what had happened 11 years before and that his lack of recall could be considered only in determining the credibility and weight to be given to the testimony.

Not only the misrepresentation of facts, but also the omission or suppression of facts that should have been submitted to the Patent Office may form the basis of a fraud charge. When the applicant in a Rule 132 affidavit chooses facts that are most favorable to his case, but conceals less favorable facts that are important in evaluating the merits of his invention, he may be flirting with fraud. This was the situation in *Monsanto Co.* v. *Rohm & Haas Co.,* 312 F.Supp. 778 (E.D. Pa. 1970), *aff'd* 456 F.2d 592 (3d Cir. 1972), *cert. denied,* 407 U.S. 934 (1972), in which the district court (at 780) stated that the plaintiff ". . . presented to the Patent Office incomplete data, carefully and intentionally chosen to support its position that [the herbicide invented] possessed herbicidal properties not possessed by closely related compound[s]. Although the affidavit contained no affirmative misrepresentations and is accurate as far as it goes, it is misleading and was intended to be misleading, in that it fails to state facts known to the applicant which were inconsistent with its position that [the herbicide invented] is a superior herbicide. It is, in short, composed of half-truths."

There appears to be general agreement in the decisions that for fraud to be actionable a fraudulent representation must have been known by the applicant to be false and must have been submitted to the Patent Office with the intent to deceive. However, there is at least one case (*Ritter* v. *Rohm & Haas Co.*, 271 F.Supp. 313, 342, n. 73, (S.D.N.Y. 1967)) which suggests that if the public interest in preventing fraud is great enough, the misrepresentation may be actionable, even though it was unintentional.

There is controversy and uncertainty over the extent of the applicant's duty to cite prior art to the Patent Office. The applicant must cite art known to him which would be pertinent under Section 102, because not to do so would constitute a material misrepresentation in most cases, the applicant having sworn in his oath that "he believes himself to be the original and first inventor." The difficult cases arise, not where anticipatory art is involved, but where the applicant becomes aware of art which might be pertinent under the obviousness provision of Section 103. There is conflict in the decisions. In *Wen Products* v. *Portable Electric Tools, Inc.*, 367 F.2d 764 (7th Cir. 1966), the court said the applicant has no duty to disclose art to the Patent Office unless it anticipates his invention. In *Scott Paper Co.* v. *Fort Howard Paper Co.*, 432 F.2d 1198 (7th Cir. 1970), the same court reaffirmed this position while invalidating a patent under Section 103 on the basis of references of which the applicant had knowledge. The court stated that the applicant was not guilty of fraudulent conduct because in good faith he disagreed with the pertinency of the art to his claimed invention.

The Court of Appeals for the Fifth Circuit, however, would apparently hold the applicant to a higher standard. In *Beckman Instruments Inc.* v. *Chemtronics Inc.*, 428 F.2d 555 (5th Cir. 1970), the court suggested that it is the applicant's duty to disclose any close prior art to the examiner, and let the Patent Office judge whether or not the art is pertinent. While the *Beckman* court held that the patent in question was anticipated by the withheld references, the language of the decision clearly indicates that an applicant is required to inform the Patent Office of any close art, whether or not he thinks it anticipates.

The question then arises of how close a reference must be before the applicant or his attorney has the duty to cite it to the Patent Office. Certainly the applicant is not required to cite everything that is somehow related to the subject matter of his invention; the MANUAL OF PATENT EXAMINING PROCEDURE, Section 707.05(b), specifically limits to five the number of references the Patent Office will accept. As stated in *United States* v. *Standard Electric Time Company,* 155 F.Supp. 949 (D. Mass. 1957), *appeal dismissed,* 254 F.2d 598 (1st Cir. 1958), neither the oath under Section 115, nor the applicant's obligation to the Patent Office in general, requires him to set up "straw men which he reasonably and in good faith believes he can knock down."

One answer to the question has been advanced by the "Proposed Guidelines Respecting Conduct in Proceedings Before the Patent Office" prepared by joint committees appointed by the National Council of Patent Law Associations and the Commissioner of Patents. Guideline No. 4 states that "He [an attorney] should disclose to the Patent Office prior art which has not been cited by the Examiner, provided he then has actual knowledge of the prior art and he recognizes that it should be considered in determining whether a claim in a patent application which he is prosecuting meets the conditions of 35 USC 103." An even more prudent course of conduct would be to cite to the Patent Office all the art that the attorney had before him while writing the patent application and which he specifically considered in drafting the claims of the application.

A related problem confronting patent attorneys is what to do with relevant prior art that is discovered after the patent has issued. If the Government's position in *U.S.* v. *Union Camp Corp.,* Crim., No. 4558 (E.D. Va., filed Nov. 30, 1967), in which the defendant pleaded nolo contendere, is accepted by the courts in future litigation, all of the sanctions that are available against one who commits fraud on the Patent Office before the issue of the patent may become available against one who commits a "fraud on the public" after the patent has issued. In *Union Camp* the Government charged that the Union Camp Company and the Bemis Bag Company were guilty of violating the antitrust laws because they were guilty of "fraudulent and deceitful assertion of patent claims [known] to be baseless and invalid. . . ." While the specific situation included an agreement that was in restraint of trade, part of the Government's theory was that a party who becomes aware, after a patent issues, of facts that prove the patent invalid commits a fraud on the public when he seeks to assert his patent and a fraud on the courts when he seeks to enforce it in a patent-infringement suit.

While the *Union Camp* rationale clearly applies to anticipating art that unquestionably invalidates a patent, it does not appear to be applicable to a patentee who becomes aware of Section 103 art after his patent issues. Nevertheless, it is conceivable that an occasion may arise when the circumstances are such that a patentee may be forced to choose between not asserting his patent and asserting it at the risk of incurring a possible fraud charge. One solution available to an attorney facing this problem is to cite the after-discovered art to the Patent Office. While the Office will do no more than place the attorney's letter in the file of the case, this may be sufficient to preclude a charge of fraud. In appropriate circumstances a reissue patent might be applied for with claims that more clearly distinguish over the newly found art.

Another area that has not been explored by the decisions is the extent of the patent attorney's duty to make inquiry of his client. Does the attorney, for instance, have the duty to ask his corporate client what prior art the corporation is aware of? If the corporation is a multidivision operation, how far does this duty extend?

In cases where corresponding patent applications have been filed in the United States and several foreign countries, is the attorney charged with the duty of translating all of the references cited in the foreign applications and analyzing them for pertinency to the claims on file in the U.S.? If he does not do this, will knowledge of such references be imputed to the applicant and his attorney to form the basis of a fraud charge at some later date? It might be argued that where the cost of such an investigation might be several thousand dollars and would outweigh the potential value of the U.S. patent, a rule of reason must be adopted. Yet what if the patentee later seeks to enforce the U.S. patent? Might not a court hold that the applicant's failure to inform the Patent Office of a close reference that had been cited in a corresponding foreign application constitute fraud? And what if one attorney prosecutes the foreign application and another attorney prosecutes the U.S. application? Is the latter excused from calling the art to the attention of the U.S. Patent Office because he was not notified of it by the former?

If the invention justifies the cost of filing and prosecuting an application abroad, it may be unlikely that a court would find that the expense of monitoring the foreign prosecution is an excuse. When a foreign patent office cites a pertinent reference, someone must study the reference and narrow the patent claims. It could be argued that in such a case the applicant would be relieved of the duty of notifying the U.S. Patent Office of pertinent prior art of which he is, or should have been, aware.

Another problem that may confront an attorney seeking to avoid fraud is what to do when faced with a public use he has reason to believe falls within the experimental-use exception to the statutory bar. If he does not inform the Patent Office of it, he may later be held to have committed fraud; if he does inform the Patent Office, perhaps by attaching a qualifying statement to the oath, he invites the Patent Office to decide a question that it may be ill-equipped to deal with. Even if the Patent Office decides favorably, the world will be alerted to the potential weakness of the patent.

A similar dilemma faces the attorney who becomes aware of a potential reference that he has good reason to believe is not "a printed publication" in the statutory sense. If he conceals the reference, he may be committing a fraud on the Patent Office. If he cites it, the Patent Office may decide that it is a printed publication and use it to defeat the application. Thus, if the applicant follows this route he may never obtain the patent and so may not have an opportunity to test the patent in an infringement suit. Despite the dilemma, if an applicant is to avoid the charge of "fraud on the Patent Office," some say that he should inform the Patent Office of a possible public use or a potential reference and give the Office an opportunity to decide whether the public use falls within the experimental-use exception or the reference is not a "printed publication." If he disagrees with the determination of the Patent Office, he may appeal to the courts.

The attorney must bear in mind that a relationship of trust exists between the applicant and the Patent Office and must not regard ex parte prosecution as an adversary proceeding. "The highest standards of honesty and candor on the part of applicants in presenting such facts to the Office are thus necessary elements in a working patent system" (*Norton* v. *Curtiss*, 433 F.2d 779 (C.C.P.A. 1970)). If the patent owner becomes aware of relevant prior art after the patent issues, he may find that he incurs the risk of a fraud charge if he asserts the patent against an infringer.

In most cases in which fraud is found, the patent is also held to be invalid over the prior art. This is so because the "but for" rule dictates that fraud will be a valid defense to a patent infringement action only if the patent would not have issued "but for" the fraud. Once the truth is known, the patent is invalidated because the basis on which it was issued is undermined. Why then, if the patent clearly can be invalidated on other grounds, should a defendant in a patent infringement suit bother to prove that the patent was fraudulently procured? Because there may be an affirmative counterclaim for treble damages under the antitrust laws. Fraud in the procurement of a patent may violate Section 1 of the Sherman Act, as in *U.S.* v. *Singer*, or Section 2, as in the *Walker Process* case. Another reason is that the proof may form a basis for an award of attorney's fees under 35 U.S.C. § 285. Also, proof of fraud will preclude the patentee's right to a reissue patent under 35 U.S.C. § 251, and proof of the fraudulent procurement of one claim of a patent will, under 35 U.S.C. § 288, prevent the patentee from sustaining an action for infringement of the remaining claims.

Notwithstanding the benefits that the defense may derive from proving that a patent has been fraudulently procured, it should be kept in mind that fraud is a serious charge. Once it is made by the defense, it may have to be heard all the way through, and could prevent a settlement that might have been beneficial to both parties. In addition, if a defendant has stated that he has a reasonable basis for believing that the patent in issue was fraudulently procured, he may not be able in good faith to take a license under the patent at a later date without implicating himself in the fraud. In *Abington Textile Machinery Works* v. *Carding Specialists (Canada) Ltd.,* 249 F.Supp. 823 (D.D.C. 1965), the court indicated that fraud which has once been called to the attention of the court by the defendant should be investigated by the court even though the defendant may seek to drop the charge at a later date.

C. PROBLEMS IN LICENSING

1. Patent Royalties

Question: *What restrictions do the antitrust and patent laws impose on royalty provisions in patent licenses?*

An owner of a patent has four ways of exploiting the patent. He can assign it to another for a consideration; he can use his invention in a manufacturing operation and take his compensation in the form of profits from sales or leases of his product; or he can license others to practice the invention and take "royalties" from the licensee. Also, he may both manufacture and license others to do so.

When the patent owner licenses for royalties, the character, rate, and measure of his compensation are primarily matters of bargaining between him and his licensee. Royalty rates and bases for calculating royalties vary. While royalties are most frequently measured as a percentage of the licensee's sales volume, they may also be tied to the licensee's costs, his profits, or the costs savings attributable to use of the invention. "Any convenient method of fixing a royalty fee may be adopted, including using the price of unpatented articles with the equipment as a basis" (*Pyrene Mfg. Co.* v. *Urquhart,* 69 F.Supp. 555, 560 (E.D. Pa. 1946)). In *Pyrene,* the patent covered a process, and the licensing provisions included a royalty expressed as a percentage of both the licensed manufacturers' sales of equipment designed to use the process and of the manufacturers' costs for key materials used in the equipment.

In *Automatic Radio Mfg. Co.* v. *Hazeltine Research, Inc.,* 339 U.S. 827 (1950), the Supreme Court permitted a patent owner to require royalties based on a percentage of the licensee's sales of radio receivers, regardless of which receivers used the patented devices and even if the licensor's patents were never used at all. Because the royalty provisions in that case made no provision for a rate reduction upon expiration of some of the patents, not all of which would last out the effective period of the licensing agreement, the case has also been cited many times as authority for the legality of a nondiminishing royalty rate on a diminishing package of patents.

Antitrust policy and the misuse-of-patent doctrine have been applied by the courts to impose some restrictions on royalty rates. In *American Securit Co.* v. *Shatterproof Glass Corp.,* 268 F.2d 769 (3rd Cir. 1959), *cert. denied,* 361 U.S. 902 (1959), it was held to be misuse of a patent to charge the same royalty for a license under that patent as the licensor wanted for his whole bundle of patents. Because the patent owner had first refused to grant a license under less than all the patents combined, the court treated the patent owner's licensing policy as one of compulsory package licensing, which was condemned not only as misuse but also as a violation of an antitrust consent decree in effect against the patent owner.

The owner of a single-process patent lost his right to enjoin infringements in *Barber Asphalt Corp.* v. *La Fera Grecco Contracting Co.,* 116 F.2d 211 (3rd Cir. 1940), 122 F.2d 701 (3rd Cir. 1941), because he applied one royalty measure to licensees who used unpatented material he manufactured and another to licensees who bought the unpatented material elsewhere. If a user of the patented concrete-curing process bought a required, unpatented bituminous emulsion from the patent owner's outlets, the price paid for the emulsion included a royalty of two cents per gallon. On the other hand, a purchaser of the emulsion from another manufacturer had to pay a royalty of one cent per square yard of concrete surface covered by the emulsion. A contractor who bought the patent owner's emulsion could spread a gallon of it as widely as possible without incurring any additional cost. A contractor buying from other producers increased his costs when he succeeded in spreading the emulsion more widely. The court saw in that arrangement an application of pressure on licensees of the patent to buy the emulsion from the patent owner's outlets.

A more direct discrimination in royalty rates was rejected by the district court in *Laitram Corp.* v. *King Crab, Inc.,* 244 F.Supp. 9 (D. Alaska 1965), 245 F.Supp. 1019 (D. Alaska 1965). The holder of the major patents on shrimp-peeling machinery was found to be charging seafood canneries in Washington, Oregon, and Alaska twice the rental rate it was charging Gulf Coast canners in leases on the patented equipment. Relying on monopolization cases under Section 2 of the Sherman Act, the court found the patents misused and denied the patent owner infringement damages during the period the double rates were in effect. The opinion cited *U.S.* v. *United Shoe Machinery Corp.,* 110 F.Supp. 295 (D. Mass. 1953), for the proposition that price discrimination in machine-leasing arrangements can be a Section 2 Sherman Act violation and is not justified by the patent laws when it results in monopolizing or attempting to monopolize trade or commerce.

The District court referred to Federal Trade Commissioner Philip Elman's concurring opinion in *Grand Caillou Packing Co., Inc.,* 65 F.T.C. 799 (1964), *aff'd in part sub nom. LaPeyre* v. *FTC,* 366 F.2d 117 (5th Cir. 1966). Commissioner Elman took the position that a patent owner has a right generally to exploit his patent monopoly by discriminatory rates, but not when the effect is to destroy or cripple a major segment of an industry. In that case, the FTC issued a cease-and-desist order banning the same patent owner's discrimination against the Northwest shrimp canners as a violation of Section 5 of the FTC Act.

An "exorbitant and oppressive" patent-royalty rate has been held a misuse of the patent (*American Photocopy Equipment Co.* v. *Rovico, Inc.,* 359 F.2d 745 (7th Cir. 1966), 384 F.2d 813 (7th Cir. 1967), *cert. denied,* 390 U.S. 945 (1968)). Impressed by indications that "the bulk of the industry" had accepted licenses at the indicated royalty rate, the court set aside a preliminary injunction the patent owner had obtained against infringement of his patent and ordered the district court to conduct a trial to determine the truth of the alleged infringer's claims of patent misuse. The license set the royalty rate at 6 percent of the retail price of the machine, which amounted to 12 percent of the licensed manufacturer's selling price. Since the patented part of the machine was half its value, the royalty rate was actually 24 percent of the selling price. In the court's view, a rate at such a level would in effect require plaintiff's licensees to fix a minimum selling price far above the price they would otherwise charge for the product containing the patented device. The court was dealing with a royalty rate set by a single patent owner. When a combination of patent owners establishes royalty rates affecting an entire industry, they are engaging in a price-fixing conspiracy violating the Sherman Act (*Standard Oil Co.* v. *U.S.,* 283 U.S. 163, 174 (1931)).

Patent royalties may be viewed as installment payments to the patent owner for his grant of a right to practice or use the invention, but in *Brulotte* v. *Thys Co.,* 379 U.S. 29 (1964), the Supreme Court made clear at least one difference between patent-license royalties and purchase-price installment payments. The court declared illegal per se the projection of patent royalties "beyond the expiration date of the patent. . . . A patent empowers the owner to exact royalties as high as he can negotiate with the leverage of that monopoly. But to use that leverage to project those royalty payments beyond the life of the patent is analogous to an effort to enlarge the monopoly of the patent by tying the sale or use of the patented article to the purchase or use of unpatented ones. . . . The exaction of royalties for use of a machine after the patent has expired in an assertion of monopoly power in the post-expiration period when . . . the patent has entered the public domain."

Justice Harlan dissented. He suggested that the majority opinion may rest on "technicalities of contract draftsmanship and not on the economic substance of the transaction." The patent licenses were given to farmers when they purchased patented hop-picking machines. The contracts signed by the parties set a flat sum for the purchase price of the machines and provided for separate royalty payments for use of the machines. While it might be possible to sell or lease unpatented machines in return for long-term payments based on use, the majority reasoned, "patents are in the federal domain; and . . . a projection of the patent monopoly after the patent expires is not enforceable." The royalties did not diminish upon expiration of individual patents, and the license agreements prevented assignment of the machines or their removal from the county after, as well as before, the expiration of the patents. To the majority, the applicability of these terms in the post-expiration period "is a telltale sign that the licensor was using the licenses to project his monopoly beyond the patent."

Justice Harlan did not think it could be assumed that a patent owner exploiting his patents by selling patented machines instead of licensing others to manufacture them could use the leverage of the patent to exact more onerous payments from farmers by gearing price to use instead of charging a flat sum. He wondered whether the result would have been different if the use payments provided for in these licenses "had been verbally disassociated from the patent licenses and described as a convenient means of spreading out payments for the machine."

The opinion in *Brulotte* distinguished *Automatic Radio Mfg. Co. v. Hazeltine Research, Inc.* by noting that not all the patents involved in that case were to expire during the period of royalties. In *McCullough Tool Co. v. Well Surveys, Inc.,* 343 F.2d 381 (10th Cir. 1965), the court decided the *Hazeltine* doctrine had not been disturbed by *Brulotte.* The Supreme Court refused to review that decision (383 U.S. 933 (1966), *rehearing denied,* 384 U.S. 947 (1966)).

The *Brulotte* decision leaves unresolved the question of whether payments based on use can lawfully run beyond the expiration date of the patent when the payments are written into the terms of the sale of the machine rather than into the terms of the patent license. Repeated references in the Court's opinion to "the patent period" and objections to attempts "to project the patent monopoly beyond the 17-year period" suggest to some antitrust lawyers that patent attorneys may be well advised to change the form of licenses granted under patent applications. Until the patent is actually granted, it may be safer to write the contract in the form of a license of trade secrets and know-how. Apprehensions of that sort may put a strained construction on the *Brulotte* opinion. Antitrust decrees with compulsory patent-licensing terms have often provided for royalties on pending patent applications.

Despite the opinion in *McCullough Tool Co.* v. *Well Surveys, Inc.*, some experts are not sure the *Hazeltine* case can be relied upon for the proposition that a non-diminishing royalty rate can be charged for a package of patents when some will expire during the term of the license. Some of the *Brulotte* opinion's reasoning about "projection of the patent monopoly" casts a shadow over that doctrine; the opinion also points out in a footnote that the review petition filed in the *Hazeltine* case "did not . . . raise the question of the effect of the expiration of any of the patents on the royalty agreements." Furthermore, in *American Securit* the court of appeals saw patent misuse in a license clause continuing the full royalty rate in effect "to the expiration of the last to expire of any" of the patents licensed.

The *American Securit* case may have set up a requirement of rate discrimination for many patent owners. Where the patent owner owns or controls a basic patent plus a series of improvement or otherwise related patents, under the *American Securit* doctrine, apparently, he may be required to differentiate in his royalty rate among his licensees, depending upon the number of his patents each wants to use. It may be that the doctrine against discrimination described in the *Barber Asphalt* and *King Crab* opinions and the antidiscrimination relief granted in *Hartford-Empire* v. *U.S.*, 323 U.S. 386 (1945), can be regarded as applicable only as between licensees under the same patent or combination of patents. The opinions in the antidiscrimination cases dwell not on the identity of the patent rights conveyed to each licensee, but on the effect or purpose of the licensor's rates to restrain or monopolize a particular part of commerce.

As for the condemnation of an "exorbitant" royalty rate in the *American Photocopy* case, the scope of the decision may be limited by the facts assumed by the court. (A trial had not yet been held.) First, the court stressed the dependence of the "bulk of the industry" on licenses under the patent. Second, the royalty rate was applied to the total price of the machine, including its unpatented parts, a feature the court seemed to regard as analogous to a tie-in; it quoted extensively from *Mercoid Corp.* v. *Mid-Continent Investment Co.,* 320 U.S. 661 (1944).

The first circumstance is one that will occur whenever the patent covers a substantial technological advance that is economically significant for an industry. The rule applied by the court would have to be regarded as an important curb on a patent owner's traditional right to charge all the traffic will bear or, as the Supreme Court put it in *Brulotte,* "to exact royalties as high as he can negotiate with the leverage of [the patent] monopoly."

Perhaps the lesson to be drawn from all these cases is that even when he is merely fixing his royalty, a patent owner must be careful not to use the royalty rate as an instrument for foreclosing competition outside the scope of his recognized patent monopoly. The restrictions placed on the patent owner are not merely those of the antitrust laws. The misuse doctrine, which is part of the patent law, can be more severe, not only in the scope of its prohibitions but also in the economic consequences of its breach. Since courts weighing misuse claims do not concern themselves with the amount of commerce restrained, the misuse doctrine operates more like a per se rule of illegality than most of the provisions in the antitrust laws. It should not be overlooked that the entry of the FTC could lead to the application of the broader and largely undefined "unfair methods of competition" ban in Section 5 of the FTC Act.

2. Patent-License Price, Territory, Quantity, and Use Limitations

Question: *To what extent has antitrust enforcement eroded the right of a patent owner to limit the scope of his grant when he licenses his patent?*

The grant of an unrestricted license by the owner of a single patent raises no antitrust problems, but the attachment of conditions limiting the licensee's use of, or dealings in, the patented product, process, or combination may.

Although legislation has been proposed from time to time to make the licensing of patents compulsory, the grantee of a single patent remains free to refuse to grant licenses. Until *Motion Picture Patents Co.* v. *Universal Film Mfg. Co.,* 243 U.S. 502 (1917), the courts took the view in patent cases that a patent owner's right to retain exclusive rights to his invention includes the right to yield it for only specified uses and on specified conditions. Decisions have upheld license clauses limiting the number of persons the licensee may employ in the manufacture of the patented article, the number of machines that may be used in its manufacture, the length of time it may be manufactured, the geographical area in which it may be manufactured and sold, the number of times a patent structure may be used, the dimensions and variety of the articles manufactured under a patented process, the price at which the patented article may be sold, and the source of the supplies or materials to be used with a patented machine.

In the *Motion Picture Patents* case the court found a "defect in this thinking" that "springs from the substituting of inference and argument for the language of the statute [R.S. 4886, now 35 U.S.C. § 101], and failure to distinguish between the rights which are given to the inventor by the patent law and which he may assert against all the world through an infringement proceeding, and rights which he may create for himself by private contract, which, however, are subject to the rules of general, as distinguished from those of the patent, law. While it is true . . . a patentee might withhold his patented machine from public use, yet if he consented to use it himself or through others, such use immediately fell within the terms of the statute, and . . . he is thereby restricted to the use of the invention as it is described in the claims of his patent." The patent-licensing condition outlawed in that case required the licensee to use only the patent owner's motion-picture films with the patented projection mechanism.

Nine years later in *U.S.* v. *General Electric Co.,* 272 U.S. 476 (1926), the Supreme Court resurrected some of the pre-1917 reasoning. It held that a patent licensor can, without violating the Sherman Act, require a licensed manufacturer of the patented article to sell at prices set by the patent owner. Noting that it is within a patent owner's rights to license the production and use of patented articles but withhold the right to sell them, the Court reasoned that, if the patent owner goes further and licenses the sale of the articles, he may "limit the selling by limiting the method of sale and the price . . . provided the conditions of sale are normally and reasonably adopted to secure pecuniary reward for the patentee's monopoly. One of the valuable elements of the exclusive right of a patentee is to acquire profit by the price at which the article is sold." The license's price-fixing term was regarded as "normally and reasonably adapted to secure pecuniary reward for the patentee's monopoly."

The Justice Department's Antitrust Division has long sought to subvert the *General Electric* doctrine. The Government has sought and obtained Supreme Court rulings that the owner of a patent cannot control the resale price of a patented product once he has sold it (*U.S.* v. *Univis Lens Co.,* 316 U.S. 241 (1942)); that a patent owner cannot control his licensee's selling price when the arrangement is part of a mutual agreement among distributors of competing products (*U.S.* v. *Masonite Corp.,* 316 U.S. 265 (1942)); that licensees' prices cannot be fixed by patent owners participating in a cross-licensing arrangement (*U.S.* v. *Line Material Co.,* 333 U.S. 287 (1948)); and that price-fixing clauses may not lawfully be included in industry-wide licensing agreements that are part of a common plan to stabilize prices in an entire industry through a network of patent licenses (*U.S.* v. *U.S. Gypsum Co.,* 333 U.S. 364 (1948)).

In the *Line Material* case, the Justice Department asked for and nearly got a complete repudiation of the *General Electric* doctrine. Four concurring justices were in favor of overruling *General Electric;* a fifth voted in the Government's favor only because of the cross-licensing arrangements that combined "competitive, noninfringing patents" for the purpose of fixing price. In *U.S.* v. *Huck Mfg. Co.,* 382 U.S. 197 (1965), the Government tried again and again narrowly failed. A district court decision (227 F.Supp. 791 (E.D. Mich. 1964)) applying the *General Electric* doctrine was affirmed by an equally divided Court. Some of the votes to affirm may have rested on the theory that the Justice Department had waived in the lower court any challenge to the *General Electric* doctrine, a matter about which the justices closely questioned Assistant Attorney General Donald F. Turner when he argued the case. During that argument, Mr. Turner expressed doubt that the *General Electric* doctrine encourages patent licensing, that licensing will in the long run produce a better competitive situation, or that the net competitive gain outweighs the economic results of price fixing in cases where licensing would have occurred without the stimulus of the right to fix prices. He suggested that a patent owner's decision whether to license turns on many factors that have nothing to do with the right to control the licensee's price.

The *General Electric* doctrine has undergone further curtailments in lower-court decisions and private lawsuits. If a patent owner puts a price-fixing clause in his license, then his licensee is no longer precluded from challenging the validity of the patent (*Sola Electric Co.* v. *Jefferson Electric Co.,* 317 U.S. 173 (1942)). Unless it is based on a valid patent, that opinion reasoned, such a price-fixing agreement is a per se Sherman Act violation. The patent owner cannot fix the price to be charged by his licensee if only part of the product involved is covered by the patent (*U.S.* v. *General Electric Co.* (Carboloy), 80 F.Supp. 989 (S.D.N.Y. 1948)) or if his patent covers the process and machine used in producing the product but not the product itself (*Barber-Colman Co.* v. *National Tool Co.,* 136 F.2d 339 (6th Cir. 1943)). Apparently the patent owner may not fix prices when he issues more than one license (*New-burgh Moire Co.* v. *Superior Moire Co.,* 237 F.2d 283 (3rd Cir. 1956)), although in the *Huck* argument Mr. Turner expressed the view that if the *General Electric* doctrine retains vitality, it should be applied to multiple licensing, since "multiple licensing would enhance the competitive advantages of licensing, if any."

In *General Talking Pictures Corp.* v. *Western Electric Co.,* 305 U.S. 124 (1938), the Supreme Court held that the owner of a patent on a sound-system device could limit its licensed use to radio speakers and that he could enjoin not only his licensee but also a buyer from the licensee from using it in motion-picture theaters. This was a step further than was permitted to the patent owner concerning control of prices or setting of territorial or customer limits. In those areas, the first sale of the patented device ends the patentee's power to impose the restriction.

Section 261 of the Patent Code (35 U.S.C. § 261) authorizes a patent owner to "convey an exclusive right under his application for patent, or patents, to the whole or any specified part of the United States." In *Deering, Milliken* v. *Temp-Resisto Corp.,* 160 F. Supp. 463 (S.D.N.Y. 1958), a patent license limiting the geographical and trade areas of use was upheld, but, as with price-fixing clauses, the courts have refused to allow a patent owner to impose territorial restrictions on a purchaser's resale of a patented product (*Keeler* v. *Standard Folding Bed Co.,* 157 U.S. 659 (1895); *Adams* v. *Burks,* 17 Wall. 453 (1873)). Moreover, the right is limited to the division of domestic markets through the licensing restrictions of a single patent owner. Combinations of patent owners dividing world markets have been outlawed under the Sherman Act (*U.S.* v. *National Lead Co.,* 63 F.Supp. 513 (S.D.N.Y. 1945), *aff'd,* 332 U.S. 319 (1947); *U.S.* v. *Singer Mfg. Co.,* 374 U.S. 174 (1963); *U.S.* v. *Imperial Chemical Industries, Ltd.,* 100 F.Supp. 504 (S.D.N.Y. 1951).

Other limitations that have been regarded by the courts as lawful are a ceiling on the quantity of production under the patent (*Baldwin-Lima Hamilton Corp.* v. *Tatnall Systems Co.,* 169 F.Supp. 1 (E.D. Pa. 1958), *aff'd,* 268 F.2d 395 (3rd Cir. 1959), *cert. denied,* 361 U.S. 894 (1959)) and a cut-off date after which the patented invention may not be used (*Mitchell* v. *Hawley,* 16 Wall. 544 (1873); *Williams* v. *Hughes Tool Co.,* 186 F.2d 278 (10th Cir. 1950), *cert. denied,* 341 U.S. 903 (1951)). The reasoning of these cases is that time and quantity restrictions merely put limits on the scope of the patent owner's waiver of his right to sue for infringement.

Until he licenses the practice of his invention, the grantee of a single patent has an unassailable monopoly in the production, use, and sale of that invention. This fact represents the premise from which both sides must start in resolving the threshold antitrust issue, whether the limitation in the license in fact has any effect on competition. There are antitrust and patent experts who take the position that to forbid the patent owner to add such limitations to his licensing contract is merely to force his royalty rate to a level above the reach of any prospective licensee. If the patent owner cannot guarantee the level of his royalty income with curbs on the activity of his licensees, they reason, he will protect it more directly in his royalty rate (although his power to do so may be curbed somewhat under *American Photocopy Equip. Co.* v. *Rovico,* 359 F.2d 745 (7th Cir. 1966), 384 F.2d 813 (7th Cir. 1967), *cert. denied,* 390 U.S. 945 (1968). A patent owner willing to issue reasonably priced but restricted licenses, this argument goes on, is not likely to impose limitations that would impair the competitive ability of his licensees any more than would the higher royalty rate he would need to compensate him for foregoing the limitations.

Some experts suggest that even price-fixing clauses can have competitive value in certain situations, for example, when the patentee owner is a small, specialized firm and the company seeking a license is large and diversified. Unless the patent owner is permitted to set a price floor, the licensee might be in a position to engage in predatory price cutting against which the patent owner could protect himself only by refusing to license large competitors.

In his argument of the *Huck* case, Assistant Attorney General Turner took the position that (1) licensing of a patent, even assuming it is induced by allowing price-fixing conditions, does not in the long run produce a better competitive situation and (2) the right to insert price-fixing clauses does not, in any event, induce licensing in situations where it would not otherwise occur. He maintained that the decision whether to license turns on many factors that have nothing to do with the right to control the licensee's price. The patent owner may have to license because his protective capacity is too small to meet the expected needs of the market, because his customers demand additional suppliers for more dependable service, because the availability of other suppliers might stimulate new demand for the patented product, or because his competitors might try to invalidate the patent or "invent around" it.

In assessing the degree to which antitrust law cuts into the rights recognized in patent cases, it is important to note that patent decisions have tended to treat the license of a patent like any other transfer of a property right. Yet current antitrust law does not permit the transferor of property to impose the use or resale restrictions allowed in the patent cases described above. In fact, even the patent cases, except for the *General Talking Pictures* case, accord a patent owner no such rights once he or his licensee has sold the patented product. For that reason, as well as the close decisions in the *Line Material* and *Huck* cases, the *General Electric* doctrine is regarded by many antitrust lawyers as a tottering base on which to predicate a patent-licensing system. Moreover, the scope of the *General Electric* doctrine may be substantially limited by the facts of the case itself. The Supreme Court described the question it was deciding as involving "patents entirely controlling the manufacture, use and sale of the tungsten incandescent lamps." While patents covering complete saleable products may still be common, particularly in the chemical industry, a rapidly growing percentage of patents cover only parts of, or improvements in, saleable products.

The scope of *GE* has been narrowed to such an extent that the advantage to be gained from the addition of a price-fixing clause to a patent license may not be worth the risk to the patent.

As far as their own antitrust legality is concerned, territorial, quantity, and field-of-use limitations do not stand on an equal footing. Territorial limits are valid under 35 U.S.C. § 261, although the Supreme Court's refusal in the *Univis Lens* case to extend the *General Electric* doctrine to permit the control of price beyond the first sale of the patented article seems to bar any territorial restriction taking effect after the licensee's sale. The decisions upholding quantity limitations predate the era of modern antitrust enforcement, and their legality may be doubtful, particularly when the patent owner competes with his licensee or licensees in the production and sale of the patented article. As for field-of-use limitations, the vitality of the *General Talking Pictures* decision upholding such a restriction is questioned by more experts than Mr. Turner.

Generally, limitations of these types are written into a patent license as limits on the grant made by the patent owner. It is possible to find in such an arrangement an implied covenant by the licensee not to use the patent outside the scope of the grant. Yet some antitrust lawyers feel that the parties to a license increase their chances of raising antitrust problems if, as sometimes happens, they take the added precaution of writing into their contract an express covenant by the licensee. Some feel that the Justice Department is less likely to investigate patent-licensing arrangements that omit the covenant by the licensee.

It is possible for antitrust problems to arise even when the restriction is not put into writing at all. A patent owner may exploit his invention by marketing the materials or supplies it uses and simply furnishing the patented machine free of charge to his customers. With the free machine goes an implied license to use, but there are no expressed restrictions on how, where, or by whom the machine is to be used. The patent owner simply makes the machine available only to customers for the materials or supplies.

In *B. B. Chemical Co.* v. *Ellis,* 314 U.S. 495 (1942), a manufacturer of shoe-insole reinforcing material gave shoe manufacturers no written licenses to his reinforcing-method patent but collected a charge per yard of reinforcing fabric used with the method. Despite the absence of a license, the Supreme Court decided that it would be contrary to public policy to permit the patent owner to enjoin others from inducing infringement of the patent by selling shoe manufacturers reinforcing materials for use with the patented method.

3. Patent-Licensing Tie-Ins

Question: *What is the antitrust status of the practice of conditioning the grant of a patent license on the licensee's agreement to purchase materials or supplies or to take a license under an additional patent or patents?*

"For our purposes a tying arrangement may be defined as an agreement by a party to sell one product but only on the condition that the buyer also purchases a different (or tied) product, or at least agrees that he will not purchase that product from any other supplier. Where such conditions are successfully exacted, competition on the merits with respect to the tied product is inevitably curbed. Indeed 'tying agreements serve hardly any purpose beyond the suppression of competition.' *Standard Oil Co. of Calif.* v. *United States,* 337 U.S. 293, 305–306 (1949). They deny competitors free access to the market for the tied product, not because the party imposing the tying requirements has a better product or a lower price but because of his power or leverage in another market. At the same time buyers are forced to forego their free choice between competing products. . . . They are unreasonable in and of themselves whenever a party has sufficient economic power with respect to the tying product to appreciably restrain free competition in the market for the tied product and a 'not insubstantial' amount of interstate commerce is affected" (*Northern Pacific Ry. Co.* v. *U.S.,* 356 U.S. 1 (1958)).

Four provisions of the antitrust laws have been applied to tying arrangements. First, in the *Northern Pacific* case, a railroad's requirement that purchasers and lessees of its land ship their products over its lines was held to be an unlawful restraint of trade violating Section 1 of the Sherman Act. Second, in *Times-Picayune Publishing Co.* v. *U.S.,* 345 U.S. 594 (1953), the Supreme Court accepted a Justice Department suggestion that a tie-in could violate Section 2 of the Sherman Act, although it threw out the Government's attempt-to-monopolize count in that case for lack of proof of "specific intent" to monopolize. Third, if the seller imposing the tie-in is selling or leasing "commodities," not land or services, his practice can be attacked under Section 3 of the Clayton Act, which the *Times-Picayune* decision recognized as imposing less stringent proof requirements on the Government. Section 3 makes it "unlawful for any person engaged in commerce, in the course of such commerce, to lease or make a sale or contract for sale of goods, wares, merchandise, machinery, supplies, or other commodities, whether patented or unpatented, . . . on the condition . . . that the lessee or purchaser thereof shall not use or deal in the goods, wares, merchandise, machinery, supplies, or other commodity of a competitor or competitors . . . , where the effect . . . may be to substantially lessen competition or tend to create a monopoly in any line of commerce." Fourth, in view of the Supreme Court's decision in *Atlantic Refining Co.* v. *FTC*, 381 U.S. 357 (1965), Section 5 of the FTC Act can be used to stop tie-ins. The majority opinion recognized authority in the FTC to stop, as a Section 5 "unfair method of competition," an arrangement that had the "competitive characteristics" of a tie-in even though it fell short of violating the Sherman or Clayton Act. See also *FTC* v. *Motion Picture Advertising Serv. Co.*, 344 U.S. 392 (1953).

While the *Times-Picayune* opinion has tended to discourage application of the Sherman Act to tying arrangements involving unpatented products, "if anything has become clear in the law on restraint of trade, it is that a tie-in to a patented product or process is virtually illegal per se, whether the Clayton Act or Sherman Act is applied" (Donald F. Turner, "The Validity of Tying Arrangements Under the Antitrust Laws," 72 HARV. L. REV. 50 (1958)). When the Sherman Act is applied, the patent is regarded as giving the seller the "economic power" or "leverage" referred to in the *Northern Pacific* opinion. On the other hand, the language used in Section 3 of the Clayton Act limits somewhat its application in a patent-licensing context. Unless the patent license accompanies a sale or lease of the patented article, Section 3 does not apply, for it speaks only to one who sells or leases a commodity.

The first Supreme Court decision striking down a tying arrangement did so on the basis of patent law rather than antitrust law. In *Motion Picture Patents Co.* v. *Universal Film Mfg. Co.*, 243 U.S. 502 (1917), the Court refused to enforce a license clause tying unpatented supplies to a patented machine. Later, in cases like *Morton Salt Co.* v. *G. S. Suppiger Co.*, 314 U.S. 488 (1942), conditioning the grant of a patent license upon agreement to buy unpatented products was declared a misuse of the patent, and it precluded the patent owner from obtaining relief even against a direct infringer of his patent. In 1944 the Supreme Court decided two cases that are now generally cited as clearly establishing the illegality of such tie-ins. In *Mercoid Corp.* v. *Mid-Continent Investment Co.*, 320 U.S. 661 (1944), it was held that a manufacturer was not guilty of contributory infringement of a combination patent on a heating-control system when he made and sold unpatented switches specifically designed to serve as part of the patented combination. It was held that the complaining patent owner was unlawfully attempting to control commerce in unpatented switches outside the grant of the combination patent. In *Mercoid Corp.* v. *Minneapolis-Honeywell Regulator* Co., 320 U.S. 680 (1944), the manufacturer of the unpatented switches was held entitled to treble damages from the patent owner under the antitrust laws.

International Salt Co. v. *U.S.*, 332 U.S. 392 (1947), is generally cited for the proposition that a tying arrangement in a patent license is "virtually illegal per se." In earlier cases such as *United Shoe Machinery Corp.* v. *U.S.*, 258 U.S. 451 (1922), and *International Business Machines Corp.* v. *U.S.*, 298 U.S. 131 (1936), the Court had looked for evidence of competitive injury. In the *International Salt* opinion it denied that there was any need for showing economic consequences if the "volume of business affected" was not "insignificant or insubstantial." International Salt's leasing of patented salt-dispensing machines on condition that the lessees purchase all their salt requirements from International was declared unlawful because "it is unreasonable, per se, to foreclose competitors from any substantial market."

Tying arrangements are created in a variety of ways. Sometimes they are written explicitly into the terms of the sale of a patented product or into the terms of a license under a process or combination patent. Others come about simply because of the patent owner's practice of granting licenses only to those who purchase the unpatented product from him. In cases like *Leitch Mfg. Co.* v. *Barber*, 302 U.S. 458 (1938); *B. B. Chemical Co.* v. *Ellis*, 314 U.S. 495 (1942); and *Barber Asphalt Corp.* v. *La Fera Grecco Contracting Co.*, 116 F.2d 211 (3rd Cir. 1940), *judgment modified*, 122 F.2d 701 (3rd Cir. 1941), an implied tying arrangement was found in practices allowing lower royalty rates to purchasers of the unpatented "tied" product.

Not all patent-licensing tie-ins have been found illegal even since the *International Salt* decision, however. In *Electric Pipe Line, Inc.* v. *Fluid Systems, Inc.*, 231 F.2d 370 (2d Cir. 1956), 250 F.2d 697 (2nd Cir. 1957), the owner of a combination patent was permitted to insist that he be the supplier of unpatented components of heating systems that he designed to each customer's needs and whose performance he guaranteed. The court stressed that there was no attempt to prevent the sale of the unpatented items for use outside the patented system. The patent owner obtained all his revenues from sales of the unpatented components, but the court pointed out that he did much more than sell those components. The patent owner's designing of the system to meet the individualized needs of his customers, his inspection of the final installation, and his guarantee of the performance of the system distinguished this case from the *Mercoid* decisions. "In this case, the sale of unpatented components is incidental to the sale of the system as a whole."

The Supreme Court made it clear in the *IBM* opinion that a patent owner is not forbidden to warn its licensees against using, with patented equipment, supplies that do not conform to the necessary specifications "or even from making its leases conditional upon the use of [supplies] which conform to them." In addition, if he is a pioneer in a new industry, he may be permitted to impose tie-ins temporarily until the technological, financial, and public-relations problems of the new endeavor can be mastered (*U.S.* v. *Jerrold Electronics Corp.,* 187 F.Supp. 545 (E.D. Pa. 1960), *aff'd,* 365 U.S. 567 (1961); see also *Dehydrating Process Co.* v. *A. O. Smith Corp.,* 292 F.2d 653 (1st Cir.), *cert. denied,* 368 U.S. 931 (1961)).

At least two federal district judges have made a distinction between conditioning the licensing of a patent upon purchase of unpatented materials and conditioning it upon the purchase of patented materials (*General Electric Co.* v. *Hygrade Sylvania Corp.,* 61 F.Supp. 531 (S.D.N.Y. 1944); *Libbey-Owens-Ford Glass Co. (L-O-F)* v. *Sylvania Industrial Corp.,* 64 F.Supp. 516 (S.D.N.Y. 1945), *appeal dismissed,* 154 F.2d 814 (2d Cir. 1946), *cert. denied,* 328 U.S. 859 (1946)). The patent owner involved in the *L-O-F* case allowed only purchasers of his patented product to use his patented process, but he was found not to have misused his patents.

In the *IBM* case, the Supreme Court called attention to the fact that Section 3 of the Clayton Act "makes tying clauses unlawful, whether the machine leased is 'patented or unpatented.'" Section 3's phrase "patented or unpatented" is used with reference to the tying product, not the tied product. In a patent-licensing context, the tying item is the patent licensed or the patented product sold or leased, not the supplies or materials whose purchase is tied to the sale, lease, or license. The language of Section 3 does not explicitly foreclose a distinction between patented and unpatented products.

In some patent-misuse and antitrust cases, the restriction on the licensee has taken the form of a prohibition against dealing in equipment or products that compete with the patented device. Since Section 3 of the Clayton Act has been applied to exclusive-dealing agreements, as well as to tying arrangements, that section is generally cited and relied on in the exclusive-dealing patent-misuse cases. In *Preformed Line Products Co.* v. *Fanner Mfg. Co.*, 328 F.2d 265 (6th Cir. 1964), *cert. denied,* 379 U.S. 846 (1964), the court, in examining patent misuse in an exclusive-dealing arrangement, applied the language of Section 3 and found a violation of that section. The court applied the standard used by the Supreme Court in *Tampa Electric* v. *Nashville Coal,* 365 U.S. 320 (1961), declaring that an exclusive-dealing contract violates Section 3 when "the court believes it probable that performance of the contract will foreclose competition in a substantial share of the line of commerce affected."

In *Berlenbach* v. *Anderson & Thompson Ski Co.,* 329 F.2d 782 (9th Cir. 1964), *cert. denied,* 379 U.S. 830 (1964), on the other hand, the court pointed out that exclusive-dealing requirements, like any other conduct of a patent owner, need not fit the antitrust mold in order to be considered misuse of the patent. That court rejected a suggestion that it must have proof of substantial lessening of competition before it can find an exclusive-dealing contract to represent misuse of a patent. The Third and Seventh Circuits showed similar attitudes in *F.C. Russell Co.* v. *Consumers Insulation Co.,* 226 F.2d 373 (3rd Cir. 1955) and *F.C. Russell Co.* v. *Comfort Equipment Corp.,* 194 F.2d 592 (7th Cir. 1952).

It seems to be well established that there is nothing in the patent or antitrust law to prevent a patent owner and his licensee from including a number of patents in a single licensing contract. In fact, multipatent licenses have become the rule rather than the exception. The Supreme Court made it clear in *Automatic Radio Mfg. Co.* v. *Hazeltine Research, Inc.,* 339 U.S. 827 (1950), that there is nothing wrong with "package licensing" when the licensee actually wants all the patents. In *American Securit Co.* v. *Shatterproof Glass Corp.,* 268 F.2d 769 (3rd Cir. 1959), *cert. denied,* 361 U.S. 902 (1959), the court held compulsory package licensing misuse of the patents. "The protection, or monopoly, which is given to the first patent stops where the monopoly in the second begins." The court took note of language in *Transparent-Wrap* v. *Stokes & Smith,* 329 U.S. 637 (1947), approving "using one legalized monopoly to acquire another" but decided to follow the rule applied in the *International Salt* case to the tying of unpatented articles to the licensing of a patent. The court also pointed out that in *Ethyl Gasoline Corp.* v. *U.S.,* 309 U.S. 436 (1940), the Supreme Court had said: "The patent monopoly of one invention can no more be enlarged for the exploitation of a monopoly of another . . . than for the exploitation of an unpatented article."

In 1964 the Supreme Court held that "the use of a royalty agreement that projects beyond the expiration date of the patent is un-

lawful *per se*" (*Brulotte* v. *Thys Co.,* 379 U.S. 29, 33 (1964)). The
Court stated that licenses for use of patented hop-picking machines
were invalid, since the annual payments were not part of the purchase price but were in effect royalties for use of the product after
the patent had expired. In *Brulotte,* the Court distinguished and
limited its decision in *Automatic Radio Mfg. Co.* v. *Hazeltine Research, Inc.,* 339 U.S. 827 (1950), approving package licensing of
patents in an agreement held enforceable where it was "a convenient mode of operation designed by the parties to avoid the necessity of determining whether each type of petitioner's product embodies any of the numerous Hazeltine patents" (339 U.S. at 833).

In *Brulotte* v. *Thys Co.,* the Supreme Court declined to extend
the *Automatic Radio* "convenience of the parties" doctrine from the
area of package licensing. When the package licensing question was
again presented in *Zenith Radio Corp.* v. *Hazeltine Research, Inc.,*
395 U.S. 100 (1969), 418 F.2d 21 (7th Cir. 1969), *rev'd,* 401 U.S.
321 (1971), the Court did not overrule *Automatic Radio,* but it
stressed the obverse of its holding: Whereas package licensing with
royalties based on the licensee's total sales is not improper when
genuine mutual convenience is served thereby, it is otherwise "where
the patentee directly or indirectly 'conditions' his license upon the
payment of royalties on unpatented products—that is, where the
patentee refuses to license on any other basis and leaves the licensee with the choice between a license so providing and no license at all" (395 U.S. at 135).

The facts in *Zenith Radio Corp.* were these: As a large domestic
manufacturer of radio and television sets for sale in the United
States and foreign countries, Zenith was a party to many patent
license agreements. It had entered into agreements with Hazeltine
Research, Inc. (HRI), a patent-owning and licensing subsidiary of
Hazeltine Corporation (Hazeltine). Until 1959, Zenith had licensed
all of HRI's domestic patents, but at that time it declined to renew
its expiring package-license agreement, although it continued to use
the processes.

In due course HRI brought suit. Zenith's answer alleged the invalidity of the patent asserted, denied infringement, and alleged
that HRI's claim was unenforceable because of unclean hands and
patent misuse. Three years later, Zenith also filed a counter-claim
for treble damages and injunctive relief under Section 1 of the
Sherman Act, on the grounds that it was damaged by a conspiracy
among HRI, Hazeltine, and foreign patent pools in Canada, England, and Australia to exclude Zenith and others from export into
those foreign markets by refusing to license the pools' patents except for manufacture in the foreign country; it also sought treble
damages for patent misuse.

Zenith prevailed below on the infringement claim, and the issue was not presented in the Supreme Court. On Zenith's counterclaim, the district court found, first, that HRI had misused its domestic patents by insisting on a five-year package license, regardless of use, with royalties on total sales of Zenith products, whether patented or unpatented, and second, that HRI and Hazeltine had conspired with the foreign pools to Zenith's injury (239 F.Supp. 51 (N.D. Ill. 1965)). Treble damages were awarded on both the patent misuse and antitrust claims, and HRI was enjoined from requiring a royalty on unpatented items as a condition of granting a patent license to Zenith and also from continued participation in foreign pools.

On appeal, the court of appeals affirmed the award of treble damages for misuse but reversed the award for conspiracy, on the ground that Zenith had not shown actual injury (388 F.2d 25 (7th Cir. 1967)). It modified the award against further misuse, struck the injunction against HRI's participation in the foreign pools, and reversed the judgment against Hazeltine, since jurisdiction had not been established over the parent.

The Supreme Court affirmed the dismissal in regard to Hazeltine, but partially reversed the finding that Zenith had failed to prove injury resulting from the pools' exclusionary tactics. It also reinstated those portions of the injunctions barring HRI from conspiring with the foreign pools, and remanded for further consideration the question of the need for injunctive relief against future antitrust violations through misuse under package licensing.

HRI had participated in Canadian, English, and Australian pools. The record showed that the chief purpose of the Canadian pool was "to protect the manufacturing members and licensees from competition by American and other foreign companies seeking to export their products into Canada." The English and Australian pools were operated on similar principles.

Justice White, for the court (Justice Harlan concurring), concluded that Zenith could recover treble damages only for the exclusionary practice of the Canadian pool, since the record showed that Zenith was not barred from entry into the other markets by the pools, but rather by technological barriers in the English television market and by high tariffs and shipping costs in Australia. (In a footnote the Court indicated that Zenith's failure to request a license from the Canadian pool during the damage period was not fatal: ". . . such a request would have been futile. The pool had made its position entirely clear . . ." (395 U.S. at 120).

Although the Court barred recovery of damages on account of the activity of the English and Australian pools, injunctive relief was allowed since treble damage cases, although "brought for private ends, . . . also serve the public interest in that they effectively pry open to competition a market that has been closed by defendants' illegal restraints" (395 U.S. at 133).

The court of appeals had relied on *Automatic Radio Mfg. Co.* v. *Hazeltine Research, Inc.,* to hold that HRI did not misuse its patent by "conditioning" the grant of a patent license upon payment of royalties on nonpatented products. Since it found no misuse, the court of appeals also considered that there could be no antitrust violation and struck that part of the injunction concerning package licensing. The Supreme Court did not reach the second point directly, but it reaffirmed the distinction between antitrust and patent concepts, citing *Morton Salt* and *Transparent-Wrap,* along with the Attorney General's Report, and various reports, articles, and treatises. It did reverse on the definitional question and held that it is patent misuse per se for a licensee to require royalties on the sale of products which do not use the "teaching of the patent."

Justice White reaffirmed the distinction, set forth in *Automatic Radio* v. *Hazeltine,* between a royalty based on a percentage of total sales when the bona fide convenience of the parties is served thereby and a total sales royalty insisted upon by the patentee. Moreover, the Court strengthened the misuse doctrine in a dictum that "patent misuse *inheres* in a patentee's insistence on a percentage of sales royalty regardless of use, and his rejection of license proposals to pay only for actual use" (395 U.S. at 139).

Many experts believe that the decision makes it desirable for a domestic patent holder to sell its foreign patent rights to a pool, rather than license them and remain liable for the acts of the licensee on a conspiratory theory. It is suggested that a small company is in any event better advised to sell its patents abroad, since, as a practical matter, the enforcement of a license agreement in foreign courts is difficult at best and inevitably very costly.

Other specialists believe that even a policy of selling each domestic patent to the foreign pool would be evidence of a continuing course of conduct binding the patentee to the pool. Although some would distinguish between a patentee's "knowledge" of the pool's exclusionary purpose and a "meeting of the minds" to that end, others point out that in *Albrecht* v. *The Herald Co.,* 390 U.S. 145 (1968), the Court did not require a showing of an agreement in order to find a combination violative of the Sherman Act. See also *United States* v. *Chas. Pfizer & Co.,* 281 F.Supp. 837 (S.D.N.Y. 1968).

When considering package licensing practices in the light of *Zenith Radio* v. *Hazeltine,* antitrust specialists are agreed that the parties to license agreements should take steps to minimize their exposure by insuring that the "mutual convenience" defense is explicitly set forth in the written agreement; in their view, the record clearly should establish the alternatives open to the licensee. It was on this point that Justice Harlan departed from the majority, arguing that the problems of proof would be too great for the "convenience" test to be of any practical value; he would have overruled *Automatic Radio* directly. To make the record clear, many practitioners would advise their clients to restrict the time period of the license to one year. They point out that Justice White's opinion called attention to the five-year term of the challenged license. Also, as they see it, there is a per se misuse of a patent, under the rationale of *Brulotte* and the holding in *Zenith,* where the patentee requires the payment of royalties on patents not actually used, but they suggest the patentee-licensor can comply with *Zenith* v. *Hazeltine* by granting an option to the licensee to choose between a higher royalty in the patent base of patents actually used and a lower royalty based on a percentage of total sales. In this connection, they observe that a patentee may properly exact what the traffic will bear for the use of its patented process, even though any attempt to extend the protection of the patent will bring trouble. Some believe, however, that the application of antitrust concepts to patent and other areas may be increasing, and that the line drawn in *Morton Salt* v. *Suppiger* may become invisible. As an example, some practitioners cite *Zenith Radio* v. *Hazeltine* and the Supreme Court's decision earlier in *Fortner Enterprises, Inc.* v. *U.S. Steel Corp.,* 394 U.S. 495 (1969), in which antitrust tying doctrine was applied to the so-called sale of credit.

Without overruling *Automatic Radio* v. *Hazeltine,* the Supreme Court appears to have changed its attitude toward package licensing of patents and to have made it more difficult for a patent holder to require a licensee to pay royalties on patents it does not use or on items not patented at all. In doing so, it materially strengthened the patent-misuse doctrine and placed heavier burdens on attorneys counselling patent-holding clients to ensure not only that package licensing is used only where it meets the genuine convenience of the parties, but also that the record reflects that fact. The alternative seems to be the loss of the patent protection.

4. No-Contest Clauses

Question: *What antitrust problems may be caused by no-contest clauses?*

The California Supreme Court, in *Adkins* v. *Lear, Inc.,* 435 P.2d 321 (Sup. Ct. of Calif. 1967), observed that "one of the oldest doctrines in the field of patent law establishes that so long as a licensee is operating under a license agreement he is estopped to deny the validity of his licensor's patent in a suit for royalties under the agreement. The theory underlying this doctrine is that a licensee should not be permitted to enjoy the benefit afforded by the agreement while simultaneously urging that the patent which forms the basis of the agreement is void" (435 P.2d at 325–326).

John Adkins, an inventor and mechanical engineer, was hired by Lear to develop a gyroscope. Lear and Adkins entered into an agreement providing that while new ideas, discoveries, and inventions related to vertical gyros were to become the property of Adkins, Lear would be granted a license, "on a mutually satisfactory royalty basis," on all ideas he might develop. Three years later, the parties executed a contract which stated the conditions upon which Lear promised to pay royalties for Adkins' improvements. The agreement provided: if "the United States Patent Office refuses to issue a patent on the substantial claims [contained in Adkins' original patent application] or if such a patent so issued is subsequently held invalid, then in any of such events Lear at its option shall have the right forthwith to terminate the specific license so affected or to terminate this entire agreement. . . ."

At the time the 1955 agreement was executed, Adkins had already filed an application with the Patent Office for his gyro improvements. Six years later he obtained a patent. During that period, Lear had become convinced that Adkins would never receive a patent and that it should not continue to pay royalties. After the patent application had been rejected twice, Lear announced that it had searched the Patent Office files and had found a patent that it believed fully anticipated Adkins' discovery. It then stated that it would no longer pay royalties on one group of gyroscopes it was producing. As soon as Adkins obtained his patent, he brought a California suit for royalties.

Lear sought to prove that, despite the grant of a patent by the Patent Office, none of Adkins' improvements was sufficiently novel. In response Adkins argued that, since Lear had entered into a licensing agreement, it was obliged to pay the agreed royalties regardless of the validity of the underlying patent. The California Supreme Court sustained Adkins' on the grounds of equitable estoppel. Justice Harlan, writing for a divided U.S. Supreme Court (395 U.S. 653 (1969)), noted the Court's earlier adherence to the doctrine in *Automatic Radio Mfg. Co.* v. *Hazeltine Research, Inc.,* 339 U.S. 827 (1950), but reconsidered this ruling "in light of our recent decisions emphasizing the strong federal policy favoring free competition in ideas which do not merit patent protection." Justice Harlan observed that "while the roots of the doctrine have often been celebrated in tradition, we have found only one 19th century case in this Court that invoked estoppel in a considered manner and that case was decided before the Sherman Act made it clear that the grant of monopoly power to a patent owner constituted a limited exception to the general federal policy favoring free competition." He emphasized that in the large number of cases in which licensing agreements contain restrictions arguably illegal under the antitrust laws, the doctrine of estoppel was a dead letter.

Justice Harlan stated that the controversy between Adkins and Lear presented a more complicated estoppel problem than the one that arises in most common licensing situations. During the period in which Adkins was attempting to obtain a patent, he found Lear gained an important benefit not generally obtained by the typical licensee. Until a patent issues, a potential licensee may not learn his licensor's ideas simply by requesting the information from the Patent Office. If a potential licensee hopes to use the ideas contained in a patent application, he must deal with the inventor himself, unless the inventor chooses to publicize his ideas to the world at large. By promising to pay Adkins royalties from the very outset of their relationship, Lear gained immediate access to ideas that it might not have learned of until the Patent Office published the details of Adkins' invention many years later.

Justice Harlan found the core of this case to be the difficult question of "whether federal patent policy bars a state from enforcing a contract regulating access to an unpatented secret idea." He held that, at least for the period subsequent to the issuance of the patent, Lear must be permitted to avoid the payment of royalties if it can prove patent invalidity. The Court did not discuss the validity of Adkins' claim to royalties accruing before the issuance of the patent. Justice Harlan noted that the California Supreme Court had not addressed itself to that issue with precision, for it believed that the estoppel doctrine provided a sufficient answer. The Court concluded that even though an important question of federal law was involved in this phase of the controversy, it should not attempt to define in even a limited way the extent, if any, to which the states might properly act to enforce the contractual rights of inventors of unpatented secret ideas.

The Court's opinion in *Lear* apparently intended to repudiate licensee estoppel retroactively concerning all patent licensees whether or not concluded prior to the *Lear* decision. The Court stated (n. 19): ". . . the public's interest in the elimination of specious patents would be significantly prejudiced if the retroactive effect of today's decision were limited in any way" (395 U.S. at 674). Nevertheless, at least one lower court seems to have disregarded the message. In *Kearney & Trecker Corp.* v. *Giddings & Lewis, Inc.,* 306 F.Supp. 189 (E.D. Wisc. 1969), *rev'd,* 452 F.2d 579 (7th Cir. 1971), the court refused to apply *Lear* to license agreements executed prior to the date of that decision, concluding that under the *Automatic Radio* case, the agreements were lawful when made. *Lear's* retroactive repudiation of licensee estoppel has, however, been followed in *Western Electric Co.* v. *Solitron,* 306 N.Y.S. 2d 624 (Sup. Ct. of N.Y. 1969), and *Cowden Mfg. Co.* v. *Koratron Co.,* 422 F.2d 371 (6th Cir.), *cert. denied,* 398 U.S. 959 (1970).

In *Bendix Corp.* v. *Balax, Inc.,* 421 F.2d 809 (7th Cir. 1970), *cert. denied,* 399 U.S. 911 (1970), the court of appeals may have defined a new, substantive antitrust offense. Bendix was successor to a suit brought for infringement of several patents. Balax counterclaimed for damages, arguing that Sherman Act Sections 1 and 2 were violated by fraudulent procurement and misuse of the patents. The patent license and sales agreements contained a broad clause prohibiting any contest of the patents' validity even after the termination of the agreements. *Lear,* it should be noted, involved an implied, not an express, estoppel. The court concluded that the licensor of a patent may not ". . . forever preclude the licensee from challenging the validity of the patent. By requiring such a condition . . . plaintiff may have placed itself in the position of unlawfully exceeding the protected area."

In *Bendix* the court held: ". . . the right to estop licensees from challenging a patent is not part of the 'limited protection' afforded by the patent monopoly. Furthermore, the reason is that it creates a danger of unwarranted monopolization. Such danger may be even greater here than in the usual licensee-estoppel case for the reason that in the instant case the licensor sought to create an irrevocable estoppel, not one merely extending during the life of the licensees and sales agreements." Since *Lear* was decided by the Supreme Court after the district court ruling on the *Balax* antitrust counterclaim, the court of appeals remanded the issue to the district court for reconsideration in light of *Lear.* The district court granted judgment for defendant on the counterclaim (321 F.Supp. 1095 (E.D. Wisc. 1971)).

The question arises whether a Sherman Act case can be premised on the mere existence of a no-contest license clause. Some think not, but the *Bendix* case seems to hold unlawful per se any patent license agreement embodying a promise not to contest validity, even if there are no other restrictive elements in the license. The Supreme Court in *Lear* expressly avoided any opinion as to whether the licensor may recover pre-issuance royalties. Though leaving the question for state court determination, Justice Harlan did recognize that the licensee obtained benefits from Adkins' disclosure to it of secret know-how prior to patent issuance. Justice Black, in his dissent, was firmly opposed to recovery.

At least one court has dealt with the trade secret problem directly (*Painton & Co.* v. *Bourns, Inc.,* 309 F.Supp. 271 (S.D.N.Y. 1970)). A British electronics component manufacturer sought a declaratory judgment recognizing its right to continue to manufacture certain items free of an American firm's trade secret and patent claims. Pursuant to a contract, the British firm had received drawings, instructions, and engineering assistance from the American firm relating to the manufacture of potentiometers. In return, it was obliged to pay royalties as specified. It also had the right to secure British or other patents at its own expense in the American firm's name and had the right to use them free of any British patent infringement claims for the term of the contract. The controversy in the federal district court was limited to the right of the British firm to continue to use the drawings, instructions, and engineering assistance to manufacture "after expiration of the contract and payment of royalties due after expiration free from any trade secret and patent claims."

Judge Constance Baker Motley ruled that plaintiff-licensee could keep the drawings free of all trade secret claims. She interpreted *Lear* to hold that "once a patent issues, regardless of what was the intention of the contracting parties, the patentee-licensor may not enforce its trade secret claims" (citing *Lear,* 395 U.S. at 672–674). Judge Motley seemed to find that the inventor may not recover royalties for secret ideas for which a patent is never sought, since "our patent policy of strict regulation of inventions would be undercut if inventors could enforce agreements for compensation for alleged secret ideas without being required to submit those ideas to the Patent Office, and, thereby, eventually have the ideas disclosed to the public. . . . Inventors would be encouraged to avoid filing applications altogether and contract for long licensing arrangements. The severely restricted areas which the Supreme Court left open to applicable State Law would become a yawning abyss. Fewer patent applications would be made. The Patent Office would soon have a less accurate view of the state of the art in a particular field. And state courts, rather than the Patent Office, would become the initial triers of whether a discovery is an invention."

The district court's summary judgment in favor of the plaintiff was reversed (442 F.2d 216 (2d Cir. 1971)). The court of appeals held that neither general considerations of public policy nor anything in federal patent law provided sufficient basis for declining to enforce trade secret agreements under all the circumstances in this case, especially where no patent application had been filed.

Judge Motley's rationale seemed to follow closely Justice Black's partial dissent in the *Lear* case. Although the Court did not deal with this issue, Justice Black concluded that "private arrangements under which self-styled 'inventors' do not keep their discoveries secret but . . . disclose them . . . for . . . payments run counter to . . . our patent laws, which tightly regulate the kind of inventions that may be protected and the manner in which they may be protected." Judge Motley declined, as did the Supreme Court in *Lear,* to decide "whether . . . an inventor, if he makes a patent application, can be compensated for his disclosure before the patent has issued."

Some find it difficult to see how *Lear* can be interpreted as invalidating royalty agreements for trade secrets unrelated to any filing of a patent application. They point out that in *Lear,* since a patent application was filed and any know-how licensed by the defendant prior to the patent issuance was clearly related to the patented invention, the question of whether pure trade secret agreements could be enforced by state or federal courts was not before the Court. They conclude that *Painton* was really concerned only with trade secrets related to the issued patent and that any language which is construed to apply to trade secrets alone may be regarded as dictum.

If the inventor does apply for a patent and grants a license prior to issuance, is he giving something of "value" should the patent later be denied or invalidated? At the time of filing he reveals to the Patent Office the secrets integral to the patent claims to the extent necessary to sustain the claim. The trade secrets will be disclosed to the public if the patent issues. This is seen by some as one reason for denying post-issuance trade secret royalties.

If royalties are not awarded for the secret revealed before filing, does a trade secret license involve a game of chance as to whether the patent will issue? Also, if "pure" trade secret or know-how licensing agreements (without patent application) are to be enforced, will a federal antitrust action lie as it would with respect to patent licenses, for restrictions employing the use of illegal price-fixing, tying, or other limitations pertaining to the products manufactured or the process used? Are there real differences between patent misuse and the misuse of a trade secret agreement?

Lear stated the public policy favoring invalidation of worthless patents. The Justice Department has a patent unit in the Antitrust Division and has challenged patent validity itself as well as patent misuse practices. See, for example, complaints in *In Re Ampicillin Antitrust Litigation,* 1972 Trade Cas. ¶ 73,966 (D. D.C. 1972); Speech of Richard Stern before the Philadelphia Patent Law Association, February 19, 1970. The *Bendix* decision may have given impetus to this program. In *Lear,* the court stated its opposition to ". . . disabling entirely all those who have the strongest incentive in showing that a patent is worthless." In *U.S.* v. *Glaxo Group Ltd.,*

302 F.Supp. 1 (D.D.C. 1969), the district court held that, absent fraudulent procurement, the Justice Department has no standing to challenge patent validity. The Supreme Court reversed (597 ATRR F-1 (1973)). (See section V-E-2, p. 404.)

Some would argue that a no-contest clause should not be actionable unless the patent it protects is subsequently held invalid; the clause would not injure the licensee since he would not be paying royalties for a worthless invention. Others would concede the applicability of a "rule of reason" but would find a no-contest clause unlawful despite patent validity, reasoning that such a clause seeks to extend an otherwise lawful patent monopoly unreasonably beyond its intended scope. Perhaps the licensor's share of the market for the applicable product may be relevant. If he is a monopolist, or oligopolist, a no-contest clause, even though related to a valid patent, might violate Section 2 of the Sherman Act.

The *Lear* court was concerned with "worthless patents," but the court of appeals in *Bendix* talked more of "unwarranted monopolization" and less about patent validity, although the validity of the patents involved was clearly at issue. Maybe the most direct explanation of the difference is that *Bendix* was an antitrust suit brought under the Sherman Act and the patentee controlled 80 percent of the market, whereas *Lear* was a royalty suit in which market impact had no relevance.

Suppose a patent license agreement contains a no-contest clause and the licensor breaches the agreement. Can he defend his contractual breach by arguing that the no-contest clause violates the Sherman Act under *Bendix* and vitiates the entire contract? The answer to this question was "no" in *Western Geophys. Co. v. Bolt Assoc.,* 50 F.R.D. 193 (D. Conn. 1970). The district court noted that "it is far from clear that *Lear* v. *Adkins* cut both ways so as to also benefit the licensor."

If the trend is toward broad application of the antitrust laws to restrictive patent license provisions and toward the invalidation of patents, it may be asked whether the licensing of a patent known to be invalid (whether or not *procured* by fraud) violates Sections 1 or 2 of the Sherman Act. Some Justice Department personnel have taken the position that such conduct is actionable under the Sherman Act if the proper market impact is shown.

D. EXCHANGES OF PATENT RIGHTS

Question: *What exchanges of patent rights are forbidden by the antitrust laws?*

"Cross-licensing" and "patent-pooling" are two types of arrangements for the interchange of patent rights. Cross-licensing is the licensing of one patent in exchange for the license back of another. A "patent-pool" is an arrangement under which one of the cooperating patent owners, or some separate patent-holding entity, is assigned the function of licensing others under the pooled patents. The "pooling" itself may be accomplished by cross licenses or by assignment or license of the patents to the entity that is to handle the licensing of others.

Statements by the Supreme Court in *Standard Oil Co.* v. *U.S. (Cracking Case)*, 283 U.S. 163 (1931), and later opinions make it clear that neither cross-licensing nor patent-pooling is necessarily a violation of the antitrust laws. As the *Standard Oil* opinion suggested, patent interchanges may promote competition. When they resolve patent conflicts, they are said to make technological advances available to more users. They make it possible to license the use of mutually dependent or "blocking" patents. The Supreme Court saw the need for exchanging patents or adjusting or settling conflicting patent claims. "Where there are legitimately conflicting claims or threatened interferences, a settlement by agreement, rather than litigation, is not precluded by the act. . . . An interchange of patent rights and a division of royalties according to the value attributed by the parties to their respective patent claims are frequently necessary if technical advancement is not to be blocked by threatened litigation. If the available advantages are open on reasonable terms to all manufacturers desiring to participate, such interchange may promote rather than restrain competition" (283 U.S. at 171).

In the *Cracking Case* the Supreme Court ordered dismissal of a Sherman Act suit brought by the Justice Department to challenge a series of agreements by which the major oil refiners exchanged their patent rights relating to the manufacture of gasoline by the cracking process. Each cross-licensing agreement empowered either party to license the process, and each agreement provided for a sharing of the royalties in fixed proportions. The cross-licensing companies retained only 55 percent of total cracking capacity. They continued to license other refiners to use their processes, and competing cracking processes were developed. Cracked gasoline represented about 26 percent of total gasoline production.

The Court noted that some interchanges of patent licenses may be antitrust violations. "Where domination exists, a pooling of competing process patents, or an exchange of licenses for the purpose of curtailing the manufacture and supply of an unpatented product, is beyond the privileges conferred by the patents and constitutes a violation of the Sherman Act. The lawful individual monopolies granted by the patent statutes cannot be unitedly exercised to restrain competition. . . . But an agreement for cross licensing and division of royalties violates the Act only when used to effect a monopoly, or to fix prices, or to impose otherwise an unreasonable restraint upon interstate commerce" (283 U.S. at 174). Under this statement of principles the Antitrust Division won a series of patent-pooling and cross-licensing cases in the Supreme Court during the 1940's beginning with *Hartford-Empire Co.* v. *U.S.*, 323 U.S. 386 (1945).

The court decisions that have found Sherman Act violations in patent interchanges have done so either on the basis of the purpose of the interchange, its effect, or the use the participants made of it. The effect of such an arrangement or the use to which it is put has sometimes been regarded as evidence of its purpose. Violations of the restraint-of-trade ban in Section 1 of the Sherman Act, the monopolization prohibition in Section 2, or both types of violations together have been found when the effect of the patent interchange was to exclude competitors from a particular market (*U.S.* v. *Singer Mfg. Co.*, 374 U.S. 174 (1963)); to regulate distribution and fix prices (*U.S.* v. *New Wrinkle, Inc.*, 342 U.S. 371 (1952)); to create monopoly power (*U.S.* v. *Imperial Chemical Industries, Ltd.*, 100 F.Supp. 504 (S.D.N.Y. 1951)); or to allocate fields of manufacture and to obtain dominance over an entire industry (*Hartford-Empire Co.* v. *U.S.*, 323 U.S. 386 (1945)).

When the restrictions imposed by the patent-interchange agreement include price fixing, the courts apply a rule of per se illegality (*U.S.* v. *General Instrument Corp.*, 87 F.Supp. 157 (D.N.J. 1949)). In *U.S.* v. *Line Material Co.*, 333 U.S. 287, 314 (1948), the Supreme Court declared that, even if a patent owner has a right under the doctrine of *U.S.* v. *General Electric Co.*, 272 U.S. 476 (1926), to fix the price at which his licensee sells the patented product, "when patentees join in an agreement . . . to maintain prices on their several products, that agreement, however advantageous it may be to stimulate the broader use of patents, is unlawful per se under the Sherman Act." See also *U.S.* v. *General Electric Co.* (Carboloy), 80 F.Supp. 989 (S.D.N.Y. 1948).

The *General Instrument* case may be said to stand for the proposition that the use to which restrictive industry power created by a patent interchange is put is immaterial. Support for the holding that mere existence of the power is unlawful was found in *American Tobacco Co.* v. *U.S.*, 328 U.S. 781 (1946). See also *U.S.* v. *Alcoa*, 91 F.Supp. 333 (S.D.N.Y. 1950).

The economic power, scope, or size of the combination has been a vital factor in patent-pooling decisions. In the *Hartford-Empire* case the pooled patents covered 94 percent of the industry; in *U.S.* v. *National Lead Co.*, 63 F.Supp. 513 (S.D.N.Y. 1945), *aff'd*, 332 U.S. 319 (1947), 90 percent of the industry was affected. In *U.S.* v.

Krasnov, 143 F.Supp. 184 (E.D. Pa. 1956), *aff'd,* 355 U.S. 5 (1957), the cooperating patent owners had 62 percent of the production in their industry.

The Justice Department's 1959 civil complaint against Singer Mfg. Co. charged Singer with violating both the restraint-of-trade provisions in Section 1 of the Sherman Act and the monopolization ban in Section 2 by entering into patent arrangements with Swiss and Italian competitors in the production of automatic zigzag sewing machines. In 1955 Singer had entered into a nonexclusive, world-wide, royalty-free, cross-licensing agreement with the Italian manufacturer to avoid litigation over conflicting claims. During negotiations with the Italian firm, Singer learned of a patent held by a Swiss manufacturer that would also raise a threat to Singer's patent claims. Singer learned later that the Swiss firm had a patent application pending in the U.S. Patent Office and had a cross-licensing agreement with the Italian producer. Singer began negotiations with the Swiss firm, using the argument that Singer would be in a stronger position to enforce the Swiss firm's U.S. patent against Japanese competition.

In April 1956, Singer executed a cross-licensing agreement with the Swiss company. The agreement covered a Singer patent and Singer's application for reissuance of the patent in the United States, the Swiss company's Italian and German patents, and an application by the Swiss firm for a United States patent. Each party promised to help the other to procure "the allowance in any country of claims as broad as possible" with regard to patent applications. A few months later the U.S. Patent Office declared an interference between the Singer reissue application and the Swiss company's application, and Singer wrote the Swiss company that the cross-licensing agreement called for settlement of this interference proceeding. Thereafter, Singer abandoned its application and the claim asserted in the Swiss Company's application was lifted verbatim from Singer's reissue claim. After issuance of the patent applied for by the Swiss firm, Singer filed two infringement suits against the largest importer of Japanese machines and obtained consent judgments in both. Singer also brought a Tariff Commission proceeding to exclude from the United States all imported machines infringing the Swiss firm's patent.

Chief Judge Ryan of the Federal District Court for Southern New York could find no antitrust violation in this series of patent arrangements (*U.S.* v. *Singer Manufacturing Co.,* 205 F.Supp. 394 (S.D.N.Y. 1962)). The Supreme Court did not go along with Judge Ryan's analysis of the evidence (374 U.S. 174 (1963)). It rejected, "as a matter of law, the inference that the attitude of suspicion, wariness, and self-preservation of the parties negated a conspiracy" violating Section 1 of the Sherman Act. (On appeal, the Government abandoned its Section 2 monopolization charge). Citing *U.S. v. Parke-Davis & Co.,* 362 U.S. 29 (1960), the Supreme Court declared that a Section 1 conspiracy can be inferred from conduct falling far short of "purely contractual arrangements." Here, according to the Court, the conduct of the parties showed a common purpose to suppress Japanese competition in the United States through the use of the patent, a purpose found to be clearly demonstrated by Singer's subsequent action before the Tariff Commission. "Singer went far beyond its claimed purpose of protecting its own 401 machine—it was protecting [the Swiss and Italian producers], the sole licensees under the patent at the time, under the same umbrella. This the Sherman Act will not permit."

Justice Harlan dissented. He took the position that the majority was not merely reversing Judge Ryan's conclusions of law but was overturning his findings of fact. Justice Harlan saw as the "true issue" in the case the issue of whether the district judge's findings were "clearly erroneous."

A footnote to the Court's opinion noted that the Government had contended that the cross-licensing agreement and the interference settlement were illegal apart from other circumstances of the case. Having concluded that "the entire course of dealings between the parties" established a Sherman Act conspiracy, the Court did not pass on those contentions, but Justice White, in a concurring opinion, advocated sustaining the Government's point on "the collusive termination of a Patent Office interference proceeding." According to Justice White, one of the Swiss company's reasons for entering into the settlement was a fear that Singer might in self-defense draw to the attention of the Patent Office earlier patents that the office was unaware of and that might cause the Swiss firm's claims to be invalidated. He pointed out that the public has an interest "in granting patent monopolies only when the progress of the useful arts and science will be furthered because as the consideration for its grant the public is given a novel and useful invention." That public interest is subordinated to private ends, he reasoned, when parties to an interference proceeding enter into a collusive settlement for the purpose of preventing the disclosures of prior inventions. "In my view, such collusion to secure a monopoly grant runs afoul of the Sherman Act's prohibitions against conspiracies in restraint of trade—if not bad per se, then such agreements are at least presumptively bad" (374 U.S. at 200).

Singer was cited by the Federal Trade Commission in *American Cyanamid Co.,* 63 F.T.C. 1747 (1963), *rev'd,* 363 F.2d 757 (6th Cir. 1966); *on remand,* 72 F.T.C. 623 (1967), *aff'd,* 401 F.2d 574 (6th Cir. 1968), to support the proposition that "misrepresentations and the intentional withholding of material information to obtain a commercially valuable patent is an unfair method of competition and an unfair act or practice." In a proceeding under Section 5 of the FTC Act against six antibiotic manufacturers, the Commission found that three of them had withheld material information from the Patent Office to procure the issuance of a patent on tetracycline to Chas. Pfizer & Co., Inc., a patent on which each of the other five firms subsequently accepted licenses with knowledge that Pfizer's claims were unpatentable. The Commission found that the misrepresentations to the Patent Office would be sufficient to sustain cancellation of the patent for fraud. Nevertheless, when the Commission got around to issuing its final order, it rejected its staff's suggestion that the drug producers be stripped of their patent rights and instead ordered compulsory licensing of the patent and unrestricted exchange of know-how.

None of these cases seems to make an distinction between patents that compete with each other or cover competing products and patents that complement each other, that is, must be used together to produce a saleable product. Decisions like the *Cracking Case, Hartford-Empire,* and *New Wrinkle* involved compromise arrangements among owners of competing patents. In the few cases that have involved interchanges of rights under noncompeting patents, the courts seem to have taken a softer line. For example, the court in *Baker-Cammack Hosiery Mills* v. *Davis Co.,* 181 F.2d 550 (4th Cir. 1950), *cert. denied,* 340 U.S. 824 (1950), saw no patent misuse in the pooling of complementary patents when the holder of the patents followed an open-licensing policy. In *U.S.* v. *Winslow,* 227 U.S. 202 (1913), the Supreme Court saw no Sherman Act violation in the pooling of complementary patents that put "from 70 to 80 percent of all the shoe machinery business . . . into a single hand."

The Supreme Court's decision in the *Singer* case may be said to suggest a retreat from the *Cracking Case* opinion's encouragement of settlements of disputes among owners of competing patents. Nevertheless, the language in the *Cracking Case* is still quoted and relied upon in patent-antitrust cases. The *Singer* case, it may be said, developed no novel doctrine. It was a "fact case," in which the district judge's findings and inferences were rejected. The Supreme Court applied well-established antitrust theories.

The most significant development in the *Singer* case may be the theory of illegality stated by Justice White in his concurring opinion. The *American Cyanamid* decision seems to indicate that the FTC, as well as the Antitrust Division, would regard collusive patent-interference settlements of the type found in Singer to be, in Justice White's words, "at least presumptively bad." Since settlement agreements must be filed with the Patent Office and are available for inspection by "government agencies," it has been suggested that they may have to be limited to interferences involving nothing more than disputes over the relative priority of the particular patent claims involved.

Later decisions conclude some of the decisions cited seem to establish the principle that even the exercise of legitimate patent rights can be regarded as an antitrust violation if that exercise is part of an overall conspiracy to restrain trade or to monopolize. In *Cutter Laboratories* v. *Lyophile-Cryochem Corp.*, 179 F.2d 80, 93 (9th Cir. 1949), it was held that a patent pool's power to exclude competition by fixing prices and charging unreasonable royalties "could not constitute unlawful monopolization unless accompanied by a purpose or intent to exclude competition," but the courts have generally held that evidence of intent or purpose is not necessary. It is sufficient if a restraint of trade or monopoly results from the cross-licensing or patent-pooling arrangement or from the use to which it is put (*Kobe, Inc.* v. *Dempsey Pump Co.*, 198 F.2d 416 (10th Cir. 1952), *cert. denied,* 344 U.S. 837 (1952); *U.S.* v. *General Instrument Corp.*, 87 F.Supp. 157 (D. N.J. 1949); *U.S.* v. *General Electric Co.* (lamps), 82 F.Supp. 753 (D. N.J. 1949)).

Perhaps the best evidence of the combining patent owners' intent is the licensing policy their pool adopts. As the Attorney General's Committee put it, "where interchanges grant licenses freely and at reasonable royalties and other terms, this should be viewed as a bona fide effort to make the patents available to all and free from conflict with the antitrust laws." When formation of a patent pool is contemplated, it is said that the participants should plan their licensing policy with the thought in mind that their licensing practices are subject to greater antitrust restrictions than those of a single patentee.

The relative scarcity of antitrust litigation involving patent pools suggests that they may no longer be a major antitrust enforcement problem. It could be that either they are being used relatively infrequently or they are being used with great circumspection. Some antitrust lawyers advise corporate clients to protect their patents by keeping clear of any patent pool that does not operate as a public utility, that is, is not open to every new patent and every patent owner in the industry. This "open-end" approach was endorsed in the *Cracking Case.*

Cross-licensing arrangements may not be subject to strictures as severe as those applied when the licensing of patents to others is delegated to a single entity. Yet even cross-licensing may be enjoined under the Sherman Act when the patent owners dominate their industry and overreach in providing for exchange of rights under future patents.

In its 1969 suit alleging that the four major automobile producers and a trade association had been parties to unlawful agreements that delayed development and installation of antipollution devices for motor vehicles, the Department of Justice attacked, among other things, a patent cross-licensing agreement alleged to restrict the price paid for patents developed by outsiders. The suit resulted in a consent decree (*U.S.* v. *Automobile Mfrs.,* 307 F.Supp. 617 (C.D. Calif. 1969), *appeal dismissed,* 397 U.S. 248 (1970)).

E. COURT ORDERS IN PATENT-ANTITRUST CASES

1. Anticompetitive Abuse

Question: *What results may follow anticompetitive abuse of patent rights?*

Antitrust violations involving the ownership and use of patents may result in the same sorts of court orders as other antitrust violations, including court injunctions, cease-and-desist orders, and treble-damage judgments. In addition, remedies have been developed by the courts to cope with the special problems of restoring competition found to have been destroyed by "abuse" or "misuse" of a patent owner's "lawful monopoly." The patentee has sometimes been forced to share his discovery by licensing its use at reasonable royalties; he has been temporarily denied income from licensees or infringers of his patent; his procurement of patents and patent licenses has been limited; and he has been stripped of his rights as patentee by injunctions, usually issued by consent, requiring him to grant royalty-free licenses or dedicating his patent rights to the public.

Temporary loss of royalties from licensees or, more frequently, damages from infringers, is the sanction invoked by assertion of the misuse-of-patent defense in patent-infringement suits brought by the patentee. Ordinarily, the patent owner's loss of income from other users of his invention continues in effect until he purges himself of the misuse. As defined by the Supreme Court in *B. B. Chemical Co.* v. *Ellis,* 314 U.S. 495, 498 (1942), the patent owner's right to demand compensation from other users of his invention is not revived until he "has fully abandoned [his] present method of restraining competition . . . and the consequences of that practice have been fully dissipated." In order to purge himself of misuse of his patent, a patent owner is not required to give the infringer a license (*Preformed Line Products Co.* v. *Fanner Mfg. Co.,* 328 F.2d 265 (6th Cir. 1964), *cert. denied,* 379 U.S. 846 (1964)).

Compulsory licensing is the most common form of remedy sought and granted in Justice Department suits to enjoin antitrust violations involving the use of patents. Since the 1940's, the Antitrust Division has followed a policy of demanding compulsory licensing in almost every antitrust suit involving patents. It has obtained more than a hundred judgments, most of them by consent, with compulsory-licensing terms. The patent owner has usually been permitted to negotiate a reasonable royalty for his license, but there have been instances, such as *U.S.* v. *Western Electric Co.,* 1956 Trade Cas. ¶68,246 (D. N.J. 1956), and *U.S.* v. *Radio Corp. of America,* 1958 Trade Cas. ¶69,164 (S.D.N.Y. 1958), in which the Government has been able to negotiate a consent decree requiring the licensing of patents on a royalty-free basis. In some cases, for example, *U.S.* v. *A. B. Dick Co.* 1948–49 Trade Cas. ¶62,233 (N.D. Ohio 1948); *U.S.* v. *Magnaflux Corp.,* 1957 Trade Cas. ¶68,707 (N.D. Ill. 1957); *U.S.* v. *The Greyhound Corp.,* 1957 Trade Cas. ¶68,756 (N.D. Ill. 1957), outright dedication of patents to the public has been agreed to. In *U.S.* v. *General Electric Co.* (lamps), 82 F.Supp. 753 (D. N.J. 1949), 115 F.Supp. 835 (D. N.J. 1953), a litigated case, there was similar dedication.

In *Hartford-Empire Co.* v. *U.S.,* 323 U.S. 386 (1945), and *U.S.* v. *National Lead Co.,* 332 U.S. 319 (1947), the Supreme Court recognized compulsory reasonable-royalty licensing as an antitrust remedy, but the propriety and the constitutionality of royalty-free compulsory licensing and outright dedication has been the subject of much disagreement. In the *Hartford-Empire* case, royalty-free licensing terms in a judgment were condemned because they would "in effect confiscate considerable portions of the appellant's property" and therefore "go beyond what is required to dissolve the combination and prevent future combinations of like character." In the *National Lead* case the Supreme Court refused to require the issuance of royalty-free licenses "without reaching the question whether royalty-free licensing or a perpetual injunction against the enforcement of a patent is permissible as a matter of law in any case. . . . We do not, in this case, face the issue of the constitutionality of such an order. That issue would arise only in a case where the order would be more necessary and appropriate to the enforcement of the antitrust act than here."

In its 1955 report, the Attorney General's National Committee to Study the Antitrust Laws was closely divided on this question. Stressing the *Hartford-Empire* opinion's use of the word "confiscate," a majority of the Committee deemed "compulsory license free of royalties and dedication penal rather than remedial in character, and hence beyond the Sherman Act's authority to 'prevent and restrain' violations." Royalty-free licensing and dedication were distinguished from divestiture requirements in antitrust judgments because "divestiture . . . allows its owner whatever recompense the market affords" (1955 Report, p. 257). In dissent, "a substantial minority" of the Committee made three points: "They feel, first, that Hartford-Empire and National Lead pronounce no blanket statutory or constitutional ban on royalty-free licensing or dedication, but merely that a court will decree no more in any one case than is needed to achieve effective competition. Second, they contend that dedication or royalty-free licensing is in principle no more 'confiscatory' than compulsory power to earn monopoly profits. Finally, in the view of these members, royalty-free licensing or dedication may in appropriate cases be essential to that competition the statute requires and the courts should have power to decree such relief, when necessary" (p. 258).

The language of district judges framing antitrust decrees shows similar disagreement. In *U.S.* v. *Vehicular Parking, Ltd.,* 61 F.Supp. 656 (D. Del. 1945), which was decided before the Supreme Court's *National Lead* decision, a district court read *Hartford-Empire* as denying it power to require royalty-free licensing. In *U.S.* v. *Imperial Chemical Industries, Ltd.,* 105 F.Supp. 215 (S.D.N.Y. 1952), the district judge had the benefit of both the *Hartford-Empire* and the *National Lead* opinions and from them concluded that his power to require royalty-free licenses "is open to serious question," in fact, to "a substantial constitutional question. . . . We hold that in the circumstances before us, compulsory royalty-free licensing may not be decreed in the absence of legislative authority and the sanction of explicit interpretation of existing statutes by higher courts affirmatively permitting such action." In the *General Electric* (lamp) case a district court concluded from reading the *National Lead* opinion that the Supreme Court had "substantially diluted its pronouncement in Hartford-Empire." *National Lead* was read as suggesting, "if it indeed does not invite," the imposition of royalty-free licensing requirements "where the circumstances of patent abuse prescribe it." The district judge went on to require actual dedication of patents for lamps and lamp parts.

Consent judgments allowing the patent owner to collect a uniform reasonable royalty establish a procedure under which competitors desiring licenses first apply to the patent owner. The royalty rate is then set by negotiations between the applicant and the patent owner. If they cannot agree, the judgment usually provides for a court hearing and determination of a reasonable rate. Ordinarily, the Attorney General must be given notice of any such hearing and a right to participate in it. In practice, most royalty rates have been set by negotiation between the parties without involvement of either the courts or the Justice Department. In 1956 a letter from the

Assistant Attorney General in charge of the Antitrust Division to
Senator Joseph C. O'Mahoney stated a Justice Department policy
"not to participate in such proceedings. . . . We feel that such matters are properly the concern only of the patentee and the applicant for a license so long as the applicant is afforded protection, by
resort to the court, against such arbitrary royalties as might amount
to a refusal to license."

Although most compulsory-licensing provisions in antitrust decrees
are made applicable to patents held by the defendant on the date
the decree becomes effective, or to existing patents specifically enumerated in the decree, there have been judgments requiring the
licensing of future patents. In *U.S.* v. *American Cyanamid Co.,* 1964
Trade Cas. ¶71,166 (S.D.N.Y. 1964), the consent judgment required
in some areas licensing of all future patents acquired within five
years of the date of the judgment. In *U.S.* v. *Besser Mfg. Co.,* 343
U.S. 444 (1952), the judgment required licensing on a reasonable-
royalty basis of all existing patents, all patents issued within the
next 10 years, and all patents issued on applications filed within the
next 10 years. The consent order in *U.S.* v. *General Motors Corp.,*
1965 Trade Cas. ¶71,624 (E.D. Mich. 1965), provided for (1) full-
term royalty-free licensing of all existing patents; (2) five-year
royalty-free licensing for patents obtained during the five years immediately after entry of the judgment, with reasonable-royalty licensing after the first five years; and (3) full-term reasonable-royalty
licensing of any patent obtained during the second five-year period
after entry of the judgment.

In the *ICI* case, the district court, in rejecting a demand for
compulsory licensing of future patents, used language that would
limit such relief to exceptional situations. "Patents which had not
been granted, and technology which had not been developed could
not have been put to misuse in the past. We may not act entirely
upon an assumption that the defendants will continue in their disregard of the law and violate the injunctions of a final judgment.
Cf. *Timken Roller Bearing Co.* v. *United States,* 341 U.S. 593, 604
(1951). . . . We may not take from the defendants all incentive for
future endeavour by depriving them in advance of the rewards
which might come to them from future patents and technology.
Such relief 'would discourage rather than encourage competitive
research.' *United States* v. *National Lead,* 332 U.S. 319, 359 (1947)."

One can find among patent-antitrust judgments special restrictions
or exceptions apparently related to unusual factual situations. There
are several making a license-all-applicants requirement operative
only in the event the defendant decides to grant someone a license
under his patent (*U.S.* v. *General Electric Co.,* 1948–49 Trade Cas.
¶62,518 (S.D. Calif. 1949); *U.S.* v. *Liquidometer Corp.,* 1950–51

Trade Cas. ¶62,867 (S.D.N.Y. 1951); *U.S.* v. *General Railway Signal Co.,* 1955 Trade Cas. ¶67,992 (W.D.N.Y. 1955). In the *American Cyanamid* decree there was a provision that the taking of a license under the terms of the judgment was not to be construed as precluding the licensee "from attacking, at any time, the validity or scope of any of said patents." In *U.S.* v. *IBM Corp.,* 1956 Trade Cas. ¶68,245 (S.D.N.Y. 1956), compulsory licensing was conditioned upon agreement by the license applicant not to bring patent-infringement suits against IBM.

Compulsory-licensing provisions are sometimes accompanied by requirements that licensees be supplied with the "know-how" necessary to make full use of the patented device or process. Such a requirement in the *ICI* decree was based on findings "that the exchange of know-how—as well as that of patents—served as a direct means for the accomplishment of the unlawful restraints" and that "the supplying of such know-how and technology is necessary to the efficient use of the licensed patents and to the production by the licensee of products comparable in quality and cost of production to that of the licensor." Besides that litigated case, there have been consent judgments requiring either the licensing of know-how or the furnishing of specific technological aids at cost. In some of these cases, it does not appear that exchange of know-how and technology, as opposed to mere exchange of patent rights, was a significant element in the illegal restraint of trade, but the transfer of know-how was apparently regarded by the Government as important to effective use of the patents that were ordered to be licensed and to the restoration of competition. For examples, see *U.S.* v. *A.B. Dick Co.,* 1948–49 Trade Cas. ¶62,233 (N.D. Ohio 1948); *U.S.* v. *Technicolor, Inc.,* 1950 Trade Cas. ¶62,586 (S.D. Calif. 1950); *U.S.* v. *Cincinnati Milling Machine Co.,* 1954 Trade Cas. ¶67,733 (E.D. Mich. 1954); *U.S.* v. *Food Machinery & Chemical Corp.,* 1954 Trade Cas. ¶67,829 (N.D. Calif. 1954); *U.S.* v. *American Steel Foundries,* 1955 Trade Cas. ¶68,156 (N.D. Ohio 1955); and *U.S.* v. *Kelsey-Hayes Wheel Co.,* 1955 Trade Cas. ¶68,093 (E.D. Mich. 1955).

There are judgment provisions which condition compulsory licensing upon the license applicant's willingness to reciprocate, to give a similar return license on any patents he may have or obtain. "Grantback" covenants can be used in ways that violate the antitrust laws, and the Antitrust Division has argued that they are illegal per se. In *U.S.* v. *Alcoa,* 91 F.Supp. 333 (S.D.N.Y. 1950), grantback clauses were stricken from Alcoa's patent licenses, even though they represented the only consideration Alcoa received for the licenses, with the result that compulsory royalty-free licensing was, in effect, decreed. The judgments finally entered in the *ICI* case and in *U.S.* v. *National Lead Co.,* 332 U.S. 319 (1947), conditioned their compulsory-licensing provisions on agreements by license applicants to grantback. In *U.S.* v. *United States Gypsum Co.*, 340 U.S. 76 (1950), without further discussion of the issue, the Supreme Court said: "In the present case there should be no requirements of reciprocal grants," apparently leaving the matter to the discretion of the district courts and the special circumstances of each case. Relying on that decision, the district court in the *General Electric* (lamp) case, 82 F.Supp. 753 (D. N.J. 1953), refused to add reciprocal-licensing conditions, agreeing with the Government that such a qualification would perpetuate GE's domination of the industry. In the consent judgment in *U.S.* v. *Western Electric Co., Inc.*, 1956 Trade Cas. ¶68,246 (D.N.J. 1956), the Government agreed to the defendant's conditioning of his patent licenses upon grantback arrangements.

In 1960, the staff of the Senate Judiciary Committee's Subcommittee on Patents, Trademarks, and Copyrights reported the results of a survey of the importance and effectiveness of compulsory-licensing provisions in antitrust decrees (Staff of Senate Committee on the Judiciary's Subcommittee on Patents, Trademarks, and Copyrights, 86th Cong., 2d Sess., COMPULSORY PATENT LICENSING UNDER ANTITRUST JUDGMENTS (1960)). "In some cases compulsory licensing has proved beneficial to licensees, particularly small business, and thus stimulated competition, while in others it has resulted in no discernible benefits. The number of licenses issued under a particular judgment ranges from zero to over 300. In those cases where licenses have been issued, licensees have reported varying degrees of success in their utilization of the licensed patents. In some cases they have stated that the patents have not contributed significantly to their operations. In others, however, licensees have indicated that the licensed patents have been very important to them, and have enabled them to make a product or expand into a field that otherwise might have been closed to them.

"The survey disclosed that among the companies which have benefited from compulsory licensing are a large number that might be classified as 'small business,' whose own research facilities are limited by comparison with those of large antitrust defendants. This comment is particularly applicable in those situations where utilization of the licensed patents did not require large capital expenditures."

After analyzing the judgments in individual cases, the staff report concluded that litigated judgments seem more likely to produce significant compulsory-licensing results than consent judgments. "This is hardly surprising since antitrust decrees entered after a trial are more likely to provide effective relief than those entered by consent before there is any litigation. A trial defines the trade restraining practices of the defendant and makes a record of the specific complaints which have led to the institution of the action. These specific complaints furnish concrete illustrations of the evils which the relief sought is intended to cure. The trial court's opinion describes the conduct which is thought to violate the law and ordinarily indicates the kind of injunction that the court believes will provide effective relief. Without such a judicial evaluation of an antitrust complaint the framing of effective patent relief is extremely difficult."

The staff report also stressed that consent-decree negotiations, being conducted in secrecy, exclude the defendant's competitors from any role in framing the decree. As a result, the Antitrust Division may sometimes unwittingly accept a defendant's offer to license patents that have no competitive significance and forego other relief that might be more effective. The Division's practice of filing proposed consent judgments 30 days before they become final and retaining the right to withdraw its consent now provides a way for competitors to be heard.

At one time the most serious sanction a patent owner had to fear if he engaged in anticompetitive misuse of his patent was loss of his right to prevent infringements. Today the infringer's misuse defense is usually accompanied by an affirmative counterclaim for treble damages under the antitrust laws. While the task of proving damages in an antitrust case is seldom a simple one, if the infringer succeeds, the financial consequences to the patent owner can be disastrous.

Lawyers seem to agree that compulsory licensing is an appropriate form of relief against a patent owner once it has been established that he has abused or misused his patent monopoly in violation of the antitrust laws, but universal compulsory licensing has few supporters. Many experts, including George E. Frost, author of a study entitled THE PATENT SYSTEM IN THE MODERN ECONOMY, prepared in 1957 for the Senate Judiciary Committee's Subcommittee on Patents, Trademarks, and Copyrights, say that in some areas effectiveness of the patent system as a device for promoting competition in research and development depends upon complete freedom from compulsory licensing.

2. Government Challenge to Patents

Question: *Does the Government have a roving commission to challenge the validity of any patent involved in an antitrust violation?*

On January 22, 1973, the Supreme Court held that when a patent is directly involved in an antitrust violation and the Government can make a substantial showing that effective relief requires some form of restriction on the patent rights, the Government may challenge the validity of the patent regardless of whether the owner relies on the patent in defending the antitrust action (*U.S.* v. *Glaxo Group Ltd.*, 597 ATRR F-1 (1973)). (Justice White wrote the majority opinion, and Justice Rehnquist, with whom Justices Stewart and Blackman concurred, dissented.)

The case arose out of a cross-licensing arrangement involving griseofulvin, the active ingredient of a drug used in the treatment of fungus infections. The bulk form of griseofulvin itself was unpatented in the United States, but appellee Imperial Chemical Corporation (ICI) held a patent on the administration of that drug internally to treat fungus diseases of the skin, and Glaxo Groups Limited (Glaxo) held various patents on a method for manufacturing the drug in bulk form, as well as a patent on an improved microsize form of griseofulvin. As part of the cross-licensing agreement between ICI and Glaxo, each party was permitted to license the other's patents. ICI agreed further "not to sell and to use its best endeavors to prevent its subsidiaries and associates from selling any griseofulvin in bulk to any independent third party without Glaxo's express consent in writing."

ICI and Glaxo granted a total of three licenses for the American market, and they each agreed with their respective distributor licensees to sell the active ingredients to them in bulk form. The licensing agreements each contained a provision prohibiting the resale of the drug in bulk form. (Although two of the licensees obtained the right to manufacture the active ingredient in bulk form as well as the right to process the bulk form into a dosage form drug and to sell it in dosage form, none of the licensees, in practice, manufactured the active ingredient in bulk form.)

The district court, citing *U.S.* v. *Arnold, Schwinn & Co.*, 388 U.S. 365 (1967), held that the bulk-sales restriction in the licensing agreement between ICI and its exclusive U.S. distributor was per se unlawful under Section 1 of the Sherman Act. The court entered similar orders holding illegal the bulk-sales restriction in the Glaxo-ICI cross-licensing agreements with its two distributors. (There was no appeal from these determinations.) Although the court enjoined further use of the bulk-sales restrictions, it denied the Government's motion to challenge the validity of the ICI and Glaxo patents when they were not relied upon as a defense to the antitrust claims. The court also refused to order compulsory, nondiscriminatory sales of the bulk form of the drug and reasonable-royalty licensing of the Glaxo and ICI patents.

The Supreme Court held that the district court erred in refusing to allow the attack on the patents and in refusing to grant the relief of compulsory sales and licensing. The Court observed that compulsory sales and licensing were well established forms of relief and that the appellees had opposed such relief on the grounds that it would " 'deny defendants an essential ingredient of their rights under the patent system,' and that there was no warrant for 'such drastic forfeiture of their rights.' " The Court stated: "[i]n this context, where the court would necessarily be dealing with the future enforceability of the patents we think it would have been appropriate, if it appeared that the Government's claims for further relief were substantial, for the court to have also entertained the Government's challenge to the validity of those patents."

The Court attempted to clarify its holding by stating that it did not grant the Government unlimited authority to attack a patent by basing an antitrust claim on the mere assertion that a patent is invalid. The majority disavowed any intention of vesting the Government with "a roving commission to question the validity of any patent lurking in the background of an antitrust case." The issue of effective relief, however, "often involves a substantial question as to whether it is necessary to limit the bundle of rights normally vested in the owner of a patent, which in itself can be a complex and difficult issue. The litigation would usually proceed on the assumption that valid patents are involved; but if this basic assumption is itself challenged, we perceive no good reason, either in terms of the patent system or of judicial administration, for refusing to hear and decide it."

The Court concluded that in this case the district court should have permitted the collateral attack on the ICI patent and on the Glaxo microsize patents and, accordingly, should have granted the additional relief of compulsory sales and licensing.

Justice Rehnquist dissented on the ground that there was an insufficient relationship between the challenged patents and the antitrust violations. He characterized the Court's ruling as being in fact a grant to the Government of a "roving commission" to attack "any patent owned by an antitrust defendant which in any way related to the background of the claimed antitrust violation." Rehnquist further asserted that there was neither statutory nor case authority for allowing collateral attacks on patent validity.

Does the Government have, as Justice Rehnquist suggested, a "roving commission" to attack patents? It seems clear that the Government cannot collaterally attack a patent merely on the assertion of patent invalidity. However, where the patent is directly involved in an antitrust violation, it would appear that the Government does have a wide range of authority. As the majority in *Glaxo* suggested, court-imposed restrictions on patents are normal forms of relief in such cases. It seems likely, therefore, that the Government will reserve the right to show that effective relief requires some restricting of patent rights to enable it to attack the patent.

What degree of involvement in the antitrust violation is necessary before a patent becomes vulnerable? In discussing the need for compulsory rules and licensing, the majority found that "it is clear from the evidence" that the "patents gave the appellees the economic leverage with which to insist upon and enforce the bulk-sales restrictions imposed on the licensees." It would appear that where an unlawful transaction depends in some degree on the market power afforded by a patent, the patent is sufficiently involved in the violation.

One might ask what relevance does the validity of a patent have if, as in *Glaxo,* compulsory sales and licensing at reasonable royalties are to be ordered anyway. The simple answer is that if the patent is invalid, then there is no need for a license.

Although it may have surprised some that the Court grounded its decision to such a great extent on the need for effective relief, the decision would seem to be consistent with the recent trend marked by *Walker Process Equip., Inc.,* v. *Food Mach. & Chem. Corp.,* 382 U.S. 172 (1965), and *Lear, Inc.* v. *Adkins,* 395 U.S. 653 (1969), in which the Court asserted a strong public policy in favor of testing the validity of patents. The teaching of *Glaxo* would seem to be that if a patent holder attempts to extend his market power beyond that inherent in the patent itself, by including unlawful provisions in his licensing agreements, the patent itself is in jeopardy.

PART VI

Regulated Industries

A. ANTITRUST IN THE REGULATED INDUSTRIES

Question: *Are public utilities exempt from the antitrust laws?*

In the early 1960's increased awareness of, and concern about, the antitrust laws brought to the fore the problem of applying antitrust policy to the regulated industries. The regulators themselves were developing a greater awareness of antitrust considerations. For example, on January 12, 1962, the Federal Power Commission issued an order "defining issues" in a matter involving an application by Southwest Gas Corp., a natural gas distributor in Arizona, California, and Nevada, to acquire the facilities of Nevada Gas Pipe Line Co. The application had previously been scheduled for a short form procedure. In ordering a full formal hearing, the Federal Power Commission made the unprecedented move of giving notice that, in addition to questions generally considered in connection with certificate applications, "it appears to be in the public interest that the Commission also consider, more specifically, whether the application, which involves a proposed merger of the applicant with an interstate pipeline, should be granted in light of the policies and provisions of the antitrust laws of the United States."

In 1955, the Attorney General's National Committee to Study the Antitrust Laws had recommended closer liaison between the Antitrust Division and the regulatory agencies. The Committee reported "no formal Antitrust Division policy" requiring "consultation with regulatory agencies regarding complaints involving matters subject to their regulation. When the Department of Justice is called upon to support administrative orders on review, however, the present Attorney General has required discussion with the agency involved before the Department determines whether or not to support the agency's order or confess error. Similarly, responses from several regulatory agencies suggest that their procedures do not require consultation with the Antitrust Division regarding agency action which may immunize conduct from the antitrust laws."

The Committee stated its belief "that broader and more formalized liaison procedures are in order" but recognized "that the

Antitrust Division, in discharging its obligations, cannot be bound by any administrative agency's view of Division jurisdiction." The Committee was far from unanimous in its analysis of antitrust considerations in the regulated industries. Some members of the Committee felt it an error to invoke a "presumption" "in favor of competition in the regulation of industries such as the railroads, motor carriers, air lines, and common carriers' communication." Other members of the Committee felt strongly that the Report did not go far enough in reexamining statutory exemptions to the antitrust laws and questioning "whether the exemption process had gone too far."

In his Report on Regulatory Agencies in December 1960, James M. Landis found "a lack of policy formulation within agencies" and "an almost complete barrenness of such formulation for those matters with which groups of agencies are concerned." Among the "many areas calling for well coordinated attacks upon problems common to many agencies," Mr. Landis included those of "transportation, communications, energy, monopoly, and unfair trade practices." Mr. Landis found that "the inability to effect interagency coordination has been responsible for the lack of any policy as to the nature of competition that should exist as between forms of transportation and also as between the carriers themselves."

The Antitrust Division has since created a separate staff section called the Public Counsel Section. In his order creating the new unit, Lee Loevinger stated that the Section would "represent public interest in competition and in the preservation of a free competitive economy in those situations that do not fall within the scope of activity of the litigating sections and other offices, and the Appellate Section. Specifically, the Public Counsel Section shall appear before executive, administrative and regulatory agencies when such appearance is authorized; shall file reports to such agencies and to Congress as required or authorized; shall conduct litigation assigned to it involving issues of antitrust or administrative law, and litigation involving kindred law enforcement, transportation, power and public utility industries, including electric, gas, water, or nuclear power, and involving the Federal Trade Commission; and shall perform other assigned functions."

Congress has decided that in some industries the Sherman Act policy of free and open competition should be modified by regulation. The regulatory body may, by its own action or by approval of private conduct, control market entry, eliminate existing competition, and fix rates or prices. For example, the Interstate Commerce Act now provides that "any carriers participating in a transaction approved or authorized are relieved from the operation of the antitrust laws" (49 U.S.C. § 5 (11)). As originally enacted in 1887, three years before the Sherman Act, the Interstate Commerce Act made no reference to antitrust prohibitions. See *U.S.* v. *Trans-Missouri Freight Association,* 166 U.S. 290 (1897). The Federal Communications Act (47 U.S.C. § 222) contains provisions comparable to the Interstate Commerce Act's present language.

Other regulatory statutes are less clear. In approving a merger of natural gas companies, the Federal Power Commission has no authority to declare the transaction immune from any antitrust law. The Packers and Stockyards Act (7 U.S.C. § 181) is in a class by itself. Section 227 states that the Federal Trade Commission shall have no jurisdiction over any matter assigned by the statute to the Secretary of Agriculture. Section 225 just as clearly and explicitly disclaims any intent to change or displace the antitrust laws. In *McCleneghan* v. *Union Stockyards Co.,* 298 F.2d 659 (8th Cir. 1962), the court decided that the Agriculture Department should be given a chance to act before antitrust action is taken against a livestock marketing practice. The court noted that the Packers Act contains "a comprehensive plan for the supervision of stockyards and market agencies," including administrative action against antitrust violations.

Antitrust problems in the regulated industries present at least three different types of questions: (1) Which tribunal decides? (2) Should the Antitrust Division and the agency both be represented at any proceedings or can action of one exclude the other? (3) What weight should be given to antitrust considerations when they are in conflict with other policies?

Because of *McLean Trucking Co* v. *U.S.,* 321 U.S. 67 (1944), the Antitrust Division apparently concedes that the Interstate Commerce Commission has plenary jurisdiction to approve mergers that otherwise would violate the Sherman Act, but the Antitrust Division has opposed railroad mergers before the ICC. The Antitrust Division has tended to prefer competition among giant systems rather than relying on ICC control over local monopolies to protect the public.

In Civil Aeronautics Board proceedings, antitrust factors may carry more weight because of statutory limitations on the CAB's approval of a merger creating a monopoly. These limitations might bar the Board from allowing two carriers on the same route to merge when a monopoly on the air traffic route would thereby be created. When the Federal Aviation Act's language was called to the court's attention in the United-Capital merger case, *Northwest Airlines, Inc.* v. *CAB,* 303 F.2d 395 (D.C. Cir. 1962), the court said it had "little to do with the problem." Nevertheless, the court considered competitive effect and held that the merger had not created a monopoly but in fact had "forestalled or at least cushioned a monopolistic development."

Section 414 of the Federal Aviation Act immunizes from antitrust liability any conduct approved by a CAB order issued under Section 408. In *Hughes Tool Co.* v. *TWA, Inc.,* 596 ATRR D-1 (1973), the Supreme Court reversed a court of appeals decision (449 F.2d 51 (2d Cir. 1971)), which had affirmed a default judgment against Hughes in an antitrust treble-damage action. The Supreme Court held that the CAB's control and surveillance of the activities of Hughes gave the transactions complained of immunity from the antitrust laws.

Two Supreme Court cases have involved the question of the appropriate tribunal for determining the role of competition in a regulated industry. One held that the proper tribunal was the court; another, that the administrative agency had exclusive jurisdiction. In the first case, El Paso Natural Gas Co. acquired 99.8 percent of the outstanding stock of the Pacific Northwest Pipeline Corp. The Department of Justice filed a suit in the U.S. District Court in Utah alleging that this acquisition of stock violated Section 7 of the Clayton Act. Two weeks later, El Paso filed an application with the Federal Power Commission for approval of a merger of Pacific's assets into El Paso's system. Section 7 (c) of the Natural Gas Act (15 U.S.C. § 717 (f)) states that no natural gas company may acquire the "facilities or extensions thereof" of another such company unless the FPC issues a certificate of public convenience and necessity. (The section does not mention the acquisition of stock in such a company.) El Paso made a motion in the district court that the Justice Department's suit be stayed, claiming the FPC had "primary jurisdiction" over this merger. Eventually, after the FPC had started its hearings, in which the Justice Department declined to participate, the motion was granted. The FPC approved the merger, stating: "Any lessening of competition, whether in the consumer markets or the producing fields, does not prevent our approving the merger because there are other factors which outweigh the elimination of Pacific as a competitor. In any case, it appears that any lessening of competition is not substantial" (22 F.P.C. 1091, 1095).

The State of California had intervened in these administrative proceedings to oppose approval of the merger. Its appeal of the FPC's ruling to the Court of Appeals for the District of Columbia Circuit was unsuccessful. The court of appeals saw no inconsistency between a ruling that the acquisition of the assets of one natural gas company by another was in the public interest and a possibility that such an acquisition might run afoul of the antitrust laws if these companies were in a normally competitive, rather than a regulated industry (*State of California* v. *FPC,* 296 F.2d 348 (D.C. Cir. 1961)).

The court of appeals was reversed by the Supreme Court (369 U.S. 482 (1962)). The FPC's order approving the asset merger was vacated. The Supreme Court, in an opinion by Justice Douglas, ruled that "orderly procedure" required the FPC to await the decision in the Justice Department's antitrust suit before taking action. The Commission, it was noted, had no statutory power under the Natural Gas Act to adjudicate antitrust issues, as did some other agencies, such as the Interstate Commerce Commission. Likewise, the FPC was not one of the agencies listed in Section 11 of the Clayton Act as empowered to enforce Section 7 of that Act.

There is a proviso in Section 7 of the Clayton Act that the section shall not apply to "transactions duly consummated pursuant to authority given by the . . . Federal Power Commission." The Justice Department's suit challenged the stock acquisition. Section 7 of the Natural Gas Act gives the FPC jurisdiction to approve asset acquisitions. The argument was made that, if the FPC's order were affirmed, it would be allowed to do indirectly what it could not do directly, i.e. approve the stock acquisition.

The case was remanded to the Utah Federal District Court. Finding the Government had failed to prove a Clayton Act violation, the district court dismissed the complaint (*U.S.* v. *El Paso Natural Gas Co.,* 1962 Trade Cas. ¶70,571 (D. Utah 1962)). The Supreme Court reversed (376 U.S. 651 (1964)) and directed the district court to order divestiture. The majority found there was sufficient evidence that the acquisition might substantially lessen competition and that the acquisition violated Section 7 of the Clayton Act.

In the *Panagra* case, Pan American and Grace entered into an agreement (in 1928) under which Panagra was to have the exclusive right to air traffic along the West Coast of South America, while Pan American was to be free from competition in the rest of South America and north of the Canal Zone. In December 1941, Grace filed a petition before the Civil Aeronautics Board requesting that Panagra's certificate be amended to provide for a terminal in continental United States. Pan American attempted to prevent this modification, and, in April 1942, Grace requested the CAB to order Pan American to divest itself of its holdings in Panagra. Grace relied on the cease-and-desist power granted the Board in Section 411 of the Civil Aeronautics Act, now the Federal Aviation Act, 49 U.S.C. § 1381, which is patterned after Section 5 of the Federal Trade Commission Act.

The CAB was unable to resolve the Pan Am-Grace conflict and twice, once in 1945 and again in 1953, requested the Attorney General to institute an antitrust suit. The Justice Department filed a suit against all three companies, alleging violations of Sections 1 and 2 of the Sherman Act. Pan American was charged with using its 50-percent control over Panagra to prevent it from extending its route north of the Canal Zone. The district court dismissed the complaint regarding Grace and Panagra but found that Pan American had violated Section 2 of the Sherman Act by blocking Panagra's certificate application to the CAB (*U.S.* v. *Pan American World Airways, Inc.,* 193 F.Supp. 18 (S.D.N.Y. 1961)).

The Supreme Court ruled that the entire complaint should have been dismissed (371 U.S. 296 (1963)). The Court concluded, in an opinion by Justice Douglas, that the questions involved had "been entrusted to the Board" by Congress when it passed Section 411 of the Civil Aeronautics Act. That tribunal had primary and exclusive jurisdiction over the transactions involved, even though they occurred before the passage of the Act in 1938, and even though antitrust issues were involved. Stressing the "unfair practices" and "unfair methods of competition" language in Section 411 of the Federal Aviation Act, the Supreme Court said: "It seems to us, therefore, that the Act leaves to the Board under Section 411 all questions of injunctive relief against the division of territories or the allocation of routes or against combinations between common carriers and air carriers."

The Court hesitated to hold that the Federal Aviation Act is "designed completely to displace the antitrust laws—absent an unequivocally declared congressional purpose so to do. While the Board is empowered to deal with numerous aspects of what are normally thought of as antitrust problems, those expressly entrusted to it encompass only a fraction of the total. Apart from orders which give immunity from the antitrust laws by reason of Section 414, the whole criminal law enforcement problem remains unaffected by the Act. . . . Moreover, on the civil side violations of antitrust laws other than those enumerated in the Act might be imagined. We, therefore, refuse to hold that there are no antitrust violations left to the Department of Justice to enforce."

When the Supreme Court heard arguments in two additional antitrust cases representing attacks on transactions that were executed under some degree of administrative supervision—a national bank merger approved by the Comptroller of the Currency (*U.S.* v. *Phila. Nat'l. Bank,* 374 U.S. 321 (1963)) and a New York Stock Exchange rule adopted without objection from the Securities and Exchange Commission (*Silver* v. *New York Stock Exchange,* 373 U.S. 341 (1963))—the *El Paso* and *Panagra* cases received only casual mention. The absence of any extensive discussion of the meaning and impact of these two decisions on application of the antitrust laws to regulated industries confirmed a conclusion that many antitrust lawyers had already drawn from the two opinions. Each regulated industry presents a unique problem when its status under the

antitrust laws needs definition or clarification. The Supreme Court
has said that Congress has the responsibility of deciding the role of
competition for each regulated industry. Therefore, each case is decided on the basis of the wording of the particular statute involved.

A natural corollary to that proposition is a general recognition
that the apparent inconsistency between the two cases is more apparent than real. The Court subordinated FPC action in the *El Paso*
case and excluded court action in the *Panagra* case because it was
dealing with regulatory statutes in which Congress said two different
things. A detailed study of legislative history and an assessment of
the "pervasiveness" of the "regulatory scheme" set out in the particular statute are emphasized in each of the Court's opinions on
the function of antitrust policy in regulated industries.

Dissenting in the *El Paso* case, Justice Harlan insisted that the
majority holding "is not limited to Federal Power Commission proceedings." In the *Panagra* case, Justice Brennan suggested that the
majority decision effected "a pro tanto repeal of the antitrust laws."
Nevertheless, although cited in passing, neither opinion appeared to
be of much significance in the disposition of the *New York Stock
Exchange* or *Philadelphia bank* cases.

The *Panagra* opinion is not generally regarded as conflicting with
the Court's 1959 decision denying the Federal Communications
Commission authority to decide antitrust issues (*U.S.* v. *RCA,* 358
U.S. 334 (1959)). The Federal Communications Act may be the
clearest of all the regulatory statutes in its references to, and coordination with, the antitrust laws. Section 313 (47 U.S.C. § 313) makes
the antitrust laws applicable to the industry and even recognizes
the power of a court to revoke a broadcasting license granted by
the FCC.

The *Panagra* case is regarded by some as a sport. There was no
real dispute between the CAB and the Justice Department's Antitrust Division over either jurisdiction or policy. Both agencies were
aiming at the same result, a split-up of Panagra, Pan American, and
Grace. Neither considered the CAB's powers adequate to accomplish that result. Another factor that may have affected the outcome
of the case was the involvement of foreign air routes, an area in
which the President's personal foreign-relations responsibilities, as
well as the "regulatory scheme," must be taken into consideration.

Early in 1973, the Supreme Court issued three decisions involving
antitrust in regulated industries. Some doubt that the decisions can
be reconciled on a doctrinal basis. In the first case, *Hughes Tool
Co.* v. *TWA, Inc.,* 596 ATRR D-1 (1973), Hughes Tool Co. (Toolco)
had acquired during the 1940's a controlling stock interest in Trans
World Airlines, Inc. (TWA). As an organization engaged in aeronautics, Toolco could not acquire control of TWA without consent

of the Civil Aeronautics Board. Pursuant to the provisions of Section 408 of the Federal Aviation Act (49 U.S.C. § 1378), which makes unlawful such an acquisition without CAB approval, the CAB in 1944 approved the *de facto* control of TWA by Toolco. In 1950, the CAB further approved Toolco's acquisition of complete control over TWA. Section 414 of the Federal Aviation Act (49 U.S.C. § 1384) immunizes from the federal antitrust laws action taken pursuant to Section 408. The CAB approvals or "control approval orders" of 1944 and 1950 were subject to certain terms and conditions. Every acquisition or lease of aircraft by TWA from Toolco and each financing of TWA by Toolco required specific CAB approval. On each occasion when Toolco applied to the CAB for approval of such a transaction, the transaction was approved after the CAB found it to be "just and reasonable and in the public interest."

Toolco surrendered control of TWA in 1960. Shortly thereafter, TWA filed a suit against Toolco, alleging violations of the antitrust laws to the injury of TWA's business. According to the complaint, the allegedly unlawful conduct arose from certain transactions between Toolco and TWA that had earlier been approved by the CAB. There were, for example, transactions relating to orders placed by Toolco for jet aircraft destined for use by TWA; these aircraft were subsequently diverted from TWA. It was asserted that Toolco had used its control over TWA to unreasonably and unlawfully dictate the manner by which TWA acquired aircraft and the necessary financing thereof. Toolco, on the other hand, claimed that CAB approval and surveillance of the transactions gave it immunity from the antitrust laws.

The Supreme Court, in a decision written by Justice Douglas, joined by Justices Brennan, Stewart, White, Powell, and Rehnquist, held that the challenged transactions, along with Toolco's control of TWA, were immunized from the operation of the antitrust laws by Section 414 of the Federal Aviation Act. Noting that competition and monopoly are "standards governing the CAB's exercise of authority in granting, allowing or expanding or contracting the control which Toolco had over TWA by reason of the various orders issued by the CAB under § 408," Justice Douglas said: "In this context, the authority of the Board to grant the power to 'control' and to investigate and alter the manner in which that 'control' is exercised leads us to conclude that this phase of CAB jurisdiction, like the one in the *Pan American* case, preempts the antitrust field." The Court also said that "it adds nothing to the analysis to characterize Toolco's exercise of power over TWA as monopolization of the TWA [aircraft] market, for it was precisely such control that the Board opted for in 1944 and 1950."

The Chief Justice, joined by Justice Blackmun, dissented. In his view, Congress did not intend the antitrust immunity afforded by Section 414 to extend "beyond the air transportation market into every market which might happen to be touched by transactions with an air carrier," for example, transactions involving the sale and financing of aircraft. He pointed out that while the Court notes that the CAB evaluated the treatment afforded TWA by Toolco, there is nothing suggesting that the Board "even remotely considered Toolco's actions as components of an antitrust conspiracy directed toward the aircraft supply and manufacturing market."

In *Ricci* v. *Chicago Mercantile Exchange,* 595 ATRR F-1 (1973), the plaintiff Ricci filed an antitrust action charging that the Chicago Mercantile Exchange transferred his membership to a third party, without notice or hearing, using a blank transfer authorization that had previously been revoked. As a result, Ricci alleged that he was excluded from trading until another membership was purchased at a considerably higher cost. The trial court dismissed the complaint. The court of appeals reversed, but ordered the trial court to stay proceedings, since the challenged conduct was deemed subject to the jurisdiction of the Commodity Exchange Commission or the Secretary of Agriculture, pursuant to the Commodity Exchange Act. The Supreme Court affirmed, in an opinion by Justice White, joined by the Chief Justice and Justices Brennan, Blackmun, Rehnquist. The Court stated that its "judgment rests on three related premises: (1) that it will be essential for the Antitrust Court to determine whether the Commodity Exchange Act or any of its provisions are 'incompatible with the maintenance of the antitrust action,' *Silver* v. *N.Y. Stock Exchange,* 373 U.S., at 358; (2) that some facets of the dispute between Ricci and the Exchange are within the statutory jurisdiction of the Commodity Exchange Commission; and (3) that adjudication of that dispute by the Commission promises to be of material aid in resolving the immunity question." As to (1), the immunity question, the Court observed that it would be necessary for the Commodity Exchange Commission to determine whether the transfer of Ricci's membership was pursuant to a valid rule of the Chicago Mercantile Exchange. If the transfer was pursuant to a valid rule, then the courts would be faced with the question of whether the rule itself and Ricci's exclusion under it are immunized from antitrust attack. If they were not, then "the antitrust action should very likely take its normal course."

Justice Marshall, joined by Justices Douglas, Stewart, and Powell, dissented on the ground that the Commodity Exchange Commission lacked the statutory power to resolve the only issue in the suit, that is, whether it has jurisdiction to determine whether the rules of the Exchange serve a legitimate self-regulatory goal.

In *Otter Tail Power Co.* v. *U.S.*, 602 ATRR D-1 (1973), Otter Tail Power Co. had been selling electric power at retail to various communities under municipally granted franchises. Upon the expiration of these franchise agreements, certain of the communities served by Otter Tail attempted to establish their own power systems. Otter Tail thereafter refused to sell power to these communities at wholesale, and refused to transmit ("wheel") power from other suppliers to the municipal power systems over its facilities. The Government charged in a civil antitrust action that such refusals to deal constituted illegal monopolization under the Sherman Act. Otter Tail argued that it was not subject to the operation of the antitrust laws by reason of the Federal Power Act, which grants the Federal Power Commission the authority under Section 202(b) to order involuntary interconnections of power.

The Supreme Court, in an opinion by Justice Douglas, joined by Justices Brennan, White, and Marshall, ruled otherwise. The court determined that "the essential thrust of § 202 . . . is to encourage voluntary interconnections of power," that "there is nothing in the legislative history which reveals a purpose to insulate electric power companies from the operation of the antitrust laws," and that the legislative history "indicates an overriding policy of maintaining competition to the maximum extent possible consistent with the public interest." Justice Douglas said: "It is clear, then, that Congress rejected a pervasive regulatory scheme for controlling the interstate distribution of power in favor of voluntary commercial relationships. When these relationships are governed in the first instance by business judgment and not regulatory coercion, the courts must be hesitant to conclude that Congress intended to override the fundamental national policies embodied in the antitrust laws." The Court concluded by observing that there was no conflict between FPC regulation and the operation of the antitrust laws. "It will be time enough to consider whether the antitrust remedy may override the power of the Commission under 202(b) as, if and when the Commission denies the interconnection and the District Court nevertheless undertakes to direct it."

Justice Stewart, joined by the Chief Justice and Justice Rehnquist, dissented. (Justices Blackmun and Powell did not participate.) According to the dissenters, the "legislative history, especially when viewed in the light of repeated subsequent congressional refusals to impose common carrier obligations in this area, indicates a clear congressional purpose to allow electric utilities to decide for themselves whether to wheel or sell at wholesale as they see fit. This freedom is qualified by a grant of authority to the Commission to order interconnection (but not wheeling) in certain circumstances. But the exercise of even that power is limited by a consideration of the ability of the regulated utility to function. The Commission may not order interconnection where this would entail an undue burden on the regulated utility." Antitrust jurisdiction, according to Justice Stewart, might interfere with this regulatory scheme.

With regard to the antitrust immunity issues, the *Hughes Tool, Ricci,* and *Otter Tail* cases may possibly be reconciled by considering various differences in the regulatory statutes. (For fuller analysis to this effect, including *Gulf States Utilities Co.* v. *FPC,* 613 ATRR E-1 (Sup. Ct. 1973), and *FMC* v. *Seatrain Lines Inc.,* 613 ATRR F-1 (Sup. Ct. 1973), see 628 ATRR B-1, 8/28/73.) In *Hughes Tool,* Section 414 of the Federal Aviation Act provides antitrust immunity for transactions approved under Section 408. The question is whether the challenged transactions, which purportedly were approved pursuant to Section 408, were properly within the scope of the express immunity provided by Section 414. In *Ricci,* where the Court found that the question of immunity could be resolved only after the Commission determined whether the transfer of membership occurred pursuant to a valid Exchange rule, the Court suggests that there is some area of immunity, since the regulatory statute "clearly contemplates a membership organization and hence the existence of criteria for the acquisition, transfer, and loss of membership." The issue would also seem to be the scope of the immunity that Congress clearly intended. On the other hand, there was no clear area of immunity in *Otter Tail,* and the issue, accordingly, was not so much the scope of the immunity but whether any immunity could be inferred at all. The defendant was faced with the presumption against implied immunity—which arises when there is no plain repugnancy between the regulatory provisions and the antitrust laws —as set forth in such cases as *U.S.* v. *Phila. Nat'l. Bank,* 374 U.S. 321 (1963), and *Calif.* v. *FPC,* 369 U.S. 482 (1962). It is also true that the Court, in *Hughes Tool,* found that there was "pervasive" control by the CAB, and that in *Otter Tail* it appeared to find a "pervasive regulatory scheme" lacking. Arguably, this is mere conclusory language. It might be argued that the Federal Power Act, which enables the FPC to order interconnections (and it did so upon application by one of the communities with which Otter Tail had refused to deal), provides no less pervasive regulation than the Federal Aviation Act did in *Hughes Tool.*

Some suggest that because the primary jurisdiction question is in a state of uncertainty, Congress is the appropriate authority to clarify it. This it could do by making clear—for each regulatory statute— when antitrust considerations are to be considered paramount and when they are not. It is more likely, however, that Congress will rely upon the courts to resolve the uncertainty. Others contend that the uncertainty is not in the formulation of the doctrine of primary jurisdiction but in its application, which involves a consideration of varying factors. Those factors include at least (1) whether there is a specific antitrust immunity provision in the regulatory statute, (2) whether there are factual questions the agency has superior competence to resolve, and (3) whether the subject matter of the agency's action is "arguably lawful" within the scope of the regulatory statute. The variances in these factors make it difficult to predict how the primary jurisdiction issue will be resolved in any particular case.

B. BANK MERGERS

Question: *Which bank mergers are permitted under the antitrust laws?*

Under the 1960 Bank Merger Act, 12 U.S.C. § 1828, bank mergers are forbidden unless approved in advance by one of three bank regulatory agencies. National banks must have the approval of the Comptroller of the Currency. State banks belonging to the Federal Reserve System must obtain clearance from the Federal Reserve Board. Insured banks not included in these two groups must have permission of the Federal Deposit Insurance Corporation. Prior to approval of any proposed merger, notice of the contemplated transaction must be published in a newspaper of general circulation in the communities where the banks' main offices are located.

In granting or withholding consent to a proposed merger or consolidation, the bank regulatory agencies are required to consider a number of factors, including earning prospects, management, the financial history and condition of the banks involved, adequacy of capital structure, and the convenience and needs of the community. The agency is also directed to "take into consideration the effect of the transaction on competition (including any tendency toward monopoly)." Approval of the transaction is to be denied unless, after considering all such factors, the agency finds the transaction to be in the public interest.

The statute provides for an exchange of information and views between the several bank regulatory agencies and the Attorney General. In the interest of "uniform standards," the banking agency asked to approve a proposed merger is directed to request "a report on the competitive factors involved" from the Attorney General and from the other two banking agencies, "unless it finds it must act immediately in order to prevent the probable failure of one of the banks involved." The statute is silent as to what the banking agency may or should do with the Attorney General's report, except that a summary of such report is to be included in the agency's annual report to Congress with "a statement . . . of the basis for its approval" of the merger.

The Supreme Court has published a decision which two dissenting Justices said "almost completely nullified" the regulatory scheme set out in the Bank Merger Act (*U.S.* v. *Phila. Nat'l. Bank,* 374 U.S. 321 (1963)). In the course of affirming an injunction against a proposed merger of the Philadelphia National Bank and the Girard Trust Corn Exchange Bank, the Court held that all bank mergers, whether approved by a regulatory agency or not, must be judged by the standards of Section 7 of the Clayton Act. The applicability of Section 7 to bank mergers was said to turn on the significance of a restriction in the asset-acquisition language added when the Clayton Act was amended in 1950 by the Celler-Kefauver Act. Unlike the pre-existing ban on stock acquisitions that substantially lessen competition, the new provision on asset-acquisitions was made applicable only to corporations "subject to the jurisdiction of the Federal Trade Commission." Section 5 of the FTC Act specifically excludes banks from FTC supervision.

As to the threshold question of classification of the conventional bank merger as either an asset-acquisition or a stock acquisition, the Court saw merit both in the Government's argument that a bank merger is "crucially different" from a pure asset acquisition and in the banks' contention that a bank merger is clearly distinguishable from a pure stock acquisition. Since "a merger fits neither category neatly," the Court examined the legislative history of the 1950 amendment to determine whether Congress intended to legislate with respect to bank mergers. In this history a majority of five justices found a primary purpose to bring such mergers within the scope of Section 7.

With regard to the phrase "corporations subject to the jurisdiction of the Federal Trade Commission," the majority found that the purpose was not to limit the transactions to be covered by the amended statute, but to make explicit the role of the FTC in enforcing Section 7. "Congress' choice of this means of underscoring the FTC's role in enforcing Section 7 provides no basis for a construction which would undercut the dominant congressional purpose of eliminating the difference in treatment accorded stock acquisitions and mergers by the original Section 7 as construed."

As to the significance of the subsequent enactment of the Bank Merger Act, the Court cited statements in House and Senate committee reports that the 1960 statute would not affect the impact of the antitrust laws on bank mergers. Citing *Pan American World Airways* v. *U.S.,* 371 U.S. 296 (1963), the Court observed that the Bank Merger Act confers no express antitrust immunity, nor does it give the broad type of competition-preserving powers that led the

Court to recognize antitrust immunity for activities regulated by the Civil Aeronautics Board.

Justice Brennan's opinion for the Court took note of the fact that, subsequent to the passage of the 1950 Clayton Act amendment, some members of Congress, as well as the Justice Department, expressed the view that bank mergers were still beyond the reach of amended Section 7. The opinion also recognized that misunderstanding of the scope of Section 7 may have played some part in the enactment of the Bank Merger Act in 1960, but stated that "the views of a subsequent Congress form a hazardous basis for inferring the intent of an earlier one" and that in 1960 the applicability of Section 7 of the Clayton Act to bank mergers "was still to be authoritatively determined; it was a subject of speculation."

Three of the "public interest" considerations that led the Comptroller of the Currency to approve the Philadelphia Bank merger were rejected by the Court. First, the Court denied that only through mergers can banks follow customers into the suburbs; it suggested that the banks resort to "de novo branching." Second, the banks' desire to achieve the strength to compete with large out-of-state banks for very large loans was denied significance; anticompetitive effects in one market cannot be justified by procompetitve consequences in another. Third, the Court refused to accept a suggestion that Philadelphia needed a larger bank to bring business into the area and stimulate economic development; this type of argument, according to the Court, was rejected by Congress when it amended Section 7 of the Clayton Act.

The Government attacked the Philadelphia Bank merger as a violation of both the Clayton Act and Section 1 of the Sherman Antitrust Act. The Sherman Act charge was the only one discussed by the Assistant Attorney General in charge of the Antitrust Division during oral argument in the Supreme Court. The Section 7 Clayton Act point had been relegated to secondary treatment in the Government's written brief. Having found a violation of the Clayton Act, the Supreme Court put aside the Sherman Act issues for future consideration.

Less than a year later the Court applied Section 1 of the Sherman Act to a bank merger (*U.S.* v. *First Nat'l. Bank & Trust Co. of Lexington*, 376 U.S. 665 (1964)). Its decision was a clear declaration that a merger having anticompetitive effects proscribed by the antitrust laws was unlawful regardless of any claimed public benefit.

Following the Justice Department's success, in *U.S.* v. *Manufacturers Hanover Trust Co.*, 240 F.Supp. 867 (S.D.N.Y. 1963), against the merger of Manufacturers Trust Co. and The Hanover Bank, agitation began in Congress to counter the impact of the Supreme

Court's decisions. In the Senate, concern seemed to concentrate on the potential threat to past bank mergers, since there is no time limit on suits to undo mergers that violate Section 7 of the Clayton Act.

Under Section 18(c)(5) of the Federal Deposit Insurance Act, as amended by the 1966 Bank Merger Act, 12 U.S.C. § 1828, none of the three bank regulatory agencies may approve any bank merger that may substantially lessen competition, tend to create a monopoly, or be in restraint of trade unless it "finds that the anticompetitive effects of the transaction are clearly outweighed in the public interest by the probable effect of the transaction in meeting the convenience and needs of the community to be served." The "public interest" factors are then listed as "the financial and managerial resources and future prospects of the existing and proposed institutions, and the convenience and needs of the community to be served."

The Justice Department has 30 days to go into court to block any approved merger it believes violates the antitrust laws. Before approval can be granted, the Justice Department and each of the other banking agencies must be given notice of the application for approval and must be given 30 days to file reports on the competitive factors involved. If the agency to rule on the merger decides there is "an emergency requiring expeditious action," the report on competitive factors can be required within 10 days, and the waiting period during which the Justice Department must bring its antitrust suit is reduced to 5 days. If the agency finds "it must act immediately to prevent the probable failure of one of the banks involved," it may dispense with the reports on competitive factors and the merger may be completed without delay.

If the Government should decide to sue, its commencement of a court action "shall stay the effectiveness of the agency's approval unless the court shall otherwise specifically order." The court in which suit is brought is directed to apply "standards . . . identical with those that the banking agencies are directed to apply," and the banking agency involved is given a right to appear as a party in the antitrust action.

Senate Antitrust Subcommittee Chairman Phillip A. Hart (D-Mich) predicted that the new statutory language would spark considerable litigation since "it has substituted a new standard that is so novel and so vague that no one understands its meaning." In two of the bank-merger cases that were in the courts when the Act was passed and two of the four cases filed afterward, four federal district courts entered decisions on substantive and vital procedural issues arising under the new statute. Few of the conclusions reached in those decisions bear any resemblance to the construction the

Antitrust Division put on the new statute, and some of them may not even have occurred to the Senators and Representatives who participated in the debate.

One of the statements repeatedly made by House Banking Committee Chairman Wright Patman (D-Tex) was that "there is no intent . . . to change the application of the antitrust laws as they apply to bank mergers." Another committee member, Congressman Henry S. Reuss (D-Wis), declared that the Act "in no way overturns any effect of the decision of the majority of the Supreme Court in the Philadelphia Bank case." In reliance on those statements, the Antitrust Division has consistently taken the position that the new Act made no substantial changes in the competitive-effects standards to be applied to bank mergers.

Any merger consistent with the Act's provisions or prior to the Supreme Court's *Philadelphia Bank* decision is exempted by the Act from all antitrust provisions except the monopolization ban in Section 2 of the Sherman Act. Mergers since the *Philadelphia Bank* decision not yet attacked by the Justice Department are granted the same exemption. The effect of these provisions was to clear one merger already held illegal, the Manufacturers-Hanover consolidation in New York, and another whose legality had not been decided, Continental Illinois National Bank and Trust Co. and City National Bank & Trust Co. in Chicago (*U.S.* v. *Continental Ill. National Bank & Trust Co.,* 1961 Trade Cas. ¶70,110 (N.D. Ill. 1961)).

In *U.S.* v. *First City National Bank of Houston,* 386 U.S. 361 (1967), the Supreme Court rejected the conclusion of several district courts that the Government has the burden of proving the absence of "public interest" elements justifying an anticompetitive bank merger. The Court saw in the legislative history of the 1966 Act an intent to make antitrust standards "the norm and anticompetitive bank mergers the exception." The Court applied the "general rule" that the burden of proof falls on the one who "claims the benefits of an exception to the prohibition of a statute."

Despite that holding and despite a ruling in the same opinion that a court reviewing a merger approved by an agency should make an "independent determination of the issues," the Government continued to lose bank-merger cases in the district courts. In *U.S.* v. *Third Nat'l. Bank in Nashville,* 260 F.Supp. 869 (M.D. Tenn. 1966), *rev'd,* 390 U.S. 171 (1968), *consent decree,* 1968 Trade Cas. ¶72,556 (M.D. Tenn. 1968), and *U.S.* v. *Crocker-Anglo National Bank,* 277 F.Supp. 133 (N.D. Calif. 1967), the district courts found the evidence insufficient to show a substantially adverse effect on competition and determined that any competitive injury that might result from the mergers was outweighed by enhancement of the merged banks' ability to compete more vigorously and to provide new or expanded services to their communities. The California court concluded that the Act's provision for considering the convenience and needs of the community reversed the doctrine of the *Philadelphia National Bank* case that an anticompetitive bank merger "is not saved because, on some ultimate reckoning of social or economic debits and credits, it may be deemed beneficial." The California court rejected the Government's suggestion that the provision for considering the "convenience and needs" of the community is but a repetition of the failing-company doctrine.

The two courts differed in finding changes made by the 1966 Bank Merger Act in the rules for testing the competitive effect of bank mergers. The Tennessee court saw in the Act an intent to return to the more permissive merger criteria of *U.S.* v. *Columbia Steel Co.,* 334 U.S. 495 (1948). The court found in the 1966 Act's provisions directing consideration of qualitative banking factors the purpose "not only to embrace the Columbia Steel criteria but also to require an even broader scope of inquiry and analysis with respect to antitrust issues." It held that the Government had not proven either a Section 1 Sherman Act or a Section 7 Clayton Act violation with statistical data intended to show that the merging banks were "major competitive factors in the Nashville area and the merger resulted in the elimination of competition between them."

One federal district judge has enjoined a bank merger approved by the Comptroller of the Currency, but he did so "reluctantly." In *U.S.* v. *Provident Nat'l. Bank,* 280 F.Supp. 1 (E.D. Pa. 1968), the court read the Supreme Court's *Houston* opinion and the Act's legislative history as indicating "that the convenience and needs test must be read restrictively. . . . It merely allows bank mergers in those cases where the needs and convenience of the community are so compelling that competition will be enhanced rather than decreased by the merger. This will occur in only a very few instances." Describing the banks' burden of proof under the Act as "indeed a heavy one," the district judge assessed the competitive-effects and public-interest evidence before him as producing "at best . . . a tie. However, in a tie situation, the banks necessarily lose." The judge pointed out that under the Bank Merger Act "a merger may be anticompetitive and yet be legal because it promotes the public interest."

No explanation was given for the court's insistence that the legality of the merger be tested under the Bank Merger Act rather than under the Clayton Act, on which the Government based its complaint. There appears to be a basic inconsistency in the language of the Bank Merger Act itself. Paragraph (5), of 12 U.S.C. § 1828(c), sets out what are apparently the only antitrust standards to be applied to bank mergers and leaves the enforcement of those standards to the responsible banking agency. Yet paragraph (7) establishes ground rules for "any action brought under the antitrust laws arising out of a merger transaction." When, in reliance on the paragraph (7) language, the Antitrust Division persisted in litigating under the Clayton Act and in refusing to assume the burden of proving the absence of public-interest factors, its complaint was dismissed.

• In *U.S.* v. *Third Nat'l. Bank of Nashville,* 390 U.S. 171 (1968), the Supreme Court reversed the judgment of the Tennessee district court. Speaking for a 5–2 majority, Justice White asserted that "securing better banking service for the community is a proper element for consideration in weighing convenience and need against the loss of competition." He conceded that the merger before the Court "would very probably end the managerial problems" that led the district judge to characterize the bank to be acquired as "not disposed to compete," but he found the district court's analysis overlooked a vital element: the possibility that "convenience and need" requirements could be satisfied without resort to merger. Although the district judge had discussed the Nashville Bank's efforts to recruit new management and had concluded that management procurement is difficult for banks in general and an "almost insoluble" problem for the Nashville Bank, Justice White said the lower court should have made it clear "just how insoluble" the problem was. The district judge was instructed on remand to ascertain whether the bank's ownership had made "concrete efforts to recruit new management" and to assess the possibility of a sale of the bank to other owners who might be willing to face the management difficulties over a more extended period.

In assessing the competitive effect of the Nashville Bank merger, the Supreme Court rejected the district judge's suggestion that the 1966 Bank Merger Act revived the *Columbia Steel* doctrine. The Supreme Court agreed with the Justice Department's position that Congress had "no intention to adopt an 'antitrust standard' for bank cases different from that used generally in the law." The Court added a footnote disposing of the relevant-market issue that had divided the district courts, and it accepted the Tennessee district court's determination that commercial banking in Davidson County, Tennessee, was the relevant market for appraising the competitive effects of the merger. The Court found in the 1966 Bank Merger Act "no intention to alter the traditional methods of defining relevant markets (390 U.S. at 182)."

The Supreme Court's decisions on the "convenience and needs" defense seem to support the Philadelphia district court's observation in *U.S.* v. *Provident Nat'l. Bank,* 280 F.Supp. 1 (E.D. Pa. 1968), that the burden of proof assumed by merging banks relying on that defense is "indeed a heavy one." The *Nashville Bank* opinion adds a requirement not explicit in the statute that the banks must show there are no less anticompetitive means of procuring the community benefits that outweigh the anticompetitive effects of the merger. The Court did say it was adopting a test that "does not demand the impossible or the unreasonable." All that is required is "a showing . . . that the gain expected from the merger cannot reasonably be expected through other means."

Implicit in the Court's reasoning seems to be acceptance of the notion that an anticompetitive bank merger can be justified. If so, the Philadelphia district court may have gone too far in saying "the needs and convenience of the community" must be "so compelling that competition will be enhanced rather than decreased by the merger." To require *enhanced* competition would impose a stricter antimerger rule than existed prior to the 1966 Act.

Without saying so, the Supreme Court may have buried a contention the Justice Department made in the *Crocker-Anglo* case, that the "convenience and needs" defense is merely a restatement of the failing-company doctrine. The Court's direction to the Nashville Federal District Court to check alternative ways of solving the acquired bank's managerial problems implies that, if no alternatives are available, the merger could be justified as a method of solving these problems, even though they fall short of putting the acquired bank in a "failing" condition. Even in *U.S.* v. *Phila. Nat'l. Bank,* 374 U.S. 321, 372, n. 46 (1963), the Court had acknowledged that "arguably, the so-called failing company defense . . . might have somewhat larger contours as applied to bank mergers because of the greater public impact of a bank failure." It may also be arguable that what the Nashville district court called the "stagnant and floundering" condition of a merging bank will be given full weight both in assessing the merger's anticompetitive effect and in balancing such effect against public-interest gains.

There appear to be two reasons why a true "failing bank" case is not likely to be litigated in court. First, the banking agencies would themselves be failing in their duties if they were to permit a bank to reach failing-company condition as that condition is defined in *International Shoe Co.* v. *FTC,* 280 U.S. 291 (1930). Second, if a bank were in such poor condition, the merger would probably be handled, under 12 U.S.C. § 1828(c) (6), on an emergency basis. Once carried out, 12 U.S.C. § 1828(c) (7)(C) provides that a bank merger is not challengeable under the antitrust laws unless in violation of Section 2 of the Sherman Act.

In 1969 a district court dismissed a suit against the proposed merger of the Phillipsburg National Bank (PNB) and the Second National

Bank of New Jersey (SNB) (*U.S.* v. *Phillipsburg Nat'l Bank & Trust Co.,* 306 F.Supp. 645 (D. N.J. 1969)). Applying provisions of the Bank Merger Act of 1966, 12 U.S.C. § 1828(c)(5), the district court concluded that the proposed merger would not have the anticompetitive effects prohibited by Section 7 and that, even assuming the existence of such adverse effects, they were outweighed by the "convenience and needs of the community" to be served by the merged bank. The Supreme Court reversed and remanded this decision, citing errors in definition of the relevant geographic and product markets (*U.S.* v. *Phillipsburg Nat'l. Bank & Trust Co.,* 399 U.S. 350 (1970)).

The towns of Phillipsburg and Easton are linked by two bridges. In Phillipsburg-Easton there were seven commercial banks; PNB and SNB were numbers three and five in market share. A proposed merger between PNB and SNB would have reduced to six the number of commercial banks in the given area, and the new PNB-SNB bank would have ranked number two. The Court stated that "mergers of directly competing small commercial banks in small communities, no less than those of large banks in large communities are subject to scrutiny." It applied the standards of the *Philadelphia National Bank* case to determine, first, whether the proposed merger would violate section 7 of the Clayton Act. Holding that commercial banking was the relevant line of commerce, despite contrary findings below, the Court defined Phillipsburg-Easton as the relevant geographic market in light of the "localized" nature of banking and despite a much broader market definition adopted by the district court that had included the city of Bethlehem.

Having defined the relevant geographic and product markets, the Court examined the competitive effects of the proposed merger. Applying the *Philadelphia Bank* doctrine that "a merger which produces a firm controlling an undue percentage . . . of the relevant market and results in a significant concentration," the Court held that the necessary anticompetitive effects had been established. Specifically, in the Phillipsburg-Easton market, of seven banks, the two largest held 49 percent of total commercial banking assets; the merged bank would become number two in the market, giving the top two of six remaining firms 55 percent of total banking assets. The Court rejected claims made regarding procompetitive effects of the merger.

The Court sought to determine whether any adverse competitive effects of the merger would be offset by a contribution to the "convenience and needs of the community." Contrary to the finding of the district court, the Court found no significant countervailing benefit. The Court asserted that the geographic market established to assess the competitive effects of the merger must also be used to assess the contribution of the merger to the convenience and needs of the "community to be served." The Court rejected the conclusion below that the proposed merger would satisfy the "convenience and needs" test since the district court's conclusion was based upon an area much larger than the Phillipsburg-Easton geographic market. Such a result, according to the Court, "would subvert the clear congressional purpose in the Bank Merger Act that convenience and needs not be assessed in only a part of the community to be served, and such a result would unfairly deny the benefits of the merger to some who sustain its direct and immediate anticompetitive effects." The Court remanded the "convenience and needs" question in light of its comments on proper market delineation.

In an opinion partly concurring and partly dissenting, Justice Harlan, joined by the Chief Justice, differed with the Court's assessment of competitive effects, arguing that the Court engaged in "antitrust numerology" (bare market concentration percentages) without considering the ease of entry into the banking market, competition from neighboring geographic markets, and the overall effect of the merger on competition in the Phillipsburg-Easton area.

There are several apparently significant aspects to the *Phillipsburg* case. First, the case indicates that Section 7 reaches bank mergers in small towns and may indicate that other types of small businesses may not lawfully grow by mergers in small towns. Secondly, the case teaches that the same Section 7 market definitions must be applied equally to assessment of "convenience and needs" under the Bank Merger Act. Third, it may be gleaned from this case that the Supreme Court will continue to strike down horizontal bank mergers, large or small; the limiting factor might be whether the Justice Department continues to seek injunctions against bank mergers of the Phillipsburg magnitude. Justice Harlan criticized the Department's interference with such a localized merger while much bigger "tigers" were "still at large." Some contend that such an arguably inefficient use of Government resources can be blamed upon the Bank Merger statute itself, which allows the Justice Department to "second-guess" the regulatory authorities and obtain an automatic injunction unavailable in other situations.

When First National Bancorporation, Inc., the second largest Colorado banking organization, obtained permission from the Federal Reserve Board to acquire a bank in Greeley, Colorado, the Justice Department sued to prevent an alleged violation of Section 7 of the Clayton Act. The district court held the acquisition would not have a significant adverse effect on competition. The district court's judgment was affirmed by an equally divided Supreme Court (*U.S.* v. *First National Bancorporation, Inc.*, 1973 Trade Cas. ¶ 74,378 (D. Colo. 1973)).

Once a bank merger violates Section 7 of the Clayton Act, the "convenience and needs" defense can apparently be defeated, even where the merger is localized in smaller communities. Some experts would argue from *Phillipsburg* that this defense is illusory; once the Court determines that Section 7 is abridged, it will find a means to strip away this defense. The Court's reference in *Phillipsburg* to the *Nashville Bank* case may require that a local bank, prior to merger, must be prepared to establish that it could not reasonably have provided better banking service to the local community other than by the merger.

Some would argue that the Court's geographic market assessment in *Phillipsburg* was incorrect because certain large loan services were unavailable from local Phillipsburg-Easton banks and could be supplied only by larger adjacent municipal banks; hence, a larger geographic area, including Philadelphia, should have been defined. Yet, in the *Philadelphia National Bank* case, this argument was rejected. Moreover, it is suggested that local banks such as PNB can and do participate with larger cooperating banks in making loans to meet local needs.

Can a bank merger be vindicated in a Government enforcement action, yet continue to provide a basis for treble-damage liability? In one sense, a bank merger unlawful under Clayton Section 7 can be justified in a Government enforcement action by the "convenience and needs" statutory defense set up by the Bank Merger Act. Arguably, that defense may not be available in a private treble-damage action under Section 7 of the Clayton Act. On the other hand, a Bank Merger Act 30-day statute of limitations for actions, 12 U.S.C. § 1828 (c) (6, 7A), may effectively kill all such private damage actions, making questions of possible defense academic.

C. INSURANCE

Question: *To what extent is the insurance industry covered by the antitrust laws?*

For 75 years prior to *U.S.* v. *South-Eastern Underwriters Assn.*, 322 U.S. 533 (1944), the Supreme Court followed the rule that the sale of insurance is not interstate commerce subject to regulation by Congress. Justice Black's opinion in that case for a four-justice majority held the insurance industry subject to the Sherman Act. Following the Court's decision, Congress was urged to return the insurance business to regulation by the states. State regulation, the industry argued, would prevent the uncertainties and insolvencies that increased competition would be sure to bring about. At the next session of Congress, in 1945, the McCarran-Ferguson Act was passed (15 U.S.C. §§ 1011–1015).

After declaring in Section 1 that "the continued regulation and taxation by the several states of the business of insurance is in the public interest," the Act declares that "the business of insurance . . . shall be subject to the laws of the several states." "No act of Congress shall be construed to invalidate, impair, or supersede any law enacted by any state for the purpose of regulating the business of insurance." Sections 2(b) and 3(b) provide two situations in which the federal antitrust laws are to be applicable, "to the extent that such business is not regulated by state law" and "to any agreement to boycott, coerce, or intimidate, or act of boycott, coercion, or intimidation." In the latter situation, Section 3(b) preserves only the applicability of the Sherman Act.

Every state has enacted some sort of insurance-regulation law. In 19 states, "Little Clayton Acts" were adopted. Some of them, based on the original Clayton Act, are aimed only at stock acquisitions and do not regulate asset acquisitions. Few of the statutes make any attempt to regulate mergers of domestic with out-of-state insurers. When they do, the regulation often takes the form of a requirement that the foreign insurer become a domestic company, that the foreign insurer be doing business in the enacting state, that the merger be authorized by the law of the other state, or that the merger be approved by the regulatory authorities of the other state.

In August 1960, the Senate Antitrust Subcommittee reported the results of a study of state laws regulating insurance and of the competitive status of the insurance market (S. Rep. No. 1834, 89th Cong., 2d Sess. (1960)). One of its conclusions was that a "most serious threat" to a free competitive market is raised by the extent to which merger activity is condoned "either because of the lack of adequate state legislation or lack of concern with this problem." As an illustration of "a serious hiatus . . . in state jurisdiction over merger activities," the Subcommittee pointed out that two insurance companies might obtain approval, in their domiciliary states, of a merger that would have serious anticompetitive effects in a different state.

The McCarran Act gives no indication how far a state must go in order to accomplish the insurance "regulation" the Act says will preclude application of the antitrust laws. In *North Little Rock Transportation Co.* v. *Casualty Reciprocal Exchange,* 181 F.2d 174 (8th Cir. 1950), *cert. denied,* 340 U.S. 823 (1950), a restraint-of-trade conspiracy action, it was enough for the court that state law authorized the licensing of rate bureaus. A state law authorizing "enforcement through a scheme of administered supervision" conformed to the Supreme Court's concept of "regulation" in *FTC* v. *National Casualty Co.,* 357 U.S. 560 (1958). The *National Casualty* case has been cited for the proposition that "a state regulates the business of insurance . . . when a state statute generally proscribes or permits or authorizes certain conduct on the part of the insurance companies" (*California League of Independent Ins. Producers* v. *Aetna Casualty and Surety Co.,* 175 F.Supp. 857, 860 (N.D. Calif. 1959)).

The question of whether insurance-company mergers are "regulated by state law" in Missouri and Illinois was presented in the Justice Department's civil suit against Chicago Title and Trust Co. (*U.S.* v. *Chicago Title and Trust Co.,* 242 F.Supp. 56 (N.D. Ill. 1965), *consent decree,* 1966 Trade Cas. ¶71,745 (N.D. Ill. 1966)). The complaint attacked, as a Section 7 Clayton Act violation, Chicago Title's 1961 purchase of a controlling stock interest in Kansas City Title Insurance Co. The district judge described Chicago as the second largest title insurance company in the United States. With its subsidiaries, it had a 1960 gross income of over $20 million and assets of over $90 million. Although Chicago Title was licensed to do business only in Illinois, its affiliates wrote title insurance in 41 other states. Their total amount of title insurance increased from less than $860 million written in 1944 to over $2.6 billion written in 1952. In 1959, Chicago Title issued 479 reinsurance policies with a coverage of about $173 million to 29 title companies located in 19 states and the District of Columbia.

Chicago Title, an Illinois corporation, acquired over 90 percent of the stock of the Kansas City Title Co., a Missouri corporation, in August 1961. According to the district judge, Kansas City was the eighth largest title company in the United States and in 1960 had premium income of almost $4 million. It was licensed to write title insurance in 25 states and the District of Columbia and operated branch offices in Arkansas, Tennessee, Mississippi, Colorado, Maryland, and North Carolina. Kansas City and the Title Insurance Corp. of St. Louis, which was acquired by Chicago Title prior to 1957, wrote 70 percent of the title insurance in Missouri in 1960. Kansas City Title and Title Guarantee Co. of Wisconsin, another Chicago Title acquisition, had over 70 percent of the title insurance business in Wisconsin in 1961.

Looking for Illinois law applicable to the merger, the district judge could find no legislation comparable to Section 7 of the Clayton Act. The Illinois antitrust statute had been construed not to apply to combinations with parties outside the state (*People* v. *Butler Street Foundry,* 201 Ill. 236 (1903)) or to the business of insurance (Op. Atty Gen. 228 (1898)). The Illinois Insurance Code was expressly made inapplicable to title insurance. The state's only title-insurance law was designed primarily to maintain the solvency of insurers.

A claim that Missouri had legislated on insurance-company mergers was based upon a requirement in that state that each title insurer file a detailed annual report, including information on the stock it owned in other title insurers and on the ownership of its own stock. Missouri law said nothing about a foreign insurer's acquisition of a domestic title-insurance company. The Missouri superintendent of insurance was authorized to make comprehensive examinations and hold hearings to satisfy himself that the insurer was complying with the law, and he could revoke a license if he found noncompliance. This power to censure an insurance company to the point of extinction was described as tantamount to regulating Chicago Title and Trust Co., even though it did no business in Missouri.

The Antitrust Division contended that the acquisition of Kansas City Title had an effect in at least 10 other states, and yet no state had power to sanction the acquisition in any other state. Of the 12 states affected, the Government urged, only four (Arkansas, Georgia, Louisiana, and Virginia) have a "Little Clayton Act," although most of them have provisions similar to the Sherman Act. The Government argued that federal law is displaced only if state law "covers the 'same ground'" as the federal legislation. Since Chicago Title was not licensed to do business in any of the other states, those states were not in a position to enforce their statutes against the merger. Chicago Title called attention to the fact that the companies had submitted all the facts on the merger to the insurance commissioners in all the states in which Kansas City Title was qualified to do business. No objection was heard from any of those states.

The district judge denied Chicago Title's motion to dismiss, concluding that there were no applicable state laws governing the merger. The court expressed doubt that the states had constitutional power to control interstate mergers, calling attention to such Supreme Court opinions as *FTC* v. *Travelers Health Assn., 362 U.S. 293 (1960); FTC* v. *National Casualty Co.,* 357 U.S. 560 (1958); and *State Board of Ins.* v. *Todd Shipyards,* 370 U.S. 451 (1962). The district judge stressed repeated statements by the Supreme Court that a state cannot "regulate activities carried on beyond its own borders" and that Congress provided for displacement of federal antitrust enforcement agencies only to the extent the insurance business is regulated "by the state where the business activities have their operative force." He also pointed to the statement of the court in *Travelers Health Assn.* v. *FTC,* 298 F.2d 820 (8th Cir. 1962): "The state must itself be legally able to do, through its own provisions, instrumentalities and processes, everything that is necessary to the effecting of control as to its situation."

The FTC since ruled that the McCarran Act does not preempt FTC challenges to mergers, and a U.S. district court has agreed *(American General Ins. Co.* v. *FTC,* 617 ATRR E-1 (S.D. Tex 1973)). In *American General Ins. Co.,* (1970–73 Transfer Binder) 3 Trade Reg. Rep. ¶20,163 (F.T.C. 1972), the administrative law judge dismissed the Commission's complaint, saying that the FTC had no jurisdiction. The Commission reversed. The opinion concluded that states cannot determine the national impact of mergers and stated: "The legislative history makes clear Congress did not intend one state, even the insurance company's home state, to control those aspects of its business which affect many states or an industry as a whole."

FTC v. *Travelers Health Assn.,* 362 U.S. 293 (1960), involved alleged deceptive practices by a mail-order insurance company with headquarters in Nebraska. Nebraska had a law prohibiting unfair or deceptive practices in the insurance business in Nebraska or "in any other state." A divided Supreme Court reversed a ruling that the advertising circulars mailed by the company to other states were "regulated by state law." Because of "doubts which constitutional limitations might create as to Nebraska's power to regulate any given aspect of extra-territorial activity," the Court read the McCarran Act's state-regulation standard as referring "only to regulation by the state where the business activities have their operative force." In other words, the existence of state regulation depended on the law of the policy-holder's home state. The next question was whether the policy-holder's state had any effective means of controlling the activities of out-of-state insurers. Cases like *Travelers Health Assn.* v. *Va.,* 339 U.S. 643 (1950), and *McGee* v. *Internat'l Life Ins. Co.,* 355 U.S. 220 (1957), established the power of a state to enforce its decisions against an out-of-state insurance company whose only contacts within the state were by mail with its policy-holders—in the *McGee* case, only one policy-holder.

The McCarran Act's "boycott" exemption has been involved in actions brought by both the Justice Department and private treble-damage claimants. A suit by the Antitrust Division under that clause produced a consent decree against the Cincinnati Insurance Board (*U.S.* v. *Cincinnati Ins. Board,* 1963 Trade Cas. ¶70,945 (S.D. Ohio 1963)). Earlier in *U.S.* v. *Ins. Board of Cleveland,* 144 F.Supp. 684 (N. Ohio, 1956), and *U.S.* v. *New Orleans Ins. Exchange,* 148 F.Supp. 915 (E.D. La.), *aff'd,* 355 U.S. 22 (1957), the Justice Department had succeeded in having the "boycott" ban applied to "direct-writer" rules enforced by insurance trade associations. Those rules barred membership to any insurance agent who solicited business for nonmember companies. In a second suit against the Cleveland Insurance Board, the Government secured an injunction against a rule barring member agents from doing business with mutual insurance companies (188 F.Supp. 949 (N.D. Ohio, 1960)).

The McCarran Act's "boycott" exemption has been interpreted in two private treble-damage actions. What the district judge called a "boycott by peaceful persuasion" was held to be a "boycott" subject to the Sherman Act in *Professional and Businessmen's Life Ins. Co.* v. *Bankers Life Co.,* 163 F.Supp. 274 (D. Mont. 1958). In *Calif. League of Independent Ins. Producers* v. *Aetna Casualty and Surety Co.,* 179 F.Supp. 65 (N.D. Calif. 1959), the district court sustained, as alleging a Sherman Act "boycott," a complaint charging automobile insurers with conspiring to refuse to do business with independent insurance agents except at commission rates the insurers had agreed upon. In defining a "boycott," the district judge refused to draw a distinction between an absolute refusal to deal and a refusal to deal except at a fixed price. The court sustained the complaint despite observations in an earlier opinion, *Calif. League of Independent Ins. Producers* v. *Aetna Casualty and Surety Co.,* 175 F.Supp. 857 (N.D. Calif. 1959), that cooperative rate making is specifically authorized by the California Insurance Code and that the rate of commission paid to agents "is a vital factor in the rate-making structure."

The McCarran Act's retention of the Sherman Act rules against "boycott, coercion, or intimidation" in the insurance industry formed the basis of the treble-damage claim asserted in *Monarch Life Ins. Co.* v. *Loyal Protective Life Ins. Co.,* 326 F.2d 841 (2d Cir. 1963), *cert. denied,* 376 U.S. 952 (1964). In 1945, when the McCarran Act became law, Section 7 of the Sherman Act provided a treble-damage remedy. That section was repealed in 1955 on the theory that Section 4 of the Clayton Act made Section 7 of the Sherman Act surplusage. Despite an argument that the McCarran Act bars application of the Clayton Act to state-regulated insurance, the Court of Appeals for the Second Circuit could find no indication that Congress had any intention to abandon the treble-damage remedy, "which was traditionally so vital to the effective enforcement of the federal right." The court read the McCarran Act as meaning that "all boycotts or agreements to boycott condemned by the Sherman Act are rendered subject to federal law; as the treble-damage provision of the Clayton Act is a significant part of that law, it remains applicable to all such conduct."

Whether the possibility of recovering treble damages in the insurance industry survived repeal of Section 7 of the Sherman Act was also considered by the district court in the *Bankers Life case,* cited above. In sustaining the suit the court reasoned that the McCarran Act adopted the Sherman Act by reference as a means of retaining control over acts of boycott, and that when a statute adopts an earlier enactment by specific reference to it, the adoption takes the statute as it is written at the time of the adoption; subsequent amendment or repeal of the adopted statute does not affect the adopting law.

Since the Federal Trade Commission has no authority to enforce the Sherman Act directly, its authority to take enforcement action under the McCarran Act's boycott exemption may be questionable. Sherman Act violations have been held to fall within the "unfair methods of competition" ban in Section 5 of the FTC Act, but the McCarran Act specifically lists the FTC Act as one that is to be applicable to the insurance business only "to the extent that such business is not regulated by state law."

When the insurance business is in fact "regulated" by state law may be a troublesome question under the McCarran Act. Some feel it is likely that the courts will construe state "regulation" to mean regulation of not merely the industry itself but of the specific practices that form the basis of the antitrust complaint. For example, few states have adopted laws restricting mergers of insurance companies. The federal courts may apply Section 7 of the Clayton Act in states that have not adopted insurance merger controls, even if there is comprehensive regulation of all other activities of insurance companies.

Many of the statutes give the state regulatory agencies wide discretionary powers of the type delegated to public utility commissions. Consequently, some antitrust lawyers feel that the test of "regulation" will be the language of the state statute, not the amount of enforcement activity under its provisions. But, others suggest, the courts may not be satisfied with the "window dressing" some states have put into the statute books. There are lawyers who reason that, while the insurance industry has an argument against application of the antitrust laws, the argument is valid only if insurance is truly a regulated industry in the same sense as the transportation and communication industries, for example. Extensive and intensive enforcement activity may not be required, but either the state law itself or the statute plus implementing regulations may have to embody a complete, comprehensive scheme of business regulation if the antitrust laws are to be held inapplicable.

D. GOVERNMENT CONTRACTING

Question: *What special antitrust problems may be presented in sales to the Government?*

Government antitrust enforcement against collusive bidding on government sales is common. See, for example, *U.S.* v. *Carnation Co. of Wash.*, 1963 Trade Cas. ¶70,695 (E.D. Wash. 1963); *U.S.* v.

Ward Baking Co., 1963 Trade Cas. ¶70,608 (M.D. Fla. 1962), *rev'd,* 376 U.S. 327 (1964); 1965 Trade Cas. ¶71,520 (M.D. Fla. 1965). Government agencies have a statutory duty to refer to the Attorney General any bid that shows violation of the antitrust laws. See 10 U.S.C. § 2305 (d); 41 U.S.C. § 252 (d). Section 4A of the Clayton Act authorizes the recovery by the United States of any actual damages "in its business or property by reason of anything forbidden in the antitrust laws," a provision the Government has sometimes invoked with success, most spectacularly in the early 1960's against manufacturers of heavy electrical equipment.

The impact of antitrust on government procurement is less clearly defined with respect to possibly anticompetitive conduct other than bid-rigging and procurement-splitting agreements. One reason is that the government contractor operates in a market created, defined, and controlled by the Government's procurement policies and practices. Some of the market factors that have competitive significance in other segments of the economy may become inoperative in government procurement.

A major development in defense procurement since World War II, given formal recognition and impetus by Secretary McNamara, is "weapons systems contracting" (DOD Directive 3200.9 (July 1, 1965)). An extension of it is "total-package procurement." See Armed Services Procurement Regulation Par. 1-330. Weapons systems procurement differs from ordinary government contracting in that the prime contractor is given full responsibility for the design and development of a total weapons system, such as a ship, aircraft, or missile, the components of which usually transcend company and even industry product lines. Under "total-package procurement" the contractor's responsibilities also include the production and support of the weapons system. By contrast, under conventional government procurement, weapons were formerly built by contractors to detailed government specifications, and major equipment components (e.g., engines for aircraft, propulsion machinery for ships, weapons and communications equipment for ships and aircraft), usually the products of other industries, were obtained by the Government by means of competitive procurement and furnished by the Government to the contractor for installation.

The scope and complexity of weapons-systems contracting and total-package procurement with their transcendence of the resources and skills of individual companies and industries made it necessary for companies to form teams, known as "contractor team arrangements," in order to compete for and perform weapons-systems and total-package contracts. Typically, the teams are formed in anticipation of the Government's request for proposals for a particular weapons system.

When a number of manufacturers pool their resources for a government contract, a specific but limited statutory antitrust exemption may be available. Section 708 of the Defense Production Act, 50 U.S.C. App. § 2158, authorizes Presidential approval "of voluntary agreements and programs to further the objectives of this Act." Also Section 708(b), 50 U.S.C. App. § 2158 (b), provides that no action taken under an approved agreement requested by the President and found by him to be in the national defense "shall be construed to be within the prohibitions of the antitrust laws." In addition, Section 11 of the Small Business Act, 15 U.S.C. § 640, exempts defense-production and research and development pools formed by small businesses with the approval of the Small Business Administration. Yet these exemptions are relatively narrow, and few approved pools have been in operation since World War II when the statutory exemption from antitrust was much broader under the Small Business Mobilization Act of 1942 (50 U.S.C. App. § 111).

Paragraph 4-118 of the Armed Services Procurement Regulation provides for Department of Defense recognition of "the integrity and validity of contractor team arrangements" that are fully disclosed, and further states that the Department "normally will not require or encourage dissolution of contractor team arrangements." ASPR 4-118(a) defines a "contractor team arrangement" to be "one whereby two or more companies from a partnership or joint venture to act as potential prime contractor or whereby a potential prime contractor agrees with one or more companies to act as his subcontractor(s) under a specified government procurement or program." That Department policy does not authorize arrangements in violation of the antitrust laws.

Lacking exemption, weapons-system team arrangements may raise antitrust problems unaffected by the contracting agency's recognition of the arrangement. These problems are not eliminated by the likelihood that the team-bidding arrangement can be considered a joint venture, for anticompetitive restrictions imposed by or inherent in joint ventures remain subject to the antitrust laws (*Timken Roller Bearing Co.* v. *U.S.,* 341 U.S. 593 (1951); *U.S.* v. *Minn. Mining and Mfg. Co.,* 92 F.Supp. 947 (D. Mass. 1950); *U.S.* v. *Imperial Chemical Industries,* 100 F.Supp. 504 (S.D.N.Y. 1951)). If an attempt is made to give the joint venture strength and continuity through the incorporation of a separate team-bidding entity or through one prime venturer's purchase of substantial or controlling ownership interest in the other participants, the combination becomes subject to the relatively broad antimerger provisions in Section 7 of the Clayton Act (*U.S.* v. *Penn-Olin Chemical Co.,* 378 U.S. 158 (1964)).

If the members of the team remain independently owned joint

venturers, their entry into a joint venture is not necessarily an anti-trust violation. If they must combine forces to have the know-how and facilities to prepare a bid or perform the contract, their combination increases competition for the procurement. A joint venture violates the antitrust laws only if the purpose or effect of its formation, or the purpose or effect of terms in the joint venture agreement, is to restrain trade or to monopolize (*U.S.* v. *Imperial Chemical Industries,* 100 F.Supp. at 557). One of the FTC's advisory opinions (No. 245, FTC ADVISORY OPINION DIGESTS 193 (1968)) condemns as a "combination to fix prices" a proposed joint venture by five producers, actual or potential competitors of each other, to bid on and perform a contract that is beyond the capacity of any of them to perform alone.

Joint ventures have been recognized as legitimate devices of doing business, an important means of financing research and development and of creating new competition (*U.S.* v. *Pan American World Airways, Inc.,* 193 F.Supp. 18 (S.D.N.Y. 1961), *rev'd on other grounds,* 371 U.S. 296 (1963)). The necessity for some ancillary restraints on the competitive activities of the joint venturers themselves has also been acknowledged (*U.S.* v. *Bausch and Lomb Optical Co.,* 45 F.Supp. 387 (S.D.N.Y. 1942), *aff'd,* 321 U.S. 707 (1944)). The lawfulness of the ancillary restraints depends on their reasonableness. Some of the "rule of reason" cases, such as *U.S.* v. *Morgan,* 118 F.Supp. 621 (S.D.N.Y. 1953), and *Appalachian Coals, Inc.,* v. *U.S.,* 288 U.S. 344 (1933), involved joint ventures with some features closely paralleling those of weapons systems teams. A key element in both the *Investment Bankers* (Morgan) and the *Appalachian Coals* ventures was combination pricing, and the factor that saved each was the absence of power to control the market's price. In each instance, there was plenty of outside competition to influence the price set by the joint venture. In the original landmark "rule of reason" case, *Chicago Board of Trade* v. *U.S.,* 246 U.S. 231 (1918), control of market price would have been possible, but the combination imposed only a temporary freeze on prices that was effective when the Board of Trade was closed. The temporary freeze substantially increased the market's efficiency.

In most weapons-system procurement situations there is competition between at least two teams that may suffice to prevent a single weapons-system team from controlling the procurement. In addition, the Government itself could become a tough potential competitor capable of producing the item itself if the winning team's price were too high or its terms of doing business otherwise appeared to stifle long-term competition. The Government is also protected by price negotiations based on the certification as to the accuracy, completeness, and currency of detailed cost data of the winning team. Reasonableness can be written into team arrangements in the form of a specific limit on the life of the team or a provision removing all restrictions on team members once some other team or prime contractor is awarded the contract. If habit of association causes the team members to come back together each time proposals for a new weapons system procurement are requested, team agreement language terminating the arrangement after each procurement may get little weight in an assessment of the reasonableness of any anticompetitive restrictions.

There are several terms or conditions that, if found in otherwise lawful team arrangements, could raise antitrust questions. A commitment by each team member that he will not quote prices to competing teams is an agreement in restraint of trade even if its only purpose is to prevent disclosure of technical know-how. An agreement by each member that he will fill particular needs for the contract exclusively by purchase from team members may be vulnerable under both Section 1 of the Sherman Act and Section 3 of the Clayton Act, unless the scope of the team's functions is limited and there is ample competition from other bidders of comparable strength. With or without any specific restrictions on team members, an understanding that the team will stick together for subsequent procurements might give the venture the stature of a conspiracy to monopolize in violation of Section 2 of the Sherman Act if the scope of the team's activities is broad and competing bidders scarce or weak. Even in the absence of that understanding, the members' "intimate association . . . in day-to-day manufacturing operations, their exchange of patent licenses and industrial know-how, and their common experience in marketing and fixing prices may inevitably reduce their zeal for competition inter sese in the [private or future government procurement] market" (*U.S.* v. *Minn. Mining and Mfg. Co.,* 92 F.Supp. at 963).

Other conditions under which team members deal with each other may create anticompetitive influences for the private, nongovernmental market for the same or related products. If team members or nonmember subcontractors and suppliers are selected for their loyalty as customers of team members (and a "not insubstantial" amount of commerce is affected) the team may be engaging in the type of "reciprocity" prohibited by Section 1 of the Sherman Act (*U.S.* v. *General Dynamics Corp.,* 258 F.Supp. 36, 48–49 (S.D.N.Y. 1966)).

It should be recognized that weapons systems procurement for large projects that transcend industry product lines makes team arrangements necessary if these contracts are not to be made on a sole-source basis. This inducement and encouragement of team arrangements, particularly by the Department of Defense, in order to create a competitive environment, may in itself lead to antitrust violations by the team members in their efforts to come together and bid on these projects. A result of this method of procurement by the Department of Defense may have been to increase the risks of antitrust violation for contractors who engage in weapons systems procurement.

In the case of the sole-source supplier, the possible antitrust violation lies in the monopoly he may have obtained in the market. Even if the Government is his only possible customer, this monopolist gets no antitrust immunity under procurement statutes such as 10 U.S.C. § 2304. The statutes regulating federal procurement practices seem to have no bearing on the behavior of the industry into which the Government goes to negotiate a contract and in which there may or may not be competition. Implied exemptions from the antitrust laws are strongly disfavored, even in federally regulated areas of business activity (*U.S.* v. *Phila. Nat'l Bank,* 374 U.S. 321 (1963)). Since the primary emphasis of 10 U.S.C. § 2304 (a) and (g) is on procurement by formal advertising or by competitive negotiation, it seems doubtful that Congress intended to confer antitrust immunity by virtue of the statutory authorization of a sole-source procurement.

The legality of the monopoly held by the Government's sole-source supplier depends on the manner of its acquisition. If the contractor is a sole-source supplier because it is the only enterprise technologically capable of producing a product that will meet the Government's needs, the only one with an essential patent, or simply a sole survivor "as a consequence of a superior product, business acumen, or historic accident" (*U.S.* v. *Grinnell Corp.,* 384 U.S. 563, 571 (1966)), presumably its monopoly is lawful. There are other ways of becoming a sole-source government supplier that may bring a contractor into collision with the antitrust laws. For example, creation of exclusive technological capability through formation of an unnecessarily broad team would produce an illegal monopoly. If the only manufacturer of a particular product has been marketing that product through distributors, he cannot safely, by halting deliveries to them, prevent those distributors from competing with him for government procurements (*U.S.* v. *Klearflax Linen Looms,* 63 F.Supp. 32 (D. Minn. 1945)). Similarly, a sole producer of an item essential to performance of the particular type of government contract probably cannot refuse to supply competing bidders with that item (*Fred Johnson Cement Block Co.* v. *Waylite Co.,* 182 F.Supp. 914 (D. Minn. 1960)).

Another way of becoming a sole source is to persuade the procuring agency to issue product specifications so narrowly drawn as to eliminate the products of competitors. Whether influence that obtains narrow specifications eliminating otherwise acceptable products is applied unilaterally by a single business enterprise or jointly by several manufacturers, questions arise as to the antitrust status of the conduct. In *U.S.* v. *Johns-Manville Corp.,* 259 F.Supp. 440, 453 (E.D. Pa. 1966), it was held that activities engaged in to influence the decisions of public procurement officials on product specifications "are constitutionally protected and cannot be the basis of a finding of violation of the antitrust laws . . . regardless of the intent with which they were undertaken." The decision was based on *Eastern Railroad Presidents' Conference* v. *Noerr Motor Freight, Inc.,* 365 U.S. 127 (1961), and *United Mine Workers* v. *Pennington,* 381 U.S. 657 (1965). (See section I-14, p. 63.)

The Justice Department elected not to take an appeal from dismissal of the Johns-Manville complaint. There are antitrust lawyers who believe that that opinion gave unwarranted scope to the *Noerr* doctrine and who predict that on further reflection the courts will extend full Sherman Act protection to the Federal Government when it is buying or selling in a commercial market.

There is no clear line of distinction between actions taken by the Government as sovereign and those it takes as a buyer. The Government often uses its massive buying power to advance policy, to discourage racial discrimination in employment, for example. In the *Pennington* case, a TVA election to use Walsh-Healey Act procurement rather than spot-market purchases could be motivated either by a desire to give full effect to the statute or by a business purpose related to advantages of doing business with larger, more dependable suppliers of coal.

Antitrust exemption has been denied to influence that took the form of bribery (*Rangen, Inc.* v. *Sterling Nelson & Sons.,* 351 F.2d 851 (9th Cir. 1965), *cert. denied,* 38 U.S. 936 (1966)). Also in *Harman* v. *Valley Natl. Bank,* 339 F.2d 564 (9th Cir. 1964), the court refused to apply the *Noerr* doctrine to a conspiracy in which the relevant government official was "a participating conspirator," although it did accord exemption to the acts of informing the official of "irregularities" in a competitor's conduct and persuading him to take enforcement action. One commentator has suggested that a distinction must be made between influencing government officials' policy or political decisions and influencing their business or "proprietary" decisions. *Noerr* granted full antitrust exemption to conduct designed to affect policy making. On the other hand, if proprietary decisions are involved, applicability of antitrust law depends upon another distinction, one between appeals to a government official based on "considerations legitimate in the formulation of government policy" and appeals to a government official who "is himself interested in, or at least aware of, the improper approach to him" (Note, "Application of the Sherman Act to Attempts to Influence Government Action," 81 HARV. L. REV. 847 (1968)).

Another way to become a sole-source supplier, or at least reduce the competition, is by acquisition of one's competitors. The manufacture and sale of products for which only the Federal Government has use apparently can represent a relevant market, national in geographical scope, for purposes of applying the antimerger provisions in Section 7 of the Clayton Act (*U.S.* v. *Ling-Temco Electronics, Inc.,* 1961 Trade Cas. ¶70,160 (N.D. Tex. 1961)). An anticompetitive merger in such a market might also constitute a combination in restraint of trade under the doctrine of *U.S.* v. *First Nat'l. Bank & Trust Co. of Lexington,* 376 U.S. 665 (1964).

Combinations that stop short of merger have also been attacked when they eliminate competition for government procurements. In *U.S.* v. *Concentrated Phosphate Export Association,* 273 F.Supp. 263 (S.D.N.Y. 1967), *rev'd,* 393 U.S. 199 (1968), the Government attacked the use of a common selling agency by five fertilizer producers to sell fertilizer to the Republic of Korea under the United States Foreign Aid Program. The complaint was dismissed on the theory that the common sales agency is entitled to antitrust exemption under the Webb-Pomerene Export Trade Association Act, 15 U.S.C. §§ 61–65. The Government persuaded the Supreme Court to review that order with a jurisdictional statement declaring that "however sweeping an agency's regulatory powers over procurement might be, they cannot supplant the antitrust laws as the basic safeguard of the competitive process." The Court reversed the order on the grounds that the transactions were not "export trade" within the meaning of the Webb-Pomerene Act.

The Comptroller General has ruled that even though the Webb-Pomerene Act may exempt combinations in restraint of trade from the application of the antitrust laws, such exemption does not authorize procuring agencies to engage in procurements of coal for export that restrict available competition (Comp. Gen. Dec. B-159868 (Nov. 7, 1967, April 18, 1968)).

There is no government procurement policy providing for the rejection of "buy-in" bids or proposals, that is, offers that knowingly quote prices below anticipated costs. The absence of such a policy has provoked congressional criticism. As a result of investigating an Army helicopter procurement said to have involved such "buying in," a House Armed Services Subcommittee for Special Investigation recommended that the Department of Defense revise its policies "to provide contracting officials with sufficient direction and authority to dispose of, by rejection or otherwise, any attempted 'buy-ins' in accordance with DOD's stated policy on the subject."

The Defense Department response to this recommendation was to restate its policy on buying in and also to stress the use of procurement methods such as multiyear procurement and priced options for additional quantities that would avoid or minimize the opportunities for buying in. The revised Department policy, set forth in ASPR 1-311, does not, however, specifically provide for the rejection of buy-in bids and proposals. In the absence of such a policy the Comptroller General has in at least three cases refused to approve the rejection of bids or proposals alleged to buy in (Comp. Gen. Decs. B-156888 (July 2, 1965), B-158326 (May 5, 1966), and B-160065 (Nov. 17, 1966)). The Comptroller General's rulings are consistent with his historical reluctance to allow exceptions to the lowest-bidder test for making awards. A price floor is usually the death of meaningful competition. At the same time, there are market situations in which drastic price cutting can be the ultimate weapon in the destruction of competition. Predatory pricing is a common element of proven violations of the monopolization ban in Section 2 of the Sherman Act (*U.S.* v. *Grinnell Corp.*, 236 F.Supp. 244 (D.R.I. 1964), *rev'd in part on other grounds,* 384 U.S. 563 (1966).

The legality of a buy-in under Section 2 of the Sherman Act depends upon a number of market and competitor characteristics. By definition, the successful bid is below the bidder's costs; if it is high enough to cover his costs, then he is not spending anything to "buy in." However, even pricing below costs is not forbidden by Section 2 when the bidder is trying merely to stay alive in a market dominated by larger competitors, to get started in a market in which he is new, or to maintain certain skills or a particular staff organization needed for later profitable contracts. Nor does below-cost price cutting violate Section 2 when it is a defensive response to competitors' pricing practices (*Union Leader Corp.* v. *Newspapers of New England, Inc.,* 180 F.Supp. 125 (D. Mass. 1959), *modified and aff'd,* 284 F.2d 582 (1st Cir. 1960), *cert. denied,* 365 U.S. 833 (1961)). Each of these circumstances negates the existence of either actual monopoly or "exclusionary intent."

Another relevant factor is the scope of the market involved. If the government procurement involves an ordinary consumer product or one widely used in private industry, success in getting the government part of the business will often not involve either monopolization or impairment of the competitive strength of the other producers in the industry. The problem is different, though, if the procurement involves a product used only by the Government. In that situation, the low bidder obtains at least a temporary monopoly in the market. Someone will win such a monopoly every time the Government satisfies its needs in a single contract.

Yet even in a market where only one competitor can survive, the successful bidder must probably avoid "unfair weapons" and must rely on "superior skill, foresight, and industry." Below-cost pricing is an "unfair weapon" whose use may show the existence of an illegal exclusionary intent, unless the price reduction was defensive (*Union Leader Corp.* v. *Newspapers of New England, Inc.,* 180 F.Supp. at 139; 284 F.2d at 586–7).

When the government procurement involves a product or service sold or used extensively by nongovernment buyers, the Robinson-Patman Act may have to be considered because of its price discrimination restrictions and prohibition against "unreasonably low prices." In a weakly reasoned and much misconstrued opinion, the Attorney General has declared the Act inapplicable to sales to the Government (38 Ops. Atty. Gen. 539 (1936)). See also *General Shale Products Corp.* v. *Struck Const. Co.,* 37 F.Supp. 598, 602–03 (W.D. Ky. 1941); *aff'd* 132 F.2d 425 (6th Cir. 1942); Rowe, PRICE DISCRIMINATION UNDER THE ROBINSON-PATMAN ACT 84 (1962).

Buying in is more likely to be treated as an antitrust problem by the Justice Department when it involves a product sold to nongovernment buyers than when it involves a product sold *only* to the Government. As a sole buyer, the Government has means of protecting itself that are not available to industry or consumers when they must buy from a seller who, by predatory procurement of a big government contract, has gained control of the market and thereafter increased his price. When the Government is the product's only user and buyer, the buying-in problem can be resolved by insuring that the contractor does not cut corners in performance and "that any amounts possibly excluded in the original contract price are not recovered in the pricing of change orders or of follow-on procurements" (Comp. Gen. Dec. B-156888 (July 2, 1965)). Some experts are skeptical about the effectiveness of that policy, although it can be argued that a government supplier always faces potential competition, since the Government has sufficient resources to develop its own production facilities or establish other sources if necessary.

Although government contractors and government contracts are generally subject to the antitrust laws even when the Government is the only buyer, the Justice Department's Antitrust Division and the Federal Trade Commission are more likely to take an interest in contracting practices that can be shown to impair competition in nongovernment markets. Where the Government alone is affected, the enforcement agencies seem inclined to view federal contractors as akin to members of a regulated industry and to leave control of their activities, at least in the first instance, to the procuring agencies and the General Accounting Office.

While both the Antitrust Division and the FTC have business review or advisory procedures that permit the solicitation of antitrust advice in advance of undertaking a proposed course of conduct, those procedures are probably too time-consuming to be of value to government contractors in most situations. By the time a contractor prepares his bid or proposal in response to a government request, there is not enough time left to clear it with the Antitrust Division or the FTC before it must be submitted. An Antitrust Division clearance letter or an FTC advisory opinion would at best give assurance only that the Government will not sue the contractor seeking advice. It would give no protection against an antitrust suit by an unsuccessful bidder for three times the profits he would have realized if the contract had not been taken from him by anticompetitive practices.

E. AUTOMOBILE DEALERS

Question: *Have the antitrust laws been superseded in automobile distribution?*

In 1956, Congress authorized suits by automobile dealers against automobile manufacturers for damages and costs of suit for any failure of the manufacturer "to act in good faith in performing or complying with any of the terms or provisions of the (dealer's) franchise, or in terminating, canceling, or not renewing the franchise" (15 U.S.C. §§ 1221–1225). Failure of the dealer "to act in good faith" is mentioned as a defense which the manufacturer "shall not be barred from asserting."

The statute, known as the "Dealer's Day in Court Act," contains a definition of "good faith," that is, "the duty of each party to any franchise, and all officers, employees, or agents thereof to act in a fair and equitable manner toward each other so as to guarantee the one party freedom from coercion or intimidation from the other party." It is further provided that "recommendation, endorsement, exposition, persuasion, urging or argument shall not be deemed to constitute a lack of good faith." There is a three-year statute of limitations and a provision that nothing in this statute "shall repeal, modify, or supersede, directly or indirectly, any provision of the antitrust laws of the United States."

What may have been the first substantial jury award of damages under the Act came five years after passage in a suit in Pittsburgh by a Ford dealer for termination of a franchise in August 1958. The dealer claimed he was given an "impossible" quota of cars to sell and that Ford had demanded an increase in sales facilities beyond the needs of the market before termination of the franchise. The jury awarded the dealer damages of $95,000, but the district judge set aside the verdict. He found no evidence that the dealer would have suffered any damages had he complied with Ford's demands for an increase in sales facilities and staff (*Milos* v. *Ford Motor Co.*, 206 F.Supp. 86 (W.D. Pa. 1962), *aff'd,* 317 F.2d 712 (3rd Cir. 1963), *cert. denied,* 375 U.S. 896 (1963).

In another case, the Court of Appeals for the Third Circuit decided that an injunction forbidding franchise termination may be granted in a suit under the Act even though the Act contains no specific provision for injunctions (*Bateman* v. *Ford Motor Co.*, 302 F.2d 63 (3rd Cir. 1962), *rev'g* 202 F.Supp. 595 (E.D. Pa. 1962)), but the district judge twice declined to grant a preliminary injunction against franchise termination, finding insufficient evidence of "bad faith, coercion, discrimination or threatened irreparable harm" (204 F.Supp. 357 (E.D. Pa. 1962), *rev'd,* 310 F.2d 805 (3rd Cir. 1962); 214 F.Supp. 222 (E.D. Pa. 1963)).

In a suit against American Motors, another judge of the same Pittsburgh court that set aside the *Milos* verdict against Ford upheld a jury verdict of $20,000 in favor of a "small-town or country" Rambler dealer who was "unable to meet the technical and detailed directives and exigencies of this mushrooming automobile manufacturer" (*Garvin* v. *American Motors Sales Corp.*, 202 F.Supp. 667 (W.D. Pa. 1962)), but the court of appeals reversed, holding the evidence insufficient to support findings of coercion and failure to act in good faith, and directing judgment for defendant (318 F.2d 518 (3rd Cir. 1963)).

In *Woodard* v. *General Motors Corp.,* GM's summary judgment in the district court was upheld by the court of appeals, 298 F.2d 121 (5th Cir. 1962). The court of appeals agreed with the conclusion of the district court that the franchise termination of a Chevrolet dealer was based, in good faith, on failure of the dealer to maintain satisfactory sales and service facilities. The court of appeals declined to rule on the Act's constitutionality, although the court acknowledged the existence of a number of "serious questions" in this regard. The Supreme Court denied certiorari (369 U.S. 887 (1962)).

Antitrust experts seem to agree that the statute and case law provide little by which to judge the future success of suits under the Act. Some feel that the result of a lawsuit will often depend on the outlook of the judge before whom the case is heard; they point to the *Milos* and *Garvin* cases.

Where the franchise agreement is properly and carefully drafted, it may provide the best guidelines for both parties. Several automobile manufacturers have provided their own internal review procedures through which a dealer can seek reversal of an administrative decision, such as termination of the franchise, without going to court. Damages will not be awarded, however. If the dealer loses, he may still go to court. Since there is no provision in the franchise for the internal review, the dealer is not required to use the procedure before bringing formal suit.

Some commentators have deplored the Act as "class legislation," seeing in it a parallel to Section 2(c) of the Clayton Act which, some argue, seeks to protect existing distribution channels through brokers without regard to general antitrust concepts of competition. Others see in the Act a legislative tendency to equalize bargaining power similar to earlier labor law developments.

A general result of the Act may be to deter automobile manufacturers from use of their power over distribution and to place the burden on them to produce some reason for cutting off a dealer, or at least a reason sufficient to satisfy the courts. In this some see a trend in public policy toward narrowing the right of large corporate enterprises to select their own customers.

PART VII

Justice Department and Court Practice

A. THE CIVIL INVESTIGATIVE DEMAND

Question: *Are there any limits to the scope of a Civil Investigative Demand?*

Noting the powerlessness of the Department of Justice to compel response to requests for information other than through grand juries, in 1955 the Attorney General's National Committee to Study the Antitrust Laws called for a law to "authorize the Attorney General in a civil antitrust investigation, to issue and have served on any corporation, partnership or association a Civil Investigative Demand [CID]. This would require the production of existing correspondence and other business records and data or copies thereof, not privileged, in the possession of the parties served. Such documents must, however, be relevant to particular antitrust offenses stated to be under investigation."

The Supreme Court furnished additional impetus for the enactment of such legislation in *U.S.* v. *Procter & Gamble Co.*, 356 U.S. 677 (1958), by stating that the Justice Department "would be flouting the policy of the law" if it were to use a grand jury to collect evidence while contemplating only a civil antitrust suit. After repeated requests by the President, in September 1962 Congress passed the Antitrust Civil Process Act, 15 U.S.C. §§ 1311–1314 (1962), which followed fairly closely the recommendations of the Attorney General's Committee.

During the debate on the floor of the House of Representatives, Congressman William M. McCulloch (R-Ohio), one of the House managers of the bill and ranking minority member of the Antitrust Subcommittee, listed 10 "safeguards" written into the Act to prevent the Attorney General from engaging in "fishing expeditions." First, the demand "must clearly state" the nature of the conduct alleged to constitute an antitrust violation and must identify the documents demanded. Second, use of civil demands is restricted to companies actually under investigation for suspected present or past violations. Third, a civil demand may be used to obtain only documents and not oral testimony. Fourth, it can be issued only to a corporation, association, or partnership; it cannot be used to obtain personal documents from a natural person. Fifth, the Justice Department ordinarily may merely inspect and make copies of documents, the originals remaining with the business concern. Sixth, the examination and copying is to be done at the company's place of business. Seventh, a demand may not be used to get documents that are privileged or that could not be obtained by grand jury subpoena. Eighth, the Attorney General is forbidden to give any other government agency access to the documents. Ninth, the demand may be used only in advance of the institution of civil or criminal proceedings. Tenth, a dual method of seeking court review is provided.

The company, association, or partnership may refuse to comply, in which case the Justice Department is authorized by Section 5(a) of the Act to seek enforcement of the demand in the district court where the company maintains its principal office. If the company wants to initiate the court test, it is permitted by Section 5(b) to apply to the district in which it does business for an order vacating or modifying the demand.

The Antitrust Division has adopted a policy of sending with each demand a letter giving the company the name and telephone number of the attorney handling the case to whom inquiries about the scope or meaning of the demand may be made. In addition, the recipient is advised that, while the statute contemplates delivery of documents at the company's place of business, it can, if it wishes, send in copies of the requested documents by mail. Some companies accept this invitation; others take the position either that they are not sure what the Government wants or do not have the time to sort out all the records demanded and invite the Division to come in and make its own selection of documents.

Court proceedings have been filed under Section 5(b) of the Act to challenge the scope of civil investigative demands. In the *Union Oil* case (*In re Union Oil of California,* 225 F.Supp. 486 (S.D. Calif. 1963)), the Justice Department served Union Oil with a demand that stated its purpose was to ascertain whether there is or has been a violation of Section 7 of the Clayton Act in "the proposed acquisitions of fertilizer companies by petroleum companies." Union Oil was to produce from its records "each survey, study, report or other writing . . . which refers or relates to the maintenance or improvement of the corporation's position in the fertilizer market, including each such document relating to any acquisition, merger, sale of assets, or consolidation consummated or considered by the corporation." In its petition to set aside the demand, Union claimed that it was not a "person under investigation" within the meaning of the Act, since it did not propose to acquire any fertilizer companies. The Government's reply was that the purpose of the Act would be defeated if recipients of demands could avoid compliance merely by stating that they are not engaged in conduct of the type under investigation.

The district court held the civil investigative demand void and set it aside. The court pointed out that, according to the statute, the demand must state the antitrust violation under investigation. The court found that in this case the investigation was of a proposed merger which, if consummated, might be a violation. There was not yet and could not be any violation, according to the court, so the demand did not meet the requirements of the Act. The decision was affirmed on appeal (343 F.2d 29 (9th Cir. 1965)).

In *Material Handling Institute* v. *McLaren,* 426 F.2d 90 (3rd Cir. 1970), *cert. denied.,* 400 U.S. 826 (1970), a trade association challenged a CID on the grounds that it failed to describe adequately the conduct under investigation. The demand said only that it was investigating a "contract or combination in unreasonable restraint of trade." The court of appeals affirmed the district court's denial of the petition to set the CID aside, finding that the Institute must have understood what conduct was under investigation since it had corresponded with the Justice Department for two years concerning the latter's desire for information on restrictive membership practices. The court held that in these circumstances the Antitrust Civil Process Act's requirement of description of the conduct under investigation was satisfied.

Hyster Co. sought to have a demand set aside on the grounds that the Antitrust Civil Process Act was unconstitutional and that the demand did not comply with the Act. The district court upheld the Act and the demand, and a court of appeals affirmed (*Hyster Co.* v. *U.S.* 338 F.2d 183 (9th Cir. 1964)).

In *In re Gold Bond Stamp Co.,* 221 F.Supp. 391 (D. Minn. 1963), *aff'd,* 325 F.2d 1018 (8th Cir. 1964), the court was asked to invalidate a demand for documents listed on seven legal-size sheets of paper. According to the brief Gold Bond filed in the court of appeals, the demand asked for 45 separate types of documents and "into its giant maw . . . swept every piece of paper in [its] relationship with, and its activities, policies, and practices with respect to, its suppliers and its customers." Before the due date Gold Bond filed a petition to set aside or modify the demand. Gold Bond contended that the demand failed to comply with the requirements of the statute and amounted to an unreasonable search and seizure violating the Federal Constitution's Fourth Amendment.

Under Section 4(b)(1) of the Antitrust Civil Process Act, each civil demand is required to "state the nature of the conduct constituting the alleged antitrust violation which is under investigation and the provision of law applicable thereto." In the demand to Gold Bond, the Antitrust Division said it was investigating "restrictive practices and acquisitions involving dispensing, supplying, sale, or furnishing of trading stamps and the purchase and sale of goods and services in connection therewith." The applicable provisions of law were listed as "Title 15 United States Code Secs. 1, 2, 3, 13, 14, and 18." The first three are the Sherman Act's restraint-of-trade and monopolization provisions, and the last three are the Clayton Act's restrictions on price discrimination, exclusive dealing, and mergers.

Gold Bond argued that the demand was being used as an adjunct to a general survey of the trading stamp industry rather than as a means of investigating specific antitrust violations. The district court's attention was called to the lack of any statement in the demand that Gold Bond was suspected of an antitrust violation. Consequently, it was contended, there was no indication that Gold Bond was "under investigation" within the meaning of Section 3(a) of the Act.

During argument before the district court, the Antitrust Division attorney stated: "This investigation arose from a series of complaints from retailers and the general public and from other sources of information that there was a pattern of acquisitions or inter-corporate relationships in the trading stamp industry which may violate the antitrust laws and that there might be a broad variety of restrictive practices which similarly may constitute violation. . . . The petition alleges we have little understanding of the trading stamp industry. That is in a large part correct. We are beginning an investigation. We do not have a great deal of information about how these companies do business and that is what we are attempting to elicit."

The district judge sustained the civil investigative demand. Treating the Fourth Amendment argument as going to the validity of the statute itself, he rejected it. In his view, the Act goes no further than the Fair Labor Standards Act or the FTC Act, the investigative provisions of which were upheld by the Supreme Court in *Oklahoma Press Publishing Co.* v. *Walling,* 327 U.S. 186 (1946), and *U.S.* v. *Morton Salt Co.,* 338 U.S. 632 (1950).

The judge agreed that the information supplied by the demand was insufficient to specify the particular offense or offenses under investigation, but he pointed out that the purpose of the statute is to enable the Attorney General to find out whether there have been any antitrust violations. "To insist upon too much specificity with regard to the requirement of this section would defeat the purpose of the Act, and an overly strict interpretation of this section would only breed litigation and encourage everyone investigated to challenge the sufficiency of the notice." He pointed out that Congress rejected an American Bar Association proposal that the demand be required to state "the particular offense which the Attorney General . . . has reason to believe may have been committed."

Despite Congressman McCulloch's statement that "fishing expeditions" are not authorized, the district court seemed to suggest that the Act may authorize just that. "Constantly the courts have been reminded of the 'no fishing' signs which have confronted some governmental agencies in their attempts to enforce civil process, but here, by the clear intent of Congress, such signs as to a proceeding under the Antitrust Civil Process Act seem to have been virtually eliminated. If the proceeding is within the purview of authority vested in the Attorney General by Congress and if the nature of the inquiry under the antitrust laws, as required by the Act, is made known to the person investigated and the list of documents demanded is reasonably relevant to the investigation, the court should recognize that this legislation comes within the broad powers of Congress."

In *Lightning Rod Mfrs. Assn.* v. *Staal,* 339 F.2d 346 (7th Cir. 1964), a trade association challenged a CID on the basis of time span. The demand covered the period from 1945 to September of 1963. The court reasoned that because courts had upheld subpoenas covering equally long periods of time, the Antitrust Civil Process Act authorized a CID's covering such a time period.

In 1963 the chief of the Antitrust Division reported that "over 140" CIDs had been issued. Addressing the Antitrust Section of the American Bar Association, Assistant Attorney General William H. Orrick, Jr., described the CID as a "useful investigative tool," but found it "difficult to say with certainty what the outer limits of the proper usage of the CID are."

Sections 5(a) and 5(b) of the Act raise some interesting procedural problems. If the company served with a demand files an objecting petition under Section 5(b), can the Government in the same proceeding obtain an order enforcing the demand? If the company does not comply with the demand but waits until the Government moves for enforcement, has the company waived its objections? If, as even some lawyers expect, the courts find it proper and expedient to dispose of the entire dispute in a single proceeding and if silent noncompliance is not treated as a waiver, the tendency may be to sit back and wait for the Justice Department to make the first move, thereby at least buying a little extra time for the collection of the documents the Government is demanding. If, on the other hand, it is eventually decided that a court order enforcing a civil demand can be secured by the Government only in a proceeding it initiates under subsection (a), the lawyer may be able to buy still more time for his client by initiating a subsection (b) proceeding.

B. CONSENT DECREES

1. Question: *Do outstanding consent decrees inhibit antitrust enforcement?*

Almost three fourths of the civil antitrust actions filed by the Justice Department have ended with decrees agreed upon by the parties without a trial. (The Government and the defendants sometimes agree upon the form and content of a decree after an adjudication of a violation. While such judgments are sometimes called consent decrees, the present discussion relates only to consent decrees entered without trial.) Decrees entered without trial ordinarily recite that they are entered without any finding that the defendants have violated any law. But see *U.S.* v. *Lake Asphalt & Petroleum Co.,* 1960 Trade Cas. ¶69,835 (D. Mass. 1960).

To the Antitrust Division, the consent-settlement procedure offers quick disposition of cases and an opportunity to appraise factual and legal considerations in the light of additional information made available during negotiations. The Division sometimes bypasses problems of lesser importance, areas where its proof is weak, or areas where it discovers that its original conception of relief would work unnecessary hardship or possible injury to third parties. The negotiated consent settlement can involve concessions to obtain those objectives the Division regards as significant.

There is no public record against which a consent judgment can be evaluated. In contrast with the broad allegations of a typical complaint, even when no real concession has been made, it may appear that the Antitrust Division has settled for a decree less restrictive than it might have obtained after litigation. As a result, some consent judgments have been criticized as ineffective instruments of antitrust policy.

In 1958, the House Antitrust Subcommittee conducted an investigation of the Justice Department's consent-decree program after receiving complaints that "consent-decree procedures essentially amounted to a compromise of the government's interest" and that consent decrees "often deprived the government of relief it could have obtained if it had litigated its case." In its printed report, the subcommittee examined two decrees in detail, *U.S.* v. *Western Electric Co.,* 1956 Trade Cas. ¶68,246 (D.N.J. 1956), known as the *AT&T* case, and *U.S.* v. *Atlantic Refining Co.,* December 23, 1941 (D. D.C.), known as the *Oil Pipe Line* decree, and found each of those decrees to have "little value as instruments of antitrust policy." "In addition to the compromise of adequate relief," the report went on, "consent settlements of antitrust cases result in a substantial lessening, if not the virtual elimination, of the deterrent effect the antitrust laws have on business operations" (Subcommittee No. 5 of the House Judiciary Committee Report on Consent Decree Program of the Department of Justice, 86th Congress, 1st Sess. (1959)).

Injunctive provisions, whether by consent or otherwise, are generally of indefinite duration. The passage of time may bring economic or market changes which make the prohibitions ineffective. Occasionally special provisions have been added to make the decree a more flexible device. For example, provision has been made for termination of the decree or some of its provisions on the occurrence of a specific event or the development of certain conditions (*U.S.* v. *Internat'l Nickel Co.*, 1948–49 Trade Cas. ¶62,280 (S.D. N.Y. 1948); *U.S.* v. *American Lead Pencil Co.*, 1954 Trade Cas. ¶67,676 (D. N.J. 1954)). Other consent decrees have included provisions for later modification upon proof of specified circumstances, e.g., *U.S.* v. *General Motors Corp.*, 1965 Trade Cas. ¶71,624 (E.D. Mich. 1965); *U.S.* v. *American Lead Pencil Co.*, 1954 Trade Cas. ¶67,676 (D.N.J. 1954); *U.S.* v. *Libbey-Owens-Ford Glass Co.*, 1948–49 Trade Cas. ¶62,323 (N.D. Ohio 1948); *U.S.* v. *Internat'l Harvester Co.*, 274 U.S. 693,697 (1927); *U.S.* v. *Columbia Artists Management, Inc.*, 1955 Trade Cas. ¶68,173 (S.D. N.Y. 1955). Following its defeat in the *International Harvester* case, the Government did not seek additional relief under a modification clause until *U.S.* v. *United Shoe Machinery Corp.*, 266 F.Supp. 328 (D. Mass. 1967), *rev'd*, 391 U.S. 244 (1968).

Many consent orders contain a "retention of jurisdiction" clause: "Jurisdiction is retained for the purpose of enabling any party to this Final Judgment to apply to this Court at any time for such further orders and directions as may be necessary or appropriate for the construction or carrying out of this Final Judgment, [or] for the modification of any of the provisions thereof." Petitions for modification under that clause have almost always failed (e.g., *U.S.* v. *Swift & Co.*, 286 U.S. 106 (1932); *U.S.* v. *Swift & Co.*, 189 F.Supp. 885 (N.D. Ill. 1960), *aff'd*, 367 U.S. 909 (1961)), although language in some Supreme Court opinions suggests that modification may be more easily obtainable by the Government than by defendants (*Chrysler Corp.* v. *U.S.*, 316 U.S. 556 (1942); *Hughes* v. *U.S.*, 342 U.S. 353, 357 (1952)).

Inclusion of the standard clause would not seem to change anything. "Whether the decree has been entered after litigation or by consent . . ., a court does not abdicate its power to revoke or modify its mandate if satisfied that what it has been doing has been turned through changing circumstances into an instrument of wrong" (*U.S.* v. *Swift & Co.*, 286 U.S. at 114–115). Except in the *Chrysler* case, however, the Government has never succeeded in obtaining modification of an antitrust consent judgment over the defendant's opposition. For example, an unsuccessful attempt was made in *Ford Motor Co.* v. *U.S.,* 335 U.S. 303 (1948).

In *U.S.* v. *RCA,* 46 F.Supp. 654 (D. Del. 1942), *appeal dismissed,* 318 U.S. 796 (1943), the Government moved to vacate a set of 10-year-old consent decrees so it could sue for stronger ones. The motion was denied on the theory that the consent decrees conferred a benefit on the defendants and were "a bar to any attempt by the government to relitigate the issues raised in the suit or to seek relief with respect thereto additional to that given by the consent decrees." Nevertheless, the Government filed a new action against RCA in 1954. The complaint's allegations of antitrust violations were limited to activities postdating the filing of the consent decree. The complaint apparently resulted from the discovery of evidence during a grand jury proceeding in which RCA pleaded the consent decree as a bar to the grand jury's subpoena. The district court refused to quash the subpoena, holding that the consent decree did not bar a subsequent grand jury investigation (*Application of Radio Corp. of America,* 13 F.R.D. 167 (S.D.N.Y. 1952)).

Another attempt to bar action against a defendant already subject to a broad consent decree was challenged in *U.S.* v. *Aluminum Co. of America,* 20 F.Supp. 608 (W.D. Pa. 1937). The second suit was allowed to continue because 62 additional defendants were named in the second complaint, a different legal theory was being advanced, and different relief was being sought. Both the rule applied by the district court and its analysis of the consent decree and the pleadings were upheld by the Supreme Court (302 U.S. 230 (1937)).

In the 1959 report of the House Antitrust Subcommittee, cited above, one of the reasons given for concern about the consent decree program was the apparent finality of the decrees. "Although antitrust consent decrees are not adjudications that defendants in fact and law have violated the antitrust statutes, they nonetheless have been held to provide, as do other civil judgments, a basis for invoking the doctrine of res judicata and the concept of estoppel associated therewith. Thus, defendants are precluded from collaterally attacking a consent decree on the ground that there are errors contained therein, and the Government is foreclosed from litigating the matters previously concluded by consent." Yet, in *U.S.* v. *Internat'l Building Co.,* 345 U.S. 502 (1953), the Supreme Court said the doctrine of res judicata or estoppel by judgment should not "become a device by which a decision not shown to be on the merits would forever foreclose inquiry into the merits."

As Assistant Attorney General, Donald F. Turner thought the Government could sue for greater relief than that afforded by an existing consent decree. He said: "Whatever may be the proper dimensions of the Government's right to secure substantial new relief without adjudication of liability, I believe that the Government should have a considerably broader right to secure further relief when it is prepared to go to trial on issues of liability, either in a reopened earlier proceeding or on the basis of a new complaint. In my view, a consent decree is no 'legal' bar at all, to, say, a new antitrust complaint by the Government, even if the new complaint contains precisely the same charges as those in the original suit. This is not to say that the Government's right to institute and proceed with a new suit is untrammeled; the propriety of permitting the renewed attack is subject to some equitable limitations imposed by the courts. But the limitations imposed by what we might call 'equitable estoppel' should be less demanding than the limitations imposed when the Government seeks modification of a consent decree because there has been no substantial change in circumstances or because the proposed relief goes beyond the 'purpose' of the original consent decree. The public interest in the effective enforcement of the antitrust laws makes it essential that the Government be reasonably free to cure anticompetitive practices or anticompetitive conditions which an earlier consent decree—for whatever reason—failed to cure" (Address by Donald F. Turner, Association of the Bar of the City of New York, Dec. 13, 1968).

On the day before Mr. Turner made this statement, the Antitrust Division had filed in the Supreme Court a memorandum defending one of its consent decrees against a charge that it sanctioned antitrust violations. Addressing the court as amicus curiae in *K-91, Inc.,* v. *Gershwin Publishing Corp.,* 389 U.S. 1045 (1968), the Government said: "We do not understand the court below to have held that the consent decree now in force against ASCAP of itself makes lawful what would otherwise be unlawful. . . . To the extent that ASCAP's activities, whether under the consent decree or unregulated, violate the antitrust laws, both the United States and private parties have a continuing remedy under the Sherman Act. . . . As conditions change or abuses are disclosed, it may become necessary . . . for the government to seek modifications of that decree or to file suit for additional relief."

(Under Section 5(b) of the FTC Act, "The Commission may at any time, after notice and opportunity for hearing, reopen and alter, modify, or set aside, in whole or in part, any report or order made or issued by it under this section, whenever in the opinion of the Commission conditions of fact or of law have so changed as to require such action or if the public interest shall so require." In *Elmo Division* v. *Dixon,* 348 F.2d 342 (D.C.Cir. 1965), the court of appeals refused to let the FTC go ahead with a new complaint proceeding on matters covered by a consent order. In such a situation, the court held, the Commission must follow the reopening procedure spelled out in its Rules. Later, the court of appeals upheld the Commission's order reopening the consent order (*Elmo Co.* v. *FTC,* 389 F.2d 550 (D.C. Cir. 1967), *cert. denied,* 392 U.S. 905 (1968)).)

In his statement to the Association of the Bar of the City of New York Mr. Turner indicated that there were some markets in which he would have liked to move but felt frustrated by outstanding consent decrees. To solve this problem it has been suggested that decrees be written to expire after a specified term of years, (e.g., 12–15 years: Victor H. Kramer, "Modification of Consent Decrees," 1 HOFFMAN'S ANTITRUST LAWS AND TECHNIQUES 385), or to expire or add specific new restrictions, upon a showing of designated future market conditions. While adoption of these techniques might eliminate the problem in the future, they offer no solution to the problem, if there is one, of outstanding decrees. As to them, it is a matter of modifying an existing decree and bringing a new suit. When the Attorney General files a new complaint, he probably need be concerned about an existing consent decree only if he seeks to enjoin conduct attacked in the original complaint but not prohibited by the decree or when he seeks a decree provision proposed during the consent order negotiations but left out of the judgment. The *Alcoa* case referred to above suggests that any conduct postdating the consent decree or not covered by the original complaint can be attacked in new litigation.

Whether the Government proceeds by complaint or petition to reopen, its attempt to resurrect decree provisions abandoned during preconsent negotiations is in a sense a default on a contractual commitment. A consent decree has many attributes of a contract, a contract approved by a court and, according to the *RCA* opinion, "binding on the government." Yet the Supreme Court has explicitly rejected "the argument . . . that a decree entered upon consent is to be treated as a contract and not as a judicial act" (*U.S.* v. *Swift & Co.,* 286 U.S. at 115). The question Mr. Turner answered in the negative is whether this "judicial act" equitably prohibits the Government from claiming what it once conceded. But the courts probably would not find the Government prohibited from enjoining an antitrust violation. It has been held that a consent decree cannot be construed as sanctioning an antitrust violation, that any decree attempting to do so would be void (*U.S.* v. *Columbia Artists Management, Inc.,* 1963 Trade Cas. ¶70,955 (S.D.N.Y. 1963)).

Many antitrust lawyers believe that an existing consent order is never a legal bar to the initiation of new antitrust litigation against a continuing violation. Yet the consent decree does raise what might be called a psychological barrier to further action. That barrier is especially strong in merger proceedings, for a consent order that stops short of divestiture could logically be read to represent an express consent by the Government to continuation of common ownership as well as a recognition that common ownership and operation would not jeopardize competition in violation of the Clayton Act once the consent order's restrictions become operative. It seems doubtful, however, that a court would bar a new government move for divestiture if it turned out that the merger, despite the restrictions of the decree, had produced unfortunate market results. The courts might distinguish between structural and behavioral violations; they might not be so willing to let the Government reopen an abandoned attack on a structural violation.

2. Question: *Do consent decrees have a purpose?*

The Supreme Court, dividing 4 to 3, ruled that Greyhound Corporation could retain the controlling interest in Armour & Co., which it had recently purchased from General Host (*U.S.* v. *Armour & Co.,* 402 U.S. 673 (1971)). The transaction between Greyhound and General Host had mooted the Government's earlier case against General Host. See *U.S.* v. *Armour & Co.,* 398 U.S. 268 (1970). The Court this time held that, although Greyhound has two wholly owned subsidiaries in the retail food business, it is not, as the acquirer of the Armour stock, subject to a 1920 consent decree that prohibits Armour (and four other packers) from "engaging or carrying on, either by concert of action or otherwise . . . the manufacturing, jobbing, selling . . . distributing, or otherwise dealing in" certain specified food and grocery products. The decree also prohibits the packers from "owning, either directly or indirectly . . . any capital stock or other interest whatsoever" in businesses dealing in those products.

The Government, pursuant to Section 5 of the Sherman Act, had brought Greyhound before the district court having jurisdiction over the 1920 decree, seeking to enjoin it from exercising control over Armour and to require divestiture of the stock. The Government's contention was "that the acquisition violates the decree since it causes Armour to be engaged in activities prohibited by the decree. The claim is that Greyhound is engaged in businesses that the decree prohibits Armour from being engaged in and the decree's purported purpose of separating the meatpackers from the retail food business is thus circumvented."

The Court, in an opinion by Justice Marshall, joined by Chief Justice Burger and Justices Harlan and Stewart, rejected the contention that the decree effected a complete "structural separation" between Armour and the retail food business. The language of the decree, as read by the Court, "prohibits particular actions and relationships not including the one here in question . . . [The] language [in the crucial provision], taken in its natural sense, bars only active conduct on the part of [Armour]."

The Court refused to construe the decree in the light of a purported purpose, as the Government had urged. The Court noted that the Government had argued "that to allow Greyhound to take over Armour would allow the same kind of anticompetitive evils which the 1920 suit was brought to prevent. In its 1920 suit, the Government sought to insulate the large meatpackers from the grocery business, both to prevent the destruction of competition in that business, and to prevent consolidation of the packers' monopoly control of the meat business by controlling commerce in products which might be substituted for meat. Those purposes, the Government says, are frustrated as much by a retail food company's acquisition of a meatpacker as they would be by a meatpacker's entry into the retail food business." In the Court's view, while this argument would have been proper "if addressed to a court which had the responsibility for formulating original relief in this case, after the factual and legal issues raised by the pleadings had been litigated," or as an "argument for modifying the original decree, after full litigation, on a claim that unforeseen circumstances now made additional relief desirable to prevent the evils aimed at by the original complaint," it was "out of place" in dealing with the construction of an existing consent decree. The Court said: "Consent decrees are entered into by parties to a case after careful negotiation has produced agreement on their precise terms. The parties waive their right to litigate the issues involved in the case and thus save themselves the time, expense, and inevitable risk of litigation. Naturally the agreement reached normally embodies a compromise; in exchange for the saving of cost and elimination of risk, the parties each give up something they might have won had they proceeded with the litigation. Thus the decree itself cannot be said to have a purpose; rather the parties have purposes, generally opposed to each other, and the resultant decree embodies as much of those opposing purposes as the respective parties have the bargaining power and skill to achieve. For these reasons, the scope of a consent decree must be discerned within its four corners, and not by reference to what might satisfy the purposes of one of the parties to it (402 U.S. at 680–681)."

In dissent, Justice Douglas, joined by Justices Brennan and White (Justices Black and Blackmun did not participate), took the position "that judges who construe, interpret, and enforce consent decrees look at the evil which the decree was designed to rectify." He went on to say: "The evil at which the present decree is aimed—combining meatpackers with companies in other food product areas—

is present whether Armour purchases a company dealing in the various prohibited food lines or whether that company purchases Armour. When any company purchases Armour they acquire not only Armour's assets and liabilities, but also Armour's legal disabilities. And one of Armour's legal disabilities is that Armour cannot be combined with a company in the various food lines set out in the decree." The dissenters would have sent the case back to the district court for a determination as to whether the businesses of the Greyhound subsidiaries are within the class which Armour, under the decree, is prohibited from engaging in or from owning.

The Court's decision applies only to consent decrees entered before litigation of the issues. Where there has been such litigation, the purpose of a final decree can be determined from the record. Some observers applaud the decision, arguing that a consent decree is often a face-saving device to conclude a weak case. They stress the fact that a consent decree entered before litigation must be construed in accordance with general contract principles, since there is no record to enlighten a court as to possible broader purposes of the decree. Despite the Court's statement that "the scope of a consent decree must be discerned within its four corners," some observers feel that it would be proper to refer to the complaint for guidance on product and market definitions and the like.

Some see in this decision an indication that the Burger Court will do less "legislating" that the Warren Court, will be more "lawyerlike" in its approach, will do less driving through to an objective regarded by the justices as desirable on policy grounds.

There are those who suggest that this decision may not remain controlling for all time, that there may yet be life in the proposition (which Justice Douglas in his dissent says is supported by the authorities) "that judges who construe, interpret, and enforce consent decrees look at the evil which the decree was designed to rectify." Otherwise, they say, what is the purpose of the court's retaining jurisdiction? They also ask, what of the theory that the decree has an estoppel effect? These observers argue that this particular case may have presented an unusual situation, having been before the Court previously, and they suggest that the Court, eager to dispose of the case, may have welcomed a rationale that might not be generally applicable.

A few consent decrees contain a statement of purpose agreed upon by the parties. It is possible that the Government (and conceivably some defendants) will press for the inclusion of such statements in future decrees.

In construing the meatpackers decree, the Court noted the absence of a "successors and assigns" clause in a critical provision. Perhaps more serious attention will be paid to such "boiler plate" language in the future.

There was no allegation that Armour, which already was subject to the decree, was itself trying to evade it. The Court observed that the Government did not contend that Greyhound had acted "in active concert or participation with" a party to the decree. Had Armour been the moving force behind the acquisition, it is possible that the result in the case might have been different.

As noted above, the Court at one point suggested that the Government's argument would have been an appropriate "argument for modifying the original decree, after full litigation, on a claim that unforeseen circumstances now make additional relief desirable to prevent the evils aimed at by the original complaint." The dissenting opinion points out, however, that as stated in *Chrysler Corp.* v. *U.S.*, 316 U.S. 556, 562 (1942), the test for reviewing a modification of a consent decree is "whether the changes served to effectuate or to thwart the basic purpose of the decree." Now that the Court has ruled that a consent decree entered before litigation has no "basic purpose," many ask: What standard now governs the *modification* of such a consent decree? Further, noting that the Court in *Armour* allows for modification "after full litigation," these observers ask whether "full litigation" refers to the original issues in the complaint; and, if so, whether a consent decree has less than full estoppel effect.

Some find these questions are largely academic. They point out that it has always been difficult to modify a consent decree and that in most instances it is easier to bring a new action than to seek a modification. Still, a new action might not always be feasible, and so the *Armour* decision may indeed have some consequences in this area. One thing is certain: the *Armour* decision places an added premium from the enforcement point of view upon meticulous care in the drafting of consent decrees. A favorable construction, in the light of an overriding purpose, cannot be relied upon to fill in any gaps.

3. Question: *Can a district court enter a consent judgment without the Government's consent?*

One of the principal purposes Congress is said to have had in enacting the Clayton Act in 1914 was to make the private treble-damage action a more effective tool for enforcement of the antitrust laws. To assist victims of antitrust violations in the task of proving a case a provision was written into Section 5 of the Act that a criminal or civil judgment obtained by the Government under the antitrust laws "shall be prima facie evidence" in a later treble-damage suit.

The provision could have impeded government enforcement efforts, since it might have discouraged capitulation by defendants in government suits. Consequently, a proviso that "this section shall not apply to consent judgments or decrees entered before any testimony has been taken" was inserted in the Act.

One of the supposed purposes of the proviso was to save the Government the expense of trying cases that could be readily settled if settlement would not wipe out defenses to damage claims. The Government's interest in avoiding a trial is not so clear when the victims of the antitrust violation are governmental agencies. In 1960, the Justice Department came up with a device for settling injunction suits and yet establishing a "prima facie" basis for government damage claims. By including in a price-fixing consent decree what came to be known as "the asphalt clause," the Justice Department prepared the way for the Commonwealth of Massachusetts and many of its cities and towns to use the decree to recover treble damages.

Massachusetts had discovered its losses in August and October of 1959 when the U.S. Justice Department had filed criminal and civil actions charging a number of companies with rigging bids on asphalt, road tar, and bituminous concrete sold to governmental bodies in the New England area. In the criminal cases, nolo contendere pleas were accepted over the objections of the Justice Department. The Attorney General of Massachusetts was denied permission to appear in opposition to the pleas. Later, however, federal officials reacted sympathetically to a request by the Commonwealth that it be given some protection in any consent decree that might be entered in the civil suits. In October 1960, consent decrees were entered in which the companies admitted the allegations of the Government's complaint and agreed to an adjudication that they had engaged in an unlawful conspiracy (*U.S.* v. *Lake Asphalt & Petroleum Co.,* 1960 Trade Cas. ¶69,835 (D. Mass. 1960)). Both terms were subject to the qualification that they were agreed to "for the sole purpose of establishing the prima facie effect of this final judgment" in any treble-damage suits already instituted by Massachusetts or any of its cities or towns. The consent decree also enjoined each of the companies "from denying that this final judgment has such prima facie effect in any such suit."

The Antitrust Division attempted a similar maneuver against a group of manufacturers charged with conspiring to rig bids on folding gymnasium bleachers sold to public school districts and state universities. In that case, (*U.S.* v. *Brunswick-Balke-Collender Co.,* 203 F.Supp. 657 (E.D. Wisc. 1962), *consent decree,* 1962 Trade Cas. ¶70,346 (E.D. Wisc. 1962)), however, the manufacturers refused to accede to the Government's proposed judgment as long as it contained a clause enjoining them "from defending—on the grounds that they have not violated the Sherman Act as charged in the goverment complaint—any damage proceeding initiated by any state or political subdivision thereof, if such suit were instituted prior to the date of entry of this final judgment." Once agreement had been reached with the Government on every term of the proposed consent judgment except the quoted clause, the manufacturers went to the federal district court and asked for entry of a judgment without the controversial provision. The court found in Section 5 of the Clayton Act "an unqualified right" of a government antitrust suit defendant to avoid the prima-facie-evidence provision of that section by capitulating to the Government's demand for injunctive relief. He concluded that the Government's insistence upon the provision protecting treble-damage claims would frustrate the clear intent of Congress to encourage settlement of government antitrust suits by consent decrees. He entered judgment against the manufacturers in the form they proposed and over the objections of the Justice Department.

Another possible device for protecting damage claims met with disapproval in the *Ward Baking* case (*U.S.* v. *Ward Baking Co.,* 1963 Trade Cas. ¶70,608 (M.D. Fla. 1962)). There, five bakeries, sued for conspiring to rig bids on Naval-base procurements, persuaded a district judge to enter a judgment the Government was not ready to consent to. A principal reason the Government would not sign a consent order was its desire to obtain an adjudication that the bakeries had in fact engaged in an illegal conspiracy. As in the *Brunswick* case, the court in the *Ward Baking* case concluded that the Government's refusal to sign a consent judgment "is frustrating the clear intent of Congress to encourage early entries of an injunction decree without long and protracted trials." All the Government was entitled to, the judge said, was a judgment "with every safeguard needful to accomplish the prevention and restraint of the violations of the Sherman Act as set forth in the complaint." In two respects, however, the judgment was narrower than the terms demanded by the Government during consent-order negotiations. It mentioned only bakery products sold to the Government, whereas the Justice Department wanted it to cover all bakery products, and it did not contain the Government's proposed prohibition against urging or requiring other bakeries to adhere to specified prices or terms of sale.

On direct appeal, the Supreme Court vacated the consent judgment and remanded the case for trial (376 U.S. 327 (1964)). The Court concluded that the additional relief sought by the Government had a reasonable basis under the circumstances and ruled that the district court had erred in entering a consent judgment without the Government's actual consent. "Where the government seeks an item of relief to which evidence adduced at trial may show that it is entitled, the District Court may not enter a 'consent' judgment without the actual consent of the government" (376 U.S. at 334). On remand the District Court entered another consent decree, 1965 Trade Cas. ¶71,520 (M.D. Fla. 1965), to which the Government agreed, having obtained what it wanted.

The existence of damage claims to be protected was unclear in the *Ward Baking* case. The Government had already announced settlement of its damage claims against the bakeries, and the injunction suit related only to rigging of bids on sales to southeastern Naval bases. However, an adjudication of a violation, unlike the asphalt clause, would have been of value in damage suits brought subsequently, as well as those pending at the time the judgment was entered.

The policy of the Justice Department in the asphalt and *Brunswick* cases was limited to the protection of damage claims asserted by governmental agencies, but the Justice Department need not restrict the protection of its asphalt clauses to the damage claims of governmental agencies. In *U.S.* v. *Paramount Pictures,* 334 U.S. 131, 171 (1948), the Supreme Court used language that might be read as entitling the Government to a requirement that the antitrust violator make restitution to his victims. In an antitrust injunction suit, the Supreme Court declared, "the problem of the District Court does not end with enjoining continuance of the unlawful restraints nor with dissolving the combination which launched the conspiracy. Its function includes undoing what the conspiracy achieved. . . . The requirement that the defendants restore what they unlawfully obtained is no more punishment than the familiar remedy of restitution."

Any extensive use of the asphalt clause would refocus attention on the conflicting policy considerations that clashed in Congress when the Clayton Act was debated. Will enforcement of the antitrust laws be facilitated more by encouraging consent decrees or by protecting damage claimants? If the consent decree is given priority, how serious an impediment does the asphalt clause really create? The answer to the second question depends, of course, on how many antitrust suits are now settled by companies that think they would have a chance of winning in court but simply do not want to spend the time, money, and additional unfavorable publicity to find out. If a company knows the Government has the goods on it, the Government's insistence on an asphalt clause may be less likely to prevent the acceptance of a consent judgment.

On the other hand, the Government's inability to get an asphalt clause may reduce the Justice Department's willingness to consider a consent order at all. In view of what happened in the *Brunswick* case, the only safe course for the Government to follow when damage claims are pending may be refusal even to begin consent-order negotiations.

There seems to be a suggestion in Judge Simpson's opinion in the *Ward Baking* case that a defendant in a government antitrust injunction suit can call for the entry of judgment as soon as he is willing to accept all the prohibitions necessary to halt the violations the Government complained of. Unlike the judgment entered in the *Brunswick* case, the *Ward Baking* judgment was entered at a time when there was still substantial disagreement between the parties as to the scope of the normal prohibitory provisions of the decree. It might be that the defendants could have moved for entry of their proposed judgment even if no consent-order negotiations had occurred.

From the point of view of the treble-damage claimant, the question might be asked whether an order of this sort can be considered a "consent judgment" within the meaning of the Section 5(a) proviso creating an exception to the "prima facie evidence" principle. Superficially, it would seem strange to classify as a "consent decree" one that is in fact entered without the Government's consent. The proviso mentions "consent judgments or decrees entered before any testimony has been taken." If this language is read as referring to two different types of orders, "consent judgments" and "decrees entered before any testimony has been taken," then the *Brunswick* and *Ward Baking* orders would fall in the second category. The Government's "consent" is essential if the phrase "entered before any testimony has been taken" is read as modifying both "consent judgments" and "consent . . . decrees." This interpretation would seem consistent with the wording of a temporary second proviso that appeared in the original Clayton Act: "Provided further, this section shall not apply to consent judgments or decrees rendered in criminal proceedings or suits in equity, now pending, in which the taking of testimony has been commenced but has not been concluded, provided such judgments or decrees are rendered before any further testimony is taken."

C. WITNESSES

1. Confidential Informants

Question: *How secret is the identity of a confidential government informant in antitrust and trade regulation matters?*

To enforce the antitrust and trade regulation laws the Government needs a constant flow of information. For the Government to receive information, someone must inform. Sometimes a potential

informer may be unwilling to supply information unless he is sure
his identity will be protected. Fear of economic retaliation is often
said to be a reason for the business informer's desire to remain
anonymous. Even where no retaliation is likely, many businessmen
simply do not like to have it known that they have "squealed" on
others in the business community. In order to encourage the flow of
information thought to be necessary, the Government offers to protect the identity of informers.

Defendants in antitrust and trade regulation cases also have a
legitimate need for information to defend themselves. The Government's informers may have information important to the defense.
In some situations, the courts will require the Government to disclose its sources. The decision of the Federal District Court for
Southern Texas (Houston) in the *National Steel* case provides an
example of how far such disclosures may go (*U.S.* v. *Nat'l. Steel
Corp.,* 49 ATRR A-1 (S.D. Texas 1962)). The court, without opinion, ordered the Government to reveal to defendants in a Clayton
Act merger case the names of business executives who had furnished to the Government information on economic conditions in
the prefabricated-metal-buildings industry. The Government had
expressed a willingness to give the defendants full information on
evidence to be used at the trial, including the names of any witnesses the Government planned to call. The Government had opposed disclosure of the informers' identity, arguing that it was not
needed by defendants and could "only serve to embarrass such informants and subject them to possible recriminations" within the
power of one of the defendants. Nevertheless, the Government did
not appeal from the district court order but elected to make the
required disclosure.

In its memorandum opposing defendants' interrogatories, the
Government asserted "privilege" to avoid revealing the names of
"confidential informants." The Government cited Federal Rule
26(b); MOORE'S FEDERAL PRACTICE, ¶26.26 [6], at 1173 (2d Ed. 1950);
and VIII WIGMORE ON EVIDENCE, § 2374 (3rd Ed. 1940). The Government also called attention to several district court decisions in
civil antitrust actions (*U.S.* v. *Kohler,* 9 F.R.D. 289 (E.D. Pa. 1949);
U.S. v. *Deere & Co.,* 9 F.R.D. 523 (D. Minn. 1949); *U.S.* v. *Lorain
Journal Co.,* 10 F.R.D. 487 (N.D. Ohio 1950); *U.S.* v. *Sun Oil Co.,* 10
F.R.D. 448 (E.D. Pa. 1950)). In each case, the court had sustained
the Government's "privilege" objections to interrogatories. The
Government claimed to enjoy a privilege of concealing the identity
of any informer not to be used as a trial witness. In the *National
Steel* case, it declared its intention to use its informers' data only as
guides for its discovery procedures against National Steel and its
officials, from whom it planned to obtain all its actual evidence.

The Government also relied upon the Supreme Court's opinion discussing the informer privilege, *Roviaro* v. *U.S.*, 353 U.S. 53 (1957), a criminal case involving narcotics. In that case, the indictment charged the defendant with selling heroin to one "John Doe." A second count charged illegal transportation of heroin. The trial court sustained the Government's refusal to disclose the identity of "John Doe," who was an undercover informer. The informer had taken a material part in bringing about the defendant's possession of the drugs, had been present with the defendant at the occurrence of the crime, and might have been a material witness as to whether defendant knowingly transported the drug as charged. For those reasons, the Supreme Court held that the failure of the trial court to require disclosure of the identity of the informer was reversible error. With respect to the "informer's privilege" the Supreme Court stated: "What is usually referred to as the informer's privilege is in reality the Government's privilege to withhold from disclosure the identity of persons who furnish information of violations of law to officers charged with enforcement of that law. Scher v. U.S., 305 U.S. 251, 254 (1938); In Re Quarles & Butler, 158 U.S. 532 (1895); Vogel v. Gruaz, 110 U.S. 311, 316 (1884). The purpose of the privilege is the furtherance and protection of the public interest in effective law enforcement. The privilege recognizes the obligation of citizens to communicate their knowledge of the commission of crimes to law-enforcement officials and, by preserving their anonymity, encourages them to perform that obligation.

"The scope of the privilege is limited by its underlying purpose. Thus, where the disclosure of the contents of a communication will not tend to reveal the identity of an informer, the contents are not privileged. Likewise, once the identity of the informer has been disclosed to those who would have cause to resent the communication, the privilege is no longer applicable.

"A further limitation on the applicability of the privilege arises from the fundamental requirements of fairness. Where the disclosure of an informer's identity, or the contents of his communication, is relevant and helpful to the defense of an accused, or is essential to a fair determination of a cause, the privilege must give way. In these situations the trial court may require disclosure and, if the Government withholds the information, dismiss the action. Most of the federal cases involving this limitation on the scope of the informer's privilege have arisen where the legality of a search without a warrant is in issue and the communications of an informer are claimed to establish probable cause. In these cases the Government has been required to disclose the identity of the informant unless there was sufficient evidence apart from his confidential communication."

Section 2.2(d) of the Federal Trade Commission's Procedures provides: "It is the general Commission policy not to publish or divulge the name of an applicant or complaining party, except as required by law or by the Commission's rules." Where the complainant is needed as a witness to prove the alleged violation complained of, his identity will be disclosed at the hearings. As a practical matter, the respondent will often be able to guess the identity of the complainant by reason of the nature of the case.

A prospective informer should not assume that his identity will or can be protected in all cases. Even where the Government assures confidentiality and does its best to maintain it, other considerations may modify the assurance when the matter is in litigation. Disclosure of identity may turn on a variety of factors, including (1) whether the matter is a civil or criminal proceeding and (2) whether the informer is a volunteer-victim, a reluctant witness-accomplice, or a disinterested third party. The best general statement available is probably that of the Supreme Court in the *Roviaro* case: "We believe that no fixed rule with respect to disclosure is justifiable. The problem is one that calls for balancing the public interest in protecting the flow of information against the individual's right to prepare his defense. Whether a proper balance renders nondisclosure erroneous must depend on the particular circumstances of each case, taking into consideration the crime charged, the possible significance of the informer's testimony, and other relevant factors."

Roviaro was a criminal case. When the Justice Department collects data from informers for an injunction suit—e.g., *National Steel* case—there may be some shifting of the weight of the elements that must be put in "proper balance." The public interest in protecting the flow of information may be just as strong, but "the individual's right to prepare his defense" may not be thought to carry as much weight in a civil proceeding. On the other hand, there is support in the antitrust bar for the proposition that the Government should be no better off in civil litigation than a private litigant. In a federal lawsuit between private parties, the defendant has a right to discover the sources of the information on which the plaintiff has based his action.

2. Immunity From Prosecution

(a) Question: *What immunity may be given to antitrust witnesses?*

In the General Appropriations Act of February 25, 1903, provisions granting funds for the enforcement of the Interstate Commerce Act, the Sherman Act, and the antitrust provisions of the

Wilson Tariff Act contained a witness-immunity proviso. The proviso stated that "no person shall be prosecuted or be subjected to any penalty or forfeiture for or on account of any transaction, matter, or thing concerning which he may testify or produce evidence, documentary or otherwise, in any proceeding, suit or prosecution under sections 1–7 of this title and all Acts amendatory thereof or supplemental thereto, and sections 8–11 of this title." (15 U.S.C. § 32).

In *U.S.* v. *Armour & Co.,* 142 F. 808 (N.D. Ill. 1906), the court applied the immunity to antitrust defendants who had given unsubpoenaed and unsworn testimony in an investigation conducted by the Commissioner of Corporations, an official of the old Department of Commerce and Labor. Following that decision, Congress enacted a new provision making it clear that the immunity from prosecution "shall extend only to a natural person who, in obedience to a subpoena, gives testimony under oath or produces evidence documentary, or otherwise, under oath" (15 U.S.C. § 33).

In *U.S.* v. *Welden,* 377 U.S. 95 (1964), Welden was seeking to derive immunity from testimony before a subcommittee of the House Small Business Committee. He argued that the failure of Congress in Section 33 to limit explicitly the immunity to witnesses in judicial proceedings demonstrates that the legislators did not intend to upset the *Armour* decision's holding that immunity could be obtained by testifying at a nonjudicial proceeding. (Justice Goldberg, speaking for a 7–2 majority, found that the only feature of the *Armour* decision Congress was concerned about and intended to reverse was the holding on unsubpoenaed and unsworn testimony. The *Armour* decision was not really based on a construction of Section 32's phrase "proceeding, suit or prosecution," and there were no manifestations of any intent by Congress to enlarge Section 32 to include nonjudicial proceedings, according to the Court. The Court found the words "any proceeding, suit and prosecution under said Acts" to refer to Justice Department proceedings for which appropriations were being made. The Court denied immunity to witnesses before congressional committees.

Restriction of Section 32 to witnesses in court proceedings did not result in discrimination against witnesses subpoenaed for FTC proceedings. Section 9 of the FTC Act had language similar to Section 32: "No natural person shall be prosecuted or subjected to any penalty or forfeiture for or on account of any transaction, matter, or thing concerning which he may testify, or produce evidence, documentary or otherwise, before the Commission in obedience to a subpoena issued by it" (15 U.S.C. § 49).

In *Hale* v. *Henkel,* 201 U.S. 43 (1906), the Court established that the statute's phrase "proceedings . . . in the courts" included grand jury investigations. In *U.S.* v. *Monia,* 317 U.S. 424 (1943), it was held that a witness who testified under oath in obedience to a subpoena need not claim his privilege against self-incrimination in order to get the benefit of the immunity statute.

The Supreme Court has repeatedly ruled that any immunity statute, if it is to be cited as a basis for compelling testimony, must give the witness protection as broad as that accorded by the Fifth Amendment. Most of the reported decisions under Section 32 tended to restrict the scope of the immunity. Finding the statute's protection to be coterminous with the privilege against self-incrimination, the Supreme Court denied immunity, in *Hieke* v. *U.S.,* 227 U.S. 131 (1913), to a grand jury witness who appeared in an antitrust investigation only to produce and identify documents taken from his company's files and was thereafter prosecuted for tax fraud. In *U.S.* v. *Swift,* 186 F. 1002 (N.D. Ill. 1911), the court decided the immunity relates to past and present, not future, crimes and refused to give a witness immunity from later prosecution for continuing the same conspiracy to which his testimony related.

Co-defendants called as witnesses for the defense in a Sherman Act injunction suit brought by the Government were denied immunity in *U.S.* v. *Standard Sanitary Mfg. Co.,* 187 F. 232 (E.D. Pa. 1911). The court thought a different holding would permit all antitrust defendants to give each other immunity. In *U.S.* v. *Consumers Ice Co.,* 84 F.Supp. 46 (W.D. La. 1949), immunity was denied a corporate officer subpoenaed to produce company records, even though the documents he produced included personal papers tending to incriminate him. The court said the witness had no one to blame but himself for mixing his personal affairs with those of the corporation.

In *U.S.* v. *Carnation Co. of Wash.,* 1965 Trade Cas. ¶71,372 (E.D. Wash. 1965), the court held that a witness would achieve no immunity by testifying in a government False Claims Act suit for double damages for bid rigging on government contracts, even though the damage complaint contained an alternative count for single damages under Section 4A of the Clayton Act. It was found that the principal cause of action was the one based on the False Claims Act and that the Clayton Act count would be abandoned if double damages could be recovered.

In *U.S.* v. *Chas. Pfizer & Co.,* 245 F.Supp. 801 (S.D.N.Y. 1965), the court allowed Sherman Act defendants to assert immunity on the basis of testimony before a federal grand jury at which Justice Department lawyers repeatedly denied any interest in antitrust matters. Whether they intended to or not, the district judge reasoned, the government lawyers did in fact elicit from the defendants a number of items of information that "would furnish a link in the chain of evidence needed to prosecute" them. The defendants were drug company officials who had been indicted for price fixing. They had appeared before a District of Columbia grand jury impaneled to investigate possible conflict of interest and illegal receipt of money by the head of the Food and Drug Administration's Antibiotic Division. The letter of authorization issued to the Criminal Division lawyers who presented evidence to the grand jury also authorized investigation of violations of "other criminal laws of the United States." The subpoenas issued to the three witnesses did not refer to any particular criminal statute, and the district judge found that many of the documents produced "would be relevant and material to an antitrust investigation." Some of the documents produced had been placed in evidence before the Senate Antitrust Subcommittee when it investigated the antibiotics industry.

The *Pfizer* opinion mentioned no documents relating directly to a price-fixing conspiracy. Nevertheless the general antibiotics marketing information supplied to the grand jury, disclosure of the marketing responsibilities of the witnesses, and the witnesses' testimony about their knowledge of antibiotics marketing all constituted evidence from which, if supported by other proof, the court thought a conspiracy could be inferred. Because the defendants had testified concerning the same market and transactions involved in the Sherman Act indictment, the court declared the D.C. grand jury investigation to be " 'proceedings under' the Sherman Act." The Justice Department took no appeal from the *Pfizer* decision.

(b) Question: *How does the Organized Crime Control Act of 1970 affect immunity in antitrust cases?*

The Organized Crime Control Act of 1970, 84 Stat. 922, contains a general immunity provision repealing immunity sections formerly scattered throughout the United States Code, including those relating to the activities of the Antitrust Division and the Federal Trade Commission. The Act does away with the automatic immunity "bath" previously given witnesses in antitrust and trade regulation proceedings. Title II of the Act, 18 U.S.C. § § 6001–6005, entitled "General Immunity," amends Title 18 of the United States Code by adding "Part V—Immunity of Witnesses." Section 6002 of that Part provides that whenever a witness refuses, on the basis of the privilege against self-incrimination, to testify in a proceeding before, or ancillary to, a federal court, grand jury, agency of the United States, or Congress, "and the person presiding over the proceeding communicates to the witness an order issued under this part, the witness may not refuse to comply with the order on the basis of his privilege against self-incrimination." However, no testimony compelled, nor "any information directly or indirectly derived from such testimony," may be used against the witness in any criminal case, "except for prosecution for perjury, giving a false statement, or otherwise failing to comply with the order."

In the case of court or grand jury proceedings, the federal district court for the judicial district in which the proceeding is, or may be, held shall issue a compelling order upon the request of the United States Attorney for such district. The United States Attorney may, "with the approval of the Attorney General, the Deputy Attorney General, or any designated Assistant Attorney General," request such an order when, in his judgment, the testimony may "be necessary to the public interest." In the case of administrative proceedings, the agency "may, with the approval of the Attorney General," issue a compelling order if, in its judgment, the testimony may be necessary to the public interest.

An "agency of the United States" is defined by Section 6001 of 18 U.S.C. as any executive department listed in 5 U.S.C. § 101, as well as, among others, the Federal Trade Commission. "Proceedings before an agency of the United States" is defined as "any proceeding before such an agency with respect to which it is authorized to issue subpoenas and to take testimony or receive other information from witnesses under oath."

The former antitrust and FTC immunity provisions, 15 U.S.C. § § 32 and 49, have been repealed. House Report No. 91-1549, 91st Cong., 2d Sess. (1970), explained that the witness must now claim his privilege to receive immunity. The immunity now granted, the Report continued, is not a "bath." The statutory immunity "is intended to be as broad as, but no broader than, the privilege against self-incrimination. It is designed to reflect the use-restriction immunity concept of *Murphy* v. *Waterfront Commission*, 378 U.S. 52 (1964), rather than the transaction immunity concept of *Counselman* v. *Hitchcock*, 142 U.S. 547 (1892)."

Title III of the Act provides for confinement of the "recalcitrant" witness, i.e., one who refuses to comply with an order to testify or provide other information. It further provides that a person so confined "shall [not] be admitted to bail pending the determination of an appeal taken by him from the order for his confinement if it appears that the appeal is frivolous or taken for delay." Title IV provides for punishment for perjury. In a prosecution for perjury under the new law, "the falsity of a declaration . . . shall be established sufficient for conviction by proof that the defendant while under oath made irreconcilably contradictory declarations material to the point in question in any proceeding before or ancillary to any court or grand jury" and that to provide a case of perjury beyond a reasonable doubt, "it shall not be necessary that such proof be made by any particular number of witnesses or by documentary or other type of evidence."

Possibly the most important change is that, under the new statute, immunity must be claimed by the witness, whereas under the old antitrust and FTC immunity statutes, immunity was automatically granted. As a consequence, lawyers may have to be more careful in advising witnesses, grand jury witnesses in particular, of their rights. *Miranda* problems may develop in antitrust grand jury investigations. (In *Miranda* v. *Ariz.*, 384 U.S. 438 (1966), the Court ruled that an individual "subjected to custodial police interrogation," in the absence of waiver, must be told of his constitutional rights before he is questioned.)

The reduction of the scope of the immunity from the "bath" to the use-restriction immunity probably will not result in many antitrust prosecutions of witnesses. In such prosecutions, the Government usually would face a heavy burden of proving that its case against a witness receiving some immunity was not "tainted" by some use of the witness's testimony. In addition, as a practical matter, the Government will probably tend not to prosecute cooperative witnesses. Even so, many think it likely that the new statute, as far as antitrust and FTC investigations are concerned, may result in less cooperation by witnesses. The old antitrust and FTC immunity statutes had a tendency to encourage the witness to volunteer information about as many transactions as possible in order to receive as broad immunity as possible. Lawyers will probably now tend to advise witnesses to answer questions precisely and to volunteer nothing. The Government, especially the FTC, may be hampered by the procedures set up in the new statute. In an FTC proceeding, the Commission must obtain the permission of the Attorney General before issuing an order requiring testimony. Sometimes this might not seem worth the trouble, and at all times it would mean some delay. Furthermore, it is not clear what the Commission is to do if the witness refuses to obey the order.

Since it requires that the Fifth Amendment claim be made before immunity can be granted, the new statute could lead to a conflict of interest between an officer of a corporation and his corporation. It may sometimes be in the interest of the officer to claim immunity in a nonsecret proceeding even though the publicity about his "taking the Fifth" would be harmful to the corporation. It is not clear whether the immunity statute will apply in treble-damage actions so as to enable the plaintiff to ask the U.S. Attorney to seek an order compelling testimony to promote the "public interest" served by the treble-damage action. The language of the statute would not seem to preclude such a procedure.

Another question concerns the provision that empowers the Attorney General or his designee to obtain an order compelling testimony from a witness who "*may* be called to testify" and who "is *likely* to refuse to testify." This would seem to imply an *ex parte* proceeding, and some would question the constitutionality of this. The advance order directed to people likely to refuse was designed to avoid delay and the interruption of the proceeding for collateral litigation about immunity. Opportunity to challenge would still be available by motion to set aside the order in advance of the relevant proceeding. Would a judge have any discretion to deny an application by the Attorney General? The statute provides that the district court "shall" issue the order upon the request from the U.S. Attorney, but some courts may be somewhat reluctant to be a rubber stamp for the Government in such matters. Issues such as jurisdiction and privilege probably could be reviewed.

The Act provides that evidence obtained by an immunity order, or any evidence "directly or indirectly derived" from such evidence, cannot be used against the witness. In *Kastigar* v. *U.S.*, 406 U.S. 441 (1972), the Supreme Court held this coextensive with the scope of the constitutional privilege against self-incrimination and, hence, despite the lack of a grant of "transactional immunity," held the Act constitutional.

D. SECRECY OF GOVERNMENT FILES

Question: *To what extent can a businessman gain access to government information collected from other businesses?*

In two court cases involving Antitrust Division files private litigants sought evidence to support their positions in treble-damage suits. Olympic Refining Co. wanted to see answers to interrogatories submitted by both sides in the Justice Department litigation that produced the 1959 Sherman Act consent judgment in *U.S.* v. *Standard Oil of Calif.*, 1959 Trade Cas. ¶69,399 (S.D. Calif. 1959). Three protective orders entered in that case by the district court required that both sides' answers be held in confidence and not divulged to anyone except the court and counsel. After filing a treble-damage suit against Standard Oil Co. of California and General Petroleum Corp., two of the defendants who signed the 1959 consent judgment, Olympic procured service of a subpoena directing the Antitrust Division's Los Angeles office to produce the answers to the interrogatories. In an effort to comply with the subpoena, the Antitrust Division filed with the district court a motion to vacate the three protective orders. The motion was denied and the subpoena quashed.

In explaining his action, the district judge noted that the three protective orders furnished the framework within which the Government "obtained a full and complete disclosure of a great mass of material. Some of the material made available to the government was sensitive, competitive information; other data produced were in the nature of trade secrets." Without the protective orders and the Government's assurances that the information would not be made public, the district judge reasoned, the oil companies would have pressed objections to the scope of the interrogatories. Both sides would have lost the advantages of the complete disclosure that was in fact made to the Government. It was also thought that the existence of the protective orders "formed an important part of the consideration which six defendants obtained in entering the consent decree."

The court of appeals saw the matter differently (*Olympic Refining Co.* v. *Carter,* 332 F.2d 260 (9th Cir. 1964), *cert. denied,* 379 U.S. 900 (1964)). "In the federal judicial system trial and pre-trial proceedings are ordinarily to be conducted in public. Rule 43(a), the Federal Rules of Civil Procedure, provides that in all trials the testimony of witnesses shall be taken orally in open court unless otherwise provided in the rules. The purpose of the federal discovery rules, as pointed out in Hickman v. Taylor, 329 U.S. 495, 501, [1947] is to force a full disclosure. . . . Neither in the express nor implied terms of the statutes or rules is there any indication that a consenting defendant could gain the additional benefit of holding under seal, or stricture of nondisclosure, for an indefinite time, information which would otherwise be available to the public or at least to other litigants who had need of it."

The court of appeals could find nothing in the Federal Rules that would authorize a federal court to protect trade secrets and sensitive competitive information "from such disclosure as is relevant to the subject matter involved in a pending action. All that may be done is to afford such protection from disclosure as is practicable, consistent with the right of access thereto for purposes of litigation." The district court was directed to modify the protective orders to give Olympic access to the interrogatory answers "subject to such reasonable restrictions as may be necessary and practicable to prevent unnecessary disclosure of any present trade secrets or presently sensitive competitive information that may be contained in such documents." It made no difference to the court that Olympic might have been able to obtain the same information by propounding its own interrogatories to Standard and General. Olympic was also entitled to know what those two companies and the alleged co-conspirators told the Government.

As an indication of a congressional aversion to keeping antitrust evidence secret, the court cited what is sometimes called "The Publicity in Taking Evidence Act," 15 U.S. C. § 30 (1913), which provides that the taking of depositions for use in civil injunction suits brought by the Attorney General under the Sherman Act "shall be open to the public as freely as are trials in open court." Congress has expressed a quite different policy toward evidence collected in criminal proceedings—at least, for that collected by grand juries. Rule 6(e) of the Federal Rules of Criminal Procedure forbids disclosure of matters occurring before a grand jury except "to the attorneys for the government for use in the performance of their duties." Any further disclosure may be made only when "directed by the court preliminarily to or in connection with a judicial proceeding."

A criminal prosecution produced the Antitrust Division file that the heavy electrical equipment manufacturers wanted to inspect in the *City of Burlington* case. The manufacturers obtained a subpoena directing the Justice Department to produce its files on the criminal price-fixing cases completed early in 1961. The Federal District Court for the District of Columbia quashed the subpoena, applying the "informer's privilege" not only to the identity of the informer but to the information he gave the Government. The court of appeals reversed (*Westinghouse Electric Corp.* v. *City of Burlington* 351 F.2d 762 (D.C. Cir. 1965)), and on remand the district court held discovery would be allowed (246 F.Supp. 839 (D. D.C. 1965)).

In those same electrical equipment cases, on the other hand, treble-damage claimants were accorded access to substantial portions of the testimony elicited by the grand jury that had indicted the manufacturers. The Federal District Court for Eastern Pennsylvania, where the grand jury sat, promulgated a standard operating procedure for nationwide use in procuring the grand jury testimony of a witness whose deposition was to be taken for a damage suit (*Phila.* v. *Westinghouse Electric Corp.*, 210 F.Supp. 486 (E.D. Pa. 1962)). That procedure was later upheld (*Allis-Chalmers Mfg. Co.* v. *Fort Pierce*, 323 F.2d 233 (5th Cir. 1963)). Subsequently, the Antitrust Division was ordered to return documents the grand jury subpoenaed from the manufacturers, but it was allowed to keep copies for its files (*U.S.* v. *General Electric Co.*, 211 F.Supp. 641 (E.D. Pa. 1962)).

In 1962, the Justice Department's data collection powers were significantly broadened by enactment of the Antitrust Civil Process Act, 15 U.S.C. § § 1311–1314; 18 U.S.C. § 1505, authorizing the issuance of civil investigative demands. (See Section VII-A above, p. 448.) Yet Section 4 (c) of that statute provides that "no material so produced shall be available for examination, without the consent of the person who produced such material, by any individual other than a duly authorized officer, member, or employee of the Department of Justice." Under subsections (d), (e), and (f), once the Justice Department has completed the case for which the documents were obtained, or once it makes its decision not to bring a proceeding, the Antitrust Division "custodian" of the documents is required to return any that have "not passed into the control of any court or grand jury through the introduction thereof into the record of such case or proceeding." However, subsection (f) relieves the Antitrust Division of any obligation to return the copies it made from the original documents.

The FTC's extensive information collecting powers are also qualified by a specific provision on publication of the material compiled. Section 6(f) of the FTC Act gives the Commission power to "make public from time to time such portions of the information obtained by it hereunder, except trade secrets and names of customers, as it shall deem expedient in the public interest." Section 10 makes it a crime for "any officer or employee of the Commission" to "make public any information obtained by the Commission" unless the Commission authorizes, or a court directs, publication. There has been little litigation involving those provisions, but the FTC has frequently cited Section 6(f) to justify refusals to allow access to its files.

Demands for access to reports obtained by the Commission under Section 6 of the FTC Act take on special weight when the Commission decides to use the reports in evidence in one of its proceedings. Two orders issued by the Commission in proceedings against *Grand Union Co.,* 62 F.T.C. 1491 (1963), and *Columbia Broadcasting System,* 62 F.T.C. 1518 (1963), acknowledged that when access to special reports its staff plans to use in evidence is essential to preparation of the defense, the reports must be made available for examination by respondent's counsel. Counsel were permitted to make one photocopy of each document and to prepare summaries of the documents, but the order specified that copies and summaries removed from the Commission's building were not to be seen by anyone other than counsel who had filed appearances in the proceedings. "And no information contained in such copies or summaries shall be disclosed to any other person, including any officer or employees of the respondent."

In both instances two commissioners dissented, expressing the view that "it would be manifestly unfair to subject the materials furnished by the various people not parties to this action to examination by their competitors."

There may be occasions when an FTC respondent wishes to see the file of its own records that the Commission has collected. In the proceeding involving *L. G. Balfour Co.,* 62 F.T.C. 1541 (1963), the jewelry manufacturer discovered that the Commission had a more complete file of some types of company records than the manufacturer itself had. Because Balfour was merely trying to recover its own documents, the Commission was prepared to be more lenient than it is in granting inspection rights with respect to other companies' records. Although Balfour was unable to identify specifically the documents it failed to keep copies of and needed for its defense to monopolization charges, the Commission did not insist upon the showing of "good cause" required by Section 1.134 of its Rules of Practice. Discussing the standards it would apply under its Rule 4.8(a)(5), the Commission said (at 1545): "In considering whether or not good cause has been shown in support of a particular request, the Commission, of course, is cognizant of the fact that a marked distinction must be drawn between discovery of a party's own documents—for example, business records peculiarly within its possession and not otherwise available to the adversary—and documents that reflect the result of investigation by lawyers in preparation for possible litigation. That distinction takes on added significance when the investigation as to which discovery is sought is by government lawyers acting in the public interest.

"It is neither necessary nor desirable," the Commission continued, "to frame a firm rule of general application defining with particularity the elements of a showing of good cause for the release of material from the Commission's files. It is impossible to anticipate the wide variety of situations which may arise and which should be met with flexibility and discretion, not rigid formula. In general, however, it may be said that an applicant must satisfy the Commission not only that the material sought is relevant and useful for defensive purposes, but also that its release would not impair any overriding public interest in preserving its confidentiality. In making its judgement the Commission will also necessarily take into account such considerations as basic fairness to the parties and the need for avoiding delay. But it must be emphasized that an effort to obtain discovery of Commission files merely for 'fishing' purposes to determine whether material might be extracted therefrom which could be exploited by the defense will not be allowed."

One type of government file the court decisions seem to say clearly is not available for inspection by businessmen involved in antitrust or trade-regulation litigation is the file of reports, memoranda, notes, and statements of witnesses drafted by a government attorney in the preparation of a case for trial. These are his "work product" exempt from production except in very unusual circumstances. In *Hickman* v. *Taylor,* 329 U.S. 495 (1947), the Supreme Court said: "We do not mean to say that all written materials obtained or prepared by an adversary's counsel with an eye toward litigation are necessarily free from discovery in all cases. Where relevant and nonprivileged facts remain hidden in an attorney's file and where production of those facts is essential to the preparation of one's case, discovery may properly be had. Such written statements and documents might, under certain circumstances, be admissible in evidence or give clues as to the existence or location of relevant facts. Or they might be useful for purposes of impeachment or corroboration . . . But the general policy against invading the privacy of an attorney's course of preparation is so well recognized and so essential to an orderly working of our system of legal procedure that a burden rests on the one who would invade that privacy to establish adequate reasons to justify production through a subpoena or court order."

There have also been court decisions according a privilege of nondisclosure to government file material on policy discussions and advice by government officials. In *U.S.* v. *Morgan,* 313 U.S. 409 (1941), the Supreme court justified nondisclosure of such files by noting that courts and administrative agencies "are to be deemed collaborative instrumentalities of justice and the appropriate independence of each should be respected by the other." Other opinions have applied an "executive privilege" to induce candor in the processes of consulting and advising responsible officials (*Kaiser Aluminum and Chemical Corp.* v. *U.S.,* 157 F.Supp. 939 (Ct. Cls. 1958), 287 F.2d 890 (Ct. Cls. 1961); *Boeing Airplane Co.* v. *Coggeshall,* 280 F.2d 654 (D.C.Cir. 1960); *NLRB* v. *Botany Worsted Mills, Inc.,* 106 F.2d 263 (3rd Cir. 1939).

An order without opinion by the Federal District Court for the District of Columbia in *William H. Rorer, Inc.* v. *FTC,* 151 ATRR A-7 (D.D.C. 1964), dismissed a drug manufacturer's suit for an order requiring the FTC to produce a copy of a memorandum submitted to the Commission by its staff during unsuccessful consent-order negotiations. In its order denying the manufacturer permission to file an interlocutory appeal from the hearing examiner's refusal to order production of the memorandum, the Commission took the position that the discovery rules developed for adjudicative proceedings are not applicable in consent negotiations (64 F.T.C. 1446 (1964)). "Like investigations, consent negotiations are distinct from the adjudication process and hence are not governed by the standards which control adjudicative procedure."

Some observers see in the *Olympic* and *Electrical Equipment* cases manifestations of a definite trend in the courts toward making more documents in government antitrust-case files available to treble-damage litigants. Yet they do not see this trend as likely to end in disclosure of antitrust defendants' business records and trade secrets to every competitor, customer, or supplier who asks for it. Generally, the courts have shown a tendency to apply the "good cause" standard set out in Rule 34 of the Federal Rules of Procedure, and the FTC has established a like criterion. To be in a position to show "good cause" for seeing government files, the competitor, customer, or supplier has to be involved in litigation in which he can point to a specific use for the documents requested. Since the FTC and Antitrust Division staffs are not permitted to reveal contents of investigative files, business records get a substantial measure of protection.

Even if limited to actual litigants, however, disclosure can have serious antitrust enforcement consequences. The view expressed by the district judge in the *Olympic* case suggests that a policy decision may have to be made to reconcile discovery practices in this area with the congressional purpose of Section 5 of the Clayton Act to encourage consent settlements of antitrust proceedings. Greater freedom of access by third parties to documents submitted to the Government during consent-order negotiations may serve to inhibit the exchange of information during such negotiations with the result that the negotiations might take longer or be unsuccessful. On the other hand, there are experts who see no clearly defined trend of this sort. They view the *Electricial Equipment* cases as representing a special combination of flagrant violations and damage claimants who themselves represented a substantial segment of the economy. In any event, it is suggested the outcome often depends on the attitude of the individual judge. In view of the secrecy clause in Federal Criminal Rule 6(e), some antitrust lawyers expect more reluctance on the part of the courts to give up grand jury records.

Until litigation begins, the language of the Antitrust Civil Process Act seems to guarantee secrecy of documents obtained by the Justice Department through civil investigative demands. Yet Section 4(e)'s provision for return of only such documents as have not "passed into the control of any court or grand jury" suggests that use of the documents in litigation may render them available to other persons to the same extent as any other papers obtained by the Government.

Part VIII

FTC Practice

A. UNFAIRNESS UNDER SECTION 5 OF THE FTC ACT

Question: *Are there any limits on the FTC's power to decide what is "unfair"?*

In 1914, dissatisfied with the Sherman Act, Congress considered two alternative proposals. The first, the original House version of the Clayton Act, would have attempted to prohibit with precision business practices thought to lead to monopoly by a series of specific and unqualified *criminal* prohibitions. The second, based on a feeling that precise statutory definition alone would not solve the problem, proposed creation of an administrative agency with power continually to re-define prohibited conduct under a general prohibition of unfair methods of competition. Congress adopted both proposals, specifying in the Clayton Act prohibitions against a variety of supposedly incipient monopoly practices, without the criminal sanctions, and creating in the Federal Trade Commission an administrative agency directed to prevent "unfair methods of competition."

Early aggressive efforts by the FTC were discouraged by the judiciary. See e.g., *FTC* v. *Gratz,* 253 U.S. 421 (1920); *FTC* v. *Sinclair Refining Co.,* 261 U.S. 463 (1923). Brandeis' dissent in the *Gratz* case and the affirmance of the Commission in *FTC* v. *Beech-Nut Packing Co.,* 257 U.S. 441 (1922), suggested another direction. In 1938 Congress broadened the FTC's charter to include the prevention of "unfair or deceptive acts or practices." The Supreme Court of the 60's encouraged the FTC to broaden the reach of Section 5 of the Federal Trade Commission Act (*FTC* v. *Brown Shoe Co.,* 384 U.S. 316 (1966); *FTC* v. *Colgate-Palmolive Co.,* 380 U.S. 374 (1965)).

In the *Brown Shoe* case, the Commission's complaint attacked contracts between Brown Shoe Co. and independent retail outlets. The contracts provided that in return for certain valuable services, including architectural plans, signs, business forms, accounting assistance, services of a field representative, and a right to participate in· group insurance rates, the retailer promised to concentrate his business within the grades and price lines of Brown Shoes and to

481

handle no competing lines of shoes. In its answer, Brown admitted that 259 retailers had executed the franchise agreements and that another 400 had in varying degrees accepted the same terms without formal agreement. Whether a formal contract had been signed or not, Brown regularly checked the performance of each participant in the franchise program, and the benefits of the agreement were denied those dealers not operating within the terms of the agreements. The Commission found that the program induced franchise stores to purchase 75 percent of their total shoe requirements from Brown and that the effect of the plan was to foreclose these retail outlets to Brown's competitors, particularly small manufacturers. On the basis of these findings, the FTC concluded that the "franchise store" program was an unfair method of competition prohibited by Section 5 of the FTC Act (*Brown Shoe Company, Inc.,* 62 F.T.C. 679 (1963)).

On review, the Commission was reversed (339 F.2d 45 (8th Cir. 1964)). The court of appeals relied primarily on *FTC* v. *Gratz,* 253 U.S. 421 (1920), in which the Supreme Court had said "the words 'unfair methods of competition' are clearly inapplicable to practices never heretofore regarded as opposed to good morals because characterized by deception, bad faith, fraud, or oppression, or as against public policy because of their dangerous tendency unduly to hinder competition or create monopoly." Because of its reliance on *Gratz,* the court of appeals was of the view that under Section 5, the FTC had the burden of proving either a specific violation of the antitrust laws or conduct "opposed to good morals because characterized by deception, bad faith, fraud or oppression." Reading the Commission's order as an attack on the agreements under Section 3 of the Clayton Act, the court ruled that the franchise agreements were neither an unlawful tying arrangement nor an exclusive-dealing agreement.

Justice Black, speaking for an undivided Supreme Court, gave short shrift to *Gratz* as a precedent (*FTC* v. *Brown Shoe Co.,* 384 U.S. 316 (1966)). He pointed out that the case had been decided soon after the FTC Act was passed and that the Court had since adopted the dissenting opinion of Justice Brandeis as the rule of law to be applied in interpreting Section 5 (*FTC* v. *R.F. Keppel & Bro., Inc.,* 291 U.S. 304 (1934)). In the Court's view, the Commission had "broad power" to declare trade practices unfair if they "conflict with the basic policies of the Sherman and Clayton Acts even though such practices may not actually violate. these laws." The Court found the obligations set out in the franchise agreements substantially limited the availability of the franchise outlets to Brown's competitors. For that reason the program was said to conflict with the central policy of the Clayton and Sherman Acts. In response to

Brown's contention that the FTC needed proof that the effect of its franchises "may be to substantially lessen competition or tend to create a monopoly," Justice Black stressed the "incipiency" theory underlying Section 5. "The Commission has broad power under Section 5 to arrest trade restraints in their incipiency without proof that they amount to an outright violation of Section 3 of the Clayton Act or other provisions of the antitrust laws."

Some antitrust experts read the opinion as recognizing a statutory grant to the FTC of broad legislative power to find business practices, especially distribution arrangements, "unfair" and to prohibit them without regard to actual proof of their relationship to competition. They feel that Justice Black's "incipiency" statement relaxes the proof requirement to what might be termed "incipient incipiency." The anticompetitive threat Justice Black mentioned in his opinion is the tendency of the franchise program to take away the freedom of purchasers to "buy" in an open market. Yet the competitive injury he had in mind is the taking away of the freedom of other manufacturers to sell to the franchised retailers. He was willing to accept the Commission's judgment on anticompetitive threat despite the Commission's finding that each franchise store was legally and "theoretically" free to quit Brown's program, giving up the free services and turning to other manufacturers for supplies. It could be argued that such an arrangement is no more effective in foreclosing competing manufacturers than is a big sale of shoes to the same number of retailers. In fact, one could reason that Brown was really helping its competitors by assisting fledgling retailers who would be free, once established, to change suppliers.

Other experts insist that the opinion merely recognized what has been clear all along, that Congress gave the Commission power to prohibit business methods, acts, and practices by quasi-legislative declarations supporting cease-and-desist orders, subject to judicial review. The holding in the *Gratz* case was undermined long ago. This is another in a series of Section 5 cases in which the Court has stressed the Commission's expertise and broad discretionary authority. See *Atlantic Refining Co.* v. *FTC,* 381 U.S. 357 (1965); *FTC* v. *Colgate Palmolive Co.,* 380 U.S. 374 (1965); and *FTC* v. *Mary Carter Paint Co.,* 382 U.S. 46 (1965). The market facts of the *Brown Shoe* case may provide the real foundation for the decision to uphold the Commission. Perhaps the foreclosure of 75 percent of the business done with 659 retailers throughout the country was enough to convince every member of the Court that, had the case been handled differently, a violation of Section 3 of the Clayton Act could have been established or at least a convincing showing of potential anticompetitive effect could have been made.

In *Sperry & Hutchinson Co.* v. *FTC*, 432 F.2d 146 (5th Cir. 1970), *modified*, 405 U.S. 233 (1972), the Commission ruled that S&H's efforts to eliminate unauthorized dealing, or "trafficking," in its stamps were "unfair methods of competition in commerce and unfair acts and practices in violation of Section 5." The Commission ordered S&H to cease and desist from preventing persons from trafficking and from instituting suits to enjoin trafficking. S&H was also ordered to notify traffickers that injunctions presently in effect in state and federal courts would not be enforced. The court of appeals vacated these portions of the Commission's order. In concluding that "Congress could not have intended to vest the Commission with such broad discretion as to allow it to hold a restraint 'unfair' without applying some judicial guidelines," the court stated: "To be the type of practice that the Commission has the power to declare 'unfair' the act complained of must fall within one of the following types of violations: (1) a *per se* violation of antitrust policy, (2) a violation of the letter of either the Sherman, Clayton or Robinson-Patman Acts, or (3) a violation of the spirit of these acts as recognized by the Supreme Court of the United States." The court of appeals concluded that efforts by S&H to restrain dealing in its trading stamps did not fall within any of these three categories. The court appears to have ignored the antitrust notion, stated in the *Schwinn* case, 388 U.S. 365 (1967), that "once the manufacturer has parted with title and risk, he has parted with dominion over the product, and his effort thereafter to restrict territory or persons to whom the product may be transferred . . . is a *per se* violation of Section 1 of the Sherman Act."

Judge Wisdom dissented. He asserted that the majority "blesses unfair anti-competitive practice against three groups," trading stamps exchanges, retailers who redeem or exchange stamps, and consumers, and that the decision "fails to give effect to the broad authority Congress granted to the FTC."

The Supreme Court, in an opinion by Justice White, remanded the case to the Commission saying that the FTC did not assume excessive powers when, in determining fairness, it considered public values beyond the letter or the spirit of the antitrust laws but had failed to articulate any rational connection between the facts found and the order issued or to provide any statement of the basis for its order.

There are two schools of thought as to whether a practice which does not violate the *letter* of the Sherman, Clayton, or Robinson-Patman Acts must be in violation of the *spirit* of those antitrust laws before the Commission can declare it to be an "unfair method of competition" in violation of Section 5 of the Federal Trade Commission Act. Those believing that the Commission's authority to find violations of Section 5 is limited to methods in conflict with the spirit of the antitrust laws cite *Atlantic Refining Co.* v. *FTC,* 381 U.S. 357 (1965), and *FTC* v. *Brown Shoe Co.,* 384 U.S. 316 (1966). In *Atlantic Refining,* the Court upheld an order prohibiting a practice that had "the characteristics of recognized antitrust violations," and in *Brown Shoe,* it held that "the Commission has power under Section 5 to arrest trade restraints in their incipiency without proof that they amount to an outright violation [of the antitrust laws]" (384 U.S. at 322). See also *FTC* v. *Motion Picture Adv. Co.,* 344 U.S. 392 (1953). According to this school, the Commission has authority only to prohibit practices that either are in the nature of recognized antitrust violations or violate the policy underlying the antitrust laws. See, for example, *R.H. Macy & Co.* v. *FTC,* 326 F.2d 445 (2d Cir. 1964). Those who hold this view concede that there is an exception where the practice, while not in violation of the antitrust laws, has, nevertheless, "met with condemnation throughout the community" or is "of the sort which the common law and criminal statutes have long deemed contrary to public policy" (*FTC* v. *Keppel & Bro.,* 291 U.S. 304, 313 (1934)).

Others hold that the Commission may declare a practice an "unfair method of competition" if it simply has a rational basis for finding the practice unfair. Support for this view also can be found in *Atlantic Refining.* There the Court said: "The Congress intentionally left development of the term 'unfair' to the Commission rather than attempting to define 'the many and variable unfair practices which prevail in commerce. . . . Where the Congress has provided that an administrative agency initially apply a broad statutory term to a particular situation, our function is limited to determining whether the Commission's decision 'has "warrant in the record" and a reasonable basis in law' " (381 U.S. at 367). The Court further seemed to suggest that it is the Commission which gives content to Section 5 and that in this respect the antitrust laws are merely useful guidelines: "As our cases hold, all that is necessary in § 5 proceedings to find a violation is to discover conduct that 'runs counter to the public policy declared in the' Act. But this is of necessity, and was intended to be, a standard to which the Commission would give substance. In doing so, its use as a guideline of recognized violations of the antitrust laws was, we believe, entirely appropriate. It has long been recognized that there are many unfair methods of competition that do not assume the proportions of antitrust violations." This school could also claim some support from language in *Keppel,* which suggests that the Commission's authority is not restricted to "incipient" violations of the antitrust laws: "It would not have been a difficult feat of draftsmanship to have restricted the operation of the Trade Commission Act to those methods of competition in interstate commerce which are forbidden at common law or which are likely to grow into violations of the Sherman Act, if that had been the purpose of the legislation" (291 U.S. at 310).

 Adherents of both schools would agree that, in declaring a practice to be an unfair method of competition, the Commission is governed by a public interest standard and that the final word belongs to the courts. Perhaps the central question is suggested by Judge Wisdom's reference to the Wheeler-Lea Act of 1938, which added to the pre-existing prohibition of unfair methods of competition, the prohibition of "unfair or deceptive acts and practices in commerce." As noted by Judge Wisdom, the Supreme Court reads the Wheeler-Lea Act as showing congressional "concern for consumers as well as for competitors." See *FTC* v. *Colgate-Palmolive Co.*, 380 U.S. 374, 384 (1965). It is well established that in declaring a practice to be a deceptive practice, the Commission has broad authority. See *FTC* v. *Mary Carter Paint Co.*, 382 U.S. 46 (1965) and *Colgate-Palmolive. Query:* Does this mean that when finding an unfair *act or practice* in commerce, as distinguished from an unfair *method of competition,* the Commission would have the same broad discretion as in finding a deceptive practice? It is hard to see how, in finding an act or practice unfair to the consumer, the Commission would be bound by the spirit of the antitrust laws, which are designed primarily to protect competition. The *S&H* decision does not seem to reach this question since neither the majority, the dissenter, nor the Commission itself considered separately the question whether S&H's practices are unfair acts and practices as distinguished from unfair methods of competition.

B. FTC FAIRNESS

1. FTC Press Releases

Question: *What measures can a businessman take to protect himself from the consequences of the FTC's public announcement of its charges before their accuracy is determined?*

The FTC prepares and distributes press releases publicizing its complaint proceedings at four stages: complaint, answer, initial decision, and final order. A computerized mailing list of over 20,000 addressees is maintained. Copies of releases are mailed to selected lists of those who have indicated a particular interest or are thought to be concerned with a particular action. For the average complaint this may mean from four thousand to fourteen thousand, depending on the issues involved. Another 200 or so copies of each release are picked up at the Commission's Public Information Office by messenger services employed by news agencies, law firms, and business enterprises. A consent order used to be publicized only once, when it and the complaint were issued. Now that the Commission has adopted a 30-day waiting period for proposed consent orders, two press releases are distributed: a full-dress announcement of the proposed order, and, at the end of the 30-day period, an abbreviated press notice of final adoption of the order, with a reference, for the details, to the original press release.

According to a Senate Subcommittee on Administrative Practice and Procedure, Congress has received many complaints that the Commission issues damning press releases while the existence and lawfulness of the conduct about which it is complaining are still matters to be determined. Senator Edward E. Long (D-Mo), Chairman of the subcommittee, reported these complaints when he and Senator Everett Dirksen (R-Ill) introduced a bill which would have amended Section 9 of the Administrative Procedure Act to require that administrative agencies give corporations and individuals "an equal opportunity" to answer charges made in press releases. The Senate passed such a bill (S. 1336) in 1966, but it was not acted on by the House. When he introduced his bill, Senator Long acknowledged that the public has a right to know about the issuance of an FTC complaint, "but the press release too often leaves the impression that the subject of the complaint has already been found guilty."

The Commission has faced litigation over its press-release policy. The Cinderella Career & Finishing School, Washington, D. C., sued to prevent the Commission from distributing a press release publicizing the complaint in a false advertising proceeding. On the day the injunction complaint was filed, the Federal District Court for the District of Columbia denied a temporary restraining order, and the next day the Commission issued its complaint, along with the regular press release. The School then amended its complaint to seek an order barring a press announcement of its answer to the Commission's charges and this time was able to persuade another judge to issue a preliminary injunction. In an opinion explaining his action (*Cinderella Career and Finishing Schools, Inc.* v. *FTC.* 1967 Trade Cas. ¶72,072 (D. D.C. 1967)), the district judge declared that the Commission's issuance of news releases prior to final adjudication in a formal complaint proceeding gives "the appearance of constituting a prejudgement of the issues." The releases were described by the opinion as "public statements appearing to support the allegations of the complaint." He said the inevitable result of any Commission news release prior to final adjudication is to "spread throughout the public and business community the impression that the respondents were guilty of unlawful and deceptive practices and were not honorable or ethical persons with whom to be doing business." He had serious doubts "that the Commission has power under Section 6(f) of the FTC Act to issue any news releases in a quasi-judicial proceeding unless and until the matter has been fully adjudicated." While an appeal from that decision was pending, an FTC administrative law judge decided that there was insufficient evidence to support the Commission's charges. (The Commission later reversed the administrative law judge; and a court of appeals vacated the Commission's decision and remanded the case (425 F.2d 583 (D.C. Cir. 1970)) on the grounds that the Commission did not comply with due process, having reversed the administrative law judge without considering the evidence adduced at the hearing.)

Meanwhile, the court of appeals vacated the preliminary injunction and instructed the district court to dismiss Cinderella's complaint (404 F.2d 1308 (D.C. Cir. 1968)). The court of appeals did not deny that an FTC press release "in this or any other complaint proceeding, is undoubtedly deleterious to the respondents' economic, business and community status." Nevertheless, the appellate court was convinced that the FTC Act gives the Commission authority to publicize its enforcement activities on its own initiative, and " 'in the discharge by Congress of a dominant trust for the benefit of the public, the possibility of incidental loss to the individual is sometimes unavoidable.' *American Sumatra Tobacco Corp.* v. *SEC,* 110 F.2d 117, 120–21 (D.C. Cir. 1940)." The court of appeals saw in the FTC Act "authority in the Commission, acting in the public interest, to alert the public to suspected violations of the law by factual press releases whenever the Commission shall have reason to believe that a respondent is engaged in activities made unlawful by the Act which have resulted in the initiation of action by the Commission." The court said that it was not ruling on situations in which the complaint contains an allegation that the Commission's charges were knowingly false, or that the Commission discriminated against the plaintiff, or that the news release did not fairly and accurately summarize the Commission's complaint.

Soon after the *Cinderella* suit, the Commission began adding to each press release announcing a complaint, immediately below the lead paragraph, a "NOTE" stating: "A complaint is issued whenever the Commission has found 'reason to believe' that the law has been violated and that a proceeding is in the public interest. It is emphasized that the issuance of a complaint simply marks the initiation of a formal proceeding in which the charges in the complaint will be ruled upon after a hearing and on the record. The issuance of a complaint does not indicate or reflect any adjudication of the matters charged." The Court of Appeals for the District of Columbia Circuit found this added warning "well intended" and "commendable" but found "its practical value in minimizing the derogatory inferences . . . at best minimal."

The Justice Department, as well as the FTC, issues press releases on every new court proceeding the Antitrust Division initiates, every proposed consent decree it negotiates, and every voluntary termination or withdrawal of one of its court actions. The Department does not ordinarily circulate the release, though, when a court decides a contested case or when a proposed consent order is entered as final. Sometimes its press releases are shorter than the Commission's and may follow more closely the language of the complaint or indictment. A Justice Department announcement of a complaint or indictment contains no caveat or "NOTE," such as the FTC adds, to disclaim a finding of guilt. Nor do the Department's announcements of consent decrees, unlike the Commission's releases on consent orders, add the reminder that the consent is not an admission or finding of guilt.

When the Justice Department first started issuing announcements of its cases in May of 1938, it submitted its policy to the American Bar Association for an opinion on propriety under Canon 20 of the ABA's Canons of Professional Ethics: "Newspaper publications by a lawyer as to pending or anticipated litigation may interfere with a fair trial in the courts and otherwise prejudice the new administration of justice. Generally they are to be condemned." The ABA Committee on Professional Ethics, in Opinion No. 199, decided that "Canon 20 does not prohibit issuance of statements by public officials." The opinion went on to state: "While we see no objection to statements reflecting departmental policy, nor to statements of fact relating to past proceedings in the nature of reports, where, as here, the statements relate to prospective or pending criminal or civil proceedings, they shall omit any assertion of fact likely to create an adverse attitude in the public mind respecting the alleged actions of the defendants to such proceedings."

A statement of news release policy by the Justice Department is found in an April 16, 1965, statement by the Attorney General that appeared at 28 C.F.R. § 50.2 (1965). That statement outlined limits on Justice Department releases announcing the initiation of criminal proceedings. The announcement was to give only (1) the defendant's name, age, residence, employment, marital status, and "similar background information;" (2) "the substance or text of the charge;" (3) the identity of the investigating and arresting agency and length of the investigation; and (4) the circumstances immediately surrounding an arrest. "Only incontrovertible factual matters" and not "subjective observations" were to be disclosed, and even ordinary background information on the arrest was to be withheld if its release would serve no law enforcement function and would be prejudicial. The release must avoid (1) observations about a defendant's character or prior criminal record although the criminal record "may be made available upon specific inquiry"; (2) statements, confessions, or alibis attributable to a defendant; (3) references to investigative procedures; (4) statements about the identity, credibility, or testimony of prospective witnesses; and (5) statements concerning evidence or argument in the case.

No one seems to question that FTC and all other administrative proceedings must be public, especially in view of the Freedom of Information Act of 1966 (56 U.S.C. § 1000 (1966)), although that statute merely prohibits federal agencies from concealing the records of their proceedings from persons who seek them. Nothing in its provisions seems to call for requiring or encouraging agencies to take the initiative in publicizing their charges. On the other hand, as the Court of Appeals for the D.C. Circuit noted, Section 6(f) of the FTC Act does authorize the Commission "to make public . . . information obtained by it." Indeed, the Commission was originally conceived as an agency for collecting and disseminating data about the business community.

The practice of issuing press releases is a common one among federal agencies. The FTC's releases on respondents' answers may be unique, and it seems to be just as thorough in publicizing the dismissal of charges as it is in publicizing a cease-and-desist order. An FTC respondent usually has advance notice of the release's contents. He has been served with a draft of a complaint and has rejected a proposed consent order. He can have an answering statement ready for the press. Some lawyers have even suggested the Commission should serve a copy of a proposed press release along with the complaint.

Many FTC proceedings, while small in economic scope and geographical area of interest, involve the marketing practices of a business whose customers and potential customers may make up a significant portion of some local newspaper's readership. The FTC's addition of the precautionary "NOTE" to its news releases is a tacit recognition of merit in Cinderella's complaint that its business would be hurt even if the charges proved to be unfounded. But in practice, the "NOTE" may serve as a warning only to editors, not the public, if it is left out of the story the public sees. A court injunction will not always solve the problem. Most newspapers keep a close watch on local court dockets. Filing an injunction suit may mean that the public's attention will be called to the Commission's action earlier and more often. In many instances an officially sanctioned press release will promote accuracy and prevent the publication of an exaggerated or emotional description of the charges. It also frequently forestalls direct questioning of the attorneys involved by reporters and thereby promotes observance of Canon 20.

If a respondent cannot persuade the FTC in precomplaint negotiations that he is innocent or that the matter should be disposed of on the basis of his assurance of voluntary compliance, then he may have no choice but to submit to whatever adverse results flow from the publicity accompanying issuance of a consent order or a complaint. An answering publicity campaign may be considered, but in most situations such campaigns call the FTC's action to the attention of a wider audience of additional potential customers who might otherwise have overlooked it.

2. Industrywide Efforts by the FTC

Question: *By what methods has the Commission sought to obtain industrywide compliance with the antitrust laws?*

If the business practice against which the FTC files a complaint is common among the accused firm's competitors, the company hit by the first cease-and-desist order may be put at a severe competitive disadvantage. In *Moog Industries, Inc.* v. *FTC*, 355 U.S. 411 (1958), the Supreme Court held that the Commission can issue cease-and-desist orders against individual firms without first proceeding against their competitors. "The decision as to whether or not an order against one firm to cease and desist from engaging in illegal price discrimination should go into effect before others are similarly prohibited depends on a variety of factors peculiarly within the expert understanding of the Commission." Even if an allegedly illegal practice appears to be widespread, the Court declared, it is up to the Commission, not the courts, to decide whether individual or industrywide treatment is appropriate. "Its discretionary determination should not be overturned in the absence of a patent abuse of discretion."

In *Universal-Rundle Corp.* v. *FTC,* one month after the Federal Trade Commission ordered a plumbing-fixtures manufacturer to cease and desist from price discrimination among its customers, the manufacturer petitioned the Commission to stay its order for a time sufficient to investigate identical industrywide practices. The Commission denied the petition for a stay, but a court of appeals set aside the order denying the stay (352 F.2d 831 (7th Cir. 1965)). The Supreme Court of the United States reversed (387 U.S. 244

(1967)). Chief Justice Warren, writing for a unanimous court, held that the order denying the stay was improperly set aside because (1) the evidence offered in the petition for a stay did not tend to show that the competitors' discounts had the required anticompetitive effect, and (2) the Commission would not be obliged to withhold enforcement even if all the manufacturer's competitors were engaged in similar illegal price discrimination practices and enforcement of the order might cause the manufacturer to suffer substantial financial injury. The Commission's order was later set aside on the merits (382 F.2d 285 (7th Cir. 1967)).

In the mid-60's the Commission's enforcement bureaus were instructed that recommendations for individual complaints should not be submitted to the Commission without advice as to whether the alleged illegal practices were general in the industry. If the alleged violation was widespread, then the staff was expected to recommend an industrywide plan for dealing with the conduct.

In the 1950's the Commission began supplementing its trade practice rules with guides covering specific practices, sometimes cutting across industry lines. Guides are said by Section 1.5 of the Commission's Rules to be "administrative interpretations of laws administered by the Commission for the guidance of the public in conducting its affairs in conformity with legal requirements." By 1965 thirteen sets of guides had been published, all dealing with deceptive practices. They covered: (1) bait advertising, (2) cigarette advertising, (3) advertising of guarantees, (4) deceptive pricing, (5) tire advertising, (6) fallout-shelter advertising, (7) shell-home advertising, (8) shoe-content labeling and advertising, (9) advertising of radiation-monitoring instruments, (10) mail-order insurers, (11) deceptive use of the word "mill" in textile industry, (12) deceptive labeling and advertising of adhesive compositions, and (13) debt-collection deception.

Guides are said not to have the force and effect of law. In *Gimbel Bros., Inc.,* 61 F.T.C. 1051 (1962), the Commission held that its staff was not required to prove the meaning of a word defined in guides. The opinion restated the proposition that guides do not have the status of substantive law. They "inform the public and the bar of the interpretation which the Commission, unaided by further consumer testimony or other evidence, will place upon advertisements using the words and phrases therein set out."

When the Federal Trade Commission announced its Enforcement Policy with Respect to Mergers in the Textile Mill Products Industry (1 Trade Reg. Rep. ¶4535 (1968)), one commissioner dissented, maintaining that the guidelines "are manifestly unfair to the industry when coupled with the simultaneously announced acceptance by the Commission of a consent order against Burlington

Industries legalizing in effect the same acquisitions which are clearly contrary to the guidelines" (at p. 6921). The policy statement promised "examination," for possible Section 7 Clayton Act enforcement action, of "any horizontal merger in a textile mill product submarket where (1) the combined firms rank among the top 4 or (2) have a combined market share of 5 percent or more of any submarket in which the four largest firms account for 35% or more of the market." According to the dissenter, the Federal Trade Commission's consent order against Burlington (*Burlington Industries, Inc.,* 75 F.T.C. 1 (1969)), "in effect puts a stamp of approval on a series of preguideline acquisitions made by Burlington which has enabled Burlington to move in the overall textile mill products industry from second to first place and similarly to advance its industry ranking to within the top four grouping in several product submarkets within this broader textile market. The Commission has been frequently criticized for adopting a merger policy which ignores or leaves untouched the largest firms in an industry and which concentrates its enforcement fire on the middle tier companies struggling to compete with their larger industry rivals. . . . The Commission's action today for the first time in my judgement gives some solid substance to this criticism."

When the Commission made final its consent order terminating the *Burlington* case, Commissioner Jones revoiced her dissent: "If the mergers described in the guidelines will give rise to possible anticompetitive consequences in the future when engaged in by the rest of the industry, all of whom rank well below Burlington in asset and sales value, I cannot understand how the Commission can conclude that identical mergers entered into by Burlington during the past decade do not also give rise to anticompetitive consequences or to the likelihood of such consequences."

The textile mill products industry is not the only one in which the Commission's consent orders have allowed retention of acquired businesses whose acquisition would be questioned by full-force application of merger-policy statements. The Commission's willingness to settle for prohibitions against future acquisitions, sometimes with partial divestiture, had produced, by the time its policy statement on mergers in the food-distribution industries was published (1 Trade Reg. Rep. ¶4525 (1967)), several consent orders in that industry appearing to sanction mergers inconsistent with the policy statement. In that policy statement, the Commission promised to give "attention and consideration" to any merger by retail food chains that resulted in combined annual food store sales in excess of $500 million. However, in two of the merger cases cited in the footnotes to the factual background for its policy statement, the Commission issued orders requiring no divestiture by leading grocery chains (*National Tea Co.*, 69 F.T.C. 226 (1966); *Winn-Dixie Stores*, 70 F.T.C. 611 (1966)). A third order, *Grand Union Co.*, 67 F.T.C. 999 (1965), required divestiture of only 10 of the 59 grocery stores whose acquisition was attacked in the complaint. And its complaint against *The Kroger Co.*, Docket 7464, was dropped after reference to "the longevity of the case," the further delays associated with additional hearings called for by a complaint amendment attacking a new grocery-chain acquisition by Kroger, and the Commission's policy-statement requirement that it be given 60 days' notice of any future acquisitions (74 F.T.C. 1129, 1134 (1968)).

The Commission's consent order in a proceeding against a major cement manufacturer's acquisitions of ready-mix concrete producers seems to fall short of the standards subsequently set out in the Commission's Enforcement Policy with Respect to Vertical Mergers in the Cement Industry (1 Trade Reg. Rep. ¶4520 (1967)). "Unless unusual circumstances in a particular case dictate to the contrary," the Commission threatened to issue a complaint challenging the acquisition by a cement manufacturer "of any ready-mixed concrete firm ranking among the leading four nonintegrated ready-mix producers in any metropolitan market." In *Lone Star Cement Corp.* 67 F.T.C. 67 (1965), the consent order required Lone Star to dispose of most of the ready-mix concrete plants of an acquired subsidiary that was the largest producer of ready-mix concrete in the Norfolk and Richmond areas of Virginia. Having disposed of 16 of its 20 Norfolk-Richmond area plants in accordance with the terms of the order, however, the Lone Star subsidiary remained one of the top four producers.

Inconsistency between policy statements or guidelines and orders terminating litigation may be explainable in terms of basic differences in the nature and goals of the two techniques of law enforcement. First, the Commission's guidelines are not restricted in their content, as are cease-and-desist orders, by any necessity for getting the approval of either a court or the merging companies. Sometimes the best allocation of resources requires settlement of litigation for something less in the way of relief than is obtainable as a matter of law. Second, guidelines or policy statements indicate that the Commission will investigate, or file complaints against, certain types of mergers; they give no commitment as to how the complaint proceedings will be terminated. The guidelines are designed to influence future business conduct, not to undo the past. A consent order apparently sanctioning a merger condemned by guidelines but prohibiting future mergers may have a purpose consistent with that of guidelines, to arrest a trend and obtain greater compliance for the future.

Some lawyers feel the FTC made a mistake in not giving an explanation of the contrast between the textile mill guidelines and the *Burlington* consent order, especially since the Commission is known to have simultaneously dropped investigations of other substantial textile-mill mergers the staff wanted to oppose. These lawyers report that in the absence of explanation, smaller mills have become resentful of the Commission's barring them from a means of growth their larger competitors have been allowed to take full advantage of. Also, the Commission's dismissal of the *Kroger* complaint is cited as proof to some expansion-minded grocery chains that the Commission can be outlasted in merger litigation.

Others insist, though, that the Commission adopted the equitable course of changing the rules only prospectively and therefore took a step toward certainty in, and more respect for, the antitrust laws. They insist that the textile mill industry is aware of this Commission purpose. The Commission's action might have been unfair if the prior mergers gave the merging companies a competitive advantage. The Commission's policy statement on the cement industry described important advantages of vertical integration there.

Like the Antitrust Division's Merger Guidelines (1 Trade Reg. Rep. ¶4225 (1968)), the FTC's policy statements may not go as far in outlawing mergers as would be possible under the Supreme Court's Section 7 Clayton Act opinions of recent years. Once it starts a complaint proceeding, the Commission may have more control over termination of that proceeding than the Justice Department can exercise in ending its injunction suits. An FTC decision to accept a consent order is probably not appealable; interveners in the Justice Department's district court suits may be able to fight for a stronger order than the Department is willing to accept.

In 1960, following recommendations of a Robinson-Patman Act Task Force composed of members of its staff, the Commission made the first extensive use of its authority to require special reports from corporations (Section 6 of the FTC Act, 15 U.S.C. § 46(b)) to assemble information of possible violations of the antitrust laws. Payment of illegal brokerage in the citrus industry was investigated by mail through the use of this reporting authority. More than 100 reports were received, resulting later in some 45 consent cease-and-desist orders. At that time the Commission also launched an extensive investigation of discriminatory allowances to food chains, directing orders to more than 400 corporations in the food industry. Looking toward enforcement proceedings, the FTC required reports from suppliers as well as from the chains. Former Chairman Paul Rand Dixon saw great potential in this investigative tool. He said to the American Bar Association: "We expect to save a good deal of professional manpower, money, and time by using the United States mails to help us get the facts. This method of investigation is not only efficient and inexpensive, but it is also, in certain circumstances, the only practicable way to bring about such fairness as may come from relatively simultaneous industry-wide enforcement" (19 ABA ANTITRUST L. J. 252, 254 (1961)).

In 1961 the Commission undertook two investigations by mail. Letters were sent to more than one hundred manufacturers of hemorrhoid products to determine whether their advertising might be exaggerating the efficacy of their products. The Commission's press release stated that on the basis of information initially supplied, "those concerns whose advertising appears to be questionable will be required by Section 6 orders to submit more detailed information pertaining to their claims." Two months later, the Commission announced an investigation "to ascertain whether drug manufacturers and distributors are giving unlawfully lower prices and other preferential treatment to any customers and are using deceptive promotional material." Orders to file special reports were mailed to 37 manufacturers and distributors requiring the respondents to furnish within forty-five days advertising and labels and detailed information concerning prices, classification of customers, and related items.

There are few court cases involving Section 6 orders. In *U.S.* v. *Morton Salt Co.,* 338 U.S. 632 (1950), the Supreme Court upheld a Commission order requiring a corporation to file a report showing how the corporation had complied with an earlier order of the Commission to cease and desist. Morton contended that Section 6(b) authorized the Commission to require reports only for the compiling of information for general economic surveys as provided in Sections 6(a) and 6(b) and was independent of the enforcement procedures of the Commission set out in Section 5. The Supreme Court rejected this contention and held that Section 6 could be used for "any purpose within the duties of the Commission, including a Section 5 proceeding." The Court's opinion, by Justice Jackson, although it sustained the Commission's authority, said: "Of course, there are limits to what, in the name of reports, the Commission may demand. Just what these limits are we do not attempt to define in the abstract. But it is safe to say that they would stop the Commission considerably short of the extravagant example used by one of the respondents of what it fears if we sustain this order—that the Commission may require reports from automobile companies which include filing automobiles. In this case we doubt that we should read the order as respondents ask to require shipment of extensive files or gifts of expensive books." The broad discretion left to the Commission on the use of the power for purposes of investigation is suggested by the following statement of the Court: "Even if one were to regard the request for information in this case as caused by nothing more than official curiosity, nevertheless law-enforcing agencies have a legitimate right to satisfy themselves that corporate behavior is consistent with the law and the public interest."

In *U.S.* v. *St. Regis Paper Co.*, 285 F.2d 607 (2d Cir. 1960), *aff'd*, 368 U.S. 208 (1961), the Commission, by orders to special file reports, had sought information to determine whether Section 7 of the Clayton Act had been violated by St. Regis' acquisition of certain other corporations. In a district court suit under Section 9 of the FTC Act, the Government sought an order of the court commanding the filing of the reports ordered by the Commission. The Government also asked for statutory penalties, provided by Section 10 of the Federal Trade Commission Act, at the rate of $200 per day against St. Regis for its failure to respond to two orders. The district judge held that the Commission had authority under Section 6(b) to order the filing of the special reports, but held further that some of the questions posed by the Commission were vague and uncertain and that therefore the statutory penalty should not be allowed (181 F.Supp. 862 (S.D.N.Y. 1960)). The court of appeals sustained the district judge concerning the Commission's authority, but reversed the determination on penalties and remanded the case to the district court with instructions to enter judgment against St. Regis in the amount of $100 a day for each day on which St. Regis was in default of the first order requiring a special report.

In the course of sustaining the Commission's authority to require special reports and adjudging penalties for failure to comply with the Commission's orders to file reports, the court of appeals held that St. Regis could have attacked the Commission's order to file a special report by seeking a declaratory judgment in the district court under Section 10(c) of the Administrative Procedure Act.

Meanwhile the Commission had adopted a new consent-order procedure to follow up investigations by mail. The present procedure of conducting consent-order negotiations in advance of the filing of a formal complaint makes it possible for the Commission to negotiate and issue simultaneous consent orders without subjecting any one of the companies to the unfavorable publicity that may accompany the filing of the first complaints.

On the basis of a mail-order investigation of cooperative-advertising arrangements in the garment industry, the Commission, in December of 1962, sent several hundred manufacturers proposed complaints and consent orders against the payment of discriminatory advertising allowances. Eventually most of them signed consent orders, and in 1965 the Commission made the consent orders effective (*Abby Keni Co.*, 68 F.T.C. 393 (1965)).

Simultaneous complaints were used by the Commission in 1959 to attack, as Robinson-Patman Act violations, cumulative annual volume discounts allowed by 12 carpet manufacturers. Eight of these manufacturers signed consent orders, which became effective early in 1964 (*Bigelow-Sanford Carpet Company*, 64 F.T.C. 704 (1964); *Mohasco Industries, Inc.*, 64 F.T.C. 709 (1964); *Magee Carpet Co.*, 64 F.T.C. 716 (1964); *C. H. Masland & Sons*, 64 F.T.C. 721 (1964); *Beattie Mfg. Co.*, 64 F.T.C. 727 (1964); *A & M Karagheusian, Inc.*, 64 F.T.C. 781 (1964); *Roxbury Carpet Co.*, 64 F.T.C. 787 (1964); *The Firth Carpet Co.*, 64 F.T.C. 793 (1964)) when the Commission completed litigation of the other three complaints and issued cease-and-desist orders in those cases (*Phila. Carpet Co.*, 64 F.T.C. 762 (1964); *Cabin Crafts, Inc.*, 64 F.T.C. 799 (1964), *order vacated*, 362 F.2d 435 (5th Cir. 1966); *Callaway Mills Co.*, 64 F.T.C. 732 (1964), *order vacated*, 362 F.2d 435 (5th Cir. 1966)). Most of the 11 companies had been defendants in the earlier Justice Department Sherman Act suit that resulted in a consent decree prohibiting them from discontinuing by agreement the very volume discount system the FTC later attacked (*U.S.* v. *Inst. of Carpet Mfrs.*, 1940–43 Trade Cas. ¶56,097 (S.D. N.Y. 1941)).

Section 1.12 of the Commission's Rules provides for "trade regulation rules," which are said to "express the experience and judgment of the Commission ... concerning the substantive requirements of the statutes which it administers." They may "cover all applications of a particular statutory provision and may be nationwide in effect, or they may be limited to particular areas or industries or to particular products or industries or to particular product or geographical markets, as may be appropriate." The Commission's authority to issue trade regulation rules has been questioned. In *Nat'l. Petroleum Refiners Ass'n* v. *FTC*, 340 F.Supp. 1343 (D.D.C. 1972), a case involving the Commission's gasoline octane rating rule, the district court found that the Commission had no such authority, but the decision was reversed on appeal (620 ATRR D-1 (D.C. Cir. 1973)).

Since its inauguration in 1962, the Federal Trade Commission's trade regulation rule procedure has been used more than 20 times. See 4 Trade Reg. Rep. ¶¶38,011–38,032. Rules restrict size representations on sleeping bags (4 Trade Reg. Rep. ¶38,011 (1963)) and tablecloths (4 Trade Reg. Rep. ¶38,015 (1965)); forbid "leakproof" claims for dry cells (4 Trade Reg. Rep. ¶38,014 (1965)); set labeling and advertising requirements for distinguishing nonprismatic from prismatic binoculars (4 Trade Reg. Rep. ¶38,013 (1964)); restrict use of the word "leather" in markings on belts made of split, ground, or shredded leather (4 Trade Reg. Rep. ¶38,016 (1965)); prohibit the use of the designation "automatic" on sewing machines (4 Trade Reg. Rep. ¶38,012 (1966)); and require disclosure of the "used" nature of re-refined lubricating oil (4 Trade Reg. Rep. ¶38,017 (1965)). A study of "long life" claims for light bulbs resulted in a trade regulation rule (4 Trade Reg. Rep. ¶38,024 (1971)).

In *Atlantic Products Corp.*, 63 F.T.C. 2237 (1963), the Commission withheld a Robinson-Patman Act cease-and-desist order in favor of moving toward a discriminatory advertising allowance rule covering the entire luggage industry, but none was ever issued. In *Motorola, Inc.*, 64 F.T.C. 62 (1964), action on a deceptive-practice charge was suspended until a rule could be considered on disclosure of foreign components in radio and television sets. The Commission's decision to study a possible rule against vertical mergers in the cement industry did not lead it, in *Permanente Cement Co.*, 65 F.T.C. 410 (1964), to delay proceedings under a Section 7 Clayton Act complaint. A Commission guideline on cement mergers was published in 1967 (1 Trade Reg. Rep. ¶4520 (1967)).

The Commission's General Procedures invite applications for trade regulation rules from any "interested person or group." The Commission has not generally indicated which, if any, of the past trade regulation rule proceedings were requested by private industry. Requests for trade regulation rule proceedings are treated as confidential by the Commission, but at least three such requests have been made public by the organizations that submitted them. In the proceeding on "long life" light bulbs industry members were asked to attend a hearing and comment on the problem in general, rather than on a specific proposed rule.

The language and form of the sleeping-bag-size rule are typical. First, the Commission made findings that "manufacturers and distributors have engaged in the practice of selling sleeping bags in commerce . . . marked as to 'cut size,' . . . without disclosing the size of the finished products," and that this practice has a tendency to deceive purchasers and "to divert business from competitors who clearly disclose the finished size of their sleeping bags. . . . Accordingly, the Commission hereby promulgates, as a Trade Regulation Rule, its findings and determinations that in connection with the sale or offering for sale of sleeping bags, any representation of the 'cut size' or the dimensions of materials used in the construction of sleeping bags, in advertising, labeling, marking, or otherwise, constitutes an unfair method of competition and an unfair and deceptive act or practice, unless—"(1) The dimensions of the cut size are accurate measurements of the yard goods used in construction of the sleeping bags; and (2) such 'cut size' dimensions are accompanied by the words 'cut size'; and (3) the 'cut size' is accompanied by a clear and conspicuous disclosure of the length and width of the finished products and by an explanation that such dimensions constitute the finished size.

"An example of proper size marking when the product has a finished size of 33″ × 68″ and a cut size of 36″ × 72″, and disclosure is made of the cut size, is—"Finished size 33″ × 68″ Cut Size 36″ × 72″.' "

In a 153-page statement justifying a proposed cigarette rule (Accompanying Statement of Basis and Purpose of Trade Regulation Rule on Cigarette Labeling and Advertising, June 22, 1964, 155 ATRR A-5 (1964)), the Commission for the first time elaborated on the legal basis for its claim of authority to issue trade regulation rules. First, the Commission pointed to what it called its "basic mandate" in Section 5(a) (6) of the FTC Act. That section empowers the Commission to "prevent" unfair methods of competition and deceptive practices in commerce. Since Section 5(b)'s explicit authorization of complaint proceedings requires the Commission to determine whether such a proceeding "would be to the interest of the public," the Commission construed Section 5 as meaning that complaint proceedings represent only one type of enforcement tool to be used by the Commission. Use of the complaint procedure, the Commission noted, presupposes a preliminary determination of an existing violation, which means that procedure "is distinctly narrower than the 5(a) (6) mandate." Second, the Commission pointed to Section 6(g) of the Act, which authorizes it "to make rules and regulations for the purpose of carrying out the provisions of this Act," and declared: "The trade regulation rule procedure is clearly embraced by the literal terms of the section, and nothing in the legislative history of the Trade Commission Act requires that the provision be read other than as written." The Commission said that it would be confident of its power to issue trade regulation rules even if Section 6(g) were not in the Act. "It is implicit in the basic purpose and design of the Trade Commission Act as a whole, to establish an administrative agency for the prevention of unfair trade practices, that the Commission should not be confined to quasi-judicial proceedings."

Suggestions at the hearings on the cigarette rule that there is no language in the FTC Act authorizing the Commission to promulgate rules "having the force and effect of law" were countered by an assertion in the cigarette-rule statement that trade regulation rules do not and will not create new law. "Trade Regulation Rules are not legislative in the sense of adding new substantive rights or obligations. Trade Regulation Rules do not broaden or expand the prohibitions contained in the statutes administered by the Commission, but, rather, define their application to specific practices or a specific industry within the jurisdiction of the Commission."

In his statement opening the hearings on the cigarette rule, Chairman Paul Rand Dixon said that, in an adjudicative proceeding based on an alleged violation of a rule, the Commission will rely on the rule "to the extent that it is fair and proper to do so." Section 1.12(c) of the Commission's Rules provides that "where a trade regulation rule is relevant to any issue involved in an adjudicative proceeding . . ., the Commission may rely upon the rule to resolve such issue, provided that the respondent shall have been given a fair hearing on the applicability of the rule to the particular case."

At the cigarette-rule hearings, the Commission heard repeated complaints from attorneys that they could not understand precisely what effect the trade regulation rule would be given in subsequent adjudicative proceedings. Although the Commission's announcement of a proposed cigarette rule said "these rules state the substantive requirements of the Act," several commissioners objected to the attorneys' characterization of the proceeding as "substantive rule making." They drew a distinction between "substantive rule making" and the Commission's publication of advice as to what specific types of conduct it regards as violative of the substantive provisions of the statutes it enforces.

In detailing its plans for trade regulation rules in factual disputes, the Commission seemed to treat the rules as devices for giving advance notice of matters it would take official notice of. The trade-regulation-rule proceeding "simply enables the systematic marshalling of the Commission's knowledge and experience in a particular area." To ascertain the nature and extent of a respondent's right to rebut findings made in reliance on prior determinations in a trade-regulation-rule proceeding, the Commission referred to Section 7(d) of the Administrative Procedure Act. Under that statute, "where any agency decision rests on official notice of a material fact not appearing in the evidence in the record, any party shall on timely request be afforded an opportunity to show the contrary." To the Commission, that language does not mean that the respondent must always have an opportunity to introduce evidence at the hearing on the complaint. In the case of a trade regulation rule, the "opportunity to show the contrary" occurs at the hearing before a trade regulation rule is promulgated. The Administrative Procedure Act guarantees a respondent at the complaint hearing "that any person or firm subject to a trade regulation rule be given an opportunity to show changed conditions, or other special circumstances, justifying a waiver of the rule as to him." In Section 1.63(c) of the Commission's General Procedures, it is provided "that the respondent shall have . . . a fair hearing on the legality and propriety of applying the rule to the particular case."

Many have found it possible to talk to the Commission's staff informally about questions that arise regarding application of the laws the Commission is responsible for enforcing. Until June 1, 1962, however, there was no formal procedure for soliciting the Commission's advice, and "informal opinions" rendered by the commissioners or the Commission's staff were not binding on the Commission in any way. On that date, with one commissioner dissenting, the Commission revised its General Procedures to initiate an advisory-opinion policy. The advisory-opinion procedure, provided in Sections 1.1–14 of the current Rules, contemplates the giving of advice only as to a proposed course of action. Request for an advisory opinion "will be considered inappropriate" if it relates to a course of action already being followed, already under investigation, or already the subject of a Commission proceeding or order, or is "the same or substantially the same" as one already the subject of an investigation, proceeding, or order. Advice will not be given "where the proposed course of action or its effects may be such that an informed decision thereon cannot be made or could be made only after extensive investigation, clinical study, testing or collateral inquiry."

Under Section 1.2, a request for an advisory opinion "should be submitted in writing to the Secretary of the Commission and should include full and complete information regarding the proposed course of action." A request is processed initially by staff attorneys who will hold conferences with the person submitting the request, after which "submittals of additional information may be required." If the staff concludes that the matter is an appropriate one for Commission consideration, it submits to the Commission a recommendation as to the action to be taken.

Section 1.3 provides that advice is given "without prejudice to the right of the Commission to reconsider the questions involved and, where the public interest requires, to rescind or revoke the advice." If an advisory opinion is to be revoked or rescinded, "notice . . . will be given to the requesting party so that he may discontinue the course of action taken pursuant to the Commission's advice." Also, the Commission makes a commitment not to "proceed against the requesting party with respect to any action taken in good faith reliance upon the Commission's advice," provided "all the relevant facts were fully, completely, and accurately presented to the Commission" and provided the course of action is discontinued promptly on notice of rescission or revocation.

During the first year of the advisory-opinion program it was the Commission's policy not to make the opinions public. While one advisory opinion, on cooperative-price advertising by retail drug-gists, did receive considerable publicity, it was first made public by the parties who had requested the advice. When the Commission revised its General Procedures in 1963, a Section 1.54 was added, stating that "texts or digests of advisory opinions of general interest will be published," and one volume of such digests was published covering the period June 1, 1962, to December 31, 1968. Under current rule 1.4, full public disclosure of the opinions and the requests therefor is made.

Many lawyers feel safer if they can get some inkling of how the FTC staff feels about a question raised by a client. The FTC advisory opinion can furnish welcome confirmation for a lawyer with a client who does not feel secure about going ahead with a transaction merely on the basis of his own counsel's advice or who rebels at negative advice. In addition, an advisory opinion can prove useful in deciding which is the better of alternative ways to carry out a particular transaction. Also, the program may be useful when an attorney's interpretation of the law does not agree with that of counsel for the client's customer, supplier, or competitor. For example, it has been suggested that a company fearful of a questionable course of conduct contemplated in its industry can submit the proposed activity to the Commission for the very purpose of obtaining a negative response and, by publicizing that response, forestalling its competitors from making the change.

On the matter of getting negative advice from the Commission, some trade regulation lawyers are hesitant. They feel that it is always the obligation of counsel to give his client a conservative opinion. They would push for a formal advisory opinion from the Commission only when they are looking for confirmation of a course of action they are confident is legal or when the proposed course of action is one whose rejection by the Commission would produce a reaction in Congress like the one that followed the opinion on cooperative price advertising by retail druggists. (See section II-A-3, p. 83.)

Some feel there is a strong case for the use of advisory opinions on Robinson-Patman Act questions. Frequently, even though the situation that leads to the issuance of an FTC order is a narrow one involving a single product, a small class of customers, a small area of the country, or a very special pricing arrangement of minor significance in the company's overall sales picture, the Commission issues a broad order, using statutory language applicable to all products or a broad range of products and to the company's entire pricing structure or its entire promotional program. Such an order can throw in doubt many facets of the company's business that were not explored at the Commission's hearings. All the troublesome questions not answered during litigation are left to plague the company when its dealings with the Commission enter the compliance stage with possible civil penalty proceedings in which potential money penalties may be substantial.

Prior to the institution of the FTC's advisory-opinion procedure it was said that some businessmen felt obliged to abandon plans for a special pricing arrangement or promotional allowance whenever counsel advised it was near the borderline. Sometimes the program abandoned would have benefited the manufacturer who initiated it as well as the manufacturer's dealers and the consumer. Even when the manufacturer was willing to test this one practice through litigation and discontinue it if he lost, the benefit from the special project may have been too small when weighed against the possibility of a broad "statutory language" or "boiler plate" order. Now, however, it is said that the projected special price or promotional allowance can be presented to the Commission for an advisory opinion without endangering other phases of the manufacturer's operations.

The Commission has stated that it will not render an advisory opinion on a course of action that is already in effect. Nevertheless, the businessman who has doubts after he executes his business decision may still be able to present his question informally to the Commission's staff and get an answer, although this can be risky. Some attorneys are sometimes successful in securing useful informal staff opinions without identifying their clients or even the products or industries involved. Even when the question submitted to the Commission relates to a truly proposed, and not existing, course of action, the businessman or lawyer seeking advice should be alert to the possibility that he may stir up Commission action on existing business practices. The authorization in Section 1.2 of the Commission's General Procedures that "submittals of additional information may be required" has in fact been used to ask the question, "what are you doing now?"

A prediction made by some experts in their initial reactions to the program, that its principal users would be small businesses and their trade associations, has not been borne out. The requests for advisory opinions have come almost as often from "big business." Nor does there appear to have been any accuracy in the conflicting forecasts that the Commisssion would be "inundated" with requests and that few businessmen or lawyers would use the new procedure. Initially, the Commission did experience the expected stampede when the gates were opened, but the flow has thinned out. The Commission seems to have kept the advisory-opinion "docket" current enough to maintain the speed essential to make the program useful.

C. OBTAINING INFORMATION FROM THE FTC

1. Pretrial Discovery in FTC Proceedings

Question: *Does the FTC, during its adjudicative proceedings, permit discovery of its files?*

In 1961, the Commission, in a major revision of its Rules of Practice, adopted a continuous-hearing policy. Under this policy, complaint counsel is supposed to be ready to proceed upon issuance by the Commission of the complaint. Discovery by complaint counsel may be limited to that necessary to "round out, extend, or supply further details" (*All-State Industries of N.C., Inc.,* 72 F.T.C. 1020 (1967)). In an interlocutory order in 1963 in *L. G. Balfour Co.,* 62 F.T.C. 1541 (1963), the Commission said one purpose of the continuous-hearing procedure is "to assure that the Federal Trade Commission's hearings are not conducted under the 'sporting theory' of litigation where the goal is to surprise and confound your opponent" (p. 1543) but instead are conducted in such a way that all parties have the facts.

Under Section 3.21 of the Rules, the administrative law judge may order a prehearing conference in any proceeding and must order one whenever it appears probable that the hearing will last more than five days. At the prehearing conference he is to consider simplification and clarification of the issues, amendments to the pleadings, stipulations and admissions, methods of expediting the presentation of evidence, and "such other matters as may aid in the orderly and expeditious disposition of the proceeding, including disclosure of the names of witnesses and of documents or other physical exhibits which will be introduced in evidence." The Commission has said that it is "the examiner's duty to exercise firm direction over adjudicative proceedings to insure that the Commission's policy of orderly, expeditious, and continuous proceedings is not thwarted by either deliberate or inadvertent actions of the parties" (*Topps Chewing Gum, Inc.,* 63 F.T.C. 2196, 2197 (1963)).

Section 3.21 speaks of "a conference," but few cases are ready for trial after only a single conference, and as a general rule, the more complex issues in antitrust (rather than deceptive practice) proceedings may require a series of conferences. Complaint counsel may come to the first conference with the documents he plans to use in evidence and a list of his witnesses. If he does not, one of the judge's first tasks is to order, and set a time limit for, their production. He may also establish a time table for discovery motions and motions directed to the complaint. At the first session there will ordinarily also be a general discussion regarding which matters might be disposed of by stipulation. Additional progress on stipulations often awaits further developments in the discovery process. As soon as there is some definition of the issues, the judge may fix a deadline for pretrial briefs. Later conferences may deal with delays and the production of documents.

Section 3.21(b) authorizes prehearing conferences "for the purpose of accepting returns on subpoenas duces tecum issued pursuant to the provisions of Section 3.34(b)." Section 3.34(b) (2) permits either party to subpoena before trial any "nonprivileged documents" which constitute or contain evidence.

In *Suburban Propane Gas Corp.,* 71 F.T.C. 1695 (1967), the Commission stressed the importance of its hearing examiners' functions at a prehearing conference. The Commission decided that the hearing examiner had an obligation, in a Robinson-Patman Act proceeding against a buyer for knowing receipt of discriminatory discounts, to respond to the buyer's request for a pretrial definition of complaint counsel's burden of proof on the issue of whether the buyer knew the discounts could not be cost-justified. "It is his responsibility to properly regulate the course of the hearing and to rule upon, as justice may require, procedural and other motions. This means that at times he may have to construe case law precedents so that the parties will know how to proceed."

Section 3.36 provides for subpoenas for records of the Commission and for appearance of Commission employees. The rule states: "No application for records, files, papers or information pursuant to Section 4 . . . (Release of Confidential Information) or the Freedom of Information Act may be filed with the Administrative Law Judge." Under Section 3.36 an application for a subpoena requiring production of Commission records or the appearance of Commission personnel is to be made in the form of a written motion specifying "the material to be produced, the nature of the information to be disclosed, or the expected testimony of the Commission official or employee." The motion shall also show the general relevance of the information sought, the reasonableness of the scope of the application, and the unavailability of the information from other sources. In this new rule the Commission has gone further than ever before in opening up the possibility of pretrial discovery as a two-way street in FTC proceedings. Previously the rules provided for little or no discovery by respondents of Commission files, and efforts to obtain such files gave rise to much collateral debate. Establishment of "good cause" for the production of "confidential" FTC records became a frequent subject of discussion in the Commission's interlocutory decisions during the 1960's. In its 1963 *Balfour* order, the Commission defined "good cause" as meaning the respondent "must satisfy the Commission not only that the material sought is relevant and useful for defensive purposes, but also that its release would not impair any overriding public interest in preserving its confidentiality. In making the judgment, the Commission will also necessarily take into account such considerations as basic fairness to the parties and need for avoiding delay." The Commission also indicated that it would require adequate identification of the documents sought, in line with court decisions applying Federal Civil Rule 34.

No mention was made in the *Balfour* order of any requirement that the respondent be unable to obtain the documents in other ways, a requirement that has sometimes been imposed under Rule 34. Such a requirement was enforced, however, in the order issued in *Crown Cork & Seal Co.*, 71 F.T.C. 1634 (1967). The Commission was not very strict with Crown's counsel on its requirement that the documents sought be identified. Counsel in fact did not know the identity of the documents but, in an attempt to develop a failing-company defense to the Commission's antimerger complaint, acted on the probability that the Commission, having conducted an extensive investigation of the relevant market, had in its files material that might be of assistance. By way of identification, Crown's counsel gave nothing more than a description of what the FTC opinion called a "broad category" of documents and a list of the firms and individuals from whom the Commission must have secured data. Turning to the "good cause" test, however, the Commission wanted "a demonstration that the material is not available directly to respondent from the same third parties from whom the Commission can receive it, through compulsory processes available to respondent." Crown's contention that many of the "third parties" were unfriendly to Crown was dismissed by the Commission with an observation that "we are not aware that friendliness and a spirit of cooperation is a necessary precondition to the effectiveness of compulsory process."

In *Grand Union Co.*, 62 F.T.C. 1491 (1963), a respondent demonstrated "good cause" for the production of competitors' reports obtained by a Section 6(b) FTC Act order by showing they were "necessary for defense." Section 6(b) reports were "confidential information" as then defined in Section 1.133. The Commission did not comment upon the meaning of its term "necessary for defense" but it did require complaint counsel to produce 180 reports, even though he planned to introduce in evidence merely a tabulation based on 20 of the reports. In allowing disclosure, the Commission divided 3–2 and imposed protective conditions limiting disclosure to counsel actually engaging in preparing the defense.

In *Graber Mfg. Co.*, 68 F.T.C. 1235 (1965), respondent requested the issuance of subpoenas and answers to interrogatories. The request included interrogatories to FTC employees covering information in documents prepared as early as 1945 pertaining to three merchandising corporations and information on the Commission's investigational sources. The Commission denied respondent's request because there was no showing of necessity; the requests went beyond what was necessary to prepare a defense; and some of the documents were the work product of the FTC's staff.

In its 1965 orders in *Texas Industries Inc.*, 67 F.T.C. 1378 (1965), and *Miss. River Fuel Corp.*, 68 F.T.C. 1173 (1965), the Commission saw as an important consideration in determining whether confidential information in its files is necessary to the defense the availability of that information for use by complaint counsel. For denying Texas Industries access to Section 6(b) reports, the FTC gave three reasons: (1) they were not obtained in the investigation preceding prosecution of the case but were "an integral and important part of a broad administrative inquiry into . . . competitive problems of the cement industry"; (2) their release would be likely to impair the Commission's ability to complete that investigation, since the companies involved did not expect them to be released; and (3) "the reports have not been and will not be made available to complaint counsel for use as evidence." Once it became known to the Commission in the *Miss. River Fuel* case that complaint counsel had had access to documents procured in that same investigation, the matter was remanded to the examiner for a determination whether those particular documents had been obtained under the Commission's Section 6(b) powers, whether they were to be used by complaint counsel, whether they were needed for the defense, and whether they contained confidential information.

In *School Services, Inc.*, 71 F.T.C. 1703 (1967), the Commission turned down an application for production of documents and the taking of the depositions of FTC officials for the purpose of establishing a respondent's claims that a Section 5 FTC Act complaint was issued without a determination either that it was in the "public interest" or that it was based on "reason to believe" that the Act had been violated. The information sought was treated as confidential because it was both the "work product" of the Commission's lawyers and "an integral part" of its decision-making process. The Commission saw in the discovery application "an attempt to probe the mental processes of this agency in investigating repondents.'

Another type of "confidential information" whose accessibility may be important to respondents is the Commission's file of memoranda prepared by its staff on meetings, interviews, and telephone conversations with prospective witnesses. The Commission has adopted a version of the Jencks Rule, 18 U.S.C. § 3500 (see section VIII-C-2, p. 510.) for the release of those memoranda for use in

cross-examination at the hearing. But, in *Viviano Macaroni Co.*, 69
F.T.C. 1104 (1966), the Commission held that such documents are
not subject to discovery in advance of the hearing. Later in *Sperry
& Hutchinson Co.*, 69 F.T.C. 1112 (1966), the Commission denied
access to complaint counsel's correspondence with customers who
were never called as witnesses. The Commission denied that it was
adopting a new discovery policy "extending the Jencks Rule to
nonwitnesses" and insisted that its decision was "confined to the
particular circumstances set forth," the inability of the respondent
company to obtain the information by any other means except by
subpoena of witnesses from far away places.

One of the Commission's reasons in the *Viviano Macaroni* case
for not allowing access to the interview reports in advance of the
hearing was that they represented the "work product" of the Commission's staff. The Commission has also applied the "work product" rule to an economic report prepared by its staff on the basis of
information collected through Section 6(b) orders. In *Sperry &
Hutchinson Co.*, the Commission decided that a report prepared by
its Bureau of Economics on "trading stamps and their effects on
prices" was confidential and not available before trial to a trad-
ing-stamp company charged with restraining competition. Should
complaint counsel decide to use the report in advance, though, the
company was told it would be given advance notice and access to
the report in time to prepare its defense.

In the Commission's discovery decisions a distinction has been
made between documents that are to be used in evidence and those
that are not. Complaint counsel's intention to use a document in
evidence has been, of itself, enough to satisfy the "good cause"
requirement. But the factual background for the discovery issue in
the *Crown Cork & Seal* case suggests that some members of the
Commission's staff of trial attorneys may oppose efforts to obtain
access to documents that they do not intend to introduce directly
into evidence but intend to use in the cross-examination of witnesses called by the respondent to establish an affirmative defense.
Complaint counsel said in *Crown* that they intended to use some
of the documents sought by Crown "to surprise respondent's witnesses," a tactic the Commission found "objectionable." In deciding that Crown had to show that the same information could not be
obtained from the Commission's original sources, the FTC did not
distinguish between the documents complaint counsel intended to
use to "surprise" witnesses and those he did not intend to so use.

Prior to the adoption of its current discovery rules, which appear
to allow complete discovery of each party by the other, the Commission was criticized by one of its own members for taking an
approach to discovery "which provides a continuing source of un-

necessary friction and delay" and "is clearly contrary to the spirit if
not the letter of the recently enacted Freedom of Information Act"
(Commissioner Elman, dissenting in *Inter-State Builders, Inc.,* 72
F.T.C. 370 (1967)). In the past, the Commission's Rule of Practice,
its largely unpublished interlocutory rulings, and the attitude of its
trial staff reflected the view that easy discovery for respondents is
not in the public interest. In addition to any litigant's instinctive
propensity for secrecy, some FTC practitioners say that they detect
feelings on the part of FTC trial lawyers (1) that respondent's counsel generally have the advantage in terms of experience, time, and
financial resources; (2) that some respondents are not above
influencing witnesses if they get information in advance about the
Commission's case; and (3) that their supervisors at the Commission judge their skills on the basis of the number of cases they win.
As long as these views prevail, some members of the private bar
seem to think, the "sporting theory" of litigation is not likely to die
out at the Commission, no matter what changes are made in the
Rules. The effect this staff attitude may have on preparation for a
particular hearing will probably vary with the administrative law
judge. Some are more inclined than others to the Federal Rules
approach and require full prehearing disclosure of complaint counsel's case as a matter of course. There are lawyers who see in the
rule changes of the 1960's the influence of the secretive attitude of
the Commission's staff. One example is said to be the requirement
in Section 3.33(a) of the Rules that the administrative law judge,
before ordering the taking of a deposition, find that "such discovery
could not be accomplished by voluntary methods." This is seen by
some lawyers as a codification of a requirement complaint counsel
have frequently sought. Complaint counsel have pressed the contention in Robinson-Patman Act cases in which the company
charged under Section 2(f) of the Clayton Act with receiving discriminatory discounts was trying to get evidence that its suppliers' pricing practices did not violate Section 2(a) of the Act. Another
codification of a position sought repeatedly in the past by complaint counsel is seen in Section 3.33(a)'s requirement that a deposition "should not be ordered to obtain evidence from a person relating to matters with regard to which he is expected to testify at
the hearing."

2. Prior Statements of a Witness

Question: *What rule is applied by the FTC to govern access to
witnesses' pretrial statements for use in cross-examination?*

Jencks v. *U.S.,* 353 U.S. 657 (1957), established the right of a
defendant in a federal criminal proceeding to production of any

pretrial statements the Government received from a witness concerning matters on which the witness has testified on direct examination at the trial. A defendant is entitled to such information for use in cross-examining the witness, even if the defendant cannot show any inconsistency between the testimony and the pretrial statements. The doctrine of that case was codified in the Jencks Act, 18 U.S.C. § 3500. The discovery right was limited to (1) a written statement made and signed or otherwise adopted by the witness or (2) "a stenographic, mechanical, electrical, or other recording, or a transcription thereof, which is a substantially verbatim recital" of an oral statement "recorded contemporaneously." In the event of a government claim that a portion of the statement bears no relationship to the witness' testimony, the trial judge is to inspect the document initially and excise the irrelevant portions.

The Jencks Rule has been held applicable to administrative proceedings as "one of the fundamentals of fair play required in an administrative proceeding" (*Communist Party* v. *SACB*, 254 F.2d 314, 327–328 (D.C. Cir. 1958). See also *NLRB* v. *Adhesive Products Corp.*, 258 F.2d 403, 408 (2d Cir. 1958), and *Great Lakes Airline* v. *CAB*, 291 F.2d 354, 364 (9th Cir. 1961). In these cases, the courts applied "the underlying principle" of the *Jencks* opinion and statute. In *Ernest Mark High*, 56 F.T.C. 625 (1959), the FTC decided it would apply the Jencks Act to its proceedings but rejected a suggestion for a broader discovery rule said to be defined in the Supreme Court's *Jencks* opinion. The Commission pointed out that the Supreme Court had declared the statute to be the exclusive means of compelling, for cross-examination purposes at criminal trials, the production of statements of a government witness to an agent of the Government (*Palermo* v. *U.S.*, 360 U.S. 343 (1959); *Rosenberg* v. *U.S.*, 360 U.S. 367 (1959)).

At the FTC, the most common manner of recording the prehearing statements of witnesses is the "interview report" prepared by an attorney-examiner when he interviews prospective witnesses. In the *High* case, the Commission refused to allow access to such reports, although it did let the respondent see signed statements of the witnesses. "Commission interview reports ordinarily are in the category of agents' summarizations," the Commission said, and therefore cannot be considered a "substantially verbatim recital" of the witness' statement. If there is any doubt about the report's "substantially verbatim character," the opinion went on, "the examiner should inspect it and make a determination."

In three earlier cases, the Commission had denied discovery of interview reports without ruling on the applicability of the Jencks Act. In *Pure Oil Co.*, 54 F.T.C. 1892, 1894–1895 (1958), the Commission held the report was not "used in any way during the course of the hearings" and was "hearsay." In *Basic Books, Inc.*, 56 F.T.C.

69, 85–86 (1959), *aff'd,* 276 F.2d 718 (7th Cir. 1960), there was no evidence that a written statement existed. The opinion in *Bakers Franchise Corp.,* 56 F.T.C. 1636 (1959), *aff'd,* 302 F.2d 258 (3rd Cir. 1962), stated that interview reports are privileged as "work product," and the investigating attorney fully described the substance of his interviews during the hearing.

In *R. H. Macy & Co., Inc.,* 69 F.T.C. 1108 (1966), the Commission applied the Jencks Act to reports prepared by one of its investigators who was himself called as a witness. Because the reports were used to refresh his recollection, the hearing examiner was directed to order complaint counsel to hand them over to the examiner for inspection and excision of the portions unrelated to the investigator's actual testimony. The Commission informed its staff that complaint counsel can elect not to comply with such production orders, but the price he must pay for such a choice is removal of the witness' testimony from the record.

In *Inter-State Builders, Inc.,* 69 F.T.C. 1152 (1966), the Commission reaffirmed its adoption of the rule of the Jencks Act, which it characterized as a mere codification of the doctrine established by the Supreme Court. It instructed a hearing examiner to determine whether the interview reports requested in that case represented "a substantially verbatim transcription of the witness' oral words as recorded by the government investigator," applying the criteria laid down by the Supreme Court in the *Palermo* case and in *Campbell* v. *U.S.,* 373 U.S. 487 (1963).

In the *Campbell* case, the Supreme Court reinstated a district court's order requiring production under the Jencks Act of an "interview report" prepared by an FBI agent. The Court felt the district judge "was entitled to infer that an agent of the Federal Bureau of Investigation of some fifteen years' experience would record a potential witness' statement with sufficient accuracy as to obviate any need for the courts to consider whether it would be 'grossly unfair to allow the defense to use statements to impeach a witness which could not fairly be said to be the witness' own.' *Palermo* v. *U.S"* (373 U.S. at 495). The FTC, however, did not choose to see its attorneys' interview reports in that light. It distinguished the result in the *Campbell* case by noting the additional finding there that the witness had adopted the interview report as an accurate reproduction of his statement.

Although the Commission in *Inter-State Builders* classified the interview reports as confidential information protected by both the attorney's work product rule and the normal privilege accorded government informants, it rejected a suggestion that respondent's counsel should have followed formal demand requirements in the Commission's Rules of Practice for release of confidential information and concluded that counsel was correct in his demand to the hearing examiner. On remand the examiner found the interview reports did not qualify as "substantially verbatim recitals." The Commission affirmed his holding when it entered its final order (72 F.T.C. 370 (1967)).

Despite statements by the courts of appeals that it is "the underlying principle" of the *Jencks* case and statute that is applicable in administrative proceedings, the FTC's two opinions in the *Inter-State Builders* case indicate an inclination to stick closely to the statute. Since the Commission recognized in a companion opinion, *L. G. Balfour Co.,* 69 F.T.C. 1118 (1966), *enforced in part,* 442 F.2d 1 (7th Cir. 1971), that "the interview reports in the Commission's files ordinarily are agents' summarizations," interview reports will probably not be made available under the Commission's interpretation of the Jencks Statute. Even if the Commission's instruction manual for its attorneys leaves them free to prepare substantially verbatim interview reports, the staff attitude toward disclosures to respondents is such that the Commission's interpretation of Jencks may be likely to discourage the preparation of verbatim reports.

Some attorneys experienced in FTC litigation suggest that the ban on access to interview reports will be of significance in only a small percentage of cases. Access is vital, they feel, in any case where the key to the defense lies in cross-examination, but such cases seldom arise at the FTC. One difference between jury trials and administrative hearings may have a bearing on eventual court resolution of the propriety of the administrative law judge's *ex parte* examination of the prehearing statement. In criminal trials, which the Supreme Court was dealing with in the *Jencks* and *Campbell* opinions, the judge who makes the inspection called for by the statute is not necessarily the trier of the facts. Would the Supreme Court be just as willing to allow *ex parte* inspection when it is to be made by an administrative law judge who does find the facts and when it is not provided for by statute?

3. Confidential Business Information

Question: *Is there any method in FTC proceedings for protecting business secrets from public disclosure even though revealed to the parties?*

Businessmen may wish to preserve as confidential a variety of facts about their operations, including marketing plans; production and distribution know-how; product formulas; cost, price, and profit data; and customer lists. Management may seek to preserve confidentiality for different reasons: to maintain a competitive edge, to allow a stronger hand in negotiation with labor unions, to avoid harassment by litigious minority stockholders, or to avoid possible government prosecution or treble-damage liability for antitrust violations.

Section 6 of the FTC Act, which grants the Commission the authority to require special reports, provides power to make public from time to time such portions of the information obtained as the Commission shall deem expedient, "except trade secrets and names of customers." This has been held to be a limitation on the publication of trade secrets and names of customers in public reports but not a limitation on what the Commission may subpoena in any proceeding or investigation under the FTC Act (*FTC* v. *Tuttle,* 244 F.2d 605 (2d Cir. 1957), *cert. denied,* 354 U.S. 925 (1957)). Section 10 of the FTC Act makes it a misdemeanor for any officer or employee of the Commission to "make public any information obtained by the Commission without its authority."

Where matters are under adjudication, problems of confidentiality become complex. Parties to court litigation, instituted either by the Government or by private plaintiffs, may secure judicial process requiring the other party to the litigation or third parties to disclose information. Confidentiality may be protected, under certain circumstances, by agreement between the parties, with the court's approval, that evidence produced will be kept under seal by the court and not disclosed to anyone not a party to the litigation. Rule 30(b) of the Federal Rules of Civil Procedure provides for the sealing of depositions and the nondisclosure of "secret processes, developments, or research." See 4 MOORE'S FEDERAL PRACTICE, Sec. 30.12. Yet this may be of little help to third parties who wish to keep facts about their business from both parties to the litigation. Also, it is not clear how such arrangements can be applied to jury cases.

Any evidence received by a court or FTC administrative law judge must, of course, be available to both sides, but one occurrence at the FTC illustrates a possible procedure to protect confidentiality even from a party to the proceedings. A witness in hearings before an examiner was reluctant to disclose the name of one of his suppliers, stating as a basis for his reluctance the fear that the supplier would be subjected to economic retaliation by the respondent to the proceedings. It was agreed that the witness would write the name on a piece of paper. This paper was then shown to respondent's counsel with instructions not to disclose the name to his client.

Although there is no provision for it in the FTC's Rules, a practice has developed at the Commission of witholding exhibits received in evidence from the public record. The Commission reviewed the practice in *H. P. Hood and Sons, Inc.*, 58 F.T.C. 1184 (1961), stating, "There can be no question that the confidential records of businesses involved in Commission proceedings should be protected insofar as possible." The Commission said, however, that "there is a substantial public interest in holding all aspects of adjudicative proceedings, including the evidence adduced therein, open to all interested persons." The Commission stated as its policy that documentary evidence may be received "in camera" only upon a "showing that the public disclosure of the documentary evidence will result in a clearly defined, serious injury to the person or corporation whose records arc involved." The Commission distinguished what it regarded as "trade secrets," such as a "secret formula or process," from "ordinary business records" and stated its conclusion that the former should be more sympathetically protected.

As to protection from possible treble-damage liability, the Commission felt that "the secretion of evidence for the purpose of frustrating possible treble-damage plaintiffs would be opposed to the public interest and the clearly expressed will of Congress. Our efforts should be directed to aiding, not hindering, private enforcement of the antitrust laws." This philosophy seems to underlie the Publicity in Taking Evidence Act, 15 U.S.C. § 30 (1913), which provides that evidence taken by deposition or by a special master in Sherman Act injunction proceedings "shall be opened to the public."

In *Grand Union Co.*, 62 F.T.C. 1491 (1963), respondent moved for permission to examine Section 6(b) reports filed with the Commission by 180 food chains. The Commission ordered that respondent's counsel could examine the documents and make one copy of each document. No additional copies were to be made; the material could only be used in the defense of the proceeding and could not be disclosed to respondent's employees except on application to the examiner showing that disclosure was necessary to respondent's defense; and all copies had to be returned to the Commission upon termination of the proceeding.

In *Miss. River Fuel Corp.* 69 F.T.C. 1186 (1966), the Commission adopted a procedure "out of an abundance of caution and in order to avoid any possibility that the allegedly confidential data will be improperly used" and ordered "that material submitted in response to the subpoenas should be submitted to a reputable and disinterested accounting firm, to be selected by the hearing examiner in consultation with the parties, which shall compile and present the material in such manner that no individual company's confidential arrangements or data will be revealed" (at 1189). In *Koppers Company, Inc.*, Docket 8755, Opinion dated January 15, 1969, the

Commission recommended that the examiner consider the procedure used in *Miss. River Fuel* and also suggested two other courses of action: "a procedure whereby the party seeking protection could be required to prepare a nonconfidential summary of the documents for inclusion in the record, or . . . a procedure whereby the Examiner may conduct an *ex parte, in camera* examination of the documents for the purpose of excising portions thereof before disclosure is made to the respondent" (75 F.T.C. 1047, 1048 (1969)).

Confidentiality may be a problem for both enforcement officials and private parties. Where protection cannot be afforded, business interests may refuse to cooperate with investigations. They may even forego the presentation of valid defenses rather than publicly disclose confidential business facts. Furthermore, confidentiality is not a problem of defendants alone. In order to defend, respondents or defendants may legitimately seek confidential information about plaintiff's business operations or information in the hands of government officials or of third parties. Market-share data for evaluation of the effects of a merger may include confidential information from many sources not parties to the litigation. If such data is received in evidence, but under seal, the right to cross-examination may be curtailed.

Some experts question whether any confidentiality should be allowed, particularly in antitrust cases. If evidence is relevant and material, it should be produced and, they say, let the chips fall where they may. Others argue that competition requires secrets and the policy favoring competition requires an attempt to protect business secrets. The common law of torts and considerations of national security are also suggested as standards to appeal to in opposing an outright denial of any confidentiality. Another approach is to start by assuming a right to privacy and to place the greater burden on the person who seeks confidential information.

The policy question cannot be answered categorically. The answer may depend on whether the facts are sought in pretrial investigation or at trial on the merits, whether the proceeding is in court or before an administrative agency, and whether the information is sought from parties to the proceeding or third parties not involved. The traditional rules of evidence offer some means of dealing with the problem. Where confidential information is involved, a stricter test of relevancy may provide appropriate protection. If essential facts can be proven by means other than the use of confidential information, it may not be material. If "trade secrets" are involved and their disclosure would constitute an unlawful taking of property right, their use as evidence may be improper.

Clearly one party to litigation can keep from the other few of the facts relevant and material to the matter in litigation. Yet both may anticipate some consideration from the court or Commission for efforts to keep some facts from the general public. Third parties may be protected to an even greater extent.

D. COURT INJUNCTIONS IN FTC CASES

1. Preliminary Court Injunctions Sought by the FTC

Question: *What cases may the FTC take to court before completion of its own proceedings?*

Section 13 (a) of the Federal Trade Commission Act, 15 U.S.C. § 53 provides:
"Whenever the Commission has reason to believe—
"(1) that any person, partnership, or corporation is engaged in, or is about to engage in, the dissemination or the causing of the dissemination of any advertisement in violation of section 12 ['any false advertisement which is likely to induce the purchase of food, drugs, devices, or cosmetics'], and
"(2) that the enjoining thereof pending the issuance of a complaint by the Commission under section 5, and until such complaint is dismissed by the Commission or set aside by the court on review, or the order of the Commission to cease-and-desist made thereon has become final within the meaning of section 5, would be to the interest of the public, the Commission, by any of its attorneys designated by it for such purpose, may bring suit in a district court . . . to enjoin the dissemination or the causing of the dissemination of such advertisement. Upon proper showing, a temporary injunction or restraining order shall be granted without bond. Any such suit shall be brought in the district in which such person, partnership, or corporation resides or transacts business."
The FTC applied to the District Court for the Eastern District of California for a temporary injunction prohibiting Medi-Hair International from making false claims for its hair replacement system, failing to disclose the potential medical risks involved, and using high pressure sales tactics. Judge Wilkins approved a temporary injunction against Medi-Hair International, franchisers of "Medi-Hair" hair replacement systems salons, and Jack I. Bauman, a director of the firm (*FTC* v. *Medi-Hair International*, 2 Trade Reg. Rep. ¶7885 (D.C. Calif. 1971)). Terms of the temporary injunction had previously been negotiated by Medi-Hair and the Commission. The temporary injunction required that Medi-Hair immediately:
"Stop making various challenged claims for the system.
"Disclose risks involved to customers before treating them, and recommend they consult with an independent physician.

"Give customers a 3-day cooling-off period to rescind the contract, and refund their money within 24 hours if they do rescind it.

"Advise each present and future franchisee to abide by these terms and warn that the franchise will be cancelled if it does not."

The temporary injunction was to remain in effect until disposition of the Commission's complaint against the parties. Specifically, the temporary injunction forbade claims that:

"The Medi-Hair system does not involve wearing a device or cosmetic which is like a hairpiece or toupee.

"The hair applied becomes part of the anatomy like natural hair, has the same appearance as and may be cared for like natural hair, and the wearer may engage in physical activity and movement with the same disregard for his hair as he would if he had natural hair.

"The wearer can care for it himself and will not have to seek professional or skilled assistance or incur maintenance costs above the application cost."

The disclosure statement was to inform the prospect that the system involved a surgical procedure resulting in the implanting of wires in his scalp, and that, because of the wires remaining in his scalp, there was a risk of discomfort, pain, infection, skin diseases, and scarring.

Referring to the "Medi-Hair" proceeding, the FTC's General Counsel stated: "The Federal Trade Commission Act gives the agency express authority to seek injunctions against false advertisements of foods, drugs, devices or cosmetics, when required by the public interest. It is my belief that the Commission will use this approach increasingly in such cases whenever it appears necessary, particularly where medical and health dangers to the public may be present."

For years the Chamber of Commerce of the U.S. has called for FTC authorization "by law to seek preliminary injunctions in the courts in all cases within FTC jurisdiction." In 1970, upon recommendation of the Antitrust Section, the American Bar Association resolved "That the Federal Trade Commission be empowered to proceed against unfair or deceptive acts or practices within Section 5 of the Federal Trade Commission Act which 'affect' commerce and that the Federal Trade Commission be empowered under appropriate standards to seek and obtain preliminary injunctive relief upon proper showing in court actions against acts or practices within Section 5 which are unfair or deceptive to the consumer."

On February 24, 1971, President Nixon stated: "I am submitting today legislation which would provide the FTC with the authority to seek preliminary injunctions in Federal courts against what it deems to be unfair or deceptive business practices. The present inability to obtain injunctions commonly results in the passage of extended periods of time before relief can be obtained. During this time the practices in question continue, and their effects multiply." Section 212 of S. 986, introduced by Senator Warren Magnuson (D-Wash) on February 25,1971, would have amended Section 13 of the FTC Act to allow the FTC to seek a preliminary injunction against "any act or practice which is unfair or deceptive to a consumer, and is prohibited by Section 5."

During the 1960's the FTC twice sought preliminary injunctions; once successfully, under the All Writs Act (*FTC* v. *Dean Foods Co.,* 384 U.S. 597 (1966)); once unsuccessfully, under Section 13 of the FTC Act (*FTC* v. *Sterling Drug, Inc.,* 317 F.2d 669 (2d Cir. 1963)). Each case, according to participating FTC officials, was a "traumatic experience" for the Commission. During 1971 it was widely reported that the FTC intended to seek a court injunction to stop the distribution of plastic-wrapped razor blades in Sunday newspapers. However, the practice was halted, and no suit was filed. Apparently the intention was to file in a U.S. district court, invoking the court's general equity powers. See *FMC* v. *Atlantic & Gulf/ Panama Canal Zone,* 241 F.Supp. 766, 774–777 (S.D.N.Y. 1965); *C. Tennant & Sons* v. *N.Y. Terminal Conference,* 299 F.Supp. 796, 800 (S.D.N.Y. 1969); 28 U.S.C. § 1337.

Experts differ over the desirability of current proposals. If the FTC makes increasing use of the practice of seeking preliminary court injunctions, either under prior law or under the new provisions of P.L. 93-153, 639 ATRR A-1 (1973), some argue that the basic character of FTC proceedings may be affected. In many cases, if the injunction is granted, the succeeding proceedings before the Commission itself may be anti-climactic. It is suggested that, when the Commission makes a strong case for a preliminary injunction, it adds fuel to the allegation that it cannot later fairly judge the merits of the case itself. On this point, some urge a breakup of the functions of prosecuting and judging; others would consider possible delegation of some functions to the Commission's staff. Some argue that the criticism is unfounded.

2. Injunctions Against FTC Proceedings

Question: *Under what circumstances will FTC action be enjoined by a federal district court?*

"The long settled rule of judicial administration is that no one is entitled to judicial relief for a supposed or threatened injury until the prescribed administrative remedy has been exhausted" (*Myers* v. *Bethlehem Shipbuilding Corp.,* 303 U.S. 41, 50–51 (1938)). The

Supreme Court has made an exception to that rule for threatened administrative action outside the scope of the agency's powers (*Allen* v. *Grand Central Aircraft Co.,* 347 U.S. 535 (1954); *Order Of Railway Conductors* v. *Swan,* 329 U.S. 520 (1947): *Leedom* v. *Kyne,* 358 U.S. 184 (1958); *Leedom* v. *International Union of Mine Workers,* 352 U.S. 145 (1956); *Skinner & Eddy Corp.* v. *U.S.,* 249 U.S. 557 (1919). These decisions are not entirely consistent with the *Myers* case, though, for it was also contended in that case that the National Labor Relations Board lacked jurisdiction to take the threatened action. The grounds cited were (1) the absence of interstate commerce and (2) the unconstitutionality of the applicable sections of the Labor-Management Relations Act. Another exception has been made when the agency action is unreasonably delayed (*Deering Milliken, Inc.* v. *Johnston,* 295 F.2d 856 (4th Cir. 1961)).

The general rule requiring exhaustion of administrative remedies has been applied to FTC proceedings; the remedy of the party claiming impropriety in FTC action is review of the Commission's final order in an appropriate court of appeals (*Ritholz* v. *March,* 105 F.2d 937 (D.C. Cir. 1939); *Crown Zellerbach Corp.* v. *FTC,* 156 F.2d 927 (9th Cir. 1946)). The jurisdiction of a U.S. court of appeals to review, set aside, or modify final FTC orders does not include power to enjoin an FTC proceeding prior to its conclusion, even if it is claimed that the Commission is acting in excess of its jurisdiction (*Chamber of Commerce of Minn.* v. *FTC,* 280 F. 45 (8th Cir. 1922)).

A federal district court has no jurisdiction to enjoin an FTC administrative law judge from holding hearings that are said to have been scheduled in an arbitrary and capricious abuse of discretion. The respondent before the Commission must first exhaust administrative appeal remedies (*Holland Furnace Co.* v. *Purcell,* 125 F.Supp. 74 (W. D. Mich. 1954)).

Until 1962, suits to enjoin most federal officials had to be brought in the District of Columbia where the officials could be served with process. In that year, Congress enacted Section 1391 (e) of the Judicial Code, permitting suits against federal officials in any district where the cause of action arises, where any real property involved in the action is located, or where the plaintiff resides. Since then, suits for injunctions against FTC activities have increased, and the courts have sometimes taken jurisdiction to enjoin specific Commission action.

The first significant case brought against the FTC under the new venue statute was that in *FTC* v. *J. Weingarten, Inc.,* 336 F.2d 687 (5th Cir. 1964), *cert. denied,* 380 U.S. 908 (1965). An injunction of the Federal District Court for Eastern Texas, 1963 Trade Cas. ¶70,790 (E.D. Texas 1963), delayed for two years issuance of a Section 5 FTC Act order against Weingarten's receipt of discriminatory advertising allowances. The district court's injunction was based on the Administrative Procedure Act's admonition against administrative delay. The district judge found that almost three and a half years after issuance of its complaint, the Commission had remanded the case to its hearing examiner for the taking of additional evidence in an area where complaint counsel's evidence had been found deficient. The Commission was given thirty days to dispose of the case on its own without remand. The court of appeals found that "This case not only proceeded at a rate comparable to that normally experienced in cases of its kind, it also proceeded at a rate satisfactory to Weingarten." An argument that the Commission's remand order shows an arbitrary prejudgment of the case was rejected with an observation that appellate courts often remand cases for "shoring up." The court of appeals assumed, without deciding, that the district court had jurisdiction to enjoin the remand proceedings

In *Lehigh Portland Cement Co.* v. *FTC,* 291 F.Supp. 628 (E.D. Va. 1968), *aff'd,* 416 F.2d 971 (4th Cir. 1969), the court rejected an FTC assertion that a district judge lacked jurisdiction but denied a request for an injunction directing the Commission to transfer a Section 7 Clayton Act antimerger proceeding to the Justice Department. The basis for the suit was a claim that the FTC had prejudged the case in a statement of enforcement policy involving the type of merger under attack. The opinion merely declared that the court "has jurisdiction to hear and determine this matter under 28 U.S.C. Sec. 1361 and 5 U.S.C. Secs. 702, 706 (formerly Administrative Procedure Act 10). See *Amos Treat & Co.* v. *SEC,* 306 F.2d 260 (D.C. Cir. 1962); *Deering Milliken* v. *Johnston,* 295 F.2d 856 (4th Cir. 1961); *Abbott Laboratories* v. *Gardner,* 387 U.S. 136 (1967); *Gardner v. Toilet Goods Assn.,* 387 U.S. 167 (1967)."

In *Bristol-Myers Co.* v. *FTC,* 284 F.Supp. 745 (D.D.C. 1968), *aff'd in part, rev'd and remanded in part,* 424 F.2d 935 (D.C. Cir. 1970), *cert. denied,* 400 U.S. 824 (1970), a drug company sought an injunction against the Commission's issuance of a proposed trade regulation rule. The court was told that the Commission has no power to conduct rule-making proceedings but may conduct only adjudicatory proceedings. The district judge declared the injunction suit "premature" since "no one can tell today what type of rule, if any, will eventually be adopted by the Commission. When one is adopted, if it is adopted at all, will be the proper time to seek court review." The same opinion rejected a request for an injunction against press releases. "The courts may no more enjoin government departments from issuing statements or making statements to the public than they can enjoin a public official from making a speech."

Although the Supreme Court has ruled that the Commission

cannot be enjoined from conducting an investigation (*FTC* v. *Claire Furnace Co.*, 274 U.S. 160 (1927)), it has indicated that the validity of an FTC investigation can be tested in a suit under the Declaratory Judgment Act (*U.S.* v. *St. Regis Paper Co.*, 368 U.S. 208 (1961)). In that case a company under investigation sought to avoid penalties under Section 10 of the FTC Act for failing to comply with Commission orders for production of file copies of census reports. St. Regis termed the penalties unfair because it had no way of testing in advance the validity of the Commission's orders. The Supreme Court said the Declaratory Judgment Act "appears sufficient to meet petitioner's needs," apparently endorsing the holding of the Court of Appeals for the Second Circuit in that case that a suit could have been brought under the Declaratory Judgment Act to challenge the Commission's orders (285 F.2d 607 (2d Cir. 1960)).

A complaint about the procedural route followed by the Commission in reopening a matter once settled by consent order was held to be within a district court's jurisdiction in *Elmo Division* v. *Dixon*, 348 F.2d 342 (D.C. Cir. 1965). The district court was directed to entertain a suit for an injunction barring prosecution of a new complaint and requiring the Commission to proceed instead by reopening the original case as provided for in the consent order and the Commission's Rules of Practice. Once the Commission had promulgated the rule and incorporated it into the consent order, the court of appeals reasoned, action at odds with the rule is indistinguishable from the ultra vires administrative actions held enjoinable in *Leedom* v. *Kyne*, 358 U.S. 184 (1958); *Skinner & Eddy Corp.* v. *U.S.*, 249 U.S. 557 (1919); and *B. F. Goodrich Co.* v. *FTC*, 242 F.2d 31 (D.C. Cir. 1957). In its *Goodrich* opinion, the court of appeals sustained the jurisdiction of a district court to enjoin enforcement of a quantity-limit rule the Commission had promulgated under the Robinson-Patman Act for the tire industry without meeting the statute's fact-finding requirements.

In *Frito-Lay, Inc.* v. *FTC*, 380 F.2d 8 (5th Cir. 1967), the court of appeals held that a district court does not have jurisdiction over a declaratory-judgment suit attacking an FTC Section 7 Clayton Act complaint as having been brought against a meat packer exempt from FTC jurisdiction. The court's per curiam opinion stated that only in extraordinary cases can there be deviation from the ordinary rule that only courts of appeals have jurisdiction to review Commission orders. "The writings of the Supreme Court are unsettled as to when a showing of jurisdictional defect will be considered as justification for such a deviation. Judicial intervention without exhaustion of administrative remedies is not justified, however, where, as here, the merit of appellant's jurisdictional attack is far from clear, the administrative body may be more qualified than the court to initially consider the jurisdictional question, and the injury sought to be avoided is merely the normal cost of administrative litigation. See Davis, Administrative Law Text Secs. 20.01–.03 (1959)" (380 F.2d at 10).

The courts have insisted that a challenge to the existence of an interstate-commerce basis for FTC jurisdiction be litigated first before the Commission (*Lone Star Cement Corp.* v. *FTC,* 339 F.2d 505 (9th Cir. 1964); *Stewart Concrete & Material Co.* v. *FTC,* 1967 Trade Cas. ¶72,098 (S.D. Ohio 1967)).

The legal standards for enjoining threatened actions by the FTC seem to have crystalized around the test set out in the *Frito-Lay* opinion. When they decide pending and future suits to enjoin FTC action, the courts are likely to be resolving only the issue of whether the threatened administrative action is a sufficiently grave dereliction of duty to make inadequate the remedy provided by eventual review of the Commission's final order.

In the light of *Sperry & Hutchinson Co.* v. *FTC,* 405 U.S. 233 (1972), some experts feel that complaints about evidentiary, discovery, or procedural matters will be given short shrift. Some lawyers practicing before the Commission attribute the trend away from the issuance of injunctions against Commission action to reforms in the Commission's own internal procedures. Since the time when a hearing examiner's findings and order might have been written by the Commission's trial attorneys, they say, the FTC has progressed to a point where it is difficult to find excesses serious enough to warrant pre-order intervention by injunction.

One area that may still have unresolved questions as to the availability of injunctive relief is that of the Commission's rule-making processes. The Commission's authority to promulgate trade regulation rules, for example, has been challenged, and one district court has sustained the challenge (*Nat'l Petroleum Refiners Assn.* v. *FTC,* 340 F.Supp. 1343 (D.D.C. 1972)), but was reversed on appeal (620 ATRR D-1 (D.C. Cir. 1973)).

E. FTC CEASE-AND-DESIST ORDERS

Question: *What standards govern the Federal Trade Commission's drafting of antitrust cease-and-desist orders?*

Except for orders of divestiture in merger cases, the cease-and-desist order is the principal means by which the Federal Trade Commission makes its interpretation of the law stick against those who do not choose to follow the Commission's suggestions voluntarily. Orders are issued under two principal statutes. Section 5(b) of the FTC Act provides for hearings by the Commission on complaint. "If upon such hearing the Commission shall be of the opinion that the method of competition or the act or practice in question is prohibited by this Act, it shall make a report in writing in which it shall state its findings as to the facts and shall issue and cause to be served . . . an order requiring . . . [the respondent] to cease and desist from using such method of competition or such act or practice."

Section 11(b) of the Clayton Act contains a similar provision: "If upon such hearing the Commission . . . shall be of the opinion that any of the provisions of [Section 2, 3, 7, & 8 of the Clayton Act] have been or are being violated, it shall make a report in writing in which it shall state its findings as to the facts, and shall issue or cause to be served . . . an order requiring . . . [the respondent] to cease and desist from such violations [and, in cases under Sections 7 and 8, to dispose of stock or assets or rid itself of directors]."

Since 1938, orders issued under the FTC Act have become "final" upon expiration of the time provided for appellate review, and violations have been subject to suits for civil penalties in the United States district courts. It was not until 1959, however, that "finality" provisions of this type were added to the Clayton Act. These 1959 amendments focused increased attention on the terms of orders issued by the Commission under the Clayton Act, particularly on those dealing with violations of Section 2 of the Act containing the 1936 Robinson-Patman amendments.

In *FTC* v. *Henry Broch & Co.* 368 U.S. 360, 367 (1962), the Supreme Court sustained a broad FTC brokerage order issued prior to the 1959 "finality" amendments, but expressly refrained from holding that such broad orders "would necessarily withstand scrutiny under the 1959 amendments." The Court stated: "The severity prescribed by the amendments for violations of orders which have become final underlines the necessity for fashioning orders which are, at the outset, sufficiently clear and precise to avoid raising serious questions as to their meaning and application." The Court spoke of "tailoring the order" to "meet the legitimate needs of the case," and "strictly to cope with the threat of future violations identical with or like or related to the violations" that the respondent "was found to have committed" (368 U.S. at 366).

The Commission has issued many Robinson-Patman Act orders that merely repeat the statutory prohibitions in a manner once described by Justice Jackson as the "undiscriminating prohibition of discrimination" (Dissenting in *FTC* v. *Ruberoid Co.,* 343 U.S. 470, 492 (1952)). The majority opinion in *Ruberoid* has often been interpreted as requiring that such blanket Commission orders be read as if they contained the statutory defenses and provisos.

In addition to the admonition as to clarity and precision contained in the *Broch* opinion, the Supreme Court has supplied several general guidelines for the drafting of Commission orders. The Court has said that the Commission's remedy must have some reasonable relationship to the unlawful practice found (*Jacob Siegel Co.* v. *FTC,* 327 U.S. 608 (1946)), but that the Commission cannot be required to confine its ban to the identical practice charged (*FTC* v. *Ruberoid Co.,* 343 U.S. 470 (1952)). The Court has repeatedly acknowledged the Commission's possession of broad discretion to formulate an order adequate to prevent repetition of the violation found. See *FTC* v. *Nat'l Lead Co.,* 352 U.S. 419 (1957).

Some courts of appeals, consistent with the Supreme Court's opinion in *Broch,* have rejected the FTC Clayton Act orders as "too broad" (*Swanee Paper Corp.* v. *FTC,* 291 F.2d 833 (2d Cir. 1961), *cert. denied,* 368 U.S. 987 (1962); *Grand Union Co.* v. *FTC,* 300 F.2d 92 (2d Cir. 1962); and *American News Co.* v. *FTC,* 300 F.2d 104 (2d Cir. 1962), *cert. denied,* 371 U.S. 824 (1962).

In arguments before the administrative law judge or before the Commission itself, respondents in FTC proceedings are sometimes reluctant to place great emphasis in their presentations on the terms of any order, not wishing to concede that they have violated the law. It is difficult to argue persuasively that no order should be issued and, at the same time, to discuss terms of an order that might be issued. Where discussion has taken place, it has frequently taken the form of "broad" versus "narrow" orders. Staff counsel have sought the broadest possible order; respondents have sought to limit the order's application by product line, by media coverage in cooperative-advertising cases, or by a variety of other specific standards.

The *Vanity Fair* and *Quaker Oats* cases (*Vanity Fair Paper Mills Inc.,* 60 F.T.C. 568 (1962), *order enforced as modified,* 311 F.2d 480 (2nd Cir. 1962); *Quaker Oats Co.,* 60 F.T.C. 798 (1962)) divided the Commission on the drafting of orders in cases under Section 2(d) of the Clayton Act. In each case the Commission issued a comparatively "broad" order. In his *Vanity Fair* dissent, Commissioner Elman distinguished three problems in the drafting of FTC orders: (1) the breadth of the order, (2) the justification for a broad order, and (3) the formulation of the order. He deplored the use of "general statutory prohibitions . . . in broad, indefinite, and ambiguous terms raising questions of interpretation and application that have not yet been resolved." In his *Quaker Oats* dissent, Commissioner Elman reemphasized his opinion that an FTC order "should inform and direct the respondent not only as to what he may not do, but as to what he may and must do in order to carry on his business without again running afoul of the statute." Commissioner Kern, writing the opinion for the majority in the *Quaker Oats* case, responded directly to the point. With the concurrence of Chairman Dixon and Commissioner MacIntyre, Mr. Kern stated for the Commission:

"Though some may argue to the contrary, we do not view the narrow language of the *Broch* decision as justification for couching orders, either in broad or detailed language, which endeavor to define what respondents may do or must do in order to comply with the statute. We believe our present compliance procedures to be adequate. We recognize an obligation to tell the respondents, with as much specificity as possible, what they must stop doing. However, to suggest that a cease and desist order is an appropriate vehicle to gratuitously guide or instruct businessmen as to what they may do and must do, we firmly believe is beyond our province."

The Supreme Court's "sufficiently clear and precise" standard may itself be far from clear. While some commentators urge that it is important to distinguish between the scope of an order and its clarity, others suggest that clarity and precision will necessarily demand some narrowing from customary boiler-plate orders. Such orders, repeating as they do only some of the ambiguous statutory provisions, may in effect be broader than the statute itself. Any attempt to make such orders clearer and more precise may tend to narrow them.

The question of whether a respondent is obligated to show some reason for narrowing any proposed FTC order or for making the order more "precise" has not been answered clearly. Commissioner Kern stated his view that the Supreme Court's *Broch* opinion is a "warning signal against the issuance of broad orders couched in the language of the statute violated, unless a clear predicate is laid in the record justifying the necessity for such an order." Once the responsibility for establishing proper scope and degree of precision is assigned, another question arises: What are the criteria to be satisfied by the party bearing that responsibility?

One solution to the problem of vagueness in Commission orders has been found practical for some respondents: the submission of a voluminous report of compliance to the FTC staff containing a statement of proposed or intended future practice based on a meaningful interpretation of the order. If the Commission receives and files the report, respondent then has at least some basis for later argument about what the order really means.

PART IX

Private Actions

A. ACTIONS FOR TREBLE DAMAGES

1. Treble Damages Under Section 7 of the Clayton Act

Question: *Does a violation of the antimerger law provide the basis for a treble-damage suit?*

Section 7 of the Clayton Act is clearly a part of the "antitrust laws" as defined in Section 1 of the Clayton Act, and Section 4 authorizes treble-damage recovery for "anything forbidden in the antitrust laws." Nevertheless, prior to *Gottesman v. General Motors*, 414 F.2d 956 (2d Cir. 1969), there was no instance of recovery of treble-damages in a litigated action under Section 7.

Between 1961 and 1965, over 40 private actions were filed for alleged violations of Section 7. The litigated cases in which plaintiffs won victories were all on the equity side; that is, injunctions were granted preventing prospective mergers or acquisitions of additional stock in the plaintiff corporation. See, e.g., *American Crystal Sugar Co.* v. *Cuban American Sugar Co.*, 152 F.Supp. 387 (S.D. N.Y. 1957), *aff'd*, 259 F.2d 524 (2d Cir. 1958); *Briggs Manufacturing Co.* v. *Crane Co.*, 280 F.2d 747 (6th Cir. 1960); *Muskegon Piston Ring Co., Inc.* v. *Gulf & Western Industries, Inc.*, 328 F.2d 830 (6th Cir. 1964). Several private actions seeking damages for alleged violations of Section 7 were dismissed by agreement between the parties. There is no way of telling whether the terms of settlement provided for the payment of damages.

In most of the litigated cases that produced formal opinions, the courts seem to have assumed that Section 4's treble-damage authorization applied to a merger violating Section 7. In each of those cases, however, some shortcoming in the allegations or in the evidence caused the court to deny recovery. Three of the four federal district courts that faced the issue decided Section 7 could not be a basis of treble-damage recovery. Judge Charles M. Metzner of the Federal District Court for Southern New York, in the *Gottesman* case (*Gottesman* v. *General Motors* 221 F.Supp. 488 (S.D.N.Y. 1963), 279 F.Supp. 361 (S.D.N.Y. 1967), *remanded*, 414 F.2d 956

(2d Cir. 1969), 310 F.Supp. 1257 (S.D.N.Y. 1970), 436 F.2d 1205 (2d Cir. 1971), *cert. denied,* 403 U.S. 911 (1971)) declared unequivocally that there can be no claim for money damages for a violation of Section 7. "The test of a Section 7 violation is whether 'there is a reasonable probability that the acquisition is likely to result in the condemned restraints.' (*U.S.* v. *E.I. duPont de Nemours & Co.,* 353 U.S. 586 at 607). Plaintiffs cannot be damaged by a potential restraint of trade or monopolization."

A year later Judge Metzner was joined by the Federal District Court for Hawaii. In *Bailey's Bakery* v. *Continental Baking Co.,* 235 F.Supp. 705 (D. Hawaii 1964), *aff'd,* 401 F.2d 182 (9th Cir. 1968), *cert. denied,* 393 U.S. 1086 (1969), Chief Judge Martin Pence pointed out that Section 7 of the Clayton Act merely "supplements the Sherman Act and was intended primarily to arrest apprehended relationships before those relationships could work their evil." Judge Pence recognized that Section 7 can be a basis for private injunction suits, but did not see how a plaintiff can recover for "anticipated invasions" of his interests, which is what a Section 7 damage suit would involve. "The prohibitory sanctions of Clayton Section 7 are triggered to explode by and at the moment of acquisition. That, after the moment of acquisition, subsequent business practices do injure competitors in that market does not, because of those subsequent injurious acts, give rise to a claim for treble damages under Clayton Section 7."

Then, in *Julius M. Ames Co.* v. *Bostitch Co.,* 240 F.Supp. 521 (S.D. N.Y. 1965), Judge Edward C. McLean of the Southern New York Federal District Court refused to follow the *Gottesman* and *Bailey* opinions. He relied on allegations that the treble-damage claimants "lost their distributorships . . . substantially at the moment when defendant acquired" the supplier from whom they had obtained the distributorships. Faced with allegations of "immediate and present damage," Judge McLean decided the distributors are persons "injured . . . by reason of anything forbidden in the antitrust laws."

In *Highland Supply Corp.* v. *Reynolds Metals Co.,* 245 F.Supp. 510 (E.D. Mo. 1965), deferring to a dictum set out by his own court of appeals in a footnote to an earlier appeal in the *Highland* case (327 F.2d 725 (8th Cir. 1964)), Judge James H. Meredith decided it is not possible for a damage claimant to allege that he has been injured "solely by a merger or acquisition which has potential prohibited effects." Rather, such a damage claimant can assert only that he has been injured by the merger and subsequent activities. Because any damages can always be attributed to subsequent, intervening activities, the prohibited acquisition standing alone causes no present, compensable injury, and there can be no damage recovery for an alleged Section 7 violation.

Judge Meredith recognized the logic of an argument based on Section 16's provision for private injunction suits "against threatened loss or damage" from a Section 7 violation. If a person can suffer threatened loss "by reason of" an illegal merger, why can't he incur actual damage "by reason of" an illegal merger? "This logic can be answered only by arguing that the enumeration of specific sections in Section 16 Clayton distinguishes it from Section 4 Clayton and that Section 4 should be strictly construed in view of the drastic and unusual nature of the treble-damage remedy."

It is difficult to conceive of situations in which a horizontal merger will produce Section 7 damage claims that could not also be asserted under the Sherman Act. In the past, however, there have been occasions when members of an industry have been so conscious of the economic disadvantages of dealing with a single source of supply that they have avoided the use of a particular raw material until several suppliers became available. When the number of suppliers, instead of growing, is reduced by a merger, there might be buyers who could prove specific dollar losses from the disappearance of the acquired supplier.

In cases like *Ames* v. *Bostitch,* some antitrust lawyers take the position that it is not necessary for cutoff distributors seeking damages to show they were injured immediately upon consummation of the horizontal acquisition. Merging companies might agree that unneeded distributors will not be dropped until six months or a year after consummation of the merger. If a distributor can obtain documents or other evidence to show that the merging firms intended to dispense with his services, he might have a cause of action under Section 7 even if he is not cut off when the merger occurs.

In 1965, the Supreme Court's decision in *Minn. Mining and Mfg. Co. (3M)* v. *N.J. Wood Finishing Co.,* 381 U.S. 311 (1965), set the stage for a reversal of the judicial trend seen in the *Gottesman, Bailey's Bakery,* and *Highland Supply* district court decisions. In the *3M* case the Court concluded that the Section 5(b) tolling provision of the Clayton Act applies to an enforcement antitrust action by the Federal Trade Commission. The Court emphasized that private litigants should be afforded maximum access to the fruits of government enforcement proceedings. Underlying this approach was the thought that treble-damage claimants play a key role in antitrust enforcement and that this is a role Congress intended them to play when it created Section 4 of the Clayton Act.

In light of the policies stated in *3M,* the Court of Appeals for the Second Circuit in *Gottesman* v. *General Motors Corp.,* 414 F.2d 956 (2nd Cir. 1969), 310 F.Supp. 1257 (S.D.N.Y. 1970), 436 F.2d 1205 (2nd Cir. 1971), *cert. denied,* 403 U.S. 911 (1971), chose to interpret the Section 4 Clayton language "any person who shall be injured" to provide for treble-damage claims arising from violations of Section 7 of the Clayton Act. The court found that threatened harm at the time a merger is consummated can provide a private cause of action if that potential reaches fruition subsequent to the merger. Recognizing that a Section 7 Clayton Act violation may not necessarily result in actual competitive injury, the court was convinced that such injury could subsequently occur and that treble damage plaintiffs were entitled to prove this injury as a matter of law. The court noted that the Supreme Court in *3M* was apparently not concerned that the treble-damage action involved in that case was based on a violation of Section 7, although the issue of whether plaintiffs could maintain a private cause of action based upon a Section 7 violation was not specifically raised. The court noted the conclusions of commentators and of the district court in *Ames* v. *Bostitch,* 240 F.Supp. 521 (S.D. N.Y. 1965). Also cited was the fact that damages have been allowed by a variety of courts for violations of Sections 2 and 3 of the Clayton Act, which are aimed at incipient violations "where the effect . . . may be . . . to lessen competition." The court of appeals referred to *3M:* ". . . if we had any real doubts on this issue, we would resolve them in favor of a broad, rather than a narrow construction of Section 4, because 'Congress has expressed its belief that private antitrust litigation is one of the surest weapons for effective enforcement of the antitrust laws.' "

Two district court cases following *Gottesman* seem to dispel any further doubts that treble-damage claimants can sue if they are adversely affected by unlawful mergers or acquisitions: *Kirahara* v. *Bendix Corp.,* 306 F.Supp 72 (D. Hawaii 1969); *Metropolitan Liquor Co.* v. *Heublein, Inc.,* 305 F.Supp. 946 (E.D. Wisc. 1969).

In *Kirahara,* the district court permitted an action for treble damages by a plaintiff whose distributorship was terminated shortly after the acquisition by Bendix Corporation of Farm Filter Corporation, the plaintiff's original supplier. While the penal nature of Clayton Section 4 and the fact that mergers are a "normal way of business life" gave the district judge pause, he concluded that *3M* decided "that the big cats are fair game for private damage guns for violations of Clayton Section 7." From a review of the pertinent legislative history, the court concluded that since "Congress has left Section 4 unchanged and uncircumscribed since 1914" it would be only reasonable to conclude that Congress intended that the deterrent effect of Section 4 be applied equally to unlawful acquisitions.

The court's inquiry in *Kirahara* did not end with the question of standing to sue but extended to the causal relationship between plaintiff's injury and the challenged acquisition. The court concluded that the plaintiff, despite his financial loss, could not recover damages. Not only must the plaintiff prove a substantive Section 7 violation which caused him immediate competitive injury, but he must also establish, according to Judge Pence in the *Kirahara* case, "that he is within that area of economy which is endangered by a breakdown of competitive conditions." Thus, the plaintiff's immediate injury must be proximately caused by the challenged acquisition, and "the injured must be one of the components of the competitive infrastructure of the relevant market"; injury to that component must reasonably be expected to affect "the viability of competition in that market." He concluded that the court must have "broad discretion" in making the determination of whether plaintiff is within the so-called target area of the substantive Section 7 violations.

Judge Pence found that plaintiff Kirahara was not within the designated area. The court noted that while plaintiff no longer distributed Fram filters after the Fram-Bendix merger, the Fram line was not removed from the Hawaiian market since the distributorship was taken over by a Bendix distributor. Furthermore, the plaintiff was free to sell filters other than Fram. Consequently, the removal of Kirahara as a Fram distributor did not have a substantial impact on the vigor of competition in the Hawaiian market, and plaintiff had no cause of action.

In the *Metropolitan Liquor* case, Judge Gordon of Wisconsin's Eastern District relied upon *Gottesman* to conclude "that there can be a cause of action for damages accruing to a private party for alleged violation of [Section 7]." Making no mention of the approach to the proximate cause issue adopted in *Kirahara,* the court simply required that "the plaintiff's injuries be proximate to the acquisition." Thus, where plaintiff's exclusive Wisconsin distributorship rights for Vintage Wines, Inc., (acquired by Heublein) were made nonexclusive three years after the acquisition, plaintiff could sue for damages arising from the acquisition. The court denied a motion to dismiss without specifically adjudicating the merits of plaintiff's Section 7 claim.

While the right to sue for treble damages for Section 7 violations now seems to be resolved, a question remains as to the proximate cause element. In *Metropolitan Liquor* the court denied a dismissal motion without elaborate reference to the proximate cause issue; it did not have before it a trial record such as that available in *Kirahara.* Under the elementary test of *Ames* v. *Bostitch,* Metropolitan was awarded damages when its distributorship was immediately terminated by the acquiring company. Under similar facts in *Kirahara,* the court found the element of causation lacking. Judge Pence's approach to this issue is precise: Not only must a plaintiff under Clayton Section 4 establish direct causation between his injury and the unlawful acquisition, but he must further prove that he was such an integral part of the relevant market that his removal or limitation by the acquisition would create a probability of injury to competition in that market.

Some commentators have suggested that courts employ the "target area" principle of causation with the intent of setting up an objective standard which emphasizes the policy nature of the proximate cause issue. Judge Cardozo, in his famous tort decision, *Palsgraf* v. *Long Island R.R. Co.,* 248 N.Y. 339, 162 N.E. 99 (1928), first formalized the concept that a negligent defendant was not liable for any injuries suffered unless the injury involved risk "within the scope of any duty" owed the plaintiff by the defendant. While no "duty" concept specifically exists under antitrust law as it does under accepted tort principles, it can be argued persuasively that decisions such as *Kirahara* have engrafted this concept onto the proximate cause issue. Thus, in a treble-damage action, a court in employing the "target area" principle may be considering policy questions such as the penal nature of the remedy, unfair windfall for incidental damages, and the danger of a litigation flood.

Should a showing of actual injury to the plaintiff's business coupled with proof of a substantive Section 7 violation create an *inference* the jury can draw that a causal link exists between the violation and the injury? In *Continental Ore* v. *Union Carbide & Carbon Corp.,* 370 U.S. 690 (1962), such an inference was indulged by the Supreme Court in a Sherman Act treble-damage action. Judge Pence in *Kirahara* saw no grounds for such an inference. Other courts, in their tendency to consider "injury" and "causation" as a single issue, may be adopting an inference of causality.

Judge Pence's test of proximate cause may require a sophisticated and costly economic analysis by treble-damage claimants. A concurrent government enforcement action in which expert analysis has established the requisite incipient effects on competition under Section 7 might not suffice for treble-damage purposes. It is possible, under Judge Pence's test, that treble-damage plaintiffs, despite their having suffered specific financial loss, would be required to establish their specific competitive role in the threatened market. The question arises whether a Section 7 treble-damage action can effectively supplement enforcement activities where a possible difference exists about standards of proof of "injury" to competition.

In considering proximate cause, the element of time plays an important role. For example, if in *Bostitch* the acquiring company had intentionally refrained from eliminating plaintiff's distributorship until six months after the acquisition, damages might not have been awarded. In *Metropolitan Liquor,* plaintiff's exclusive distributorship was not terminated until 3 years after the acquisition and plaintiff retained a nonexclusive agency. The court's order denying defendant's motion to dismiss suggests that the court was not particularly disturbed by the intervening time between the acquisition and termination of the exclusive agency, but in *Burkhead* v. *Phillips Petroleum Co.*, 308 F.Supp. 120 (N.D. Calif. 1970), the court held that Section 7 based damage actions can be brought only at the time the acquisition is "actually consummated and not thereafter."

The *Ames* v. *Bostitch* test of causation appears to be widely applied. It might have resulted in liability under the *Kirahara* facts, but there may be a general reluctance to grant damages to private litigants suing for Section 7 violations. This is suggested by *Walder* v. *Paramount Publix Corp.*, 132 F.Supp. 912 (S.D.N.Y. 1955), where the officers of an acquired firm who lost their positions subsequent to a challenged merger were not permitted to recover lost income from the loss of salary since this was held not to be "injury to one's business or property" under Section 4 of the Clayton Act. Perhaps there is a significant distinction between this case and the loss of a going distributorship as the result of an acquisition. In *Daily* v. *Quality School Plan, Inc.*, 380 F.2d 484 (5th Cir. 1967), a salesman whose territory was eliminated by an acquiring firm was permitted to sue for treble damages. The court distinguished the loss of a sales territory (which the court classified as a business) from the loss of salary as a corporate employee.

2. Standing to Sue for Treble Damages

(a) Question: *Who is a "person injured" by an antitrust violation?*

Section 4 of the Clayton Act provides for treble-damage suits by "any person who shall be injured in his business or property by reason of anything forbidden in the antitrust laws." The courts have not given a literal interpretation to Section 4's phrase, "any person . . . injured," in determining the classes of persons who can maintain damage suits. They have denied recovery for the "secondary," "derivative," or "indirect" injuries suffered by individual stockholders and creditors of a company allegedly injured by antitrust violations (*Loeb* v. *Eastman Kodak Co.*, 183 F. 704 (3rd Cir., 1910)); officers, directors, and employees of an injured corporation (*Bookout* v. *Schine Chain Theaters*, 253 F.2d 292 (2d Cir. 1958)); a partner in an injured business partnership (*Coast* v. *Hunt Oil Co.*, 195 F.2d 870 (5th Cir. 1952)); a landlord of an injured lessee (*Erone Corp.* v. *Skouras Theaters Corp.*, 166 F.Supp. 621 (S.D.

N.Y. 1957)); a supplier of an injured customer (*Volasco Products Co.* v. *Fry Roofing Co.*, 308 F.2d 383 (6th Cir. 1962)); a patent owner claiming royalty losses attributable to injuries to his licensee (*Productive Inventions Inc.* v. *Trico Products Corp.*, 224 F.2d 678 (2d Cir. 1955)); an insurance agent representing an injured underwriter (*Miley* v. *John Hancock Mutual Life Ins. Co.*, 148 F.Supp. 299 (D. Mass. 1957)); and members of an injured association (*Schwartz* v. *Broadcasting Music Inc.*, 180 F.Supp. 332 (S.D. N.Y. 1959)).

At least one court, on the other hand, has accorded a landlord standing to sue where his tenant was a participant in, rather than a victim of, an antitrust violation that reduced the landlord's rental income (*Congress Building Corp.* v. *Loew's, Inc.*, 246 F.2d 587 (7th Cir. 1957)). Earlier another court had twice denied standing in that type of situation (*Melrose Realty Co.* v. *Loew's, Inc.*, 234 F.2d 518 (3rd Cir. 1956); *Harrison* v. *Paramount Pictures, Inc.*, 211 F.2d 405 (3rd Cir. 1954)).

In *Karseal Corp.* v. *Richfield Oil Corp.*, 221 F.2d 358 (9th Cir. 1955), the test applied was whether the damage claimant "was within the target area of the illegal practices." A supplier frozen out of part of his potential market by a competitor's exclusive-dealing arrangements "was not only hit, but was aimed at" and therefore was allowed to sue. Similar reasoning has been employed in *Elyria-Lorain Broadcasting Co.* v. *Lorain Journal Co.*, 298 F.2d 356 (6th Cir. 1961), and in *Productive Inventions Inc.* v. *Trico Products Corp.*, cited above. "Target area" was the expression for the standard applied earlier in *Conference of Studio Unions* v. *Loew's, Inc.*, 193 F.2d 51 (9th Cir. 1951), that is, whether the damage claimant is "within that area of the economy which is endangered by a break-down of competitive conditions in a particular industry."

Whether the "target area" or "direct-injury" test is used, decisions in 1966 suggested that the courts were relaxing somewhat the barriers to standing to recover treble damages. Standing was accorded a supplier (*South Carolina Council of Milk Producers* v. *Newton*, 360 F.2d 414 (4th Cir. 1966), *cert. denied*, 385 U.S. 934 (1966)) and a customer (*Schulman* v. *Burlington Industries*, 255 F.Supp. 847 (S.D. N.Y. 1966)) of businesses injured directly by antitrust violations. Each opinion found the damage claimant to be one of the "targets" of the antitrust violation. In the *Newton* opinion, the court saw standing to sue for anyone "within the sector of the economy in which the violation threatened a breakdown of competitive conditions." The *Schulman* opinion expressed impatience with the "legal subtleties" of the direct-injury rule.

Recovery has been denied to stockholders of an injured company (*D'Ippolito* v. *Cities Service Co.*, 1966 Trade Cas. ¶71,792 (S.D.

N.Y. 1966), *rev'd in part,* 374 F.2d 643 (2d Cir. 1967)) and to insurance agents representing an insurance company said to have suffered antitrust damages (*Young* v. *Security Benefit Life Ins. Co.,* 279 ATRR A-10 (D. Kans. 1966)).

In *Snow Crest Beverages* v. *Recipe Foods,* 147 F.Supp. 907 (D. Mass. 1956), a supplier of extracts used in the manufacture of syrup was denied standing to sue a syrup manufacturer for attempting to monopolize the syrup market. The court pointed out that "the gist of the complaint turns upon competitive practices in the market for the sale of syrup," a "field of competition" the extract supplier did not operate in.

The court in *Sanitary Milk Producers* v. *Bergjans Farm Dairy, Inc.,* 368 F.2d 679 (8th Cir. 1966), followed the *Newton* opinion and distinguished the *Snow Crest* case in allowing standing to a milk processor whose sales company lost business because of the antitrust violations of a wholesale milk company. The court reasoned that the milk processor and its sales company did not occupy the relationship of raw-material supplier and manufacturer. The processor put out the finished product, and his product moved intact through the sales company, which did no processing or manufacturing. These factors persuaded the court that there was directness of competition between the processor and the wholesaler; that any recovery by the processor would not be in the nature of a windfall; that the processor's injury is something more than remote, is not derivative but direct, and is the proximate result of the wholesaler's misdoing.

In *Schulman* v. *Burlington Industries, Inc.,* the district court was unimpressed by "legal subtleties generated by rules couched in terms of 'direct' versus 'indirect' consequences." The court refused to dismiss an antitrust claim of retailers who were complaining about conduct aimed at their wholesaler-supplier. The retailers alleged that a manufacturer of hosiery conspired with a retail chain to pressure their wholesaler-supplier into purchasing all or substantially all his hosiery requirements from the manufacturer. The complaint further asserted that the manufacturer first induced the other retail chain to stop buying from the wholesaler and to buy instead directly from the manufacturer. In addition, the retail chain allegedly agreed to and did open retail stores close to the complaining retailers for the purpose of injuring them and bringing further pressure on the wholesaler to deal exclusively with the manufacturer.

To the manufacturer's motion to dismiss, the court replied that the cases make it clear that one qualifies as a private antitrust plaintiff either when the violation is directly aimed at him or when he has been directly harmed by it. The opinion described the conspiracy alleged as one "expressly and purposefully aimed at coercing and injuring the plaintiffs as identified targets." It made no difference to the court that the conspirators were alleged to have combined to produce the restraints hurting the retailers only as part of an over-all scheme to reach bigger game (255 F.Supp. 847, 851).

The test for determining treble-damage "standing" was couched in new terms by the Federal District Court for Southern New York in *Epstein* v. *Dennison Mfg. Co.*, 1966 Trade Cas. ¶71,852 (S.D. N.Y. 1966). Since many antitrust violations are defined in terms of "relevant market," the court suggested that the more sensible method of resolving the standing issue is to allow standing to all those who are within the sector of the economy threatened by a breakdown in competitive conditions. Using a relevant-market test to determine directness of injury, the court saw no reason why an inventor claiming that a manufacturer of inventory-ticket printing machines stole his ticket-fastener invention should have standing to sue the manufacturer for monopolizing the ticket-fastener market. The court perceived no significant relationship between the market restricted by the manufacturer's anticompetitive acts, the market in ticket fasteners, and the inventor's claimed damages. The inventor claimed that the manufacturer's illegal acts restricted competition in the fastener and inventory-ticket markets, but he made no claim that he was a competitor or customer or was otherwise involved in those markets. It was clear to the court that he was not a potential competitor. The inventor cited *La Chappelle* v. *United Shoe Machinery Corp.*, 90 F.Supp. 721 (D. Mass. 1950), to support his contention that because he invented a device useful in the ticket-processing market, he was directly injured by any monopolizing within that market. The district judge saw a clear distinction between the facts of *La Chappelle* and those of the inventor's suit. In *La Chappelle*, an inventor of shoe machinery was held to have standing to sue when he alleged that he had been forced to sell his invention to the manufacturer at an unreasonably low price because of the manufacturer's power over the entire shoe-machinery industry. Here, the inventor did not allege an attempt by the manufacturer to monopolize the market for ticket-processing inventions.

These decisions indicate that the courts have often applied a relevant market test to determine whether a particular treble-damage claimant had standing to sue. A raw-material supplier does not sell in the same market as his manufacturer-customer and therefore has no standing to complain about antitrust violations affecting the manufacturer's sales. A patent owner who licenses his inventions, being in the invention-marketing business, cannot recover for violations affecting the sales of his licensee in the market for the ultimate product made under the patent, even though patent royalties are also affected. Stockholders, creditors, officers, directors, and employees can be regarded as sellers of capital or personal services and hence as operators in markets different from that of their corporation. When companies deal in the same product, they may be treated as being in the same market, even if they are not at the same distribution level. In *South Carolina Council* v. *Newton,* which allowed dairy farmers standing to sue retail grocers for conduct aimed at dairies, the court emphasized that the milk sold by the farmer "is essentially the equivalent" of the product sold by the dairies (360 F.2d 414 at 419).

Some antitrust experts are satisfied that a "relevant market" test simply will not fit more than a small portion of the "standing" issues that arise. They feel the relevant-market language was used in opinions like *Epstein* v. *Dennison* as another way of expressing the target-area concept as it applied in those particular situations. Even the Ninth Circuit's *Karseal* decision, generally cited as the source of the target-area test, relied on the "area of the economy" rationale of the *Conference of Studio Unions* case, cited above.

Since "relevant market" is a term of art for substantive merger and monopolization issues, perhaps "target area" is a better name for the test of standing to sue for damages. If "target area" is defined as the sector of the economy in which the antitrust violation threatened a breakdown of competitive conditions, there is no need to concern courts with the problem of whether the damage claimant was aimed at or accidentally hit. If he has been operating in the proper "sector of the economy," he is within the "target area." Adjectives such as direct, indirect, derivative, and secondary may be out of place in that context.

Many antitrust lawyers are convinced that if a treble-damage claimant gets by a motion to dismiss on the standing question, he will have little trouble in convincing a jury that he is within the "target area." Jury decisions will probably have a tendency to increase the size of the target.

(b) Question: *What is "business or property" damage?*

To recover damages under Section 4 of the Clayton Act a claimant must be a "person injured" in his "business or property." The Supreme Court held in *Chattanooga Foundry and Pipe Works* v. *City of Atlanta,* 203 U.S. 390 (1906), that "a person whose property is diminished by a payment of money wrongfully induced is injured in his property" for purposes of Section 4. It has been held that interference with a valid contract constitutes an actionable injury to "property" (*North Texas Producers Assn.* v. *Young,* 308 F.2d 235 (5th Cir. 1962), *cert. denied,* 372 U.S. 929 (1963)). "Property" has been held not to exist in negotiations that have not yet ripened into a contract *(Peller* v. *Internat'l. Boxing Club, Inc.,* 227 F.2d 593 (7th Cir. 1955), and *Brownlee* v. *Malco Theaters,* 99 F.Supp. 312 (W.D. Ark. 1951)). In *Peller,* the lack of a license from state authorities was also emphasized.

The term "business" includes a commercial or industrial enterprise *(Broadcasters, Inc.,* v. *Morristown Broadcasting Corp.,* 185 F.Supp. 641 (D. N.J. 1960); *Image & Sound Serv. Corp.* v. *Altec Serv. Corp.,* 148 F.Supp. 237, (D. Mass. 1956)). Also included in "business" may be the employment or occupation by which a persons earns a living *(Nichols* v. *Spencer International Press, Inc.,* 1967 Trade Cas. ¶71,974 (7th Cir. 1967), *rehearing granted,* 371 F.2d 332 (7th Cir. 1967); *Roseland* v. *Phister Mfg. Co.,* 125 F.2d 417 (7th Cir. 1942); *Vines* v. *General Outdoor Adv. Co.,* 171 F.2d 487 (2nd Cir. 1948). In the *Roseland* case, the court read the word "in its ordinary sense and with its usual connotations. It signifies ordinarily that which habitually busies, or engages, time, attention or labor, as a principal serious concern or interest. In a somewhat more truly economic, legal and industrial sense, it includes that which occupies the time, attention, and labor of men for the purpose of livelihood or profit—persistent human efforts which have for their end pecuniary reward. It denotes 'the employment or occupation in which a person is engaged to procure a living.' "

The "business" question comes up in lawsuits brought by potential competitors, suppliers, or customers who claim to have been excluded from an industry by reason of an antitrust violation. In *Thomsen* v. *Union Castle Mail S.S. Co.,* 166 F. 251 (2d Cir. 1908), the court thought it is "as unlawful to prevent a person from engaging in business as it is to drive him out of business." In such situations, decisions on whether the damage claimant had "business" have been grounded on the degree of preparation made toward entering the market or industry. In *Deterjet Corp.* v. *United Aircraft Corp.,* 211 F.Supp. 348 (D. Del. 1962), the court concluded that the damage claimant had satisfied the "business" requirement by investing $8,000, by leasing a building, by obtaining necessary production machinery, and by obtaining additional financing commitments. Similarly, in *Penna. Sugar Ref. Co.* v. *American Sugar Ref. Co.,* 166 F. 254 (2d Cir. 1908), the court concluded that there was an injury to "business" when a recently constructed sugar refinery was rendered useless by an antitrust violation. A would-be broadcaster's mere filing of an application for a broadcast license was found insufficient preparation to create a "business" within the meaning of Section 4. *Broadcasters, Inc.,* v. *Morristown Broadcasting Corp.,* 185 F. Supp. 641 (D. N.J. 1960). The damage claimant's incurrence of little, if any, expense was the deciding factor in *Duff* v. *Kansas City Star Co.,* 299 F.2d 320 (8th Cir. 1962).

The court held in *Martin* v. *Phillips Petroleum Co.,* 365 F.2d 629 (5th Cir. 1966), *cert. denied,* 385 U.S. 991 (1966), that an independent oil and gas operator who did no more than obtain an oral sub-option on a gasoline plant and enter into loan negotiations with a bank did not acquire a "business or property" whose loss would give him standing to sue. The court reasoned that there must be a showing of both intention and preparedness to enter business and concluded that the damage claimant was prepared neither to enter a new business nor to expand an existing business. The damage claimant had no experience in the operation of a gas plant, did not have the ability to finance the business, had made no investment in facilities or equipment, and had no contract with the bank. Moreover, his sub-option for the plant, being oral, was a nullity under the Louisiana statute of frauds. In addition, neither the relationship with the bank nor the loan application qualified as "property." There was no obligation under the circumstances from which legal rights and duties might flow. The court emphasized that the sub-option was a nullity.

In *Waldron* v. *British Petroleum Co., Ltd.,* 231 F.Supp. 72 (S.D. N.Y. 1964), *aff'd,* 361 F.2d 671 (2d Cir. 1966), *aff'd,* 391 U.S. 253 (1968), 324 F.Supp. 1348 (S.D.N.Y. 1971), the district court drew a distinction between business and property. "Property" has "wider scope and is more extensive than the word 'business.'" It includes any interest the law protects, the court declared. If the "rights, privileges and powers possessed" by the damage claimant are entitled to judicial sanction, then the claimant possesses Section 4 "property." The court found an allegation of injury to "property" in a prospective foreign-oil trader's claim that several oil companies conspired to thwart his efforts to sell Iranian oil pursuant to a contract with the National Iranian Oil Co. The claim was that negotiations between his group and Cities Service Oil Co. to have that company manage and operate the Iranian oil industry broke down because conspiring oil companies "bought off" Cities Service. The damage claimant maintained that he could have sold the Iranian oil or sold his "inherently valuable" contract with the Iranian Government.

Since the damage claimant asserted that he was prevented from entering a business, the court stated that he must show that he had the intention and was prepared to engage in that business. The court listed four factors to be considered in determining intention and preparedness: (1) the background and experience of the damage claimant in the prospective business; (2) some affirmative action by the damage claimant to engage in the proposed business; (3) the financial ability of the damage claimant to purchase the necessary equipment and facilities to engage in the business; and (4) the consummation of contracts by the damage claimant. The court found no evidence that the damage claimant was financially able to engage in the business of importing and selling oil; he did not have sufficient capital or other assets to carry out such a business. "Other than the letter of credit and the . . . minimum expenses," the court declared, the damage claimant "has failed to produce any evidence which would support a finding that he did, could, or was willing to invest enough money to operate the alleged oil business successfully."

A distinction between "business and "property" was recognized in *Utah Gas Pipelines Corp.* v. *El Paso Natural Gas Co.,* 233 F.Supp. 955 (D. Utah 1964). The court viewed the word "business" as "a word of broad connotation" and said "a business need not be fully developed to sustain injury." A company formed to construct and operate a natural gas pipeline had partially implemented its plans when, it asserted, a conspiracy deprived it of sources of supply and prevented it from completing arrangements. The defendants insisted there was no "business" subject to injury, since, until it got a certificate from the Utah Public Service Commission, the new company had only a "hope" of beginning operation. The court would not accept that proposition, reasoning that it would permit established enterprises to "pick off" potential competitors before they can be certificated. In any event, it was decided that the matter could not be disposed of without a trial, that even if there were no "business," the evidence might show injury to the treble-damage claimant's "property."

With the possible exception of *Duff* v. *Kansas City Star,* which made the unqualified declaration that "loss of anticipated profits in an anticipated business" is not recoverable, recent decisions tend to reinforce earlier rulings that, in theory at least, injury to an embryonic enterprise is just as actionable as injury to an actual one. The problem for plaintiff is to establish that he has reached a sufficiently advanced state of preparation for entering a market. Perhaps the best statement of the factors to be considered is that given in *Waldron* v. *British Petroleum.* The tests of intention and preparedness listed there dovetail with those applied in *Deterjet* v. *United Aircraft, Penna. Sugar* v. *American Sugar,* and *Duff* v. *Kansas City Star.*

Contract rights qualify as Clayton Act "property," and an existing contract can be a major factor in proving the intention and preparedness elements in a claim for injury to "business." Yet the precedents do not make clear whether the absence of contractual commitments is fatal to a finding that a damage claim relates to "business." The cases involving claims based on loss of employment were asserted by persons who clearly had not gotten job-tenure contractual commitments from their employers. Yet an employee who has lost his job has, in effect, lost an already existing business.

One question that has not been discussed in earlier cases is: Has there been injury to a damage claimant's "business or property" if he has been prevented from getting a job? Although the issue was not discussed, the Supreme Court in *Radovich* v. *Nat'l. Football League,* 352 U.S. 445 (1957), apparently assumed that a professional football player who was unable to get a job because of a conspiracy to monopolize professional football suffered compensable injury.

There has been an easing of the strictures on establishing standing to sue for treble damages. Antitrust lawyers see a similar trend in determinations of whether the claimed damages were inflicted on "business or property." Both issues ordinarily arise on motions for summary judgment, a form of relief favored by judges concerned about crowded dockets. Antitrust litigation is not known for its brevity, and a district judge can save a good deal of time by using either the "target area" test or the "business or property" test as a shorthand expression of his view that no valid claim exists. In addition, these tests often serve as a shortcut in disposing of claims for losses, such as those of creditors and stockholders of corporations hurt by antitrust violations, that are recoverable in other ways.

(c) Question: *Does a franchisor have standing to sue for damages resulting from antitrust violations affecting his franchisees?*

In *Billy Baxter, Inc.* v. *Coca-Cola Co.,* 431 F.2d 183 (2d Cir. 1970), *cert. denied,* 401 U.S. 923 (1971), the court of appeals applied the target-area test to deny standing to a franchisor seeking to recover treble damages for his own injuries resulting from alleged antitrust violations that injured his franchisees. The Second Circuit thus joined the Tenth Circuit (*Nationwide Auto Appraiser Service, Inc.* v. *Assn. of Casualty and Surety Companies,* 382 F.2d 925 (10th Cir. 1967)) in denying standing to such a franchisor. In view of the rapid expansion of franchising as a means of distribution, *Billy Baxter* would appear to be a decision affecting many potential plantiffs. Does it mean that the door is now closed to the franchisor seeking his own recovery for antitrust violations that first affect his franchisees?

In *Billy Baxter,* the plaintiff, owner of trademarks used in the sale of soft drinks, franchised four bottlers to manufacture and sell beverages under the Billy Baxter trademarks. Plaintiff sold to these bottlers flavored extracts purchased from other sources and provided advertising and promotional services. The bottlers mixed the extracts with other ingredients according to secret recipes supplied

by plaintiff, sold the beverages to retail outlets, and paid royalties
to plaintiff on the basis of the number of cases sold. In the normal
course of its business, aside from the sale of extracts to the bottlers,
the plaintiff "neither manufactured, bottled, distributed nor sold
products."

Plaintiff sued under Section 4 of the Clayton Act seeking treble
damages from the defendants Coca-Cola Company and Canada
Dry Corporation, claiming that it had lost profits because of certain
of the defendants' activities allegedly unlawful under the Sherman,
Clayton, and Robinson-Patman Acts. The complaint alleged that
defendants had used improper methods to persuade retail outlets to
buy products other than those manufactured and sold by the franchised bottlers, and that, as a result, the plaintiff lost royalties.

The court of appeals held that plaintiff lacked standing to sue,
applying the rule that under Section 4 of the Clayton Act "A
plaintiff must allege a causative link to his injury which is 'direct'
rather than 'incidental' or which indicates that his business or property was in the 'target area' of the defendants' illegal act." Noting
that the complaint had alleged only unlawful interference with
sales by plaintiffs franchised bottlers to retailers and not interference in the relationship between the plaintiff and its franchised bottlers, the court found that the only target area in this case was the
"marketing of bottled beverages." In rejecting the plaintiff's contention that the line of Billy Baxter products, rather than a specific
area of economic activity, was the target in this case, the court said:
"Reference to the products as a target simply points to the
self-evident fact that antitrust violations might do some damage to
all the entities connected with their production and distribution."

Having located the target area, the court found that the plaintiff
was outside it not only because the plaintiff was one link away
from the link in the production-distribution chain receiving the first
impact of the alleged anticompetitive activity, but also because
plaintiff did not have "comprehensive responsibilities for and
identification with the beverages." As to the latter point, the court
said: "[The plaintiff] manufactured no products, and the bottlers
did not act as its agents in doing so. The franchisor merely licensed
the information needed for the manufacture of the beverages, supplied ingredients which still others had manufactured, and left
further production activities to its franchisees. It would be meaningless to state that Billy Baxter, Inc. simply elected to carry on its
business by authorizing others to bottle and sell the beverages, because the franchisor consciously structured the production distribution process in a way which limited its own activities in order to
gain the benefits of certain specific rights and liabilities."

The court ruled that plaintiff's standing would not be improved
even if the defendants were regarded as rival franchisors competing

with plaintiff and even if they knew that their allegedly unlawful activity was harmful to the plaintiff. In the court's view, there is no significant difference between this case and cases in which courts denied standing to patent licensors seeking treble damages for royalties lost because of injuries to licensees, and to suppliers of ingredients seeking treble damages for profits lost because of injury to the manufacturers and sellers of the ultimate products.

In a dissent the view was expressed that courts have too uncritically applied the "standing" doctrine in barring suit by a plaintiff one link away on the production-distribution chain from the link receiving the primary impact. The dissenter, Judge Waterman, favored the more liberal approach taken in *Karseal Corp.* v. *Richland Oil Corp.,* 221 F.2d 358 (9th Cir. 1955). In *Karseal,* the manufacturer of a product sold under a trade name sold his products to franchised distributors which in turn sold them to retail outlets. The court held that the manufacturer had standing under Section 4 of the Clayton Act to sue for treble damages even though the basis of the suit was a claim that the defendant's exclusive dealing agreements with the retail outlets had reduced the franchised distributors' sales to those outlets and thus in this indirect way reduced the manufacturer's sales to the distributors. Judge Waterman found persuasive this passage from the *Karseal* opinion: "To say to a manufacturer of wax that he may have the protection of the antitrust laws in private litigation if he hires salesmen for his product. and not have such protection if he decides to contract with a distributor, would appear to be an unequal application of the law and unjustified dictation as to how he operated his business." Judge Waterman did not accept the distinction suggested by the majority that a franchisor "cannot claim to be a firm with comprehensive responsibilities for and identification with" the final product. According to Judge Waterman, "Billy Baxter, as was Karseal, is the nerve center or the center of operations for the production and marketing of a 'brand name' product. Billy Baxter's franchisees, as did Karseal's franchisees, perform functions ancillary to and in furtherance of their franchisor's primary function and purpose, that of providing the consumer public a different and distinct product line and of promoting its products' good will and acceptability in a competitive market." Judge Waterman pointed out that the plaintiff's franchise agreements with its bottlers preserved rights of quality control and that, under the Lanham Act, the owner of a trademark must exercise such rights or risk loss of his trademark.

Judge Waterman would distinguish this case from the Second Circuit's previous decision, *Productive Inventions. .Inc.* v. *Trico Products Corp.,* 224 F.2d 678 (2d Cir. 1955), denying standing to a patent licensor: "Billy Baxter is directly in the retail market where it alleges defendants' violations occurred because it presells its trade named products in the consumers' mind and, presumably in order to protect its own interest, makes available business advice and promotes product quality control through inspections of its franchisees; the franchisee-bottlers, therefore, do not have the inalienable right to mismanage their own businesses. . . . In contrast, the licensor in Trico Products was passive in the relevant market and left every aspect of the business to the manufacturer licensee."

Most experts seem to doubt whether *Billy Baxter* is the last word on the subject of the franchisor's standing. Some deem standing merely a problem of common-law causation. It has been suggested that where it is clear someone should be allowed to sue for treble damages, the courts scan the possibilities and permit suit by the first seriously injured person in the chain. Thus, the standing doctrine, which sorts out plaintiffs according to whether their injuries are direct or indirect, becomes a more or less "mechanical" (or rule-of-thumb) means of finding a plaintiff. The development of the doctrine has apparently been strongly influenced by fear of windfalls. Some question whether this "pro-defendant" concern is consistent with the strong "pro-plaintiff" trend of Supreme Court decisions, in which the Court has repeatedly stressed the deterrent effect of private treble-damage actions. For instance, in both *Perma Life Mufflers, Inc.* v. *Internat'l. Parts Corp.*, 392 U.S. 134 (1968) (rejecting an in pari delicto defense) and in *Hanover Shoe, Inc.* v. *United Shoe Machinery Corp.*, 392 U.S. 481 (1968) (rejecting a "passing-on" defense), the Court clearly subordinated concern about windfalls to the objective of deterring violations. If there is such a trend, the *Billy Baxter* case may be inconsistent with it, especially because, in some situations, it may be the franchisor who is harder hit than any of his franchisees and, hence, the franchisor would sometimes be the most likely person to sue.

A comparison of two "standing" cases, one in the Second Circuit and the other in the Ninth Circuit (neither of which involves a franchisor as plaintiff), indicates that the Ninth Circuit more liberally defines the target area. On September 8, 1970, the Second Circuit, simply citing *Billy Baxter* in a per curiam decision, upheld a denial of standing to a licensor of movie rights seeking to recover treble damages because his licensee engaged in "block booking" that resulted in a reduction of royalties to the licensor (*Fields Productions, Inc.* v. *United Artists Corp.*, 432 F.2d 1010 (2d Cir. 1970), *aff'g* 318 F.Supp. 87 (S.D.N.Y. 1969). In denying standing, the lower court had reasoned as follows: "Block booking is a form of tying agreement. The reason that a tying agreement violates Section 1 is that it injures buyers and competitors of the seller. As applied to licensing motion pictures, this means that the block booking injures the television stations who are compelled to accept motion pictures that they do not want and it also injures other distributors who are deprived of an opportunity to license their pictures to television stations who have been forced to accept defendant's pictures . . . It is thus the television stations and the other distributors who are in the 'target area'. If the block booking in fact causes any injury to the producer of the pictures which are thus block booked, that injury is only incidental."

In the Ninth Circuit case, the plaintiff sold his movie rights to a distributor and claimed that his return, which was calculated according to the distributor's net receipts, was reduced by the distributor's "block booking." That court, on October 20, 1970, reversed the lower court's finding that he lacked standing (*Mulvey* v. *Samuel Goldwyn Productions, Inc.*, 433 F.2d 1073 (9th Cir. 1970), *cert. denied*, 402 U.S. 923 (1971), citing its own *Karseal* decision; *Hoopes* v. *Union Oil Company of Calif.*, 374 F.2d 480 (9th Cir. 1967); and *Twentieth Century Fox Film Corp.* v. *Goldwyn*, 328 F.2d 190 (9th Cir. 1964). The court ruled that a plaintiff is in the "target area" if he is within the area " 'which it could reasonably be foreseen would be affected' by block booking." This test of whether the plaintiff's injury was reasonably foreseeable seems significantly different from the test adopted by the Second Circuit. If the Second Circuit had applied the *Mulvey* rule, *Fields* and *Billy Baxter* might have gone the other way.

In addition to the apparent "pro-plaintiff" Supreme Court trend in antitrust cases, there seems to be another trend toward relaxing the standing requirements in general. See *e.g. Flast* v. *Cohen*, 392 U.S. 83 (1968); *Assn. of Data Processing Service Organizations, Inc.* v. *Camp*, 397 U.S. 150 (1970); *Scanwell Laboratories, Inc.* v. *Shaffer*, 424 F.2d 859 (D.C. Cir. 1970); but see *Sierra Club* v. *Hickel*, 433 F.2d 24 (9th Cir. 1970), *aff'd subnom. Sierra Club* v. *Morton*, 405 U.S. 727 (1972).

Whether or not the tough approach to standing reflected in the *Billy Baxter* decision will ultimately go the way of the "in pari delicto" and "passing-on" defenses is as yet uncertain; but in view of the recent trends, there is the possibility, as one expert puts it, that "standing may be on its last legs."

3. Proof of Damages

(a) Question: *How does the claimant show damages?*

The increase in private antitrust suits after World War II resulted primarily from prior government action. Section 5 of the Clayton Act provides that "a final judgment or decree . . . in any civil or criminal proceeding brought by or on behalf of the United States under the antitrust laws to the effect that a defendant has violated said laws shall be prima facie evidence against such defendant in any action or proceeding brought by any other party against such defendant under said laws . . . as to all matters respecting which said judgment or decree would be an estoppel as between the parties thereto . . ." The section further provides that it shall not apply to consent judgments or decrees "entered before any testimony has been taken." This provision has provided powerful motivation to many defendants in government antitrust suits to accept consent decrees. Where defendants have litigated and lost, a rash of private treble-damage suits has sometimes resulted. One example is the motion-picture-industry litigation resulting from the Government's decree in *U.S.* v. *Paramount Pictures,* 66 F.Supp. 323 (S.D. N.Y. 1946), 70 F.Supp. 53 (S.D. N.Y. 1947), *modified,* 334 U.S. 131 (1948), 85 F.Supp. 881 (S.D. N.Y. 1949). The Philadelphia electric-equipment convictions (*U.S.* v. *Westinghouse Electric Corp.,* 1960 Trade Cas. ¶69,699 (E.D. Pa. 1960)) resulted in an even greater number of private damage actions.

Once the private treble-damage claimant has proven defendant's violation of the antitrust laws either independently or by prior government judgment or decree, the claimant has two additional hurdles. He must show, first, injury to his business or property caused by defendant's violation; secondly, he must make some showing of the amount of his damage in dollars and cents. Courts have required a degree of certainty in proof of damage and in proof that the damage actually resulted from the antitrust violation. Yet where the fact and cause of damage have been proven with certainty, courts have been willing to leave to reasonable inferences the actual extent and amount of damage. In addition, where the defendant's wrong has made difficult "the ascertainment of the precise damages suffered by the plaintiff, [defendant] is not entitled to complain that they cannot be measured with the same exactness and precision as would otherwise be possible" (*Eastman Kodak Co.* v. *Southern Photo Materials Co.,* 273 U.S. 359, 379 (1927)). The plaintiff has been required to offer all the evidence available to him (*William Goldman Theaters* v. *Loew's, Inc.,* 69 F.Supp. 103, 106 (E.D. PA., 1946), *aff'd,* 164 F.2d 1021 (3rd Cir. 1948), *cert denied,* 334 U.S. 811 (1948).

Cases prior to World War II generally adhered to the doctrine requiring certainty in proving the existence and cause of damage but tended in the direction of a more liberal attitude with respect to proof of amount of damage. In *Bigelow* v. *R.K.O. Radio Pictures, Inc.,* 327 U.S. 251 (1946), with its roots in *Story Parchment Co.* v.

Paterson Parchment Papers Co., 282 U.S. 555 (1931), the Supreme Court is supposedly to have endorsed a liberal attitude toward proof of the fact, as well as the amount, of damage. Since the *Bigelow* decision plaintiffs have had less difficulty in getting to the jury on the question of damages, but the route has not been an entirely easy one. Depending on the type of violation and the type of injury to business or property, plaintiffs have sought to prove the amount of damages with the use of a number of different theories including increased cost incurred, decreased sale prices, capital loss suffered, and loss of anticipated profits.

The jury, or the judge if no jury is requested, determines the actual amount of damages. This amount is then automatically trebled. In 1955, the Attorney General's National Committee to Study the Antitrust Laws favored "vesting in the trial judge discretion to impose double or treble damages." Some have suggested the possibility of legislation to prescribe a minimum amount of damage to be granted automatically to the plaintiff upon proof of the fact of damage and without any further proof of the actual amount.

The question of the quantity and type of evidence needed to show a causal relationship between the plaintiff's damages and the alleged antitrust violation was reviewed by the Supreme Court in *Continental Ore Co.* v. *Union Carbide & Carbon Corp.*, 370 U.S. 690 (1962). In that case, the treble-damage claimant contended, on the authority of the *Bigelow* and *Story Parchment* cases, that the causal connection can be inferred from (1) the fact of an antitrust violation and (2) the occurrence of otherwise unexplained losses. That argument was rejected by the Court of Appeals for the Ninth Circuit, which held (289 F.2d 86 (9th Cir. 1961)) that the claimant must present evidence demonstrating the causal connection between the claimant's losses and the defendants' creation of a monopoly. The Supreme Court reversed on the ground that there was sufficient evidence for the jury to infer a causal connection.

In *Union Carbide and Carbon Corp.* v. *Nisley,* 300 F.2d 561 (10th Cir. 1961), *cert. pet. dismissed,* 371 U.S. 801 (1962), the court held that plaintiff must establish that damages suffered were the proximate result of the antitrust violation. The violation and damages had been proven. The court found there was sufficient evidence to support the jury's finding of proximate cause and affirmed the judgment.

Some commentators despair at drawing any conclusions from the cases, feeling that cases involving damages may all be "sports" and not capable of revealing any pattern. Others see some clear trends. The cases illustrate problems of three types: the existence, the cause, and the amount of injury. Perhaps the central question is whether treble-damage awards must be limited to existing business concerns or whether damages may be recovered by one who has been kept out of business by an illegal monopoly or other antitrust violation. With a single exception, the federal courts that have been faced with this issue have decided that the would-be entrepreneur, lacking a going business, cannot have suffered damage to "business or property" within the meaning of the Clayton Act. Such was the holding in *Duff* v. *Kansas City Star,* 299 F.2d 320 (8th Cir. 1962). In *Delaware Valley Marine Supply Co.* v. *American Tobacco Co.,* 184 F.Supp. 440 (E.D. Pa. 1960), *aff'd,* 297 F.2d 199 (3rd Cir. 1961), *cert. denied,* 369 U.S. 839 (1962), however, the district court could see no reason why a person frozen out of the market should have fewer rights than one already in business. That problem was not raised in the appellate courts.

It has been suggested that, as a result of *Siegfried* v. *Kansas City Star,* 193 F.Supp. 427 (W.D. Mo. 1961), *aff'd,* 298 F.2d 1 (8th Cir. 1962), *cert. denied,* 369 U.S. 819 (1962), plaintiffs may now have some second thoughts before requesting a jury in certain cases where they might previously have done so with alacrity. In his Supreme Court review petition, Siegfried claimed that the only issue contested at the trial was the amount of damages, that the actual occurrence of an injury as the result of an antitrust violation was not disputed. After extended deliberations interrupted by requests for more instructions, the jury called the damages "speculative," which the district judge interpreted as entitling Siegfried to only nominal damages.

The plaintiff in *Herman Schwabe, Inc.,* v. *United Shoe Machinery Corp.,* 26 F.R.D. 228 (E.D. N.Y. 1960), *aff'd,* 297 F.2d 906 (2d Cir. 1962), *cert denied,* 369 U.S. 865 (1962), had difficulty showing damages since defendant's violation began before plaintiff was incorporated. Thus plaintiff could not prove his profits before the commencement of the unlawful activity. The court of appeals held that plaintiff could have demonstrated that its profits went down as defendant's went up. However, plaintiff did not succeed in producing sufficient evidence from which the jury could approximate damages.

In *Goldsmith* v. *St. Louis-San Francisco Ry. Co.,* 201 F.Supp. 867 (W.D. N.C. 1962), plaintiff had made a short sale of railway stock. Defendant purchased stock in the railway in violation of the Interstate Commerce Act. Defendant's purchases drove up the price of the stock and plaintiff lost money on his sale. Plaintiff brought suit alleging that defendant's action was an antitrust violation and caused plaintiff's stock losses. The district court found there was no causal connection proven between the violation and the loss.

(b) Question: *What evidence is necessary to get to the jury on the question of damages?*

Almost every antitrust damage action has sought recovery for one or more of three types of economic injury: (1) overcharges paid by complaining customers to suppliers participating in a price-fixing conspiracy; (2) loss of profits, actual or anticipated, by a competitor or customer frozen out of a market by a boycott, monopoly, or conspiracy to monopolize; (3) loss of capital—good will or, in some instances, loss of an entire business. In the *Electrical-Equipment* cases, the measure of damages was the amount by which the manufacturers' price-fixing conspiracy had increased the prices paid by utilities and government agencies over the prices they would otherwise have paid.

Proof of anticipated profits has caused damage claimants and the courts the greatest amount of difficulty. Yet, common-law courts have been entertaining loss-of-profit suits based on business torts for more than three centuries. One author has said that the American courts' requirement that damages be proved with certainty originated in the middle of the nineteenth century "as a development of an earlier doctrine that damages for breach of contract could not be measured by loss of 'profits'" (McCORMICK ON DAMAGES (Hornbook Series, 1935), p. 98). Initially, that requirement was carried over into antitrust damage litigation.

The earliest Supreme Court decision on proof of antitrust damages was *Chattanooga Foundry & Pipe Works* v. *City of Atlanta*, 203 U.S. 390 (1906). The city bought cast-iron pipe for its waterworks at a price inflated by an illegal conspiracy (See *U.S.* v. *Addyston Pipe and Steel Co.*, 175 U.S. 211 (1899)). The Supreme Court, in sustaining a jury verdict for the city, held that the measure of damages is the difference between the price paid as a result of the conspiracy and the market or fair price.

In *Thomsen* v. *Cayser*, 243 U.S. 66 (1917), shippers were attempting to collect an overcharge resulting from a rate-fixing conspiracy by ocean carriers. The Court again sustained a jury verdict, one that had been set aside by the court of appeals, and held that the amount of the overcharge was a jury question. The shippers also sought to recover anticipated profits on business lost to them because of the conspiracy. The Supreme Court rejected the carriers' contention that the damages sought were speculative and therefore not recoverable. "There were different sums stated, resulting from the loss of particular customers, and the fact of their certainty was submitted to the jury. They were told that they 'ought not to allow any speculative damages,' that they were not 'required to guess' as to what damages 'plaintiff claimed to have sustained.' And further, that the burden of proof was upon plaintiffs and that, from the evidence, the jury should be able to make a calculation of what the damages were."

In *Eastman Kodak Co.* v. *Southern Photo Materials Co.,* 273 U.S. 359 (1927), a wholesaler of photographic materials sought damages sustained by reason of his supplier's unlawful refusal to deal. He wanted to recover profits he would have realized in the four years covered by the suit had he been able to continue the purchase and sale of the supplier's goods. His proof related exclusively to the loss of these anticipated profits. In rejecting the supplier's claim that the damages were purely speculative, the Court ruled that the wholesaler's future profits could be shown through his past experience by deducting from the gross profits of an earlier period an estimated expense of doing business. The Supreme Court endorsed the court of appeals' rule that "damages are not rendered uncertain because they cannot be calculated with absolute exactness. It is sufficient if a reasonable basis for computation is afforded, although the result be only approximate" (295 F. 98 (5th Cir. 1923)).

Story Parchment Co. v. *Patterson Parchment Paper Co.,* 282 U.S. 555 (1931), involved a conspiracy by three manufacturers of parchment paper to drive another manufacturer out of business. There was evidence that the three manufacturers had sold their goods below the point of profit and finally below the cost of production. Two types of damages were claimed. The first was the difference between the amount actually realized by the damage claimant at the conspiracy-depressed prices and what would have been realized from sales at reasonable prices. The second was the extent to which the value of the damage claimant's property had diminished as a result of the unlawful acts. The Supreme Court held that the two items were properly submitted to the jury, which awarded damages. "The trial court fairly instructed the jury in substance, that, if they were satisfied that the old prices were reasonable, and that they would not have changed by reason of any economic condition, but would have been maintained except for the unlawful acts of the respondents, the jury might consider as an element of damages the difference between the prices actually received and what would have been received but for the unlawful conspiracy." The court distinguished between the measure of proof necessary to establish that the claimant had sustained some damage and the measure of proof necessary to enable the jury to fix the amount. "The rule which precludes the recovery of uncertain damages applies to such as are not the certain result of the wrong, not to those damages which are definitely attributable to the wrong and only uncertain in respect of their amount."

The Supreme Court dealt directly with the measurement of anti-trust damages in *Bigelow* v. *RKO Radio Pictures,* 327 U.S. 251 (1946). The violation asserted was a conspiracy by motion-picture distributors and theater operators whereby the damage claimants' theater was discriminated against in the distribution of feature films, and the conspirators' theaters were favored. Two lines of proof were relied upon to show damages. The first was a compari-son of the earnings by the claimants' theater with those of a com-parable competitor who was able to secure the films denied to the claimants. The second was a comparison between the claimants' net receipts during a four-year period when it had been able to procure some films that had not already been shown in the conspirators' theaters and the claimants' receipts during a five-year period when the conspiracy was fully operative. The Supreme Court reversed the court of appeals and accepted the jury verdict, treating the loss of admission receipts as a fair measure of damages.

Lower court opinions reflect in general the standard adopted by the Supreme Court. In the motion-picture industry, theater owners have been permitted to recover the profits the theaters would have earned if a Sherman Act conspiracy had not prevented satisfactory film bookings. Damages have been calculated on the basis of earn-ings realized by comparable established theaters *(William Goldman Theater* v. *Loew's, Inc.,* 69 F.Supp. 103 (E.D. Pa. 1946), *aff'd,* 164 F.2d 1021 (3rd Cir. 1948); *Milwaukee Towne Corp.* v. *Loew's, Inc.,* 190 F.2d 561 (7th Cir. 1951); *Charles Rubenstein, Inc.,* v. *Columbia Pictures Corp.,* 176 F.Supp. 527 (D. Minn. 1959), *aff'd,* 289 F.2d 418 (8th Cir. 1961)).

Kobe, Inc. v. *Dempsey Pump Co.,* 198 F.2d 416 (10th Cir. 1952) sustained a judgment for the amount of profit a new oil pump would have made for its manufacturer if a boycott had not kept it off the market. The court of appeals stressed evidence that the pump was already on the market, a market survey prepared by experts predicting a large demand for the new pump, and testi-mony by a marketing expert that, in the light of these factors, sales of the new pump were likely to grow to an extent in excess of the trial court's findings.

In *Mechanical Contractors Bid Depository* v. *Christiansen,* 352 F.2d 817 (10th Cir. 1965), a construction contractor was allowed to recover boycott damages measured by his loss of net income on a single job, even though his business, over-all, earned profits during the period of the boycott. The defendant sought Supreme Court review, contending that the complaining contractor had in fact suffered no loss "in the aggregate of his business." The Supreme Court refused to review the court of appeals' decision (384 U.S. 918 (1966)).

Under the Supreme Court's *Bigelow* opinion permitting a jury to "make a just and reasonable estimate of the damage based on relevant data" the court in *Elyria-Lorain Broadcasting Co.* v. *Lorain Journal Co.,* 358 F.2d 790 (6th Cir. 1966), permitted recovery of profits that would have been earned by a radio station if a local newspaper had not organized an advertisers' boycott of the station, and it allowed damages to be set on the basis of "probable and inferential as well as direct and positive proof."

Not all of the reported decisions have found evidence on the amount of damages adequate. In *Emich Motors Corp.* v. *General Motors Corp.,* 181 F.2d 70 (7th Cir. 1950), *rev'd on other grounds,* 340 U.S. 558 (1951), the court of appeals upset a damage verdict in favor of a terminated Chevrolet dealer alleging a conspiracy to control the financing of wholesale and retail sales of General Motors cars. The dealer put an accountant on the stand to testify on the value of the good will destroyed by termination of the dealership. He used 7.5 percent of the dealership's tangible assets as a normal rate of return for the five years preceding termination. Subtracting that 7.5 percent from actual average annual returns during the five-year period, the accountant treated the excess as earnings attributable to good will. These earnings he then capitalized at 10 percent to establish the value of good will. The court of appeals found the testimony worthless because the percentages were not based on custom or usage. According to the court, they were simply what the witness considered reasonable under the circumstances, and he never stated what those circumstances were. Another element of damages claimed was reduction of profits during the last two years of the dealership's existence. The accountant estimated the value of new-car sales lost by using lost-sales figures furnished by the dealer. He also stated average profits of the dealership before deducting federal taxes and salaries of officer-owners. This testimony was rejected because he had no original records such as would have been used if he had performed an audit. There were no records for the damage period except book entries, which were not authenticated, and the accountant did not prepare a balance sheet and did not consider liabilities.

Flintkote Co. v. *Lysfjord,* 246 F.2d 368 (9th Cir. 1957), involved the exclusion from the market of a would-be acoustical-tile contractor. Some commission salesmen who once worked for a tile contractor decided they could make as much for themselves as they and their former employer had made together. Because of a conspiracy they were kept from entering the business. The court of appeals agreed that the lack of prior business history was not fatal to proving damages, but it found in the record made by the former salesmen insufficient evidence to support a computation of the amount of their lost profits. "There are three chief types of evidence which the decisions have approved as the basis for the award of damages," the court observed. "(1) Business records of the plaintiff or his predecessor before the conspiracy arose. (2) Business records of comparative but unrestrained enterprises during the particular period in question. (3) Expert opinion based on items (1) or (2)." The damage claimants, besides asserting that they could make as much for themselves and their own business as they had with their former employer, estimated that their profits would increase as much as 50 percent annually. The evidence showed the highest commission they had received during an unspecified period and the amount of profits that their former employer had made on those sales. The evidence showed only their segment of their former employer's sales.

The court of appeals reversed a jury verdict in favor of the damage of the claimants, pointing out that nothing had been shown as to whether their former employer had prospered or whether the former employer had made more or less profit on the damage claimant's sales to compensate for other gains or losses in other parts of the business. No comparison was made between their former employer and their own company as to size or financial resources. No testimony was introduced concerning the experience of any other comparable acoustical-tile business during the period involved or, for that matter, during any period.

In *Herman Schwabe* v. *United Shoe Machinery,* 297 F.2d 906 (2d Cir. 1962), the court of appeals affirmed the lower court's directed verdict in favor of the defendant, United Shoe Machinery Corp. The court noted that because of United's total domination of the shoe-machinery market the damage claimant could not show how much of his sales and profits had diminished as a result of the antitrust violation. Yet the court saw no reason why the damage claimant could not, instead, show an increase of sales and profits after the unlawful practices had ceased. Damages were claimed in the form of lost sales of the single machine produced by the damage claimant. To prove the amount of lost earnings, the claimant estimated United's share of the sales of those machines in both the shoe market and nonshoe market, which used the machines but was not alleged to have been affected by United's antitrust violations. Plaintiff presented evidence of his percentage of the nonshoe market and asked for damages on the theory that he was entitled to the same percentage of both markets. The court rejected the figures because the shoe and nonshoe markets were not parallel. There was no evidence that United had made an effort to penetrate the nonshoe market comparable to its lawful activity in the shoe market or that, barring United's unlawful acts, the damage claimant would have had the same success in the shoe market as he had in the nonshoe market. It was undisputed that part of United's shoe-market percentage resulted from lawful activity. The damage claimant did not adduce any evidence that his machine competed or would have competed with all 24 types of United's machines.

The Supreme Court decisions on damages leave little doubt that determination of the amount of damages is within the province of the jury. As long as there is probative evidence that furnishes "a reasonable basis for computation," the treble-damage claimant is entitled to get to the jury on the question of damages. It is clear that exact proof of the amount recoverable is unnecessary. The claimant must produce the best available evidence. The source of the best evidence varies with the circumstances, but more often than not the best evidence will be found in the financial records of the treble-damage claimant and comparable business enterprises. Statistical and financial data regarding the particular industry in general will often be useful in proving the amount of anticipated profits and value of goodwill.

If an expert witness is used, a proper foundation must be laid. Expert testimony as to lost profits or competitive prices may be rejected as a substitute for basic data from which the court and the jury may draw their own conclusions. The amount of damages is determined by comparing what actually happened to the treble-damage claimant's business with what would have happened to it "but for" the defendant's violation of the antitrust laws.

(c) Question: *What showing must be made that plaintiff's injury was "by reason of" defendant's violation?*

If plaintiff has shown that he is a "person injured" and that he has been injured in his "business or property," he may still have a problem showing that his injury was "by reason of" defendant's forbidden conduct. Was plaintiff's injury caused by defendant's violation?

Many of the antitrust court opinions treat injury and causation as a single issue. An example is *Bigelow* v. *RKO Radio Pictures,* 327 U.S. 251 (1946). The suit was brought by a theater operator complaining about a conspiracy to discriminate against him in the distribution of first-run motion picture films. To show his damages, he compared his theater's earnings with those of a comparable theater able to secure first-run films and compared his net receipts during a period when the conspiracy was fully operative with his receipts during a period when he had been able to procure first-run films. The court of appeals reversed a jury verdict for the theater operator holding that neither of these lines of proof established what the theater's earnings would have been in the absence of the conspiracy. The Supreme Court reversed, applying the rule that "the wrongdoer may not object to the plaintiff's reasonable estimate of the cause of injury . . . because not based on more accurate data which the wrongdoer's misconduct has rendered unavailable."

The Supreme Court's opinion in *Continental Ore Co.* v. *Union Carbide & Carbon Corp.,* 370 U.S. 690 (1962), seems to deal only with the problem of causation; the injury claimed was the complete destruction of the damage claimant's business, which was apparently not contested. It was claimed that failure of the claimant's business was caused by a conspiracy controlling the supply of a vital raw material. The court of appeals held that the damage claimant had to show not only the conspiracy and a failure of his business for lack of the material but also that he had made timely demands for the raw material from the defendants and that he had exhausted all other possible sources of the material. The Supreme Court found "sufficient evidence for a jury to infer the necessary causal connection between respondent's antitrust violations and petitioners' injury." The Court quoted its statement in *Bigelow* that "in the absence of more precise proof, the jury could conclude as a matter of just and reasonable inference from the proof of defendants' wrongful acts and their tendency to injure plaintiff's business, and from the evidence of the decline in prices, profits, and values, not shown to be attributable to other causes, that defendants' wrongful acts had caused damage to the plaintiffs."

In *Richfield Oil Corp.* v. *Karseal Corp.,* 271 F.2d 709 (9th Cir. 1959), the court agreed with a damage claimant's assertion that, "having shown the illegal restraint applied to its product" by a competing seller, "it had proved the causal connection between the defendant's wrongful act and the loss of revenue." The Section 1 Sherman Act restraint was an exclusive-dealing arrangement under which Richfield Oil Corp. supplied all its service stations with their requirements of tires, batteries, and accessories. Later in another TBA case, *Lessig* v. *Tidewater Oil Co.,* 327 F.2d 459 (9th Cir. 1964), *cert. denied,* 377 U.S. 993 (1964), the court pointed to an additional item of evidence as proving that the exclusive-dealing requirement hurt the complaining retailer. "Evidence that a merchant has been required to pay more for goods which he resells is sufficient to establish, prima facie, that he has been damaged; tested by common experience, such proof is adequate to 'establish with reasonable probability' that profits on resale were less." To the oil company's argument that higher costs of sponsored TBA would not necessarily mean lower retailer profits, the court responded that the oil company's illegal activity made production of such evidence impossible by preventing the retailer from dealing in a competing line of TBA.

Another example of a Sherman Act conspiracy whose intended and natural result was the injury complained of by the damage claimant is seen in *Emich Motors Corp.* v. *General Motors Corp.*, 340 U.S. 558 (1951). The claimant had no trouble proving a Sherman Act violation; he showed a criminal conviction of General Motors for coercing its automobile dealers into exclusive use of General Motors' financing subsidiary and for terminating the franchises of those dealers who did not comply. The court of appeals held (181 F.2d. 70 (7th Cir. 1950)) that the criminal judgment could not be used as evidence that the conspiracy of which General Motors had been convicted caused the franchise cancellation complained of in the damage suit. The Supreme Court reversed, treating the criminal judgment as prima facie evidence of not only the general conspiracy to monopolize automobile financing but also the effectuation of the conspiracy by coercing dealers to use General Motors financing. "It therefore was necessary for petitioners only to introduce, in addition to the criminal judgment, evidence of the impact of the conspiracy on them, such as the cancellation of their franchises and the purpose of General Motors in cancelling them, and evidence of any resulting damages."

The *Emich* case was distinguished in *Monticello Tobacco Co.* v. *American Tobacco Co.*, 197 F.2d 629 (2d Cir. 1952), in which the court held that the criminal conviction affirmed in *American Tobacco Co.* v. *U.S.*, 147 F.2d 93 (6th Cir. 1944), *aff'd*, 328 U.S. 781 (1946), could not be used as evidence that a cigarette marketer's failure was caused by the restraint-of-trade and monopolization attempt of which the major tobacco companies had been convicted. It was the court's view that "the mere fact of conviction cannot make the major tobacco manufacturers liable for every business casualty in the cigarette field." The major manufacturers' control of their market was found to have no impact on the damage claimant, since he always had ready access to cigarettes and had never sought to buy leaf tobacco for his own manufacturing purposes. In addition, major manufacturers' price-fixing activities could not have affected the damage claimant, since there was no suggestion that the major manufacturers had dictated the prices to be charged by nonparticipants in their conspiracy.

The issue of the sufficiency of proof of the fact of damage seems to have been considered independent of causation by the court in *Wolfe* v. *Nat'l. Lead Co.*, 225 F.2d 427 (9th Cir. 1955). As in the *Continental Ore Case*, a manufacturing enterprise was complaining about a conspiracy that deprived it of an essential raw material. The district judge dismissed the suit for failure to show any injury, pointing to evidence (1) that the years of shortage were profitable for the damage claimants, (2) that a later year was less profitable even though they had an abundance of the raw material, (3) that the damage claimants were newcomers to the industry, (4) that all members of the industry had been limited in their supplies of the critical raw material during the period of the alleged conspiracy, and (5) that the damage claimants had received their share of the short material (15 F.R.D. 61 (N.D. Calif. 1953)). The court of appeals agreed with the district judge that these circumstances were illustrative "of the completely speculative nature of the evidence as to any hurt or damage claimed to have been suffered."

Decisions like those in the *Monticello Tobacco* and *Wolfe* cases make it clear that despite some of the courts' broad language suggesting that juries can infer the fact of damage from proof of the violation, the burden of proving that he was hurt and that his injury was the result of the antitrust violation remains on the damage claimant. The court's statement in *Fox West Coast Theatres Corp.* v. *Paradise T. Building Corp.*, 264 F.2d 602 (9th Cir. 1958), that "the mere unlawful combination over a period of time to eliminate competition is proof of damage" was made in a context of clear evidence of injury and causation. More typical, perhaps, is the language in *McCleneghan* v. *Union Stock Yards of Omaha*, 349 F.2d 53 (8th Cir. 1965): "Proof of monopoly or restraint of trade and evidence that plaintiff was a customer or competitor of the wrongdoer is not sufficient in itself to support a recovery. Proof of damage to the public or to others will not without more support a finding of fact of damage caused by the defendants' wrongful acts" (349 F.2d at 56).

The weight of the burden of proving a causal relationship between a proven violation and a proven loss or injury seems to vary from one type of antitrust violation to another. It may be easier, for example, to establish that a price-fixing conspiracy was the cause of a higher price paid by a complaining customer during the period of the conspiracy than it is to show that a monopolization attempt by a few large producers in an industry caused the failure of one of their competitors. When damage suits are based on the price-discrimination provisions in Section 2(a) of the Clayton Act, the task of proving a causal connection between the violation and the claimed damage will often be easier when the complaint comes from a buyer who was discriminated against than when the complaint comes from a competitor of the seller who discriminated. One of the elements the damage claimant has to prove to establish a violation is probable injury to competition. Consequently, a buyer suing because he was discriminated against will have furnished most of his "causation" proof by the time he finishes his proof of the violation. A competing seller, on the other hand, can often prove the competitive-injury element of a Section 2(a) violation without evidence of matters that directly affect him. See *Utah Pie Co.* v. *Continental Baking Co.*, 386 U.S. 685 (1967). In any type of case, one of the best means of showing "causation" is proof of the violator's intent to cause the injury complained of.

Although the Supreme Court's opinion in the *Utah Pie* case deals with the problem of proving probable competitive injury as an element of a Section 2(a) violation, the opinion contains the suggestion that a treble-damage claimant need not prove that his profit-and-loss statement shows a minus figure. A business enterprise can be in good economic shape and still prove losses recoverable under the antitrust laws by proving it would have made larger profits but for the antitrust violation. See *Mechanical Contractors Bid Depository* v. *Christiansen,* 352 F.2d 817 (10th Cir. 1965), *cert. denied,* 384 U.S. 918 (1966).

Even after he has presented prima facie proof of injury and causation, the damage claimant is not always home free. The defendant can counter with evidence that the damages claimed were the result of economic factors other than his conduct. He can point to such factors as the damage claimant's inefficiency, poor management decisions, or inferior product, to special conditions prevailing in the market at the time the injury was suffered, to cost increases that would have boosted prices as much as the price-fixing conspiracy proven by the damage claimant, or to a new technological development that made the plaintiff's product obsolete.

Some antitrust experts believe that alternative explanations supplied by a defendant for the plaintiff's losses are effective only when they completely eliminate the antitrust violation as a possible reason for the losses. If the damage claimant is able to show clearly that he was hurt and that the antitrust violation was at least one of the causes, they say, federal judges tend to allow recovery. The *Electrical-Equipment* cases are cited to illustrate this point. There the manufacturers seemed to have little success with their contentions that such factors as higher costs and limited production capacity would have pushed prices to at least the level they reached during the price-fixing conspiracy even if there had been no conspiracy. In *Ohio Valley Electric Corp.* v. *General Electric Co.,* 244 F.Supp. 914 (S.D. N.Y. 1965), one federal district judge attempted to separate the portion of the price increase attributable to changed economic conditions, but even he allocated less than one sixth of the price increase to the factors relied on by the defendant manufacturers.

The defendant may present rebuttal evidence showing that the damage claimant in fact suffered no economic loss at all. The most common is proof that the losses or added costs were passed on to customers in the form of higher prices. (See section IX-A-6(b), p. 593.)

(d) Question: *Must plaintiff have dealt directly with defendant to recover treble damages?*

In *Hanover Shoe, Inc.* v. *United Shoe Mach. Corp.,* 392 U.S. 481 (1968), the Supreme Court disallowed a "passing-on defense." It had been determined that defendant's monopolistic practices had resulted in an overcharge to the plaintiff for the use of shoe-making machinery leased by the defendant to the plaintiff. Defendant claimed that plaintiff had passed on this overcharge to those who purchased plaintiff's shoes. In disallowing this defense, the Court said (at 493): "Even if it could be shown that the buyer raised his price in response to, and in the amount of, the overcharge and that his margin of profit and total sales had not thereafter declined, there would remain the nearly insuperable difficulty of demonstrating that the particular plaintiff could not or would not have raised his prices absent the overcharge or maintained the higher price had the overcharge been discontinued. Since establishing the applicability of the passing-on defense would require a convincing showing of each of these virtually unascertainable figures, the task would normally prove insurmountable."

The Court asserted that permitting the defense would have an adverse effect on the private enforcement of the antitrust laws (at 494): "In addition, if buyers are subjected to the passing-on defense, those who buy from them would also have to meet the challenge that they passed on the higher price to their customers. These ultimate consumers, in today's case the buyers of single pairs of shoes, would have only a tiny stake in a lawsuit and little interest in attempting a class action. In consequence, those who violate the antitrust laws by price fixing or monopolizing would retain the fruits of their illegality because no one was available who would bring suit against them. Treble damage actions, the importance of which the Court has many times emphasized, would be substantially reduced in effectiveness."

The Court did suggest, however, that "there might be situations, for instance, when an overcharged buyer has a pre-existing 'cost-plus' contract, thus making it easy to prove that he has not been damaged, where the considerations requiring that the passing-on defense not be permitted in this case would not be present."

A Colorado district court has ruled that, as a corollary to the *Hanover Shoe* decision, only direct purchasers may normally recover from price-fixing sellers (*City and County of Denver* v. *American Oil Co.,* 53 F.R.D. 620 (D. Colo. 1971)). This case was brought as a class action charging the defendants with price fixing in the sale of asphalt. The ruling as to the *Hanover Shoe* issue came at the class-determination stage of the proceeding and was the basis of the court's rejection of a proposed class consisting of 126 governmental units, most of which were only indirect purchasers of asphalt from the defendants. Since it ruled that only direct purchasers could normally recover, the court concluded that there were significant differences as to the defendants' liability to each of the members of the proposed class and that, accordingly, the common issues in the case were not predominant. (Having disallowed the class, the court set forth "a rather loose intervention" procedure to allow members of the disallowed class to intervene individually.)

In ruling that only direct purchasers may normally recover, the court first noted the *Hanover Shoe* doctrine that the direct purchaser can normally recover regardless of whether he passed on the illegal overcharge. The court observed that to allow an indirect purchaser to recover when the direct purchaser can also recover would subject the defendant to "multiple liability trebled." The court also noted that it would be extremely difficult to trace and measure the effect of an illegal overcharge down the distribution chain, taking into account the markups at each link of the chain. The court cited a situation where there is an overcharge for a product which is used in the manufacture of another product: "Would anyone be so bold as to suggest that a purchaser of an automobile would have standing to bring an antitrust action against the steel companies, either for himself or in behalf of some massive class? There has to be a cutoff somewhere, and we think that *Hanover Shoe* coupled with the cases it cites makes the cutoff point that of privity of contract between wrongdoer and original victim, unless the "cost-plus" exception discussed by Justice White [in Hanover Shoe] can be shown."

The Colorado court distinguished *W.Va.* v. *Chas. Pfizer & Co.,* 440 F.2d 1079 (2d Cir. 1971), *cert. denied,* 404 U.S. 871 (1971), in which the court of appeals rejected the claim of retailers and wholesalers who were the direct buying customers of the defendants that they and not the consumers were entitled to a settlement fund. After noting the policy expressed in *Hanover Shoe* and other Supreme Court decisions favoring private enforcement of the antitrust laws, the court said (at 1088): "Keeping these comments in mind, there are then several obvious distinctions between the principles laid down in *Hanover Shoe* and the present case, First, the passing-on doctrine is not here being used as a defense to permit the defendants to escape liability, but rather as an attempt to award damages, insofar as is possible, to those who ultimately paid higher prices as a result of the collusive pricing, and to avoid giving a windfall gain to those who rather clearly were not injured. Secondly, to permit the use of the doctrine in the present circumstances will not act to limit or frustrate private treble-damage claims, but will, if anything, do the opposite."

The court in *Pfizer* also went on to find, however, that the court below had properly determined that the situation was "much like" the cost-plus exception mentioned in *Hanover Shoe*, since the products were "in virtually all cases" sold pursuant to a set percentage mark-up. The Colorado court distinguished *Pfizer* on this ground.

In support of its holding, the Colorado court cited *Phila. Housing Authority* v. *American Radiator and Standard Sanitary Corp.*, 50 F.R.D. 13 (E.D. Pa. 1970), *aff'd sub nom., Mangano* v. *American Radiator and Standard Sanitary Corp.*, 438 F.2d 1187 (3d Cir. 1971). In that case, there were several links in the distribution chain between the defendant manufacturers of plumbing fixtures, and the plaintiffs, who were purchasers of houses in which the plumbing fixtures were those made and sold by the defendants. The court held that the plaintiffs could not recover because of the extreme difficulty in tracing the overcharge to them. The court was influenced also by the fact that the plumbing fixtures were only a small part of the houses which the plaintiffs purchased. (To the same effect was *Phila. Housing Authority* v *American Radiator and Standard Sanitary Corp.*, 323 F.Supp. 381 (E.D. Pa. 1970), dismissing claims of public bodies which entered into fixed price contracts, including cost of installed plumbing fixtures for public buildings.)

One's assessment of the Colorado decision may depend to some extent upon one's judgment as to the proper weight to be given each of the conflicting interests. Those believing that more weight should have been given to the policy favoring private enforcement of the antitrust laws would argue that the dislodgement of a violator's ill-gotten "pot-of-gold" is of primary importance and that the distribution of the "pot-of-gold" is a problem of secondary importance which can generally be satisfactorily worked out later in the proceeding. Those holding this view would argue that it was wrong for the court to pass upon the remoteness issue at the class determination stage of the proceeding. They would urge that *Hanover Shoe* should be read as holding no more than that the first purchaser can normally recover and should not be read as precluding those down the distribution chain from some share in the recovery. In support of this position, it is pointed out that the first purchaser, who often has a valuable continuing relationship with the prospective defendant, would for that reason often be less likely to sue than would later purchasers.

On the other hand, there are those who would argue that the difficulty of tracing the effects of an unlawful overcharge was at least as much a factor in the *Hanover Shoe* decision as the policy favoring private enforcement of the antitrust laws, and that the Colorado court properly gave great weight to that consideration as well as to the risk of "multiple recovery trebled" and, by implication, to the risk of windfall recoveries. According to this school of thought, the Colorado court also was correct in passing on the remoteness issue at the class-determination stage of the proceeding, because such a basic issue should be determined early in order to avoid wherever possible some of the heavy litigation costs that go with class actions.

Perhaps an accommodation between the opposing points of view will be hammered out as the scope of the "cost-plus" exception is determined. The Third Circuit, in the plumbing-fixtures case, spoke of a "pre-existing cost-plus contract or analogous fixed markup type of arrangement" as embraced within the exception (*Mangano v. American Radiator and Standard Sanitary Corp., supra*). The Second Circuit, in the *Pfizer* case, in the context of a decision relating to the distribution of an existing settlement fund, upheld the trial court's finding that set percentage mark-ups were enough to bring the case within the "cost-plus" exception.

It would appear from the cases that one important factor in determining whether a case falls with the "cost-plus" exception is whether the product involved is resold in its original form, as it was in the *Pfizer* case, or resold as a component or ingredient in another product. In a decision affecting several of the unsettled antibiotic cases, Judge Miles W. Lord has ruled that because of the extreme difficulty of tracing an overcharge, purchasers of animal feed could not recover for an overcharge included in the original price of a drug which was used as an ingredient in the animal feed. (The court also noted that the original purchasers of the drugs used for the animal feed were present in the case as a separate class of plaintiffs.) *(In re Coordinated Pretrial Proceedings in Antibiotic Antitrust Actions,* S.D. N.Y., April 13, 1971 (unreported)).

Likewise, the Colorado court in the *Denver* case observed that "the asphalt here was in most instances but a material included in an overall contractor's bid, and with perhaps some few exceptions, there is little chance that the cost-plus analogy can be drawn here." Also, the court in the plumbing case was influenced by the fact that plumbing fixtures were only a small part of the house sold to each plaintiff. Finally, it might be argued that some such consideration was present in *Hanover Shoe,* in which the unlawful overcharge was included in the price for the use of shoe-making machinery and defendant's contention was that the overcharge was passed on in the price of the plaintiff's shoes.

The most significant aspect of the Colorado decision may turn out to be its conclusion that the proper time to pass upon the remoteness issue is at the class-determination stage of the proceeding. A class which passes the certification stage may have a good chance to get a share of the "pot-of-gold" when and if the time comes to divide it. In any case it seems possible that the "cost-plus" exception, which can be an obstacle to recovery by direct purchasers, may be the key to the hopes of many of the more remote classes in consumer class actions.

4. Public Injury

Question: *Must plaintiff allege and prove public injury?*

Contrary to earlier decisions by lower federal courts, the Supreme Court ruled in *Klor's, Inc.* v. *Broadway-Hale Stores,* 359 U.S. 207 (1959), that a private antitrust treble-damage claimant complaining about a boycott violating Sections 1 and 2 of the Sherman Act need not allege or offer proof that the boycott caused injury to the public. Placing boycotts among those "classes of restraints which from their 'nature or character' were unduly restrictive, and hence forbidden," the Court declared: "As to these classes of restraints, . . . Congress had determined its own criteria of public harm and it was not for the courts to decide whether in an individual case injury had actually occurred."

In *Atlantic Heel Co.* v. *Allied Heel Co.,* 284 F.2d 879 (1st Cir. 1960), the court declared, "the question for our decision is whether or not the allegation of a conspiracy to destroy a competitor . . . is a per se violation of Section 1 so that the rationale of the Klor's case applies, and, thus, no allegations of further facts showing the basis of public harm and consequent unreasonableness of the restraint are necessary." The court eliminated the requirement of alleging and proving public injury only after it had concluded that the damage complaint had alleged a per se violation of the Sherman Act.

In *Radiant Burners, Inc.* v. *People's Gas Light & Coke Co.,* 364 U.S. 656 (1961), the Supreme Court stated the rule as follows: "To state a claim upon which relief can be granted under [Section 1 of the Sherman Act], allegations adequate to show a violation and, in private treble damage action, that plaintiff was damaged thereby are all the law requires." That language was read in *Syracuse Broadcasting Corp.* v. *Newhouse,* 295 F.2d 269 (2d Cir. 1961), and

Switzer Bros., Inc. v. *Locklin,* 297 F.2d 39 (7th Cir. 1961), *cert. denied,* 369 U.S. 851 (1962), 335 F.2d 331 (7th Cir. 1964), *cert. denied,* 379 U.S. 962 (1965), 429 F.2d 873 (7th Cir. 1970), *cert. denied,* 400 U.S. 1020 (1970), as eliminating public injury as a separate element in private damage suits based on conduct that does not violate the antitrust laws unless its unreasonableness or anticompetitive effect is proven. In *In re McConnell,* 370 U.S. 230, 231 (1962), the Supreme Court interpreted *Klor's* and *Radiant Burners* as holding "that the right of recovery . . . in a treble damage antitrust case does not depend at all on proving an economic injury to the public."

In *Donlan* v. *Carvel,* 209 F.Supp. 829 (D. Md. 1962), however, a district court concluded that specific allegation and proof of public injury is necessary for anything but a per se antitrust violation. The court went on to find that public injury had been sufficiently alleged in the complaint it had been asked to dismiss. The court made no reference to *Radiant Burners, Syracuse Broadcasting,* or *Switzer Bros.* but relied entirely on its reading of *Klor's* as applicable only to per se violations.

Without mentioning any distinction between per se and other Sherman Act violations, a New York district court has found a treble-damage complaint "fatally defective since it does not allege any facts which show injury to the public." (*Epstein* v. *Dennison Mfg. Co.,* 1966 Trade Cas. ¶71,852 (S.D.N.Y. 1966)).

The *Epstein* and *Donlan* opinions apparently do not reflect the prevailing view. *Epstein* is the only surviving precedent for requiring separate allegation and proof of public injury in any private antitrust action. The statements in the *Atlantic Heel* and *Donlan* cases limiting the *Klor's* doctrine to per se violations were not necessary to the decisions reached there. In *Atlantic Heel,* a per se violation was found to be alleged, and in *Donlan* there were found to be separate allegations of public injury. The appellate court decisions in *Syracuse Broadcasting* and *Switzer Bros.* stand as precedents in which separate public-injury evidence was held unnecessary to show violations of the Sherman Act in conduct that was not unlawful per se, but those opinions do not contain an exposition of the rule. Nevertheless, the logic of the courts of appeals' holdings seems clear. If, as the Supreme Court has said, Congress has determined there is public injury in every violation of the Sherman Act, then every allegation of a Sherman Act violation necessarily encompasses an allegation of injury to the public. It makes no difference whether the conduct in question is alleged to violate the Act because such conduct is, by its very nature, always in unreasonable restraint of trade or is alleged to violate the Act because it is unreasonable in the particular context in which it occurred. Similarly, evidence sufficient to establish a violation necessarily establishes public harm under the theory that Congress has determined that public injury is inherent in every antitrust violation.

This theory may be just as applicable to the Clayton Act as to the Sherman Act, although all the reported decisions dealing with the public-injury issue have been Sherman Act cases.

5. Assistance From Prior Government Action

(a) Grand Jury Proceedings

Questions: *Can plaintiff obtain grand jury transcripts and witness debriefing memoranda?*

To what extent and subject to what criteria may a potential plaintiff obtain transcripts of grand jury proceedings and memoranda of debriefing of grand jury witnesses? This question was answered by Judge Bernard Decker in *Illinois* v. *Harper & Row Publishers, Inc.,* 50 F.R.D. 37 (N.D. Ill. 1969), but his decision with respect to debriefing memoranda was substantially overruled on appeal (*Harper & Row Publishers, Inc.* v. *Decker,* 423 F.2d 487 (7th Cir. 1970)). An equally divided Supreme Court affirmed the decision of the court of appeals (400 U.S. 348 (1971)).

Judge Decker presided over many treble-damage actions by schools and state and local governments seeking damages allegedly arising from a conspiracy by several publishers to fix the prices of children's books. These actions were consolidated for pretrial procedures. The plaintiffs made a substantial effort to depose nearly 100 witnesses, but many of the events had occurred six to 10 years earlier. Plaintiffs sought to examine the transcripts of testimony of 11 witnesses who had testified three years earlier before a grand jury investigating the practices involved in the treble-damage action. (The Department of Justice had not sought indictments.) These witnesses were officers or employees of the defendant companies. Plaintiffs also sought production by the defendants of all debriefing memoranda summarizing the deponent's grand jury testimony. The defendants objected to the discovery of debriefing memoranda on the basis (a) that the documents fell within the attorney-client privilege and (b) that the documents were shielded by the "work product" doctrine of *Hickman* v. *Taylor,* 329 U.S. 495, 509 (1947). Questions were also raised under Rule 6 (c) of the Federal Rules of Criminal Procedure as to violations of traditional grand jury secrecy by disclosure of the transcripts. The district court rejected defendant's contentions and permitted broad discovery of both the grand jury transcripts and the debriefing memoranda, treating the two categories separately in its opinion.

Rule 6(e) of the Federal Rules of Criminal Procedure provides: "Disclosure of matters occurring before the grand jury other than its deliberations and the vote of any juror may be made to the attorneys for the government for use in the performance of their duties. Otherwise a juror, attorney, interpreter, or stenographer may disclose matters occurring before the grand jury only when so directed by the court preliminarily to or in connection with a judicial proceeding or when permitted by the court at the request of the defendant upon a showing that grounds may exist for a motion to dismiss the indictment because of matters occurring before the grand jury. No obligation of secrecy may be imposed upon any person except in accordance with this rule."

Recognizing a "long-established policy of grand jury secrecy" in interpreting Rule 6(e), Judge Decker noted that, within the trial court's discretion, grand jury secrecy can be lifted "discreetly and limitedly" where "particularized need" for the transcript exists. Thus, in *U.S.* v. *Procter & Gamble,* 356 U.S. 677, 683 (1958), the Court held that the use of the grand jury transcript at trial to impeach a witness or to refresh his recollection constituted a permissible particularized need warranting discovery. In *Procter & Gamble* the Supreme Court stated that the policy of grand jury secrecy can be outweighed by a showing (a) of a particular need, (b) compelling necessity, or (c) that the demands of justice require disclosure. In the *Illinois* v. *Harper & Row* case, plaintiffs wished to use the transcript as evidence, not merely for discovery, since several witnesses were beyond the subpoena power of the court, yet Judge Decker found no difference between the introduction of the transcripts into evidence and their use in *Procter & Gamble* as an impeaching or refreshing device. Citing *U.S.* v. *Rose,* 215 F.2d 617, 628–629 (3rd Cir. 1954), the judge explored five traditional reasons for imposing secrecy upon grand jury proceedings: (a) to prevent the escape of a witness whose indictment is contemplated, (b) to ensure freedom of deliberation for the grand jury, (c) to prevent witness tampering or subornation of perjury, (d) to encourage free disclosure by witnesses, and (e) to protect the accused from disclosure of the fact that he was investigated by the grand jury. In the court's opinion only the policy of encouraging free disclosure was relevant to the *Harper and Row* situation. The first three reasons were made inapplicable by the termination of the grand jury proceedings without returning indictments. See *U.S.* v. *Socony-Vacuum Oil Co.,* 310 U.S. 150 (1940). The fifth reason did not apply.

In weighing the "particularized need" for the grand jury transcript against the policy of secrecy, Judge Decker noted that the question hinged on the importance of maintaining secrecy. See *Dennis* v. *U.S.*, 384 U.S. 855 (1966). He saw no compelling need for secrecy (a) because the witness deposed would be asked to testify in the trial of the damage action, thus exposing the witness to the same dangers created by the disclosure of grand jury testimony, and (b) because little secrecy surrounded the grand jury proceedings since most witnesses from the defendant companies were immediately debriefed, and the notes of these debriefings were widely circulated throughout their corporations. On the other hand, in the face of minimal necessity for secrecy, there was said to be a strong need for the release of the transcripts because witnesses deposed in the current action had great difficulty in recalling significant facts and their testimony contradicted other documentary evidence.

The information sought was relevant and useful, but the Supreme Court has held this to be an insufficient showing of need (*U.S.* v. *Procter & Gamble Co.*, 356 U.S. 677, 682 (1958)). In *Harper & Row*, there was the inability of hostile witnesses to recall the facts as well as defendant's own extensive internal publication and circulation of debriefing memoranda. The fact that the plaintiffs were governmental agencies may also have influenced Judge Decker to grant broad discovery. No review was sought with respect to the grand jury transcripts.

The trial court's exercise of its own discretion requires a balancing of the need for secrecy against the need for disclosure. Judge Decker's opinion discloses an unwillingness to tolerate antiquated arguments for secrecy. This may signal increasing judicial reluctance to inhibit grand jury disclosure without a compelling need for secrecy or a seriously deficient showing of "particularized need." This has been restated as a "growing tendency to limit secrecy after the grand jury has completed its work to those cases where secrecy serves legitimate policy considerations" (*U.S.* v. *Hughes*, 413 F.2d 1244 (5th Cir. 1969), *dismissed as moot sub nom.*, *U.S.* v. *Gifford-Hill-American, Inc.*, 397 U.S. 93 (1970)).

Another case illustrates the point that unlimited access to grand jury transcripts will not be allowed. In *ABC Great States, Inc.* v. *Globe Ticket Co.*, 309 F.Supp. 181 (E.D. Pa. 1970); 316 F.Supp. 449 (E.D. Pa. 1970), the district court refused to make available to the plaintiff sentencing memoranda containing excerpts from grand jury testimony. The court required the party seeking disclosure to show "a more compelling and particularized need than merely expediting civil discovery," and held that the plaintiff had failed to make such a showing.

Judge Decker refused to consider in camera treatment of the grand jury transcripts. He released the minutes along with the transcripts. The fact that the votes or deliberations of the grand jurors did not appear in the minutes may have explained the court's willingness to make them available along with the transcripts. In *Phila.* v. *Westinghouse Electric Corp.,* 210 F.Supp. 486 (E.D. Pa. 1962), the court ordered in camera inspection of the grand jury transcripts by the deposition judge to determine whether material discrepancies existed between the deposed testimony and that revealed in the transcript. Only then, "to uncover full and complete facts," did the court permit access to the transcripts. In contrast, Judge Decker allowed free access upon a showing of inconsistent or incomplete testimony at the deposition without a thorough comparison of deposition testimony with the grand jury transcript.

As to the question of plaintiff's discovery of memoranda prepared by defendant's attorneys upon their debriefing of witnesses who had previously testified before the grand jury, Judge Decker, faced with attorney-client and work-product objections to the release of these memoranda, nevertheless ordered that they be made available to plaintiffs seeking to depose these defense witnesses in the current action. Judge Decker first defined two varieties of the attorney-client privilege: (a) a personal attorney-client relationship between the witness and the debriefing attorney, and (b) a corporate attorney-client privilege. There was no personal privilege, according to the Court, because "The attorneys did not (1) render personal legal advice after the witnesses completed their grand jury testimony, (2) advise them on other personal matters, or (3) bill the witnesses for their services." Apparently, the debriefing was alleged to have been conducted as a favor to the defendant corporations by their outside legal counsel who were not acting as counsel for the witnesses themselves.

As to a possible attorney-client relationship between the attorney and the corporation whose employee was debriefed, the court noted that the privilege would attach only when "a responsible member of the corporation's management or control group must seek legal advice about corporate affairs," and the official "must be in a position to influence the decision about which legal counsel is sought" (hereafter the "control group test"). Since only two debriefed witnesses were in a position to influence their company's legal strategy, all other memoranda were held not privileged, despite the fact that several witnesses helped to shape pricing policies investigated by the grand jury.

Judge Decker also rejected objections to the release of the debriefing memoranda under the work-product doctrine. This doctrine, according to the court, "does not, however, insulate nonlegal services rendered by persons who happen to be attorneys." Many of the memoranda, Judge Decker noted, were prepared by attorneys whose function was merely to reconstruct the witness' grand jury testimony as would an "investigator." This factual summation was not regarded as work product by an attorney in his "true professional capacity." While other memoranda did include counsel's comments and impressions about the witness' report, these documents, said Judge Decker, "are only entitled to limited protection since they remain basically summaries of testimony." The court was not satisfied that the fact that the debriefing memoranda were physically prepared by an attorney was enough to convert them to "work product" in the absence from the memoranda of any legal analysis or discussion of defense strategy. While some of this material was arguably privileged as work product, the privilege was conditioned by a showing of "good cause" for production under Rule 34 of the Federal Rules of Civil Procedure. Since Judge Decker found the privilege "weak" here, he concluded that the requisite showing of good cause was correspondingly reduced. Thus, he found that in light of the witness' lack of memory about events occurring six to 10 years before, and because conflict existed between their depositional testimony and existing documentary evidence, "good cause" for production of the debriefing memoranda was shown.

The defendants sought to perfect an appeal of Judge Decker's discovery rulings, but the district court refused to make the necessary certification. The defendants presented on appeal the question of discovery of debriefing memoranda by means of a mandamus action to compel the court to vacate its order for production. In a *per curiam* decision, the court of appeals reversed the district court's order to produce several of the debriefing memoranda and questioned some of the criteria employed by the court below (*Harper & Row Publishers, Inc.* v. *Decker,* 423 F.2d 487 (7th Cir. 1970)). The appellate court agreed that no personal attorney-client privilege attached to the debriefing memoranda. However, some of the witnesses who were debriefed had made disclosures to the corporation's counsel "at the direction of his corporate employer and on its behalf." The court indicated that the witness' grand jury testimony was "germane to the duties of his employment." Noting that Judge Decker had applied the "control group test," the court of appeals found this test inadequate as applied to questions of corporate attorney-client privilege, concluded that the corporation's attorney-client privilege "protects communications of some corporate agents who are not within the control group," and found that the privilege should apply "where the employee makes the communication at the direction of his superiors . . . and where the subject matter upon which the attorney's advice is sought . . . and dealt with in the communication is the performance by the employees of the duties of his employment." As to several debriefing memoranda of key corporate operating personnel, it was held that they should not be released to the plaintiffs.

The court of appeals did not wholly agree with Judge Decker's concepts of "work product." The court said that "where an attorney personally prepares a memorandum of an interview of a witness with an eye toward litigation such memorandum qualifies as work product even though the lawyer functioned primarily as an investigator."

In a later opinion, *U.S.* v. *Hart, Schaffner, & Marx,* 451 ATRR A-27 (N.D. Ill. 1970), Judge Decker indicated a possible change of thought on "work product." There, the reports of a government economist, though not legal analysis, were held to be "work product" because the economist was an integral part of the Government's trial staff. Discovery of a portion of the economist's memoranda was granted because good cause for production of the economist's reports was established.

The court of appeals in *Harper & Row* indicated that "the less the lawyer's mental processes are involved, the less will be the burden to show good cause." While the court was reluctant to overturn Judge Decker's finding of good cause, it disapproved of his general conclusion that a six-year time lapse would inevitably fade the deponent's memory and justify production of a debriefing memo. Rather, the court suggested that it was preferable to have specific findings based upon the trial court's inspection of the deposition to determine whether discrepancies existed between the deposition testimony and the witness' account in the debriefing memorandum. Other courts may be inclined towards more liberal access to debriefing statements than was the court of appeals in the *Harper & Row* case. If so, defense attorneys may need to exercise special care in their debriefing methods. Witnesses may be debriefed by tape recording their own recollection of their testimony, but such tapes might be subject to later disclosure. Oral debriefing and reliance by the attorney upon his memory might avoid later disclosure, but the deposition of the debriefing attorney could be requested to obtain his recollection of what the debriefed witness told him. If the court makes available grand jury transcripts of the witness' testimony, it could be argued that there is no cause for granting access to debriefing memoranda. But, if the witness has made a statement before the grand jury which he attempts to modify or retract during debriefing, some say the plaintiff's attorney should be given the opportunity to explore this conflict.

One view, somewhat antique, is that any debriefing involves the obstruction of justice by the invasion of grand jury secrecy, and he who engages in such a practice deserves little consideration. On the other hand, unlimited access by plaintiffs to debriefing documents could, in the view of some practitioners, do basic harm to the attorney-client privilege.

Several questions are left unanswered by the *Harper & Row* decisions. Can debriefing memoranda, if obtained, be used as evidence? It would seem that these memoranda, made out of court by a lawyer rather than the witness, are clearly hearsay and hence inadmissible, in contrast to transcripts of testimony before the grand jury under oath. This may explain why Judge Decker specifically referred to the evidentiary value of transcripts while making no such allusion to debriefing memoranda. Where the witness has subsequently died or is beyond the court's subpoena power, great need for any form of prior testimony, perhaps even in the form of debriefing memos, may exist. This could incline the courts to admit the memoranda into evidence in some qualified way, perhaps limiting the weight they will carry.

The court of appeals did not review the correctness of Judge Decker's finding that no personal attorney-client privilege existed with respect to the debriefing memoranda. The witness' request for counsel and his statement that such counsel, in fact, represented him had not convinced Judge Decker that a privileged relationship existed absent a showing that a fee was paid by the witness. Perhaps, some suggest, it might have made a difference had the witness-employees retained control of the memoranda rather than circulating them throughout the corporations. The defendant corporations and their counsel retained the documents, and it was the corporate defendants, not the employee-witness, who claimed the privilege.

(b) Prior Judgment Based on Guilty Plea

Question: *Are antitrust criminal convictions based on guilty pleas "consent judgments"?*

In January 1914, President Wilson urged Congress to enact legislation that would allow an antitrust plaintiff to base his suit on facts proved in actions brought and won by the Government. Later that year, Congress passed language substantially similar to that now found in Section 5(a) of the Clayton Act, 15 U.S.C. § 16(a). Under Section 5(a), "a final judgment or decree," in any government action under the antitrust laws, "that a defendant has violated said laws" is to be regarded, in a private treble-damage action, as "prima facie evidence against such defendant . . . as to all matters respecting which said judgment or decree would be an estoppel as between the parties" in the initial action brought by the Government.

During the debates on the bill, it was pointed out that many defendants had consented without litigation to antitrust decrees, with substantial savings in government time and money. It was argued that, unless some inducement were held out to consenting defendants, the proposed bill would probably end such capitulations in future proceedings. As a result, two provisos were added. The first was substantially the same as that now found in Section 5(a), which states "that this section shall not apply to consent judgments or decrees entered before any testimony has been taken." The second was temporary legislation, designed to enable defendants in cases then pending before the courts to withdraw pleas of not guilty and capitulate, thereby enabling them to escape the impact of the prima facie evidence rule even if testimony had already been taken in their cases. This proviso stated: "This section shall not apply to consent judgments or decrees rendered in criminal proceedings or suits in equity, now pending, in which the taking of testimony has been commenced but has not been concluded, provided such judgments or decrees are rendered before any further testimony is taken."

In *Twin Ports Oil Co.* v. *Pure Oil Co.,* 36 F.Supp. 366 (D.Minn. 1939), *aff'd,* 119 F.2d 747 (8th Cir. 1941), *cert. denied,* 314 U.S. 644 (1941), a gasoline jobber sued an oil company for treble damages. The complaint alleged that a criminal antitrust judgment had previously been entered against the oil company upon a plea of nolo contendere. The oil company moved to strike this allegation, arguing that a judgment based on a plea of nolo contendere was a "consent judgment" within the meaning of the Section 5(a) proviso. Granting the oil company's motion, the district court held that a judgment based on a plea of nolo contendere did not create an estoppel between the Government and the defendant and was therefore not the type of judgment contemplated by Section 5(a), and that the legislative history of the act indicates that a judgment based on a plea of nolo contendere is to be deemed a "consent judgment" within the meaning of the proviso. The court placed heavy emphasis on legislative history showing a congressional intent to encourage consent judgments in government cases. The judge also added his view that judgments based on pleas of guilty are also "consent judgments" protected by the proviso. In reaching this conclusion the court relied on statements made by several Senators during debate on the proviso, and on a comparison of the language in the general proviso with that found in the temporary proviso. The court quoted Senator Norris, who had opposed the exception, as saying, "the real effect of that proviso is to make the Section inapplicable to cases in which consent judgments have been taken in cases where pleas of guilty have been entered by the defendant." The court also noted that although the proviso used only the words "consent judgments or decrees," the temporary proviso referred to consent judgments "rendered in criminal proceedings," as well as those rendered in "suits in equity." Thus, although the court admitted that the term "consent judgment" was anomalous when used in reference to a criminal proceeding, Congress had used the term in that very context in the temporary proviso pertaining to pending cases, and the court saw no reason why later cases should be treated differently.

Other district courts have followed the holding that a judgment based on a plea of nolo contendere is a "consent judgment." See, e.g., *Barnsdall Refining Corp.* v. *Birnamwood Oil Co.,* 32 F.Supp. 308 (E.D. Wis. 1940).

In *U.S.* v. *Standard Ultramarine & Color Co.,* 137 F.Supp. 167 (S.D.N.Y. 1955), the indictment charged six corporate defendants with violations of the Sherman Act. The defendants pleaded not guilty but later moved for leave to change their pleas to nolo contendere. The court denied the motion, noting that the plea of nolo contendere is not one to which defendants are entitled as a matter of right, but one which the court can, in its discretion, accept or reject. The reason given for rejecting the nolo pleas was that judgments based on such pleas, having been held to be "consent judgments," would not be usable in treble-damage suits. The court noted that the purpose behind the proviso was to encourage defendants' capitulation, but it placed greater stress on the underlying policy behind the section itself—to lighten the burden of private parties in expensive antitrust litigation. The court was unwilling to deprive future plaintiffs of this benefit by allowing the defendants to plead nolo contendere. The court also noted that the nolo plea was coming into extended use in antitrust suits brought by the Government because it gained for the defendant the benefit of the exemption from Section 5(a), an advantage that was uncertain if the defendant pleaded guilty.

Two district courts have faced the question of whether a judgment based on a plea of guilty is a "consent judgment" falling within the proviso of Section 5(a); the courts have split. In *Atlantic City Electric Co.* v. *General Electric Co.,* 207 F.Supp. 613 (S.D.N.Y. 1962), plaintiffs in 418 of the treble-damage actions brought against the electrical-equipment manufacturers alleged in their complaints that the February 1961 convictions and sentences had been entered, in some instances, on pleas of guilty. The manufacturers moved to strike these allegations. The Federal District Court for Southern New York (Manhattan) granted the motion as to the judgments entered on nolo pleas, citing the *Twin Ports Oil* and *Barnsdall* cases, and denied the motion as to the judgments entered on guilty pleas. The court took issue with the dictum in *Twin Ports Oil;* it looked at the same legislative history and drew the opposite conclusions. The court recognized that the language used in the temporary proviso was "consent judgments . . . in criminal proceedings," and that the words "criminal proceedings" were absent in the general proviso. Unlike the Minnesota Federal District Court, however, it concluded that this variation in language showed a congressional intent to exclude criminal proceedings from the scope of the proviso. The Manhattan Federal District Court quoted Senator Walsh as saying, "I am not able to agree with Senator Reed that in the future the judgment entered upon a plea of guilty in a criminal action would not be available under the proposed statute."

The Manhattan court drew support, by way of inference, from the *Standard Ultramarine* opinion's rejection of a tendered plea of nolo contendere. The court reasoned that the decision to thwart Standard Ultramarine's attempt to take advantage of Section 5(a) must have been based on the premise that a plea of guilty, which the court had no power to reject, did not fall within the proviso. It was clear to the Manhattan court that "opposing policy considerations" were involved in Congress' attempt, at the same time, to aid the private litigant and encourage capitulation of defendants in government cases. Of the two purposes, the former is paramount and the latter can be served by allowing pleas of nolo contendere when they are justified by the facts of the case. Besides, the court noted, to hold otherwise would erase the long-standing common-law distinction between a plea of nolo contendere, which is not admissible in evidence in later civil actions, and a plea of guilty, which is admissible.

In *Commonwealth Edison Co.* v. *Allis-Chalmers Mfg. Co.,* 211 F.Supp. 712 (N.D. Ill. 1962), *aff'd in part, rev'd in part,* 323 F.2d 412 (7th Cir. 1963), the electrical-equipment manufacturers moved to strike from another set of complaints allegations that prior judgments against them had been entered on pleas of either guilty or nolo contendere. The district court granted the motion and ordered that all references to the criminal judgments, whether on pleas of nolo contendere or on pleas of guilty, be stricken. A divided court of appeals affirmed the exclusion from evidentiary use of judgments based on nolo pleas but reversed as to judgments based on pleas of guilty.

Two other district courts ruled on motions to strike the electrical equipment complaints' references to the pleas in the Philadelphia cases. In *Phila.* v. *Westinghouse,* 1961 Trade Cas. ¶70,143 (E.D. Pa. 1961), the district court struck references to nolo pleas, and in *Sacramento Utility District* v. *Westinghouse,* 1962 Trade Cas. ¶70,552 (N.D. Calif. 1962), the court refused to strike references to guilty pleas, holding them not to be "consent judgments." In the *Commonwealth Edison* case, Judge Robson struck from the pleadings all references to "nolo pleas, guilty pleas, judgments, sentences and summaries of, and quotations from the indictments." Yet he specifically pointed out: "The court is not at this time ruling upon questions of evidence." If convictions are admissible as evidence of violations, what difference does it make to plaintiff's case if references to them are stricken from the pleadings? References in the pleadings may enable plaintiff's counsel to force responsive answers from the defendants and focus attention sooner on the real issues in the case as they see them. Plaintiff's counsel may thus be able to concentrate their efforts on the procurement of proof that the plaintiff suffered damages that resulted from the antitrust violation.

Aside from the question of what constitutes a "final judgment or decree" under Section 5(a) and what constitutes a "consent judgment or decree" under the proviso, should all references to earlier judgments be stricken from the complaint under the generally accepted theory that only facts should be alleged in the pleadings and evidence should be reserved for the trial? Apparently the law is far from settled on the point. Some district judges permit the pleading of such judgments, and others do not.

Apart from questions of pleading, what real effect did the enactment of Section 5(a) have? A guilty plea in a prior criminal proceeding is generally regarded as usable in evidence, without the help of Section 5(a), as an admission against the defendant's interest. There appears to be general agreement that the statute has at least three results. First, it provides a uniform federal rule of evidence in place of what otherwise might be a rule varying from state to state. Second, it makes admissible as prima facie evidence prior judgments or decrees that would not otherwise be admissible. Third, where it applies, Section 5(a) gives to plaintiff an opportunity to place greater emphasis upon defendant's violation in arguments to the court and the jury and transfers to the defendant the burden of going forward with the evidence on the issue of violation of the antitrust laws.

(c) Prior Judgment Based on Consent or Nolo Plea

Question: *What help can treble-damage claimants get from Justice Department antitrust cases terminated by consent decrees or nolo contendere pleas?*

The Supreme Court has seen in Section 5(b) of the Clayton Act a congressional intent "to assist private litigants in utilizing any benefits they might cull from government antitrust actions" (*Minn. Mining & Mfg. Co.* v. *N.J. Wood Finishing Co.,* 381 U.S. 311, 317 (1965)). Noting that in most instances the pleadings, transcripts of testimony, exhibits, and other documents of the Government's cases are available to a damage plaintiff, the Court described government cases "as a major source of evidence for private parties" (381 U.S. at 319).

Congress has declared a policy that government antitrust litigation is not to be conducted in secrecy. The Publicity in Taking Evidence Act of March 3, 1913, 15 U.S.C. § 30 (1913), provides that the taking of depositions in government Sherman Act injunction suits "shall be open to the public as freely as are trials in open court; and no order excluding the public from attendance on any such proceedings shall be valid or enforceable." A general intention to keep the activities of administrative and executive agencies open to the public has also been expressed in the Freedom of Information Act, 5 U.S.C. § 552, but there is an exception in the Act that makes it largely inapplicable to the law enforcement activities of the Antitrust Division and the FTC. Subsection(b)(7) preserves the secrecy of "investigatory files compiled for law enforcement purposes." This exemption is not limited to criminal investigations (*Clement Brothers Co.* v. *NLRB,* 282 F.Supp. 540 (N.D. Ga. 1968).

Section 4(c) of the Antitrust Civil Process Act, 15 U.S.C. § 1311–1314, authorizing the issuance of civil investigative demands, provides that "no material so produced shall be available for examination, without the consent of the person who produces such material, by an individual other than a duly authorized officer, member, or employee of the Department of Justice." If the Government's case, whether civil or criminal, is tried and won, not only is a judgment available as "prima facie evidence" of an antitrust violation, but the entire record of the proceeding is available to prove the scope and nature of the violation. Occasionally, a defendant will succeed in convincing the district judge that some of the information furnished the Government during discovery proceedings is sufficiently confidential or privileged to be segregated from the public record.

In *Olympic Refining Co.* v. *Carter,* 332 F.2d 260 (9th Cir. 1964), *cert. denied,* 379 U.S. 900 (1964), a damage claimant wanted to see interrogatory answers that were subject to protective orders. In an effort to cooperate with the plaintiff, the Antitrust Division filed a motion to vacate the protective orders; the district judge denied the motion and quashed the plaintiff's subpoena. In the district court's view it was the protective orders that had enabled the Government to obtain "full and complete disclosure" in the first place. The court of appeals reversed the district judge, finding nothing in the Federal Rules of Civil Procedure that would authorize a court to protect trade secrets and sensitive competitive information "from such disclosure as is relevant to the subject matter involved in a pending action. All that may be done is to afford such protection from disclosure as is practicable, consistent with the right of access thereto for purposes of litigation." The district court was directed to modify the protective orders to give the damage-suit plaintiff access to the interrogatory answers "subject to such reasonable restrictions as may be necessary and practicable to prevent unnecessary disclosure."

Fear of developing a record for use by damage claimants may be a strong motivating factor in a defendant's election to accept a consent decree rather than litigate the Government's charges. As described above, Congress added to Section 5(a) of the Clayton Act a proviso "that this section shall not apply to consent judgments . . . entered before any testimony has been taken." Like its investigations, the Antitrust Division's consent-decree negotiations are treated as confidential. That rule of confidentiality has not been applied, though, to documents exchanged by the parties in the post-decree mechanics of compliance with the decree.

Shortly after entry of the consent decree in *U.S.* v. *United Fruit Co.*, 1958 Trade Cas. ¶68,941 (E.D. La. 1958), the district court granted United Fruit's motion for a protective order prohibiting inspection by outsiders of "any document submitted by either party in this case," apparently because the court feared that disclosure of the documents would create problems in the foreign relations of the United States. A request by a United Fruit competitor for leave to inspect and copy compliance programs and reports was denied in *U.S.* v. *United Fruit Co.*, 1968 Trade Cas. ¶72,630 (E.D. La. 1968). In a petition to the Supreme Court for a writ of mandamus, the competitor alleged that the Government was interested in obtaining the competitor's view as to the compliance program. The Supreme Court denied mandamus without comment (*Standard Fruit and Steamship Co.* v. *Lynne*, 393 U.S. 974 (1968)) and dismissed an appeal (393 U.S. 406 (1969)), citing *Shenandoah Valley Broadcasting, Inc.* v. *ASCAP*, 375 U.S. 39 (1963), which rejected direct appeals in private controversies outside the "mainstream" of government litigation.

In criminal antitrust cases, nolo contendere pleas are accepted as "consent judgments" within the Section 5(a) proviso. When a defendant is convicted and sentenced on the basis of a nolo contendere plea, there is often information developed before entry and acceptance of the plea, as well as later in the determination of the sentence to be imposed. Federal Rule of Criminal Procedure 6(e) forbids disclosure of matters occurring before the grand jury except

"to the attorneys for the use in the performance of their duties."
Any further disclosure may be made only when "directed by the
court preliminarily to or in connection with a judicial proceeding."
In the *Electric-Equipment* cases, damage claimants were accorded
access to substantial portions of the transcripts of testimony elicited
by the grand jury that had indicted the manufacturers. The Federal
District Court for Eastern Pennsylvania, where the grand jury sat,
promulgated a standard operating procedure for nationwide use in
procuring the grand jury testimony of any witness whose deposition
was to be taken for a damage suit (*Phila.* v. *Westinghouse Electric
Corp.,* 210 F.Supp. 486 (E.D. Pa. 1962)). That procedure was
upheld later by the Court of Appeals for the Fifth Circuit in *Allis-Chalmers Mfg. Co.* v. *Fort Pierce,* 323 F.2d 233 (5th Cir. 1963).

Documents subpoenaed by several grand juries during an antitrust investigation of the publishing industry were ordered produced for inspection by treble-damage plaintiffs in *Harper & Row*
v. *Decker* 423 F.2d 487 (7th Cir. 1970), *aff'd,* 400 U.S. 348 (1971).
The production order was entered by the Federal District Court for
Northern Illinois, *Ill.* v. *Harper & Row Publishers, Inc.,* 308 F.Supp.
1207 (N.D. Ill. 1969), in which the Judicial Panel on Multi-District
Litigation had consolidated, for pretrial purposes, 21 treble-damage
suits filed against publishers and wholesalers of library editions of
children's books. (See section IX-A-5(a), p. 565.)

When a damage claimant is denied access to the grand jury transcript and documents procured by the grand jury, he may be able
to find a less direct route to the information he wants through
identification of the witnesses who appeared before the grand jury.
A list of the names of the grand jury witnesses may be obtained in
several ways. The returns to the subpoenas served on the witnesses
should be available in the office of the clerk of the district court,
since they are public records. While some courts seem to impede
access to those returns, there does not appear to be any reason why
the names of the grand jury witnesses known to the defendant cannot be obtained through interrogatories under Federal Civil Rule
33.

After indictment, if there are discovery and other pretrial proceedings before nolo pleas are tendered, information helpful to
damage claimants may get into the public record of the case or the
defendants themselves may come into possession of evidence that is
subject to discovery in a suit for damages. Before the nolo contendere pleas were accepted in *U.S.* v. *Union Camp Corp.,* 353 ATRR
A–12 (E.D. Va. 1968), there were several acknowledgments by the
defendants that they were admitting the allegations of the indictment "in open court." However, admissions of guilt made in connection with entry of a nolo plea have sometimes been treated as
"part and parcel of the plea" and therefore not usable in subse-

quent damage litigation (*Polychrome Corp.* v. *Minn. Mining & Mfg. Co.*, 263 F.Supp. 101 (S.D.N.Y. 1966)).

Even after a nolo contendere plea has been tendered to the court, government counsel often makes statements helpful to potential damage claimants in open court either at the time of acceptance of the plea or at the time of sentencing. The Government often files a sentencing memorandum with the court or with the probation officer for inclusion in his presentence report. Under Rule 32(c) of the Federal Rules of Criminal Procedure, as amended in 1966, the court "may disclose to the defendant or his counsel all or part of the material contained in" the "pre-sentence investigation and report by the probation service of the court." While this language indicates that the report is not to become part of the public record of the case, portions of it may be subject to discovery from a defendant who obtains a copy of it.

In *U.S. Industries, Inc.* v. *U.S. District Court,* 345 F.2d 18 (9th Cir. 1965), the Government admitted that its presentencing memorandum to the probation officer contained information that related to the grand jury proceedings and was protected by Rule 6(e) of the Criminal Rules. Therefore, when damage plaintiffs sought access to the government memorandum, the court of appeals deleted those portions whose exclusion it considered necessary to respect "the policy considerations behind the rule of secrecy of grand jury investigations." Having done so, the Court ordered the document unsealed and made available to the damage plaintiffs. Because the *U.S. Industries* case was decided before the 1966 amendment adding the Federal Criminal Rule 32(c) language quoted above, it was distinguished by the district judge who decided *Hancock Bros., Inc.* v. *Jones,* 293 F.Supp. 1229 (N.D. Calif. 1968). The Antitrust Division was willing there to have its presentencing reports made part of the public record so they could be disclosed to treble-damage claimants. One of the convicted defendants in the criminal case sued for a declaratory judgment, and the district judge decided that the presentencing reports "should remain under the seal of confidentiality." Much of the information contained in the presentencing reports was procured in the grand jury proceedings. The district court declared: "it is a firmly established policy of the law that acts of the grand jury and evidence taken before it are to be protected from public scrutiny." Since the only reason given by the damage-suit plaintiffs for disclosure was that they would be able to avoid expense and additional work, the district judge could not see the "compelling necessity" that must be shown for disclosure of grand jury records.

Despite all the rules of secrecy protecting criminal investigations and proceedings, a criminal prosecution terminated by nolo pleas often offers a damage claimant more avenues of access to evidentiary materials than a civil case producing a consent order. One antitrust lawyer has suggested that the advantages of a nolo contendere plea over a guilty plea "can be overrated at least insofar as the consequences in subsequent treble-damage actions are concerned" (Victor H. Kramer, "Subsequent Use of the Record and Proceedings" 38 ABA ANTITRUST L. J. 300 (1969)). An antitrust defendant who wants to get the maximum benefit out of a nolo contendere plea should submit that plea to the court at the earliest possible moment. Demands for bills of particulars and efforts at discovery of the Government's case too often bring into the defendant's possession information or documents that are easier to get from the defendant by Rule 34 motion or Rule 33 interrogatories than they would be to get from the Government or the court. In addition, government counsel may be sympathetic to private damage claimants and therefore not reluctant to take advantage of opportunities in open court or in memoranda to make relevations that can be used by damage claimants. The generally cooperative attitude of government counsel, antitrust lawyers also report, often makes it possible for damage plaintiffs to derive valuable information from direct conversations with government counsel. While the Antitrust Division's policy in this regard is not entirely clear, its attorneys seem to be given considerable leeway in cooperating with state and local agencies that file treble-damage actions. Experiences reported by plaintiff's lawyers indicate that the amount of cooperation varies from lawyer to lawyer.

(d) Consent Judgment After Testimony Taken

Question: *Can treble-damage claimants derive any support from consent judgments after testimony?*

Additional issues have arisen under Section 5(a) of the Clayton Act: (1) Under what circumstances will a consent judgment entered after the taking of testimony be regarded as covered by the proviso? (2) What effect under Section 5(a) is to be given a consent judgment that expressly recites it is without adjudication of any issues?

In *Dalweld Co.* v. *Westinghouse,* 252 F.Supp. 939 (S.D. N.Y. 1966), the district judge adhered to the rule that criminal convictions entered on nolo contendere pleas are "consent decrees," even though he was dealing with a nolo plea that was not accepted until after a trial had produced a hung jury. The nolo contendere plea had been tendered before the trial, and the judge insisted that the exclusion of the conviction was in line with the purpose of the "consent judgment" proviso, to encourage settlement of antitrust litigation without the expense of trial.

There was a related issue in *Mich.* v. *Morton Salt Co.,* 259 F.Supp. 35 (D. Minn. 1966), *aff'd sub nom., Hardy Salt Co.* v. *W. Va.,* 377 F.2d 768 (8th Cir. 1967), *cert. denied,* 389 U.S. 912 (1967). After the defendants had been acquitted on criminal antitrust charges, one of the defendants signed a consent decree in the Government's parallel civil action on the same day as the remaining defendants stipulated that the civil action would be submitted to the court on the basis of the record in the criminal base plus answers to certain government interrogatories. In the civil action, it was determined that a price-fixing conspiracy had existed. In a treble-damage action based on this conspiracy, the Minnesota court held that the consent decree entered into by one of the defendants was admissible in evidence because the Government had not been saved the time and expense of a trial. The court discounted arguments that neither the consent decree nor the final judgment against the other defendants in the civil action contained an explicit adjudication that the consenting defendant had violated the antitrust laws. On the basis of the complaint, the court's memorandum decision, and the final judgment, it was concluded that there existed a litigated finding that all the defendants, including the consent-decree defendant, had conspired to fix prices.

The district judge ruled that the judgment could be used by all plaintiffs located in the six-state area named in the indictment and the complaint, rather than merely by those identified in the evidence. Plaintiffs located outside the six-state area could not use the judgment as evidence, however, and the judgment was not admitted into evidence against co-conspirators identified in the Government's pleadings but not named as defendants.

The Minnesota court distinguished *Dalweld* because the defendant in *Dalweld* had attempted to enter a nolo plea before any evidence had been taken in the first trial. In *Barnsdall Refining Corp.* v. *Birnamwood Oil Co.,* 32 F.Supp. 308 (E.D. Wis. 1940), which the *Dalweld* opinion cited and the *Morton Salt* opinion refused to follow, a new trial was granted after the jury returned a guilty verdict but before judgment was entered. Before the new trial commenced, a plea of nolo contendere was entered. The defendant was later successful in arguing that the plea was entered "before any testimony [was] taken" within the meaning of Section 5(a). As read by the Minnesota judge, the *Barnsdall* opinion "fails to recognize that defendant is given a double advantage, while private litigants receive no benefit if a consent decree entered after a first trial is held not to be within the proviso clause" (259 F.Supp. at 64).

The purpose of Section 5(a)'s consent-judgment proviso is to prevent trial records from being started in the first place. Although the first trial was not prevented in either *Dalweld* or *Barnsdall,* the nolo plea did prevent a second trial. In the *Morton Salt* case, the consent decree did save the Government the trouble of proving the conspiracy in the civil suit concerning International, although the second trial went ahead because other defendants litigated. Perhaps the most significant difference between the *Morton Salt* case and the two earlier district court rulings is that International Salt was acquitted at the criminal trial. In a sense, the Minnesota federal district judge seems to have reasoned that one purpose of the Section 5(a) proviso is to encourage capitulation in a criminal case even when the defendant cannot be proven guilty under the criminal law's more stringent burden-of-proof rule.

It is uncertain what scope is to be given to Section 5(a)'s "estoppel" standard for determining the matters settled by the government proceeding. Section 5(a) applies only to judgments "to the effect that a defendant has violated said [antitrust] laws" and provides that such judgments shall constitute prima facie evidence "as to all matters respecting which said judgment or decree would be an estoppel as between the parties thereto." In *Emich Motors* v. *General Motors Corp.*, 340 U.S. 558 (1951), the Supreme Court held that "such estoppel extends only to questions 'distinctly put in issue and directly determined.' " Nevertheless, the district court in the *Morton Salt* case held that prima facie effect would be given to a consent judgment that, like the typical consent judgment, specifically recites that it was being entered without adjudication of any issue of law or fact.

The district court in the *Morton Salt* case also broke new ground in determining what the scope of the estoppel would be. In the *Emich* case, which dealt with a litigated government judgment, the Supreme Court held that a damage claimant relying upon the prior judgment had to show the impact of the antitrust violation on his business. In the *Morton Salt* case, the court ruled that the prior judgment "must be taken to determine that the conspiracy existed in localities throughout these states and had an impact on them." When that ruling is combined with the proof-of-damage test applied in *Bigelow* v. *RKO Radio Pictures, Inc.*, 327 U.S. 251 (1946), all government agencies in the area seem to be left with the necessity of proving nothing more than a reasonable estimate of overcharges.

In addition to its *Emich Motors* opinion, the Supreme Court has applied the "estoppel" standard to limit the use of a government judgment in *Theatre Enterprises, Inc.*, v. *Paramount Film Distributing Corp.*, 346 U.S. 537 (1954). The *Paramount* decrees, 334 U.S. 131 (1948), "were only prima facie evidence of a conspiracy covering the area and existing during the period there involved." The Court refused to disturb jury instructions that required the damage claimant to prove, with other evidence, that the conspiracy was operative in his city during the post-decree time covered by his complaint.

(e) FTC Orders

Question: *Does an FTC order have prima facie effect?*

In *Carpenter* v. *Central Ark. Milk Producers,* 1966 Trade Cas. ¶71,817 (W.D. Ark. 1966), the district judge decided an issue the Supreme Court reserved in *Minn. Mining & Mfg. Co.* v. *N.J. Wood Finishing Co.,* 381 U.S. 311 (1965). He held that an FTC order is an antitrust "judgment or decree" under Section 5(a) of the Clayton Act "as prima facie evidence" in a damage suit. The key factor for the district court seemed to be that under the 1959 finality amendments to the Clayton Act, an FTC order becomes final after 60 days if a court review petition is not filed within that period. Regardless of whether court review is sought, "the proceeding resulting in such final order or decree is a proceeding in equity and a civil proceeding within the meaning of Section 5 and an adjudication of a violation of the Clayton Act."

The FTC order in question was a "consent order" negotiated while cross appeals were pending from the hearing examiner's initial decision. In refusing to treat such an order as a "consent judgment" within the meaning of Section 5(a)'s proviso, the district court relied on a statement in *Emich Motors* v. *General Motors Corp.,* 340 U.S. 558 (1951), "that Congress intended to confer, subject only to a defendant's enjoyment of its day in court against a new party, as large an advantage as the estoppel doctrine would afford if the government brought suit."

Defense counsel in the *Carpenter* case requested the FTC to intervene, pointing out that admission of the consent order would reduce the Commission's chances of negotiating consent orders in the future once hearings begin. The Commission, without expressing any opinion on the merits, declined the request. (Commissioner Elman did not agree. It was his opinion that the Commission had entered a consent order to which Section 5(a) did not apply.) The treble-damage claimant eventually decided not to put the consent order in evidence.

In *Farmington Dowel Prods. Co.* v. *Forster Mfg. Co.,* 421 F.2d 61 (1st Cir. 1969), the court of appeals faced the question whether an FTC order relating to a violation of Section 2(a) of the amended Clayton Act ("Robinson-Patman Act") is a "final judgment or decree" within the language of Clayton Section 5(a). The district court had granted plaintiff treble damages for defendant's violation of Section 2(a) and, during trial, the court had admitted as prima facie evidence of a prior violation a portion of an FTC order based upon a finding that Forster had violated Section 2(a). Forster appealed on the propriety of admitting the FTC order as prima facie evidence under Section 5(a) of the Clayton Act and also raised questions as to the extent of admissibility of the FTC order. Whether FTC orders should be given prima facie effect, the court noted, was expressly left open by the Supreme Court in the *3M* case. The court examined reasons traditionally cited by the majority of courts in other actions refusing to accord FTC orders the prima facie effect attached to court decrees. The first reason was that FTC orders lacked finality and were not operative until acted upon by a reviewing court of appeals. Second, an FTC proceeding was not brought "by or on behalf of the United States." The court of appeals was satisfied that this reasoning was no longer compelling. First, the court noted from the *3M* case that any ambiguities in Sections 5(a) and 5(b) of the Clayton Act must be interpreted to assist private litigants in obtaining the benefits of government antitrust enforcement actions. "Because the assistance to the private litigant may even be greater under Section 5(a), [*prima facie* provision] we would think that only a strong countervailing policy should limit the application of Section 5(a)." The court concluded that a Commission proceeding is a "civil or criminal proceeding brought by the United States" within the meaning of Clayton Section 5(a) since virtually the same language in Section 5(b) was held applicable to FTC proceedings in *3M*.

The court then turned to the question: Is an FTC order a "final judgment or decree"? The court saw the passage of the Finality Act of 1959 as "the most significant indication of the Commission's maturation." Prior to 1959, three steps were required for the enforcement of an FTC order relating to the Clayton Act: (1) FTC order upon proof of a Clayton Act violation, (2) order of enforcement by a court of appeals upon a violation of the given FTC order, and (3) contempt proceeding following a violation of the court-sanctioned FTC order. The Finality Act of 1959 made Commission orders final unless appealed to the court of appeals within 60 days. "Final" orders were made enforceable by civil penalty proceedings. As the court said, "Implicit in the thinking behind this change was a belief that the Commission had come of age: its orders now have legal significance without the necessity of court appearance."

Given a "final" FTC order, the court still had to determine whether that order was a "judgment or decree" under Section 5(a).

The court examined the legislative history of the Clayton Act and noted in several instances the use of the term "day in court." It refused, however, to limit the applicability of Section 5(a) to court decrees, holding, rather, that the term must have been used by Congress "in the generic sense of a full opportunity to be heard and have one's case determined with finality in a proceeding in which fairness is assured." Finding congressional history of no aid, the court examined FTC procedures to determine whether a defendant could rely on a fair hearing. "The Commission's Rules of Practice today, while not so extensive as the Federal Rules of Civil Procedure, provide for litigants a substantial body of rights and privileges," stated the court. While hearsay evidence is admissible in FTC proceedings, the court noted in *U.S.* v. *United Shoe Machinery*, 89 F.Supp. 349, 355 (D. Mass. 1950), a civil antitrust court action without jury (analogous to an FTC proceeding), that hearsay evidence was also admitted. The court rejected Forster's challenge to the incomplete separation between the Commission's decision-making and prosecutorial functions, noting that the FTC separation of functions was internal, as was that of the Interstate Commerce Commission, whose orders had prima facie effect in damage actions.

The court concluded, "All we say is that the difference in ground rules facing defendants in court and Commission proceedings is not so significant as to warrant the exclusion of final decisions in the latter from the *prima facie* evidentiary effect of section 5(a)." Conversely, according to the court, "unfairness to injured plaintiffs would result from a holding excluding final Commission orders from Section 5(a). Given arbitrary allocation of antitrust enforcement powers between the FTC and the Justice Department, any differentiation between them for purposes of Section 5 is unfair to potential treble damage litigants. The unfairness is multiplied in the case of Robinson-Patman violations, where the Justice Department defers to substantially exclusive enforcement by the FTC."

In *Purex Corp. Ltd.* v. *Procter & Gamble Co.,* 308 F.Supp. 584 (C.D. Calif. 1970), *aff'd*, 453 F.2d 288 (9th Cir. 1971), *cert. denied*, 405 U.S. 1065 (1972), Purex brought an action under Section 4 of the Clayton Act for treble damages arising from Procter and Gamble's acquisition of Clorox Chemical Company in alleged violation of Section 7 of the Clayton Act. Prior to this suit, the Federal Trade Commission's ruling that the acquisition violated Section 7 was upheld by the Supreme Court, 386 U.S. 568 (1967). Purex sought to offer the FTC order as prima facie proof that Procter and Gamble violated the federal antitrust laws; defendant argued that the FTC order was not a "final judgment or decree" within the meaning of Section 5(a) of the Clayton Act. Plaintiff further contended that not only is the FTC order prima facie proof of liability but that "such order conclusively settles the issue of Procter's violation of Section 7, under the common law principle of collateral estoppel."

Judge Gray held that the FTC divestiture order was admissible as prima facie evidence in the damage action, but he concluded that the common law principle of collateral estoppel did not serve here to increase the effect of the Commission order beyond that accorded by Section 5(a). He referred with approval to the decision in *Farmington Dowel,* noting simply that, "Inasmuch as I agree with the conclusion reached by Judge Coffin . . . I shall, for the most part, simply state the general proposition and incorporate by reference Judge Coffin's explanations in justification thereof." Judge Gray found that an FTC proceeding is a "civil or criminal proceeding brought by the United States" under 5(a), citing *Farmington Dowel* and *3M.* He agreed with the *Farmington Dowel* holding that an FTC order is a "judgment or decree," reciting Judge Coffin's conclusion that nothing in the legislative history of 5(a) indicated an intention to preclude FTC orders from having the same evidentiary effect as court decrees. Judge Gray further concluded, in light of the Finality Act, that FTC orders are "final" and that the Act "gives significant indication of the Congressional conviction that Commission orders are worthy of being enforced, even in the absence of judicial review thereof." Judge Gray concluded: "In this case . . . the order of the Commission was reviewed by the court of appeals and by the Supreme Court. . . . I do not see how any Commission order could have more finality. . . ."

The court rejected defendant's argument that a determination of finality based upon judicial review of FTC orders would penalize defendants for seeking review because they would do so at the peril of having the order later introduced against them in a treble-damage action. Judge Gray answered that "the defendant's cries of pain are much louder than warranted by the nature and extent of the wound." Noting that it could not ignore the fact that the FTC order was vigorously contested at the administrative level and that the prima facie use of the FTC order creates only a rebuttable presumption cutting off no defenses, the court rejected defendant's "penalty" argument.

Judge Gray rejected plaintiff's assertion as to collateral estoppel. He pointed out that "the Commission order cannot be both prima facie and conclusive; and it having been determined that the statute applies, the statute must govern. Accordingly, the principle of collateral estoppel is adjudged not to be applicable to this case." But he ended with a note of caution: "The matter and extent to which evidentiary use may be made of the Commission order is for another day."

The court of appeals affirmed the district judge's denial of defendant's motion to exclude the Commission order. The court of appeals emphasized that it, like the trial judge, was reserving for another day the matter of the extent of use of the judgment in question and stated (453 F.2d at 291): "The trial judge referred to the Commission's order. As we have pointed out, the order is merged in the decree of the Court of Appeals. It is the decree, therefore, that we hold admissible. We leave to the trial judge the question as to the extent to which the underlying record, made before the Commission, may be referred to to shed light on the evidentiary effect of the decree. We also leave to another day the question whether an FTC order, final under the Finality Act, but not merged into a decree or judgment of a court of appeals, is admissible under § 5 of the Clayton Act."

The *Forster* and *Purex* decisions leave unanswered the question of whether FTC orders enjoining violations of Section 5 of the FTC Act will be given prima facie effect for treble-damage purposes. The Supreme Court has held in *Nashville Milk Co.* v. *Carnation Co.,* 355 U.S. 373 (1958), that Section 5 of the FTC Act is not an "antitrust law" as the term is used in Section 5(a) of the Clayton Act. It has also been held that Section 5 of the FTC Act creates no private right of action (*Holloway* v. *Bristol-Myers Corp.,* 624 ATRR A-1 (D.C. Cir. 1973); *Carlson* v. *The Coca-Cola Co.,* 625 ATRR A-5 (9th Cir. 1973)). In *Lippa's, Inc.* v. *Lenox, Inc.,* 305 F.Supp. 182 (D. Vt. 1969), a Section 5 FTC Act proceeding was held to toll the statute of limitations under Section 5(b) of the Clayton Act, which uses the term "antitrust laws." The district court ruled that Section 5 FTC Act actions were designed to prevent incipient antitrust violations, making them actions under "an antitrust law." (See section IX-A-6(c), p. 600.) The breadth of Section 5 of the FTC Act allows for wide potential vulnerability of respondents for practices which may never have been previously challenged. (See section VIII-A above, p. 481.) In contrast, Clayton Act Sections 2, 3, and 7 are thought to provide more specific rules.

One result of the *Farmington* and *Purex* rulings may be to encourage respondents to settle cases with the FTC to avoid the increased danger of treble-damage vulnerability which may flow from the prima facie effect of the FTC decision. Dependence on a prior FTC decision alone will probably present a weaker case. On the other hand, with a good case through live witnesses, the prior FTC order may lend an added factor which could be crucial. The conclusion in *Farmington Dowel* that FTC orders are prima facie proof of liability in subsequent damage actions left a further question for consideration: What portion of the Commission's decision and order should be admitted into the record? The district court instructed the jury to give prima facie effect to only two FTC findings: (a) that a price discimination had been granted and (b) that the discrimination caused injury to competition between purchasers. The plaintiff argued the examiner's initial decision and opinions of the FTC on appeal and on remand should also have been admitted, and that other findings should have been given prima facie effect.

In *Emich Motors* v. *General Motors Corp.,* 340 U.S. 558, 568–569 (1951), the Supreme Court stated that "the evidentiary use of prior judgments under Section 5(a) is to be determined by reference to the general doctrine of collateral estoppel," and "a prior judgment constitutes *prima facie* evidence of 'all matters of fact and law necessarily decided' by an earlier adjudication." This decision was modified by the Court in *Yates* v. *U.S.,* 354 U.S. 298, 338 (1957), which concluded that collateral estoppel "only operates to estop a party on ultimate facts in the subsequent proceeding." The *Farmington* court accepted the "necessarily decided" test of *Emich,* but formulated its own test: "when two adversaries concentrate in attempting to resolve an issue importantly involved in a litigation, there is no unfairness in considering that issue settled for all time between the parties and those in their shoes. But since parties can be expected to exert their full effort only on what seems essential at the time, it is unfair to close the door to issues which have not been on stage center, for there is no knowing what the white light of controversy would have revealed."

Applying this test to the facts in *Farmington,* the court concluded that the FTC findings of price discrimination and injury to competition were required for a valid cease-and-desist order under Section 2(a) of the amended Clayton Act. "These were the foci of controversy," stated the court, "necessarily decided," whereas the bulk of the other items, "while putting flesh on the bones . . could not be said to be essential to the Commission's decision."

6. Defenses

(a) The "In Pari Delicto" Defense

Question: *Can plaintiff prevail even where he participated in defendant's antitrust violation?*

The doctrine of "in pari delicto" (equally at fault) was regarded as applicable to antitrust litigation in *Eastman Kodak Co.* v. *Blackmore,* 277 F. 694 (2d Cir. 1921). Two situations in which a treble-damage claimant's participation in the antitrust violation did not foreclose his recovery have been recognized: (1) when disparity

of economic bargaining power forced him into the participation
(*Eastman Kodak* v. *Sou. Photo Materials,* 273 U.S. 359 (1927))
and (2) when he had severed his relationship with the unlawful
scheme and claimed damages sustained only after such severence
(*Victor Talking Machine Co.* v. *Kemenay,* 271 F.810 (3rd Cir. 1921)).

In *Crest Auto Supplies, Inc.* v. *Ero Mfg. Co.,* 246 F.Supp. 224
(N.D. Ill. 1965)), and *Perma Life Mufflers, Inc.* v. *Internat'l. Parts
Corp.,* 1966 Trade Cas. ¶71,801 (N.D. Ill. 1966), the district court,
finding the parties equally at fault, denied two groups of "exclusive
franchisees" the right to maintain antitrust suits against their suppliers for losses claimed as a result of exclusive-dealing provisions
in the franchise agreements. Relying on its own 1964 decision in
Rayco Mfg. Co. v. *Dunn,* 234 F.Supp. 593 (N.D. Ill. 1964), the court
said that a litigant cannot "complain of injuries which resulted
from alleged antitrust violations to which it was a voluntary party."
Lessig v. *Tidewater Oil Co.,* 327 F.2d 459 (9th Cir. 1964), and *Osborn* v. *Sinclair Refining Co.,* 286 F.2d 832 (4th Cir. 1960), cited by
the franchisees, were distinguished by the district judge on the
grounds that while these cases affirmed the proposition that alleged
illegal conduct by plaintiff does not automatically immunize defendant from liability, the defense had been disallowed only where the
damage claimant had not violated the antitrust laws in combination
with the defendant.

The *Crest Auto* decision was affirmed (360 F.2d 896 (7th Cir.
1966)). The court of appeals rejected without discussion the dealers' contention that whether they were "in pari delicto" is a question of fact which should not be decided without a trial. The court
was satisfied on the pleadings and depositions that the district judge
properly granted summary judgment to the supplier. The court also
affirmed the district court's decision in *Perma Life Mufflers, Inc.,*
376 F.2d 692 (7th Cir. 1967), with one dissent. The damage claimant had relied on the Supreme Court's decision in *Simpson* v.
Union Oil Co. of Calif., 377 U.S. 13 (1964), but the majority observed that the Supreme Court's opinion "does not mention pari
delicto and we think it did not intend to annihilate a principle so
long imbedded in the law."

The dissenter based his objection on "a close study of the Simpson case, including the briefs filed therein." In *Simpson,* the Court
of Appeals for the Ninth Circuit denied recovery on the basis of the
"in pari delicto" doctrine. That point was fully briefed in the Supreme Court, and, since plaintiff prevailed in the Supreme Court,
the dissenter was "forced to conclude that the Supreme Court rejected the in pari delicto defense." The dissenter also concluded that
the public policy justifying the denial of the defense in a case like
Perma Life was stated by the Supreme Court in *Kiefer-Stewart Co.*

v. *Jos. E. Seagram & Sons, Inc.,* 340 U.S. 211 (1951). (In *Kiefer-Stewart,* the Supreme Court held that allegations of horizontal price fixing by liquor wholesalers were no defense to one wholesaler's damage suit charging two distillers with a price-fixing conspiracy. The Court stated that "if [the damage claimant] and others were guilty of infractions of the antitrust laws, they could be held responsible in appropriate proceedings brought against them by the government or by injured private persons. The alleged illegal conduct of [the damage claimant] however, could not legalize the unlawful combination by [defendants] nor immunize them against liability to those injured.")

The Supreme Court reversed the lower courts in *Perma Life Mufflers, Inc.* v. *Internat'l Parts Corp.,* 392 U.S. 134 (1968). In an opinion by Justice Black. the Court asserted that the law encourages plaintiff's suit even if his action is as reprehensible as defendant's and ruled that "in pari delicto" should not be recognized as a defense to an antitrust action. The Court did not decide whether "truly complete involvement and participation in a monopolistic scheme could ever be a basis, wholly apart from the idea of pari delicto, for barring a plaintiff's cause of action." The facts of the *Perma Life* case made it unnecessary to go that far. The damage claimants were retail dealers operating "Midas Muffler Shops" under franchise agreements obligating each dealer to purchase all his exhaust-system parts from the franchisor, to carry a complete line of the franchisor's products, and to resell Midas at prices and locations specified by the franchisor. In return the franchised dealer received permission to use registered trademarks and service marks and was granted an exclusive right to sell "Midas" products within his defined territory. In these circumstances, the Court asserted, there could not have been complete involvement by the dealers in the illegal restraints of trade created by the exclusive-dealing and full-line requirements. for neither of those provisions could be in a dealer's self-interest. There was evidence that the dealers tried to get out from under these two restrictions. It made no difference that the complaining dealers sought their franchises enthusiastically; they did not actively seek each and every clause of the agreement. They accepted many of the restraints "solely because their acquiescence was necessary to obtain an otherwise attractive business opportunity." The courts were said to have no power "to undermine the antitrust acts by denying recovery to injured parties merely because they have participated to the extent of utilizing illegal arrangements formulated and carried out by others." Nor was it regarded as significant that the territorial restrictions benefited the complaining dealers. "They cannot be blamed for seeking to minimize the disadvantages of the agreement once they had been forced to accept its more onerous terms as a condition of doing business." These "possible beneficial by-products," on the other hand, "can of course be taken into consideration in computing damages."

Justice White joined in the majority opinion, rejecting "the in pari delicto defense in its historic formulation" but filing a concurring opinion. "I would deny recovery where plaintiff and defendant bear substantially equal responsibility . . . but permit recovery in favor of the one least responsible where one is more responsible than the other." He saw the issue before the Court as being a causation problem, maintaining that a damage claimant equally responsible with the defendant for the antitrust violation should be denied recovery "for failure of proof that [defendant] was the more substantial cause of the injury."

Justice Fortas concurred only in the result. He agreed that "private attorneys general" "cannot be denied [recovery] on the basis of the doctrine of in pari delicto." Yet he insisted that the doctrine does have "a significant if limited role in private antitrust law. If the fault of the parties is reasonably within the same scale—if the 'delicto' is approximately 'pari'—then the doctrine should bar recovery."

Justice Marshall, too, concurred only in the result. His reasons for refusing to join the majority opinion "are, perhaps, less related to the public interest in eliminating all forms of anticompetitive business conduct and more related to the equities as between the parties." He would look not only for substantial equality of fault but also for active participation by the complaining party in the formation and implementation of the illegal scheme. He would deny recovery to the claimants who "actually participated in the formulation of the entire agreement, trading off anticompetitive restraints on their own freedom of action (such as the tying and exclusive dealing provisions) for anticompetitive restraints intended for their benefit (such as resale price maintenance or exclusive territories)."

Justices Harlan and Stewart concurred in part and dissented in part. They held out for application of "the true in pari delicto standard." "Plaintiffs who are truly in pari delicto are those who have themselves violated the law in cooperation with the defendant." They saw the *Kiefer-Stewart* decision (that a supplier sued for resale price maintenance cannot defend by proving the complaining buyer's participation in a horizontal price-fixing conspiracy) as different from true in pari delicto because there the defendants' illegal actions were taken in reprisal against altogether independent illegal actions by the plaintiff. They would deal with large supplier-small customer situations like those involved in the *Simpson* case, *Albrecht* v. *Herald Co.*, 390 U.S. 145 (1968), and possibly the

Perma Life case "on the theory of a 'coercion' exception to the in pari delicto doctrine."

There are at least three indications in the *Perma Life* decision that an "in pari delicto" doctrine will continue to function in private antitrust litigation. First, Justice Black excluded the in pari delicto doctrine only as it was defined and applied at common law, "with its complex scope, contents, and effects." Like the passing-on defense, in pari delicto, as traditionally used, has ramifications that would frustrate antitrust policy. If the plaintiff "aggressively support[ed] and further[ed] the monopolistic scheme as a necessary part and parcel of it," even Justice Black would have denied him damages. Second, after disqualifying any plaintiff who "aggressively support[ed] and further[ed] the monopolistic scheme," the majority opinion clears one who merely engages in "understandable attempts to make the best of a bad situation." Between these two degrees of participation by the plaintiff there are conceivable levels of involvement on which the Supreme Court majority has not spoken. For plaintiffs in those categories, the best guidelines available are those set out, in somewhat different terms, by Justice White, who would disqualify the "equally responsible" plaintiff; Justice Fortas, who would apply the "in pari delicto" label to "equality of position"; and Justice Marshall, who would find the plaintiff "substantially equally at fault" to be in pari delicto. Indeed, since Justice White joined in the majority opinion, his "equally responsible" test must be regarded as consistent with the majority view.

Third, seven of the justices agreed the facts of the case before them clearly established that the franchisees were not real "collaborators" or "co-adventurers" (Justice Fortas' terms) in the exclusive-dealing requirements they were complaining about. If the case had involved "collaborators" or "co-adventurers" who were "equally responsible" with the defendant for the illegal conduct, at least five justices would probably have found the "collaborators" in pari delicto and have denied them damages.

Some suggest that the most persuasive criteria in "pari delicto" or "equal fault" cases will be the relative size of the parties. Franchisees are merely one example of the type of damage claimant who, because dwarfed individually in size by the defendant he sues, may be able to avoid a finding of "equal responsibility" for restrictions inserted in a contract. On those less frequent occasions when the defendant is overmatched in size by the plaintiff, it is said, it will be correspondingly easier to prove "equal responsibility" or "in pari delicto," if that term should continue in use, as at least four justices in the *Perma Life* case apparently would prefer. It is also important to remember, though, that *Perma Life* is a franchise case.

In a franchising context, the problem of relative degree of fault or responsibility becomes immediately pertinent, not as a matter of post-contract conduct, but more as a matter of the way in which the contract relationship is established in the first place. In most instances, establishment of the franchise relationship involves promises by the franchisor that are anticompetitively beneficial to the franchisee and are given in exchange for covenants by the franchisee to confer benefits upon the franchisor. While the small reseller will often have similar post-contract claims against a large manufacturer, the frequency of claims such as those asserted by *Perma Life* will probably be greatest in the franchise setting.

The *Perma Life* decision was one of a number during the 1960's which indicated a continuing lively interest of the Court in the effectiveness of private damage actions as an antitrust enforcement tool. Other examples were: *Leh* v. *General Petroleum Corp.*, 382 U.S. 54 (1965); *Minn. Mining and Mfg. Co.* v. *N.J. Wood Finishing Co.*, 381 U.S. 311 (1965); *Continental Ore Co.* v. *Union Carbide & Carbon Corp.*, 370 U.S. 690 (1962); *Poller* v. *CBS*, 368 U.S. 464 (1962); *Radiant Burners, Inc.* v. *Peoples Gas Light & Coke Co.*, 364 U.S. 656 (1961).

(b) The "Passing-On" Defense

Question: *Can the antitrust violator defend with evidence that the damage claimant passed along to his customers any higher costs resulting from defendant's violation?*

One who is able to add cost increases to his selling price without losing sales, it may be argued, has not lost anything and, hence, has not been "injured in his business or property." If he can follow the common practice of setting his price at a fixed percentage above cost, without losing sales, a cost increase will boost his margin and he may actually come out ahead. But the increase may cause him to lose sales. If he sues for loss of that business, however, he is not relying on the overcharge or increased-costs theory of damages.

The Supreme Court dealt with the passing-on issue in an antitrust case in *Keogh* v. *Chicago & Northwestern Ry.*, 206 U.S. 156 (1922). A manufacturer who had charged a railroad with conspiring to fix freight rates in violation of the Sherman Act was held to be alleging damages that "are purely speculative." The Court reasoned that the allegedly excessive freight rates "may not have injured Keogh at all," since his competitors presumably had to pay the same freight rate. "Under these circumstances no court or jury could say that, if the rate had been lower, Keogh would have enjoyed the difference between the rates or that any other advantage would have accrued to him. The benefit might have gone to his customers, or conceivably, to the ultimate consumer."

Earlier, in *Southern Pacific Co.* v. *Darnell-Taenzer Co.,* 245 U.S. 531 (1918), the Court rejected a passing-on defense in a suit to enforce a reparation award made by the Interstate Commerce Commission. That decision was specifically distinguished by the Supreme Court in the *Keogh* case. An antitrust treble-damage action, the *Keogh* opinion declared, "is not like those cases where a shipper recovers from the carrier the amount by which its exaction exceeds the legal rate."

In another antitrust case the Supreme Court, while not dealing with the passing-on defense, used language suggesting that the total amount of overcharge is an appropriate measure of damages. In a suit based on the Robinson-Patman Act, "if petitioner can show price discrimination, . . . it would establish its right to recover three times the discriminatory difference without proving more than the illegality of the prices. If the prices are illegally discriminatory, petitioner has been damaged, in the absence of extraordinary circumstances, at least in the amount of that discrimination" (*Bruce's Juices* v. *American Can Co.,* 330 U.S. 743 (1947)). The court did not discuss the significance of the deletion from the Robinson-Patman Act of language in the original bill that would have designated as the "presumed" measure of damages "the pecuniary amount or equivalent of the prohibited discrimination."

Most court of appeals decisions on price-discrimination damages have denied damages in the amount of the prohibited discrimination without proof that the discriminatorily higher price has not been passed on to the consumer. The Eighth Circuit first allowed recovery of the pecuniary amount of the discrimination in *Elizabeth Arden Sales Corp.* v. *Gus Blass Co.,* 150 F.2d 988 (8th Cir. 1945), but apparently changed its rule later in *American Can Co.* v. *Russellville Canning Co.,* 191 F.2d 38 (8th Cir. 1951). The Second Circuit has twice held that the discrimination is not a proper measure of the plaintiff's loss (*Sun Cosmetic Shoppe* v. *Elizabeth Arden Sales Corp.,* 178 F.2d 150 (2d Cir. 1949); *Enterprise Industries* v. *Texas Co.,* 240 F.2d 457 (2d Cir. 1957)). During the 1940's in the "oil jobber cases," jobbers suing for Section 1 Sherman Act violations were denied recovery of overcharges that were passed along to their customers (*Clark Oil Co.* v. *Phillips Petroleum Co.,* 148 F.2d 580 (8th Cir. 1945); *Northwestern Oil Co.* v. *Socony-Vacuum Oil Co.,* 138 F.2d 967 (7th Cir. 1943); *Twin Ports Oil Co.* v. *Pure Oil Co.,* 119 F.2d 747 (8th Cir. 1941)). In the *Clark* case, the jobber's margin was guaranteed by his supplier. In the *Twin Ports* and *Northwestern* cases, it was held that the plaintiff had the burden of showing that the increase in the price he had to pay was not passed on to his customers. In the absence of such proof, it was inferred that the increase was passed along. Similar results were reached in *Miller Motors, Inc.* v. *Ford Motor Co.*, 252 F.2d 441 (4th Cir. 1958), and *Wolfe* v. *Nat'l. Lead Co.*, 225 F.2d 427 (9th Cir. 1955). In *Hanover Shoe, Inc.* v. *United Shoe Machinery Corp.*, 185 F. Supp. 826 (M.D. Pa. 1960), *aff'd,* 281 F.2d 481 (3rd Cir. 1960), the district court rejected a motion to dismiss based on evidence that the complaining shoe manufacturer had passed on the excessive machinery costs to its customers. The district court declared that "the plaintiff's injury occurred when he was charged too much for the machinery," citing the Supreme Court's decision in *Southern Pacific Co.* v. *Darnell-Taenzer Lumber Co.* The *Hanover* decision was affirmed by the Court of Appeals for the Third Circuit on the opinion of the district court.

Later, in *Freedman* v. *Phila. Terminals Auction Co.*, 301 F.2d 830 (3rd Cir. 1962), the Third Circuit backed off somewhat from its rule in the *Hanover* case. Fruit brokers were denied recovery of excess auction-market charges that had been passed on to customers. The *Hanover* case was distinguished on the theory that it was based on findings that the shoe manufacturer was a consumer and not a middleman. Implicit in that finding in the *Hanover* case, the court stated, is the "doctrine enunciated in earlier cases that middlemen cannot recover damages when they suffered no injury by reason of their payment of proscribed charges."

The issue came up in the *Electrical-Equipment* cases. In *Commonwealth Edison Co.* v. *Allis-Chalmers Mfg. Co.*, 335 F.2d 203 (7th Cir. 1964), the court applied the rule of the *Darnell-Taenzer* case that "the general tendency of the law, in regard to damages . . . is not to go beyond the first step." Therefore, it decided that "the pass-on doctrine as enunciated in the oil jobber cases . . . should be given limited application and is the exception rather than the rule." The court rejected the idea "that the applicability of the defense should . . . depend entirely on whether plaintiffs are classified as middlemen or consumers." The oil jobber cases were distinguished on the theory that the jobbers' service-station customers "or at least the ultimate consumers" had independent rights to recover damages under the antitrust laws. In the *Electrical-Equipment* cases, on the other hand, "the possibility of plaintiffs' present and future customers recovering against defendants are nonexistent." The court had already denied the State of Illinois leave to intervene on behalf of consumers.

An even stronger opinion against the passing-on defense was released in *Atlantic City Electric Co.* v. *General Electric Co.*, 226 F. Supp. 59 (S.D.N.Y. 1964), *interlocutory appeal denied,* 337 F.2d 844 (2nd Cir. 1964). The issue was stated as "whether plaintiff may use increased costs as a separate and distinct measure of damages without regard to gain or loss of revenue." After listing the three normal theories of recovery (loss of profits, increased costs, and decrease in value of investment), the court insisted that "no two categories of injury are necessarily mutually exclusive" and reasoned that "as a practical matter, recognition of the passing-on doctrine is tantamount to a repudiation of the 'increased costs' measure of damages and a limitation on the extent of recovery primarily to lost profits." For that court, "the most significant consideration is the strong policy in favor of private treble-damage actions, which are intended not only to compensate those injured by violations of the antitrust laws, but also to function as an independent method of enforcing antitrust policy."

In a sense, it was the passing-on theory that was the basis of recovery in *Armco Steel Corp.* v. *North Dakota*, 376 F.2d 206 (8th Cir. 1967). In a suit charging construction-steel suppliers with a price-fixing conspiracy, the court allowed the State of North Dakota to recover the amounts by which construction contractors increased their bids to cover the conspiratorial price increase. It made no difference that some of the contractors might actually have paid less for the steel once it was delivered than the price quotations on which they based the bids submitted to state highway authorities. In *Washington* v. *American Pipe & Constr. Co.*, 274 F.Supp. 961 (D. Hawaii 1967), the district court accorded states standing to sue for overcharges on pipe bought by general contractors for installation in public projects. A suggestion that an injury to "end-users" is too remote to support recovery was rejected.

When the *Hanover Shoe* case reached the Supreme Court (392 U.S. 481 (1968)), an 8–1 Supreme Court majority declared the passing-on defense inoperative in almost all buyer-supplier situations. "If in the face of the overcharge the buyer does nothing and absorbs the loss, he is entitled to treble damages. This much seems conceded. The reason is that he has paid more than he should and his property has been illegally diminished, for had the price paid been lower his profits would have been higher. It is also clear that if the buyer, responding to the illegal price, maintains his own price but takes steps to increase his volume or to decrease other costs, his right to damages is not destroyed. Though he may manage to maintain his profit level, he would have made more if his purchases from the defendant had cost him less. We hold that the buyer is equally entitled to damages if he raises the price for his own product. As long as the seller continues to charge the illegal price, he takes from the buyer more than the law allows. At whatever price the buyer sells, the price he pays the seller remains illegally high, and his profits would be greater were his costs lower."

The Supreme Court was "not impressed by" a suggestion that sometimes it is the illegal overcharge that makes it possible for the buyer to increase the price he charges his customers, for example, when the overcharge is imposed equally on all the buyer's competitors and the demand for the buyer's product is so inelastic that the buyer and his competitors are all able to increase their prices by the amount of their cost increase without suffering a sales decline. "A wide range of factors influence a company's pricing policies," the Court observed, and "normally the impact of a single change in the relevant conditions cannot be measured after the fact." It is difficult to determine what effect a change in price will have on total sales and how costs will be affected by a change in sales volume. Even if total sales and unit costs remain unaffected by a buyer price increase matching his supplier's overcharge, there still remains "the nearly insuperable difficulty of demonstrating that the particular plaintiff could not or would not have raised his prices absent the overcharge or maintained the higher price had the overcharge been discontinued."

The Court expressed fear that injection of the passing-on issue into treble-damage litigation would mean that damage actions "would be substantially reduced in effectiveness." Although the task of showing that the particular plaintiff could not or would not have raised his prices in the absence of the overcharge "would normally prove insurmountable," the Court thought it "not unlikely that if the existence of the defense is generally confirmed, antitrust defendants will frequently seek to establish its applicability." As a result, "treble damage actions would often require additional long and complicated proceedings involving massive evidence and complicated theories," and the damage claim would pass along to ultimate consumers with "only a tiny stake in a lawsuit and little interest in attempting a class action."

The Court asserted that it was following the rule in *Chattanooga Foundry & Pipe Works* v. *Atlanta,* 203 U.S. 390 (1906), and *Southern Pacific Co.* v. *Darnell-Taenzer Lumber Co.,* 245 U.S. 531 (1918). The contrary rule in *Keogh* v. *Chicago & N.W. Ry.,* 260 U.S. 156 (1922), was said to be a dictum after the Court had already determined that ICC approval of the alleged conspirators' rates gave those rates immunity from antitrust attack. "We ascribe no general significance to the Keogh dictum for cases where the plaintiff is free to prove that he has been charged an illegally high price."

Justice White's majority opinion did acknowledge that there might be situations where the passing-on defense could succeed, "for instance when an overcharged buyer has a pre-existing 'cost plus' contract, thus making it easy to prove that he has not been damaged—where the considerations requiring that the passing-on defense not be permitted in this case would not be present. We also recognize that where no differential can be proved between the price unlawfully charged and some price that the seller was required by law to charge, establishing damages might require a showing of loss of profits to the buyer. (Some courts appear to have treated price discrimination cases under the Robinson-Patman Act in this category. See, e.g., *American Can Co.* v. *Russellville Canning Co.,* 191 F.2d 38 (8th Cir. 1951); *American Can Co.* v. *Bruce's Juices,* 187 F.2d 919 (5th Cir. 1951), *opinion modified,* 190 F.2d 73 (5th Cir. 1951), *cert. dismissed,* 342 U.S. 875 (1951))."

An important factor in the *Hanover Shoe* opinion was the Court's outspoken desire to avoid any impairment of the effectiveness of treble-damage actions as an antitrust enforcement tool. The Court's emphasis of this element left open the possibility that it may not regard the amount of an illegal overcharge as the exclusive measure of the buyer's lost profits. Conceivably, the buyer could show that the actual economic effects of increased prices went beyond the amount of the overcharge. He might prove, as examples, added carrying charges involved in financing a more expensive inventory, loss of profits on further sales he would have made if he had not had to raise his own prices, or increased selling costs incurred in attempting to prevent a drop in sales. Yet Justice White said that in most commercial contexts the seller cannot reduce recovery below the amount of the overcharge, whether by proof of passing-on, cost reduction, or increased sales volume. It makes no difference what happens to the buyer's profit level. Through his overcharge, the seller took "more than the law allows," and the buyer is entitled to full reimbursement plus the full benefit of any measures he took to mitigate his damage. Since he had a right to, and might have, taken those mitigating steps even in the absence of the alleged overcharge, the gains he realized from them are not related to, and hence do not reduce his damage from, the antitrust violation.

Neither of the Court's two types of exceptional situations that might allow application of the passing-on defense creates a very broad exception. The Court itself recognized there would not be many instances when it is "easy to prove that [the buyer] has not been damaged"; earlier it had called that burden of proof "normally . . . insurmountable." Situations "where differential can be proved between the price lawfully charged and some price that the seller was required by law to charge" are rare by definition.

Is there any set of facts that will fit the definition except the price-discrimination example mentioned by the Court? The complaining buyer in a Robinson-Patman Act case is the one who paid the higher of the two discriminatory prices. He complains that one of his competitors was given a discount that enabled his competitor.

to lure away some customers with price cuts. The antitrust violation here does not involve the seller's taking from the complaining buyer "more than the law allows." There is no overcharge. Dozens of other buyers might have been charged the higher price and yet have no right of action for damages; they may not have had to compete with the favored buyer. Rather, what the seller did was to take less from the favored buyer than the law required him to take. Yet this benefit to his competitor can in no sense be regarded as a measure of the damage suffered by the buyer who brought suit. The damage he is ordinarily complaining about is loss of profits on sales he would have made if his competitor had not been given an unfair price advantage, so he must prove that he lost sales and profits. This analysis may not be reconcilable with the dictum in *Bruce's Juices, Inc.* v. *American Can Co.*, 330 U.S. 743, 757 (1947), that "If the prices are illegally discriminatory [plaintiff] has been damaged, in the absence of extraordinary circumstances, at least in the amount of that discrimination." Similarly, it may not be reconcilable with the dictum in *Fowler Manufacturing Co.* v. *Gorlick*, 415 F.2d 1248 (9th Cir. 1969), *cert. denied*, 396 U.S. 1012 (1969).

Aside from the problem of measuring damages, evidence that a price differential was passed along to the complaining buyer's customers may have a significant role in treble-damage suits based on the Robinson-Patman Act. In a price-discrimination case, proof of passing-on is relevant to an issue other than damages. The defendant seller can rebut proof of competitive injury with evidence that the buyer was able to pass along the price differential to his customer without suffering a loss of profits, even if introduction of this evidence will cause "additional long and complicated proceedings." Once the passing-on evidence is introduced, there would appear to be no reason for not considering it in determining damages. There is authority requiring a buyer to show that he mitigated his damages by lowering his own resale prices or developing his own promotions before claiming injury to himself (*Sun Cosmetic Shoppe, Inc.*, v. *Elizabeth Arden Sales Corp.*, 178 F.2d 150 (2d Cir. 1949); *Enterprise Industries* v. *Texas Co.*, 240 F.2d 457 (2d Cir. 1957)). In the *Enterprise Industries* case, the court refused to give literal effect to the dictum from the *Bruce's Juices* opinion, pointing out that a provision making the price differential the measure of damages was eliminated in conference from the Senate bill that became the Robinson-Patman Act.

How may the Supreme Court's reasoning in *Hanover Shoe* affect recovery in a series of treble-damage suits by successive buyers? If Hanover Shoe, a shoe manufacturer, recovers the full amount of excessive rentals for shoe machinery supplied by United Shoe Machinery Co., can Hanover's wholesale and retail customers sue

United Shoe for the amounts by which their costs were increased when Hanover passed on the machinery costs? If it is a "normally . . . insurmountable" task to trace an illegal overcharge as the cause of a corresponding price increase by the buyer, then a subsequent buyer may have a "normally . . . insurmountable" burden in attempting to prove that the original overcharge, and hence the antitrust violation, was the proximate cause of his cost increase. This time the "additional long and complicated proceedings involving massive evidence and complicated theories" would be introduced at the election of the damage claimant and would be action in furtherance of the damage suit, not something that would substantially reduce the effectiveness of treble-damage actions.

The City of Philadelphia sued plumbing fixture manufacturers for treble damages arising from overcharges plaintiff allegedly paid as a result of defendants' price-fixing conspiracy. The district court granted defendants' motion for summary judgment on the grounds that plaintiff was too remote in the chain of distribution to recover (*Phila. Housing Authority* v. *American Radiator and Standard Sanitary Corp.*, 1971 Trade Cas. ¶73,410 (E.D. Pa. 1970)). The court held that plaintiff would be unable to prove injury to its business or property since the necessary figures were unascertainable. Successive actions of this nature are subject to objections against "double recovery," although as tort actions, not litigation over title to a specific fund or res, one could argue that they do not call for "double recovery." It is difficult, however, to see how the first buyer could recover the overcharge on the ground that it cannot be traced to his own price increase and then the second buyer recover it as traceable to the same price increase. If multiple claims of this sort come before different juries, all plaintiffs could conceivably win.

(c) The Statute of Limitations and Its Tolling

(1) Question: *Must allegations in a treble-damage complaint duplicate those made in government litigation if the government action is to be relied upon to toll the statute of limitations?*

Section 4B of the Clayton Act provides a four-year statute of limitations. Private antitrust actions are "forever barred unless commenced within four years after the cause of action accrued." Under Section 5(b) of the Clayton Act, "whenever any civil or criminal proceeding is instituted by the United States to prevent, restrain, or punish violations of any of the antitrust laws, . . . the running of the statute of limitations in respect of every private right of action arising under said laws and based in whole or in part on any matter complained of in said proceeding shall be suspended during the pendency thereof and for one year thereafter."

Most federal courts have construed strictly the requirement that the private action must be "based in whole or in part on any matter complained of in" the government proceeding. Dealing most often with Section 1 Sherman Act conspiracy cases, the lower-court decisions generally require that the private treble-damage complaint set forth the same acts to accomplish the same conspiracy alleged in the government proceeding. "A greater similarity is needed than that the same conspiracies are alleged. The same means must be used to achieve the same objectives of the same conspiracies by the same defendants" (*Steiner* v. *Twentieth Century-Fox Film Corp.*, 232 F.2d 190 (9th Cir. 1956). But cf. *Union Carbide and Carbon Corp.* v. *Nisley*, 300 F.2d 561 (10th Cir. 1962)).

In the *Steiner* case, and later in *Leh* v. *General Petroleum Corp.*, 330 F.2d 288 (9th Cir. 1964), one court of appeals determined the scope of Section 5(b) of the Clayton Act by the principles of collateral estoppel applicable under Section 5(a). Subsection (a) provides for the use of government judgments as "prima facie evidence" in subsequent damage suits. (See section IX-A-5, p. 565.) This reasoning of the *Steiner* and *Leh* decisions was rejected by the Supreme Court in *Minn. Mining & Mfg. Co.* v. *N.J. Wood Finishing Co.*, 381 U.S. 311 (1965). In deciding that FTC proceedings under Section 7 of the Clayton Act extend the damage-suit time limit, the Supreme Court rejected an argument that a government proceeding suspends the running of the limitations period only when a final order in that proceeding would be admissible under Section 5(a).

Another question in the *Minnesota Minning* case was whether the FTC antimerger proceeding, having been held effective to suspend the running of limitations on the damage claimant's Section 7 Clayton Act claim, could be treated as having the same effect on claims asserted under Sections 1 and 2 of the Sherman Act. The treble-damage complaint against 3M was filed by a producer of electrical insulation materials. Section 1 and 2 counts alleged a conspiracy and a monopolization attempt whose purposes were: (1) control of an insulation-material distributor whose acquisition was the subject of the FTC complaint, (2) prevention of that company's distribution of the complaining producer's products, (3) assurance that the acquired distributor would buy its supplies from 3M's electrical-supplies subsidiary, and (4) tie-in sales of products handled by the distributor with other products of the 3M subsidiary.

A 5–2 Supreme Court majority held that these allegations were based "in part" on the FTC proceeding, which charged that this acquisition and one other placed in 3M's hands two of the three largest distributors of the products manufactured by its subsidiary,

that after the acquisitions the acquired distributors stopped buying
the products of several other manufacturers, and that the effects of
the acquisitions were "the actual and potential lessening of competition" and the foreclosure of other manufacturers from a substantial share of the market. The variation between the FTC complaint's allegation of conduct that "may" substantially lessen
competition, and the damage complaint's necessary allegation of
activity that has actually done so "is a distinction without a
difference," the Court declared. "The fact that [the damage
complaint] claims that the same conduct has a greater anticompetitive effect does not make the conduct challenged any less a matter
complained of in the government action."

In reviewing the Ninth Circuit's decision in *Leh* v. *General Petroleum Corp.,* 382 U.S. 54 (1965), the Supreme Court elaborated
further on the relationship that must exist between the treble-damage complaint and the government proceeding. Both pieces
of litigation involved allegations based on Sections 1 and 2 of the
Sherman Act. In the treble-damage suit, an independent gasoline
wholesaler charged seven West Coast oil companies with a conspiracy to eliminate independent jobbers and retailers. To extend the
limitations period applicable to his suit, the wholesaler relied on a
1950 civil injunction suit filed against the refiners in *U.S.* v. *Standard Oil of Calif.,* 1959 Trade Cas. ¶69,399 (S.D. Calif. 1959), which
also charged a conspiracy to eliminate independent marketers. Both
the complaining wholesaler and the Government charged the companies with fixing prices at wholesale and retail. According to the
Government's complaint, the refiners intended to eliminate independent operators by acquiring them, limiting the supply of crude
oil available to them, and inducing them to shut down their
refining facilities. The wholesaler asserted that the companies had
refused to sell to him and had prevented him from obtaining gasoline from other sources.

There were several differences between the allegations in the two
complaints. The damage complaint alleged a conspiracy beginning
in 1948 and continuing until the complaint was filed in 1954; the
Government alleged a conspiracy beginning in 1936 and running
until the filing of its complaint in 1950. The damage complaint
spoke of a Southern California conspiracy; the Government described a conspiracy covering the entire "Pacific States area." While
most of the defendants named were the same in both actions, two
of the eight defendants named by the Government were not named
in the damage complaint, and one of the companies named in the
damage suit was not involved in the Government's action. The
Supreme Court attached no significance to these differences. The
period of time covered by the damage-suit allegations naturally

corresponded to the period of time the damage claimants were in business. Also, said the Court, "the absence of complete identity of defendants may be explained on several grounds unrelated to the question whether the private claimant's suit is based on matters of which the government complained. In the interim between the filing of the two actions it may have become apparent that a company named by the government was in fact not a party to the antitrust violation alleged. Or the private plaintiff may prefer to limit his suit to the defendants named by the government whose activities contributed most directly to the injury of which he complains. On the other hand, some of the conspirators whose activities injured the private claimant may have been too low in the conspiracy to be selected as named defendants or co-conspirators in the government's necessarily broader net. . . . To require more detailed duplication of claims would be to resurrect the collateral estoppel approach declared in Steiner and rejected by this court in Minnesota Mining."

The Supreme Court brushed off a contention that during discovery proceedings the damage claimant had made certain concessions establishing that his claim was not based at all on any matter complained of by the Government. "In general, consideration of the applicability of Section 5(b) must be limited to a comparison of the two complaints on their face. Obviously suspension of the statute of limitations pending resolution of the government action may not be made to turn on whether the United States is successful in proving the allegations of its complaint. . . . Equally, the availability of Section 5(b) to the private claimant may not be made dependent on his ability to prove his case, however fatal failure may prove to his hope of success on the merits."

For some antitrust lawyers, the key to both the *Leh* and the *3M* cases is a statement that appears in both: "Congress has expressed its belief that private antitrust litigation is one of the surest weapons for effective enforcement of the antitrust laws." Both decisions must be read in the light of the Court's determination to make sure the law on treble-damage suits facilitates enforcement of the antitrust laws. The *Leh* decision added two significant principles to the law of antitrust treble-damage litigation. (1) The allegations of the complaint are the sole basis for determining whether the damage claim bears sufficient relationship to the government action to activate the tolling provision in Section 5(b) of the Clayton Act. (2) Once activated, the tolling provision is effective against co-conspirators not named as either defendants or co-conspirators in the government action. Under the first doctrine, any damage complaint reciting the allegations of the earlier government complaint or indictment forestalls application of the statute of limitations. Lawyers representing treble-damage claimants often phrase their complaints in the same language the Government used. For that reason, the Court's discussion of similarities in, and differences between, the scope and purposes of the conspiracies alleged seems to be relatively insignificant. The Court's application of the tolling provision to damage-suit defendants who are not named in the Government's complaint suggests the existence of an interesting problem when the government litigation is terminated earlier for some defendants than for others. Does the suspension of the running of the limitations period continue for all defendants until the litigation is completed for all of them or does the early execution of a consent decree entitle a defendant to an earlier cut-off date on damage claims? Unless a co-conspirator named in the government action is to get more favorable treatment than one who is not named, which does not seem logical, the tolling of the statute would seem to continue until the last defendant is disposed of in the government litigation.

(2) Question: *Must defendant in a private action have been named as a defendant in the prior government action for tolling to be effective?*

The *Morton Salt* case involved a series of Section 5(b) issues relating to multiplicity of defendants in both government and related private litigation. The Morton, Diamond Crystal, International, and Carey salt companies were indicted by a Minnesota federal grand jury for conspiring to fix the price of rock salt. Before the trial began, the Minnesota Federal District Court accepted from Carey a plea of nolo contendere. The remaining three defendants were tried and found not guilty. In the meantime, the Government had also filed a civil suit, which was stayed during the trial of the criminal case, but resulted in a judgment against the defendants Morton and Diamond (*U.S.* v. *Morton Salt Co. and Diamond Crystal Salt Co.,* 1964 Trade Cas. ¶71,304 (D. Minn. 1964)). Carey entered into a consent decree in the civil action the same day it pleaded nolo to the criminal charge (*U.S.* v. *Morton Salt Co.,* 1962 Trade Cas. ¶70,276 (D. Minn. 1962)), and International consented to a similar consent judgment (1963 Trade Cas. ¶70,907 (D. Minn. 1963)). The judgment against Morton and Diamond Crystal was affirmed by the Supreme Court (*Morton Salt Co.* v. *U.S.,* 382 U.S. 44 (1965)).

The Government's civil complaint and the indictment named five other salt companies as co-conspirators but not as defendants. All nine of the companies were named as defendants in treble-damage suits filed late in 1964 and early in 1965 by the states of Illinois, Indiana, Iowa, Michigan, Minnesota, Missouri, and Wisconsin and some of their political subdivisions. In those damage actions the Minnesota Federal District Court held that the government suit was effective under Section 5(b) in postponing the deadline for filing damage actions against co-conspirators who were neither sued by the Government nor identified in the Government's complaint or indictment as co-conspirators; that the tolling period began when the indictment was handed down in the criminal case, not when the grand jury proceedings began; and that the tolling period created by the parallel criminal and civil proceedings did not end for any of the salt companies until conclusion of the civil case against the last remaining defendant, that is, until the Supreme Court's affirmance of the judgment against Morton and Diamond Crystal (*Mich.* v. *Morton Salt Co.,* 259 F.Supp. 35 (D. Minn. 1966), *aff'd sub nom. Hardy Salt Co.* v. *W.Va.* 377 F.2d 768 (8th Cir. 1967), *cert. denied,* 389 U.S. 912 (1967)).

The district judge could find no decision as to the effect of the tolling provision upon co-conspirators not mentioned by the Government, but he concluded that "the broad interpretation given Section 5(b)" by the Supreme Court in *Minn. Mining & Mfg. Co.* v. *N.J. Wood Finishing Co.,* 381 U.S. 311 (1965), and *Leh* v. *General Petroleum Corp.,* 382 U.S. 54 (1965), "suggests that the Supreme Court would hold that it tolls the statute on a cause of action asserted against a non-Government defendant" (259 F.Supp. at 54).

The states and their subdivisions had argued that the tolling period began upon initiation of grand jury proceedings by the Justice Department, but this contention was rejected. In finding the tolling provision effective against all the companies throughout the life of the government litigation, the district judge refused to follow a series of cases calculating the end of the suspension period on a defendant-by-defendant basis. In *Sun Theatre Corp.* v. *RKO Radio Pictures,* 213 F.2d 284 (7th Cir. 1954), the court of appeals could see no purpose in continuing to toll the statute of limitations once a final judgment or decree is entered with respect to one defendant. It viewed Section 5(b) as designed to protect Section 5(a)'s provisions on using government judgments as prima facie evidence in private actions.

According to the Minnesota district judge, this line of reasoning had been repudiated in the *Leh* and *3M* decisions. The *3M* opinion rejected a suggestion that the tolling provision has no further purpose once a judgment or decree is available, he observed, and pointed out "that the private litigant may receive invaluable aid from the pleadings, transcript, exhibits and documents in the government suit, apart from the prima facie effect, if any, of these materials" (259 F. Supp. at 48). Even when one defendant in a government lawsuit capitulates before the others, the judge said, "it is quite reasonable to assume that as the proceedings continue, that defendant will be referred to in subsequent testimony, documents and exhibits" (*id.*).

Another argument rejected in the *Morton Salt* case was that termination of the criminal prosecution ended the tolling period. Morton and Diamond Crystal argued that it was not proper under Section 5(b) to "tack together two government proceedings to prolong the suspension until the last action has been completed." The district judge found no case law on the point, so he followed the same reasoning here as he did in rejecting the defendant-by-defendant approach for ending the tolling period. One factor that may have influenced the district judge to give broad scope to Section 5(b) in the rock-salt case was the identity of the damage claimants, all of whom were governmental agencies. Also it is easier for the courts to be generous with the benefits of Section 5(b) than with the "prima facie evidence" benefits of Section 5(a).

The rock-salt decision may have been significant for its relationship to class actions. (See section IX-C, p. 626.) The rulings made by the district judge make it possible for all damage claimants to wait for the conclusion of government litigation and then sue all the co-conspirators at once, instead of filing separate earlier complaints against those conspirators who were not sued by the Government or were sued and settled early. Another effect of the decision may be to complicate record retention problems of some corporations. The district court's holding that the tolling provision is applicable even to defendants who were not named by the Government either as defendants or as co-conspirators means that a company in an industry hit by Sherman Act conspiracy litigation may have to retain its old files several years longer than usual despite the fact that it was not associated with the conspiracy in the Government's pleadings and that it believes itself innocent of any wrongdoing.

In *Leh* v. *General Petroleum Corp.,* 382 U.S. 54 (1965), the Supreme Court indicated that a comparison of the complaints in the government and private actions was the only significant criterion to use in evaluating whether the two proceedings were sufficiently related to activate the tolling provision and that substantial, rather than virtual, identity of parties and issues would suffice. This reasoning was extended in *Lippa's, Inc.* v. *Lenox, Inc.,* 305 F.Supp 182 (D. Vt. 1969). To determine whether a pending FTC action under Section 5 of the FTC Act tolled a related treble-damage action against Lenox, the court was required to determine whether the allegations of the private action were "based on any matter complained of" in the FTC proceeding. Recognizing that "the tolling statute does not require almost total identity of issues" between public and private suit, the district court noted that in *Leh* the tolling statute was invoked even though both the time period and the purpose of the conspiracies charged differed. The requirements of Section 5(b) are satisfied if, "treating the allegations as a whole, the complaints set up substantially the same claim." Since both complaints in the Lenox matters charged unlawful resale price maintenance, though only the treble-damage action mentioned specific prohibition by Lenox of "transshipping" by customers (selling to unauthorized retailers), the district court found a "substantial identity of claims." The court determined from the "realities of the situation" that the transshipping prohibition, although not specifically alleged in the FTC complaint, was an integral part of the price-maintenance scheme alleged in both complaints. The "thrust" of both complaints was deemed identical.

In *Russ Togs, Inc.* v. *Grinnell Corp.,* 304 F.Supp 279 (S.D.N.Y. 1969), *aff'd,* 426 F.2d 850 (2d Cir. 1970), *cert. denied,* 400 U.S. 878 (1970), a district court held for treble-damage claimants on the question of when the tolling period terminates. Defendant asserted that plaintiff's claims were barred by the statute of limitations. Plaintiff argued that a concurrent government injunction suit against Grinnell had tolled the statute. The Government's action had been upheld in the district court (236 F.Supp. 244 (D.R.I. 1964)), but the Supreme Court, while affirming the judgment, remanded the matter for further hearings on the nature of the relief (384 U.S. 563 (1966)). Grinnell argued in the treble-damage action that the tolling period terminated when the Supreme Court affirmed the judgment, regardless of the remand on the remedy question. Plaintiff maintained that the statute was tolled until a final decree by the district court was issued after subsequent hearings on the question of relief.

The district court rejected defendant's distinction between liability and relief, indicating that *3M* "requires us to re-examine the prior law," and held that the statute of limitations was tolled until the government action was fully terminated, including the final resolution of remedy. Noting that the Senate Report accompanying Section 5(b), as amended, extended the tolling effect "for the *duration* of the government's antitrust suit," the court made reference to the "Supreme Court's broad application of the policy of § 5(b)" in the *3M* case. The district court noted that should certain documents and testimony develop during the hearing on the relief question, these benefits, as outlined by the Supreme Court in *3M,* would be unavailable to treble-damage litigants unless the statute of limitations were tolled.

U.S. v. *Grinnell Corp.,* 305 F.Supp. 285 (S.D.N.Y. 1969), poses and answers the question of whether the Government, in its own civil damage actions, can make use of the tolling effect of a concurrent government enforcement suit against one or more of the same defendants. Under Section 5(b), the statute of limitations is tolled only "in respect of every private right of action arising under said laws." Defendants contended that only an action by a private party is eligible for the Section 5(b) tolling exemption; the Government urged that the phrase applies to action by any party where the cause of action is for "private injury." Refusing to extend the tolling privilege to government damage actions, the district court noted that persons of small means "must rely on the government's extensive resources for investigating antitrust violation," whereas "the government itself does not have this excuse for delay" in its own damage actions.

The court noted that Congress had amended Section 4 of the Clayton Act in 1955 in order to allow the Government to bring single damage suits, following a previous Supreme Court holding that the Government was not a "person" under Section 4 and could not sue for damages (*U.S.* v. *Cooper Corp.,* 312 U.S. 600 (1941)). Congress carried over to the new Section 5(b) the language of the original Section 5, which tolled the statute of limitations only "in respect of each and every private right of action." Since Congress in the 1955 amendment was concerned with the definition under Section 4 of the term "person," but left untouched the "private right" language of the original Section 5, the district court concluded that Congress intended that the tolling provision of Section 5(b) was not to apply to damage actions by the Government. The court acknowledged the emphasis in *3M* upon the benefits of government enforcement actions that should be available to treble-damage litigants but pointed out that in that case the Supreme Court noted that Congress enacted the tolling provision "to assist *private litigants* in utilizing any benefits they might cull from government antitrust actions" (Emphasis added).

In a suit brought by Hazeltine in 1959 for patent infringement, Zenith counter-claimed for treble damages for loss of business during the years 1959–1963 as a result of Hazeltine's conspiring with foreign patent pools. In the first of two decisions in this case *(Zenith Radio Corp.* v. *Hazeltine Research, Inc.,* 395 U.S. 100 (1969)), the Supreme Court sustained the trial court's finding that Zenith had been damaged in the Canadian market. Zenith proved damages by comparing its actual share of that market in the years 1959–1963 with what its share probably would have been absent the conspiracy, computing that probable share on the basis of its contemporaneous penetration of the domestic market.

In its second decision the Supreme Court dealt with two important issues left open earlier: (1) to the extent that the 1959–1963 damages were the result of conduct which took place before 1959, whether the recovery sought in the 1963 counterclaim was barred

by the four-year statute of limitations, and (2) whether recovery
was barred by a general release given by Zenith in another civil
action to certain of Hazeltine's co-conspirators *(Zenith Radio Corp.*
v. *Hazeltine Research, Inc.,* 401 U.S. 321 (1971)).

Hazeltine belatedly raised these defenses before the trial court.
The trial court rejected both defenses, but it was not clear whether
it did so on their merits or on the ground that they had been
waived. The court of appeals, upon remand after the first Supreme
Court decision, held that the trial court had not rejected them on
waiver grounds and that it had erroneously rejected them on their
merits. The Supreme Court, without any further remand, reversed
the court of appeals and held, without determining which of the
two grounds the trial court had relied upon, that the trial court's
decision was sustainable on either ground. After ruling that the trial
court could properly have held that the defenses had been waived,
the Court went on to reject each of the two defenses on their merits.

The Government had brought suit against companies participating in the patent pool but not against Hazeltine itself. This suit was
brought in 1958 and was terminated in 1962. Zenith counter-
claimed in 1963, within one year of the termination of the Government's suit. If the statute of limitations was tolled by the Government's suit, it was clear that Zenith was not barred from recovery
for damages resulting from activities taking place after 1954, i.e.
taking place within the four-year period preceding the initiation of
the Government's suit in 1958. The court of appeals concluded "that
tolling takes place only with respect to parties to a government suit
and hence that tolling did not occur here because [Hazeltine] was
not a party." The Supreme Court rejected this reasoning by broadly
construing the protection afforded to private plaintiffs by section
16(b): "The language of 15 U.S.C. Sec. 16(b) expressly provides for
tolling of the statute of limitations 'in respect of *every* private right
of action . . . based in whole or in part on any matter complained
of' in the proceeding instituted by the government. [Emphasis
added.] On the face of this section, a private party who brings suit
for a conspiracy against which the government had already brought
suit is undeniably basing its claim in whole or in part upon the
matter complained of in the government suit, even if the defendant
named in the private suit was named neither as a defendant nor as
a co-conspirator by the government. If, that is, the government sues
only certain conspirators, the fact of the tolling of the statute
against those so proved but not sued can hardly be denied. Nor
could tolling be denied if a defendant has never been shown to be
a conspirator by the evidence offered in the earlier government suit,
but then had been proved to be such in the subsequent private

suit." In reaching this result, the Court expressly overruled several lower court decisions, including *Sun Theatre Corp.* v. *RKO Radio Pictures, Inc.,* 213 F.2d 284, 290–292 (7th Cir. 1954), and *Momand* v. *Universal Film Exchanges, Inc.,* 172 F.2d 37, 48 (1st Cir. 1948).

Having determined that the statute was tolled and that Zenith was not barred from recovery at least for the post-1954 conduct, the Court went on to determine that Zenith likewise was not barred from recovery for pre-1954 conduct, holding that a cause of action for damages for loss of business in the years 1959–1963 did not accrue before 1954, since in 1954 the damages for the 1959–1963 period were too speculative to be proven: "In antitrust and treble damage actions, refusal to award future profits as too speculative is equivalent to holding that no cause of action has yet accrued for any but those damages already suffered. In these instances, the cause of action for future damages, if they ever occur, will accrue only on the date they are suffered; thereafter the plaintiff may sue to recover them at any time within four years from the date they were inflicted. Otherwise future damages which could not be proved within four years of the conduct from which they flowed would be forever incapable of recovery, contrary to the congressional purpose that private actions serve as a bulwark of antitrust enforcement and that the antitrust laws fully protect the victims of the forbidden practices as well as the public." The Court found that in 1954 Zenith would not have been able to prove damages for the 1959–1963 period and that the statute of limitations with respect to the 1959–1963 damages had not begun to run before 1954.

In 1957, Zenith, in settlement of a civil action against Hazeltine's co-conspirators, gave a release to those co-conspirators for all past and future damages resulting from their pre-1957 conduct. Hazeltine, which was not a party in that civil action, was not named in the release. The court of appeals held that since Zenith had failed to reserve expressly any rights against Hazeltine, that company was released along with the others. The Supreme Court rejected the rule that such rights had to be reserved expressly, and also rejected the ancient common-law rule that the release of one tortfeasor releases all the joint tortfeasors. It adopted instead the rule proposed in the tentative draft of the Second Restatement of Torts that "the effect of a release upon co-conspirators shall be determined in accordance with the intentions of the parties." The Court said that the rule adopted "is most consistent with the aims and purposes of the treble damage remedy under the antitrust laws." The rule applied by the court of appeals, it said, "would create a trap for unwary plaintiffs' attorneys."

The Court avoided determining whether the statute of limitations and the release of defendants had been waived by the defendant, though Justices Harlan and Stewart, in their concurring opinion, stated their view that the trial court had indeed rested its decision on the ground that the defenses had been waived. The Court decided the statute of limitations and the release issues on their merits. It may be, of course, that the Court was reluctant to base a multimillion dollar judgment on waiver grounds. However, in volunteering to confront the ticklish questions, the Burger-Blackmun court has, according to some observers, indicated a tough attitude toward antitrust violations. Justice White, speaking for the majority, underscored this in his reference to "the congressional purpose that private actions serve 'as a bulwark of antitrust enforcement' and that the antitrust laws fully 'protect the victims of the forbidden practices as well as the public' " (citing *Perma Life Mufflers, Inc.* v. *Internat'l Parts Corp.,* 392 U.S. 134, 139 (1968)).

(3) Question: *Do FTC proceedings suspend the running of the statute of limitations in related damage actions?*

A conflict between two courts of appeals was resolved by the Supreme Court's decision in *Minn. Mining & Mfg. Co.* v. *N.J. Wood Finishing Co.,* 381 U.S. 311 (1965), that the four-year limit on private treble-damage actions is tolled by Federal Trade Commission proceedings "to the same extent and in the same circumstances as it is by Justice Department actions." In *Highland Supply Corp.* v. *Reynolds Metals Co.,* 327 F.2d 725 (8th Cir. 1964), a court of appeals had decided that an FTC proceeding does not toll the damage-suit limitations period, concluding that the reference in the tolling provision in Section 5(b) of the Clayton Act to "any civil or criminal proceeding . . . instituted by the United States" means any *court* proceeding. The Supreme Court affirmed a holding to the contrary by the Court of Appeals for the Third Circuit (*N.J. Wood Finishing Co.* v. *Minn. Mining & Mfg. Co.,* 332 F.2d 346 (3rd Cir. 1964)). Writing for a 5–2 majority (Justices Harlan and Stewart did not participate), Justice Clark conceded that "the precise language of Section 5(b) does not clearly encompass Commission proceedings." He also found "little in the legislative history to suggest that Congress consciously intended to include Commission actions within the sweep of the tolling provision." Justice Clark argued from two elements in the legislative history of Section 5(b) that the literal wording of the statute should not be regarded as controlling. First, Congress gave no indication of its intent concerning Section 5(b)'s coverage of FTC proceedings. "It seems that Congress simply did not consider the extent of its coverage in the course of its deliberations." But there was a clearly stated desire expressed by Congress that private parties be permitted the benefits of prior government litigation. The Supreme Court made this clearly expressed congressional purpose the overriding consideration.

The Court refused to examine whether FTC proceedings also come within Section 5(a) of the Act, which makes "a final judgment or decree" obtained by the United States "in any civil or criminal proceeding" under the antitrust laws "prima facie evidence against such defendant" in a subsequent damage action. Noting the use in Section 5(a) of the terms "final judgment or decree," the Court did deny that the two subsections are necessarily coextensive. The opinion pointed out that Section 5(b) takes effect regardless of whether a final judgment or decree is ultimately entered. Moreover, under Section 5(a) the judgment may be used as "prima facie" evidence only in matters respecting which it would operate as an estoppel between the parties. No such limitation appears in Section 5(b), which applies to every private right of action based in whole or in part on "any matter" complained of in the government suit. In Section 5(b), the Court continued, Congress meant to assist private litigants in utilizing any benefits they might cull from government antitrust actions, not merely to give them full advantage of the estoppel doctrine mentioned in Section 5(a).

Justices Black and Goldberg, the dissenters, argued that both the language and the legislative history of the statute "clearly show that Congress did not intend the statute of limitations . . . to be tolled by the institution of the Federal Trade Commission administrative proceedings." Justice Black quoted statement after statement, by members of both Houses of Congress, in which the terms "jury," "court," "verdict," "judgment," "trial," and "day in court" were used in referring to the proceeding that would toll the statute of limitations. Other statements on the floor of Congress listed Federal Trade Commission proceedings as an additional method of enforcement after the speaker had already spoken of actions by "the government of the United States" in a "criminal court or a civil court" and of the private damage actions that could follow the court proceeding.

Lawyers active in private antitrust litigation anticipated from the Court's decision that the number of informal complaints filed with the FTC would be likely to increase; that the amount of damages in suits based on conduct whose illegality under the antitrust laws initially is not clear might be likely to be substantially increased; that the lengthening of the time period covered by the suit would also broaden the pretrial discovery process in the damage suit, by making documents and records covering a longer period of time subject to discovery; and that the pleadings, the transcript of testimony, exhibits, and documents used in the FTC proceeding would now be available for use by the private-suit plaintiff. Just as significant, in the view of many lawyers, was the opinion's strong support for private antitrust enforcement and what that support portended for related issues still undecided. Some lawyers thought that if Justice Black's impressive quotations from legislative history would not sway the majority on legislative intent, then the Court might even apply Section 5(a) to FTC orders when that question was presented. On this point, though, it must be remembered that Justice Clark's opinion expressly treated the two subsections as "governed by different considerations as well as congressional policy objectives."

Whatever the validity of all these conclusions about the tenor of the decision and its effect on treble-damage litigation related to FTC proceedings, there are some factors dealt with by the Supreme Court that may limit the impact of its decision. Even as applied by the Court, Section 5 of the Clayton Act is worded in such a way that some attorneys think the only FTC proceedings it can cover are Clayton Act cases (mergers, price discrimination, exclusive dealing, and interlocking directorates). The Commission has no authority, they note, to enforce any provisions of the Sherman Act except indirectly through application of Section 5 of the FTC Act. Section 5(b) of the Clayton Act suspends the statute of limitations only during the pendency of a government proceeding to stop or punish violations of "any of the antitrust laws," and the FTC Act is not one of the "antitrust laws." Other attorneys point out that a Section 5 complaint aimed at a Sherman Act violation (and in *FTC* v. *Cement Institute*, 333 U.S. 683 (1948), the Supreme Court said the Commission could see Section 5 that way) is in fact and in law a proceeding to stop a violation of the "antitrust laws."

In *Lippa's, Inc.* v. *Lenox, Inc.*, 305 F.Supp. 182 (D. Vt. 1969), Lenox moved for dismissal of plaintiff's treble-damage suit, arguing, in part, that the statue-of-limitations period had expired. Plaintiff asserted that the statutory period had been tolled by a pending FTC action for violation of Section 5 of the FTC Act. Defendant maintained that the Section 5(b) Clayton tolling provision did not apply to government actions based upon Section 5 of the FTC Act. Since FTC Act Section 5 was not an "antitrust law" for purposes of prima facie effect under Section 5(a) of the Clayton Act, it could not, Lenox argued, be considered a "proceeding . . . to prevent, restrain or punish violations of any of the antitrust laws" under the 5(b) tolling provision. The district court recognized that two decisions had held that actions under Section 5 of the FTC Act had no tolling effect (*Rader* v. *Balfour*, 1969 Trade Cas. ¶72,709 (N.D. Ill. 1968), *rev'd*, 440 F.2d 469 (7th Cir. 1971); *Laitram Corp.* v. *Deepsouth Packing Co.*, 279 F.Supp. 883 (E.D. La. 1968)), but the court

chose not to follow these decisions, relying on the policy directive
of the *3M* case to resolve ambiguities in the tolling statute in favor
of damage claimants. The court emphasized congressional intent to
provide treble-damage claimants with all possible fact-finding resources and legal expertise available to government antitrust agencies. The court reasoned that an action under Section 5 of the FTC
Act can be brought to restrain "in their incipiency practices which,
if allowed to continue, would grow into antitrust violations" (*FTC*
v. *Cement Institute,* 333 U.S. 683,708 (1948)). Section 5 can be
used to prevent potential, but as yet unfulfilled, violations of Sections 1 or 2 of the Sherman Act, which is an "antitrust law." The
court concluded that all FTC antitrust proceedings under Section 5
of the FTC Act are brought to restrain incipient violations of the
"antitrust laws," as in the case at bar, and are sufficient to toll
the statute of limitations.

B. THE ATTORNEY'S FEE

1. Question: *How is the attorney's fee in a treble-damage action
determined?*

Section 4 of the Clayton Act provides that a person injured
in his business or property by reason of a violation of the antitrust laws may sue therefor "and shall recover threefold the damages
by him sustained, and the cost of suit, including a reasonable
attorney's fee." Section 7 of the Sherman Act has a similar, but
seldom cited, provision, which uses the phrase "costs of suit,"
instead of "cost of suit." Black's Law Dictionary attributes to "cost"
the broad, general meaning of "expense" and defines only "costs"
as designating those items traditionally taxed to the unsuccessful
litigant and now listed, for the federal courts, in Sections 1920,
1921, and 1923 of the Federal Judicial Code (28 U.S.C.). Apparently Congress had nothing specific in mind when the "s" was
dropped in the Clayton Act, for House Report 627, 63rd Cong.,
2d Sess. (1914), said the new provision "is supplementary to the
existing law, and extends the remedy under Section 7 of the Sherman Act." The usual rule is that "the only costs recoverable by a
successful plaintiff in a private antitrust suit are those which are
normally allowable under 28 U.S.C. § 1920 and Rule 54 (d)"
(*Twentieth Century-Fox Film Corp.* v. *Goldwyn,* 328 F.2d 190, 222
(9th Cir. 1964)).
   The statement in *Twentieth Century-Fox* v. *Goldwyn* was challenged in *Advance Business Systems* v. *SCM Corp.,* 287 F.Supp.
153 (D. Md. 1968), by a plaintiff who sought to expand the usual
categories of taxable costs by stressing the Act's use of the phrase

"cost of suit." It was pointed out that "costs" is the word used in Rule 54 (d) of the Federal Rules of Civil Procedure. While the Maryland district court did not adopt plaintiff's argument, it did say: "In a private antitrust suit a court should not exercise . . . niggardly" its "broad discretionary powers in the allowance or disallowance of costs within the category set out in Section 1920" of the Judicial Code.

This concept that "cost" means the full expense of litigation has been rejected by the courts not only in awarding taxable "costs" but also in applying the Clayton Act's provision that "cost" is to be regarded as "including a reasonable attorney's fee." In setting the attorney-fee allowance, the courts make no attempt to reimburse a successful plaintiff for the fee he has contracted to pay his counsel. The plaintiff's fee agreement with his attorney is "wholly immaterial to the issue before the court" (*Milwaukee Towne Corp.* v. *Loew's, Inc.*, 190 F.2d 561, 570 (7th Cir. 1951); see also *Twentieth Century-Fox Film Corp.* v. *Brookside Theatre Corp.*, 194 F.2d 846, 859 (8th Cir. 1952)). Conversely, the fee allowance granted by the court does not limit the fee that plaintiff's attorney can charge his client under their contractual arrangements. In the *Milwaukee Towne* case, the fee allowance awarded by the court was substantially less than the fee plaintiff had contracted to pay, but nothing was said to relieve the plaintiff of his fee contract.

Another approach was taken in *American Federation of Tobacco Growers* v. *Allen*, 186 F.2d 590, 591–92 (4th Cir. 1951), in which the court used language indicating that it assumed the right to the "reasonable attorney's fee" referred to in the Clayton Act accrued to the attorney rather than to the plaintiff.

Fee arrangements between plaintiffs' attorneys and their clients generally assume that the allowance set by the court bears no relationship to the fee to be paid. Often the fee contract calls for inclusion of the attorney-fee allowance in the amount of damages and for payment to the attorney of a percentage of the total. Sometimes the plaintiff contracts to pay a percentage of damages plus the amount the court allows as "a reasonable attorney's fee."

One plaintiff's treble-damage lawyer has said that he doubts "that there is any basic difference in the financial arrangement between lawyer and client in this field and in any other field. The usual agreement, with variations, involves a retainer within a range of $5,000 to $25,000, a percentage arrangement on damage recovery, and some understanding on the attorney's fee which is ordered by the court to be paid by the defendant. All clients should be given the opportunity to take an arrangement which provides for a straight hourly rate in lieu of the contingency. Costs must always be paid by the client on regular monthly billings. The plaintiff who accepts an hourly rate should still pay the retainer since, more often than not, the plaintiff is accepting the benefits of a good deal of work already done in the same industry by the particular lawyer involved" (Alioto, "The Economics of a Treble Damage Case," 32 ABA ANTITRUST L. J. 87, 93 (1966)).

In *W. W. Montague & Co.* v *Lowry,* 193 U.S. 38 (1904), the Court sustained an allowance of $750 for a fee to an attorney who had recovered a judgment for trebled damages in the amount of $1,500, stating: "The amount of the attorney's fee was within the discretion of the trial court, reasonably exercised." The Court was dealing with the damage provision in Section 7 of the Sherman Act, but the "discretion of the trial court" theme has carried over into the many federal district court and court of appeals' opinions rationalizing attorney-fee allowances under the Clayton Act.

In *Bal Theatre Corp.* v. *Paramount Film Distributing Corp.,* 206 F.Supp. 708 (N.D. Calif. 1962), the district court listed four criteria to be followed in fixing an allowance for an attorney's fee: "1. The nature of the questions involved, their novelty and difficulty, and the skill and competence of counsel required to properly conduct the cause; 2. The customary charges of the bar for similar services; 3. The standing of counsel in the community; and 4. The amount recovered in the controversy and the beneficial result obtained by counsel." A longer list of "factors considered" was set out in *Hanover Shoe, Inc.* v. *United Shoe Machinery Corp.,* 245 F.Supp. 258 (M.D. Pa. 1965). Except for "time and labor spent," those factors seem to fall within the four general criteria listed in the *Bal Theatre* case.

In considering the difficulty of the questions involved, the courts have sometimes indicated that antitrust cases should be regarded as requiring greater "variety and rarity of skill" than other types of litigation. "It is doubtful whether any type of legal work requires a higher degree of professional competence and need of ability than the presentation to a jury of complicated economic questions" (*Cape Cod Food Products, Inc.* v. *National Cranberry Assn.,* 119 F.Supp. 242, 244 (D. Mass. 1954)). In *Milwaukee Towne Corp.* v. *Loew's, Inc.,* 190 F.2d 561 (7th Cir. 1951), however, the court declared that "the uniqueness which perhaps formerly attached to such a case has been largely dissipated."

The availability or nonavailability of a relevant government antitrust decree has been listed as an important fact bearing on the difficulty of the lawyer's task and hence on the size of a reasonable-fee allowance. In *Cape Cod Food Products* v. *National Cranberry Assn.,* 119 F.Supp. (at 244), the absence of a government decree and of concomitant investigatory assistance to the plaintiff was a factor stressed by the court when it pointed to the difficulties of presenting "complicated economic questions" to a jury. In *Twentieth*

Century-Fox Film Corp. v *Brookside Theatre Corp.*, 194 F.2d 846,
859 (8th Cir. 1952), the existence of a government decree serving
as prima facie evidence of an antitrust violation was given prominence as a consideration for reducing the fee allowance.

In looking at "the customary charges of the bar for similar
services," the courts tend to compare the size of fee allowances
with the amount of recovery in other cases. The ratios of recovery to
fee allowance vary greatly. A table of cases footnoted in the *Hanover Shoe* opinion contains a list of fee allowances ranging from less
than 8 percent to 33⅓ percent of the amount of treble damages
recovered. *Hanover Shoe,* having recovered over $4 million, was
allowed $650,000 for attorney's fees. The *Bal Theatre* opinion, after
examining a similar table taken from other cases, allowed $55,000
for fees to attorneys who had obtained a judgment of $438,900.
In *Courtesy Chevrolet, Inc.* v. *Tenn. Walking Horse Breeders,* 393
F.2d 75 (9th Cir. 1968), *cert. denied,* 393 U.S. 938 (1968), the court
ordered a fee allowance increased from $5,000 to $10,000, about
equal to the $10,200 recovered as treble damages.

Sometimes members of the bar are called to testify as to the
customary charges for the type and amount of services involved
in the damage suit. Such testimony has apparently not carried
much weight, however. Courtesy Chevrolet, for example, presented
testimony of "a highly respected and competent member of the
Los Angeles Bar" that a reasonable fee would be from $140,000
to $150,000. Yet the court of appeals increased the fee allowance
to only $10,000. In the *Milwaukee Towne* case, three Chicago
lawyers estimated a reasonable fee at $175,000-$250,000, so the
district judge set the fee allowance at $225,000. The court of appeals
cut it to $75,000. In *Darden* v. *Besser,* 147 F.Supp. 376 (E.D. Mich.
1956), there was a fee allowance of only $10,000 after a "highly
respected and competent member of the local bar" testified that
$72,000 would be reasonable. On appeal, 257 F.2d 285 (6th Cir.
1958), the allowance was increased to $30,000.

Mention is sometimes made of the hourly rate reflected in the
fee allowance. Hanover Shoe's allowance was described by the
Court as reflecting $74 per hour for partners and $37 for associates
in the nonresident law firm that had primary responsibility for the
litigation, and $50 per hour for the senior partner of a local firm
retained to satisfy the court's rule requiring local association. Even
when expressed in terms of hourly rates, the "customary" charge
is not easily ascertained. In *Bal Theatre,* the hourly rate averages
out to less than $24 and in the Century Chevrolet case the hourly
rate comes to an average of only about $4.37 per hour.

As for "the amount recovered," the courts are not in agreement
on how that factor in setting a fee allowance is to be defined. As
indicated by the above references to the *Hanover Shoe* and *Bal*

Theatre opinions, the district judges tend to measure fee allowance against trebled damages. The Massachusetts district court in the *Cape Cod Food* case specifically held that "ordinarily . . . reference is made to the total amount in issue between the parties, or to the total amount recovered by one of them." Yet in *Twentieth Century-Fox Film Corp.* v. *Brookside Theatre Corp.,* 194 F.2d 846, 859 (8th Cir. 1952), the court of appeals declared that single damages are "the only recovery that may be attributable to the services of counsel for plaintiff as it was through no effort of theirs that these damages were trebled" (Accord: *Milwaukee Towne Corp.* v. *Loew's. Inc.,* 190 F.2d at 571.) On at least one occasion, the large size of the damage award was given as a basis for reducing the attorney-fee allowance. "It should not be made more profitable than it is for a person to become the victim of a conspiracy in restraint of trade" (*Milwaukee Towne Corp.* v. *Loew's,* 190 F.2d at 570).

Seldom do the courts attempt to weigh the skill of counsel, referring rather to his "reputation" or "experience" *(Bal Theatre Corp.* v. *Paramount Film Distributing Corp.* 206 F.Supp. at 718). An exception is the impression a lawyer of less than seven years' experience made on the district court in the *Cape Cod Food Products* case. Such was counsel's "indefinable distinction which breathes excellence" that even the relatively little time he spent on the case was regarded as proof of "economy of counsel's methods" and hence of his "outstanding talent" (119 F.Supp. at 242, 244).

Additional commentary on the "reasonable fee" is provided by *TWA* v. *Hughes Tool Co.,* 312 F.Supp. 478 (S.D.N.Y. 1970), *aff'd,* 449 F.2d 51 (2nd Cir. 1971), *rev'd on other grounds,* 596 ATRR D-1 (1973). Plaintiff had successfully maintained a treble-damage action and was awarded over $137 million in damages. Plaintiff moved for counsel fees of $10.5 million and costs of $2.2 million. The district judge reviewed the factors for determining the fee set forth in the *Hanover Shoe* case, 245 F.Supp. 258, 302 (M.D. Pa. 1965). These were: (a) whether plaintiff had the prima facie benefit of a prior judgment; (b) standing at the bar of counsel for all parties; (c) time and labor spent; (d) magnitude and complexity of the litigation; (e) responsibility undertaken; (f) amount recovered; (g) court's actual knowledge of actual work done by the attorneys involved; (h) what it would be reasonable for counsel to charge a victorious plaintiff.

The district judge characterized the suit as one "of great magnitude and complexity" and as "bitterly contested." Monumental discovery was employed by both sides, including 80 days of deposition testimony and extensive maneuvering by Hughes to prevent the taking of his deposition. Twenty-one pretrial hearings were held. In a second phase of the litigation subsequent to a default judgment on the liability issue, 11,000 additional pages of testimony by a number of experts and witnesses were recorded before a special master on the issue of damages, and 800 exhibits were introduced in evidence. At the conclusion of this phase, the parties submitted 745 pages of briefs. In total, plaintiff's attorneys claimed an expenditure of 64,000 hours on the case. The court adjusted this figure to 58,600 hours (20,000 hours were partner's time).

The court rejected defense counsel's reliance upon the fact that a default judgment was involved, observing that several years of litigation preceded this judgment and that the damage issue was strenuously contested. The court recognized that counsel's time to obtain equitable (injunctive) relief against Hughes was not compensable under Section 4 of the Clayton Act, but noted that "the development of the facts was the same for both [damages and injunction] grounds of claimed relief." Such time for the injunction claim was "minimal" but "will be taken into account." The court disposed similarly of defendant's argument that plaintiff's attorneys' time devoted to defending the counterclaim could not be considered.

The court rejected as "unfair," in the light of counsel's success and the complexity of issues, defendant's argument that plaintiff's fee claim for 64,000 hours amounted to $164 per hour. Judge Metzner recognized that the local New York City average "mix" rate for partner-associate time is $75, but such a rate as well as a fee based on a percentage of recovery is inappropriate because it "ignores professional skill and the complexity of the work involved." The court awarded $7,500,000 as a "reasonable attorney's fee."

The court concluded its choice of key factors in this manner: "It seems to me that the major factors bearing on the fixing of attorney's fees in antitrust cases are the complexity of the problems presented, the skill of counsel, and the measure of success achieved by counsel. The other factors are subsidiary to these and may be helpful in evaluating them, but neither separately nor collectively do these other factors constitute the basis for fixing the fee. In measuring the success of counsel, only single damages should be considered, since that is the amount produced through the efforts of counsel. Trebling is a penalty imposed by law and automatically attaches to the damages found." The judge rejected plaintiff's claim for $2.2 million as "costs of suit".

One other case, *Phila. Elec. Co.* v. *Anaconda Am. Brass Co.,* 47 F.R.D. 557 (E.D. Pa. 1969), should be noted for its definition of the criteria to be used in setting a reasonable attorney's fee. The opinion dealt with a petition requesting that damage awards of 90 recalcitrant plaintiffs be impressed with liens for counsel fees and expenses. The court had to evaluate petitioner's claims for a

25-percent contingent fee based on the damages awarded, and the court awarded such fee, citing the following factors: (1) the ability and standing of counsel; (2) the favorable results achieved in the interest of class members; (3) the effect of counsel's efforts in preserving the rights of class members against possible defeat by the statute of limitations; (4) the treble-damage feature of antitrust recoveries that means counsel can be generously paid without actual cost to the claimants—i.e., the fees of counsel merely reduce a windfall; and (5) the percentage fee already agreed to by all of the claimants.

Other federal statutes provide for court allowances for attorneys' fees. A few of them, such as the Federal Tort Claims Act, 28 U.S.C. § 2678; Section 28 of the Longshoremen's and Harbor Workers Compensation Act, 33 U.S.C. § 928; and Section 206(b) (1) of the Social Security Act, 42 U.S.C. § 406 (b) (1), appear designed solely to prevent exorbitant fees for collecting federal statutory claims. These statutes generally set a maximum fee (25 percent of recovery under the Social Security Act and 10 percent under the Federal Tort Claims Act) and forbid the collection by the attorney of any amount in excess of that awarded by the court. Among those that, like Section 4 of the Clayton Act, merely authorize the recovery of a "reasonable attorney's fee," are the Packers and Stockyards Act, 7 U.S.C. § 210(f); the Copyright Law, 17 U.S.C. § 116; the Fair Labor Standards Act, 29 U.S.C. § 216(b); the 1934 Communications Act, 47 U.S.C. § 206; and the Interstate Commerce Act, 49 U.S.C. § 8. The fee determination under those statutes is left to the discretion of the federal district judge, and there is a similar lack of uniformity or consistency in the results.

One Fair Labor Standards Act opinion, *Hutchinson* v. *William C. Barry, Inc.,* 50 F.Supp. 292, 298 (D. Mass. 1943), declares: "The spirit of the law is that the plaintiff gets as part of his recovery, if he wins, his whole reasonable counsel fees, not some fraction of them." No such rule has been followed in antitrust cases. Indeed, at least two federal district judges have decided it is their function to determine the amount the defendant should be required to pay as a "contribution" toward the fee of plaintiff's counsel (*Webster Motor Car Co.* v. *Packard Motor Car Co.,* 166 F.Supp. 865, 866 (D. D.C. 1955); *Courtesy Chevrolet, Inc.,* v. *Tenn. Walking Horse Breeders, unreported opinion of a district court in California,* September 13, 1966, *reversed,* 393 F.2d 75 (9th Cir. 1968)).

In antitrust litigation, the right to recover "a reasonable attorney's fee" does not extend to a successful defendant (*Byram Concretanks, Inc.,* v. *Warren Concrete Products Co.,* 374 F.2d 649 (3rd Cir. 1967)). It has been held, too, that even a successful plaintiff must prove he has been damaged; he cannot recover an attorney's fee if he established only that he is entitled to injunctive relief against future injury (*Alden-Rochelle, Inc.,* v. *ASCAP,* 80 F.Supp. 888, 899 (S.D.N.Y. 1948)). When a plaintiff has proved that he has been injured in some amount but fails to prove the amount of damages with sufficient certainty to support the entry of a judgment for damages, the courts have divided over his right to an allowance for attorney's fees *(Alden-Rochell, Inc.* v. *ASCAP,* 80 F.Supp. 888, 899 (no allowance); *Ledge Hill Farms, Inc.,* v. *W. R. Grace & Co.,* 1964 Trade Cas. ¶71,105 (S.D.N.Y. 1964) (no allowance); *Finley* v. *Music Corp. of America,* 66 F.Supp. 569, 571 (S.D. Calif. 1946) (allowance granted)). If the plaintiff recovers only a portion of the damages he claimed, he is not entitled to an allowance for the fee he owes his counsel for work on the items of damages unrecovered (*Union Leader Corp.* v. *Newspapers of New England, Inc.,* 218 F.Supp. 490, 492 (D. Mass. 1963)).

In declaring that a successful plaintiff is not entitled to an attorney-fee allowance if he wins only an injunction, the courts are probably speaking only of the scope and effect of Section 4 of the Clayton Act. It is within the traditional powers of a court of equity to allow attorneys' fees and other additional expense items to a successful litigant, although it is done only "in exceptional cases and for dominating reasons of justice" (*Sprague* v. *Ticonic National Bank,* 307 U.S. 161, 167 (1939)).

The cases suggest many arguments for each side over the amount a successful treble-damage claimant is to be allowed for his attorney's fee. Almost every argument available to one side has its counterpart for the other. Plaintiff's counsel asserts the difficulties of antitrust litigation in general, and the defense replies that in the last decade antitrust litigation, and especially private damage suits, have become commonplace. Emphasis on the special complexities of a particular case may be answered with a reminder that a preexisting government decree greatly eased the task of the plaintiff's lawyer. Lists of cases awarding substantial percentages of recovery or high hourly rates of compensation produce lists of other cases setting smaller allowances. Plaintiff's lawyer relies on the public interest in encouraging private antitrust suits as important law-enforcement tools, and defense counsel points to the provision for treble damages as already establishing more than ample incentives for the plaintiff and a heavy penalty on the defendant.

Extreme variations in the degrees to which each of these arguments appeals to federal judges are apparent in the widely fluctuating results they reach. The lawyer who must prepare a case for or against a fee allowance will not have the assistance of findings, conclusions, or opinions explaining the weight given the various fee-level determinants. Most court opinions in private antitrust suits concentrate on violation and damage issues, leaving the attorney-fee allowance for summary treatment in the last few sentences. As a practical matter, development of certainty or uniformity in fee allowances may have limited public-interest value. Since fee allowances have not been tied to fees paid or contracted for, the only function of the fee allowance seems to be the encouragement of private antitrust enforcement suits. Yet most private damage suits are brought with an eye on the Clayton Act's provision for treble recovery. Only in that minority of private suits brought for little or no damages but for an injunction is the attorney-fee allowance likely to be a significant incentive to a potential plaintiff. The plaintiff's attorney can then contend that the congressional purpose implicit in the Clayton Act's provision for attorney's fees is the "exceptional" circumstance justifying a full allowance for attorneys' fees under the traditional rules of equity. When a potential plaintiff and his attorney are discussing the advisability of filing an antitrust suit for substantial damages, they may be less likely to be concerned with eventual reimbursement for expenses than with initial financing of the litigation.

The fees awarded in *TWA* and *Philadelphia Electric* seem generous to some, yet if the fee is regarded as part of the penalty under the Clayton Act for violating the antitrust laws, such large awards may have the deterrent effect on defendants some say was intended by Congress. A trend of generosity to plaintiffs as well as to their counsel may add additional incentive towards settlement. For a running battle over fees, see *Perkins* v. *Standard Oil Co. of Calif.*, 602 ATRR A-4 (9th Cir. 1973).

Of the factors given emphasis by the courts in setting reasonable attorney's fees, three appear to stand out: (a) skill and standing of counsel; (b) measure of success in the suit; and (c) difficulty of the litigation. Some suggest that the courts should also concern themselves with the size and record of the corporate defendant, its ability to pay and still remain a viable entity, and the effect, if any, that the result of the suit may have upon the relevant market.

2. Question: *Does a contractual fee arrangement between plaintiff and his attorney have any effect on the court's determination of a "reasonable" fee under the statute?*

In *Farmington Dowel Prods. Co.* v. *Forster Mfg. Co.*, 421 F.2d 61 (1st Cir. 1969), plaintiff sought treble damages for an alleged violation of Section 2(a) of the Clayton Act as amended by the Robinson-Patman Act, 15 U.S.C. § 13(a). Much of the plaintiff's case was built around a prior FTC Clayton Act cease-and-desist order dealing with the same practices. Plaintiff sought and was granted the benefit of prima facie effect of the FTC order under Section 5(a) of the Clayton Act. The jury found for plaintiff on all questions of liability and awarded plaintiff $109,000 in damages, trebled to $327,000. Plaintiff had agreed with its attorneys in advance of trial that the attorneys would receive one third of the trebled damages plus all of the amount awarded as a "reasonable attorney's fee." The district court concluded that $85,000 would be a "reasonable attorney's fee" but noted that the fee arrangement would yield counsel a $194,000 total fee ($85,000 plus one third the damage award of $327,000). The court ruled that an award of $85,000 as a reasonable attorney's fee would be "both excessive and contrary to the language" of Section 4 of the Clayton Act. Thus, the court awarded no fee, despite what might be contended was a consequent windfall of $85,000 to defendant Forster. Plaintiff was left with $327,000 less $109,000 in fees which it was obligated to pay its counsel (297 F.Supp. 924 (D. Maine 1969)).

The court of appeals disagreed. Courts "generally are not without power to modify excessive fee arrangements," stated Judge Coffin, and "there is no evidence that Section 4 was intended to inhibit this power." The court did not question the discretionary right of lower courts to inject themselves into fee controversies, but the appellate court rejected what it considered to be the lower court's conclusion that "any fee arrangement between plaintiff and his counsel by which the 'reasonable attorney's fee' awarded by the court goes directly to counsel is contrary to . . . Section 4." Rather, the court held: " . . . we believe that the district court should award Farmington $327,000 as trebled damages and the $85,000 found to be a 'reasonable attorney's fee' under section 4 in this case. We believe that section 4 not only contemplates recovery of a reasonable attorney's fee by a successful plaintiff but also payment of that fee by a losing defendant as a part of his penalty for having violated the antitrust laws. We cannot believe that the imposition of this penalty was meant to turn in any way on the nature or amount of the plaintiff's fee arrangement, a fortuity wholly unrelated to defendant's illegal conduct."

The court stated that this portion of Section 4 was designed to protect the successful plaintiff from a diminished recovery through having to pay attorney's fees by giving counsel court-awarded fees, leaving to the client full trebled damages. A combined "fees awarded" and contingency arrangement also satisfies the intent of the statute, according to the court. Judge Coffin stated that "some important differences" may exist between "reasonableness" of fees under Section 4 of the Clayton Act and Canon 12 of the Canons of Professional Ethics: ". . . there is a difference in over all complexity between the court's role in awarding a fee under section 4 and in exercising its supervisory power over the bar. The first is commonly exercised; the second is reserved for exceptional circumstances. The first requires the court to arrive at a figure it considers reasonable; the second requires it to arrive at a figure which it considers the outer limit of reasonableness. The first determination is made without reference to any prior agreement between the parties, the second must take account of the fact that an agreement, if freely made, is not lightly set aside. A section 4 award has only economic impact; a supervisory decision is an ethical judgment. For all these reasons, particularly when the two kinds of decisions arise in the same case, the setting of the maximum fee which can ethically be accepted requires its own deliberate articulation of rationale."

Judge Coffin would limit the court's role in the setting of maximum attorney's fees under Canon 12 of the Canons of Ethics to "exceptional circumstances," and directed that once the court chooses to invoke its discretionary power of review, it must set the maximum fee so as "not to exceed the outer limits of reasonableness." The court appeared reluctant to inject itself into ethical questions of "reasonableness," having satisfied its statutory duty to set a "reasonable fee" under Section 4 of the Clayton Act. The *Farmington* appellate court did not by its remand of the fee issue to the district court rule out a determination that fees beyond $109,000 in that case might be unreasonable under Canon 12. The fact that counsel would receive more than 30 percent of what was deemed reasonable for Section 4 purposes is not dispositive. Should the district court hold $194,000 in total fees excessive, concluded the First Circuit, "the proper resolution would be simply to indicate the maximum fee which Farmington's counsel can accept consistent with the Canons of Ethics."

A Utah District Court considered the *Farmington* guidelines on somewhat different facts in *Gossner* v. *Cache Valley Dairy Assn.,* 307 F.Supp. 1090 (D. Utah 1970). Prior to successful litigation, plaintiff had agreed to pay counsel one third of any recovery, excluding the court's award of "reasonable attorney's fees." The court determined $42,500 to be a "reasonable fee" in addition to $90,000 awarded by the jury as treble damages, totalling $132,500. The defendant argued that the agreed contingent fee for plaintiff's counsel of one third of $90,000 or $30,000 was the maximum fee which counsel could be awarded under Section 4 of the Clayton Act. The court concluded that defendant's reliance on the district court holding in *Farmington,* later reversed, was misplaced because there the plaintiff arranged to pay counsel one third of its recovery plus a "reasonable attorney's fee" which that court found "antipathetic to the spirit of the Clayton Act." The district court there limited Farmington's award of damages to the one-third contingency and awarded no fee.

The *Gossner* court found that no case holds that a contingent fee arrangement may restrict the plaintiff to the recovery under Section 4 of the Clayton Act of less than a reasonable fee, but it concluded that this appeared to be the law since "the statute authorizes an attorney's fee, not a litigant's fee." Nevertheless, said the Utah court, ". . . a contingent fee avails the defendant nothing here for at best it would be only a limiting factor and not the measure of a reasonable fee . . ." The court held that the private contingency fee arrangement in this case was not a limiting factor in determining the award to the plaintiff of a "reasonable attorney's fee" under Section 4 of the Clayton Act. The court awarded treble damages of $90,000 plus a reasonable attorney's fee of $42,500 despite the contingent arrangement. As to how much of the total fee awarded under Section 4 should be distributed to plaintiff's attorney, the court chose not to interfere with any private arrangements between plaintiff and counsel. This choice was apparently based upon a brief consideration of Canon 12, although this is not clear from the opinion.

Judge Coffin of the First Circuit again reviewed a fee determination in the second *Farmington Dowel* case, 436 F.2d 699 (1st Cir. 1970). Plaintiff requested an additional award of fees for its cross-appeal of the district court's decision. The attorney's fees for the appeal were granted by the court of appeals because the "goal to be obtained by the cross-appeal" was to secure reversal, a new trial, and greater damages, not to defend against Forster's claim for reversal. Thus, according to the court, whether or not plaintiff's cross-appeal was successful, it was entitled to those additional attorney's fees under Section 4 of the Clayton Act upon the ultimate successful conclusion of the case.

The courts, in their discretion and coincident to the award of attorney's fees under Section 4 of the Clayton Act, may inquire into the reasonableness of fee arrangements between treble-damage plaintiffs and their counsel. In the *Farmington* case, the court suggested that a contingent fee arrangement plus a "reasonable attorney's fee" might permit an unconscionable gain for plaintiff's counsel. Yet, to avoid a windfall to the guilty defendant, the court proposed a flexible test, first establishing a "reasonable fee" to go to the plaintiff in addition to treble damages under Section 4 of the Clayton Act. Were the court to refuse to grant a "reasonable attorney's fee" to the plaintiff where a contingent arrangement existed, the court would be diminishing plaintiff's return and giving defendant a break. But the court could examine the total fee received by plaintiff's attorney to consider whether it was "within the outer limits of reasonableness" under the Canons of Ethics. If plaintiff himself has chosen to make such an arrangement with counsel, should the court cut it back?

The *Gossner* holding, although not entirely clear, seems to follow the policy in *Farmington* and does not give defendant a windfall where plaintiff has a contingency arrangement which turns out to provide less than the court-awarded attorney's fee. By setting and awarding a "reasonable fee" to plaintiff, the defendant has been properly penalized, according to the court, and the penalty seems to conform to the language of Section 4. The court appears to take a "hands off" position on whether plaintiff must pay counsel the contingent fee only, even if the agreed fee is less than the amount the court awards as a "reasonable fee." This may be a risk assumed with contingency arrangements.

C. CLASS ACTIONS FOR TREBLE DAMAGES

1. Question: *Can every antitrust plaintiff claim he is suing on behalf of a class of persons injured by defendant's violation?*

Class actions may be brought in the federal courts under special procedures set out in Rule 23 of the Federal Rules of Civil Procedure. Until July of 1966, when amendments promulgated by the Supreme Court in February of that year became effective (383 U.S. 1047 (1966)), Rule 23 seemed to provide for three types of class actions for which the federal courts had developed three different standards on jurisdiction and scope. Claims by or against a class of persons "so numerous as to make it impracticable to bring them all before the court" could be asserted by representative plaintiffs if the claims (1) were "joint, or common, or secondary" to a primary right whose owner refused to enforce it (a "true" class action); (2) were "several" and related to specific property (a "hybrid" class action); or (3) were "several" but involved "a common question of law or fact" and "common relief" (a "spurious" class action).

All antitrust class actions brought in reliance on the last rule were "spurious" class actions. Few were allowed to proceed as class actions during the first decade of the post-World War II surge in antitrust litigation. In *Weeks* v. *Bareco Oil Co.,* 125 F.2d 84 (7th Cir. 1941), the court of appeals saw "strong and persuasive reasons" for extending the class-suit theory to antitrust conspiracies, which have "a singleness of object" and an "integral core." The turning point seemed to come in 1952 with the decision in *Kainz* v. *Anheuser-Busch,* 194 F.2d 737 (7th Cir. 1952). Using the principle established in the *Weeks* case, the court recognized as a legitimate class a group of retailers complaining about prices said to discriminate against them. In *Nagler* v. *Admiral Corp.*, 248 F.2d 319 (2d Cir. 1957), the court established lenient standards for antitrust plaintiffs claiming to be acting for a "spurious" class.

With the amendment of Rule 23 determination of the propriety of a purported "class action" assumed a different complexion. "The amended rule describes in more practical terms the occasions for maintaining class actions; provides that all class actions maintained to the end as such will resolve in judgments including those whom the court finds to be members of the class, whether or not the judgment is favorable to the class; and refers to the measures which can be taken to assure the fair conduct of those actions" (Advisory Committee's Notes, Proposed Rules of Civil Procedure, 39 F.R.D. 69, 99).

No longer does the rule recognize three types of class actions; nor does it concern itself with the sort of rights, "joint" or "several," to be enforced. It simply lists the circumstances under which a class action may be brought. Its provision for judgments binding on all members of the class in effect wipes out the concept of "spurious" class actions. Under the old rule, judgments in such suits were effective only as to those parties who actually participated in the litigation. "Spurious" class actions were frequently characterized as mere devices for permissive joinder of additional plaintiffs or additional defendants. The new rule sets out six prerequisites to the type of class action that arises in the antitrust field. First, the rule retains the old requirement that the class must be "so numerous that joinder of all members is impracticable." In such pre-amendment cases as *Harris* v. *Palm Spring Alpine Estates, Inc.*, 329 F.2d 909 (9th Cir. 1964), and *Advertising Specialty National Assn.* v. *FTC*, 238 F.2d 108 (1st Cir. 1956), the courts said that "impracticable" does not mean impossible but merely extremely difficult or inconvenient. Second, there must be "questions of law or fact common to the class." The old rule spoke of "question," rather than "questions," of law or fact, but the Advisors' Notes make no comment on the change. Third, "the claims or defenses of the representative parties" must be typical of the claims or defenses of the class. Fourth, the "representative parties" who sue must be such as "fairly and adequately protect the interests of the class." This requirement seems to be a carryover from the old rule, although it may now assume more importance. Since in spurious class actions the old rule provided for judgments binding only on those who actually appear as parties and intervened in the action, the courts often passed up any inquiry into the adequacy of the representation of the class. An extensive inquiry is now likely to be regarded as necessary in view of the new rule's provisions making the judgment binding on all members of the class.

Fifth, the court must find that "the questions of law or fact common to the members of the class predominate over any questions affecting only individual members." Sixth, the court must find "that a class action is superior to other available methods for the fair and efficient adjudication of the controversy." Each of these last two requirements is new. In making these two findings, the court is to consider: "(A) the interest of members of the class in individually controlling the prosecution or defense of separate actions; (B) the extent and nature of any litigation concerning the controversy already commenced by or against members of the class; (C) the desirability or undesirability of concentrating the litigation of the claims in the particular forum; (D) the difficulties likely to be encountered in the management of a class action."

One requirement plaintiffs had to meet under the old rule has been eliminated. It is no longer necessary to establish that "a common relief is sought." The court is to determine the propriety of the class action "as soon as practicable after the commencement of an action." The court's order allowing the class action "may be conditional, and may be altered or amended before the decision on the merits."

Once it has been determined that the court is entertaining a proper class action, "the court shall direct to the members of the class the best notice practicable under the circumstances, including individual notice to all members who can be identified through reasonable effort." In that notice, each member of the class is to be told: first, that the court will exclude him from the class if he so requests by a specified date; second, that the judgment will be binding on all members who do not request exclusion; and, third, that any member of the class who does not request exclusion may enter an appearance through counsel.

These notice provisions embody changes of great significance for antitrust litigation. The spurious class action is no longer an invitation to other members of the class to come in and participate in the litigation. Now each is told that he is a party to the lawsuit unless he takes affirmative action to stay out. Although some doubt has been expressed on the point, it would appear that any person who receives notice and demands that the court exclude him from the class affected remains free to bring a separate lawsuit to enforce his own claim. One who receives notice and does not object, on the other hand, apparently gets the benefit of the earlier filing of the complaint, even if he had neglected to file suit himself within the period of time allowed him by the statute of limitations.

The last few paragraphs of the rule give the federal district judges broad powers in the administration of class actions. The court can issue orders "determining the course of proceedings or prescribing measures to prevent undue repetition or complication," requiring notice to each member of the class of any particular development in the litigation, imposing conditions on the original plaintiffs or on intervenors, requiring amendment of pleadings to eliminate allegations concerning representation of absent persons, and "dealing with similar procedural matters." Finally, a class action cannot be dismissed or compromised without the court's approval and advance notice to all members of the class.

The new rules were not promulgated without dispute. Justice Black dissented, commenting: "It seems to me that they place too much power in the hands of the trial judges and that the rules might also as well simply provide that 'class suits can be maintained for or against particular groups whenever in the discretion of a judge he thinks it is wise.' The power given to the judge to dismiss such suits or to divide them up into groups at will subjects members of classes to dangers that could not follow from carefully prescribed legal standards enacted to control class suits."

In *School District of Phila.* v. *Harper & Row,* 267 F.Supp. 1001 (E.D. Pa. 1967), all "class action" references were stricken from a price-fixing treble-damage complaint filed by the State of Pennsylvania and the City of Philadelphia against 17 book publishers on behalf of more than 1,300 public school systems and public libraries. Not persuaded that questions of law and fact common to all members of the asserted class of claimants predominated over questions affecting individual members, the court treated the lawsuit "as an ordinary civil action, with liberal allowance of permissive joinder and intervention under Federal Rules 20 and 24." Having thus disposed of the "class action," the district judge went on to express doubts about the "propriety" of several aspects of the new rule. One of the changes at which the court looked askance is Rule 23(c) (2)'s provision for "the best notice practicable under the circumstances" to all members of the class, "including individual notice to all members who can be identified through reasonable effort." This "onerous task" plus "the ensuing detail of the consequent record keeping" are functions the court was "loath to impose on the already overburdened clerical facilities of this court."

Although the damage claimants' counsel offered to undertake the task of sending notices to all members of the class, the court rejected that suggestion as one that would seriously impair the court's "appearance of detached impartiality." Service of notice upon all the hundreds of school districts and other library-operating public agencies that might have claims against the book publishers "is more likely to be the beginning, rather than the end of frustrating complexities." Inquiries would inevitably come in, and the answers would involve the court in direct correspondence with prospective litigants in a pending case, "a very questionable judicial undertaking."

Criticism was also directed at the provision that a class-action judgment is binding on every member of the class who receives individual notice of the action even if he simply ignores the notice. Clearly this provision extends the court's jurisdiction to persons not previously within the court's power, the opinion observed. "Such a radical extension of this court's jurisdiction by the mere inaction of the nonappearing, nonresident citizen is, in our view, unprecedented. By its silence, a proposed class member not only forfeits its previously unfettered right to choose its own forum and to initiate its own litigation, but apparently waives any objections it might have concerning the lack of personal jurisdiction and venue of this court."

The court also had doubts "of the propriety of a rule which extends the binding, substantive effect of a judgment to absent, but 'described,' class members as well as to 'identified' class members. Conceivably, after trial, unsuccessful antitrust defendants could find themselves liable to unidentified, but 'described,' class members, against whom they had no fair opportunity to pursue pre-trial discovery, to define and refine issues in pre-trial conference or to cross-examine upon trial."

Difficulty in promulgating the notice required by Rule 23(c) was characterized in *Phila. Electric Co.* v. *Anaconda American Brass Company,* 43 F.R.D. 452 (E.D.Pa. 1968) as one of the factors to be considered in weighing the feasibility of managing a proposed class action, i.e., in determining whether "a class action is superior to other available methods for the fair and efficient adjudication of the controversy," within the meaning of Rule 23(b) (3). That court attempted "to reduce the likely difficulties of management to a tolerable level" by limiting its definition of the class. One form of notice the courts are apparently willing to accept in difficult situations is publication in prominent newspapers. See WALL STREET JOURNAL, May 20, 1968, p. 27.

In *Eisen* v. *Carlisle & Jacquelin,* 41 F.R.D. 147 (S.D.N.Y. 1966), the district court saw little difference between the requirements spelled out in the amended rule and the old judge-made requirements for a spurious class action. Substantially all the new rule's requirements were found to have existed under the old rule. The district judge's reason for striking class-action allegations from a complaint attacking the brokerage differential charged on odd-lot transactions on the New York Stock Exchange was the lack of a showing that the complaining trader would adequately protect the interests of all other odd-lot traders. Because the amended rule purports to abandon the old distinctions between "true," "hybrid," and "spurious" class actions, the district judge took the position that it is more important than ever to make sure the plaintiff will be able to represent adequately all members of his class. The papers filed in the case were said to give "no compelling reasons" why the complaining odd-lot trader could adequately protect the interests of "possibly hundreds of thousands" of odd-lot traders. It was not enough, the court declared, to assert that the complaining trader's lawyers are well qualified antitrust specialists, a factor that would not serve as a basis for a class action even under the old rule (*Austin* v. *Warner Bros.*, 19 F.R.D. 93 (S.D.N.Y. 1953)). The district judge seemed even more concerned about the problems that would arise in complying with Rule 23(c)'s requirement that the best notice practicable must be furnished to all members of the class. The complaining trader had not suggested, he pointed out, that a single other person had expressed any interest in the lawsuit. Also the judge rejected a suggestion of plaintiff's counsel that press advertisements plus notices to stock-exchange files would constitute satisfactory notice to the class. In fact, the suggestion raised the "suspicion" that the complaining trader "is more interested in notice for the sake of undesirable solicitation of claims than for proper protection of the interests of the other members of the class."

Recognizing that the change made in Rule 23 "received somewhat less than an enthusiastic reception" in the early district court decisions, the Court of Appeals for the Second Circuit reversed the district court and insisted on "a liberal rather than a restrictive interpretation" of the new rule (391 F.2d 555 (2d Cir. 1968)). The court of appeals agreed that a more careful inspection of the adequacy of representation was called for under the amended rule, in view of the "res judicata effects given to the judgments in those suits." Yet it did not agree with statements that a small number of claimants cannot adequately represent a large class. "One of the primary functions of the class suit is to provide 'a device for vindicating claims which, taken individually, are too small to justify legal action but which are of significant size if taken as a group.' *Escott* v. *Barchris Construction Corp.*, 340 F.2d 731, 733 (2d Cir. 1965), *cert. denied*, 382 U.S. 816 (1966). Individual claimants who may initially be reluctant to commence legal proceedings may later join in a class suit, once they are assured that a forum has been provided for the litigation of their claims" (391 F.2d at 563).

The court of appeals was not concerned, as the district judge seemed to be, at the failure of other members of the class to show an interest in the litigation by seeking to intervene. Noting that absent class members would be able to share in the recovery in the event of a favorable judgment and might for various reasons wish to avoid the binding effect of a possible adverse judgment, the court declared: "If we have to rely on one litigant to assert the rights of a large class then rely we must." See also *Mersay* v. *First Republic Corp. of America*, 43 F.R.D. 465 (S.D.N.Y. 1968); *Dolgow* v. *Ander-*

son, 43 F.R.D. 472 (E.D.N.Y. 1968); *Hohmann* v. *Packard Instrument Co.,* 43 F.R.D. 192 (N.D. Ill. 1967).

As discussed above, one of the reasons given in *School District of Phila.* v. *Harper & Row Publishers, Inc.,* 267 F.Supp. 1001 (E.D. Pa. 1967), for a reluctance to apply the new Rule 23 was the "onerous task" of giving notice to all members of the class. The court in the case rejected a suggestion that the job of giving the notice could be delegated to counsel for the plaintiff seeking to represent a class of claimants. The Second Circuit, on the other hand, adopted the view that this task "must rest upon the representative party when he is the plaintiff." In *Richland* v. *Cheatham,* 272 F.Supp. 148 (S.D. N.Y. 1967), the plaintiff's reluctance to accept the burden of sending notices was one of the reasons the court gave for refusing to allow maintenance of the suit as a class action.

Chief Judge Lumbard dissented from the holding in *Eisen,* maintaining that the amounts of individual recoveries were going to be so small and the administrative problems so vast that "obviously the only persons to gain from a class suit are not potential plaintiffs, but the attorneys who will represent them." The suit was brought by a securities investor alleging a conspiracy to fix brokerage differential for "odd lots" on the New York Stock Exchange. He estimated his damages at only $70. The majority, too, was reluctant to permit actions that "are not likely to benefit anyone but the lawyers who bring them." Consequently, the court of appeals directed the district court, before allowing this suit to proceed, to conduct a further inquiry into the problems of administration of the suit.

The district judge in the *Eisen* case was directed to explore the feasibility of carrying out Rule 23's direction that all members of the class be given the "best notice practicable." If it is feasible to identify an adequate number of members of the class who may be given individual notice, then the plaintiff must assume the burden of giving them such notice or suffer dismissal of the class suit.

On remand of the *Eisen* case the district judge held that Eisen's suit on behalf of odd-lot investors was maintainable as a class action and ordered *defendants* to bear 90 percent of the costs of notice (52 F.R.D. 253 (S.D.N.Y. 1971)). On the appeal the court of appeals again reversed, holding that "If identification of any number of members of the class can readily be made, individual notice to these members must be given and Eisen must pay the cost. If this cannot be done, the case must be dismissed as a class action" (*Eisen* v. *Carlisle & Jacquelin,* 612 ATRR F-1 (2d Cir. 1973)).

Amended Rule 23 was considered in *Knuth* v. *Eric-Crawford Dairy Coop.,* 395 F.2d 420 (3rd Cir. 1968). The Third Circuit was not so ready as was the Second to rely on one litigant to represent a large class of small claimants. Its answer was to instruct the district court to use the rule's notice procedure to test the interest of other class members. The district judge had dismissed a single dairy farmer's claim to represent 1200 other milk producers after 98 members of the class had filed affidavits saying they did not wish to be represented by the plaintiff. In the court's view, this was "an inadequate factual basis" for dismissal. "We think the use of the procedure provided by new F.R. Civ. P. 23(c) would have been more likely to have provided trustworthy evidence for deciding whether, numberwise at least, the plaintiff could fairly and adequately protect the interests of the class." The district judge was in effect instructed to see that all class members were given notice of the action and an opportunity to respond before any determination was made on the adequacy of representation by the class plaintiff.

Another problem under Rule 23 was discussed in *Kronenberg* v. *Hotel Governor Clinton, Inc.,* 41 F.R.D. 42 (S.D.N.Y. 1966), a securities-fraud suit brought for the benefit of a class consisting of all purchasers of the securities who relied on the fraudulent misrepresentations. "The court is handicapped somewhat by having to decide 'as soon as practicable after the commencement of the action brought as a class action. . .' whether it may be maintained as such." Forced to make the decision on a motion to dismiss the suit's "class" aspects before any discovery had been had and with only the motion papers for guidance, the district judge denied the motion but made his order conditional, as permitted by Rule 23(c)(1). He reserved the right to reverse his decision later if it turned out that the fraudulent representations were so varied as to render the action unmanageable.

Another class-action requirement that has been the subject of litigation is Rule 23(a) (2)'s provision that there must be "questions of law or fact common to the class." In *Iowa* v. *Union Asphalt,* 281 F.Supp. 391 (S.D. Iowa 1968), the district court found common issues despite the fact that some members of the purported class purchased directly from the alleged price-fixing conspirators while others employed contractors who made the purchases from the alleged price fixers. In the *Eisen* case, the court had said that differences relating only to the computation of damages are not enough, in and of themselves, to justify dismissal of a class action. Variations in application of the statute of limitations, brought about by application of the fraudulent-concealment doctrine, were held not to preclude a finding of common issues of fact in *Zeigler* v. *Gibraltar Life Ins. Co. of America,* 43 F.R.D. 169 (D.S.D. 1967).

Does the filing of a class action serve to toll the running of the statute of limitations against members of the class who are not participating and have not intervened? The Philadelphia Federal District Court ruled members of a class of claimants may wait for the court's determination of the validity of the class action even though the limitations period expires in the meantime (*Phila. Electric Co.* v. *Anaconda American Brass Co.,* 43 F.R.D. 452 (E.D. Pa. 1968)). If the court determines that a class action may be maintained, the district judge reasoned, that determination relates back to the date of the filing of the complaint, and all members of the class can participate in the judgment. If the court determines that there are not common questions or there is not a proper class, that determination, too, relates back to the date of the suit, and inactive members of the purported class have lost their rights. If, on the other hand, the reasons for dismissing the class action are matters of "judicial housekeeping," then the determination does not relate back, and members of the class should have an opportunity to prove "reliance upon the pendency of the purported class action sufficient to toll the statute of limitations." Otherwise, every class member would have to file a separate action within the limitation period as a precautionary measure. In the *Phila. Electric* case, having decided that it had a class action, the court went on to announce that it would set a deadline for members of the class who did not elect to be excluded from the suit to come forward and file proof of claim or be forever barred.

Rule 23(e)'s provision for court approval of any proposed dismissal, compromise, or settlement was applied to a settlement negotiated with several of the named defendants well in advance of any definition of the class of plaintiffs and of any determination that the suit was in fact a proper class action (*Phila. Electric Co.* v. *Anaconda American Brass Co.,* 42 F.R.D. 324 (E.D. Pa.1967)).

Use of the class-action technique on behalf of franchisees complaining of antitrust violations by their franchisor was encouraged by the decision in *Siegel* v. *Chicken Delight, Inc.,* 271 F.Supp. 722 (N.D. Calif. 1967), 311 F.Supp. 847 (N.D. Calif. 1970), *aff'd in part,* 448 F.2d 43 (9th Cir. 1971), *cert. denied,* 405 U.S. 955 (1972). Five franchisee plaintiffs were held adequate to represent a class of more than 600 "Chicken Delight" franchisees scattered across the country.

If the Second Circuit's attitude toward the class action rule is accepted generally, it supplies answers to two important questions presented in applications of the rule. First, it shows a willingness to permit the aggregation and representation of a multitude of treble-damage claims by one or a few persons asserting the claims. Apathy on the part of other members of the class would be of little or no importance. Second, it resolves the conflict over the mechanics of serving notice on class members by putting the burden on plaintiff. Other authorities indicate that only the mechanics of sending the notice are delegated to the plaintiff; the notice sent is the court's, not any party's (*Kronenberg* v. *Hotel Governor Clinton, Inc.,*

41 F.R.D. 42 (S.D.N.Y. 1966); Frankel, "Some preliminary observations concerning Civil Rule 23," 43 F.R.D. 39 (1967)).

While these rulings would broaden the use of class actions in antitrust litigation, there are other factors to counter such a trend. One factor is difficulty in giving adequate notice, which apparently was assigned significant weight by the Second Circuit in its directions to the district court regarding the mandated inquiry into the problems of administering a class action. A new element may have been added to the district judge's determination of whether a class action is superior to other available methods of litigating the claims. The Multi-District Litigation Act, 28 U.S.C. § 1407, could be regarded by the court as an improvement in the "other available methods" and hence reduce the appeal of class actions as a means of court management of multiclaim litigation.

Rule 23 has been applied in a manner that has significantly increased the use of class actions in antitrust litigation. Some types of antitrust violations, particularly those involving the Robinson-Patman Act, may be ideally suited to class actions because they may inflict harm on a large number of small claimants, no one of whom suffers damage in an amount approaching that needed to support the substantial expense of proving a treble-damage claim. This development has probably caused some lawyers to conclude that the threat of increased treble-damage liability calls for even more care in observance of the antitrust laws. The new provisions may allow combining claims extending antitrust into new areas that have been closed to the Antitrust Division and the Federal Trade Commission because of budget limitations.

The rule's advantages and disadvantages for both the parties and the courts were discussed in some detail at the American Bar Association symposium, "Amended Federal Rule 23" (32 ABA ANTITRUST L. J. 251 (1966)). There seem to be a number of advantages for plaintiffs. First of all, the notice provisions promise to develop financial backing for the plaintiff not only in the initial litigation but also in any subsequent appeal. Similarly, this mandatory device for soliciting additional participants in the litigation makes it easier to gather intelligence about the transactions complained of and, presumably, builds up the volume of evidence available against the defendant. Third, members of the class who do not elect at the outset to be excluded from the litigation have to stick with the suit and are less likely to lose interest when and if the outcome becomes doubtful.

While each of these advantages for plaintiffs can be considered disadvantages for defendants, the rule can have its benefits for some defendants. It is possible more often to get all antitrust claims of the same sort determined in a single lawsuit instead of dozens or hundreds of smaller ones. Determination of a multitude of claims in this fashion might avoid the possibility of a defendant's being burdened with incompatible standards of conduct in his dealings with various plaintiffs.

The rule is not an unmixed blessing for antitrust damage claimants. Counsel who decides to file his client's suit as a class action may have to give up much of the control he would otherwise be able to exercise over the litigation. He is inviting the participation not only of other plaintiffs but also of other plaintiffs' counsel. The loss of control is likely to be most noticeable when serious settlement negotiations near a satisfactory conclusion. Also, a federal district judge pointed out at the ABA symposium that the very specificity with which the rule spells out the prerequisities for maintenance of a class action may create "potentially significant obstacles" to such actions.

The revisors of Rule 23 probably had uppermost in their minds not the interests of litigants but the advantages that might accrue in the administration of justice. Their basic purpose was to avoid duplication of effort on the part of the judiciary and to speed the disposition of litigation. While the new rule works toward those goals by providing for concentration of all the litigation in one court, it does not really stick entirely to its concept of a class action as a "representative" suit. After requiring in paragraph (a) that the class must be "so numerous that joinder of all members is impracticable," in paragraph (c) (2) it invites the actual participation, with counsel, of all members of the class. Purely representative actions may have been possible under the old rule in a "spurious" class suit. In *Union Carbide & Carbon Corp.* v. *Nisley,* 300 F.2d 561 (10th Cir. 1962), antitrust damage claimants were permitted to intervene after rendition of a verdict in favor of the named plaintiffs and to claim the benefits of the favorable judgment, even though they would not have been bound by an unfavorable judgment rendered against the named plaintiffs.

2. Question: *Will the courts allow recovery to a class even if difficulties of distribution among the members of the class may be forbidding?*

In a treble-damage action on behalf of several classes of consumers alleging that defendant oil companies conspired to fix prices in a three-state area, Chief Judge Augelli of the U.S. District of New Jersey refused to certify the largest of the classes, the one consisting of at least six million gasoline consumers (The other classes were certified.) (*City of Phila.* v. *American Oil Co.,* 53 F.R.D. 45 (D.N.J. 1971)). The six-million-member class (and each of the

other classes) did meet, according to the court, the standards of
Rule 23(a) of the Federal Rules of Civil Procedure in that (1) its
membership was so numerous that joinder of all members was
impracticable; (2) there were questions of law or fact common
within the class; (3) the claims of the representative parties were
typical; and (4) the representative parties would fairly protect the
interests of the members of the class. The court found that this
class also met the first of the two standards of Rule 23(b) in that
the common questions of law and fact predominated over the questions affecting only individual members of the class. "The predomi-
nance requirement is met if there is one underlying conspiracy alleged to have affected all members of the class, and damages are
ascertainable on a general level."

According to the court, the six-million-member class did not
meet the second standard of Rule 23(b), which requires that the
class action be "superior to other available methods for the fair and
efficient adjudication of the controversy," taking into account the
manageability of the class action. The court stated that "it is readily
apparent that no matter how easy it is to establish damages on a
class level, if it is extremely difficult or impossible to distribute
these sums to their rightful recipients, the class is unmanageable"; it
found that in this case it would be impossible to sort out claims of
individual consumers who made "cash purchases at many different
stations, at many different times, at many different prices."

The court rejected a proposed "fluid class recovery" as a solution
to the problem of distribution. A "fluid class recovery" would provide, first, for recovery for the class as a whole and, later, some sort
of roughly just distribution among members of the class. Precision
in the distribution would not be rigorously required. As noted by
Judge Augelli, the principle of the "fluid class recovery" was accepted in *Eisen* v. *Carlisle & Jacquelin,* 52 F.R.D. 253 (S.D.N.Y.
1971), *rev'd* 612 ATRR F-1 (2d Cir. 1973).

In *Eisen,* the district court had discussed the "fluid class recovery" concept in the following terms. "To emphasize individual recovery is to unduly stress considerations not totally relevant to the considerations of this case, especially the small amounts of potential
recoveries by most members, which, absent the class device, would
effectively bar suit by the majority of odd-lot investors. Perhaps
fortuitously, the repetitive activity of the principals in odd-lot transactions makes it possible to fashion a procedure which will assure
that the benefits of any recovery will flow in the main to those who
bore the burden of defendants' allegedly illegal acts. Indeed, there
is respectable precedent for such a 'fluid class recovery'. [Citations
omitted] This does not mean, of course, that individual recovery is
to be entirely ruled out. Individual claims may be satisfied to the

extent they are filed, but the fluid class recovery might then be appropriate for distribution of the unclaimed remainder."

Judge Augelli refused to allow a "fluid class recovery" in *American Oil* on the ground that the class in this case was simply too fluid. "Such a solution to the problems of awarding damages to individual claimants is not realistically available for the group here under consideration. The motorist who purchased gasoline from a retail station during the relevant period is still likely, if he has not moved out of the trading area, to continue his purchases of gasoline. However, he will be joined by many persons who were either not old enough to have had a driver's license or were not residing in the trading area between 1955 and 1965. Any fluid class recovery would be a windfall to them and a deprivation to the motorist entitled to recovery. This Court, believing that the composition of the motoring public which purchased from retail stations has changed considerably during and since the alleged conspiracy ended, concludes that there can not be a fluid class recovery for this group of the Philadelphia-New Jersey class."

Judge Augelli went on to point out the consequences of the decision: "The argument that defendants should not be permitted to profit by the enormity as well as the magnitude of their conspiracy has been carefully considered. Assuming that there was a price-fixing conspiracy which affected all ultimate users of gasoline, this Court is well aware of the consequences of not certifying as a class the motorists who purchased from retail stations. These particular individuals purchased more gasoline than all other ultimate users put together. Not being able to sue as a class, their interests in maintaining an antitrust action are so minimal that no action will probably ever be commenced. Hence, the bulk of the illgotten gains reaped by defendants through their assumed conspiracy will remain untouched within their corporate coffers. Although this Court recognizes the importance of private antitrust actions to help enforce the antitrust laws, *Hanover Shoe, Inc.* v. *United Shoe Machinery Corp.*, 392 U.S. 481 (1968), it is not believed that Rule 23 was intended to permit a redress for all wrongs committed under the antitrust laws."

In the passage quoted from *Eisen*, the district court envisioned a "fluid class recovery" as a solution to the problem of distribution which would be fair "in the main" to each of the injured members of the class. In later holding the suit unmanageable as a class action, the Court of Appeals for the Second Circuit said that "no 'fluid recovery' procedures are authorized by any reasonable interpretation of amended Rule 23." The court distinguished *Bebchick* v. *Public Utilities Commission*, 318 F.2d 187 (D.C. Cir. 1963), *cert. denied*, 373 U.S. 913 (1963); *W.Va.* v. *Chas. Pfizer & Co.*, 314

F.Supp. 710 (S.D.N.Y. 1970), *aff'd,* 440 F.2d 1079 (2d Cir. 1971); and *Daar* v. *Yellow Cab Co.,* 67 Cal. 2d 695, 433 P. 2d 732 (1967). In *American Oil,* a "fluid class" was rejected, apparently because in the court's view the class was too "fluid" for fair distribution "in the main," even though the result would be to allow the defendants to retain their allegedly ill-gotten gains. Some observers see inconsistencies among *American-Oil, Eisen,* and the other class-action cases, and see a need for guidelines from the Supreme Court. Others point out that certification of a class is essentially a subjective matter and that Rule 23 provides for an exercise of discretion by the court. Some think that the size of the potential recovery, which can be overwhelming, and the character of the alleged violation are factors which influence courts on the certification question. It may be that a major stumbling block is sometimes simply the determination of which class should recover, the middlemen or the ultimate consumers.

The "fluid class recovery" is generally seen as a way of deferring to the end of the case difficult problems of distribution. The probable effect of certification of a class on a "fluid class recovery" basis may be to facilitate settlement; there does not yet appear to be a single instance of a consumer class action which has been fully litigated.

The decisions in *American Oil* and *Eisen* notwithstanding, many see a trend in class actions away from a concern for the victim and toward a concern to see that ill-gotten profits are disgorged. In other words, according to these observers, the "private attorney general" aspect of the class action now receives the emphasis. While some applaud this trend, others think that a "fluid class recovery" is improper because it may provide recovery to persons who were not injured by the conspiracy, despite Section 4 of the Clayton Act which restricts recovery to one "who shall be injured in his business or property" by a violation of the antitrust laws, and because it is contrary to the principle that the antitrust laws "create new rights and remedies which are available only to those on whom they are conferred by the act[s]" (*U.S.* v. *Cooper Corp.,* 312 U.S. 600 (1941)).

Arguably, the "fluid class recovery" should be limited to per se violations common to the entire class, where the fact of injury to the class may be inferred from proof of a conspiracy and where the stereotyped nature of the transaction makes it easy to establish damages for the class by use of a simple formula. According to this argument, in other cases where the injury to each class member is based on individual circumstances that are not subject to a formalized approach, the "fluid class recovery" would appear to be inappropriate, since the jury would not be capable of determining the aggregate injury to the class without first determining the disparate individual damages resulting from injury to the business or property of each of the plaintiffs. Consistent with this view, it may be that the deferral of questions of individual damages to the end of the case would not be possible, since, except for those per se violations where injury can be inferred, injury must be proved along with conspiracy in order to establish liability, and these elements are usually so intertwined as to preclude separate trials. See *Beacon Theatres, Inc.* v. *Westover*, 359 U.S. 500 (1959).

On the other hand, it could be said that the problem of computing damages is just the problem which the "fluid class recovery" has been designed to solve. Some think that damages normally can be well enough estimated so that the "fluid class recovery" is a fair solution, considering the alternative. This is the consideration that impressed Judge Miles W. Lord in the *Antibiotics* case. He said: "The court would be hesitant to conclude that conspiring defendants may freely engage in predatory price practices to the detriment of millions of individual consumers and then claim the freedom to keep their ill-gotten gains which, once lodged in the corporate coffers, are said to become a 'pot of gold' inaccessible to the mulcted consumers because they are many and their individual claims small" (*In Re Coordinated Pretrial Proceedings in Antibiotic Antitrust Actions* (consumer class actions), 333 F.Supp. 267 (S.D.N.Y. 1971)). According to the court in the *American Oil* case, the propriety of "fluid class recovery" seems to turn upon whether the class is simply too fluid for substantial justice to be achieved in the distribution of the award.

3. Question: *Have class actions reached a high water mark?*

Several decisions have dealt adversely with two issues concerning class action plaintiffs: (1) the certification of classes in cases based upon the Truth in Lending Act (15 U.S.C. § 1601) and (2) the plaintiff's right to interlocutory review of adverse preliminary decisions related to the certification of the class.

Judge Marvin Frankel of the Southern District of New York, an early supporter of Rule 23, refused to certify a class consisting of as many as 130,000 charge card holders in a suit charging the defendant bank with failure to make the full disclosure required by the Truth in Lending Act. The complaint sought the statutory minimum damage of $100 for each of the 130,000 alleged violations (*Ratner* v. *Chemical Bank New York Trust Co.,* 54 F.R.D. 412 (S.D.N.Y. 1972)). Judge Frankel noted that the plaintiff suffered little or no actual damage and that the total liability, if the class were allowed and if plaintiff were to prevail on the merits, would amount to about $13 million. He concluded: "Students of the

Rule[23] have been led generally to recognize that its broad and open-ended terms call for the exercise of some considerable discretion of a pragmatic nature. Appealing to that kind of judgment, defendant points out that (1) the incentive of class-action is unnecessary in view of the Act's provisions for a $100 minimum recovery and payment of costs and a reasonable fee for counsel; and (2) the proposed recovery of $100 each for some 130,000 class members would be a horrendous, possibly annihilating punishment, unrelated to any damage to the purported class or to any benefit to defendant, for what is at most a technical and debatable violation of the Truth in Lending Act. These points are cogent and persuasive. They are summarized compendiously in the overall conclusion stated earlier: the allowance of this as a class action is essentially inconsistent with the specific remedy supplied by Congress and employed by plaintiff in this case."

This point of view was adopted four days later in *Rogers* v. *Coburn Finance Corp.,* 54 F.R.D. 417 (N.D. Ga. 1972), dismissing a class action based upon the Truth in Lending Act. On the other hand in *La Mar* v. *H & B Novelty & Loan Co.,* 55 F.R.D. 22 (D. Ore. 1972), in which violations of the Truth in Lending Act are alleged, the court allowed a class consisting of 33,000 borrowers from several defendant pawnbrokers. This case is noteworthy since the defendants acted independently of each other in their alleged violations of the Act and since the individual plaintiff seeking to represent the class had dealings with only one of the defendants. The court treated the problem as one under Rule 23 for the determination of a class rather than as a problem of the standing of the individual plaintiff to sue those of the defendants he had not himself dealt with.

In a suit brought against seven bakers who had pleaded nolo contendere to an indictment for price fixing in the Philadelphia market and who had previously settled a treble-damage class action brought on behalf of governmental and nongovernmental entities, the Third Circuit (with two judges dissenting) dismissed an appeal from the trial court's refusal to certify a class of plaintiffs consisting of about one and one-half million purchasers of bread in Philadelphia (*Hackett* v. *General Host Corp.,* 455 F.2d 618 (3rd Cir. 1972)). The remaining individual claim was for about nine dollars. In dismissing the appeal, the court refused to follow the "death knell" rule adopted by the Second Circuit in *Eisen* v. *Carlisle & Jacquelin,* 370 F.2d 119 (2d Cir. 1966). In *Eisen,* the court assumed that "no lawyer of competence is going to undertake this complex and costly case to recover $70 for Mr. Eisen [the remaining individual claim]," and ruled that "where the effect of a district court's order, if not reviewed, is the death knell of the action, review should be allowed."

Having noted that the "death knell" rule operates only in favor of the plaintiff who fails to receive designation as the representative of a class, the Third Circuit in *Hackett* ruled that the policy favoring class actions as a deterrent to violations of the antitrust laws is outweighed by "the policies which have historically protected the federal appellate courts from being overwhelmed by interlocutory appeals." According to the court's analysis, the "core issue, though conventional pieties about the role of the legal profession might suggest its obfuscation," is whether "the attorney deprived of the quixotic opportunity of representing one and one-half million potential claimants should be recognized as a private attorney general with standing of his own to appeal the adverse class action decision." (By "quixotic," the court meant "the sense that for many attorneys it would be the impossible dream come true.")

"Realistically, when we are asked to grant interlocutory appellate review of an adverse class action determination we are asked to recognize a separate interest of the attorney sufficient to bring the class action determination within the 'collateral order' doctrine, or to recognize the standing of the attorney's client to assert such an interest on his behalf. We decline to do either. Those typical consumer class actions in which the Eisen rule would be likely to operate involve areas of federal law in which public enforcement co-exists with private remedies. There is no compelling need to go beyond those inducements to the bar which already encourage a lively pursuit of private enforcement remedies" (455 F.2d at 625).

Conceding that the case was not likely to go forward without the class action, the *Hackett* court said: "If the public interest issue involved in the individual suit is so insignificant that neither a private nor a public attorney deems it worthy of pursuit, despite the availability of an award of attorneys' fees in the event of success, then the public interest issue may well be so insignificant that the redress of the nine-dollar wrong should from a policy viewpoint be left to the realm of private ordering. Our scarce federal judicial resources cannot be allocated on the assumption that they must provide a forum for the vindication of every individual wrong however slight. . . . If in some cases as Judge Rosenn suggests the individual claim often will be so small that neither private nor public lawyers think it should be litigated, then that decision of the legal marketplace may be the best reflection of a public consciousness that the time of the lawyers and of the court should best be spent elsewhere" (455 F.2d at 625–626).

In the course of its discussion of the "death knell" rule, the court quoted a passage from a concurring opinion in *Korn* v. *Franchard Corp.*, 443 F.2d 1301 (2d Cir. 1971), expressing reservations about that rule. In *Weight Watchers of Phila.* v. *Weight Watchers Internat'l.*, 455 F.2d 770 (2d Cir. 1972), there was further indication that the Second Circuit may be backing away from its earlier position favorable to plaintiffs seeking review.

In *Weight Watchers,* the plaintiff was seeking review of an order allowing defendant to communicate with members of the proposed class. It was possible that the defendant might thereby be able to settle with enough members of the class to render the proposed class too small for certification. Having expressed concern about a possible "flood of appeals" if review were granted in this instance, the court stated: "Here, even if defendant should succeed in settling with so many franchisees that the court will be forced to deny class action status, plaintiff's complaint will remain untouched. As we have, in essence, already noted, plaintiff has no legally protected right to sue on behalf of other franchisees who prefer to settle; F.R. Civ. P. 23(3), requiring court approval of the dismissal or compromise of a class action, does not bar non-approved settlements with individual members which have no effect upon the rights of others. [citation omitted.]"

The ruling in the *Chemical Bank* case that the class action is essentially incompatible with the Truth in Lending Act could be significant. This point was not fully considered in the Oregon pawnbroker case. If *Chemical Bank* becomes the rule and the Second Circuit is followed in other jurisdictions, the class action plaintiff would be foreclosed from a potentially large category of cases. Also possibly significant is the Third Circuit's refusal to review the order dismissing the class action. On several occasions in recent years courts of appeals have reviewed and reversed such orders. Some observers think that there is more hostility to class actions among district court judges than among appellate judges.

Perhaps more significant than the decisions themselves, are the considerations that influenced the courts in reaching these decisions. These considerations may suggest that the courts are beginning to have serious reservations about the class action itself. Thus, as noted, in *Hackett* the court stated that the "core issue" was whether the plaintiff's attorney would have the "quixotic opportunity" of representing one and one-half million plaintiffs rather than just the one; and, having expressed earlier the concern that the appellate courts might be "overwhelmed" with appeals, it concluded with equanimity that if no lawyers could be found to prosecute a small claim even if reasonable attorneys' fees are awarded, "then that decision of the legal market-place may be the best reflection of a public consciousness that the time of the lawyers and the court should best be spent elsewhere." In the *Chemical Bank* case, Judge Frankel contrasted the small amount of injury to each member of the proposed class with the "horrendous, possibly annihilating punishment" of a damage award of many millions of dollars.

In the dissent by Judge Rosenn in *Hackett* and in the Oregon pawnbroker decision great weight is given to those opposing considerations that have promoted class actions in the past. The Oregon court states: "One important function of the class action is to afford meaningful legal rights to persons who may be ignorant of such rights or to those whose individual claims are too small to support custom-tailored litigation. If the Rule is to be effective, the courts should not restrict class membership by narrow and grudging rules. Unduly restrictive limitations upon the class may have the effect of denying legal remedies to the ignorant and the poor while creating windfall immunities for law violators. [Citations omitted.]"

In *Eisen* v. *Carlisle & Jacquelin,* 612 ATRR F-1 (2d Cir. 1973), Judge Medina expressed what may be a widespread disaffection among the judiciary with class actions and suggested that the "problem is really one for solution by the Congress." (For fuller analysis, see 624 ATRR B-1, 7/31/73.) Indications of this attitude could be seen in *City and County of Denver* v. *American Oil Co.* 53 F.R.D. 620 (D. Colo. 1971) and *City of Phila.* v. *American Oil Co.,* 53 F.R.D. 45 (D. N.J. 1971). Class action status has been denied in *Andrucci* v. *Gimbel Bros., Inc.,* 614 ATRR A-16 (W.D. Pa. 1973); *Graybeal* v. *American Saving & Loan Assn.,* 611 ATRR A-1 (D.D.C. 1973); *Hettinger* v. *Glass Specialty Co.,* 610 ATRR A-8 (N.D. Ill. 1973); *Greisler* v. *Hardee's Food Systems, Inc.,* 609 ATRR A-22 (E.D. Pa. 1973); *County of Custer* v. *Wilshire Oil Co.,* 608 ATRR A-7 (W.D. Okla. 1973); *Gneiting* v. *Taggares,* 607 ATRR A-20 (D. Idaho 1973); *Yanai* v. *Frito-Lay, Inc.,* 607 ATRR A-20 (N.D. Ohio 1973); *Wilcox* v. *Commerce Bank of Kansas City,* 602 ATRR A-24 (10th Cir. 1973).

On the other hand, class action proponents may find some encouragement in *Hawaii* v. *Standard Oil Co. of Calif.,* 405 U.S. 251 (1972). In that case, while holding that a state cannot recover treble damages under Section 4 of the Clayton Act in a *parens patriae* capacity, both the Supreme Court majority and Justice Douglas in dissent spoke approvingly of the class action as an alternative to an action by a state in its *parens patriae* capacity.

D. THE ANTITRUST DEFENSE TO A BREACH-OF-CONTRACT SUIT

Question: *If sued for breach of contract, can defendant avoid his obligation if the contract violates the antitrust laws?*

"Highly debatable . . . to say the least," is the way Justice Harlan has characterized federal law on the availability to a defendant in a breach-of-contract action of the claim that enforcement of the contract would sanction or further an antitrust violation (*American Mfrs. Mutual Ins. Co.* v. *American Broadcasting-Paramount Theaters, Inc.*, 87 S.Ct. (1966) not officially reported). Under the common law on illegal contracts, "The well-established general rule is that an agreement which violates a provision . . . of a constitutional statute, or which cannot be performed without violating such a provision, is illegal and void. . . . The general rule applies equally where the consideration to be performed or the act to be done is unlawful and where an agreement with respect to the subject matter is prohibited. A contract for an object prohibited by a penal law is void." However, "the rule that an agreement in violation of law is invalid does not always apply where the existence of the thing in question is due to a violation of law only in the sense that incidentally some law was violated in its production, where it might have been created without such violation" (17 Am. Jur. 2d *Contracts* § 165 (1964)).

In antitrust litigation, the general rule has been applied to "inherently illegal" contracts, that is, contracts that are either unlawful on their face (*Bement* v. *National Harrow Co.*, 186 U.S. 70, 88 (1902)) or are part of an unlawful scheme or conspiracy (*Sola Electric Co.* v. *Jefferson Electric Co.*, 317 U.S. 173 (1942)). "The courts are averse to holding contracts unenforceable on the ground of public policy unless their illegality is clear and certain. Since the right of private contract is no small part of the liberty of the citizen, the usual and most important function of courts of justice is to maintain and enforce contracts rather than to enable parties thereto to escape from their obligations on the pretext of public policy, unless it clearly appears that they contravene public right or the public welfare" (17 Am. Jur. 2d *Contracts* § 178). This reluctance to let an informed, competent party avoid his commitments seems to have influenced the development of the law on the right of antitrust violators to enforce their contracts. "As a defense to an action based on contract, the plea of illegality based on violation of the Sherman Act has not met with much favor in this Court," the Supreme Court observed in *Kelly* v. *Kosuga*, 358 U.S. 516 (1959).

One of the devices the courts have used to allow recovery of damages for breach of contracts containing or related to antitrust violations is to find illegal portions of the transaction severable from the portion on which suit has been brought. The courts are particularly apt to find severability when the illegal aspect of the transaction relates to a subsidiary rather than the main purpose of the contract and when the plaintiff has already performed his obligations under the contract. Application of these rules on severability is not simple. The validity of the severability doctrine when antitrust issues are involved has been put in doubt by a series of

Supreme Court opinions in actions to collect patent royalties. Although a patent licensee is ordinarily not permitted to challenge the validity of the patent, the inclusion in the licensing agreement of a price-fixing provision whose legality under the Sherman Act depends on the validity of the patent has been held by the Court to remove that estoppel and, upon proof of the patent's invalidity, to render the whole contract void, including the obligation to pay royalties (*Sola Electric Co.* v. *Jefferson Electric Co.,* 317 U.S. 173 (1942); *Katzinger Co.* v. *Chicago Metallic Mfg. Co.,* 329 U.S. 394 (1947); *MacGregor* v. *Westinghouse Electric & Mfg. Co.,* 329 U.S. 402 (1947).

Most Supreme Court opinions dealing directly with the antitrust defense to contract damage actions have discussed the problem of distinguishing between a contract that is part of a Sherman Act conspiracy and therefore illegal and a contract that is merely collateral to the illegal conspiracy and therefore enforceable by either party. In *Connolly* v. *Union Sewer Pipe Co.,* 184 U.S. 540 (1902), the Court was asked to bar a suit for the purchase price of delivered goods because the seller was involved in an illegal price-fixing conspiracy. The Court refused, declaring that "the plaintiff, even if part of a combination illegal at common law, was not for that reason forbidden to sell property it acquired or held for sale. The purchases by the defendant had no necessary or direct connection with the alleged illegal combination" (184 U.S. at 549). *Continental Wall Paper Co.* v. *Voight & Sons Co.,* 212 U.S. 227 (1909), was a similar case except that the Supreme Court found that the plaintiff had admitted, by its demurrer to the antitrust defense, that the account sued on "has been made up in execution of the agreements" that formed the Sherman Act combination, that the plaintiff itself was the illegal combination of competitors, and that a part of the illegal conspiracy was to compel all jobbers, including defendant, to sign exclusive-dealing agreements. To give judgment for the plaintiff in this case, the Supreme Court reasoned, would "be to give the aid of the court in making effective the illegal agreements that constituted the forbidden combination." The *Connolly* decision was distinguished as involving a defendant who had no connection with the operations of the illegal combination except for the purchase contract sued on.

In *D.R. Wilder Mfg.* v. *Corn Products Refining Co.,* 236 U.S. 165 (1915), defendant tried to take advantage of the *Continental Wall Paper* decision by arguing that his supplier had no legal existence but was an illegal combination of competitors charging unreasonably high and noncompetitive prices. The controlling precedent was found to be the *Connolly* case; *Continental Wall Paper* was distinguished since in *Wilder* the sale contract was not inherently unlawful and was not directly related to the alleged illegal organization of the selling corporation. See also *A.B. Small Co.* v. *Lamborn & Co.*, 267 U.S. 248 (1925).

The "collateral contract" issue has also arisen in a Robinson-Patman Act context. In *Bruce's Juices, Inc.*, v. *American Can Co.*, 330 U.S. 743 (1947), the Supreme Court sustained a judgment for the price of goods sold and delivered, even though the buyer was ready to prove that he was being charged a discriminatorily higher price than his competitors. Listing the sanctions imposed by the statute, the Supreme Court pointed out that uncollectability of purchase price was not one of them. The Court concluded that the Robinson-Patman Act must be applied, in contract actions, on a different basis than the Sherman Act, since no single sale can violate the Robinson-Patman Act. At least two transactions must occur, it reasoned, and a court does not approve the sale made at the discriminatorily lower price when it allows recovery of the higher price called for by the other sale.

This test, based on whether the court is giving its approval of, or assistance in making effective, an illegal agreement, was stated in the *Continental Wallpaper* case and is the basis for the Supreme Court's decision in *Kelly* v. *Kosuga*, 358 U.S. 516 (1959). In that case, both the sales contract sued on and the alleged conspiracy in restraint of trade involved the same two groups of parties. A group of onion growers agreed to buy 287 of 600 carloads of onions from two onion marketers who had threatened to dump the onions on the futures market. Both the sellers and the buyers agreed not to deliver any of the 600 carloads on the futures market for the remainder of the season. The Supreme Court decided that giving legal effect to the completed sale of onions at a fair price would not enforce a violation of the Sherman Act. By this time the period of market stabilization the parties had bargained for had long since passed.

Calling attention to the observation in the *D.R. Wilder* case "that the Sherman Act's express remedies could not be added to judicially by including the avoidance of private contracts as a sanction," the Court endorsed a dissenting statement in the *Continental Wall Paper* case that courts are to be guided by the overriding general policy of "preventing people from getting other people's property for nothing when they purport to be buying it." An attempt to distinguish *Connolly*, *Wilder*, and *Small* as involving situations where the defense was asserted by a person who was not party to the unlawful conspiracy was rejected as "paradoxical" and as creating "a very strange class of private attorneys general."

The Supreme Court's repeated refusal to treat the illegal-contract defense as an additional antitrust enforcement tool seems to forestall, in the law relevant to that defense in antitrust cases, any trend comparable to the one that has increased recoveries in treble-damage actions. In both *Bruce's Juices* and the *Kelly* case, the Court clearly stated its intent to rely on direct actions, whether private or governmental, to enforce the antitrust laws.

A reluctance to decide antitrust issues is particularly noticeable in state courts, where most breach-of-contract suits are litigated. See *American Broadcasting-Paramount Theaters, Inc.* v. *American Mfrs. Mutual Ins. Co.,* 249 N.Y.S. 2d 481 (1963), *aff'd* 271 N.Y.S. 2d 284, 218 N.E. 2d 324 (1966). The general rule of the common law applies; if a contract in and of itself (or "inherently") violates antitrust law, it will not be enforced in any kind of litigation (*Merchant Suppliers Paper Co.* v. *Photo-Marker Corp.,* 1967 Trade Cas. ¶72,325 (N.Y. App. Div. 1967)). Also, if the issue is raised by a defendant who is not trying to keep something he has not paid for, the Supreme Court's interest in promoting compliance with antitrust policy may affect the result. Court opinions disallowing the illegality-of-contract defense have generally decided suits for damages; different considerations may arise in a suit under equity jurisdiction for specific enforcement of a contract. A defendant able to point to illegal conduct on the part of the plaintiff is probably in a stronger position in a court of equity than he is in a court of law. It has been suggested that it is the equitable nature of the proceedings that accounts for the Supreme Court's refusal, in the patent-royalty suits described above, to consider the price-fixing agreements severable from the patent license. In some damage actions the antitrust defense has failed because of circumstances that cause the court to "suspect that the claim of the Sherman Act illegality was an afterthought to justify having broken a contract that turned out sour" (*American Mfrs. Ins. Co.* v. *American Broadcasting-Paramount Theaters, Inc.,* 388 F.2d 272, 279 n. 9 (2d Cir. 1967)). In the view of many antitrust experts, this explains the result in *Tampa Electric Co.* v. *Nashville Coal Co.,* 365 U.S. 320 (1961).

Defendant in a contract suit for either damages or specific enforcement can counterclaim for plaintiff's antitrust violation. Conceivably, a contract-suit defendant denied an antitrust defense by reason of the "severance" or "collateral contract" rule could, nevertheless, prove an antitrust violation and satisfy the other prerequisites to damage recovery. If the plaintiff in the *D. R. Wilder* case, for example, had been able to show the existence of an illegal conspiracy and the amount by which the price of the corn syrup he bought had been increased by the conspiracy, perhaps he could have counterclaimed and recovered, either as an offset or as an affirmative judgment, three times the amount of the price increase he paid on all corn syrup purchases, including the purchase contract sued on. But cf. *American Mfrs. Ins. Co.* v. *American Broad-casting-Paramount Theaters, Inc.*, 388 F.2d 272 (2d Cir. 1967).

On the other hand, a defendant with an acceptable antitrust defense to the contract suit does not necessarily have a claim for damages or an injunction, although the successful defendant in *Continental Wall Paper* may have been able to prove that the illegal combination actually caused him injury or "threatened" injury (§ 16, Clayton Act) to his business or property. Since state courts have no jurisdiction over federal antitrust treble-damage claims, counterclaims arise only in contract suits brought in the federal courts. If a federal court is selected by a plaintiff, the defendant's failure to assert a treble-damage claim by counterclaim may foreclose him from ever recovering his damages. See Rule 13(a), Federal Rules of Civil Procedure, and *Hancock Oil Co.* v. *Union Oil Products Co.*, 115 F.2d 45 (9th Cir. 1940). In *Channel Marketing, Inc.* v. *Telepro Industries, Inc.*, 45 F.R.D. 370 (S.D.N.Y. 1968), a state-court action on a contract was brought after a federal antitrust treble-damage suit had already been filed by the other party to the contract. After the contract action had been removed to the federal court, the two proceedings were consolidated on the theory that each would be a compulsory counterclaim under Rule 13(a).

E. SUPPLIER'S REFUSAL TO DEAL WITH CUSTOMER WHO SUES

Question: *May supplier cut off a customer when the customer sues the supplier for an antitrust violation?*

Sellers are entitled to choose their own customers, but refusals to deal may be illegal when carried out in a particular business setting or market context. Concerted refusals to deal, often referred to as boycotts, have long been held to be combinations or conspiracies in restraint of trade and violations of Section 1 of the Sherman Act (*Eastern States Retail Lumber Dealers' Ass'n.* v. *U.S.*, 234 U.S. 600 (1914)), as well as "unfair methods of competition" in violation of Section 5 of the Federal Trade Commission Act (*Fashion Originators Guild* v. *FTC,* 312 U.S. 457 (1941)). Individual refusals to deal have, in general, been considered legitimate, but when the purpose behind the refusal to deal is the maintenance of a manufacturer's resale price, the manufacturer's conduct may violate Section 1 of the Sherman Act. He may not go beyond a "mere announcement of his policy and the simple refusal to deal" (*U.S.* v. *Parke, Davis & Co.,* 362 U.S. 29, 44 (1960)).

Other motivations may subject refusals to deal to antitrust scrutiny. If one refusing to deal is said to have monopoly power in a particular market and the evidence shows that the purpose behind the refusal is an attempt to extend or perfect that power, Section 2 of the Sherman Act may be violated (*Lorain Journal Co.* v. *U.S.*, 342 U.S. 143 (1951); *Eastman Kodak Co.,* v. *Southern Photo Materials Co.,* 273 U.S. 359 (1927)). Section 3 of the Clayton Act may be violated if the seller refuses to continue dealing with a distributor who takes on competing lines (*Carter Carburetor Corp.* v. *FTC,* 112 F.2d 722 (8th Cir. 1940); *U.S.* v. *J. I. Case Co.,* 101 F.Supp. 856 (D. Minn. 1951)) or if the seller refuses to sell one of its products unless another, or "tied" product, is also purchased (*Times-Picayune Publishing Co.,* v. *U.S.,* 345 U.S. 594 (1953)).

In *P.W. Husserl, Inc.* v. *Simplicity Pattern Co.,* 191 F.Supp. 55 (S.D.N.Y. 1961), the court suggested an additional limitation on the right of refusal to deal. The limitation was rejected by the court of appeals (298 F.2d 867 (2d Cir. 1962)) but appeared again in *Bergen Drug Co.* v. *Parke, Davis & Co.,* 307 F.2d 725 (3rd Cir. 1962). The Federal Trade Commission had found that Simplicity Pattern Co. had violated Section 2(e) of the Clayton Act, as amended by the Robinson-Patman Act, by furnishing discriminatory services and facilities to some of its larger customers (*Simplicity Pattern Co., Inc.,* 53 F.T.C. 771 (1957). The Supreme Court affirmed (*FTC* v. *Simplicity Pattern Co.,* 360 U.S. 55 (1959)). Within a month of that decision three retail stores filed a private treble-damage action against Simplicity. Thereafter, some 43 additional plaintiffs were allowed to intervene. Plaintiffs sold yard-good fabrics and notions. They purchased dress patterns from Simplicity for sale in their stores, primarily as an accommodation to their customers and for the purpose of selling fabric. Each 25-cent pattern sale generally resulted in an additional sale of several dollars worth of material. Simplicity was said to be the nation's largest manufacturer of tissue patterns used in home sewing. It sold these patterns to its retailers under five-year contracts that were automatically renewed "unless terminated by either party by written notice served 60 days prior to the expiration of the initial or any succeeding term." More than half of the patterns sold in the fabric stores were Simplicity patterns. Five of the fabric stores were near the end of their five-year terms, and, soon after the treble-damage action was commenced, Simplicity without explanation gave these five written notice of the termination of their contracts. These five fabric shops sought from the court a preliminary injunction to restrain Simplicity from refusing to deal with them.

The trial court granted the motion, finding that Simplicity's sole motive for termination of these contracts was the "exertion of economic pressure to deter plaintiffs from pursuing their legal rights and remedies." Although he could cite no authority for holding this an invalid reason for refusing to deal, the judge reasoned "that the right to choose one's customers and to refuse to deal is not unlimited and must under appropriate circumstances give way to considerations of public policy which require its reasonable restriction in the public interest" (191 F.Supp. at 61). Since Congress had indicated a public policy in favor of enforcement of the antitrust laws by private suits, and since this refusal to deal was contrary to that policy, the court held this was itself an antitrust violation entitling the fabric shops to the injunctive relief provided for in Section 16 of the Clayton Act. The court issued the preliminary injunction and directed that the complaint be amended to include a count alleging Simplicity's refusal to deal.

The Court of Appeals for the Second Circuit reversed this decision (*House of Materials, Inc.* v. *Simplicity Pattern Co.,* 298 F.2d 867 (2d Cir. 1962)). Noting that the lower court had failed to specify which provision of the antitrust laws Simplicity had violated by its refusal to deal, the court of appeals surveyed the possibilities and concluded that there had been no violation and that the district court had no power to issue an injunction under Section 16 of the Clayton Act. The court expressed doubt that there had been any type of joint action, but felt that, even if this were found, Simplicity's conduct was "of such Doric simplicity" as to come within the protection of the *Colgate* doctrine, (discussed in section II-A-7, p. 103.). See *Warner & Co.* v. *Black & Decker Mfg. Co.,* 277 F.2d 787, 790 (2nd Cir. 1960). The court concluded Simplicity's conduct had not resulted in any violation of Section 1 of the Sherman Act. It distinguished resale price maintenance schemes. Simplicity's refusal to deal was found not to have been pursuant to an attempt to achieve a monopoly in violation of Section 2. On the contrary, the court suggested that such action created more markets for Simplicity's competitors.

In addition to holding that the lower court had no power to issue the injunction under Section 16 of the Clayton Act, the court of appeals found that it was not an appropriate case for the exercise of general equity power to issue an injunction. Simplicity was said to be doing more than coercing the fabric shops to discontinue a lawsuit; it was exercising a decision to terminate a contract that had come to the end of its term. The court said: "The issuance of the injunction, however, would have the effect of extending appellee's contractual right to do business with Simplicity for the duration of the litigation. . . . It is apparent to us that the effect of such temporary injunctive relief is singularly inappropriate."

Seven months after the decision in the *Simplicity Pattern* case, the Court of Appeals for the Third Circuit issued its decision in *Bergen Drug Co.* v. *Parke, Davis & Co.,* 307 F.2d 725 (3rd Cir. 1962). Bergen Drug, a wholesaler of pharmaceuticals and drug

sundries, had filed a complaint against Parke, Davis & Co., a manufacturer of drug products, alleging discriminatory dealing, monopolization, and attempting to monopolize. Bergen asked for both
treble damages and a permanent injunction to enjoin Parke, Davis
from refusing to sell its products to Bergen upon the same terms as
to other purchasers. Shortly after the complaint was filed, Parke
Davis sent a letter to Bergen stating that Bergen's account was
being permanently closed and that Parke, Davis did "not wish to
make further use of the distribution facilities of Bergen. . . ." Bergen then moved for an injunction, which was denied.

On appeal, this decision was reversed. The court of appeals held
that the district court, "as a court of equity," did possess power to
issue the preliminary injunction. This was a case of an alleged attempt to monopolize, the appellate court declared, and Parke, Davis' refusal to deal would further that monopoly. Furthermore, according to the court, the preliminary injunction sought would be
identical to the permanent relief to which Bergen would be entitled,
if successful. The court found a danger of irreparable loss to Bergen because retail drug stores prefer to purchase from wholesalers
who can meet all their needs in one order. The court stated: "Many
of defendant's products are indispensable to the operation of a retail pharmacy. A large number of defendant's drugs are specified in
physicians' prescriptions and under the law substitution is forbidden. Other products of defendant are trademarked drugs, and some
of those not sold under a trademark have no functional equivalent.
On the average, 25 percent of the orders received by plaintiff call
for at least one of defendant's products. If plaintiff is unable to fill
the retail druggist's needs for one item, the druggist will turn to
another wholesaler who can do so, thereby causing a permanent
loss of business."

As a further reason for granting the injunction, the court found
that the injunction was necessary to permit Bergen's prosecution of
its claim under the antitrust laws. "The point plaintiff convincingly
makes is that it will be unable to secure the cooperation of other
wholesalers and of retailers to be witnesses because they fear the
same sort of retaliatory action that plaintiff has experienced. Certainly a court can act where a party's conduct is calculated to frustrate litigation."

Are the *Simplicity* and *Bergen* cases in direct conflict, or can they
be reconciled? A number of distinctions between the two cases can
be made.

1.) The alleged initial violations of the defendants were different.
In the *Simplicity* case, the pattern maker already had been held to
have violated Section 2 of the Clayton Act as amended by the Rob-

inson-Patman Act. In *Bergen,* Parke, Davis was charged not only with a Robinson-Patman Act violation but also with monopolization and attempt to monopolize in violation of the Sherman Act.

2.) The treble-damage complaints did not seek the same relief. In *Simplicity,* there were 46 plaintiffs initially seeking money damages only. *Bergen* involved only one plaintiff asking for both money damages and a permanent injunction to stop Parke, Davis from refusing to sell its products to Bergen upon the same terms as they were sold to other wholesalers.

3.) The refusals to deal took different forms. In the *Simplicity* case, the pattern maker precluded automatic renewal of five-year contracts by terminating those contracts that had reached the end of their terms. In the *Bergen* case, Parke, Davis closed the Bergen account.

4.) The cases involved different products and industries. In the *Simplicity* case, the fabric shops were cut off from obtaining tissue dress patterns; in the *Bergen* case, a wholesale druggist was refused the entire line of Parke, Davis drugs. A special problem was said to result from a retail druggist's obligation not to substitute for prescribed drug products.

5.) The relative market positions of the defendants were dissimilar. Although Simplicity was "the nation's largest manufacturer of tissue patterns," the court found its refusal to deal was not an attempt to achieve or further a monopoly. The court in the *Bergen* case, noting that Parke, Davis had been charged with an attempt to monopolize, held that the manufacturer's refusal to deal would further any such monopoly.

6.) The treble-damage claimants were subjected to different types of pressure. While the fabric shops in the *Simplicity* case claimed that economic pressure was being brought to bear on them to make them discontinue suit, Bergen alleged, and the court of appeals agreed, that it would be unable to conduct its suit properly without the injunction because it would be unable to secure witnesses.

Experts disagree on the relative importance of these distinctions between the two cases. Some say flatly that the two cases cannot be reconciled but are opposite holdings on the question of whether a defendant in a private treble-damage action can cut off a customer who files suit. These experts see the touchstone as defendant's monopoly power and feel that if such power is possessed in any great degree, a preliminary injunction follows from the *Bergen* case rationale even if the refusal to deal consists of a contract termination. This view is based on the premise that even the right to terminate a contract may, in some instances, have antitrust implications. Other antitrust lawyers think the cases can be reconciled. This group feels that the main distinction between the cases is the right of a contracting party to refuse to renew his contract no matter what the reason.

Some experts, while they incline toward the view that the cases are not reconcilable, point to practical considerations that may have influenced the decisions. This group emphasizes the nature of the drug industry, its customs, and its legal restrictions, as noted by the *Bergen* opinion. To these factors they add the contemporary feeling toward drug manufacturers resulting from publicity over thalidomide, hearings in Congress, and resulting legislation and the relatively "hard-core" antitrust violations with which Parke, Davis had been charged initially. They also note that, at the time of its refusal to deal, Simplicity was attempting to comply with an FTC Robinson-Patman Act order that had been affirmed by the Supreme Court. Such a defendant may be given greater latitude to choose its customers in order to avoid prohibited discriminatory practices. Also, some say, a defendant charged with a Robinson-Patman violation may be accorded more sympathy in the courts than one charged with monopolization or an attempt to monopolize.

The question arises: Should a manufacturer about to be sued for treble damages cut off the "soon-to-be" plaintiff before suit? Opinion is divided on the advisability of doing so. If an injunction of the *Bergen*-case sort is issued, the defendant may seek from the court an inclusion of the condition found in *P. W. Husserl, Inc.* v. *Simplicity Pattern Co.* that the plaintiff cannot assert any claims for damages "by reason of defendant having continued to deal . . . during the period this order is in effect" (191 F.Supp. at 64). A like provision was inserted in the *Bergen* order issued by the district judge on remand.

May a manufacturer cut-off a customer who complains to the Government about the manufacturer's alleged antitrust violation? In *Dart Drug Corp.* v. *Parke, Davis & Co.*, 344 F.2d 173 (D.C. Cir. 1965), the court of appeals held that the customer had no claim against the manufacturer, but, in a concurring opinion, one judge stated: "Antitrust drug violators are no more immune than other defendants from the criminal statutes concerning obstruction of justice" (344 F.2d at 187).

Table of Cases

249
Gulf States Utilities Co. v. FPC   418

H

Hackett v. General Host Corp.   641, 642, 643, 644
Hale v. Henkel   469
Hamilton Watch Co. v. Benrus Watch Co. 10, 236
Hancock Bros., Inc. v. Jones   579
Hancock Oil Co. v. Union Oil Products Co. 649
Hanover Shoe, Inc. v. United Shoe Machinery Corp.
—185 F.Supp. 826 (M.D.Pa. 1960), aff'd, 281 F.2d 481 (3rd Cir. 1960)   595
—245 F.Supp. 258 (M.D.Pa. 1965)   616, 617, 618
—392 U.S. 481 (1968)   544, 559, 560, 561, 595, 596, 598, 599, 638
Hardy Salt Co. v. W. Va.   581, 605
Harman v. Valley Natl. Bank   441
Harper & Row Publishers, Inc. v. Decker 565, 567, 569, 570, 571, 578
Harris v. Palm Spring Alpine Estates, Inc. 627
Harrison v. Paramount Pictures, Inc.   534
Hart, Schaffner, & Marx; U.S. v.   570
Hartford-Empire Co. v. U.S.
—323 U.S. 382 (1945)   14, 356, 370, 393, 396, 399, 400
—324 U.S. 570 (1945)   15, 356
Hat Corp.; U.S. v.   248, 249
Hawaii v. Standard Oil Co. of Calif.   644
Hawaiian Oke and Liquors, Ltd. v. Joseph E. Seagram and Sons, Inc.   29
Hazel-Atlas Glass Co. v. Hartford-Empire Co.   353
Hazeltine (see Automatic Radio Mfg. Co. v. Hazeltine Research, Inc.)
Hearst Corp.   51
Hecht v. Pro-Football, Inc.   73
Herff Jones Co.; U.S. v.   249
Hertz Corp.; U.S. v.   18
Hettinger v. Glass Specialty Co.   644
Hichman v. Taylor   475, 478, 565
Hieke v. U.S.   470
High (see Ernest Mark High)
Highland Supply Corp. v. Reynolds Metals Co.   528, 529, 611
Hohmann v. Packard Instrument Co.   632
Holland Furnace Co. v. Purcell   520
Holloway v. Bristol-Myers Corp.   587
Hood, H. P., & Sons, Inc.
—U.S. v.   349
—58 F.T.C. 1184 (1961)   515
Hooker Chemical Corp.   243, 254

Hoopes v. Union Oil Company of Calif. 545
House of Materials, Inc. v. Simplicity Pattern Co.   111, 651
Houston opinion (see First City National Bank of Houston; U.S. v.)
Hruby Distributing Co.   283
Huck Mfg. Co.; U.S. v.   373, 375, 376
Hughes
—U.S. v.   567
—v. U.S.   454
Hughes Tool Co. v. TWA, Inc.   411, 414, 418
Husserl, P. W., Inc. v. Simplicity Pattern Co. 650, 654
Hutcheson; U.S. v.   52
Hutchinson v. William C. Barry, Inc.   620
Hutzler Bros. v. Remington-Putnam Book Co.   113
Hyster Co. v. U.S.   450

I

IBM (see International Business Machine Corp.)
ICI (see Imperial Chemical Industries, Ltd.; U.S. v.)
Illinois v. Harper & Row Publishers, Inc.
—50 F.R.D. 37 (N.D.Ill. 1969)   565, 566
—308 F.Supp. 1207 (N.D.Ill. 1969)   578
Image & Sound Serv. Corp. v. Altec Serv. Corp.   538
Imperial Chemical Industries, Ltd.; U.S. v.
—100 F.Supp. 504 (S.D.N.Y. 1951)   40, 374, 393, 437, 438
—105 F.Supp. 215 (S.D.N.Y. 1952)   176, 177, 400, 402
Indiana General Corp. v. Krystinel Corp. 360
Ingersoll-Rand Co.; U.S. v.   162, 208, 226, 227, 233
Instant Delivery Corp. v. City Stores   21, 22, 23
Institute of Carpet Manufacturers; U.S. v. 48, 498
Interborough News Co. v. Curtis Publishing Co.   21
International Brotherhood of Teamsters, Local 24, v. Oliver   56
International Building Co.; U.S. v.   455
International Business Machines Corp.
—U.S. v.   402
—v. U.S.
——298 U.S. 131 (1936)   141, 379, 380
——1973 Trade Cas. ¶74,293 (2d Cir. 1972) 235, 236
International Fishermen, Local 36 of; U.S. v.   36

Y

Z

Topical Index